Understanding the Bible

(An Independent Baptist Commentary)

I Kings through Esther

By
David H. Sorenson
B.A., M. Div., D. Min.

Northstar Ministries
(A ministry of Northstar Baptist Church)
1820 W. Morgan St.
Duluth, MN 55811
218-726-0209

Printed 2008

Second Edition
Copyright 2008
Northstar Ministries
1820 W. Morgan St.
Duluth, MN 55811

Printed in U.S.A.

An Overview of
Understanding the Bible
(An Independent Baptist Commentary)

Understanding the Bible has one purpose: to help the reader understand the Word of God. It seeks to accomplish what Nehemiah wrote, "*So they read in the book in the law of God distinctly, and gave the sense, and caused them to understand the reading*" (Nehemiah 8:8). This work endeavors to give the *sense* of any given passage of Scripture and help the reader to *understand* the reading.

THE FIRST BOOK OF THE
KINGS

COMMONLY CALLED
THE THIRD BOOK OF THE KINGS

Introduction to I Kings: The book of I Kings is also commonly called the third book of the kings of Israel. It continues the divinely inspired record of Old Testament history from the time of the death of David through the division of the kingdom to the reign of Jehoram over Judah and Ahaziah in Samaria. The ministry of Elijah is also contained therein.

The Jews commonly consider both I Kings and II Kings to be merely divisions of the greater book of the history of the Jewish kings. Jewish tradition commonly ascribes Jeremiah to be the author. Ussher estimated that the chronology of I Kings covers a period of 118 years.

Overview of I Kings 1: The first chapter of the book presents the final days of David and the intrigue by Adonijah to succeed him. Solomon is anointed as king amidst the attempted coup d' etat by his brother Adonijah.

1:1-2 The book of Kings begins with record of David's final days. **Now king David was old *and* stricken in years; and they covered him with clothes, but he gat no heat.** The latter phrase likely refers to terminal exhaustion in David. He was perennially chilled. **2 Wherefore his servants said unto him, Let there be sought for my lord the king a young virgin: and let her stand before the king, and let her cherish him, and let her lie in thy bosom, that my lord the king may get heat.** David's servants, concerned for their old, battle-scarred leader, sought a young woman who could nurse him and even lie beside him to give warmth to his old body. Though improper by standards of this day, there was no hint of impropriety in this plan. David's servants only sought to help their ailing king.

1:3-4 Therefore, **they sought for a fair damsel throughout all the coasts of Israel, and found Abishag a Shunammite, and brought her to the king.** Shunem was a town in central Israel, of the tribe of Issachar, about five miles south of Mount Tabor. Morever, **4 the damsel *was* very fair, and cherished the king, and ministered to him: but the king knew her not.** Abishag was a beautiful young woman. However, her service to David was as a nurse. David made no improper advance toward her.

1:5-6 Meanwhile, knowing that David's days were numbered, **Adonijah the son of Haggith exalted himself, saying, I will be king: and he prepared him chariots and horsemen, and fifty men to run before him.** Adonijah was a son of David whose mother was Haggith, one of David's several wives. Developing here is a classic illustration of Matthew 23:12. There, Jesus warned how one who exalts himself shall be abased. Before long, that is exactly what would happen to Adonijah. Regarding chariots, horsemen, and fifty men to run with him, it is of interest that Absalom had done the same thing some years earlier. See II Samuel 15:1. It would appear that his motive in doing so was to impress the people that he was a man of leadership.

Understanding I Kings

Furthermore, **6 his father had not displeased him at any time in saying, Why hast thou done so? and he also *was a* very goodly *man*; and *his mother* bare him after Absalom**. It is apparent at the least that David had not rebuked him for this behavior. In fact, some think that David never disciplined his son, leaving it up to the mothers of his respective sons. This is one of the great weakness of polygamy. In any event, David did not challenge Adonijah who portrayed himself as if he were king. Moreover, he was a handsome young man. Adonijah's mother was not the same woman as Absalom's, but he was born shortly after Absalom.

1:7-9 Adonijah thus sought to build his political base. **And he conferred with Joab the son of Zeruiah, and with Abiathar the priest: and they following Adonijah helped *him*.** Adonijah was able to enlist Joab, David's general, as well as Abiathar the priest. However, **8 Zadok the priest, and Benaiah the son of Jehoiada, and Nathan the prophet, and Shimei, and Rei, and the mighty men which *belonged* to David, were not with Adonijah.** Certainly not all of the notables of Israel joined with Adonijah.

In the meantime, **Adonijah slew sheep and oxen and fat cattle by the stone of Zoheleth, which *is* by Enrogel, and called all his brethren the king's sons, and all the men of Judah the king's servants**. Adonijah prepared a great feast on the northern outskirts of Jerusalem. Though he was not king as yet, he was acting like it. It would seem that he sought to curry the favor of the men of Judah as well as the rest of his brothers. He was clearly campaigning for the office of king in seeking to gain the support of those of influence.

1:10 Conspicuous in his absence was Solomon along with those loyal to him. **But Nathan the prophet, and Benaiah, and the mighty men, and Solomon his brother, he called**

not. Solomon his brother was the heir apparent to the throne. Adonijah was surreptitiously seeking to usurp his brother's place. Thus, he carefully did not let Solomon in on his plans.

1:11-14 However, **Nathan spake unto Bathsheba the mother of Solomon, saying, Hast thou not heard that Adonijah the son of Haggith doth reign, and David our lord knoweth *it* not?** 12 **Now therefore come, let me, I pray thee, give thee counsel, that thou mayest save thine own life, and the life of thy son Solomon.** Nathan's loyalties clearly were to David. He promptly warned Bathsheba of what Adonijah was up to. Adonijah was portraying himself as king and David evidently did not know it. Nathan was thus concerned for the life of both Bathsheba and Solomon, her son.

He thus counseled her, 13 **Go and get thee in unto king David, and say unto him, Didst not thou, my lord, O king, swear unto thine handmaid, saying, Assuredly Solomon thy son shall reign after me, and he shall sit upon my throne? why then doth Adonijah reign?** 14 **Behold, while thou yet talkest there with the king, I also will come in after thee, and confirm thy words.** Nathan's plan was for Bathsheba to have David openly re-affirm his choice of Solomon to succeed him. (This event evidently took place before David's public announcement of Solomon as his successor as recorded in I Chronicles 28.) Bathsheba had approached David on this matter, Nathan then would show up immediately thereafter and remind David of the same.

1:15-21 Bathsheba thus agreed to Nathan's plan. **And Bathsheba went in unto the king into the chamber: and the king was very old; and Abishag the Shunammite ministered unto the king.** 16 **And Bathsheba bowed, and did obeisance unto the king. And the king said, What wouldest thou?** Both David and Bathsheba were advanced in years. That likely is why Abishag was employed as David's nurse. David therefore inquired as to what his wife of many years sought.

Bathsheba thus reminded David of the promise he had made to her at some earlier time. **17 And she said unto him, My lord, thou swarest by the LORD thy God unto thine handmaid,** *saying*, **Assuredly Solomon thy son shall reign after me, and he shall sit upon my throne.** The fact that David at some point had vowed to her in the name of Jehovah made his promise binding. His public announcement of Solomon's succession was made a short time later in I Chronicles 28:5.

Bathsheba therefore informed David of what was going on. **18 And now, behold, Adonijah reigneth; and now, my lord the king, thou knowest** *it* **not: 19 And he hath slain oxen and fat cattle and sheep in abundance, and hath called all the sons of the king, and Abiathar the priest, and Joab the captain of the host: but Solomon thy servant hath he not called.**

Bathsheba thus implored David to make a statement as to who should succeed him. **20 And thou, my lord, O king, the eyes of all Israel** *are* **upon thee, that thou shouldest tell them who shall sit on the throne of my lord the king after him. 21 Otherwise it shall come to pass, when my lord the king shall sleep with his fathers, that I and my son Solomon shall be counted offenders.** Moreover, Bathsheba was worried about what would become of her and Solomon should Adonijah succeed with his plot.

Once again, the great weakness of polygamy is revealed. The several factions of David's wives were clearly in competition against each other. Rather than unity of family, David's sons had become political enemies. Though this certainly can occur in monogamous families, polygamy seems to magnify such strife.

1:22-27 As planned and on cue, Nathan showed up with the same story. **And, lo, while she yet talked with the king,**

Nathan the prophet also came in. 23 And they told the king, saying, Behold Nathan the prophet. And when he was come in before the king, he bowed himself before the king with his face to the ground. 24 And Nathan said, My lord, O king, hast thou said, Adonijah shall reign after me, and he shall sit upon my throne?

25 For he is gone down this day, and hath slain oxen and fat cattle and sheep in abundance, and hath called all the king's sons, and the captains of the host, and Abiathar the priest; and, behold, they eat and drink before him, and say, God save king Adonijah.

26 But me, *even* me thy servant, and Zadok the priest, and Benaiah the son of Jehoiada, and thy servant Solomon, hath he not called. 27 Is this thing done by my lord the king, and thou hast not shewed *it* unto thy servant, who should sit on the throne of my lord the king after him?

Nathan methodically rehearsed all that had taken place with Adonijah. Moreover, he added further detail how that those at Adonijah's party were invoking God to "save king Adonijah." Twice Nathan asked David if he had so endorsed Adonijah. It may be that the Lord had revealed to Nathan and thus to David that Solomon should be the next king. He therefore was perplexed why David had not informed him if Adonijah should be next king.

1:28-30 Upon hearing all of this, king David answered and said, **Call me Bathsheba. And she came into the king's presence, and stood before the king. 29 And the king sware, and said,** *As* **the LORD liveth, that hath redeemed my soul out of all distress, 30 Even as I sware unto thee by the LORD God of Israel, saying, Assuredly Solomon thy son shall reign after me, and he shall sit upon my throne in my stead; even so will I certainly do this day.**

Understanding I Kings

Bathsheba had evidently left the room when Nathan entered. David thus recalled her. As she stood by his bed, he vowed to her again that Solomon would succeed him as king. Moreover, he promised that he would transfer the crown to him that very day.

1:31 Upon hearing that, **Bathsheba bowed with *her* face to the earth, and did reverence to the king, and said, Let my lord king David live for ever.** Evident is the respect that Bathsheba gave her aged husband. Though she knew his days were numbered, nevertheless, she invoked endless life to him. Bathsheba no doubt was sincere in her adulation. David was her husband of many years and she no doubt loved him.

1:32-35 David therefore issued orders. **And king David said, Call me Zadok the priest, and Nathan the prophet, and Benaiah the son of Jehoiada. And they came before the king.** The old king thus summoned top leaders of the nation. Zadok was a chief priest. Nathan was the long established prophet. Benaiah, one of David's mighty men, was the captain of David's palace guard.

Therefore, **33 the king also said unto them, Take with you the servants of your lord, and cause Solomon my son to ride upon mine own mule, and bring him down to Gihon: 34 And let Zadok the priest and Nathan the prophet anoint him there king over Israel: and blow ye with the trumpet, and say, God save king Solomon.**

David directed that Solomon was to be mounted upon the king's white mule. Evidently, this animal was distinctive not only in its color, but also as belonging to the king. This regal procession was directed by David to go to the spring of Gihon where he was to be anointed as king. Why David directed them to Gihon is debatable. It may be that this was a place of public assembly because of the spring of water there. By way of contrast, at En-rogel where Adonijah was celebrating was also a spring of water which fed the pool of Siloam. Some Jewish tradition holds that a Hebrew king must be anointed by a spring of running water. There is no scriptural indication of this and this apparently was the only incident thereof.

It may also be that Gihon, on the west side of the city, was away from where Adonijah was having his party on the north side at En-rogel. In any event, Adonijah's partisans would not be able to interfere with the anointing of Solomon as king.

David further directed that his trusted lieutenants were to there publicly anoint Solomon as king, blowing a trumpet (shofar) to signal the moment of the occasion. They then were to publicly invoke God to "save king Solomon."

Having accomplished that, David directed, **35 Then ye shall come up after him, that he may come and sit upon my throne; for he shall be king in my stead: and I have appointed him to be ruler over Israel and over Judah.** The newly anointed king was thus to be brought to David and officially set upon his throne with David's full blessing. In so doing, it would be made clear to all that Solomon was the new king over Israel.

1:36-37 Thus Benaiah, perhaps as a spokesman for the rest replied, **Amen: the LORD God of my lord the king say so *too*. 37 As the LORD hath been with my lord the king, even so be he with Solomon, and make his throne greater than the throne of my lord king David.** Benaiah thus placed his approval upon the king's decision and invoked God's blessing upon Solomon. Speaking perhaps prophetically and certainly presciently, Benaiah asked God to make Solomon's throne to exceed even that of his father, David.

1:38 These three appointed by David immediately got on with the task given them. **So Zadok the priest, and Nathan the**

prophet, and Benaiah the son of Jehoiada, and the Cherethites, and the Pelethites, went down, and caused Solomon to ride upon king David's mule, and brought him to Gihon. As directed by David, Solomon was brought upon the king's white mule to the spring of Gihon. (The "Cherethites, and the Pelethites" were mercenary bodyguards hired as David's palace guard. Benaiah apparently was their commander. Accordingly, the ceremony of anointing Solomon was under the watchful force of David's palace guard.)

1:39-40 Solomon was thus anointed king. **And Zadok the priest took an horn of oil out of the tabernacle, and anointed Solomon. And they blew the trumpet; and all the people said, God save king Solomon.** To make Solomon's anointing official, the oil whereby he was anointed was from the Tabernacle. It undoubtedly was of the holy recipe for divine office. The blowing of the trumpet (shofar) was the public announcement of the new king. To that the people present cried out, "God save king Solomon." Their invocation was specifically assigned to Solomon. The phrase essentially means, "May God preserve (or give life to) king Solomon."

Thereafter, **40 all the people came up after him, and the people piped with pipes, and rejoiced with great joy, so that the earth rent with the sound of them.** As the newly anointed king rode upon David's white mule back up into the city to where David's throne was, the throngs of the city followed after him. They clearly were cheering loudly while others played upon musical instruments. The cheering and roar of the crowds were such that the ground virtually shook. The common people rejoiced to know of their new king, Solomon. They thus very publicly celebrated in the streets.

1:41 Meanwhile across town, the roar of the crowds and the sound of the blowing of the shofar (trumpet) were heard. **And**

Adonijah and all the guests that *were* with him heard *it* as they had made an end of eating. And when Joab heard the sound of the trumpet, he said, Wherefore *is this* noise of the city being in an uproar? Joab, as a general, clearly understood the significance of the blowing of the trumpet. It was the official system of public signals. Something was up and he knew it.

1:42-43 And while he yet spake, behold, Jonathan the son of Abiathar the priest came: and Adonijah said unto him, Come in; for thou *art* a valiant man, and bringest good tidings. 43 And Jonathan answered and said to Adonijah, Verily our lord king David hath made Solomon king. Joab, perhaps with wishful thinking, invited the young messenger hoping he brought good news. However, the son of Abiathar quickly rained on their parade. He dropped the news like a bombshell. "Verily our lord king David hath made Solomon king."

1:44-46 No doubt panting and out of breath, the young man continued rehearsing what had happened. **And the king hath sent with him Zadok the priest, and Nathan the prophet, and Benaiah the son of Jehoiada, and the Cherethites, and the Pelethites, and they have caused him to ride upon the king's mule: 45 And Zadok the priest and Nathan the prophet have anointed him king in Gihon: and they are come up from thence rejoicing, so that the city rang again. This *is* the noise that ye have heard. And also Solomon sitteth on the throne of the kingdom.** Adonijah's worst dream had come true. While they partied, David his father had anointed his half-brother, Solomon, as king. Moreover, he already was seated upon the throne.

1:47-48 The young messenger continued, **And moreover the king's servants came to bless our lord king David,**

saying, God make the name of Solomon better than thy name, and make his throne greater than thy throne. And the king bowed himself upon the bed. 48 And also thus said the king, Blessed *be* the LORD God of Israel, which hath given *one* to sit on my throne this day, mine eyes even seeing *it*. The news got worse for Adonijah. David's servants had put their blessing upon Solomon and David himself had bowed upon his bed to Solomon, putting his formal blessing upon him. David's official blessing upon Solomon as king clinched it. The old king had formally passed his sceptre to Solomon. The deed was done. It could not be changed.

1:49-50 Adonijah's party was over. **And all the guests that *were* with Adonijah were afraid, and rose up, and went every man his way.** The guests clearly understood the implications of what had happened. They had backed the wrong man. Solomon had the authority and perhaps the inclination to wreak vengeance upon his rival. Adonijah's guests therefore quickly melted away.

Furthermore, 50 **Adonijah feared because of Solomon, and arose, and went, and caught hold on the horns of the altar.** The altar clearly was the brazen altar still at the old Tabernacle. To grab hold upon the horns thereof was a custom which had no basis in the Mosaic Law. However, it was supposed that none would presume to defile with human blood such a sacred place. Adonijah realized his life was in jeopardy and thus went and clung to the horns of the altar as a presumed sanctuary from Solomon's anticipated revenge.

1:51-53 Word got back to Solomon of what Adonijah had done. **And it was told Solomon, saying, Behold, Adonijah feareth king Solomon: for, lo, he hath caught hold on the horns of the altar, saying, Let king Solomon swear unto me to day that he will not slay his servant with the sword.**

Solomon thus replied, 52 **If he will shew himself a worthy man, there shall not an hair of him fall to the earth: but if wickedness shall be found in him, he shall die.**

Therefore, 53 **king Solomon sent, and they brought him down from the altar. And he came and bowed himself to king Solomon: and Solomon said unto him, Go to thine house.** In being taken to Solomon, the new king sternly admonished Adonijah to go home. Implied is that his behavior would determine later judgment.

* * * * *

Overview of I Kings 2: The second chapter of II Kings is climactic. David, the elderly king emeritus, gave charge to Solomon the new king. The death of David is recorded followed by the account of the execution of Adonijah. The chapter also records the flight and death of Joab as well as the execution of Shimei. Solomon thus consolidated power as the new king.

2:1 In David's final days, he straitly advised his son Solomon as new king. **Now the days of David drew nigh that he should die; and he charged Solomon his son, saying**. The word translated as **charged** (צוה *tsavah*) essentially means to 'command.' David therefore directed Solomon in the following.

2:2 David thus charged Solomon, **I go the way of all the earth: be thou strong therefore, and shew thyself a man**. His reference to going the way of all the earth was an euphemistic way of indicating that he was about to die. He thus *charged* Solomon to be (1) **strong** of character and to (2) **shew thyself a man**. The latter likely has the sense of being courageous, wise, and mature.

Understanding I Kings

2:3-4 David therefore directed Solomon to **keep the charge of the LORD thy God, to walk in his ways, to keep his statutes, and his commandments, and his judgments, and his testimonies, as it is written in the law of Moses, that thou mayest prosper in all that thou doest, and whithersoever thou turnest thyself.**

David advised Solomon in summary of God's ways. Specifically, that included God's "statutes, and his commandments, and his judgments, and his testimonies." God's statues and commandments likely refer to the comprehensive law of Moses in which not only the ceremonial regulations for Israel were set forth, but more importantly the moral, spiritual, and judicial laws of God. His testimonies likely refer to the greater sum of truth regarding God.

Of particular note is David's intimation that by obeying the totality of God's will and way, God would prosper Solomon in all that he did. The greater principle is that God has promised to specially bless those who obey His Word. That was made clear in Deuteronomy 28. God likewise promised Joshua the same in Joshua 1:8. That principle remains to this day. God will bless and prosper those who obey Him. See Revelation 1:3 and 22:7,14.

David continued, **4 That the LORD may continue his word which he spake concerning me, saying, If thy children take heed to their way, to walk before me in truth with all their heart and with all their soul, there shall not fail thee (said he) a man on the throne of Israel.** The word which the Lord spake to David (referenced here) likely was that of the Davidic Covenant made in II Samuel 7. The simple condition to God's promised blessing for David's posterity was *if* (1) they took heed to their way (2) to walk before God in truth (3) and to do so with all their heart and soul. Though the context clearly was of the lineage of David and his dynasty to come, by way of principle, the promise is universal. God will prosper and bless those who take heed to walk before Him in truth with all their heart and soul.

2:5-6 Having thus established lofty principles by which Solomon should reign, David now shifted to settling personal accounts. He thus warned Solomon, **Moreover thou knowest also what Joab the son of Zeruiah did to me,** *and* **what he did to the two captains of the hosts of Israel, unto Abner the son of Ner, and unto Amasa the son of Jether, whom he slew, and shed the blood of war in peace, and put the blood of war upon his girdle that** *was* **about his loins, and in his shoes that** *were* **on his feet**.

Joab was David's nephew and for many years had been his trusted general. However, in later years, Joab's loyalty to David had evaporated. He had killed Absalom contrary to orders. He had been insolent to David in mourning for Absalom's death. Moreover, he had joined in with the attempted *coup d' etat* against Solomon in the matter of Adonijah. It was Joab who had unlawfully and cruelly murdered Abner, Saul's cousin and commander. (See II Samuel 3: 27.) Joab had likewise dealt harshly in killing Amasa who was a lieutenant of Absalom. In his later years, Joab had become a loose cannon who had not been loyal to either David or to Solomon.

Therefore, David counseled Solomon regarding Joab, **6 Do therefore according to thy wisdom, and let not his hoar head go down to the grave in peace**. It is evident that Joab, like David, was an elderly man by this time. The word translated as **hoar head** (שיבה *seybah*) essentially means 'aged.' Though David, himself, had not dealt with Joab in his final years, he counseled his son in so many words to execute the man.

2:7 In contradistinction, David directed Solomon to **shew kindness unto the sons of Barzillai the Gileadite, and let them be of those that eat at thy table: for so they came to me**

Understanding I Kings

when I fled because of Absalom thy brother. Barzillai, as intimated in the text, was he who had at great risk shown exceptional loyalty to David during the uprising of Absalom. David thus counseled Solomon to show perpetual kindness to the sons of Barzillai.

2:8-9 However, David had one other account to settle. He reminded Solomon, **behold,** *thou hast* **with thee Shimei the son of Gera, a Benjamite of Bahurim, which cursed me with a grievous curse in the day when I went to Mahanaim: but he came down to meet me at Jordan, and I sware to him by the LORD, saying, I will not put thee to death with the sword.**

David hearkened back to the traumatic time of Absalom's rebellion. Shimei at that time had publicly and defiantly sided with Absalom against David. See II Samuel 16:5 *ff.* After David returned in victory, Shimei sang a different tune and David magnanimously promised to spare him. See II Samuel 19:18 *ff.* Though not recorded, it is apparent that Shimei's repentance at the time was feigned and that he never was loyal to David. Though David had promised that he would not kill Shimei, he never promised that another would not. He evidently feared that Shimei's disloyalty would undermine young Solomon's reign.

Therefore, David directed, **9 Now therefore hold him not guiltless: for thou** *art* **a wise man, and knowest what thou oughtest to do unto him; but his hoar head bring thou down to the grave with blood.** It may be surmised that David was not ordering judgment upon his enemies out of revenge. Rather, he likely was counseling Solomon to remove known pockets of disloyalty which had potential to destabilize the reign of the new, young king. Therefore, he counseled Solomon to use his own judgment in removing Shimei.

2:10-11 The sacred historian thus notes the demise of David. **So David slept with his fathers, and was buried in the**

city of David. His death is euphemistically referred to as sleeping with his fathers. The city of David, of course, is Bethlehem. To this day, there is a shrine marking the presumed site of David's tomb.

The sacred writer thus cryptically summarized David's career. **11 And the days that David reigned over Israel *were* forty years: seven years reigned he in Hebron, and thirty and three years reigned he in Jerusalem**. The initial seven-year reign of David in Hebron was that over Judah. The final thirty-three years was over the entire nation of Israel.

2:12 Summary note is thus made of Solomon's ascension to the throne. **Then sat Solomon upon the throne of David his father; and his kingdom was established greatly**. It is clear that God providentially established Solomon's reign. His kingdom thus from the start prospered.

2:13-18 Evidently not long after David's death, Adonijah began to scheme again. **And Adonijah the son of Haggith came to Bathsheba the mother of Solomon. And she said, Comest thou peaceably? And he said, Peaceably**. Thinking he could curry favor through the king's mother, Adonijah approached Bathsheba and sought to enlist her help.

14 He said moreover, I have somewhat to say unto thee. And she said, Say on. 15 And he said, Thou knowest that the kingdom was mine, and *that* all Israel set their faces on me, that I should reign: howbeit the kingdom is turned about, and is become my brother's: for it was his from the LORD. 16 And now I ask one petition of thee, deny me not. And she said unto him, Say on.

In briefly rehearsing his earlier ambitions, Adonijah made a revealing comment. He acknowledged that the kingdom was given to Solomon by the Lord. However, he had one request.

Understanding I Kings

17 And he said, Speak, I pray thee, unto Solomon the king, (for he will not say thee nay,) that he give me Abishag the Shunammite to wife. 18 And Bathsheba said, Well; I will speak for thee unto the king. It is apparent that Abishag had caught the eye of Adonijah. They may have even developed a relationship of some sorts. Therefore, he asked Bathsheba to intercede with Solomon on his behalf. Some have assumed that Abishag had in fact become a wife of David though there is no specific record to that end. However, if that was the case, then Adonijah's request would have been in violation of Leviticus 18:8, which see. However, that scenario does not seem to have been the case.

Bathsheba's reply of **well** likely has the more modern idiom of 'very well.' She agreed to take the matter to Solomon, the king.

2:19-21 Bathsheba therefore went unto king Solomon, to speak unto him for Adonijah. And the king rose up to meet her, and bowed himself unto her, and sat down on his throne, and caused a seat to be set for the king's mother; and she sat on his right hand. Of note is the formal courtesy which Solomon showed unto his mother. He rose, bowed to her, and then had a seat brought for her at his right hand. Of interest is that the word translated **seat** (כסא *kicce'*) is the same as translated as **throne** elsewhere in the verse. The greater thought is the deference and respect Solomon showed to his mother.

Bathsheba thus broached the purpose of her audience with the king. **20 Then she said, I desire one small petition of thee; *I pray thee*, say me not nay. And the king said unto her, Ask on, my mother: for I will not say thee nay. And she said, Let Abishag the Shunammite be given to Adonijah thy brother to wife**.

2:22-23 Though Solomon as a courtesy had indicated he would grant his mother's request, upon hearing it; his response was in so many words, "no way!" **And king Solomon answered and said unto his mother, And why dost thou ask Abishag the Shunammite for Adonijah? ask for him the kingdom also; for he *is* mine elder brother; even for him, and for Abiathar the priest, and for Joab the son of Zeruiah. 23 Then king Solomon sware by the LORD, saying, God do so to me, and more also, if Adonijah have not spoken this word against his own life.**

Some have thought that Adonijah was trying to marry the king's widow (assuming that Abishag had in fact become David's wife). If that were the case (the text does not so indicate), then Adonijah conceivably had even greater intentions of still seizing the throne via Abishag. Solomon may have therefore have seen the request by Adonijah to marry Abishag as a threat to his throne. Abiathar had supported the ill-fated *coup d' etat* of Adonijah as had Joab. All three were therefore suspect by Solomon. The king therefore vowed that Adonijah had thus spoken his own death sentence.

2:24-25 Solomon therefore sentenced Adonijah to death on the spot. **Now therefore, *as* the LORD liveth, which hath established me, and set me on the throne of David my father, and who hath made me an house, as he promised, Adonijah shall be put to death this day.** The solemnity of Solomon's edict is magnified by his swearing by Jehovah that Adonijah would die that day.

Accordingly, **25 king Solomon sent by the hand of Benaiah the son of Jehoiada; and he fell upon him that he died**. The Benaiah mentioned was one of several by the same name during the time of David. This one likely was one of David's mighty warriors, the son of Jehoiada, the priest. He had remained loyal to David and then Solomon through all the troubled waters of the transition of the throne. Of interest is the phrase translated "and he fell upon him." That is the most literal rendering. However, it is clear that it is idiomatic and can also have the sense in this context of striking or assaulting another. Benaiah thus executed Adonijah. The latter had made the fatal error of threatening his brother's young reign by seeking Abishag as wife.

2:26-27 Abiathar, Adonijah's supporter, was either near at hand or was immediately summoned. **And unto Abiathar the priest said the king, Get thee to Anathoth, unto thine own fields; for thou *art* worthy of death: but I will not at this time put thee to death, because thou barest the ark of the Lord GOD before David my father, and because thou hast been afflicted in all wherein my father was afflicted.**

Anathoth was a city allocated to the priests. It was located in the tribe of Benjamin about three miles north of Jerusalem. Though priests had their duties at the Tabernacle, they usually also had a homestead elsewhere. Abiathar's home was at Anathoth. Because of his support of Adonijah's attempted *coup*, Solomon considered him worthy of death. However, because he had been loyal to David at the troubled time of Absalom's rebellion and had helped carry the Ark of the Covenant with David then, Solomon gave him a reprieve from execution. However, his days as high priest were over.

27 So Solomon thrust out Abiathar from being priest unto the LORD; that he might fulfil the word of the LORD, which he spake concerning the house of Eli in Shiloh. The latter comment hearkens back to the vow made by God in I Samuel 2:31-35 and 3:12-14. The mills of God grind slow, but they grind exceedingly fine. The vow of God to remove the priestly lineage from the house of Eli had been made approximately 150 years earlier. God in his providential wisdom did not accomplish the same until now. It is not clear if Solomon's decision was to intentionally fulfill God's purpose regarding the house of Eli or if God used this event to providentially effect

His will. The latter seems more likely. The context seems to lean toward the latter.

2:28-29 Word quickly reached Joab of what had happened to Adonijah and Abiathar. **Then tidings came to Joab: for Joab had turned after Adonijah, though he turned not after Absalom. And Joab fled unto the tabernacle of the LORD, and caught hold on the horns of the altar.** Joab had been loyal to David during the uprising of Absalom, but he certainly had not supported Solomon for king. Hearing what happened to Adonijah, Joab therefore fled to the Tabernacle and grabbed hold upon the horns of the altar. See notes thereto for I Kings 1:50-51. It may be that he well recalled how Solomon had shown mercy to Adonijah when he did so (I Kings 1:50-51). **29 And it was told king Solomon that Joab was fled unto the tabernacle of the LORD; and, behold,** *he is* **by the altar. Then Solomon sent Benaiah the son of Jehoiada, saying, Go, fall upon him.** Notwithstanding, Solomon sent Benaiah to execute Joab.

2:30-34 And Benaiah came to the tabernacle of the LORD, and said unto him, Thus saith the king, Come forth. And he said, Nay; but I will die here. And Benaiah brought the king word again, saying, Thus said Joab, and thus he answered me. Though having the authority of the king to execute Joab, Benaiah had enough respect to the Tabernacle to hesitate executing Joab there.

Notwithstanding, **31 the king said unto him, Do as he hath said, and fall upon him, and bury him; that thou mayest take away the innocent blood, which Joab shed, from me, and from the house of my father. 32 And the LORD shall return his blood upon his own head, who fell upon two men more righteous and better than he, and slew them with the sword, my father David not knowing** *thereof, to wit,* **Abner** the son of Ner, captain of the host of Israel, and Amasa the son of Jether, captain of the host of Judah.** Solomon thus ordered Benaiah to execute Joab not only for his suspected disloyalty, but especially for his murder of Abner and Amasa in the past. It may well be surmised that God providentially wrought vengeance for Joab's crimes. Indeed, God does repay.

Continuing, Solomon noted, 33 **Their blood shall therefore return upon the head of Joab, and upon the head of his seed for ever: but upon David, and upon his seed, and upon his house, and upon his throne, shall there be peace for ever from the LORD. 34 So Benaiah the son of Jehoiada went up, and fell upon him, and slew him: and he was buried in his own house in the wilderness.** Thus Benaiah executed Joab.

2:35 Solomon therefore ordered structural changes in his government. **And the king put Benaiah the son of Jehoiada in his room over the host: and Zadok the priest did the king put in the room of Abiathar.** Benaiah was promoted from being captain of the palace guard to general of the army. Zadok the priest was also promoted to being high priest.

2:36-38 As for Shimei, the king sent and called for him and said unto him, **Build thee an house in Jerusalem, and dwell there, and go not forth thence any whither. 37 For it shall be,** *that* **on the day thou goest out, and passest over the brook Kidron, thou shalt know for certain that thou shalt surely die: thy blood shall be upon thine own head. 38 And Shimei said unto the king, The saying** *is* **good: as my lord the king hath said, so will thy servant do. And Shimei dwelt in Jerusalem many days.**

The brook Kidron flowed along the eastern edge of Jerusalem between the city and the Mount of Olives. Solomon therefore offered Shimei a degree of clemency on the condition that he did not leave the city of Jerusalem. He was essentially under house arrest with orders not to leave town. Shimei therefore agreed.

2:39-41 However, it came to pass at the end of three years, that two of the servants of Shimei ran away unto Achish son of Maachah king of Gath. And they told Shimei, saying, Behold, thy servants *be* in Gath. 40 And Shimei arose, and saddled his ass, and went to Gath to Achish to seek his servants: and Shimei went, and brought his servants from Gath. 41 And it was told Solomon that Shimei had gone from Jerusalem to Gath, and was come again. Shimei had a problem and seeking to resolve it, he had violated the terms of his agreement.

2:42-46 And the king sent and called for Shimei, and said unto him, Did I not make thee to swear by the LORD, and protested unto thee, saying, Know for a certain, on the day thou goest out, and walkest abroad any whither, that thou shalt surely die? and thou saidst unto me, The word *that* I have heard *is* good. 43 Why then hast thou not kept the oath of the LORD, and the commandment that I have charged thee with?
44 The king said moreover to Shimei, Thou knowest all the wickedness which thine heart is privy to, that thou didst to David my father: therefore the LORD shall return thy wickedness upon thine own head; 45 And king Solomon *shall be* blessed, and the throne of David shall be established before the LORD for ever. 46 So the king commanded Benaiah the son of Jehoiada; which went out, and fell upon him, that he died. And the kingdom was established in the hand of Solomon.

Because (1) Shimei had broken his word to Solomon and (2) because of his open disloyalty to David, he was ordered executed. However, in so doing, Solomon had systematically rooted out individuals who held potential to destabilize his reign. As noted, the kingdom was thus established in his hand.

* * * * *

Overview of I Kings 3: *After having consolidated his power, the record of Solomon's reign begins in this chapter. Noted are his dalliances with Egypt. Then the sacred writer notes Solomon's great sacrifice at Gibeon. The incident of Solomon seeking God's wisdom and God's response thereto are recorded. That wisdom is noted in the classic episode of Solomon and the two harlots fighting over the one child.*

3:1 After Solomon had consolidated his political power base as noted in the preceding two chapters, the sacred historian now begins to record the actual reign of Solomon. **And Solomon made affinity with Pharaoh king of Egypt, and took Pharaoh's daughter, and brought her into the city of David, until he had made an end of building his own house, and the house of the LORD, and the wall of Jerusalem round about.**

Even at this early stage in his reign, Solomon already was sowing the seeds of his own destruction. Notwithstanding the clear intent in the Law of Moses regarding separation from pagan gentiles, Solomon nevertheless ignored that in marrying the daughter of Pharaoh. That pattern would be repeated many times over in later years as Solomon married many foreign women. In this case, he brought her to Jerusalem to a temporary home in the city of David while his major construction projects, including his own house, the Temple, and the extension of the city wall were completed. The city of David was a section of Jerusalem overlooking the valley of Kidron west of the Mount of Olives.

3:2 The text further records, **Only the people sacrificed in high places, because there was no house built unto the name of the LORD, until those days.** The law of Moses clearly directed that Israel was to offer sacrifices only in the place which God chose. That was where the Tabernacle was located. After occupation of the land, it had rested in various places and David had brought it finally to Jerusalem. Notwithstanding, the nation of Israel disregarded that injunction and offered sacrifices on convenient hilltops which was the custom of the pagans of the region. Though the Temple itself had not as yet been built, the Tabernacle still remained. Evident therefore was a spiritual carelessness across the land. Solomon evidently did nothing to abate it.

3:3 Notwithstanding, **Solomon loved the LORD, walking in the statutes of David his father: only he sacrificed and burnt incense in high places.** In the early years of Solomon's reign, he clearly loved the Lord and emulated the example of his father David. However, once again, Solomon tolerated compromise by sacrificing to God in high places. A pattern of compromise and accommodation with the world is established in Solomon's reign which would soon corrupt him altogether. David *never* offered sacrifices of burnt incense in high places. It was common practice in Israel learned from neighboring gentile nations. But David never did so.

3:4 Accordingly, **the king went to Gibeon to sacrifice there; for that *was* the great high place: a thousand burnt offerings did Solomon offer upon that altar.** Gibeon was a place about five miles northwest of Jerusalem. There was a particularly prominent high place. Thus at Gibeon, Solomon offered a thousand burnt offerings. Never before in Israel had there been such a public display of worship. Some commentators believe that this massive sacrifice to God was done over a period of several days. In any event, it was an extraordinary occurrence.

3:5 The time was still evidently early in Solomon's reign. Thus, while at Gibeon, **the LORD appeared to Solomon in a dream by night: and God said, Ask what I shall give thee.** The famous incident of God offering Solomon whatever he wished is about to unfold.

3:6-9 Recorded is the wise and humble prayer of Solomon to God in response to God's gracious offer. **And Solomon said, Thou hast shewed unto thy servant David my father great mercy, according as he walked before thee in truth, and in righteousness, and in uprightness of heart with thee; and thou hast kept for him this great kindness, that thou hast given him a son to sit on his throne, as** *it is* **this day.**
Solomon began his prayer with gratitude to God, reminding Him how David his father had walked before Him in truth and righteousness. Of interest is that Solomon ascribed to his father the two forms of righteousness commonly defined in the Old Testament. The word translated as **righteousness** (צדקה *tsadaqah*) derives from the more basic 'tsadiq' which refers to righteousness as a principle. He also noted how David had walked in "uprightness of heart."

The word translated as **uprightness** (ישרה *yishrah*) derives from the more basic *yashar* which refers to uprightness of living (i.e., integrity). David exemplified both. Solomon thus praised God for his great mercy to David and His kindness in placing him upon David's throne.

Solomon thus exemplified a humble spirit before God. **7 And now, O LORD my God, thou hast made thy servant king instead of David my father: and I** *am but* **a little child: I know not** *how* **to go out or come in.** Though king, Solomon humbled himself before God. Moreover, **8 thy servant** *is* **in the** midst of thy people which thou hast chosen, a great people, that cannot be numbered nor counted for multitude.** Of further interest is that Solomon referred to himself as God's servant. He realized the great burden of responsibility which rested upon his shoulders as king over God's chosen nation.

He thus pled, **9 Give therefore thy servant an understanding heart to judge thy people, that I may discern between good and bad: for who is able to judge this thy so great a people?**

Of interest is that the word translated as **understanding** (שמע *shama'*), in its most basic meaning, has the sense of 'hearing.' By extension, it had the sense of hearing to the degree of understanding. The word translated **judge** (שפט *shaphat*) has the basic sense to 'discern,' or the ability to 'make sound decisions,' or to 'govern.' In essence, Solomon asked God for the ability to be a good king—for the ability to make sound judgments and right decisions in governing. Though he could have asked for personal gain, he rather asked God for the ability to rule righteously and wisely.

3:10-11 The humility and wisdom of Solomon's request was pleasing to God. **And the speech pleased the Lord, that Solomon had asked this thing. 11 And God said unto him, Because thou hast asked this thing, and hast not asked for thyself long life; neither hast asked riches for thyself, nor hast asked the life of thine enemies; but hast asked for thyself understanding to discern judgment.** Of note is that God refers to himself here as **Lord** (אדני *Adonay*) rather than **Lord** (יהוה *Jehovah*). The former is a more generic term whereas the latter is His proper name. Nevertheless, Adonay is a title used to refer to Jehovah-God numerous times in the Old Testament.

God recognized that Solomon's request was not selfish. He had not asked for any personal gain or revenge against his en-

Understanding I Kings

emies. Rather, he had sought for understanding to righteously make wise decisions as king.

3:12-14 God therefore continued, **Behold, I have done according to thy words: lo, I have given thee a wise and an understanding heart; so that there was none like thee before thee, neither after thee shall any arise like unto thee.** God gave Solomon the wisdom for which he sought. Moreover, God promised that the degree of wisdom given would be such as never before or thereafter given.

Furthermore, God promised, **13 I have also given thee that which thou hast not asked, both riches, and honour: so that there shall not be any among the kings like unto thee all thy days.** Because of the righteous and unselfish request made by Solomon, God promised also wealth and honor such as no other king of his day possessed. Indeed, in the course of events, Solomon became the wealthiest man of his day.

On top of that, God added one stipulation. **14 And if thou wilt walk in my ways, to keep my statutes and my commandments, as thy father David did walk, then I will lengthen thy days.** If Solomon would be utterly obedient to God's Word even as his father did, God promised to give him extra length of life. Sadly, as the story will unfold, Solomon was never fully obedient. It seems that with age, he drifted farther and farther from the Lord. God promised additional blessing for obedience. Solomon never received that blessing because of his developing disobedience.

3:15 And Solomon awoke; and, behold, *it was* **a dream.** Notwithstanding that he had dreamed, it is evident, that God did speak to him through that dream. Thus, apparent is one of the ways in which God often spoke to His people especially in that day. **And he came to Jerusalem, and stood before the ark of the covenant of the LORD, and offered up burnt offerings,**

and offered peace offerings, and made a feast to all his servants. Evident is that the ark of the covenant remained in Jerusalem which David had brought there before. It was there that Solomon should have offered sacrifice and there he now did so. He then invited all his servants to join with him in celebrating God's blessing.

3:16-22 Solomon's newly received wisdom was soon tested. Two immoral women showed up with a bitter dispute. **Then came there two women, *that were* harlots, unto the king, and stood before him. 17 And the one woman said, O my lord, I and this woman dwell in one house; and I was delivered of a child with her in the house. 18 And it came to pass the third day after that I was delivered, that this woman was delivered also: and we *were* together; *there was* no stranger with us in the house, save we two in the house. 19 And this woman's child died in the night; because she overlaid it**.

The story is self-evident. The mothers of these infants came with a dispute over the dead child. Obvious indeed is the bitter life of those given to immorality. Furthermore, the first woman alleged, **20 the other arose at midnight, and took my son from beside me, while thine handmaid slept, and laid it in her bosom, and laid her dead child in my bosom. 21 And when I rose in the morning to give my child suck, behold, it was dead: but when I had considered it in the morning, behold, it was not my son, which I did bear. 22 And the other woman said, Nay; but the living *is* my son, and the dead *is* thy son. And this said, No; but the dead *is* thy son, and the living *is* my son. Thus they spake before the king**. Bitter indeed was the dispute between these two harlots. They thus came to the king to judge between them.

3:23-25 Solomon thus summarily rehearsed the dispute. **Then said the king, The one saith, This *is* my son that liveth,**

and thy son *is* the dead: and the other saith, Nay; but thy son *is* the dead, and my son *is* the living. He therefore said. **24 Bring me a sword. And they brought a sword before the king. 25 And the king said, Divide the living child in two, and give half to the one, and half to the other.** The wisdom of Solomon's judgment is apparent. It would immediately reveal the true mother.

3:26-27 Then spake the woman whose the living child *was* unto the king, for her bowels yearned upon her son, and she said, O my lord, give her the living child, and in no wise slay it. But the other said, Let it be neither mine nor thine, *but* divide *it*. 27 Then the king answered and said, Give her the living child, and in no wise slay it: she *is* the mother thereof. With wisdom remembered from that day to this, Solomon forced the issue. The true mother deferred whilst the imposter was ambivalent. Solomon thus wisely discerned the truth of the matter and justly adjudicated the case.

3:28 Word quickly spread of Solomon's wise decision. **And all Israel heard of the judgment which the king had judged; and they feared the king: for they saw that the wisdom of God *was* in him, to do judgment.** Such wisdom caused Solomon's realm to fear him for they perceived he had the wisdom of God in making righteous judgments.

* * * * *

Overview of I Kings 4: *The sacred historian records how Solomon organized his government. The chapter then proceeds to record the prosperity and blessing which befell Israel in Solomon's reign. Further comment is made regarding the wisdom of Solomon, his writing, his music, and his fame.*

4:1-5 The chapter begins noting the complete consolidation of Solomon as king over Israel. **So king Solomon was king over all Israel**. The sacred historian thus proceeds to enumerate the high-level officials of Solomon's government. 2 **And these were the princes which he had; Azariah the son of Zadok the priest, 3 Elihoreph and Ahiah, the sons of Shisha, scribes; Jehoshaphat the son of Ahilud, the recorder. 4 And Benaiah the son of Jehoiada *was* over the host: and Zadok and Abiathar *were* the priests: 5 And Azariah the son of Nathan *was* over the officers: and Zabud the son of Nathan *was* principal officer, *and* the king's friend: And Ahishar *was* over the household: and Adoniram the son of Abda *was* over the tribute**.

In more modern thought, what is listed here would be the equivalent of Solomon's cabinet. Zadok was the high priest of the land, apparently assisted by Abiathar. Ahiah and the sons of Shisha were those who wrote the official records of the realm. Jehoshaphat was the official historian. Benaiah was the chief military officer. And, a man named Azariah was chief of staff over other servants to the king.

Of interest is that one of the prophet Nathan's sons, Zabud, is described as "principal officer, *and* the king's friend." The word translated as **principal officer** (כֹּהֵן *kohen*) is the common word for priest. Indicative is that both Zabud and Nathan may have been priests. Zabud may have served as a personal 'chaplain' to the king. Moreover, he is noted as the king's friend. Implicit is that he was the king's confidant. One named Ahishar was steward of Solomon's house and a man named Adoniram was his secretary of revenue.

4:7-19 The sacred historian therefore sets forth twelve officials in Solomon's government which were assigned to procure necessary provisions for the royal household. Each of these was on duty for one month of the year. It would seem that each perhaps spent the other eleven months preparing their royal order and then one month of the year actually administering it.

And Solomon had twelve officers over all Israel, which provided victuals for the king and his household: each man his month in a year made provision. 8 And these *are* their names: The son of Hur, in mount Ephraim: 9 The son of Dekar, in Makaz, and in Shaalbim, and Bethshemesh, and Elonbethhanan: 10 The son of Hesed, in Aruboth; to him *pertained* Sochoh, and all the land of Hepher:

11 The son of Abinadab, in all the region of Dor; which had Taphath the daughter of Solomon to wife: 12 Baana the son of Ahilud; *to him pertained* Taanach and Megiddo, and all Bethshean, which *is* by Zartanah beneath Jezreel, from Bethshean to Abelmeholah, *even* unto *the place that is* beyond Jokneam: 13 The son of Geber, in Ramothgilead; to him *pertained* the towns of Jair the son of Manasseh, which *are* in Gilead; to him *also pertained* the region of Argob, which *is* in Bashan, threescore great cities with walls and brasen bars: 14 Ahinadab the son of Iddo *had* Mahanaim: 15 Ahimaaz *was* in Naphtali; he also took Basmath the daughter of Solomon to wife:

16 Baanah the son of Hushai *was* in Asher and in Aloth: 17 Jehoshaphat the son of Paruah, in Issachar: 18 Shimei the son of Elah, in Benjamin: 19 Geber the son of Uri *was* in the country of Gilead, *in* the country of Sihon king of the Amorites, and of Og king of Bashan; and *he was* the only officer which *was* in the land.

These various officers of provisions for Solomon were not necessarily over respective tribes of Israel, though some were. Others rather were over various regions, including distant places such as Bashan. Evidently each region of greater Israel was responsible to provide a monthly provision for Solomon's royal household. The officials mentioned above were over each of the respective areas noted to ensure the provision was duly supplied to the king's household on schedule.

4:20 The sacred historian pauses to make note the prosperity and blessing in Israel in that day. **Judah and Israel *were* many, as the sand which *is* by the sea in multitude, eating and drinking, and making merry**. The fulfillment of the promise which God made to Abraham more than eight-hundred years earlier was completely fulfilled. See Genesis 22:17. Evident is that under the wise leadership of Solomon, there were prosperous times. Of further note is the ongoing distinction between Judah and Israel. Though one nation, the old distinction is still noted.

4:21 The extent of Solomon's kingdom is noted. **And Solomon reigned over all kingdoms from the river unto the land of the Philistines, and unto the border of Egypt: they brought presents, and served Solomon all the days of his life**. In Solomon's day, Israel for a brief time was a 'superpower' in the Middle East. The kingdom of Solomon extended from the Euphrates River in the northeast to the region of Philistia and Egypt to the southwest. The various lessor kingdoms included in this region paid tribute to Solomon during his reign and served him throughout his lifetime.

4:22-23 Specific note is made of the provisions needed to operate Solomon's royal household for one day. **And Solomon's provision for one day was thirty measures of fine flour, and threescore measures of meal, 23 Ten fat oxen, and twenty oxen out of the pastures, and an hundred sheep, beside harts, and roebucks, and fallowdeer, and fatted fowl**. By one estimation, a measure of flour was more than six bushels. Thus, in one day, Solomon's household consumed approximately two-hundred bushels of the finest flour, four-hundred

Understanding I Kings

bushels of more common flour (perhaps for his servants), ten fattened steers, twenty more common head of beef cattle (again perhaps for his household servants), one-hundred sheep, not counting numerous kinds of wild meats hunted and served each day. Truly Solomon's fare was fit for a king. Moreover, this regimen was provided to his royal household 365 days a year.

4:24 Further detail of the extent of his realm is noted. **For he had dominion over all *the region* on this side the river, from Tiphsah even to Azzah, over all the kings on this side the river: and he had peace on all sides round about him.** The river noted again undoubtedly is the Euphrates River to the north and east. **Tiphsah** is thought to be a crossing on the Euphrates River and marked the furthermost terminus of his kingdom in that direction. **Azzah** was another name for Gaza which is located in Philistia to the southwest. Not only were the borders of Israel larger than at anytime in history, both in the past to this day, there was peace on all sides.

4:25 The reign of Solomon in many ways was typical of what it will be in the day when Jesus will reign from Jerusalem. **And Judah and Israel dwelt safely, every man under his vine and under his fig tree, from Dan even to Beersheba, all the days of Solomon.** Dan is the northernmost portion of Israel proper (to this day) and Beersheba to the south historically have been the extremities of Israel proper. From one end of the land to the other, Israel was at peace and prosperous. The metaphor of dwelling under one's fig tree is a symbol of domestic tranquility and prosperity.

4:26 Note is made of Solomon's stables. **And Solomon had forty thousand stalls of horses for his chariots, and twelve thousand horsemen.** Though not commented thereon in the sacred text, another insight into the compromise of obedience to the Word of God by Solomon is at hand. In Deuteronomy 17:16, the law of Moses clearly prescribed that any future king of Israel was to "not multiply horses unto himself." Solomon was in direct violation of that scriptural injunction.

Some have thought there to be a contradiction between this passage and II Chronicles 9:25. In the latter, record is made of four-thousand stalls of horses. The answer to the seeming contradiction however is simple. Solomon had a total of 40,000 horses. However, in II Chronicles is the number of stables which were 4,000. Ten horses were typically quartered at each stable. There thus quite apparently were stables for Solomon's vast herd of horses all throughout his realm.

4:27-28 Record is therefore noted for the provisions necessary for Solomon's herds of livestock in addition to his household. **And those officers provided victual for king Solomon, and for all that came unto king Solomon's table, every man in his month: they lacked nothing. 28 Barley also and straw for the horses and dromedaries brought they unto the place where *the officers* were, every man according to his charge**. The word translated as **dromedaries** (רכש *rekesh*) might imply camels. However, it actually refers to steeds. These evidently were the finest of Solomon's equestrian heads. The officers noted in verses 8-19 evidently also saw too it that the king's vast herd of horses received due provisions each month.

4:29-31 The sacred writer pauses to record the widespread knowledge of Solomon's wisdom. **And God gave Solomon wisdom and understanding exceeding much, and largeness of heart, even as the sand that *is* on the sea shore**. The metaphor of the sand of the sea shore is used to describe the immeasurable wisdom which God gave Solomon. The mention of his largeness of heart may refer to the goodness and kindness of the man. God gave him great wisdom and kindness.

Moreover, 30 **Solomon's wisdom excelled the wisdom of all the children of the east country, and all the wisdom of Egypt**. In that day, the other centers of civilization and learning were to the east in Mesopotamia and Egypt to the west. Solomon's wisdom and brilliance exceeded the highest levels of human education and learning anywhere else in the world.

Furthermore, 31 **he was wiser than all men; than Ethan the Ezrahite, and Heman, and Chalcol, and Darda, the sons of Mahol**. Precisely who these men were is not clear. A similar list of names in found in I Chronicles 2:6. However, there they were the sons of one named Zerah. Here they are called the sons of one named Mahol. There apparently were two different families. However, these men evidently were men esteemed to be of great wisdom in Solomon's day as well. Whether the Ethan and Heman noted are the same as the composers of several Psalms is not clear. However, they well may have been. The following text refers to the music and poetry of Solomon.

In any event, Solomon's **fame was in all nations round about**. The renown of Solomon's name quickly spread throughout the nations of the day.

4:32-33 Not only was Solomon a wise ruler and political leader, he also was accomplished in the arts. **And he spake three thousand proverbs: and his songs were a thousand and five**. Many of these proverbs were divinely inspired as they were collected and written in the Book of Proverbs. Likewise some of his songs were recorded in the books of Ecclesiastes and the Song of Solomon.

In his works, Solomon 33 **spake of trees, from the cedar tree that *is* in Lebanon even unto the hyssop that springeth out of the wall: he spake also of beasts, and of fowl, and of creeping things, and of fishes**. Implied is that Solomon also spoke (or perhaps wrote) of the natural sciences, specifically noting the flora and fauna of the region.

4:34 Accordingly, **there came of all people to hear the wisdom of Solomon, from all kings of the earth, which had heard of his wisdom**. As the fame of this remarkable king spread across the civilized world, emissaries and even kings came to hear of his wisdom and knowledge.

Solomon's reign, in many ways, is a type of Christ in His millennial reign. However, as will be soon noted, Solomon would miserably fail. The difference between his majestic reign and that of Christ is that Solomon was a sinner. Moreover, he from the beginning compromised specific prohibitions in the Word of God as it pertained to him. That compromise and incipient disobedience would eventually bear its bitter fruit.

The last half of Solomon's life would be one of emptiness and frustration. He had all that any man could ever wish. Yet, he ended as utterly miserable. The reason lay in (1) his sinful nature and (2) his compromise of obedience to the Word of God. Though profoundly wise, his sin nature was his undoing. When Christ returns to rule and reign, none of these imperfections will be present.

* * * * *

***Overview of I Kings 5**: This next chapter of I Kings presents Solomon's preparations to build the Temple at Jerusalem. It describes his league with Hiram and him raising the necessary work force.*

5:1 After having fully established his kingdom, Solomon then turned his attention to building the Temple for which David his father had made preliminary preparation. **And Hiram king**

Understanding I Kings

of Tyre sent his servants unto Solomon; for he had heard that they had anointed him king in the room of his father: for Hiram was ever a lover of David. Hiram, king of Tyre, is mentioned previously in the Bible once in II Samuel 5:11. There is no record of hostilities between David and Hiram. Moreover, Hiram had provided materials and men to help build David's palace. Tyre was a principal city in Lebanon to the north. Thus, upon hearing of David's death, Hiram sent a diplomatic mission to Solomon because of his respect for David, Solomon's father.

5:2-4 In reply, **Solomon sent to Hiram, saying, 3 Thou knowest how that David my father could not build an house unto the name of the LORD his God for the wars which were about him on every side, until the LORD put them under the soles of his feet.** Solomon rehearsed to Hiram how that God would not allow David his father to build the Temple because of his bloody years as a warrior. David had thus built the kingdom, but God directed that his son rather than he would build the Temple at Jerusalem.

Solomon continued, **4 But now the LORD my God hath given me rest on every side, *so that there is* neither adversary nor evil occurrent.** Solomon was at peace with all nations. Not only had he no international adversaries, there was no "evil occurrent." The latter refers to no wars or hostilities taking place.

5:5-6 Continuing, Solomon indicated to Hiram, **behold, I purpose to build an house unto the name of the LORD my God, as the LORD spake unto David my father, saying, Thy son, whom I will set upon thy throne in thy room, he shall build an house unto my name.** Solomon was well aware that God had directed that he should be the one to build a permanent Temple to Jehovah God at Jerusalem. He therefore intended to do just that.

He thus requested Hiram to **6 command thou that they hew me cedar trees out of Lebanon; and my servants shall be with thy servants: and unto thee will I give hire for thy servants according to all that thou shalt appoint: for thou knowest that *there is* not among us any that can skill to hew timber like unto the Sidonians.** Solomon requested that Hiram cut of the famed cedars of Lebanon for the looming Temple construction project. Moreover, he offered to send a labor force to assist the Lebanese workers. He further offered to pay Hiram whatever he requested for services rendered. He also complimented the Lebanese for their skill in the timber and lumber industry, acknowledging that none in Israel could match their skills.

5:7-9 And it came to pass, when Hiram heard the words of Solomon, that he rejoiced greatly, and said, Blessed *be* the LORD this day, which hath given unto David a wise son over this great people. Hiram replied by first praising Jehovah God for giving David such a wise son. It is evident that Solomon wisely approached Hiram. Rather than irritating his neighbor, he made a friend.

Hiram therefore **8 sent to Solomon, saying, I have considered the things which thou sentest to me for: *and* I will do all thy desire concerning timber of cedar, and concerning timber of fir**. He further sent word back to Solomon that after considering Solomon's request that he would provide all that Solomon wished regarding cedar or fir timber. The latter (fir) can also refer to pine or cypress wood.

In addition, Hiram agreed that his **9 servants shall bring *them* down from Lebanon unto the sea: and I will convey them by sea in floats unto the place that thou shalt appoint me, and will cause them to be discharged there, and thou shalt receive *them*: and thou shalt accomplish my desire, in giving food for my household**. Hiram indicated that he would

Understanding I Kings

ship the required timber by rafts along the coast from Lebanon down to Israel. II Chronicles 2:16 indicates that the port of entry for the rafted timbers was at Joppa. In return, Hiram requested of Solomon payment in foodstuffs.

5:10-11 Therefore, **Hiram gave Solomon cedar trees and fir trees** *according to* **all his desire.** 11 **And Solomon gave Hiram twenty thousand measures of wheat** *for* **food to his household, and twenty measures of pure oil: thus gave Solomon to Hiram year by year.**

Solomon received the timber and lumber he needed for the Temple construction project. He in return provided 20,000 measures of wheat to Hiram. The word translated as **measure** (כֹּר *kor*) refers to 6.25 bushels of English dry measure. That translates into 125,000 bushels of wheat. In addition, Solomon agreed to send twenty measures of pure olive oil to Hiram. A 'kor' of liquid measure approximated 58 gallons. Thus, twenty measures thereof approximated 1,160 gallons of pure olive oil. The final phrase "year by year" apparently refers to the duration of the contract. As long as Hiram was providing the needed lumber, Solomon made payment in foodstuffs to Hiram accordingly.

In II Chronicles 2:10 others numbers are given. There, 20,000 measures of *beaten* wheat along with 20,000 measures of barley are noted. Also, 20,000 baths of oil and 20,000 baths of wine were provided. Some have imagined a discrepancy between these two records. A bath of liquid measure approximated ten gallons. Therefore, the account in II Chronicles speaks of approximately 200,000 gallons of olive oil.

The resolution of the problem however is simple. In the account in I Kings 5, the record is of payment of food for the *household* of Hiram. It amounted to a royalty to him. However, the account in II Chronicles recorded the payment of food for his workforce "the hewers that cut timber" sent by Hiram for the project. Solomon thus was to provide the provisions needed by Hiram's workforce in addition to paying him a royalty for his services rendered.

5:12 The sacred historian records, **And the LORD gave Solomon wisdom, as he promised him: and there was peace between Hiram and Solomon; and they two made a league together**. Evident is the wisdom given by God. Kings of lessor wisdom would be tempted to simply take what they wanted by force. Solomon certainly had the military power to do so. However, he rather wisely chose to work out a contractual agreement with his neighbor Hiram. The result of the wise agreement was peace between them. They accordingly made a **league** together. The latter is translated from the word (ברית) *berith* which has the sense of a 'covenant,' 'treaty,' or 'contract.'

5:13-14 Meanwhile, **king Solomon raised a levy out of all Israel; and the levy was thirty thousand men**. The word translated as **levy** (מס *mac*) in this context refers to a work force. Implied is that Solomon 'drafted' 30,000 men out of Israel for the impending construction project.

He thus **14 sent them to Lebanon, ten thousand a month by courses: a month they were in Lebanon, *and* two months at home: and Adoniram *was* over the levy**. Of this drafted workforce, 10,000 were on duty at a time while the other 20,000 remained at home tending to affairs at home. The Adoniram mentioned likely is the same noted as over the tax collection in Israel, noted in 4:16. These 30,000 men evidently were Israelites sent to Lebanon to assist in the work of felling the requisite timber there.

5:15-16 In addition to these, **Solomon had threescore and ten thousand that bare burdens, and fourscore thousand hewers in the mountains**. Solomon also employed 70,000

Understanding I Kings

men who were common laborers in the work. He also employed 80,000 quarrymen who quarried, dressed, squared, and shipped the massive amount of stone work necessary for the Temple. These were gentile workers according to II Chronicles 2:17. Furthermore, even the immediate foremen at the quarries were gentile in nature according to the account in II Chronicles.

These were **16 beside the chief of Solomon's officers which *were* over the work, three thousand and three hundred, which ruled over the people that wrought in the work**. Solomon thus employed 3,300 foremen over the work in the quarries. The mountains likely were in areas not distant from Jerusalem wherein was fine Dolomite limestone. Solomon provided his own officers as construction managers of the project. Precisely who the gentile laborers were and what their arrangements were is not noted either here or in II Chronicles. They are only noted there as "strangers that *were* in the land of Israel." Thus, 153,300 gentile laborers were employed in preparing the stonework for the Temple.

5:17-18 After the massive quarrying project, **the king commanded, and they brought great stones, costly stones, *and* hewed stones, to lay the foundation of the house**. The foundation stones of the Temple were massive and very expensive because of the enormous labor invested into their preparation and transportation to Jerusalem. These were for the foundation of the Temple on Mount Moriah.

18 And Solomon's builders and Hiram's builders did hew *them*, and the stonesquarers: so they prepared timber and stones to build the house. It appears that Hiram sent men to assist Solomon in the finishing and squaring of the blocks of stone for the Temple in addition to timber work. The stonework was finely finished and planed square in all dimensions. There was nothing rough or unfinished in the materials used for the Temple. The finest craftsmanship in the world of that day was employed in the preparation of the stonework and lumber for the Temple.

* * * * *

***Overview of I Kings 6:** This sixth chapter of I Kings provides the details of the Temple construction. Interjected is a message from God to Solomon during its construction promising His fullest blessing if Solomon would walk in His ways. The chapter then provides considerable particulars of the architectural details.*

6:1 Precise dating of when the construction of the Temple began is provided. **And it came to pass in the four hundred and eightieth year after the children of Israel were come out of the land of Egypt, in the fourth year of Solomon's reign over Israel, in the month Zif, which *is* the second month, that he began to build the house of the LORD.**

Dating from when Israel departed from Egypt, 480 years had elapsed. John Gill enumerates the chronology accordingly: 40 years in the wilderness; 17 years under Joshua; 299 years under the Judges; 80 years under Eli, Samuel, and Saul; 40 years under David; and 4 years under Solomon. That totals 480 years. Solomon was established in his kingdom. Preparations had been wisely made. Construction began in the second month of the ancient Hebrew calendar which would be analogous to the month of May. Thus, in the loveliness of springtime, work began on the Temple. (It is noteworthy that this one of a number of very specific date markers in the Bible.) The date of the exodus was 1491 B.C. The specific date thereof likely was the spring of the year 1011 B.C.

6:2 The general dimensions of the Temple proper are given. **And the house which king Solomon built for the**

Understanding I Kings

LORD, the length thereof *was* **threescore cubits, and the breadth thereof twenty** *cubits***, and the height thereof thirty cubits**. The dimensions given are of the Temple proper, not including its side chambers or massive courtyards. In modern measure, it was approximately 90 feet long, 30 feet wide, and 45 feet tall. The height evidently was not the same for the porch on the front. It was 120 cubits or 150 feet high.

6:3-6 Other architectural dimensions are given. **And the porch before the Temple of the house, twenty cubits** *was* **the length thereof, according to the breadth of the house;** *and* **ten cubits** *was* **the breadth thereof before the house. 4 And for the house he made windows of narrow lights.**

5 And against the wall of the house he built chambers round about, *against* **the walls of the house round about,** *both* **of the Temple and of the oracle: and he made chambers round about: 6 The nethermost chamber** *was* **five cubits broad, and the middle** *was* **six cubits broad, and the third** *was* **seven cubits broad: for without** *in the wall* **of the house he made narrowed rests round about, that** *the beams* **should not be fastened in the walls of the house.**

There was a porch across the front of the Temple structure adding another 15 feet to the overall length. There were narrow windows presumably along the length of the holy place, but apparently not in the holy of holies. These presumably had some sort of shuttering devices. Around the outer perimeter of the Temple structure were built rooms abutting the main structural walls. There is varying opinion as to the placement and size of these apartments. It is thought that there were three stories of these chambers built up around the outer perimeter of the Temple structure itself. These chambers apparently were for the use of the priests as well as other appurtenant uses.

Evidently, on the ground floor were the smallest rooms. (The word translated as **nethermost** {תחתון *tachtown*} simply means 'lowest.') These were about 7.5 feet wide. The second floor of apartments were slightly larger being 9 feet wide. The top story was 10.5 feet wide. The depth of the rooms is not noted. The design was such that with each story, the main structural wall of the Temple itself provide 'nests' or bearing places for the beams of the side stories. This evidently was by means of a gradation of the thickness of the wall as it rose up. It became narrower with each story allowing a ledge for the support timbers of each floor. No holes for structural support were thus made into the Temple itself.

6:7 Detail of the material and construction methods are noted. **And the house, when it was in building, was built of stone made ready before it was brought thither: so that there was neither hammer nor axe *nor* any tool of iron heard in the house, while it was in building.** The masonry stonework of the Temple was prepared offsite. The cutting, squaring, and finishing of the stonework was not done at the Temple site. Therefore, there was no sound of iron tools during the construction of the Temple proper. The masonry stones were completely finished when they arrived at the Temple site. They only had to be laid in their proper sequence. Various reasons have been advanced as to why this was accomplished.

One thing seems clear however. The building stones were perfectly fitted before they arrived. Great skill and craftsmanship is evident. There may be spiritual truth hinted at as well in how the church, as a Temple to God is "fitly framed together" (Ephesians 2:20). The work of God is always perfect. It might even be assumed that there was providential intervention in seeing that there was absolute perfection in the craftsmanship of the work.

6:8-10 Further dimensions regarding the architectural details are noted. **The door for the middle chamber *was* in the**

Understanding I Kings

right side of the house: and they went up with winding stairs into the middle *chamber*, and out of the middle into the third. Regarding the chambers built around the perimeter of the holy place, there was a door on the right (south) side of the structure. Also there was a winding staircase to second level which continued on up to the third story.

In rising the structure to its height, **9 so he built the house, and finished it; and covered the house with beams and boards of cedar.** The roof system of the structure was with beams and boards of cedar lumber.

10 And *then* he built chambers against all the house, five cubits high: and they rested on the house *with* timber of cedar. Apparently, the chambers on the side of the Temple had ceilings 7.5 feet high. These were framed and built with cedar lumber. Implied is that the floor above was cedar as well.

6:11-13 Apparently during the construction of the Temple, **the word of the LORD came to Solomon, saying, 12 *Concerning* this house which thou art in building, if thou wilt walk in my statutes, and execute my judgments, and keep all my commandments to walk in them; then will I perform my word with thee, which I spake unto David thy father: 13 And I will dwell among the children of Israel, and will not forsake my people Israel.**

In a fashion not described, God spoke to Solomon, warning him to utterly obey Him. God specified in threefold fashion His condition for fulfilling the covenant He had made with David. Those three conditions were if Solomon would (1) "walk in my statutes" and (2) "execute my judgments" and (3) "keep all my commandments to walk in them."

Then, God promised that he would perform His word to Solomon which He had promised David. He furthermore would dwell amongst Israel and not forsake them. But notice that the fundamental condition for God's promised blessing was simple obedience to His Word. There was nothing complicated about it. See II Samuel 7:12-16.

6:14 Summary is therefore made of the completion of the project. **So Solomon built the house, and finished it.**

6:15-18 The sacred historian therefore proceeds with the details of the actual construction of the Temple. **And he built the walls of the house within with boards of cedar, both the floor of the house, and the walls of the cieling:** *and* **he covered** *them* **on the inside with wood, and covered the floor of the house with planks of fir.** 16 **And he built twenty cubits on the sides of the house, both the floor and the walls with boards of cedar: he even built** *them* **for it within,** *even* **for the oracle,** *even* **for the most holy** *place***.** 17 **And the house, that** *is***, the Temple before it, was forty cubits** *long***.** 18 **And the cedar of the house within** *was* **carved with knops and open flowers: all** *was* **cedar; there was no stone seen.**

Though the structural building material was primarily of finely-crafted masonry stonework, the interior trim work is noted here. The interior surfaces of the Temple were of inlaid cedar with framing of fir. This cedar inlay evidently rose up to a height of 30 feet to the ceiling. The holy place was forty cubits (60 feet) long and the oracle (the holy of holies) was twenty cubits (30 feet) in all dimensions. The finely crafted trim work of the interior was carved with intricate circular patterns (**knops**) as well as delicate carved flowers. The entire interior was covered with finely finished and exquisitely carved work so that no stonework was seen from the inside.

6:20 The dimensions of the holy of holies are thus noted. **And the oracle in the forepart** *was* **twenty cubits in length, and twenty cubits in breadth, and twenty cubits in the height thereof: and he overlaid it with pure gold; and** *so*

covered the altar *which was of* cedar. The word translated as **oracle** (דביר *dabiyr*) is another name for the holy of holies of the Temple. It was thirty feet in all dimensions. This entire room was overlaid or covered with pure gold. The mention to the altar of cedar being covered with gold is somewhat enigmatic. Some have suggested that it was the altar of incense. However, no other pieces of interior furniture are here noted. Furthermore, such an implement for fire would not be constructed of cedar wood with a thin veneer of gold. What rather may be in view is the area where the altar of incense would be placed.

6:21-22 Further description of the gold overlay is described. **So Solomon overlaid the house within with pure gold: and he made a partition by the chains of gold before the oracle; and he overlaid it with gold. 22 And the whole house he overlaid with gold, until he had finished all the house: also the whole altar that *was* by the oracle he overlaid with gold.**

The entire interior of the Temple itself was covered with pure gold. This included all the fine carved woodwork therein. II Chronicles 3:8 notes that 600 talents of gold were used for just this portion of the project. Where the veil would be placed, gold chains were prepared for further ornamentation of that area. Again the mention of the altar may refer to the altar of incense, but more likely refers to the area wherein that piece of furniture would be placed. It may have been a raised platform.

6:23-28 Details of the golden cherubim to be placed in the holy of holies is noted. **And within the oracle he made two cherubims *of* olive tree, *each* ten cubits high. 24 And five cubits *was* the one wing of the cherub, and five cubits the other wing of the cherub: from the uttermost part of the one wing unto the uttermost part of the other *were* ten cubits. 25 And the other cherub *was* ten cubits: both the cherubims**

were **of one measure and one size. 26 The height of the one cherub** *was* **ten cubits, and so** *was it* **of the other cherub.**

27 And he set the cherubims within the inner house: and they stretched forth the wings of the cherubims, so that the wing of the one touched the *one* **wall, and the wing of the other cherub touched the other wall; and their wings touched one another in the midst of the house. 28 And he overlaid the cherubims with gold.**

The cherubims were likenesses of angels. They were carved from olive wood each and were twenty feet in height. Their outstretched wings extended inward from each side so that their combined wingspans reached from one side of the sanctuary to the other. These angelic likenesses were completely overlaid with gold.

6:29-30 Further details regarding the artwork into the interior woodwork is noted. **And he carved all the walls of the house round about with carved figures of cherubims and palm trees and open flowers, within and without. 30 And the floor of the house he overlaid with gold, within and without.** The interior of the woodwork of the Temple was further adorned with fine carvings of cherubims and the flora of the region. The reference to "within and without" may indicate that such exquisite artwork was on both the interior of the holy of holies as well as the rest of the interior of the Temple. The entire interior of the Temple was overlaid with gold including the floor.

6:31-35 Further details regarding the doors and their ornamentation are noted. **And for the entering of the oracle he made doors** *of* **olive tree: the lintel** *and* **side posts** *were* **a fifth part** *of the wall*. Though the final entrance into the holy of holies (the oracle) was the veil, evidently there were two doors made of olive wood in front of the veil. The reference to it being the "fifth part *of the wall"* may mean that they were four cubits (six feet) in height or perhaps in width. Though not specifically stated, it may well be assumed that they were covered with gold as well.

32 The two doors also *were of* olive tree; and he carved upon them carvings of cherubims and palm trees and open flowers, and overlaid *them* with gold, and spread gold upon the cherubims, and upon the palm trees. 33 So also made he for the door of the Temple posts *of* olive tree, a fourth part *of the wall.*

34 And the two doors *were of* fir tree: the two leaves of the one door *were* folding, and the two leaves of the other door *were* folding. 35 And he carved *thereon* cherubims and palm trees and open flowers: and covered *them* with gold fitted upon the carved work.

These doors evidently were the main gates into the Temple itself. These had finely carved cherubims, palm trees, and flowers carved into the woodwork as well. These also were overlaid with gold. The door frames were apparently of olive wood though the actual doors themselves were of fir. These are noted as being "a fourth part *of the wall.*" This gate was apparently five cubits in width or 7.5 feet wide. Evidently the two leaves of the doors folded into themselves. This gateway was again finely carved with similar carvings and all was overlaid with gold.

6:36 Some details of the courtyard are mentioned. **And he built the inner court with three rows of hewed stone, and a row of cedar beams.** The inner court likely refers to the court of the priests in distinction to the court of the people. This courtyard wall was of fine cut masonry stonework and trimmed along the top with cedar trim. Jewish authorities indicate that this wall was only 4.5 feet in height so that the common people could see into the inner court.

6:37-38 Final details pertaining to the construction time is noted. **In the fourth year was the foundation of the house of the LORD laid, in the month Zif: 38 And in the eleventh year, in the month Bul, which *is* the eighth month, was the house finished throughout all the parts thereof, and according to all the fashion of it. So was he seven years in building it.**

In May of the fourth year of Solomon's reign, the work on the Temple of Jehovah commenced. It was finished seven and one-half years later. The writer rounds the number off to seven years of construction. That number will take added significance in the next chapter when compared to the length of time Solomon spent in building his own palace.

* * * * *

Overview of I Kings 7: *Record is made of some of the details of the building of Solomon's own house as well as further details of the fixtures of the Temple of God.*

7:1 In distinction to the final comment of chapter 6, the sacred writer makes a revealing statement: **But Solomon was building his own house thirteen years, and he finished all his house**. Hinted at is the coming spiritual declension of Solomon. He spent seven years building God's house, but thirteen in building his own. Some have argued that he merely made haste in building the Temple. However, it rather seems that Solomon invested more time and energy in his own personal construction project. It portended his later self indulgence and his turning away from serving the Lord.

7:2-12 Considerable detail is given of the architectural grandeur of Solomon's palace. **He built also the house of the forest of Lebanon; the length thereof *was* an hundred**

Understanding I Kings

cubits, and the breadth thereof fifty cubits, and the height thereof thirty cubits, upon four rows of cedar pillars, with cedar beams upon the pillars.

His palace at Jerusalem was designed and built with cedar timbers from Lebanon. (Some have thought that this palace was actually built in Lebanon as a 'summer' home. However, it would rather seem that the structure detailed below was his palace at Jerusalem and built primarily with timber from Lebanon.) Translated into modern dimensions, this palace occupied 11,250 square feet and was about four stories high. Its apparent primary structural system was that of cedar beams.

Moreover, 3 *it was* **covered with cedar above upon the beams, that** *lay* **on forty five pillars, fifteen** *in* **a row.** This may refer to at least a second floor and possibly higher. In any event, his home was built both structurally as well as finished in cedar wood. It must have been beautiful both in its scent and woodwork.

Further architectural details are presented in that **4** *there* **were windows** *in* **three rows, and light** *was* **against light** *in* **three ranks. 5 And all the doors and posts** *were* **square, with the windows: and light** *was* **against light** *in* **three ranks.** It appears that there were many large windows in this palace. It apparently had three floors with windows on each level.

Also, **6 he made a porch of pillars; the length thereof** *was* **fifty cubits, and the breadth thereof thirty cubits: and the porch** *was* **before them: and the** *other* **pillars and the thick beam** *were* **before them.** Attached to the main house was a porch which extended out 45 feet and apparently was 75 feet in length. **7 Then he made a porch for the throne where he might judge,** *even* **the porch of judgment: and** *it was* **covered with cedar from one side of the floor to the other.** In addition to the fore-mentioned porch, Solomon built another one in which he apparently placed his throne of ivory. See I Kings

10:18. This court for judgment was finished in exquisite cedar woodwork.

In addition, **8 his house where he dwelt *had* another court within the porch, *which* was of the like work**. The latter may have been his own personal living quarters. **Solomon made also an house for Pharaoh's daughter, whom he had taken *to wife*, like unto this porch**. As mentioned in 3:1, Solomon's first wife evidently was Pharaoh's daughter. She seemed to hold a place higher than his many later additional wives. He constructed a palace just for her like unto his own quarters.

In addition to the evident structural cedar and trim work, these palaces also had substantial cut stone masonry. **9 All these *were of* costly stones, according to the measures of hewed stones, sawed with saws, within and without, even from the foundation unto the coping, and *so* on the outside toward the great court**. The mention of "costly stones" has the thought of expensive stone work. These were not rough hewn, but finely cut, trimmed, polished, and finished. It is not known if there was marble available. However, there is an abundance of Dolomite limestone in this region of Israel which can be cut and finished to an elegant appearance. This evidently was interspersed architecturally throughout the structures.

10 And the foundation *was of* costly stones, even great stones, stones of ten cubits, and stones of eight cubits. The description of foundation stones measuring ten and eight cubit indicates huge stonework. These foundation stones were 12 by 15 feet in dimension. The weight of such stones without doubt was immense indicating the massive number of men needed to cut, fit, and place them.

Moreover, **11 above *were* costly stones, after the measures of hewed stones, and cedars**. His palace was erect-ed of very expensive stone masonry and cedar woodwork. **12 And the great court round about *was* with three rows of hewed stones, and a row of cedar beams, both for the inner court** of the house of the LORD, and for the porch of the house. Surrounding Solomon's palace were three rows of pil-lars with a structural cap of cedar beams. There is similar description made of the Temple in I Kings 6:36. Implied is that Solomon's palace may have been adjacent to the Temple.

7:13-14 The focus of the text now shifts back to details regarding the erection of the Temple. **And king Solomon sent and fetched Hiram out of Tyre.** 14 **He** *was* **a widow's son of the tribe of Naphtali, and his father** *was* **a man of Tyre, a worker in brass: and he was filled with wisdom, and understanding, and cunning to work all works in brass. And he came to king Solomon, and wrought all his work.** The Hiram mentioned here in all likelihood is not the same as Hiram king of Tyre. From II Chronicles 2:13, it appears that this Hiram was a skilled brass worker with the same name as the king of Tyre. His mother was an Israelite. His specialty seems to have been as a brass founder.

7:15-20 Details of his workmanship are further noted. **For he cast two pillars of brass, of eighteen cubits high apiece: and a line of twelve cubits did compass either of them about.** 16 **And he made two chapiters** *of* **molten brass, to set upon the tops of the pillars: the height of the one chapiter** *was* **five cubits, and the height of the other chapiter** *was* **five cubits.**
The two brass pillars described evidently were two tall decorative pillars set before the main door into the Temple. Eighteen cubits would approximate twenty-seven feet high. The mention of "a line of twelve cubits did compass either of them about" evidently refers to their circumference. The *chapiters* mentioned refer to the 'capitals' (decorative crowns) atop the pillars. (In II Chronicles 3:15, these same pillars are described as being thirty-five cubits tall. The apparent discrepancy is resolved in that the dimension there apparently includes

the stone bases upon which each brass pillar sat. The brass pillar itself was eighteen cubits tall, but its stone base was another seventeen cubits in height. Atop all of this was the capitals {chapiters} of an additional five cubits.) Thus, the overall height of the pillars and including their bases and capitals was forty cubits (sixty feet). That approximates the height of a six story building. This front 'porch' with its massive pillars towered above the rest of the Temple itself.

Further architectural details are provided. **17 And nets of checker work, and wreaths of chain work, for the chapiters which *were* upon the top of the pillars; seven for the one chapiter, and seven for the other chapiter.** The details describe the ornamental carving of the capitals. The motif was of treetops intertwined (wreaths of chain work) together. There apparently were seven *wreaths* or treetops carved onto each capital.

Furthermore, **18 he made the pillars, and two rows round about upon the one network, to cover the chapiters that *were* upon the top, with pomegranates: and so did he for the other chapiter.** Further decorative ornamentation is described. There apparently were two rows of figures like pomegranates upon the branch work that covered the capitals atop each of the pillars. In addition, **19 the chapiters that *were* upon the top of the pillars *were* of lily work in the porch, four cubits.** Intertwined in the carved artwork of the capitals were open flowers like lilies. These evidently were on the lower four cubits of each capital.

Also, **20 the chapiters upon the two pillars *had pomegranates* also above, over against the belly which *was* by the network: and the pomegranates *were* two hundred in rows round about upon the other chapiter.** Intertwined amidst the rest of this intricate artwork were two-hundred carved pomegranates on each capital. Thus, the pillars and their capitals were strikingly intricate in their artistic work.

Understanding I Kings

7:21-22 Finally, Hiram **set up the pillars in the porch of the Temple: and he set up the right pillar, and called the name thereof Jachin: and he set up the left pillar, and called the name thereof Boaz. 22 And upon the top of the pillars** *was* **lily work: so was the work of the pillars finished**. These massive ornamented pillars were placed at the porch of the front of the Temple on each side of the main entrance thereof. The pillar to right he named **Jachin** which means 'established' or 'he shall establish (it).' The thought likely is that God would establish the Temple. The pillar to the left was named **Boaz** which means 'strength' or 'in it is strength.' A final note of further ornamentation of lily work is noted. The text will now move on to other details.

7:23-26 The detailed description now moves to the large basin (reservoir) constructed for the new Temple. **And he made a molten sea, ten cubits from the one brim to the other:** *it was* **round all about, and his height** *was* **five cubits: and a line of thirty cubits did compass it round about**. Referred to is a large **sea** or vessel for water which was of cast brass. It is described as being fifteen feet in diameter, seven and one-half feet deep with a circumference of forty-five feet.

Critics have quickly pointed out that circumference is 3.1412 times the diameter and hence the biblical description is in error. However, there are several comments to that. (1) The noted circumference may be in round numbers rather than a precise measurement. (2) Or, as John Gill notes, "The circumference given may be for the inside circumference and the diameter may be the diameter including the thickness of the rim. This would yield a very accurate mathematical result for the inside circumference of thirty cubits. The outside circumference would be about 31.4 cubits giving a rim thickness of four inches or an hand breadth agreeing with 1Kings 7:26." (3) Gill also comments, "In 1Kings 7:26 we read the vessel 'was wrought like the brim of a cup.' That is the brim on the top of the vessel was wider than the main part of the vessel. The diameter would be given for the brim. If the brim or lip extended about four inches past the main body of the vessel then the outside circumference of the main part of the vessel would be exactly thirty cubits."

This molten sea (laver) was placed beside the main Temple structure as a source of water for ceremonial cleansings. Further details are noted. **24 And under the brim of it round about *there were* knops compassing it, ten in a cubit, compassing the sea round about: the knops *were* cast in two rows, when it was cast**.

A *knop* was a spherical or egg-shaped ornament. These evidently were cast all around the circumference of the *sea* with ten such decorative embellishments per cubit. Furthermore, there were two parallel rows of this ornamentation.

The entire massive laver rested upon **25 twelve oxen, three looking toward the north, and three looking toward the west, and three looking toward the south, and three looking toward the east: and the sea *was set* above upon them, and all their hinder parts *were* inward**. The twelve oxen evidently were of cast brass and were the support upon which the laver rested. It has been estimated that the *sea* and its supporting brazen oxen weighed more than 837,500 pounds. That apparently was all solid brass.

This elaborate vessel is additionally described as being **26 an hand breadth thick, and the brim thereof was wrought like the brim of a cup, with flowers of lilies: it contained two thousand baths**. Apparently, the thickness of the sea was about four inches (a hand breadth). Its brim was also intricately decorated with graven lilies. The sea is described as *containing* 2,000 baths. A bath of liquid measure approximates forty liters or roughly ten gallons. Hence, the sea was filled to a measure of approximately 20,000 gallons of water.

Understanding I Kings

In II Chronicles 4:5 it is noted that this sea held 3,000 baths of water. This apparent discrepancy is resolved in the simple solution that the sea ordinarily was not filled to the brim. It normally *contained* 2,000 baths of water though if filled to the brim, it could hold 3,000 baths. Other skeptics have claimed a vessel of such dimensions could not hold that amount of water. However, their criticism is based on the assumption that the 'sea' was a shallow bowl or saucer in its shape. It very well may have been more like unto a rounded 'pot.' In that configuration, it surely could hold such quantities of water. Though not noted, because of the height of the 'sea' (it surely must have been at least ten feet atop its base), there may have been 'spickets' from whence to draw water from the reservoir above.

7:27-39 Following is a description of ten smaller lavers around the large sea. These evidently were the working lavers from whence the priests washed themselves and the various sacrifices. **And he made ten bases of brass; four cubits *was* the length of one base, and four cubits the breadth thereof, and three cubits the height of it**. These bases (or pedestals) were made of solid brass and were approximately six feet square and four and one half feet tall. Upon these pedestals the working lavers were placed.

Details regarding these bases follows. **28 And the work of the bases *was* on this *manner*: they had borders, and the borders *were* between the ledges: 29 And on the borders that *were* between the ledges *were* lions, oxen, and cherubims: and upon the ledges *there was* a base above: and beneath the lions and oxen *were* certain additions made of thin work**. These pedestal bases of the lavers were also intricately decorated with graven artwork. Part of the ornamentation were carvings of lions, oxen, and cherubims. The lion may refer to royalty of the Messiah, the oxen to His servant status and possibly His self-sacrifice. The cherubims were depictions of angelic creatures and thus the heavenly nature of God Himself. The word translated as **ledges** (שלב *shalab*) essentially refers to joints. Gill suggests that the reference to **thin work** refers to "shelving plates of brass at the bottom of the borders and bars, where the priests washed the sacrifice; the filth of which ran off the easier, through the angle of them."

30 And every base had four brasen wheels, and plates of brass: and the four corners thereof had undersetters: under the laver *were* **undersetters molten, at the side of every addition**. Under each pedestal base of the lavers were brass wheels. There remains debate whether these wheels were functional or were merely ornamental. It would seem that they served some functional purpose to move the lavers as needed. The succeeding descriptions will lend credence to them being mobile. The word translated as **undersetters** (כתף *katheph*) simply refers to 'undercarriages.'

Further details of the pedestals are noted. 31 **And the mouth of it within the chapter and above** *was* **a cubit: but the mouth thereof** *was* **round** *after* **the work of the base, a cubit and an half: and also upon the mouth of it** *were* **gravings with their borders, foursquare, not round**. Described apparently is the actual receptacle of which the lavers themselves rested upon each pedestal base. This evidently was a hemispheric well into which the laver was placed.

Further details regarding the undercarriage and wheels of these bases are noted. 32 **And under the borders** *were* **four wheels; and the axletrees of the wheels** *were joined* **to the base: and the height of a wheel** *was* **a cubit and half a cubit. 33 And the work of the wheels** *was* **like the work of a chariot wheel: their axletrees, and their naves, and their felloes, and their spokes,** *were* **all molten. 34 And** *there* **were four undersetters to the four corners of one base:** *and* **the undersetters** *were* **of the very base itself**. It appears that the lavers and their bases were designed to be moved. All of the mentioned hardware was of solid brass. Notice the mention of axletrees, naves, felloes, and spokes. These were the running gear referring to hubs, spokes, pivot points, and axles. All of the undercarriages were of solid brass and apparently worked so that the lavers could be moved.

Final details are given of the top of the bases themselves. **35 And in the top of the base *was there* a round compass of half a cubit high: and on the top of the base the ledges thereof and the borders thereof *were* of the same. 36 For on the plates of the ledges thereof, and on the borders thereof, he graved cherubims, lions, and palm trees, according to the proportion of every one, and additions round about. 37 After this *manner* he made the ten bases: all of them had one casting, one measure, *and* one size.** Recall that the *ledges* refers to joints. At the various joints of the design were engraved further ornamentation of cherubims, lions, and palm trees. Thus the bases were all made of identical dimension and design.

Atop these intricately designed pedestal bases were placed the working lavers for the use of the priests. **38 Then made he ten lavers of brass: one laver contained forty baths: *and* every laver was four cubits: *and* upon every one of the ten bases one laver. 39 And he put five bases on the right side of the house, and five on the left side of the house: and he set the sea on the right side of the house eastward over against the south.**

Five solid brass lavers were placed on each side of the main Temple structure. Each laver contained approximately 400 gallons of water. Each was six feet in diameter.

Final comment is made regarding the *sea*. It was apparently placed on the north side of the main Temple structure which from the east is called the right. The phrase "over against the south" has the idea of the opposite direction—in this case from the south. Apparently from this large reservoir, water was routinely drawn to supply the ten smaller lavers used in the day-to-day operations of the Temple.

7:40-45 Summary is thus made of the brass castings made by Hiram for Solomon. **And Hiram made the lavers, and the shovels, and the basons. So Hiram made an end of doing all the work that he made king Solomon for the house of the LORD.** Even smaller utensils of brass such as shovels for utility work and basins are mentioned. Some have suggested that the lavers mentioned here were actually pots to collect ashes.

The sacred writer thus summarizes Hiram's work: **41 The two pillars, and the *two* bowls of the chapiters that *were* on the top of the two pillars; and the two networks, to cover the two bowls of the chapiters which *were* upon the top of the pillars; 42 And four hundred pomegranates for the two networks, *even* two rows of pomegranates for one network, to cover the two bowls of the chapiters that *were* upon the pillars;**

43 And the ten bases, and ten lavers on the bases; 44 And one sea, and twelve oxen under the sea; 45 And the pots, and the shovels, and the basons: and all these vessels, which Hiram made to king Solomon for the house of the LORD, *were of* bright brass. The mention of *bright brass* has the idea of polished or furbished brass. It was bright and shiny.

7:46 The place whence Hiram did his founding is noted as **in the plain of Jordan did the king cast them, in the clay ground between Succoth and Zarthan.** These locales were in the Jordan River valley. Succoth was thought to be on the east side and Zarthan the place whence Joshua led Israel across the Jordan River. Implicit is the considerable transportation engineering which must have been required. First, the Jordan River had to be bridged or ferried. Then, these substantial castings, especially the molten sea, had to be transported on the

Understanding I Kings

circuitous route up through the mountains to Jerusalem. That in itself must have been a marvel of engineering of that day.

7:47 Further note is made that **Solomon left all the vessels *unweighed*, because they were exceeding many: neither was the weight of the brass found out**. Though the price of such vast of amounts of brass work must have been substantial, Solomon never bothered to determine the weight thereof.

7:48-50 And Solomon made all the vessels that *pertained* unto the house of the LORD: the altar of gold, and the table of gold, whereupon the shewbread *was*, 49 And the candlesticks of pure gold, five on the right *side*, and five on the left, before the oracle, with the flowers, and the lamps, and the tongs *of* gold, 50 And the bowls, and the snuffers, and the basons, and the spoons, and the censers *of* pure gold; and the hinges *of* gold, *both* for the doors of the inner house, the most holy *place, and* for the doors of the house, *to wit*, of the Temple.

Of interest is that though considerable detail was presented regarding the brass fixtures of the Temple, the more valuable fixtures of gold are only mentioned in summary fashion. Implicit is that these were made as exact duplicates of that which had originally been in the Tabernacle. Also implied is that they still remained to that day. However, Solomon remade them anew for the new Temple. These were described in detail in the book of Exodus. Also mentioned here were the gold hinges for both the inner and outer doors of the Temple. Significant again is that the most sacred utensils and fixtures of the Temple were pure gold.

7:51 So was ended all the work that king Solomon made for the house of the LORD. And Solomon brought in the things which David his father had dedicated; *even* the

silver, and the gold, and the vessels, did he put among the treasures of the house of the LORD. All the gold and silver which David had accumulated for the Temple were now placed into its treasuries. The later years of Solomon surely would manifest spiritual declension. It would seem that his backsliding took place not too long after he finished the construction of the Temple. He then got away from doing God's work and then got busy building his own palace. It likely was then that he began building his harem. A simple lesson remains. When a person gets away from doing God's work, he is easy prey to be distracted by the devil. That seems to have been the case with Solomon.

* * * * *

Overview of I Kings 8: *This lengthy chapter records the ark of the covenant being brought into the completed Temple. This is followed by the sermon and prayer of dedication by Solomon along with his praise to God for His goodness. Finally, record is made of the great sacrifice made by Solomon and the rejoicing of the people.*

8:1-3 Then Solomon assembled the elders of Israel, and all the heads of the tribes, the chief of the fathers of the children of Israel, unto king Solomon in Jerusalem, that they might bring up the ark of the covenant of the LORD out of the city of David, which *is* Zion. Upon completion of the Temple, record is made of Solomon gathering the leadership of the nation of Israel together to formally move the ark of the covenant to its new place. Of interest is the notation that the ark of the covenant had formerly rested in the city of David. That was a section of east Jerusalem facing the Mount of Olives whence David had originally built his palace. However, now

Understanding I Kings

the Temple had been completed atop Mount Moriah just to the north which was the highest hill in Jerusalem.

2 And all the men of Israel assembled themselves unto king Solomon at the feast in the month Ethanim, which *is* the seventh month. It would appear that not only did the leadership of the nation assemble at Jerusalem, but all the men of the nation were invited as well. The month *Ethanim* is the seventh Jewish month, corresponding to modern October or early November. It was so named because permanent streams still flowed. The word literally means *enduring*. In any event, in the mid-Autumn of that year, all adult men of the nation gathered at Jerusalem for the official moving of the ark to the Temple. That must have been hundreds of thousands if not more than a million men.

As prescribed by the Law of Moses, **3 all the elders of Israel came, and the priests took up the ark.** Solomon did not make the initial error of his father in attempting to move the ark. The priests of God, the descendants of Aaron, took the ark upon their shoulders and carried it up to the Temple.

8:4-5 And they brought up the ark of the LORD, and the tabernacle of the congregation, and all the holy vessels that *were* in the tabernacle, even those did the priests and the Levites bring up. What is evident is that not only was the ark moved to its new location in the recently finished Temple, but also all that remained of the Tabernacle as well (its sacred furniture and utensils). Implicit is that the old Tabernacle had been kept throughout the 450 years since Joshua entered the land. It likely was not in good condition. However, a new Temple was now ready. Also implied is that the various pieces of furniture and utensils dedicated for use at the Tabernacle still existed and they were brought to the new Temple as well.

Thus, **5 king Solomon, and all the congregation of Israel, that were assembled unto him, *were* with him before the**

ark, sacrificing sheep and oxen, that could not be told nor numbered for multitude. On this great day in Israel, innumerable sacrifices were offered to Jehovah God. So great was the worship and rejoicing on that day.

8:6-9 And the priests brought in the ark of the covenant of the LORD unto his place, into the oracle of the house, to the most holy *place,* *even* **under the wings of the cherubims**. The word translated as **oracle** (דביר *dabiyr*) refers to the holy of holies. There, the ark was placed between the outstretched wings of the golden cherubim(s). **7 For the cherubims spread forth** *their* **two wings over the place of the ark, and the cherubims covered the ark and the staves thereof above**. It should not be inferred that the cherubim(s) were alive, but rather they were made of gold. However, the manner in which they were designed was such that their wings spread out over the ark from above.

Thus, **8 the priests drew out the staves, that the ends of the staves were seen out in the holy** *place* **before the oracle, and they were not seen without: and there they are unto this day**. The final thought here likely is that the priests withdrew the staves of the ark and placed them such that the ends thereof could be seen in the antechamber (the holy place). This may have been so that a small portion of the staves were visible should the ark ever have to be moved.

Comment is also made that **9** *there was* **nothing in the ark save the two tables of stone, which Moses put there at Horeb, when the LORD made** *a covenant* **with the children of Israel, when they came out of the land of Egypt**. Note should be made that all that was *in* the ark were the tables of stone which contained the Ten Commandments. Hebrews 9:4 indicates that at some other time other sacred items (Aaron's rod that budded, a golden pot of manna, and a golden censer) were also located in the holy of holies, but not in the ark.

8:10-11 With the installation of the ark of the covenant in the completed Temple, **it came to pass, when the priests were come out of the holy *place*, that the cloud filled the house of the LORD, 11 So that the priests could not stand to minister because of the cloud: for the glory of the LORD had filled the house of the LORD.** The *cloud* mentioned in conjunction with the "glory of the Lord" mentioned next undoubtedly refers to the Shekinah glory of God. Though the word "Shekinah" does not appear as such in the Bible and is an interpretation of Jewish commentators, it refers to the abiding presence of God's glory. God placed His approval upon the proceedings just taken place and sent a manifestation of His glory into the Temple. The priests could only flee for safety lest they be consumed thereby.

8:12-13 Upon witnessing the proceedings, Solomon rose to make introductory comments. **The LORD said that he would dwell in the thick darkness. 13 I have surely built thee an house to dwell in, a settled place for thee to abide in for ever.** Solomon's reference to thick darkness may refer to the darkness of the uninhabited holy of holies. The room was without windows or light and thus dark. However, as the Shekinah glory of God descended, it filled that holy room with the brilliant light of the glory of God. Solomon thus notes that he had built such a permanent house for God's earthly presence to dwell in perpetuity.

8:14-16 And the king turned his face about, and blessed all the congregation of Israel: (and all the congregation of Israel stood;) 15 And he said, Blessed *be* the LORD God of Israel, which spake with his mouth unto David my father, and hath with his hand fulfilled *it*. In respect to their king, the assembled throng of Israel rose to their feet as he began to speak unto them. Solomon thus began his remarks by praising the Lord God of Israel. He recalled how that God first described the building of the Temple with David, his father. Now, by God's permission, the work of the Temple was complete. Solomon continued, speaking on behalf of God that 16 **since the day that I brought forth my people Israel out of Egypt, I chose no city out of all the tribes of Israel to build an house, that my name might be therein; but I chose David to be over my people Israel**. Though God had not officially chosen a city in which to dwell amongst His people, He had chosen a king. Through that king (David), He made known His choice of a city.

8:17-19 Continuing to speak on behalf of God, Solomon recounted, **And it was in the heart of David my father to build an house for the name of the LORD God of Israel. 18 And the LORD said unto David my father, Whereas it was in thine heart to build an house unto my name, thou didst well that it was in thine heart. 19 Nevertheless thou shalt not build the house; but thy son that shall come forth out of thy loins, he shall build the house unto my name**. Solomon thus rehearsed the history how that God would not allow David to build the Temple, but rather that his son would be allowed to do so. See II Samuel 7: 3-13.

8:20-21 Solomon therefore verified how that God fulfilled the promise which He made to David. **And the LORD hath performed his word that he spake, and I am risen up in the room of David my father, and sit on the throne of Israel, as the LORD promised, and have built an house for the name of the LORD God of Israel. 21 And I have set there a place for the ark, wherein *is* the covenant of the LORD, which he made with our fathers, when he brought them out of the land of Egypt**.

The reference to Solomon being in the "room of David" essentially refers to him being David's successor. He thus accomplished that which was not only the desire of his father,

David, but also of the Lord His God. The Temple with the now active Shekinah glory of God was a testimony to the covenant God had made with their forefathers.

8:22 Solomon therefore prepared to pray a great prayer of dedication for the inauguration of the new Temple. **And Solomon stood before the altar of the LORD in the presence of all the congregation of Israel, and spread forth his hands toward heaven**. The altar in question evidently was the great brasen altar in the court of the priests. The sacred historian speaks of all the congregation of the Israel being present. First, that refers to only males. Secondly, detail is not provided whether or not the *congregation* was in that court or could only see and hear through open gates what was going on therein.

Dimensions are not given of the size of the outer courts of the Temple. In the later Temple of Herod, the overall complex occupied thirty-six acres. Solomon's Temple complex undoubtedly was smaller, but still likely substantial. The phrase "all the congregation of Israel" literally has the sense of simply "the assembly of Israel." Whether that included all the males of the nation or just its assembled leadership is not clear. However the crowd was assembled, it must have been a spectacular event. Solomon thus stood and "spread forth his hands toward heaven."

8:23-24 His great prayer of dedication began with praise to Jehovah God. **And he said, LORD God of Israel, *there is* no God like thee, in heaven above, or on earth beneath, who keepest covenant and mercy with thy servants that walk before thee with all their heart: 24 Who hast kept with thy servant David my father that thou promisedst him: thou spakest also with thy mouth, and hast fulfilled *it* with thine hand, as *it is* this day**. This great prayer began with Solomon praising God for keeping His Word and for His great mercy to

His servants who obeyed Him. Moreover, Solomon acknowledged that there is only one true God. All heathen gods were fake and never could fulfill their presumed word. Solomon thus reflected upon how God had specifically kept His Word to David his father.

8:25-26 Solomon moved immediately to his first request. **Therefore now, LORD God of Israel, keep with thy servant David my father that thou promisedst him, saying, There shall not fail thee a man in my sight to sit on the throne of Israel; so that thy children take heed to their way, that they walk before me as thou hast walked before me.** He directly asked God to fulfill the Davidic Covenant in which He had promised David that his descendants would sit upon his throne in perpetuity. **26 And now, O God of Israel, let thy word, I pray thee, be verified, which thou spakest unto thy servant David my father.** Moreover, Solomon added that in so doing, his descendants might be careful to walk before God as David had. He thus publicly and officially petitioned God to fulfill that promise. See Psalm 132:11-12.

8:27 Solomon thus paused to interject a profound question. **But will God indeed dwell on the earth? behold, the heaven and heaven of heavens cannot contain thee; how much less this house that I have builded?** Solomon realized the potential folly of what he had just done. Though massive and spectacular, the Temple he had just finished was for the Almighty God of this universe. Would God so humble himself to dwell in such a tiny place and so honor one people thereby? Solomon freely acknowledged how that the heaven of the heavens could not contain God. His questions revealed the humility of Solomon and the proper perspective he held. He understood the infinite omnipresence of God. For God to so enter the Temple he had built was an honor unsurpassed.

8:28-30 Fully realizing the magnitude of what God was doing, Solomon asked, **Yet have thou respect unto the prayer of thy servant, and to his supplication, O LORD my God, to hearken unto the cry and to the prayer, which thy servant prayeth before thee to day: 29 That thine eyes may be open toward this house night and day,** *even* **toward the place of which thou hast said, My name shall be there: that thou mayest hearken unto the prayer which thy servant shall make toward this place. 30 And hearken thou to the supplication of thy servant, and of thy people Israel, when they shall pray toward this place: and hear thou in heaven thy dwelling place: and when thou hearest, forgive.**

In profound eloquence, Solomon asked God to hear his prayer. Notice also how Solomon routinely referred to himself as "thy servant." Though the most powerful king on the earth of that day, Solomon realized how small he was compared to the majesty of God. He could only refer to himself as a servant of God.

He thus prayed that God would hear his prayer and continue to watch over that hallowed place. In so doing, Solomon reminded God of the promise He had previously made that His name would be there. In Deuteronomy 16:2 and 6, God had promised to place His name whence He directed the Passover to be sacrificed. That clearly would be at this new Temple. Solomon again pled with God to hear the prayer of His people from that place though He altogether dwelt in heaven. He thus pled that in hearing the prayer of His people that God would forgive their sin. There was no question in Solomon's mind of the ultimate purpose of the Temple—a place for reconciliation with God.

8:31-32 The king therefore moved on to another section of his prayer. **If any man trespass against his neighbour, and an oath be laid upon him to cause him to swear, and the oath**

come before thine altar in this house: 32 **Then hear thou in heaven, and do, and judge thy servants, condemning the wicked, to bring his way upon his head; and justifying the righteous, to give him according to his righteousness**.

Solomon noted the undoubted coming situation whence two Israelites had a quarrel and it became a lawsuit (in modern terms). When that question for judgment ultimately came to the priest at the Temple for adjudication, he prayed that God would hear from heaven. It was his prayer that such cases would be judged righteously—the one who had wrought fraud to be condemned and the just person exonerated. Clearly implied is God's help for those who sought His face at the Temple seeking wisdom in judgment.

8:33-34 Solomon then moved on to another matter of crisis which undoubtedly would come. **When thy people Israel be smitten down before the enemy, because they have sinned against thee, and shall turn again to thee, and confess thy name, and pray, and make supplication unto thee in this house: 34 Then hear thou in heaven, and forgive the sin of thy people Israel, and bring them again unto the land which thou gavest unto their fathers**.

Solomon foresaw the day when Israel would backslide away from their God and be chastened by Him in being taken from the land. That had been foretold in Leviticus 27:32-33 and Deuteronomy 28:63-64. Notwithstanding, Solomon besought God that if they in their captivity would repent, confess God's name, and pray toward the Temple that God would forgive them and allow them to return to the land. Daniel certainly took this promise to heart. See Daniel 6:10 and 9:3 *ff*

8:35-36 Solomon posed another calamity which he foresaw happening. **When heaven is shut up, and there is no rain, because they have sinned against thee; if they pray**

Understanding I Kings

toward this place, and confess thy name, and turn from their sin, when thou afflictest them: 36 **Then hear thou in heaven, and forgive the sin of thy servants, and of thy people Israel, that thou teach them the good way wherein they should walk, and give rain upon thy land, which thou hast given to thy people for an inheritance.**

Solomon no doubt was well aware of Leviticus 26:19-20 as well as Deuteronomy 28:23-24. He foresaw such sin coming upon Israel followed by God's chastisement against His people. He thus pled with God that if they would pray toward the Temple in repentance and confession that God would have mercy upon them and return the rains.

8:37-40 Likewise when God was forced to further judge for their sin, **If there be in the land famine, if there be pestilence, blasting, mildew, locust,** *or* **if there be caterpiller; if their enemy besiege them in the land of their cities; whatsoever plague, whatsoever sickness** *there be*; 38 **What prayer and supplication soever be** *made* **by any man,** *or* **by all thy people Israel, which shall know every man the plague of his own heart, and spread forth his hands toward this house:** 39 **Then hear thou in heaven thy dwelling place, and forgive, and do, and give to every man according to his ways, whose heart thou knowest; (for thou,** *even* **thou only, knowest the hearts of all the children of men;)** 40 **That they may fear thee all the days that they live in the land which thou gavest unto our fathers.**

When chastening came upon the land because of their sin, if God's people would repent in prayer toward the Temple, Solomon implored God to hear and deal righteously with each man according to his ways. He then paused to make a profound comment. "For thou, *even* thou only, knowest the hearts of all the children of men." Truly only God knows our hearts. The devil can only find out what is in our heart when we open our mouth. God knows already. Moreover, He knows when one is truly repentive. Furthermore, in chastening and being forgiving upon repentance, Israel would come to "fear thee all the days that they live in the land which thou gavest unto our fathers." Solomon thus petitioned God to so hear the prayer of his people as they were truly repentive.

8:41-43 He thence moved on to another category. **Moreover concerning a stranger, that *is* not of thy people Israel, but cometh out of a far country for thy name's sake; 42 (For they shall hear of thy great name, and of thy strong hand, and of thy stretched out arm;) when he shall come and pray toward this house; 43 Hear thou in heaven thy dwelling place, and do according to all that the stranger calleth to thee for: that all people of the earth may know thy name, to fear thee, as *do* thy people Israel; and that they may know that this house, which I have builded, is called by thy name**.

Solomon foresaw righteous gentiles in other nations who, hearing of Jehovah God, would come to pray to God at the Temple. He thus besought God to hear all such who came in true faith and repentance. He thus hoped that all nations would come to know the name of Jehovah and fear Him as did Israel. A classic example of that is the Ethiopian Eunuch as recorded in Acts 8. In Herod's Temple, a special court of the gentiles was constructed for just such supplicants. See Acts 21:19. Solomon thus besought God to hear gentile pilgrims. Clear is the view that Solomon did not harbor the prejudice against gentiles which later generations of Jews would develop.

8:44-45 Still another situation is addressed. **If thy people go out to battle against their enemy, whithersoever thou shalt send them, and shall pray unto the LORD toward the city which thou hast chosen, and *toward* the house that I**

Understanding I Kings

have built for thy name: 45 **Then hear thou in heaven their prayer and their supplication, and maintain their cause.** Solomon foresaw occasions when Israel would need to go to war. However, he asked God that in so doing, that if Israel would pray toward the Temple, that He would hear their prayer and prosper the battle in their favor.

8:46-50 With prophetic prescience, Solomon again foresaw the day whence Israel would be taken from their land. **If they sin against thee, (for *there is* no man that sinneth not,) and thou be angry with them, and deliver them to the enemy, so that they carry them away captives unto the land of the enemy, far or near; 47 *Yet* if they shall bethink themselves in the land whither they were carried captives, and repent, and make supplication unto thee in the land of them that carried them captives, saying, We have sinned, and have done perversely, we have committed wickedness; 48 And *so* return unto thee with all their heart, and with all their soul, in the land of their enemies, which led them away captive, and pray unto thee toward their land, which thou gavest unto their fathers, the city which thou hast chosen, and the house which I have built for thy name:**
49 Then hear thou their prayer and their supplication in heaven thy dwelling place, and maintain their cause, 50 And forgive thy people that have sinned against thee, and all their transgressions wherein they have transgressed against thee, and give them compassion before them who carried them captive, that they may have compassion on them.

Solomon clearly understood the universal sinful condition of the human heart—"for *there is* no man that sinneth not." He foresaw the sinful rebellion of Israel against God and their eventual dispersion as a result. Nevertheless, he besought God that if and when they would truly repent, confess their sin, and pray toward the Temple at Jerusalem that God would be merciful to them. He pled with God to forgive them, prosper them, and cause their captors to have compassion upon them. Sadly, when that captivity did take place, it seems that only Daniel took this provision to heart. See Daniel 9:3 *ff.*

8:51-53 Solomon thus concluded his great prayer by reminding God how He had heretofore chosen Israel to be His people. **For they *be* thy people, and thine inheritance, which thou broughtest forth out of Egypt, from the midst of the furnace of iron: 52 That thine eyes may be open unto the supplication of thy servant, and unto the supplication of thy people Israel, to hearken unto them in all that they call for unto thee. 53 For thou didst separate them from among all the people of the earth, *to be* thine inheritance, as thou spakest by the hand of Moses thy servant, when thou broughtest our fathers out of Egypt, O Lord GOD.**

Of interest is how that Solomon referred to Israel's sojourn in Egypt as a furnace of iron. See Deuteronomy 4:20. However, the greater thought here is Solomon's plea for God to hear His people as they would pray to Him at the new Temple. He reminded God how that He had separated them from all other nations to be His people and inheritance. This profound, eloquent prayer is thus concluded by his plea, "O Lord GOD."

8:54 It is clear that Solomon's great prayer had been made on his knees. **And it was *so*, that when Solomon had made an end of praying all this prayer and supplication unto the LORD, he arose from before the altar of the LORD, from kneeling on his knees with his hands spread up to heaven.** Verse 22 of this chapter indicates that he at first stood. Here, he is described as kneeling. Evidently, Solomon had stood before the congregation and then fell upon his knees with his arms outstretched to heaven. In II Chronicles 6:13, mention is also

Understanding I Kings

made how that he prayed upon a platform of brass, three cubits high.

8:55-58 Solomon then **stood, and blessed all the congregation of Israel with a loud voice, saying, 56 Blessed be the LORD, that hath given rest unto his people Israel, according to all that he promised: there hath not failed one word of all his good promise, which he promised by the hand of Moses his servant. 57 The LORD our God be with us, as he was with our fathers: let him not leave us, nor forsake us: 58 That he may incline our hearts unto him, to walk in all his ways, and to keep his commandments, and his statutes, and his judgments, which he commanded our fathers**.

Though the text says that he blessed the people, he actually blessed the Lord more. Noted is how that God had given rest (peace) to Israel as He had promised. Furthermore, not one single word of God's promises had ever failed. He thus invoked the Lord to be with Israel as a nation not ever leaving them or forsaking them. Moreover, he invoked Israel to turn their hearts to their God to utterly obey all He had commanded them. Implicit is the profound importance of obedience to God.

8:59-60 Solomon therefore concluded his great benediction by noting, **And let these my words, wherewith I have made supplication before the LORD, be nigh unto the LORD our God day and night, that he maintain the cause of his servant, and the cause of his people Israel at all times, as the matter shall require: 60 That all the people of the earth may know that the LORD is God, *and that there is* none else.**

He invoked his prayer to therefore remain before God day and night. Implicit is the proposition that one's prayer may linger at length before God. He thus besought God again to maintain the cause of His people at all times that all other peoples might know that He was God and none else. Sadly,

Israel largely prevented that testimony from ever being fully known.

8:61 He thus enjoined Israel, **Let your heart therefore be perfect with the LORD our God, to walk in his statutes, and to keep his commandments, as at this day.** The word translated as **perfect** (שָׁלֵם *shalem*) in this context has the idea of 'complete.' The greater thought was for Israel to be wholehearted or totally dedicated to God and be utterly obedient to His Word. A lesson remains to this day for gentile believers. The greater context was that others would see God's hand upon His people and thus realize His mighty power.

8:62-64 After Solomon's great prayer of dedication, **the king, and all Israel with him, offered sacrifice before the LORD. 63 And Solomon offered a sacrifice of peace offerings, which he offered unto the LORD, two and twenty thousand oxen, and an hundred and twenty thousand sheep. So the king and all the children of Israel dedicated the house of the LORD.**

The degree of sacrifices is utterly astounding. There were 22,000 oxen and 120,000 sheep sacrificed as free-will peace offerings. As verse 65 will note, there were festivities for fourteen days. This astonishing sacrifice likely was spread out over these two weeks. These were the dedicatory sacrifices for the official dedication of the Temple. (Implicit also is a well organized system of sacrifice by the priests and Levites not to mention a properly designed system to remove the carcasses and blood.)

64 The same day did the king hallow the middle of the court that *was* before the house of the LORD: for there he offered burnt offerings, and meat offerings, and the fat of the peace offerings: because the brasen altar that *was* before the LORD *was* too little to receive the burnt offerings,

and meat offerings, and the fat of the peace offerings. Because such massive offerings could not be accomplished on only one altar be is ever so large, Solomon ordered that the outer court of the Temple be sanctified. There, evidently other temporary altars were used to offer the large numbers of sacrifices offered.

8:65-66 And at that time Solomon held a feast, and all Israel with him, a great congregation, from the entering in of Hamath unto the river of Egypt, before the LORD our God, seven days and seven days, *even* fourteen days. 66 On the eighth day he sent the people away: and they blessed the king, and went unto their tents joyful and glad of heart for all the goodness that the LORD had done for David his servant, and for Israel his people.

For this monumental time in the nation's history, Solomon declared a two week holiday. The full extent of his kingdom is noted ranging from Hamath, which was well into Syria to the north and east, to Egypt (either the Nile River itself or a tributary thereof). On the eighth day after the second week of this national holiday, the people were sent back to their normal schedules and homes. They thus rejoiced in all that God had done for David's son (Solomon) and for Israel. (Some have thought that the eighth day refers to the end of the feast of Tabernacles which it may have been.)

* * * * *

Overview of I Kings 9: *The narrative of the reign of Solomon continues. Record is here made of God's second appearance to Solomon with a conditional promise to bless Him. The final portion of the chapter records the success and fame of King Solomon.*

9:1-2 And it came to pass, when Solomon had finished the building of the house of the LORD, and the king's house, and all Solomon's desire which he was pleased to do, 2 That the LORD appeared to Solomon the second time, as he had appeared unto him at Gibeon.

There is diversity of opinion as to when this event took place. At first glance, it would seem that it was after Solomon had constructed the Temple and his own palace. However, if that be the case, then it would have been thirteen years after his prayer of dedication recorded in the preceding chapter. It may be that this event took place soon after his great prayer of praise and dedication as the next verse will intimate. However, it also may be that by the time the twenty years of his major construction projects were complete that Solomon needed a stern warning from God. The greater context as well as the text itself however leans toward the former.

9:3 And the LORD said unto him, I have heard thy prayer and thy supplication, that thou hast made before me: I have hallowed this house, which thou hast built, to put my name there for ever; and mine eyes and mine heart shall be there perpetually.

God clearly is responding to Solomon's eloquent prayer of dedication recorded in the preceding chapter. The word translated as **supplication** (תחנה *techinnah*) has the sense to 'seek favor.' That Solomon did as he prayed. The word translated as **hallowed** (קדש *qadash*) has the basic sense to 'set apart as holy.' Solomon did just that as he dedicated the Temple exclusively for the work of God. God therefore promised His name would be there forever.

The final phrase "and mine eyes and mine heart shall be there perpetually" likely is a metaphor referring to how God would watch over it and His heart would be there in perpetuity. With the perspective of history, we know that God allowed the

Temple to be destroyed on several occasions. It still remains unbuilt. However, it someday will be rebuilt. The word translated as **perpetually** (יוֹם *yowm*) is the word commonly translated as 'day.' The idea is that God's eyes and heart would be there each day.

9:4-5 God therefore promised to Solomon, **And if thou wilt walk before me, as David thy father walked, in integrity of heart, and in uprightness, to do according to all that I have commanded thee,** *and* **wilt keep my statutes and my judgments: 5 Then I will establish the throne of thy kingdom upon Israel for ever, as I promised to David thy father, saying, There shall not fail thee a man upon the throne of Israel.**

There is here a conditional reaffirmation of the Davidic Covenant. God presented to Solomon a classic *if/then* proposition. The condition was threefold. *If* Solomon would walk (or live) before God (1) "in integrity of heart." The word translated as **integrity** (תֹּם *tom*) in this context essentially has the idea of dedication—of heart. *If* he would walk (2) "in uprightness." The latter has to do with righteous living. And. *if* he would (3) "do according to all that I have commanded thee, *and* wilt keep my statutes and my judgments." The condensed essence is obedience to God's Word.

Thus, *if* Solomon would keep this threefold condition, God promised *then* He would establish his throne forever as He had promised David. In essence, God promised that if Solomon would be completely dedicated, upright, and obedient that He would fulfill the Davidic Covenant through him. Solomon's sons would reign as a continuation of the Davidic dynasty in perpetuity. See II Samuel 7:12-13.

9:6-7 To the contrary, God warned, *But* **if ye shall at all turn from following me, ye or your children, and will not**

keep my commandments *and* my statutes which I have set before you, but go and serve other gods, and worship them: 7 Then will I cut off Israel out of the land which I have given them; and this house, which I have hallowed for my name, will I cast out of my sight; and Israel shall be a proverb and a byword among all people.

God presented Solomon with another *if/then* proposition. *If* (1) he (or his children) would turn away from Jehovah God and (2) be disobedient to God's Word and (3) turn to other gods, *then* God would turn against them. He warned that *then* (1) Israel would be removed from the land. (2) The Temple would be overturned. And, (3) Israel would become a name of derision to other nations.

9:8-9 Furthermore, **at this house,** *which* **is high, every one that passeth by it shall be astonished, and shall hiss; and they shall say, Why hath the LORD done thus unto this land, and to this house?**

God foretold further that if Solomon or his descendants would depart from Him, that all which passed by the then destroyed Temple would be in astonishment. The word translated as **hiss** (שׁרק *sharaq*) has the sense of 'whistling' as in amazement or astonishment. Moreover, God foretold that there would be no question that He Himself had allowed such destruction to the land and to the Temple. Reference is made to this height of the Temple. II Chronicles 3:4 notes that it was 120 cubits (180 feet) high. A building approximating eighteen stories tall in that day was an amazing structure. Yet God foretold if they would turn from Him, then that magnificent structure would be laid waste.

To the question posed above, God continued, **9 And they shall answer, Because they forsook the LORD their God, who brought forth their fathers out of the land of Egypt, and have taken hold upon other gods, and have worshipped** them, and served them: therefore hath the LORD brought upon them all this evil.** The day was coming that it would be common knowledge why God so had judged His people. It would be because they had forsaken Him and worshiped other gods. When that time came, that is exactly what happened. See Jeremiah 19:1 *ff*.

Solomon was thus offered the continuation of the Davidic Covenant as well as a stern warning of what would happen should he depart from serving the Lord. No record is given of his response. However, it very well may be that Solomon was already beginning to manifest the spiritual declension which would mark his later life. This would be especially so if this event took place after the completion of his own palace rather than after the completion of the Temple. God in seeing this thus gave him fair warning.

9:10-14 Record is made of the events taking place after the completion of Solomon's major building projects. **And it came to pass at the end of twenty years, when Solomon had built the two houses, the house of the LORD, and the king's house, 11 (*Now* Hiram the king of Tyre had furnished Solomon with cedar trees and fir trees, and with gold, according to all his desire,) that then king Solomon gave Hiram twenty cities in the land of Galilee.**

This passage leaves no question that Solomon's two major building projects (the Temple and his palace) were built consecutively and not concurrently. See I Kings 6:38 - 7:1. Note is also made again of all the materiel which Hiram, king of Tyre, had provided Solomon. Therefore, Solomon gave Hiram twenty cities in the Galilee region near to Tyre.

12 And Hiram came out from Tyre to see the cities which Solomon had given him; and they pleased him not. It may be that there was nothing wrong with the cities, but rather the economy of them was agrarian and the Lebanese of Tyre were merchants. They therefore may not have been interested in becoming farmers. That seems more likely than the possibility that Solomon gave him cities in disrepair. Therefore, Hiram sent word and said, **13 What cities *are* these which thou hast given me, my brother? And he called them the land of Cabul unto this day**. The word *Cabul* in Phoenician may means 'displeasing.' II Chronicles 8:2 seems to indicate that Hiram eventually gave them back to Solomon.

Comments is also made, **14 And Hiram sent to the king sixscore talents of gold**. The thought is that Hiram *had* sent 120 talents of gold, evidently over the preceding years in the building of the Temple and of Solomon's palace. No further word is given of how Solomon and Hiram reconciled their differences over the twenty cities. Evidently, they worked it out agreeably for there is no other record of acrimony regarding this.

9:15-16 Other endeavors of Solomon are noted. **And this *is* the reason of the levy which king Solomon raised; for to build the house of the LORD, and his own house, and Millo, and the wall of Jerusalem, and Hazor, and Megiddo, and Gezer**. The **levy** mentioned refers to (1) taxes being levied as well as (2) men being drafted to work. See I Kings 5:13 *ff*. Funds as well as manpower were raised to build first the Temple and then Solomon's palace. But he had other major construction projects as well. Mentioned is **Millo** which was a fortified portion of Jerusalem between the city of David and the upper city whence was the Temple. Implicit is that this was a major military installation. He also rebuilt the wall of Jerusalem which must have been a major project.

Solomon also built or rebuilt the cities of "Hazor, and Megiddo, and Gezer." There were several cities named Hazor. However, this one probably was located in Naphtali to the north of the Sea of Galilee. Megiddo was an ancient city located at the southern edge of the valley of Jezreel not far from Mount Carmel. Gezer was to the west of Jerusalem near the beginning of the coastal plain. These cities were undoubtedly rebuilt for military reasons establishing a strong strategic presence in each direction. They also likely had significant commercial activity.

The sacred historian goes on to give further detail regarding the city of Gezer. 16 *For* **Pharaoh king of Egypt had gone up, and taken Gezer, and burnt it with fire, and slain the Canaanites that dwelt in the city, and given it** *for* **a present unto his daughter, Solomon's wife.** Solomon's first wife was the daughter of the sitting Pharaoh of Egypt. Evidently, Gezer was a city of Canaanites (Palestinians) which had never been expunged from the land. This Pharaoh (evidently with permission of Solomon) had gone and captured the city from the Canaanites, destroyed it, and given it to Solomon and his wife as a present. Solomon thus rebuilt the city, perhaps as a country home for his wife. It also was closer to Egypt wherein she might receive family.

9:17-19 Further summary is made of Solomon's public works. **And Solomon built Gezer, and Bethhoron the nether, 18 And Baalath, and Tadmor in the wilderness, in the land, 19 And all the cities of store that Solomon had, and cities for his chariots, and cities for his horsemen, and that which Solomon desired to build in Jerusalem, and in Lebanon, and in all the land of his dominion.**

Bethoron the nether refers to a lower city, perhaps at a lower elevation than the main city of Bethoron. Baalath is thought to have been in Dan. Tadmor is thought to have been in Syria which David had conquered. Each of these cities no doubt had strategic purposes. Also mentioned are the cities of storage as well as cities for his cavalry. His kingdom stretched from Lebanon in the north and across all which had traditionally been Israel. Thus, Solomon established major installations both for military purposes as well as for commercial activity across his kingdom.

9:20-22 Record is made regarding taxation in his realm. **And all the people *that were* left of the Amorites, Hittites, Perizzites, Hivites, and Jebusites, which *were* not of the children of Israel, 21 Their children that were left after them in the land, whom the children of Israel also were not able utterly to destroy, upon those did Solomon levy a tribute of bondservice unto this day.** Remnants of Canaanites still in the land were not only taxed but forced to be servants to Israel. They were forced to be the common labor and slaves of the kingdom.

However, **22 of the children of Israel did Solomon make no bondmen: but they *were* men of war, and his servants, and his princes, and his captains, and rulers of his chariots, and his horsemen**. Solomon used no true Israelites as bondmen. Rather, they were his soldiers and officers, personal servants, and rulers in the land.

9:23 More details of Solomon's government are noted. **These *were* the chief of the officers that *were* over Solomon's work, five hundred and fifty, which bare rule over the people that wrought in the work**. Evidently, there were 550 rulers who served as job superintendents on Solomon's various construction projects. II Chronicles 8:10 mentions 250 rulers, but there only a portion of them are noted. Here, the grand total is presented.

9:24 Record is also made of Solomon's Egyptian wife's move to her new palace. **But Pharaoh's daughter came up out of the city of David unto her house which *Solomon* had built for her: then did he build Millo.** II Chronicles 8:11 indicates that he would not let her live there until the Temple had been built. Thereafter, he built the fortifications between the upper city and the city of David.

9:25 And three times in a year did Solomon offer burnt offerings and peace offerings upon the altar which he built unto the LORD, and he burnt incense upon the altar that *was* before the LORD. So he finished the house. II Chronicles 8:13 notes that these three feasts were Unleavened Bread, Pentecost, and Tabernacles. These were the three major convocations of the Jewish calendar.

9:26-28 Record is also made of Solomon's far reach, his navy, and a source of his wealth. **And king Solomon made a navy of ships in Eziongeber, which *is* beside Eloth, on the shore of the Red sea, in the land of Edom. 27 And Hiram sent in the navy his servants, shipmen that had knowledge of the sea, with the servants of Solomon. 28 And they came to Ophir, and fetched from thence gold, four hundred and twenty talents, and brought *it* to king Solomon.**

Eloth is the modern city of Elat at the head of the Red Sea. From there, Solomon commissioned a navy to sail to Ophir. Hiram sent experienced sailors to man Solomon's navy. The site of ancient Ophir is not certain. It may have been along the southwestern coast of what is today Saudi Arabia. Or, it may have been across into the adjacent region of the horn of Africa. In any event, Solomon took large amounts of gold therefrom. Noted are 420 talents of gold from this source alone. Translating that in modern money is unsure. However, that sum alone would be in the hundreds of millions of dollars, if not more in modern currency.

* * * * *

Overview of I Kings 10: *Record is made of the meeting of Solomon and the queen of Sheba. The remainder of the chapter describes the vast wealth which Solomon came to accumulate and the prosperity which reigned in Israel during his rule.*

10:1-3 And when the queen of Sheba heard of the fame of Solomon concerning the name of the LORD, she came to prove him with hard questions. The location of ancient Sheba is uncertain. Some have suggested that it was a region of southern Arabia. However, Josephus claims that Sheba was Ethiopia. Ethiopians to this day claim that distinction. (Moreover, Ethiopian tradition holds that Solomon and the queen of Sheba had a liaison during her visit and she conceived a son as a result.)

Ethiopian tradition therefore holds that much of their nation are therefore descended from Solomon. There certainly has been an affinity between Jews and Ethiopia through the centuries including the Ethiopian Eunuch. However, there is absolutely no scriptural basis for the claim that there was intimacy between Solomon and her.) The sacred record notes that she had heard of the name of Jehovah as well as the fame of Solomon. She therefore journeyed to Jerusalem to meet him and to find answers to serious questions which she had.

She thus came with a great caravan. **2 And she came to Jerusalem with a very great train, with camels that bare spices, and very much gold, and precious stones: and when she was come to Solomon, she communed with him of all that was in her heart.** She came with great gifts for the famous Solomon. Thus, upon arrival at Jerusalem, she met with Solomon and spoke to him of all that was on her heart. There is indication to believe that the queen of Sheba did in fact become a proselyte to Judaism and returned as a believer in Jehovah God. The Ethiopian Eunuch of Acts 8 was likely a spiritual descendant. Knowledge of the God of Israel evidently was taken back to Ethiopia by her and she spread the truth of Jehovah in her land.

Morever, 3 **Solomon told her all her questions: there was not** *any* **thing hid from the king, which he told her not.** Solomon was able to answer all of her questions. Nothing that she brought was hid from his understanding. He was able to answer her every question. These very well may have pertained to the things of God.

10:4-7 And when the queen of Sheba had seen all Solomon's wisdom, and the house that he had built, 5 And the meat of his table, and the sitting of his servants, and the attendance of his ministers, and their apparel, and his cupbearers, and his ascent by which he went up unto the house of the LORD; there was no more spirit in her.
The queen of Sheba saw the grandeur and splendor of Solomon's kingdom. She saw his royal palace. She saw the regal bearing of even his servants. She also saw the food upon which he dined. She saw the magnificent Temple, though she no doubt was not allowed into it. But she saw the intricately designed stairs designed for the king to enter the Temple. Seeing the regal realm of Solomon took all the starch out of her sails. Though she was a queen, she had never seen anything like this. Any aspersions of pomp and ceremony on her part were deflated on seeing the realm of Solomon.

Therefore, 6 **she said to the king, It was a true report that I heard in mine own land of thy acts and of thy wisdom. 7 Howbeit I believed not the words, until I came, and mine eyes had seen** *it***: and, behold, the half was not told me: thy wisdom and prosperity exceedeth the fame which I heard.** She had heard fabulous stories of Solomon and his royal city. Now she had seen with her own eyes. She confessed that prior to seeing for herself, she had not believed the tales she had heard. Moreover, the half of his greatness, wisdom, wealth, and power were not told her. His wisdom and prosperity exceeded anything she had heard.

10:8-9 She continued, **Happy *are* thy men, happy *are* these thy servants, which stand continually before thee, *and* that hear thy wisdom. 9 Blessed be the LORD thy God, which delighted in thee, to set thee on the throne of Israel: because the LORD loved Israel for ever, therefore made he thee king, to do judgment and justice**. She noted the happiness of even his servants. She therefore blessed Jehovah God and noted that God had made him king to righteously judge His people.

There possibly is a foreview of how events will be in the Millennium when Jesus Christ rules and reigns. Solomon's reign, at least the first half thereof, very well may typify Christ's millennial reign. In that day, there will be great peace, happiness, and prosperity such as the world has never seen. God blessed David's son with such blessings of righteousness. David's greater Son will someday exhibit even greater blessing.

10:10-12 Description of the queen's gift to Solomon is noted. **And she gave the king an hundred and twenty talents of gold, and of spices very great store, and precious stones: there came no more such abundance of spices as these which the queen of Sheba gave to king Solomon**. This evidently was the initial gift she brought. This included a large sum of gold, jewels, and large amounts of exotic spices. She evidently continued to supply Solomon with gifts after her departure.

11 And the navy also of Hiram, that brought gold from Ophir, brought in from Ophir great plenty of almug trees, and precious stones. 12 And the king made of the almug trees pillars for the house of the LORD, and for the kings house, harps also and psalteries for singers: there came no such almug trees, nor were seen unto this day.

Understanding I Kings

There is uncertainty as to what almug trees were. However, some think that they were ebony trees. Solomon thus used these for decorations to the Temple as well as to make musical instruments. The wood thereof evidently was of exquisite quality.

10:13 And king Solomon gave unto the queen of Sheba all her desire, whatsoever she asked, beside *that* which Solomon gave her of his royal bounty. So she turned and went to her own country, she and her servants. Anything she wanted prior to her departure, Solomon granted. She thus returned home.

10:14-17 Further details of Solomon's wealth is recorded. **Now the weight of gold that came to Solomon in one year was six hundred threescore and six talents of gold.** Again, determining how much this is in modern terms is difficult. It may have approximated a half-billion dollars in modern terms. This was just the gold bullion which came into his possession. 15 **Beside *that he had* of the merchantmen, and of the traffick of the spice merchants, and of all the kings of Arabia, and of the governors of the country.** In addition to his income in gold, he also had the proceeds of other vast business interests of his kingdom. (It should be interesting to read the book of Ecclesiastes at this point. In spite of all this wealth, Solomon became a miserable man. See Ecclesiastes 1:14.)

With some of the gold which came to him, 16 **king Solomon made two hundred targets *of* beaten gold: six hundred *shekels* of gold went to one target.** These **targets** were a type of shield. In this case, they were wrought of pure gold. Moreover, 17 *he made* **three hundred shields *of* beaten gold; three pound of gold went to one shield: and the king put them in the house of the forest of Lebanon.** These shields were evidently of a lessor size and character. Precisely what the house of the forest of Lebanon was is not clear. It very well may be that Solomon had constructed a summer palace there to escape the heat. He apparently decorated that palace with these three-hundred gold shields.

10:18-20 Description is made of Solomon's magnificent throne. **Moreover the king made a great throne of ivory, and overlaid it with the best gold. 19 The throne had six steps, and the top of the throne *was* round behind: and *there were* stays on either side on the place of the seat, and two lions stood beside the stays. 20 And twelve lions stood there on the one side and on the other upon the six steps: there was not the like made in any kingdom.**

This great throne of pure ivory was evidently trimmed with pure gold. It apparently was of some height because six steps were required to mount it. Behind the throne itself evidently was a semicircular alcove. On each side of the throne were armrests (i.e., **stays**). On each side of the throne was a golden lion. Alongside the six steps up to the throne were twelve golden lions, one on each side of each step. No throne was ever like his.

10:21 More regarding Solomon's wealth is noted. **And all king Solomon's drinking vessels *were of* gold, and all the vessels of the house of the forest of Lebanon *were of* pure gold; none *were of* silver: it was nothing accounted of in the days of Solomon**. In Solomon's palaces, all the eating and drinking utensils were of pure gold. Silver was so common in his day, it was not even counted.

10:22 Further mention is made of his navy. **For the king had at sea a navy of Tharshish with the navy of Hiram: once in three years came the navy of Tharshish, bringing gold, and silver, ivory, and apes, and peacocks**. Precisely where *Tharshish* (Tarshish) was is uncertain. Some have thought it to be somewhere along the coast of North Africa which would fit

Understanding I Kings

with the navy of Hiram. Others think it on the coast of the Indian Ocean. In any event, Solomon's fleet assisted by Hiram brought vast wealth to him every three years. With that amount of turnaround time, it may be that this refers to other than the Mediterranean Sea.

10:23-27 So king Solomon exceeded all the kings of the earth for riches and for wisdom. 24 And all the earth sought to Solomon, to hear his wisdom, which God had put in his heart. 25 And they brought every man his present, vessels of silver, and vessels of gold, and garments, and armour, and spices, horses, and mules, a rate year by year. No king was greater than Solomon. The entire earth came to court his favor and hear the wisdom which God had given him. In so coming, they brought additional wealth to him as gifts. Once again, there likely is a foreview of the millennial reign of Christ.

Solomon's wealth extended to his military. **26 And Solomon gathered together chariots and horsemen: and he had a thousand and four hundred chariots, and twelve thousand horsemen, whom he bestowed in the cities for chariots, and with the king at Jerusalem.** He placed chariots of war and cavalry throughout his kingdom in strategic places. His forces had 1,400 chariots and 12,000 horsemen (cavalry).

Furthermore, **27 the king made silver *to be* in Jerusalem as stones, and cedars made he *to be* as the sycomore trees that *are* in the vale, for abundance.** Jerusalem is a city of stones. Everything there tends to be constructed of stone. However, during Solomon's reign, the silver of the city was as common as the ubiquitous stones. It was everywhere. Moreover, cedar trees were considered of greatest value. The common indigenous tree of the day were sycamores. However, during Solomon's reign, cedar trees were as common as sycamore trees.

10:28-29 Morever, **Solomon had horses brought out of Egypt, and linen yarn: the king's merchants received the linen yarn at a price**. Solomon also had considerable commercial interaction with Egypt. From there he obtained more horses. The word translated as **linen yarn** (מִקְוֵה *miqveh*) literally refers to a 'collection.' It may be the thought is that Solomon bought a *collection* of horses from Egypt for a specified price. See Deuteronomy 17:16 wherein God forbad kings of Israel to multiply horses to himself. The backsliding of Solomon was already well underway. He already had either forgotten what God's Word said or he simply ignored it.

The prices for which he purchased horses and chariots is noted. **29 And a chariot came up and went out of Egypt for six hundred *shekels* of silver, and an horse for an hundred and fifty: and so for all the kings of the Hittites, and for the kings of Syria, did they bring *them* out by their means**. It is difficult to ascertain the going rate for such transactions in that day. However, the implication is that Solomon paid 'top dollar' for horses and chariots he purchased in Egypt. He apparently likewise paid such prices to other rulers of the region. The wealth of Solomon thus was immense.

＊ ＊ ＊ ＊ ＊

Overview of I Kings 11: *Recorded herein is the turning point in the life of Solomon. Because of his ignoring of God's Word, God's blessing began to pass from him. God begins to chasten him. Then recorded is the rise of Jeroboam and finally the death of Solomon.*

11:1-2 Though wise in many areas, it was the lust of the flesh which was the downfall of Solomon. **But king Solomon loved many strange women, together with the daughter of**

Pharaoh, women of the Moabites, Ammonites, Edomites, Zidonians, *and* Hittites;

Some think he did this with political views to get intelligence of the state of those countries or to neutralize their hostility. Rather, it seems to be the lust of the flesh or pride which so motivated him. Solomon did not need additional wives to help with the housework. He rather usurped his position as king to build a large 'harem.' He likely added any and every beautiful woman which caught his fancy.

Though polygamy was grudgingly tolerated under the Old Testament Law, it never has been God's perfect plan for any home. Solomon abused this tolerance to the greatest degree ever. It seems clear that his basic motive was sexual lust. Because he had the power to do so, he took virtually any woman he desired.

Moreover, there was an even worse sin. In so doing, he directly violated God's Word. Deuteronomy 7:1 commanded, "When the LORD thy God shall bring thee into the land whither thou goest to possess it, and hath cast out many nations before thee, the Hittites, and the Girgashites, and the Amorites, and the Canaanites, and the Perizzites, and the Hivites, and the Jebusites, seven nations greater and mightier than thou." Furthermore, God said, in Deuteronomy 7:3, "Neither shalt thou make marriages with them; thy daughter thou shalt not give unto his son, nor his daughter shalt thou take unto thy son." Solomon directly violated this charge of God's Word. He had introduced paganism into his own home.

As the sacred historian warned, 2 **Of the nations *concerning* which the LORD said unto the children of Israel, Ye shall not go in to them, neither shall they come in unto you:** *for* **surely they will turn away your heart after their gods: Solomon clave unto these in love.** Because of his disobedience of God's Word, Solomon's reign had already passed its peak.

11:3 And he had seven hundred wives, princesses, and three hundred concubines: and his wives turned away his heart. Solomon, simply put, had a harem; some of which were daughters of kings of neighboring nations. Precisely what the distinction between this large amount of wives and concubines might be is not clear. One thing however is clear, if he visited only one of his wives a day, it would take three years to be with them all. Here is a man who had an almost endless resource for the lusts of his flesh. Yet, in reading the book of Ecclesiastes, it is clear that he was a miserable man. This again was in direct disobedience to God's Word for Deuteronomy 17:17 said regarding kings of Israel, "Neither shall he multiply wives to himself, that his heart turn not away: neither shall he greatly multiply to himself silver and gold." Solomon certainly had done both in direct violation of God's laws.

11:4-5 As God had forewarned, **For it came to pass, when Solomon was old, *that* his wives turned away his heart after other gods: and his heart was not perfect with the LORD his God, as *was* the heart of David his father. 5 For Solomon went after Ashtoreth the goddess of the Zidonians, and after Milcom the abomination of the Ammonites.**

Solomon's sin was not so much the lust of the flesh as it was in marrying the women of the world from neighboring pagan nations. In due season, these wives turned his heart away from Jehovah God. The word translated as **perfect** (שׁלם *shalem*) has the sense here of 'whole.' Or to put it another way, Solomon was no longer wholly dedicated to God. Furthermore, he himself began to dabble in the idolatry of "Ashtoreth the goddess of the Zidonians, and after Milcom the abomination of the Ammonites." Ashtoreth was the female goddess of fertility (sex) of the Zidonians. She was also called 'Ishtar' of Assyria and 'Astarte' by the Greeks and Romans. Milcom was also Molech, the god of the Phoenicians, to which infants were sacrificed. Solomon therefore was not only dabbling in idolatry, but it was some of the most perverse idolatry ever.

11:6-8 Accordingly, **Solomon did evil in the sight of the LORD, and went not fully after the LORD, as** *did* **David his father.** Though David had his faults, he never *once* wavered in his whole-hearted dedication to Jehovah God. Tragically, Solomon did not continue that dedication. **7 Then did Solomon build an high place for Chemosh, the abomination of Moab, in the hill that** *is* **before Jerusalem, and for Molech, the abomination of the children of Ammon. 8 And likewise did he for all his strange wives, which burnt incense and sacrificed unto their gods.**

It is thought that Chemosh was the same god as Baal-peor, also called Baal-zebub, Mars, or Saturn of various ancient nations. It is here called the abomination of Ammon. The "hill that is before Jerusalem" likely is the Mount of Olives which is the hill immediately to the east of the city. Solomon thus built a "high place" or place of worship for this wicked idol as well as for other of the pagan deities of the many wives he had married.

Clearly implicit is the consequences of the breach of separation. Solomon may have been motivated by the lust of the flesh in obtaining the many foreign wives which he had. However, it also was a violation of the biblical principle of separation. From the lust of the flesh, he surely reaped corruption.

11:9-10 Not surprisingly, **the LORD was angry with Solomon, because his heart was turned from the LORD God of Israel, which had appeared unto him twice, 10 And had commanded him concerning this thing, that he should not go after other gods: but he kept not that which the LORD commanded.**

God had blessed Solomon more than any other one man. He had appeared to him twice, both promising to bless and warning against idolatry. Notwithstanding such privilege and direct orders, Solomon disregarded God's command and utterly disobeyed Him.

11:11-13 God evidently appeared to Solomon again. Or, it may rather be that God sent a prophet. **Wherefore the LORD said unto Solomon, Forasmuch as this is done of thee, and thou hast not kept my covenant and my statutes, which I have commanded thee, I will surely rend the kingdom from thee, and will give it to thy servant.**

In its distilled essence, Solomon's sin was simply disobedience to God. He ignored God's Word. Therefore, God curtly informed him that He was about to take his kingdom from him. The servant mentioned was Jeroboam. Solomon had utterly disregarded God's condition of blessing and perpetuity. See I Kings 9:4-5. Rather, he had already fulfilled the cause for God's judgment found in 9:6-9.

12 **Notwithstanding in thy days I will not do it for David thy father's sake:** *but* **I will rend it out of the hand of thy son.** 13 **Howbeit I will not rend away all the kingdom;** *but* **will give one tribe to thy son for David my servant's sake, and for Jerusalem's sake which I have chosen**.

Because of David's great dedication and service to God, God promised that he would not strip the kingdom from Solomon in his lifetime. However, after his son ascended the throne, the kingdom would be stripped from Rehoboam, Solomon's heir apparent. Of interest is the word translated as **rend** (קרע *qara*). It essentially means to 'rip.' God promised to 'rip' the majority of the kingdom out of the hand of Solomon's son. However, He did promise to leave at least one tribe to Solomon's son in deference to the promise He had made to David to always have a descendant of David on his throne.

The reference to one tribe being given to Solomon's son may well refer to one tribe in addition to the tribe of Judah whence he was. Others have suggested that because the two tribes of Benjamin and Judah were so closely related in their inheritance with both having part of Jerusalem, that they were essentially viewed as one.

11:14-18 God wasted no time in effecting the beginning of chastening against Solomon. The background to that judgment is begun here. **And the LORD stirred up an adversary unto Solomon, Hadad the Edomite: he** *was* **of the king's seed in Edom**. The same Jehovah God which had so blessed Solomon now began stir up trouble against him. He who had established the kingdom of Solomon now began to unravel it. Of interest is the word translated as **adversary** (שטן *satan*). Though not referring to the devil himself, that very word has also become one of the proper names of the devil in Satan.

The adversary which God raised up against Solomon was *Hadad the Edomite*. Background into this man is thus provided. **15 For it came to pass, when David was in Edom, and Joab the captain of the host was gone up to bury the slain, after he had smitten every male in Edom; 16 (For six months did Joab remain there with all Israel, until he had cut off every male in Edom:) 17 That Hadad fled, he and certain Edomites of his father's servants with him, to go into Egypt; Hadad** *being* **yet a little child.**

The history involved here likely hearkens back to II Samuel 8:14, which see. That had taken place at least fifty years earlier. In the war with Israel then, Joab had spent six month after their victory in a mopping-up action. As far as he was concerned, Joab had killed every male Edomite. That clearly was not the case as indicated by those who fled to Egypt. Among these one little boy named Hadad.

Further details of Hadad's sojourn in Egypt are noted. **18 And they arose out of Midian, and came to Paran: and they took men with them out of Paran, and they came to Egypt,**

unto Pharaoh king of Egypt; which gave him an house, and appointed him victuals, and gave him land. Their journey from Edom took them through Midian and Paran and they ultimately came into Egypt. The Pharaoh, upon being informed who little Hadad was, gave him provisions and land upon which to live. Implied is that Hadad was of the royal lineage of Edom. Thus, God saw to it that Hadad remembered what had happened to him and his people at the hand of David. Though David was long gone, the focus of this man's hatred was upon Solomon, David's son.

11:19-22 The history of Hadad is continued. **And Hadad found great favour in the sight of Pharaoh, so that he gave him to wife the sister of his own wife, the sister of Tahpenes the queen.** 20 **And the sister of Tahpenes bare him Genubath his son, whom Tahpenes weaned in Pharaoh's house: and Genubath was in Pharaoh's household among the sons of Pharaoh.** Pharaoh took a liking to Hadad and gave him his sister-in-law as a wife. A son born to them was brought up in Pharaoh's court as if he were a son of the Pharaoh. Thus there was clear affinity and bond between Hadad of the Edomites and Egypt.

However, 21 **when Hadad heard in Egypt that David slept with his fathers, and that Joab the captain of the host was dead, Hadad said to Pharaoh, Let me depart, that I may go to mine own country.** Upon learning his powerful enemies were dead, Hadad sought permission to return to his own country. Pharaoh was not happy with the request and **said unto him, But what hast thou lacked with me, that, behold, thou seekest to go to thine own country? And he answered, Nothing: howbeit let me go in any wise.** He tried to dissuade Hadad from leaving, but he insisted.

Implicit is that Hadad therefore became an implacable foe of Solomon, causing him trouble from Edom. However, verse

14 makes it very clear that this trouble had been stirred up against Solomon by God. It was the beginning of the chastening of God against Solomon for his sin.

11:23-25 Furthermore, **God stirred him up *another* adversary, Rezon the son of Eliadah, which fled from his lord Hadadezer king of Zobah: 24 And he gathered men unto him, and became captain over a band, when David slew them *of Zobah*: and they went to Damascus, and dwelt therein, and reigned in Damascus. 25 And he was an adversary to Israel all the days of Solomon, beside the mischief that Hadad *did*: and he abhorred Israel, and reigned over Syria.**

To the northeast, God helped another vanquished foe of David rise to power against Solomon. This was one Rezon of Syria who gathered forces to himself in Damascus. There was trouble for Solomon from the southeast in Hadad (with his implicit allies in the Egyptians). To his northeast, God enabled Rezon and the Syrians to become an implacable foe against him. It is again clear that these enemies were allowed and even helped by God against Solomon. The magnificent kingdom of Solomon was beginning to unravel. He had taken God's blessing for granted. That is a terrible place to be.

11:26 God was not only helping the enemies of Solomon rise to power outside his kingdom, He also stirred opposition from with. **And Jeroboam the son of Nebat, an Ephrathite of Zereda, Solomon's servant, whose mother's name *was* Zeruah, a widow woman, even he lifted up *his* hand against the king.**

Little if anything is known of Jeroboam's background other than he apparently was of the tribe of Ephraim and the town of Zereda of Ephrath. However, Jeroboam had been appointed by Solomon to be a servant or 'officer' in his government. In the course of events, as will be noted below, Jeroboam became disloyal to Solomon, stirring trouble from within his own kingdom. Though Solomon would try to kill Jeroboam, it is apparent that his authority in his own realm was weakened in that Jeroboam could be disloyal and initially get away with it. God's blessing was no longer upon Solomon. Everything now seemed to be going wrong. It was and the reason was simple. God was now working against him rather than blessing him.

11:27-28 The story behind the story of Jeroboam and his ascension to prominence is here begun. **And this *was* the cause that he lifted up *his* hand against the king: Solomon built Millo, *and* repaired the breaches of the city of David his father**. Early in the reign of Solomon, he had built Millo, which were military fortifications between the city of David and the upper city of Jerusalem. He also repaired the city of David, a section of eastern Jerusalem whence David had originally lived. Mention is made of this in I Kings 9:24. Implied is that Jeroboam was involved in this work.

28 **And the man Jeroboam *was* a mighty man of valour: and Solomon seeing the young man that he was industrious, he made him ruler over all the charge of the house of Joseph**. Solomon apparently saw that young Jeroboam had leadership ability and was diligent. Solomon therefore made him governor over the tribes of Ephraim of Manasseh.

11:29-31 The time of the following event is not clear. It may be when Solomon had appointed Jeroboam to his new post. Or, it may have been later, perhaps after he had been to Jerusalem and was returning home. It most likely was after God had turned against Solomon. **And it came to pass at that time when Jeroboam went out of Jerusalem, that the prophet Ahijah the Shilonite found him in the way; and he had clad himself with a new garment; and they two *were* alone in the**

field: **30 And Ahijah caught the new garment that *was* on him, and rent it *in* twelve pieces.**

Whenever this event took place, God sent a prophet by the name of Ahijah to confront Jeroboam. Mention of him being a Shilonite likely refers to Shiloh. See I Kings 14:2. The prophet that day was wearing a new suit of clothes. In meeting Jeroboam out in the countryside, Ahijah took his new clothing and tore it into twelve pieces. That surely got the attention of Jeroboam

31 And he said to Jeroboam, Take thee ten pieces: for thus saith the LORD**, the God of Israel, Behold, I will rend the kingdom out of the hand of Solomon, and will give ten tribes to thee: (But he shall have one tribe for my servant David's sake, and for Jerusalem's sake, the city which I have chosen out of all the tribes of Israel:).**

God clearly spoke through the prophet with the familiar, "Thus saith the LORD." God was direct to Jeroboam. He intended to rip the kingdom from Solomon and give ten tribes to Jeroboam. (Again, the usage of the word **rend** {קרע *qara*} or 'rip' is instructive.) God had lost all respect for Solomon. He therefore would rip his kingdom apart even as Ahijah had ripped his garment into pieces. However, God made clear to Jeroboam that He would reserve one tribe (in addition to Judah) to him because of His promise to David. It may be that Benjamin is included by implication in as much as Jerusalem was partially located in the inheritance of Benjamin.

11:33 God made clear to Jeroboam the reason why he would so deal against Solomon and Israel. **Because that they have forsaken me, and have worshipped Ashtoreth the goddess of the Zidonians, Chemosh the god of the Moabites, and Milcom the god of the children of Ammon, and have not walked in my ways, to do *that which is* right in mine eyes, and *to keep* my statutes and my judgments, as *did* David his father.** God enumerated the idolatry which Solomon had introduced into Israel. Moreover, Solomon had (1) not walked in His ways. (2) He had not done that which was right before Him. And, (3) he had flagrantly disobeyed God's Word unlike David his father. Solomon's sin was therefore a combination of idolatry, unrighteousness, and disobedience. God had had enough.

11:34-37 God therefore carefully spelled out to Jeroboam the precise character in which He intended to act. First, God said, **I will not take the whole kingdom out of his hand: but I will make him prince all the days of his life for David my servant's sake, whom I chose, because he kept my commandments and my statutes**.

These events would not come to pass during the lifetime of Solomon. He would remain king throughout his lifetime. God made clear that he would honor his word to David, Solomon's father. Of note is that God's respect to David was because he kept his commandments altogether. God characterized David's life as one of obedience. (Though David had sinned grievously in the matter of Bathsheba, his overall life had been one of total dedication and obedience to His God.) Therefore, God carefully kept His Word to David.

Second, God informed Jeroboam that 35 **I will take the kingdom out of his son's hand, and will give it unto thee,** *even* **ten tribes**. After the death of Solomon, God would take ten tribes from Solomon's son and successor and give them to Jeroboam.

Third, God told Jeroboam that to Solomon's son, 36 **will I give one tribe, that David my servant may have a light alway before me in Jerusalem, the city which I have chosen me to put my name there**. Again, the reference to one tribe likely alludes to how that God would give one additional tribe to Solomon's son. It likely was assumed that he would retain leadership over Judah. In any event, Jerusalem was located in both Judah and Benjamin.

Finally, God announced to Jeroboam that **37 I will take thee, and thou shalt reign according to all that thy soul desireth, and shalt be king over Israel**. With God's approval, Jeroboam would become the king of greater Israel in the foreseeable future.

11:38-39 God however, gave to Jeroboam a clear condition for His blessing. It was not dissimilar to what He had told either David or Solomon. **And it shall be, if thou wilt hearken unto all that I command thee, and wilt walk in my ways, and do *that is* right in my sight, to keep my statutes and my commandments, as David my servant did; that I will be with thee, and build thee a sure house, as I built for David, and will give Israel unto thee**.

God's condition of blessing for Jeroboam was simple: (1) walk in my ways, (2) obey me, and (3) do that which is right. If Jeroboam would so comply, God promised to build him a "sure house." The latter has the idea of a lasting posterity (i.e., a perpetual dynasty) even as God had promised David.

Moreover, if Jeroboam would meet God's simple conditions, He would give him Israel altogether to rule over. Sadly, Jeroboam like Solomon soon ignored God's conditions for blessing.

God also noted to Jeroboam, **39 And I will for this afflict the seed of David, but not for ever**. Because that Solomon had ignored His warning, God promised to afflict his posterity. However, He also warned Jeroboam that His chastening upon the seed of David would not be forever. The time was coming when His full blessing would return to the house of David. That ultimately will be fulfilled when Christ returns.

11:40 Word of this incident evidently reached Solomon. **Solomon sought therefore to kill Jeroboam. And Jeroboam arose, and fled into Egypt, unto Shishak king of Egypt, and**

was in Egypt until the death of Solomon. Jeroboam sought refuge in Egypt beyond the reach of Solomon.

11:41-43 The inspired historian therefore summarizes the reign of Solomon. **And the rest of the acts of Solomon, and all that he did, and his wisdom, *are* they not written in the book of the acts of Solomon?** Reference to these additional books are mentioned in II Chronicles 9:29. This may also be an oblique reference to the Book of Proverbs as well as the Song of Solomon and Ecclesiastes.

Therefore, 42 **the time that Solomon reigned in Jerusalem over all Israel *was* forty years. 43 And Solomon slept with his fathers, and was buried in the city of David his father: and Rehoboam his son reigned in his stead**. The mention of the "city of David" is unclear. Both Bethlehem as well as a part of Jerusalem were so named. Jewish tradition holds that David was buried in Bethlehem and that may be where Solomon was buried as well. One thing is clear: the wisest wealthiest man who ever walked upon this earth died like everyone else. His great wealth and wisdom could not prevent that ignoble end. Upon Solomon's death, his son, Rehoboam acceded the throne.

* * * * *

Overview of I Kings 12: *Chapter 12 of I Kings is a turning point in the history of Israel. Rehoboam ascended the throne and through his folly promptly split the kingdom. Record is then made of the accession of Jeroboam over the northern ten tribes of Israel. The chapter concludes with Jeroboams's idolatrous altars being erected at Bethel and Dan.*

12:1 And Rehoboam went to Shechem: for all Israel were come to Shechem to make him king. The question as to

Understanding I Kings

why Rehoboam went to Shechem to be anointed king seems apparent. It may be that the nation had become aware of what the prophet Ahijah had foretold in 11:31-39. The following context will make clear that Jeroboam had returned from Egypt. Pressure from the 'public' likely forced Rehoboam thence. If so, it reflected a mounting mood of insurrection.

Moreover, Shechem was Jeroboam's area of strength. (It also was considered by the Jews to be an ominous place in Jewish history. It was at Shechem where Dinah was ravished. There, Joseph was sold into slavery. There, Abimelech had exercised his tyranny. Now, the kingdom would divide there. Shechem was about thirty-four miles north of Jerusalem in the tribe of Manasseh.

12:2-4 Meanwhile, **it came to pass, when Jeroboam the son of Nebat, who was yet in Egypt, heard** *of it,* **(for he was fled from the presence of king Solomon, and Jeroboam dwelt in Egypt;)**. Recall the details of Jeroboam's exile found in the previous chapter (11:40). Of interest is that the *people* of Israel had brought Jeroboam back—likely to be a spokesman for them against Rehoboam. It may well be that they had already seen arrogance and tyranny in Rehoboam as a young prince in the land.

Therefore, **3 they sent and called him. And Jeroboam and all the congregation of Israel came, and spake unto Rehoboam, saying, 4 Thy father made our yoke grievous: now therefore make thou the grievous service of thy father, and his heavy yoke which he put upon us, lighter, and we will serve thee**. The majority of Israel, aware of Jeroboam's insurgency against Solomon, now turned to him as a spokesman against the crown prince. Also, it is apparent that Solomon's later years had been one of heavy taxation and governmental oppression. The people therefore called upon Jeroboam to be their spokesman to Rehoboam. He brought to the young prince's attention how they had been oppressed by his father. They therefore offered a deal to Rehoboam. Lighten the taxation and the oppressive government regulations and they would receive him as king.

12:5-7 Rehoboam thus **said unto them, Depart yet *for* three days, then come again to me. And the people departed**. He asked for three days to think it over. Meanwhile, **6 king Rehoboam consulted with the old men, that stood before Solomon his father while he yet lived, and said, How do ye advise that I may answer this people? 7 And they spake unto him, saying, If thou wilt be a servant unto this people this day, and wilt serve them, and answer them, and speak good words to them, then they will be thy servants for ever**. In consulting with the elders of the kingdom, they counseled him to deal kindly with the people and their request. If he did so, they told him the people would submit themselves to him.

12:8-11 In one of the greatest acts of folly of all time, **Rehoboam forsook the counsel of the old men, which they had given him, and consulted with the young men that were grown up with him, *and* which stood before him: 9 And he said unto them, What counsel give ye that we may answer this people, who have spoken to me, saying, Make the yoke which thy father did put upon us lighter?** Rehoboam rejected the wise counsel of the elders of the land. Rather, he turned to the young 'punks' he had grown up with.

10 And the young men that were grown up with him spake unto him, saying, Thus shalt thou speak unto this people that spake unto thee, saying, Thy father made our yoke heavy, but make thou *it* lighter unto us; thus shalt thou say unto them, My little *finger* shall be thicker than my father's loins. 11 And now whereas my father did lade you

with a heavy yoke, I will add to your yoke: my father hath chastised you with whips, but I will chastise you with scorpions**. Not only was there folly in their advice, it was arrogant, impudent, and brash. Insight into the harsh treatment by Solomon is apparent in the reference to him using whips against people. Rehoboam's buddies counseled he should be even more authoritarian.

12:12-15 So Jeroboam and all the people came to Rehoboam the third day, as the king had appointed, saying, Come to me again the third day. 13 And the king answered the people roughly, and forsook the old men's counsel that they gave him. Not only did Rehoboam reject the wise counsel of the elders of the land, he replied to them harshly. Few men have ever been a greater fool than Rehoboam. He proceeded to insult his people with the moronic advice of his fellows. **14 And spake to them after the counsel of the young men, saying, My father made your yoke heavy, and I will add to your yoke: my father *also* chastised you with whips, but I will chastise you with scorpions**.

The sacred writer therefore comments, **15 Wherefore the king hearkened not unto the people; for the cause was from the LORD, that he might perform his saying, which the LORD spake by Ahijah the Shilonite unto Jeroboam the son of Nebat**. God had clearly foretold that He would rend the kingdom from Solomon's son for the sin of the elder. See I Kings 11:11-12 and 11:29-39. That was about to happen. God allowed the foolish son of Solomon to tear the nation apart. Moreover, it is evident that the wisdom which Solomon once had certainly had not been imparted to his impudent son.

12:16-17 The inevitable split occurred. **So when all Israel saw that the king hearkened not unto them, the people answered the king, saying, What portion have we in David?**

neither *have we* inheritance in the son of Jesse: to your tents, O Israel: now see to thine own house, David. So Israel departed unto their tents.** The vast majority of the nation of Israel rejected the dynasty of David. They wanted nothing more to do with the descendants of him. Solomon had been oppressive, especially in his latter years. Now his son had shown himself an arrogant fool. They thus seceded from the union of Israel. However, **17 *as for* the children of Israel which dwelt in the cities of Judah, Rehoboam reigned over them.** Rehoboam's kingdom was reduced to the tribe of Judah. Benjamin remained loyal to the house of David, Judah's favorite son. There thus remained the historic tie between Judah and Benjamin.

12:18-19 Then king Rehoboam sent Adoram, who *was* over the tribute; and all Israel stoned him with stones, that he died. Therefore king Rehoboam made speed to get him up to his chariot, to flee to Jerusalem. Sophomoric Rehoboam still had not gotten the message. He sent a tax agent out to collect taxes to himself. (There also was an Adoram who was over tribute in David's kingdom. However, more than forty years had passed and it is unlikely that they were the same individual, though it is conceivable they may have been the same.) The population caught this hapless agent of Rehoboam's internal revenue service and stoned him to death. Then the folly of his decisions began to soak in. Rehoboam thence hightailed it back to Jerusalem. As a result, **19 Israel rebelled against the house of David unto this day**. The kingdom was thus divided until the time of the Assyrian conquest about 250 years later. As noted in the introduction to the notes on I Kings, the author of I Kings may have been Ezra or Nehemiah.

12:20 And it came to pass, when all Israel heard that Jeroboam was come again, that they sent and called him

Understanding I Kings

unto the congregation, and made him king over all Israel: there was none that followed the house of David, but the tribe of Judah only. Upon hearing that Jeroboam had returned from Egypt, the northern ten tribes of Israel called him before them and made him their king. Though Judah is noted singularly here, it is evident from the next verse that Benjamin had cast its lot with Judah. The two tribes were closely joined to each other and actually shared Jerusalem in their territories. However, from thence onward the combined tribes of Benjamin and Judah would ever be known simply as Judah.

12:21 Rehoboam still was determined to restore his kingdom, by force if necessary. Therefore, **when Rehoboam was come to Jerusalem, he assembled all the house of Judah, with the tribe of Benjamin, an hundred and fourscore thousand chosen men, which were warriors, to fight against the house of Israel, to bring the kingdom again to Rehoboam the son of Solomon**. Upon arriving back in Jerusalem, Rehoboam assembled an army of 180,000 men from both Judah and Benjamin. As far as Rehoboam was concerned, if it meant a civil war to restore his kingdom, then so be it.

12:22-24 However, God put a stop to this folly. **But the word of God came unto Shemaiah the man of God, saying, 23 Speak unto Rehoboam, the son of Solomon, king of Judah, and unto all the house of Judah and Benjamin, and to the remnant of the people, saying, 24 Thus saith the LORD, Ye shall not go up, nor fight against your brethren the children of Israel: return every man to his house; for this thing is from me. They hearkened therefore to the word of the LORD, and returned to depart, according to the word of the LORD.**

God had spoken to Jeroboam earlier through the prophet Ahijah. Rehoboam no doubt was aware of that and would have rejected his counsel. However, God now spoke through another prophet, presumably someone whom Rehoboam did not suspect of being partial to his adversary. Shemaiah therefore apparently appeared before Rehoboam and announced, "Thus saith the LORD." He thence proceeded to pronounce God's injunction against going to war against the northern ten tribes.

What is significant is that God made clear to Rehoboam through the prophet that this whole matter was of Him. See 11:11-12 and 11:29-39. Rehoboam more than likely had been aware of Ahijah's prophecy before his father died. Now, he heard it again from another prophet, presumably loyal to him. Therefore, the considered judgment of Judah and Benjamin was to suspend military operations against the north. The greater tribes of Judah and Benjamin therefore obeyed God's Word in the matter.

12:25 Meanwhile, to the north, **Jeroboam built Shechem in mount Ephraim, and dwelt therein; and went out from thence, and built Penuel.** Shechem was in Manasseh, the region which Solomon had originally given oversight to Jeroboam earlier. Therefore, he rebuilt the city, making it his initial capital. He also rebuilt the city of Penuel which was east of the Jordan River in Gilead.

12:26-27 However, Jeroboam, though established as king of the northern ten tribes, began to worry about his influence being eroded by Jerusalem whence was the Temple of God. **And Jeroboam said in his heart, Now shall the kingdom return to the house of David: 27 If this people go up to do sacrifice in the house of the LORD at Jerusalem, then shall the heart of this people turn again unto their lord,** *even* **unto Rehoboam king of Judah, and they shall kill me, and go again to Rehoboam king of Judah.** The historic capital of Israel since the time of David had been Jerusalem. Moreover, it

Understanding I Kings

was there that the Temple of Jehovah was. Jeroboam feared (and rightly so) that his people would still gravitate back to Jerusalem to worship Jehovah and make sacrifices to Him. He feared the people would therefore come under the influence of Rehoboam and he (Jeroboam) would eventually be ousted as king of the north.

12:28-30 Whereupon the king took counsel, and made two calves *of* gold, and said unto them, It is too much for you to go up to Jerusalem: behold thy gods, O Israel, which brought thee up out of the land of Egypt.

Jeroboam already had rejected the offer made to him by Jehovah God as recorded in 11:38-39. He knew the Law of God. Yet, for political expediency, he rejected it. His sojourn in Egypt had perhaps exposed him to the idolatry of the pagans. Baal worship usually involved the erection of statues of calves or young oxen. Moreover, Jeroboam must have been aware of the sin of Aaron and the people during the exodus when they made the golden calf. Notwithstanding, he made two golden calves. He thus informed his people that it was too much for them to make the long journey to Jerusalem to worship God. Rather, he proclaimed the two golden calves to be the gods which had delivered them from Egypt.

It was blatant blasphemy of the most outrageous character. Moreover, it was religion politically motivated. It was a striking parallel to the blasphemous statement made by Aaron when he made the golden calf. See Exodus 32:4. Jeroboam therefore **29 set the one in Bethel, and the other put he in Dan.** Bethel, ironically means 'house of God.' It was at the southern edge of northern kingdom near the border of Benjamin. Dan was to the far north. To this day, ruins of the city of Dan and the remnants of the pagan altar for the golden calf remain.

In one of the great understatements of the Bible, the sacred writer records, **30 And this thing became a sin: for the people** went *to worship* before the one, *even* unto Dan. It was sin of the worst character. It blatantly violated the first three commandments. Nevertheless, many of the northern kingdom went to worship at these two pagan shrines, even as far north as the one in Dan.

12:31 Not only that, but Jeroboam **made an house of high places, and made priests of the lowest of the people, which were not of the sons of Levi**. The word translated as **lowest** (קצה *qatsah*) can also have the sense of 'extremity' or 'end.' Some have suggested that he rather took some of the aristocracy of the nation at the other end of the social scale and made them priests. See also comments for 13:33.

12:32-33 In any event, **Jeroboam ordained a feast in the eighth month, on the fifteenth day of the month, like unto the feast that *is* in Judah, and he offered upon the altar. So did he in Bethel, sacrificing unto the calves that he had made: and he placed in Bethel the priests of the high places which he had made**. Jeroboam shrewdly made a high holy day in the north to correspond with the feast of Tabernacles at Jerusalem. He also placed his high priests at the shrine he had built at Bethel. Apparently, the shrine at Dan became secondary.

33 **So he offered upon the altar which he had made in Bethel the fifteenth day of the eighth month, *even* in the month which he had devised of his own heart; and ordained a feast unto the children of Israel: and he offered upon the altar, and burnt incense**. Here is a classic illustration of false religion. It was politically motivated and counterfeited the true. Many religions to this day have the same characteristics. But it was an abomination to God as will soon be seen.

* * * * *

Understanding I Kings

Overview of I Kings 13: This next chapter records God's warning of judgment against the blasphemous altar at Bethel. There is then a lengthy account of an old prophet who became disobedient to God. Notwithstanding evident judgment by God, Jeroboam continued in his apostasy.

13:1-3 God's wrath against the blasphemous altar at Bethel is made evident. **And, behold, there came a man of God out of Judah by the word of the LORD unto Bethel: and Jeroboam stood by the altar to burn incense.** Apparently at the same time that Jeroboam was offering incense as noted in the previous verse, God sent a "man of God" from Judah. Notwithstanding God's direction to him, it must have taken great courage for this prophet to come and withstand an arrogant king.

2 **And he cried against the altar in the word of the LORD, and said, O altar, altar, thus saith the LORD; Behold, a child shall be born unto the house of David, Josiah by name; and upon thee shall he offer the priests of the high places that burn incense upon thee, and men's bones shall be burnt upon thee.** With eloquence, yet divine authority, this prophet announced that the day was coming when a king would be born in Judah by the name of Josiah. In his reign, he would offer the very priests of this pagan altar upon it for sacrifice. The pointed statement "and men's bones shall be burnt upon thee" is foreboding in its forewarning. Approximately, 350 years later, this prophecy would be fulfilled when Josiah did the same. See II Kings 23:15,16, and 20.

Moreover, the prophet 3 **gave a sign the same day, saying, This *is* the sign which the LORD hath spoken; Behold, the altar shall be rent, and the ashes that *are* upon it shall be poured out.** The clear implication is that God would destroy this altar. It would not merely be damaged, but split down the middle such that its contents spilled out on the ground.

13:4-5 This arrogant king did not take kindly to the prophet who had so rebuked him. **Therefore, it came to pass, when king Jeroboam heard the saying of the man of God, which had cried against the altar in Bethel, that he put forth his hand from the altar, saying, Lay hold on him. And his hand, which he put forth against him, dried up, so that he could not pull it in again to him.** Jeroboam therefore angrily ordered the prophet to be arrested on the spot. However, when the king went to remove his hand from the altar, it shriveled up. Furthermore, he could no longer move it. It was shriveled in a distended position. God's judgment was evident.

In addition, **5 the altar also was rent, and the ashes poured out from the altar, according to the sign which the man of God had given by the word of the LORD**. God clearly authenticated the ministry of this prophet. The idolatrous altar was broken in half. His prophecy came to pass moments after he had uttered it. The greater truth is that it had been given by the "word of the LORD."

13:6 Jeroboam then had the audacity to seek the help of the God he had so blatantly offended. **And the king answered and said unto the man of God, Intreat now the face of the LORD thy God, and pray for me, that my hand may be restored me again. And the man of God besought the LORD, and the king's hand was restored him again, and became as *it was* before**. It was clear that the golden calf had no power. And in distinct contrast, the power of Jehovah God had been forcibly demonstrated. God in mercy healed this corrupt king.

13:7-10 Thereafter, Jeroboam quickly changed his tune toward the prophet. **And the king said unto the man of God, Come home with me, and refresh thyself, and I will give thee a reward**. Jeroboam invited the unnamed prophet to come home for dinner and he would handsomely reward him. However, the prophet replied, **8 If thou wilt give me half thine house, I will not go in with thee, neither will I eat bread nor drink water in this place: 9 For so was it charged me by the word of the LORD, saying, Eat no bread, nor drink water, nor turn again by the same way that thou camest.** God had given him strict orders to not have any fellowship with anyone at Bethel. Furthermore, he was instructed to turn around and go home when his ministry was finished though not by the same route which he had come. Therefore, the prophet turned upon his heel and **10 he went another way, and returned not by the way that he came to Bethel.**

13:11-13 Meanwhile, **there dwelt an old prophet in Bethel; and his sons came and told him all the works that the man of God had done that day in Bethel: the words which he had spoken unto the king, them they told also to their father. 12 And their father said unto them, What way went he? For his sons had seen what way the man of God went, which came from Judah. 13 And he said unto his sons, Saddle me the ass. So they saddled him the ass: and he rode thereon.** It is apparent that God had chosen to not use this old prophet who already lived in Bethel. However, upon hearing of what had happened, he pursued after the man of God as he journeyed back south.

13:14-17 The old prophet therefore **went after the man of God, and found him sitting under an oak: and he said unto him,** *Art* **thou the man of God that camest from Judah? And he said, I** *am***. 15 Then he said unto him, Come home with me, and eat bread.** Upon finding the now famous man of God, the old prophet invited him home to eat. To this, the man of God replied, **16 I may not return with thee, nor go in with thee: neither will I eat bread nor drink water with thee in this place: 17 For it was said to me by the word of the LORD,**

Thou shalt eat no bread nor drink water there, nor turn again to go by the way that thou camest. The man of God turned down his offer, noting he had been straitly charged not to do any such thing while in the northern kingdom.

13:18-19 He said unto him, I *am* a prophet also as thou *art*; and an angel spake unto me by the word of the LORD, saying, Bring him back with thee into thine house, that he may eat bread and drink water. *But* **he lied unto him. 19 So he went back with him, and did eat bread in his house, and drank water.** The prophet from Judah was being tested. The old prophet from Bethel 'twisted' his arm and claimed that an angel had given him a new revelation directing the prophet from Judah to come home with him. However, the text is clear, *"But* he lied unto him." Therefore, the prophet disobeyed his orders and went home with the man.

13:20-22 God evidently tested this fellow and he flunked the test. Therefore, **it came to pass, as they sat at the table, that the word of the LORD came unto the prophet that brought him back: 21 And he cried unto the man of God that came from Judah, saying, Thus saith the LORD, Forasmuch as thou hast disobeyed the mouth of the LORD, and hast not kept the commandment which the LORD thy God commanded thee, 22 But camest back, and hast eaten bread and drunk water in the place, of the which *the LORD* did say to thee, Eat no bread, and drink no water; thy carcase shall not come unto the sepulchre of thy fathers**.

While still at dinner with the old lying prophet, God spoke through him nevertheless and informed his disobedient man that because of his direct disobedience, he would die a premature death. A clear lesson is at hand of how important obedience to God is. This man's sin was simply disobedience. Yet, it would cost him his life. He was in a position of spiritual influ-

Understanding I Kings 123

ence. But he disobeyed the God who had sent him. Therefore, God chose to deal severely with him.

13:23-25 Thereafter, **it came to pass, after he had eaten bread, and after he had drunk, that he saddled for him the ass,** *to wit,* **for the prophet whom he had brought back. 24 And when he was gone, a lion met him by the way, and slew him: and his carcase was cast in the way, and the ass stood by it, the lion also stood by the carcase.** God chose to take this prophet to heaven early for his disobedience. A lesson is at hand illustrating the fear of the Lord.

25 And, behold, men passed by, and saw the carcase cast in the way, and the lion standing by the carcase: and they came and told *it* **in the city where the old prophet dwelt.** It is apparent that God allowed the lion to kill the prophet, but it devoured neither him nor his donkey. Ironically, God spared the donkey but not the disobedient prophet. Word thus reached the old prophet at Bethel of what had happened.

13:26 And when the prophet that brought him back from the way heard *thereof,* **he said, It** *is* **the man of God, who was disobedient unto the word of the LORD: therefore the LORD hath delivered him unto the lion, which hath torn him, and slain him, according to the word of the LORD, which he spake unto him.** The old compromising prophet rightly judged. The prophet from Judah had been slain for direct disobedience to God. God may not always intervene and so severely judge one disobedient to him. But in this case, a prophet who had direct instructions from him violated them anyway. God dealt severely with him. A lesson in obedience and the fear of the Lord remains.

13:27-30 The old prophet therefore **spake to his sons, saying, Saddle me the ass. And they saddled** *him.* **28 And he**

went and found his carcase cast in the way, and the ass and the lion standing by the carcase: the lion had not eaten the carcase, nor torn the ass.** God quite evidently had prevented the lion from desecrating the body of his man.

29 And the prophet took up the carcase of the man of God, and laid it upon the ass, and brought it back: and the old prophet came to the city, to mourn and to bury him. Furthermore, God caused the lion to just stand and watch as the old prophet took the body of the disobedient man of God and brought him back to town for burial.

There, **30 he laid his carcase in his own grave; and they mourned over him,** *saying***, Alas, my brother!** Though the old prophet did the slain man of God a service in burying him, it was his deceit that provoked the entire incident. He was a compromiser altogether.

13:31-32 Notwithstanding his part in provoking the death of the prophet from Judea, **it came to pass, after he had buried him, that he spake to his sons, saying, When I am dead, then bury me in the sepulchre wherein the man of God** *is* **buried; lay my bones beside his bones: 32 For the saying which he cried by the word of the LORD against the altar in Bethel, and against all the houses of the high places which** *are* **in the cities of Samaria, shall surely come to pass.**

He wanted his body placed next to the bones of this man of God. He had that much respect unto him. He realized the truth which this poor fellow had pronounced against the apostasy of Jeroboam's kingdom. The deceased prophet may have had more to say about "the high places which *are* in the cities of Samaria" or it may be that the old prophet by implication made application to them as well. He remained a prophet of Jehovah in the north, though certainly not a vocal one. Eventually, God would judge all the apostasy of the north as well in due season.

13:33-34 After this thing Jeroboam returned not from his evil way, but made again of the lowest of the people priests of the high places: whosoever would, he consecrated him, and he became *one* of the priests of the high places. Notwithstanding the evident judgment of God before his very eyes, Jeroboam refused to repent of his sin. He placed anyone into his corrupt priesthood. See comments on 12:31 regarding the lowest of the people. However, the comments here would seem to indicate that the lowest of the people were in fact just that.

34 And this thing became sin unto the house of Jeroboam, even to cut *it* off, and to destroy *it* from off the face of the earth. The allowance of the idolatrous blasphemy in Israel by Jeroboam became a great sin, especially his refusal to destroy it. The implication is that it became the cause for further judgment of God. In the next chapter, we read of the illness of his son. It likely was not coincidental!

* * * * *

Overview of I Kings 14: *The sacred writer chronicles the conclusion of the reign of Jeroboam and Rehoboam. Record is made of a portion of the fulfillment of the prophecy against Jeroboam. Also note is made of the apostasy of Judah under Rehoboam's reign with the invasion of Egypt as a result. Note is also made of the deaths of both Jeroboam and Rehoboam.*

14:1-3 The chapter commences with what is evident chastening of God against Jeroboam and the apparent initial fulfillment of God's judgment against him as noted in the previous chapter.

At that time Abijah the son of Jeroboam fell sick. 2 And Jeroboam said to his wife, Arise, I pray thee, and disguise

thyself, that thou be not known to be the wife of Jeroboam; and get thee to Shiloh: behold, there *is* Ahijah the prophet, which told me that *I should be* king over this people. 3 And take with thee ten loaves, and cracknels, and a cruse of honey, and go to him: he shall tell thee what shall become of the child. The illness of Jeroboam's son was perceived to be God's hand. He therefore directed his wife to disguise herself and go to Shiloh whence was Ahijah the prophet who had told him that he would someday be king. See I Kings 11:29 *ff*.

14:4-6 Meanwhile, God clued Ahijah in as to what was going on. **And Jeroboam's wife did so, and arose, and went to Shiloh, and came to the house of Ahijah. But Ahijah could not see; for his eyes were set by reason of his age.** Though Mrs. Jeroboam came incognito, it made little difference. Ahijah by now was blind in his old age. **5 And the LORD said unto Ahijah, Behold, the wife of Jeroboam cometh to ask a thing of thee for her son; for he *is* sick: thus and thus shalt thou say unto her: for it shall be, when she cometh in, that she shall feign herself *to be* another *woman*.**

God informed old Ahijah who was coming and why. Furthermore, **6 when Ahijah heard the sound of her feet, as she came in at the door, that he said, Come in, thou wife of Jeroboam; why feignest thou thyself *to be* another? for I *am* sent to thee *with* heavy *tidings*.** When Jeroboam's wife arrived in her disguise, Ahijah immediately acknowledged who she was and informed her that he had bad news. Indeed, what Ahijah would foretell would be bad news.

14:7-9 Ahijah began his austere prophecy by reminding Jeroboam why he was king and who had put him there. **Go, tell Jeroboam, Thus saith the LORD God of Israel, Forasmuch as I exalted thee from among the people, and made thee prince over my people Israel.** It was Jehovah God who had exalted Jeroboam to be king over the northern ten tribes. **8 And rent the kingdom away from the house of David, and gave it thee: and** *yet* **thou hast not been as my servant David, who kept my commandments, and who followed me with all his heart, to do** *that* **only** *which was* **right in mine eyes**.

It was Jehovah God who had removed most of David's kingdom from Rehoboam. God speaking through the prophet thus noted how that David had faithfully kept His commandments, doing that which was right before God. Jeroboam had not. **9 But hast done evil above all that were before thee: for thou hast gone and made thee other gods, and molten images, to provoke me to anger, and hast cast me behind thy back**. The message of God confronted Jeroboam with his blatant idolatry. It may be that this message was delivered through his wife because she may have been a major influence upon her husband's idolatry.

14:10-11 Ahijah thus delivered a scathing pronouncement against the house of Jeroboam from God. **Therefore, behold, I will bring evil upon the house of Jeroboam, and will cut off from Jeroboam him that pisseth against the wall,** *and* **him that is shut up and left in Israel, and will take away the remnant of the house of Jeroboam, as a man taketh away dung, till it be all gone**. The essence of the above judgment is that God would soon kill every male of the house of Jeroboam. (The word translated as **pisseth** {שתן *shathan*} refers to male urination. Though the word today is considered coarse, that was not the case when the Authorized Version was translated.) The greater point is that God warned he was about to destroy the house of Jeroboam, especially every male thereof. When He was through, the house of Jeroboam would be thrown out like garbage or sewage. This is sharp and harsh language. It revealed the anger of God which had been kindled by Jeroboam's flagrant breaking of God's covenant with him.

Ahijah continued on behalf of God, **11 Him that dieth of Jeroboam in the city shall the dogs eat; and him that dieth in the field shall the fowls of the air eat: for the LORD hath spoken *it*.** God was about to violently deal with the utter blasphemy of Jeroboam. The judgment pending would find the house of Jeroboam being eaten by scavenging animals. They would not even have the dignity of burial—so harsh was the coming judgment of God. God had graciously given Jeroboam leadership over ten tribes. Jeroboam in return had utterly and flagrantly blasphemed Him by his idolatry.

14:12-13 Because it was to Mrs. Jeroboam that such a harsh pronouncement was made concerning her family, it may well be assumed that she was part and parcel to the sin of her husband. She well may have influenced him in the direction that he went. Ahijah therefore gave her more bad news in sending her away. **Arise thou therefore, get thee to thine own house: *and* when thy feet enter into the city, the child shall die.** When Jeroboam's wife set foot back in Tirzah, the seat of Jeroboam's throne, her son would die. Ahijah thus ordered her home. She had come to receive word from the prophet regarding her sick son. She did. It was not good news.

The only good news was that **13 all Israel shall mourn for him, and bury him: for he only of Jeroboam shall come to the grave, because in him there is found *some* good thing toward the LORD God of Israel in the house of Jeroboam.** Of the impending judgment upon the house of Jeroboam, only this young son would have the dignity of a decent burial. Jewish tradition holds that the good mentioned in the house of Jeroboam was that in the death of his son, the guards were removed which had hindered Israelites from going to the feasts of Jehovah at Jerusalem.

14:14-16 Before Jeroboam's wife left, God through the prophet delivered more stern tidings. **Moreover the LORD**

Understanding I Kings

shall raise him up a king over Israel, who shall cut off the house of Jeroboam that day: but what? even now. The day was coming when God would raise up a new king in Israel who would destroy the dynasty of Jeroboam in one day. That would happen about five years later when Baasha would overthrow Nadab, Jeroboam's son, and kill him the same day. See I Kings 15:25-30.

Ahijah's prophecy became even worse. He looked far beyond Jeroboam to the day of the Assyrian captivity. **15 For the LORD shall smite Israel, as a reed is shaken in the water, and he shall root up Israel out of this good land, which he gave to their fathers, and shall scatter them beyond the river, because they have made their groves, provoking the LORD to anger.**

Clearly foretold is the dispersion of Israel from their land because of their sin of idolatry. The land beyond the river undoubtedly refers to the Euphrates River. This was fulfilled in II Kings 17:4 *ff* which see. God had clearly forbad His people in Deuteronomy 16:21-2 to make groves or set up idols therein. They had flagrantly ignored that. As foretold in Leviticus 26:34 *ff* and Deuteronomy 28:58 *ff*, God now warned again of them being dispersed from the land because of their sin.

Ahijah warned, **16 And he shall give Israel up because of the sins of Jeroboam, who did sin, and who made Israel to sin.** God was about to judge Israel because of the sin introduced into the land by Jeroboam. Mrs. Jeroboam no doubt was influential in this and she was the one who received the blunt news.

14:17-18 And Jeroboam's wife arose, and departed, and came to Tirzah: *and* **when she came to the threshold of the door, the child died.** Upon arriving back in Tirzah, the town where Jeroboam had established residence, as his wife crossed the threshold of the city gate, her son died. God's warning through Ahijah was already coming to pass. **18 And they**

buried him; and all Israel mourned for him, according to the word of the LORD, which he spake by the hand of his servant Ahijah the prophet. Jeroboam soon learned that Ahijah's was God's servant and not his.

14:19-20 And the rest of the acts of Jeroboam, how he warred, and how he reigned, behold, they *are* written in the book of the chronicles of the kings of Israel. 20 And the days which Jeroboam reigned *were* two and twenty years: and he slept with his fathers, and Nadab his son reigned in his stead.

The final years of Jeroboam's reign are thus summarized. He certainly warred against Rehoboam and his son Abijam, as noted in II Chronicles 13. The reference to the "chronicles of the kings of Israel" may refer to non-inspired histories apart from the biblical books of Chronicles. In any event, Jeroboam's tenure as king was twenty-two years. A typical euphemism of death is used in describing him as have "slept with his fathers." Mention is briefly made of Nadab his son acceding the throne upon the death of his father.

14:21-24 The focus of the book now shifts back to Rehoboam and the southern kingdom. **And Rehoboam the son of Solomon reigned in Judah. Rehoboam *was* forty and one years old when he began to reign, and he reigned seventeen years in Jerusalem, the city which the LORD did choose out of all the tribes of Israel, to put his name there. And his mother's name *was* Naamah an Ammonitess.** Rehoboam's reign is thus briefly summarized. He was forty one when he became king. He reigned for seventeen years in Jerusalem. His mother was from Ammon.

Moreover, under Rehoboam's reign as king, **22 Judah did evil in the sight of the LORD, and they provoked him to jealousy with their sins which they had committed, above**

all that their fathers had done. 23 For they also built them high places, and images, and groves, on every high hill, and under every green tree. The chief evil wrought by Judah under Rehoboam was the sliding back into idolatry. Baal worship and other pagan gods were typically worshiped upon hilltops where groves of trees had been planted. It became so flagrant in Judah that such idolatry was practiced under "every green tree."

With the spiritual apostasy followed moral perversity. **24 And there were also sodomites in the land:** *and* **they did according to all the abominations of the nations which the LORD cast out before the children of Israel.** With the idolatry of the pagans came their immoral practices. When spiritual apostasy sets in, homosexuality often is not far behind. Judah was thus not far from where the Canaanites had been before Israel entered the land hundreds of years earlier.

14:25-26 In what clearly is chastening by God, **it came to pass in the fifth year of king Rehoboam,** *that* **Shishak king of Egypt came up against Jerusalem: 26 And he took away the treasures of the house of the LORD, and the treasures of the king's house; he even took away all: and he took away all the shields of gold which Solomon had made.** Not only did Rehoboam lose God's blessing, he now faced God's wrath. God sent Shishak of Egypt who looted Jerusalem and the Temple of its wealth. It is clear that God was not impressed with the gold of the Temple.

14:27-28 And king Rehoboam made in their stead brasen shields, and committed *them* **unto the hands of the chief of the guard, which kept the door of the king's house.** Undeterred, Rehoboam replaced the gold shields taken by the Egyptians with brass ones. However, **28 it was** *so,* **when the king went into the house of the LORD, that the guard bare them, and brought them back into the guard chamber.** It seems that thereafter, Rehoboam lived in fear. Even when he went to the Temple, he had to do so with an armed body guard. They then carried the brass shields as they escorted the king.

14:30-31 The sacred writer concludes his record of Rehoboam. **Now the rest of the acts of Rehoboam, and all that he did, *are* they not written in the book of the chronicles of the kings of Judah? And there was war between Rehoboam and Jeroboam all *their* days.** Regarding the chronicles of the kings of Judah, see II Chronicles 12:15. There, additional historians are noted in Shemaiah the prophet and Iddo the seer. The lack of God's blessing is apparent in that Rehoboam was in a state of perpetual war with Jeroboam throughout his reign as king.

The epitaph of his reign is thus summarily noted, **31 And Rehoboam slept with his fathers, and was buried with his fathers in the city of David. And his mother's name *was* Naamah an Ammonitess. And Abijam his son reigned in his stead.** His son Abijam (or Abijah as written in II Chronicles 13) reigned after him.

* * * * *

Overview of I Kings 15: *This next chapter chronicles the life and reign of Abijam in Judah followed by the same of Asa, his successor. The focus then shifts back to the northern kingdom and presents brief detail of Nadab. This is followed by record of him being deposed by Baasha and his accession to the throne of Israel.*

15:1-2 The sacred historian now presents an overview of Abijam and his reign over Judah. **Now in the eighteenth year of king Jeroboam the son of Nebat reigned Abijam over**

Understanding I Kings

Judah. 2 **Three years reigned he in Jerusalem. And his mother's name** *was* **Maachah, the daughter of Abishalom**. His reign was short—three years. It is thought that **Abishalom** is another name for Absalom. See II Chronicles 11:20-21.

15:3-5 As the successive kings of Judah and Israel will be chronicled, there usually will be a brief description of their reign. Here is it noted that Abijam (Abijah) **walked in all the sins of his father, which he had done before him: and his heart was not perfect with the LORD his God, as the heart of David his father**. Here is illustrated: like father like son. More descriptive, Abijam's "heart was not perfect with the LORD his God." The word translated as **perfect** (שלם *shalem*) here essentially means 'complete' or 'whole.' In other words, Abijam's heart was not dedicated to the Lord. His sentiments lay elsewhere. He thus was unlike David who sought the Lord with his whole heart. See Psalm 119: 10.

The text continues, 4 **Nevertheless for David's sake did the LORD his God give him a lamp in Jerusalem, to set up his son after him, and to establish Jerusalem: 5 Because David did** *that which was* **right in the eyes of the LORD, and turned not aside from any** *thing* **that he commanded him all the days of his life, save only in the matter of Uriah the Hittite**. Comment is again made of God's promise to David to maintain his descendants upon his throne. David's life is thus summarized as having done that which was right in the eyes of the Lord with the exception of what he did to Uriah. Righteousness (or the lack thereof) is a simple defining characteristic used to described most of the kings of Israel and Judah.

15:6-7 Abijam's reign is thus summarized, **And there was war between Rehoboam and Jeroboam all the days of his life**. The bitter dispute caused by Rehoboam continued through his son as proxy throughout his reign. 7 **Now the rest of the acts**

of Abijam, and all that he did, *are* they not written in the book of the chronicles of the kings of Judah? And there was war between Abijam and Jeroboam**. See II Chronicles 13:22. Also, the state of hostilities between Abijam and Jeroboam is reiterated. See II Chronicles 13:3, 17.

15:8 Again, the euphemism of sleeping with one's fathers is used for death. **And Abijam slept with his fathers; and they buried him in the city of David: and Asa his son reigned in his stead**. He was succeeded by his son Asa. Though the English pronunciation usually is *AYsa*. The Hebrew pronunciation thereof is *AhSAW*.

15:9-10 Historical markers of the reign of Asa are noted. **And in the twentieth year of Jeroboam king of Israel reigned Asa over Judah. 10 And forty and one years reigned he in Jerusalem. And his mother's name *was* Maachah, the daughter of Abishalom**. His tenure would be the longest as a king in either Judah or Israel to date at forty-one years. The mention of his mother being the daughter of *Abishalom* likely refers to her being his grandmother. This same woman, though not his mother, may have been the one who brought him up.

15:11 The moral and spiritual character of Asa is thus succinctly noted. **And Asa did *that which was* right in the eyes of the LORD, as *did* David his father**. All that he did was summarized into the short statement, "He did that which was right in the eyes of the LORD." A lesson remains there for us to this day. Though not sinless, the character of his reign was similar to that of his great, great grandfather David.

15:12-13 The courage and moral fortitude of Asa are noted. **And he took away the sodomites out of the land, and removed all the idols that his fathers had made. 13 And also**

Understanding I Kings

Maachah his mother, even her he removed from *being* queen, because she had made an idol in a grove; and Asa destroyed her idol, and burnt *it* by the brook Kidron. In ways unspecified, Asa got rid of the homosexuals in his kingdom. He even had the courage to remove his grandmother as the queen mother. She had erected a pagan idol in a grove near Jerusalem. Asa therefore destroyed that pagan idol. He also burnt it in by the brook Kidron. That latter is in the deep valley between Jerusalem proper and the Mount of Olives to the east of the city.

15:14-15 Notwithstanding, **the high places were not removed: nevertheless Asa's heart was perfect with the LORD all his days.** Unlike his father Abijam, the heart of Asa was totally dedicated to the Lord. He, like David, sought the Lord with his whole heart. See comments for 15:3. However, he did fail to remove the high places scattered throughout his kingdom. However, **15 he brought in the things which his father had dedicated, and the things which himself had dedicated, into the house of the LORD, silver, and gold, and vessels.** His father Abijam had apparently dedicated the spoils of a victory over Jeroboam to the Temple, but never got around to actually giving it. See II Chronicles 13:19. Asa made sure that booty was taken to the Temple. He himself prevailed in a war against the Ethiopians. (See II Chronicles 14:13-14.) Asa thus also dedicated the gold and silver taken in that war to the Temple.

15:16-17 However, there remained war with the northern kingdom throughout the reign of Asa. **And there was war between Asa and Baasha king of Israel all their days. 17 And Baasha king of Israel went up against Judah, and built Ramah, that he might not suffer any to go out or come in to Asa king of Judah.** The war described likely was a 'cold war' through much of Asa's life. II Chronicles 14:1 speaks of peace in Asa's reign for ten years. However, eventually, Baasha (in the thirty-six year of the reign of Asa) built fortifications along the border between Judah and Israel at the place called Ramah which was about five miles north of Jerusalem. His purpose was to impede any communication or commerce between the two states. It in effect was a land 'blockade' against Judah.

15:18-20 Therefore, **Asa took all the silver and the gold** *that were* **left in the treasures of the house of the LORD, and the treasures of the king's house, and delivered them into the hand of his servants: and king Asa sent them to Benhadad, the son of Tabrimon, the son of Hezion, king of Syria, that dwelt at Damascus, saying,** 19 *There is* **a league between me and thee,** *and* **between my father and thy father: behold, I have sent unto thee a present of silver and gold; come and break thy league with Baasha king of Israel, that he may depart from me**.

Rather than seek God's deliverance from his trouble, Asa foolishly turned to human help—Benhadad, king of Syria. He therefore looted the treasuries of the Temple to hire Benhadad as a mercenary army. In fact, with the money sent, he enticed Benhadad to break his alliance with Baasha. Thus, 20 **Benhadad hearkened unto king Asa, and sent the captains of the hosts which he had against the cities of Israel, and smote Ijon, and Dan, and Abelbethmaachah, and all Cinneroth, with all the land of Naphtali**. Benhadad accordingly attacked cities in northern Israel near to Syria.

15:21-22 As hoped, **it came to pass, when Baasha heard** *thereof*, **that he left off building of Ramah, and dwelt in Tirzah**. Tirzah was farther north and Baasha moved his throne there to keep an eye on the Syrians who had doubled crossed him. 22 **Then king Asa made a proclamation throughout all Judah; none** *was* **exempted: and they took away the stones**

Understanding I Kings

of Ramah, and the timber thereof, wherewith Baasha had builded; and king Asa built with them Geba of Benjamin, and Mizpah. Asa thus ordered *every* able-bodied man in Judah to Ramah and they thus destroyed the fortifications Baasha had there made. They took the timbers thereof and used them to build defensive installations in Geba and Mizpah, cities in Benjamin along the border with Israel.

15:23-24 The life and reign of Asa are thus summarized. **The rest of all the acts of Asa, and all his might, and all that he did, and the cities which he built, *are* they not written in the book of the chronicles of the kings of Judah? Nevertheless in the time of his old age he was diseased in his feet.** More details about his reign are found in II Chronicles 14:1-16:14. The disease in his feet may have been gout or it conceivably may have been complications of diabetes.

Thus, 24 **Asa slept with his fathers, and was buried with his fathers in the city of David his father: and Jehoshaphat his son reigned in his stead.** The narrative of the life of Jehoshaphat will not begin until I Kings 22:41. The focus now turns back to Israel in the north.

15:25-26 The sacred writer now will returns his attention to events in the northern kingdom. **And Nadab the son of Jeroboam began to reign over Israel in the second year of Asa king of Judah, and reigned over Israel two years.** Though the preceding paragraphs have jumped over to Baasha, the sacred writer hearkens back to 14:20. Nadab's reign however was short lived. Moreover, 26 **he did evil in the sight of the LORD, and walked in the way of his father, and in his sin wherewith he made Israel to sin.** The reign of Nadab is characterized as unrighteous in that its primary moral and spiritual distinction was evil in the sight of the Lord. He, like his father Jeroboam, continued to lead Israel into pagan idolatry.

15:27-28 Record is made how Nadab was overthrown in an insurrection. **And Baasha the son of Ahijah, of the house of Issachar, conspired against him; and Baasha smote him at Gibbethon, which *belonged* to the Philistines; for Nadab and all Israel laid siege to Gibbethon. 28 Even in the third year of Asa king of Judah did Baasha slay him, and reigned in his stead.** Gibbethon was a city to the north in Dan. Evidently, Baasha's conspiracy to oust Nadab had reached his ears. He therefore had gone north to deal with Baasha. However, in the ensuing battle, Baasha killed him. He thus became king in the third year of Asa's reign.

15:29-30 And it came to pass, when he reigned, *that* he smote all the house of Jeroboam; he left not to Jeroboam any that breathed, until he had destroyed him, according unto the saying of the LORD, which he spake by his servant Ahijah the Shilonite. Baasha made sure there were no descendants left of Jeroboam. He destroyed the entire family of Jeroboam. In so doing, he fulfilled the prophecy made by Ahijah in I Kings 14:10, 14. The mills of God grind slow, but they grind exceedingly fine. God judged Jeroboam's apostasy in his son. Furthermore, the text makes it very clear that this judgment was from God because of the sin of Jeroboam.

The destruction of the house of Jeroboam was **30 because of the sins of Jeroboam which he sinned, and which he made Israel sin, by his provocation wherewith he provoked the LORD God of Israel to anger.** Jeroboam's provocation was his introduction of idolatry into Israel.

15:31 Nadab's reign is here summarized. **Now the rest of the acts of Nadab, and all that he did, *are* they not written in the book of the chronicles of the kings of Israel?** See notes for I Kings 14:19.

Understanding I Kings

15:32-33 The reign of Baasha is thus briefly summarized. **And there was war between Asa and Baasha king of Israel all their days. 33 In the third year of Asa king of Judah began Baasha the son of Ahijah to reign over all Israel in Tirzah, twenty and four years.** That war at times was cold and at other times hot. But there was hostility between the southern and northern kingdom continually. Baasha is thus noted as reigning over Israel in the north for twenty-four years. See comments for II Chronicles 16:1 for an explanation pertaining to an *assumed* error in the chronologies noted here.

15:34 The moral and spiritual character of his reign is thus characterized. **And he did evil in the sight of the LORD, and walked in the way of Jeroboam, and in his sin wherewith he made Israel to sin.** Like his predecessors, Baasha did evil before God. He continued the pagan idolatry of Jeroboam in Israel.

* * * * *

***Overview of I Kings 16**: The focus of this next chapter remains in the northern kingdom. Chronicled are a succession of kings of Israel from Baasha to Ahab. All were apostate.*

16:1 The chapter begins with God stirring a young prophet by the name of Jehu to go and deliver a stinging prophecy against Baasha, king of the northern kingdom. **Then the word of the LORD came to Jehu the son of Hanani against Baasha, saying.**

16:2-4 Forasmuch as I exalted thee out of the dust, and made thee prince over my people Israel; and thou hast walked in the way of Jeroboam, and hast made my people Israel to sin, to provoke me to anger with their sins; 3

Behold, I will take away the posterity of Baasha, and the posterity of his house; and will make thy house like the house of Jeroboam the son of Nebat. 4 Him that dieth of Baasha in the city shall the dogs eat; and him that dieth of his in the fields shall the fowls of the air eat.

God through the prophet reminded Baasha that his position as king of Israel was by His dispensation. Notwithstanding, Baasha had walked in the ways of Jeroboam in leading Israel into the same sin as Jeroboam. He thus had provoked God to anger. Therefore, God informed him that He was about to remove all posterity of Baasha from ever succeeding him as king. He would destroy his house even as he had destroyed that of Jeroboam. Moreover, his royal family would die like dogs without proper burial.

16:5-7 The reign of Baasha is thus summarily described. **Now the rest of the acts of Baasha, and what he did, and his might, *are* they not written in the book of the chronicles of the kings of Israel? 6 So Baasha slept with his fathers, and was buried in Tirzah: and Elah his son reigned in his stead.** Mention is again made of other unspecified historical records which evidently were not inspired. Upon the death of Baasha, his son, Elah, succeeded him upon his throne. His untimely death is linked to God's judgment against him for his sin.

7 And also by the hand of the prophet Jehu the son of Hanani came the word of the LORD against Baasha, and against his house, even for all the evil that he did in the sight of the LORD, in provoking him to anger with the work of his hands, in being like the house of Jeroboam; and because he killed him. Baasha had killed the son of Jeroboam (Nadab). Though God's retribution was long in coming, it certainly came.

16:8 The brief reign of Elah is thus noted. **In the twenty and sixth year of Asa king of Judah began Elah the son of**

Baasha to reign over Israel in Tirzah, two years. The beginning of his reign is referenced against the twenty-sixth year of king Asa to the south. His reign was actually less than two years for in verse 10, he is noted as dying in the twenty-seventh year of Asa.

16:9-10 And his servant Zimri, captain of half *his* chariots, conspired against him, as he was in Tirzah, drinking himself drunk in the house of Arza steward of *his* house in Tirzah. 10 And Zimri went in and smote him, and killed him, in the twenty and seventh year of Asa king of Judah, and reigned in his stead. The degenerate character of Elah is evident. While purposefully getting drunk; one of his subordinates, Zimri, murdered him and seized the throne. The beginning of the fulfillment of the prophecy which the prophet Jehu had uttered was beginning to come to pass. Sin begets sin. The corrupt foundation of the northern kingdom was already reaping what it had sown.

16:11-14 The prophecy of Jehu against Baasha was now fulfilled altogether. **And it came to pass, when he began to reign, as soon as he sat on his throne, *that* he slew all the house of Baasha: he left him not one that pisseth against a wall, neither of his kinsfolks, nor of his friends.** After establishing himself as the new king, Zimri proceeded to murder the entire family of Baasha. Not one male was left alive of the greater family of Baasha. Moreover, Zimri killed even the friends of Baasha. Regarding the comment about "one that pisseth against a wall," see notes for I Kings 14:10.

The reason for this slaughter is made clear. **12 Thus did Zimri destroy all the house of Baasha, according to the word of the LORD, which he spake against Baasha by Jehu the prophet, 13 For all the sins of Baasha, and the sins of Elah his son, by which they sinned, and by which they made**

Israel to sin, in provoking the LORD God of Israel to anger with their vanities. The mills of God grind slow, but they grind exceedingly fine. God's judgment always comes in His perfect time. Furthermore, when God promises judgment, it will come to pass. Here, the sin of not only Baasha but also of Elah was judged. The reign of Elah is thus summarized. **14 Now the rest of the acts of Elah, and all that he did, *are* they not written in the book of the chronicles of the kings of Israel?**

16:15 However, Zimri's reign lasted only seven days. **In the twenty and seventh year of Asa king of Judah did Zimri reign seven days in Tirzah. And the people *were* encamped against Gibbethon, which *belonged* to the Philistines.** Tirzah was a city in the northern kingdom sometimes used as its capital. Meanwhile, when Zimri had executed his conspiracy, the rest of the nation was involved in a war against the Philistines at Gibbethon.

16:16-20 Word soon reached the forces of the northern kingdom at Gibbethon. **And the people *that were* encamped heard say, Zimri hath conspired, and hath also slain the king: wherefore all Israel made Omri, the captain of the host, king over Israel that day in the camp. 17 And Omri went up from Gibbethon, and all Israel with him, and they besieged Tirzah.** When the main body of Israelites learned what Zimri had done; they rather appointed another officer, Omri, as king over Israel. They therefore marched back to Tirzah and besieged the city.

18 And it came to pass, when Zimri saw that the city was taken, that he went into the palace of the king's house, and burnt the king's house over him with fire, and died, 19 For his sins which he sinned in doing evil in the sight of the LORD, in walking in the way of Jeroboam, and in his sin which he did, to make Israel to sin. In seeing that he was

Understanding I Kings

surrounded with no hope for escape, Zimri committed suicide by burning the palace down upon himself. The sacred writer makes clear that his demise was in fact judgment from God for the sin of his life. Though he had fulfilled the prophecy against the house of Baasha, nevertheless, he had done so by cruel murder. The cycle of corruption continued.

The action and brief reign of Zimri is thus noted as treasonous. **20 Now the rest of the acts of Zimri, and his treason that he wrought, *are* they not written in the book of the chronicles of the kings of Israel?**

16:21-22 Then were the people of Israel divided into two parts: half of the people followed Tibni the son of Ginath, to make him king; and half followed Omri. 22 But the people that followed Omri prevailed against the people that followed Tibni the son of Ginath: so Tibni died, and Omri reigned.

Though Omri had been hurriedly made king, he too faced opposition. A fellow by the name of Tibni thought that he should be king. There thus was division among the nation. About half of the population supported each man for king. Though not noted as such, implicit is that a brief civil war erupted and the forces of Omri prevailed. Tibni evidently was slain in the battle. Omri was thus without opposition and became king of the northern kingdom altogether.

16:23-24 In the thirty and first year of Asa king of Judah began Omri to reign over Israel, twelve years: six years reigned he in Tirzah. The reference to Omri's reign in the north as being in the thirty-first year of Asa actually refers to when he was first appointed king at Gibbethon. The transitional, political battle with Tibni took four years. Omri's undisputed reign was only twelve years. During his first six years, he set his throne at Tirzah.

However, 24 **he bought the hill Samaria of Shemer for two talents of silver, and built on the hill, and called the name of the city which he built, after the name of Shemer, owner of the hill, Samaria.** For undisclosed reasons, maybe because of the political upheaval associated with Tirzah, Omri decided to move his capital. He bought a hill from a man named Shemer about nine miles to the west of Tirzah and there built a new city. Its name, Samaria, derived from its former owner Shemer.

16:25-28 Omri, however, proved to be the worst king of the northern kingdom to date as far as God was concerned. **But Omri wrought evil in the eyes of the LORD, and did worse than all that *were* before him.** No king of the north did as wickedly as Omri. **26 For he walked in all the way of Jeroboam the son of Nebat, and in his sin wherewith he made Israel to sin, to provoke the LORD God of Israel to anger with their vanities.** He did as Jeroboam had done, only worse. He continued in the tradition of provoking the Lord God to anger.

His reign is thus summarized: **27 Now the rest of the acts of Omri which he did, and his might that he shewed, *are* they not written in the book of the chronicles of the kings of Israel? 28 So Omri slept with his fathers, and was buried in Samaria: and Ahab his son reigned in his stead.** As other of the kings of Israel, additional chronicles were kept which have been lost. Upon the death of Omri, his son Ahab acceded his throne.

16:29 The reign of Ahab is thus summarized. **And in the thirty and eighth year of Asa king of Judah began Ahab the son of Omri to reign over Israel: and Ahab the son of Omri reigned over Israel in Samaria twenty and two years.** Ahab was to reign over Israel in Samaria for the next twenty-two years.

16:30-33 Ahab however soon proved to be even spiritually worse than his father. **And Ahab the son of Omri did evil in the sight of the LORD above all that *were* before him.** Though Omri had utterly provoked the Lord by his apostasy, Ahab soon surpassed him. Specifically, **31 it came to pass, as if it had been a light thing for him to walk in the sins of Jeroboam the son of Nebat, that he took to wife Jezebel the daughter of Ethbaal king of the Zidonians, and went and served Baal, and worshipped him.** Ahab married a pagan Lebanese woman by the name of Jezebel. She introduced Ahab to Baal worship to which he quickly resorted.

Moreover, Ahab **32 reared up an altar for Baal in the house of Baal, which he had built in Samaria. 33 And Ahab made a grove; and Ahab did more to provoke the LORD God of Israel to anger than all the kings of Israel that were before him.** Ahab built a Temple to Baal in Samaria and placed a major altar for sacrifice there. He thus did more to provoke God than all of the previous wicked kings before him.

16:34 Meanwhile, **in his days did Hiel the Bethelite build Jericho: he laid the foundation thereof in Abiram his firstborn, and set up the gates thereof in his youngest *son* Segub, according to the word of the LORD, which he spake by Joshua the son of Nun.**

Jericho was a part of the northern kingdom. During the reign of Ahab, one named Hiel from Bethel went down to the ruins of Jericho and proceeded to rebuild the city. He may have been ignorant of the curse made by Joshua in Joshua 6:26 or he may have been aware of it but ignored it. (Joshua in destroying Jericho more than five-hundred years earlier had placed a curse upon whoever sought to rebuild the city. Joshua had further foretold that whoever would rebuild the city would "lay the foundation thereof in his firstborn, and in his youngest *son* shall he set up the gates of it." That is precisely what happened. As soon as he began rebuilding the city, his firstborn (oldest son) died. However, Hiel continued. Meanwhile, the rest of His children died with his youngest son dying as he completed the gates of the city. It is apparent that Hiel's rebuilding of Jericho was with the approval of Ahab. He as well may have been aware of the curse of Joshua, but encouraged Hiel to ignore God's Word as well. Though five-hundred years had passed, God's promise still came to pass.

* * * * *

Overview of I Kings 17: *The focus of the book now turns to the ministry of Elijah. The chapter commences with Elijah's announcement to Ahab that the rain was now stopped according to his word. The narrative then gives details about Elijah at the brook Cherith, his visit to Zarephath, as well as him raising the widow's son at Zarephath.*

17:1 The northern kingdom was at a crisis. They had altogether turned their back on their God. The nation was on the verge of becoming altogether pagan. Therefore, God raised up a powerful prophet by the name of Elijah. It will be during this time of crisis in Israel that God works a flurry of miracles through Elijah and his successor, Elisha. We thus are introduced to Elijah.

And Elijah the Tishbite, *who was* **of the inhabitants of Gilead, said unto Ahab,** *As* **the LORD God of Israel liveth, before whom I stand, there shall not be dew nor rain these years, but according to my word**. Of interest is that the name **Elijah** (or 'Elias') literally means "Jehovah is my God." His home area was Gilead which is east of the Jordan River. His hometown may have been a village by the name of Tishbi which has been lost to history.

Elijah evidently was sent by God to Ahab with the stern message that there would be neither dew nor rain upon Israel in the coming years except at his word. This warning was solemnized in the name of Jehovah (**LORD**). As it will turn out, God stopped all rain in the land for the following three and one-half years. A drought that lasts for one season is bad enough. But one which continued that long would be catastrophic. God was in the process of getting Ahab's attention.

17:2-4 No record is made of Ahab's reaction. It probably was one of scorn and irritation that an unknown prophet would be so brazen as to thus confront him as king. Evidently, Ahab did not take Elijah's warning seriously nor did he order him arrested. Elijah apparently just left after having delivered his ultimatum from God.

Thus, **the word of the LORD came unto him, saying, 3 Get thee hence, and turn thee eastward, and hide thyself by the brook Cherith, that** *is* **before Jordan. 4 And it shall be,** *that* **thou shalt drink of the brook; and I have commanded the ravens to feed thee there**. God directed Elijah to head east, evidently to the Jordan River valley. He then was to head south to the brook Cherith which flowed into the Jordan River just below of the area of Jericho. The highlands which form the west ridge of the Jordan valley here are some of the most rugged and inhospitable places on earth. There, Elijah found refuge. Furthermore, the brook provided the water he needed. Meanwhile, God would have ravens bring the necessary food to him which he needed. A raven, of course, is a crow-like bird, though larger than a crow.

17:5-7 Therefore, **Elijah he went and did according unto the word of the LORD: for he went and dwelt by the brook Cherith, that** *is* **before Jordan. 6 And the ravens brought him bread and flesh in the morning, and bread and flesh in**

the evening; and he drank of the brook. Elijah thus obeyed God. Meanwhile, God miraculously directed ravens to bring both bread and meat to Elijah twice a day. Ravens are by nature scavengers who selfishly grab any and all food they can get their beaks on. However, God so directed these wild creatures to not only find good food for Elijah, but to bring it to him and release it.

However, the drought was beginning to take effect. 7 **And it came to pass after a while, that the brook dried up, because there had been no rain in the land.** Though God could have miraculously kept water in the brook for Elijah, he had other plans. Through a time of testing, God had greater things in store for His servant.

17:8-9 Therefore, **the word of the LORD came unto him, saying,** 9 **Arise, get thee to Zarephath, which** *belongeth* **to Zidon, and dwell there: behold, I have commanded a widow woman there to sustain thee.** God directed Elijah to Zarephath. This city was in Lebanon, to the north, and out of Israel. It was near the coastal city of Zidon. There, God directed Elijah to go and be supported by a widow woman. Widows in ancient times were almost always in poverty. There was no social or welfare support systems, much less life insurance or pensions. When a woman found herself widowed, it usually meant a lifetime of poverty. Yet, it was through such an unlikely source that God promised to take care of His prophet.

17:10-11 Elijah thus made his journey north to Lebanon and the city of Zarephath. **So he arose and went to Zarephath. And when he came to the gate of the city, behold, the widow woman** *was* **there gathering of sticks: and he called to her, and said, Fetch me, I pray thee, a little water in a vessel, that I may drink.** 11 **And as she was going to fetch** *it*, **he called to her, and said, Bring me, I pray thee, a morsel of bread in thine hand.**

It may be that widows wore distinctive clothing identifying them as such. In any event, upon arriving at the gate of the city, a woman apparent to Elijah as a widow was gathering wood, presumably for a fire. He therefore requested of this woman a cup of water. (It was the women of middle-eastern cities which drew water and had access to local wells. Elijah rightly assumed this woman would have permission to use the well and so he asked her for a drink of water.) As she went, he also asked in effect, "Oh, by the way, could you also give me a little bread as well?" Though perhaps forward for a stranger, God had informed Elijah that a widow at Zarephath would provide for him. He thus put the first widow he met to the test.

17:12-14 The woman replied, *As* **the LORD thy God liveth, I have not a cake, but an handful of meal in a barrel, and a little oil in a cruse: and, behold, I** *am* **gathering two sticks, that I may go in and dress it for me and my son, that we may eat it, and die.**

Several comments are at hand. (1) It is apparent that this woman recognized Elijah as an Israelite. It may have been from his distinctive dress or perhaps through his accent. (2) She referred to the Lord as *his* God. She was a gentile and aware of Jehovah God, but apparently did not serve Him. (3) It also is apparent that she was in abject poverty. She had no food in her house other than a little flour in a container and a small amount of olive oil with which she intended to bake a loaf of bread. After that, she thought her son and her would die of starvation. They had nothing else. It was to this woman that God sent Elijah for provision. What a test!

13 And Elijah said unto her, Fear not; go *and* **do as thou hast said: but make me thereof a little cake first, and bring** *it* **unto me, and after make for thee and for thy son. 14 For thus saith the LORD God of Israel, The barrel of meal shall not waste, neither shall the cruse of oil fail, until the day** *that* the LORD **sendeth rain upon the earth.** Now Elijah put the woman to the test. Acknowledging her dire straits, he nevertheless instructed her to bake him bread *first*. Then, she could provide for herself and her son.

This was not selfishness on the part of Elijah, but rather a test and a lesson for this poor widow. She was about to learn first-hand how God provides for those who trust Him. Elijah thus informed her of God's promise that her meager container of floor and small amount of cooking oil would not fail until the day that God sent rain once again. It also is apparent that the drought had reached up into Lebanon. Sin always affects others. The sin of Israel also brought drought to their neighbors.

17:15-16 This poor widow woman there did as she was instructed. **And she went and did according to the saying of Elijah: and she, and he, and her house, did eat** *many* **days. 16** *And* **the barrel of meal wasted not, neither did the cruse of oil fail, according to the word of the LORD, which he spake by Elijah.** The woman clearly took God at His word. She trusted Him. Thus God provided not only for her but also for the prophet throughout the remainder of the drought. Her supply of flour and cooking oil did not fail. God miraculously provided for His servant.

17:17-18 In the meantime, **it came to pass after these things,** *that* **the son of the woman, the mistress of the house, fell sick; and his sickness was so sore, that there was no breath left in him.** After some time, the son of the widow fell ill and quite apparently died.

The distraught mother therefore **18 said unto Elijah, What have I to do with thee, O thou man of God? art thou come unto me to call my sin to remembrance, and to slay my son?** The woman however, in her distress accused Elijah of coming to her to bring some past, unknown sin to account. She thought that the death of her son was judgment for former sin.

17:19-21 Elijah therefore **said unto her, Give me thy son. And he took him out of her bosom, and carried him up into a loft, where he abode, and laid him upon his own bed.** It is apparent that Elijah was embarrassed at what had happened to this poor widow. He therefore 20 **cried unto the LORD, and said, O LORD my God, hast thou also brought evil upon the widow with whom I sojourn, by slaying her son?** He therefore asked God if He was bringing such trouble upon her son in return for the good which she had done to him.

Elijah thus **stretched himself upon the child three times, and cried unto the LORD, and said, O LORD my God, I pray thee, let this child's soul come into him again.** Evident is the effectual, fervent prayer of a righteous man. Its fervency is emphasized in that Elijah stretched himself out upon the child and prayed. It might be presumed that he also prayed this urgent prayer thrice as well.

17:22-23 And the LORD heard the voice of Elijah; and the soul of the child came into him again, and he revived. 23 **And Elijah took the child, and brought him down out of the chamber into the house, and delivered him unto his mother: and Elijah said, See, thy son liveth.** God hears the effectual, fervent prayer of righteous men. Evident is the faith of Elijah. In a time of crisis, his only recourse was to ask God to intervene and work powerfully. That He did. It should not be thought that Elijah raised the boy to life. God did that. However, God acted upon the faith and fervent prayer of Elijah. He thus delivered the boy to his mother.

17:24 Thus **the woman said to Elijah, Now by this I know that thou** *art* **a man of God,** *and* **that the word of the**

LORD in thy mouth *is* truth. She had witnessed the power of God at Elijah's hand. She was convinced of both the truth of Jehovah God and that Elijah was a man of God. She also now had no question that what Elijah spoke was the truth of God.

* * * * *

Overview of I Kings 18: The ministry of Elijah is further presented. The primary focus is the confrontation of Elijah with the prophets of Baal on Mount Carmel.

18:1-2 In the preceding chapter (17:1) and at God's direction, Elijah had announced that all rainfall would cease in Israel. Therefore, **it came to pass *after* many days, that the word of the LORD came to Elijah in the third year, saying, Go, shew thyself unto Ahab; and I will send rain upon the earth. 2 And Elijah went to shew himself unto Ahab. And *there was* a sore famine in Samaria**. Almost three years had passed since the drought had begun. God thus directed Elijah to go back and confront Ahab. Not surprisingly, there was a **sore famine** in the land.

18:3-4 Further background information is provided. **And Ahab called Obadiah, which *was* the governor of *his* house. (Now Obadiah feared the LORD greatly: 4 For it was *so*, when Jezebel cut off the prophets of the LORD, that Obadiah took an hundred prophets, and hid them by fifty in a cave, and fed them with bread and water.)**

Of interest is the introduction here of Obadiah. Jewish tradition holds that this is one and the same as the prophet who wrote the small book by the same name. There is no scriptural proof of that however. In any event, this Obadiah is noted as fearing the Lord greatly. Here is a strange enigma. How could one who

Understanding I Kings

feared the Lord greatly be directly involved with the likes of Ahab and Jezebel? Though he may have been true to Jehovah, it is apparent that the man compromised any conviction of separation from the apostasy of Ahab.

However, to his credit, he had hidden one-hundred prophets of Jehovah still in the northern kingdom. Through his efforts, they were sustained by bread and water sent to them at his hand. Also noted is how that Jezebel had in the meantime killed as many prophets of Jehovah still in the northern kingdom as she could locate. The spiritual condition of the time is evident.

18:5-6 Because of the severity of the famine, **Ahab said unto Obadiah, Go into the land, unto all fountains of water, and unto all brooks: peradventure we may find grass to save the horses and mules alive, that we lose not all the beasts. 6 So they divided the land between them to pass throughout it: Ahab went one way by himself, and Obadiah went another way by himself.** It would appear that to save his own personal livestock, Ahab sent Obadiah in search of water. Obadiah went one way. Ahab went another.

18:7-8 Thus, **as Obadiah was in the way, behold, Elijah met him: and he knew him, and fell on his face, and said, *Art* thou that my lord Elijah? 8 And he answered him, I *am*: go, tell thy lord, Behold, Elijah *is here*.** As Obadiah was out searching for water, he came face to face with Elijah. Of note is that he immediately recognized him and even called him 'lord.' Elijah therefore directed him to go and inform Ahab that he was back.

18:9-14 Obadiah was terrified at the prospect of informing Ahab regarding Elijah. **And he said, What have I sinned, that thou wouldest deliver thy servant into the hand of Ahab, to**

slay me? As far as Obadiah was concerned, God must have been exacting judgment against him to announce such news to Ahab. He feared Ahab would kill him.

Obadiah continued, **10 *As* the LORD thy God liveth, there is no nation or kingdom, whither my lord hath not sent to seek thee: and when they said, *He is* not *there*; he took an oath of the kingdom and nation, that they found thee not. 11 And now thou sayest, Go, tell thy lord, Behold, Elijah *is here*.** It is apparent that an arrest warrant had long been out for Elijah. In fact, Obadiah intimated that Ahab had sought Elijah in neighboring countries, asking the leadership of them to swear that Elijah was not there. Elijah had become public enemy number one. Ahab had spared no expense to find him. And now Obadiah mused about showing up and informing Ahab that Elijah was right beneath their noses.

Obadiah feared, **12 And it shall come to pass, *as soon as* I am gone from thee, that the Spirit of the LORD shall carry thee whither I know not; and *so* when I come and tell Ahab, and he cannot find thee, he shall slay me: but I thy servant fear the LORD from my youth.** Obadiah's fear was that after informing Ahab where Elijah was that he would not be there when they came to get him. The compromised prophet therefore feared for his own life. But He reminded Elijah how he had feared Jehovah from his youth.

Moreover, Obadiah reminded Elijah, **13 Was it not told my lord what I did when Jezebel slew the prophets of the LORD, how I hid an hundred men of the LORD'S prophets by fifty in a cave, and fed them with bread and water?** Obadiah sought to remind Elijah of the good he had done for the prophets of Jehovah. (Elijah evidently was already so aware.) Why would Elijah therefore send him to his death? **14 And now thou sayest, Go, tell thy lord, Behold, Elijah *is here*: and he shall slay me.**

Understanding I Kings

18:15-16 And Elijah said, *As* the LORD of hosts liveth, before whom I stand, I will surely shew myself unto him to day. Elijah assured Obadiah that he would surely present himself to Ahab. **16 So Obadiah went to meet Ahab, and told him: and Ahab went to meet Elijah.** Of interest is that Ahab the king went to meet Elijah and not the other way around. Ahab had learned to not take Elijah lightly.

18:17-18 And it came to pass, when Ahab saw Elijah, that Ahab said unto him, *Art* thou he that troubleth Israel? Some have thought that Ahab was not sure who he was meeting was in fact Elijah and thus asked this question. It would seem rather that he recognized him and with sarcasm and prejudice so addressed him. Elijah was not intimidated in the least.

Without missing a beat, **18 he answered, I have not troubled Israel; but thou, and thy father's house, in that ye have forsaken the commandments of the LORD, and thou hast followed Baalim.** There is amazing boldness in Elijah. He was addressing the king of Israel. He feared not to point his finger at Ahab and inform him that he was the one who had brought the drought to Israel. The real problem is that Ahab had forsaken the commandments of God and followed **Baalim**. (The latter word is plural and refers to multiple idols of Baal, no doubt scattered across the land.)

18:19-20 Elijah therefore gave orders to Ahab. **Now therefore send, *and* gather to me all Israel unto mount Carmel, and the prophets of Baal four hundred and fifty, and the prophets of the groves four hundred, which eat at Jezebel's table.** Elijah ordered the king to have all the prophets of Baal in Israel gathered to him at Mount Carmel. That in itself is amazing. Though he had been public enemy number one, Elijah was now ordering Ahab what to do. Mount Carmel is near the coast of the Mediterranean Sea in north-central Israel. It is a forested low mountain with a fairly large summit. Apparently there were 450 prophets of Baal in the land in addition to another 400 prophets of the groves supported by Jezebel. It has been suggested that the latter were some sort of domestic chaplains for her. So 20 **Ahab sent unto all the children of Israel, and gathered the prophets together unto mount Carmel**. Thus, 850 'clergymen' of Baal were rounded up and sent to Mount Carmel for a climactic showdown with Elijah.

18:21 With poetic eloquence, Elijah threw down the gauntlet to the nation of Israel. **And Elijah came unto all the people, and said, How long halt ye between two opinions? if the LORD *be* God, follow him: but if Baal, *then* follow him. And the people answered him not a word**. It is apparent that a large assembly of ordinary Israelites had gathered atop Mount Carmel to watch the proceedings as well. Elijah thus challenged them. If Jehovah was God, then follow Him. But if Baal was God then follow him. Much of Israel had turned to worshiping Baal. They were on the spot. They therefore answered nothing.

18:22-24 Elijah thus laid down the ground rules for the coming challenge. **Then said Elijah unto the people, I, *even* I only, remain a prophet of the LORD; but Baal's prophets *are* four hundred and fifty men**. As far as Elijah was concerned, he was the last prophet of Jehovah. He did not even give Obadiah that credit. His opponents were the 450 prophets of Baal.

He therefore proposed, 23 **Let them therefore give us two bullocks; and let them choose one bullock for themselves, and cut it in pieces, and lay *it* on wood, and put no fire *under* : and I will dress the other bullock, and lay *it* on wood, and put no fire *under***. Elijah's plan was simple. Take two bullocks. Butcher them and place one on an altar to Jehovah and the other on an altar to Baal. Put no fire under either sacrifice. Further-

Understanding I Kings

more, **24 call ye on the name of your gods, and I will call on the name of the LORD: and the God that answereth by fire, let him be God. And all the people answered and said, It is well spoken**. The true God would reveal Himself by fire from heaven. The assembled congregation of Israel agreed that that was a fair contest. (It is unclear what the prophets of Baal thought of the plan.)

18:25-29 The contest thus began. **And Elijah said unto the prophets of Baal, Choose you one bullock for yourselves, and dress** *it* **first; for ye** *are* **many; and call on the name of your gods, but put no fire** *under*. Elijah allowed the prophets of Baal to go first. He let them take first choice of the bullocks available. There were 450 of them. "So go first and call down fire from heaven."

26 And they took the bullock which was given them, and they dressed *it***, and called on the name of Baal from morning even until noon, saying, O Baal, hear us. But** *there was* **no voice, nor any that answered. And they leaped upon the altar which was made**. All that morning, the prophets of Baal desperately tried to have Baal respond. They even leaped upon their altar to entreat Baal. Nothing happened.

27 And it came to pass at noon, that Elijah mocked them, and said, Cry aloud: for he *is* **a god; either he is talking, or he is pursuing, or he is in a journey,** *or* **peradventure he sleepeth, and must be awaked**. Elijah got tired of waiting and began to mock his adversaries. He sarcastically suggested that maybe they needed to yell louder for Baal to hear them. He mocked further. Maybe Baal was busy talking to someone else. Some have suggested the reference to him **pursuing** may refer to being in the bathroom which the word so translated may suggest. Maybe old Baal was taking a nap.

The prophets of Baal were becoming desperate. **28 And they cried aloud, and cut themselves after their manner**

with knives and lancets, till the blood gushed out upon them. Still nothing happened. **29 And it came to pass, when midday was past, and they prophesied until the *time* of the offering of the *evening* sacrifice, that *there was* neither voice, nor any to answer, nor any that regarded.** They continued their futile attempts until the middle of the afternoon.

18:30-35 Meanwhile, **Elijah said unto all the people, Come near unto me. And all the people came near unto him. And he repaired the altar of the LORD *that was* broken down.** He beckoned the congregation of Israel to where his altar was and to ignore the sideshow of the prophets of Baal. That they did. He thus repaired an old altar of the Lord that had long been in disrepair. (The latter apparently had been a holdover from the days when Israel sacrificed to Jehovah upon various high places before the Tabernacle had been established at one place.)

31 And Elijah took twelve stones, according to the number of the tribes of the sons of Jacob, unto whom the word of the LORD came, saying, Israel shall be thy name: 32 And with the stones he built an altar in the name of the LORD: and he made a trench about the altar, as great as would contain two measures of seed. In addition to rebuilding the altar of Jehovah, he ordered a trench be dug around it such that two measures of seed could be placed therein. How much that was is unclear. The point however is that a substantial trench was dug around the altar.

33 And he put the wood in order, and cut the bullock in pieces, and laid *him* on the wood, and said, Fill four barrels with water, and pour *it* on the burnt sacrifice, and on the wood. 34 And he said, Do *it* the second time. And they did *it* the second time. And he said, Do *it* the third time. And they did *it* the third time. 35 And the water ran round about the altar; and he filled the trench also with water.

Understanding I Kings

After preparing his sacrifice upon his altar, Elijah ordered that it be drenched with water. How much water a **barrel** of that day contained is not clear. The word so translated (כד *kad*) most often refers to the large pottery jars used to carry water in that day. The greater question however is from whence came so much water in a time of great drought. Mount Carmel is not far from the Mediterranean Sea and Elijah may have ordered men to go and fetch sea water therefrom. That is the likely source. In any event, his altar was drenched with the water running down and filling the trench he had built.

(In knowing what he was going to do ahead of time, Elijah may have made preparations before for this showdown. It may be that he made sure there were two bullocks ready on the mount as well as firewood. Most importantly, he may have stockpiled the seawater ahead of time for just this occasion.)

18:36-38 Now it was Elijah's turn. By now it was late afternoon. **And it came to pass at *the time of* the offering of the *evening* sacrifice, that Elijah the prophet came near, and said, LORD God of Abraham, Isaac, and of Israel, let it be known this day that thou *art* God in Israel, and *that* I *am* thy servant, and *that* I have done all these things at thy word**. With poetic eloquence, Elijah called upon the God of Abraham, Isaac, and Israel—the patriarchs of Israel. He thus besought the Lord to make clear that He was the God of Israel and that Elijah had acted at His direction.

He further implored the Lord, **37 Hear me, O LORD, hear me, that this people may know that thou *art* the LORD God, and *that* thou hast turned their heart back again**. The latter phrase likely refers to how that God would thus turn the heart of Israel from idolatry back to Him again.

38 Then the fire of the LORD fell, and consumed the burnt sacrifice, and the wood, and the stones, and the dust, and licked up the water that *was* in the trench. Fire from heaven fell with such intensity that not only was the sacrifice and the wood consumed, but even the stones of the altar were vaporized along with all the water which had been poured thereupon. There was nothing left. God had shown His power before their eyes.

18:39-40 The assembly of Israel got the message. **And when all the people saw *it*, they fell on their faces: and they said, The LORD, he *is* the God; the LORD, he *is* the God**. In witnessing the mighty power of God before their eyes, the throng could only fall upon their face in worship of the God of heaven. They cried out twice, "The LORD, he *is* the God." It is significant that they added the definite article to the word God (Elohim). Jehovah was not just 'a' God, He was 'the' God. Implicit is their reaffirmation that "the LORD our God *is* one LORD" (Deuteronomy 6:4).

Elijah therefore **40 said unto them, Take the prophets of Baal; let not one of them escape. And they took them: and Elijah brought them down to the brook Kishon, and slew them there**. Elijah thus ordered the prophets of Baal to be slain. He thus sent them down into the valley below whence was the streambed of the brook Kishon. There they were slain.

18:41 And Elijah said unto Ahab, Get thee up, eat and drink; for *there is* a sound of abundance of rain. With prophetic prescience, Elijah warned Ahab to go back up on the mountain and eat. They had not had time to do so all day long. Moreover, he foretold a storm was coming. It is unlikely as yet that they could hear any thunder or the sound of rain. But Elijah prophetically foretold it.

18:42-44 Therefore, **Ahab went up to eat and to drink. And Elijah went up to the top of Carmel; and he cast himself down upon the earth, and put his face between his**

knees. Ahab may have returned to Carmel where there his royal provisions had been brought. Elijah, however went to the summit of the mount and began to fervently pray. He had announced rain as God had told him in 18:1. Now, he besought the Lord to fulfill His Word. Implicit is the intensity of his prayer in praying with his face between his knees. He apparently was kneeling with his head all the way down between his knees. See James 5:16-18.

After a season of such effectual, fervent prayer; Elijah **43 said to his servant, Go up now, look toward the sea. And he went up, and looked, and said,** *There is* **nothing. And he said, Go again seven times**. Not only did Elijah pray fervently, he persevered in his praying. When his servant came back from the summit overlooking the Mediterranean Sea to the west, he returned and said **nothing**. Of note is that weather systems bringing rain to Israel to this day come off the Mediterranean. Elijah knew where to look. Also noteworthy is that his servant came back and tersely said **nothing**. The words *'there is'* are interpolated. This continued for seven times.

44 And it came to pass at the seventh time, that he said, Behold, there ariseth a little cloud out of the sea, like a man's hand. And he said, Go up, say unto Ahab, Prepare *thy chariot*, **and get thee down, that the rain stop thee not**. After having been sent to the top seven times, his servant returned with word that there was a small cloud developing to the west. Elijah therefore directed Ahab to leave soon before the rain prevented him from so doing. Great faith is evident therein.

18:45-46 And it came to pass in the mean while, that the heaven was black with clouds and wind, and there was a great rain. And Ahab rode, and went to Jezreel. 46 And the hand of the LORD was on Elijah; and he girded up his loins, and ran before Ahab to the entrance of Jezreel. The rain Elijah had foretold now descended with great fury. Ahab meanwhile rode down the mountain and up the valley of Jezreel to the city by that name. The distance by ground is approximately twenty-five miles. God evidently girded Elijah with supernatural strength for he ran before Ahab that entire distance. By now it must have been sundown, perhaps in the summer when the days are the longest. It had been an eventful day. Elijah in one day had destroyed public support for Baal worship and had also restored rain to Israel.

* * * * *

Overview of I Kings 19: *The aftermath of the events at Mount Carmel are noted with Jezebel seeking the life of Elijah. God sent him to Horeb where He supernaturally spoke to His discouraged prophet. The chapter concludes with details of the call of Elisha.*

19:1-2 Ahab arrived home that evening and **told Jezebel all that Elijah had done, and withal how he had slain all the prophets with the sword**. It was Jezebel who more than anyone else had introduced Baal worship into Israel. See I Kings 17:31. Hearing what had happened, 2 **Jezebel sent a messenger unto Elijah, saying, So let the gods do** *to me*, **and more also, if I make not thy life as the life of one of them by to morrow about this time**. Ahab had seen firsthand what had happened on Mount Carmel. But Jezebel was unrepentant. She thus sent word to Elijah that she would see to it that he was like unto the prophets of Baal by that time the next day. In other words, she ordered his execution.

19:3-4 Upon learning that Jezebel intended to kill him, **when he saw** *that*, **he arose, and went for his life, and came to Beersheba, which** *belongeth* **to Judah, and left his servant**

Understanding I Kings

there. Evidently, that very night, Elijah fled, heading south toward Beersheba. The latter is more or less the southern extremity of Judah. He left his servant there and continued on.

4 But he himself went a day's journey into the wilderness, and came and sat down under a juniper tree: and he requested for himself that he might die; and said, It is enough; now, O LORD, take away my life; for I *am* not better than my fathers. In traveling into the Negev, he found a juniper tree. He likely was not only exhausted physically but emotionally as well. Though he had, with God's power upon him just days before, boldly wrought some of the most powerful of miracles, now he was discouraged. As far as he was concerned, God could just take him to heaven on the spot.

19:5-7 And as he lay and slept under a juniper tree, behold, then an angel touched him, and said unto him, Arise *and* eat. 6 And he looked, and, behold, *there was* a cake baken on the coals, and a cruse of water at his head. And he did eat and drink, and laid him down again. While he rested, God sent an angel who miraculously provided sustenance for him. He thus woke up to eat and drink. But then he laid down to sleep more. However, **7 the angel of the LORD came again the second time, and touched him, and said, Arise *and* eat; because the journey *is* too great for thee.** God knew what was ahead. Elijah did not. But God therefore made provision for him ahead of time.

19:8-9 And he arose, and did eat and drink, and went in the strength of that meat forty days and forty nights unto Horeb the mount of God. God miraculously enabled Elijah to continue for forty days from the health food He had provided for him. He thus journeyed on southward to Horeb which is another name for Mount Sinai. There, **9 he came thither unto a cave, and lodged there; and, behold, the word of the LORD *came***

to him, and he said unto him, What doest thou here, Elijah? In a cave on Mount Sinai, God spoke to Elijah and asked him what he was doing there. From his answer, it is evident that he was still discouraged.

19:10 In self pity, Elijah complained to God, **I have been very jealous for the LORD God of hosts: for the children of Israel have forsaken thy covenant, thrown down thine altars, and slain thy prophets with the sword; and I, *even* I only, am left; and they seek my life, to take it away.** Elijah rehearsed how Israel had turned their backs on Jehovah God. As far as he was concerned, he was the only one left who still served Jehovah. And on top of that, they sought his life to kill him.

19:11-14 God therefore directed Elijah to **go forth, and stand upon the mount before the LORD. And, behold, the LORD passed by, and a great and strong wind rent the mountains, and brake in pieces the rocks before the LORD; *but* the LORD *was* not in the wind: and after the wind an earthquake; *but* the LORD *was* not in the earthquake.** God brought a succession of powerful events of nature. He sent a powerful wind storm against Mount Sinai, but His presence was not in the wind. He then sent an earthquake, but the presence of the Lord was not in the earthquake.

However, 12 **after the earthquake a fire; *but* the LORD *was* not in the fire: and after the fire a still small voice.** After the earthquake, God sent a fire, perhaps a terrible lightning storm. But God's presence was not in the lightning. However, after all of this, Elijah perceived within him a "still small voice." God does not need the forces of nature to make known His presence. It is within and can be as simple as a "still small voice." The lesson for Elijah was that God's presence was always at hand.

Therefore, **13 it was *so*, when Elijah heard *it*, that he wrapped his face in his mantle, and went out, and stood in the entering in of the cave. And, behold, *there came* a voice unto him, and said, What doest thou here, Elijah?** Perhaps in reverence to God whom he now perceived to be present or perhaps in shame and confusion for his doubt, Elijah thus wrapped his face in his mantle (a portion of his garment) and stood at the entrance of the cave. Once again as before, God asked him the same question, "What doest thou here, Elijah?"

Elijah once again rehearsed his complaint. **14 And he said, I have been very jealous for the LORD God of hosts: because the children of Israel have forsaken thy covenant, thrown down thine altars, and slain thy prophets with the sword; and I, *even* I only, am left; and they seek my life, to take it away.**

19:15-17 God therefore gave Elijah new instructions. **And the LORD said unto him, Go, return on thy way to the wilderness of Damascus: and when thou comest, anoint Hazael *to be* king over Syria.** God now sent him eastward into Arabia and then northward toward Syria and the wilderness near Damascus. There, he would meet one named Hazael. Elijah was thus to anoint him king of Syria. Elijah thus was directed to be a king maker. In due season, Hazael would indeed become king of Syria. See II Kings 8:13.

Furthermore, **16 Jehu the son of Nimshi shalt thou anoint *to be* king over Israel: and Elisha the son of Shaphat of Abelmeholah shalt thou anoint *to be* prophet in thy room.** Elijah would then anoint one named Jehu to be the next king over the northern kingdom of Israel. Moreover, Elijah was then to anoint his successor Elisha, the son of Shaphat. It may be that Jehu was in fact anointed by Elisha unless he was anointed as king twice. See II Kings 9:3.

God added further ominous warning. **17 And it shall come to pass, *that* him that escapeth the sword of Hazael shall Jehu slay: and him that escapeth from the sword of Jehu shall Elisha slay.** The implication is that many would eventually be slain in Israel by Hazael as well as by Jehu. See II Kings 10:32-33 and II Kings 9:24,33.

19:18 God also in so many words added, "Oh, by the way;" **Yet I have left *me* seven thousand in Israel, all the knees which have not bowed unto Baal, and every mouth which hath not kissed him.** Though Elijah thought he was the last one to serve Jehovah God, the Lord informed him that there were seven thousand in Israel who had not bowed to Baal. It would seem that a part of Baal worship was actually kissing the idol of him. God said, seven thousand in Israel had refused to do so. Elijah was not alone after all.

19:19-21 Thus, Elijah **departed thence, and found Elisha the son of Shaphat, who *was* plowing *with* twelve yoke *of oxen* before him, and he with the twelfth: and Elijah passed by him, and cast his mantle upon him**. As Elijah journeyed, he came upon Elisha, the son of Shaphat, who had twelve separate plows being pulled by twelve yoke of oxen. When Elijah came to the one Elisha was using, he cast his mantle upon him.
  20 And he left the oxen, and ran after Elijah, and said, Let me, I pray thee, kiss my father and my mother, and *then* I will follow thee. And he said unto him, Go back again: for what have I done to thee? Elisha understood the significance of what Elijah had done. He had not only called him 'into the ministry' but had tapped him to be his successor. Therefore, Elisha asked leave to bid farewell to his parents. Elijah in effect said, if that be case, go back to plowing. He in effect asked, do you not realize what I have done to you? God has called you to be my successor.

Therefore, Elisha 21 **returned back from him, and took a yoke of oxen, and slew them, and boiled their flesh with the instruments of the oxen, and gave unto the people, and they did eat. Then he arose, and went after Elijah, and ministered unto him.** It seems that Elisha did in fact bid farewell to his parents and then returned to Elijah. He then butchered one of the yoke of oxen, cooked its meat, and gave to perhaps his servants and family who came to honor his departure. He then departed with Elijah, becoming his servant. He thus became a student of the great prophet whom God had so mightily used.

* * * * *

Overview of I Kings 20: *In this chapter is record of the war between Ahab and Syria. Ahab is warned by a prophet of Syria's further intentions. Finally, record is made of Ahab's sin in sparing Benhadad.*

20:1-3 And Benhadad the king of Syria gathered all his host together: and *there were* thirty and two kings with him, and horses, and chariots: and he went up and besieged Samaria, and warred against it. 2 And he sent messengers to Ahab king of Israel into the city, and said unto him, Thus saith Benhadad, 3 Thy silver and thy gold *is* mine; thy wives also and thy children, *even* the goodliest, *are* mine.

The king of Syria, Benhadad, gathered thirty-two lessor chieftains and attacked Samaria the provisional capital of Israel. Benhadad thus taunted Ahab, king of Israel, in effect saying, give up. All you have is going to be mine.

20:4 And the king of Israel answered and said, My lord, O king, according to thy saying, I *am* thine, and all that I have. Amazingly, Ahab was willing to surrender to Benhadad.

It also very well may be that Ahab realized his relative impotence against his power adversary.

20:5-6 And the messengers came again, and said, Thus speaketh Benhadad, saying, Although I have sent unto thee, saying, Thou shalt deliver me thy silver, and thy gold, and thy wives, and thy children; 6 Yet I will send my servants unto thee to morrow about this time, and they shall search thine house, and the houses of thy servants; and it shall be, *that* whatsoever is pleasant in thine eyes, they shall put *it* in their hand, and take *it* away.

Benhadad therefore sent messengers back and informed Ahab that he would send his men the next day and they would search through Ahab's house and the city. They then would take whatever caught their fancy.

20:7-8 Meanwhile, **the king of Israel called all the elders of the land, and said, Mark, I pray you, and see how this *man* seeketh mischief: for he sent unto me for my wives, and for my children, and for my silver, and for my gold; and I denied him not. 8 And all the elders and all the people said unto him, Hearken not *unto him*, nor consent.** In consulting with the leaders of the rest of the nation, they urged Ahab to not allow Benhadad to pillage the city.

20:9-10 Wherefore he said unto the messengers of Benhadad, Tell my lord the king, All that thou didst send for to thy servant at the first I will do: but this thing I may not do. And the messengers departed, and brought him word again. Ahab therefore sent word back to Benhadad, reneging on his initial surrender. He essentially informed him that his lieutenants had rejected the idea.

10 **And Benhadad sent unto him, and said, The gods do so unto me, and more also, if the dust of Samaria shall**

Understanding I Kings

suffice for handfuls for all the people that follow me. Benhadad thus threatened Ahab telling him that when he was done with them, there would not be enough dust left of Samaria for his people to take handfuls thereof.

20:11-12 And the king of Israel answered and said, Tell him, Let not him that girdeth on *his harness* boast himself as he that putteth it off. Ahab shot back to the effect, don't boast of your victory until after you have won and taken your armor off. Or, don't count your chickens before your eggs hatch. In other words, Ahab taunted Benhadad that he would not win the coming fight.

12 **And it came to pass, when *Benhadad* heard this message, as he *was* drinking, he and the kings in the pavilions, that he said unto his servants, Set *yourselves in array*. And they set *themselves in array* against the city.** Meanwhile, Benhadad was having a drinking party. When he received word of Ahab's insolence, he ordered his men to prepare for battle.

20:13-14 It seems that though Ahab had used bravado against Benhadad, he really did not have a clue as to how he was going to win the battle. Thus, **there came a prophet unto Ahab king of Israel, saying, Thus saith the LORD, Hast thou seen all this great multitude? behold, I will deliver it into thine hand this day; and thou shalt know that I *am* the LORD.** The prophet informed Ahab on behalf of God that the Syrians would be delivered to them that very day.

Incredulous, Ahab asked, 14 **By whom? And he said, Thus saith the LORD, *Even* by the young men of the princes of the provinces. Then he said, Who shall order the battle? And he answered, Thou**. To Ahab's question, "by whom" the battle would be won, the prophet informed him that the princes of his provinces would rise up against Benhadad. Ahab therefore wanted to know who would lead the battle, and to his astonishment, the prophet told him that he would.

20:15-16 Then he numbered the young men of the princes of the provinces, and they were two hundred and thirty two: and after them he numbered all the people, *even* all the children of Israel, *being* seven thousand. Ahab therefore hastily counted his potential forces. He had 232 princes and 7,000 soldiers at his disposal. **16 And they went out at noon. But Benhadad *was* drinking himself drunk in the pavilions, he and the kings, the thirty and two kings that helped him**. At noon of that day, Ahab's modest force marched out of Samaria to engage the Syrians. However, Benhadad and his chieftains were drinking themselves drunk under open tents.

20:17-18 And the young men of the princes of the provinces went out first; and Benhadad sent out, and they told him, saying, There are men come out of Samaria. As the Israelite force marched out to battle, Benhadad was informed thereof. In his drunken judgment, he ordered, **18 Whether they be come out for peace, take them alive; or whether they be come out for war, take them alive**. For reasons unexplained, he ordered the Israelites to be captured alive—maybe to find out what Ahab was up to. He made a fundamental military mistake in underestimating his enemy.

20:19-21 So these young men of the princes of the provinces came out of the city, and the army which followed them. 20 And they slew every one his man: and the Syrians fled; and Israel pursued them: and Benhadad the king of Syria escaped on an horse with the horsemen. 21 And the king of Israel went out, and smote the horses and chariots, and slew the Syrians with a great slaughter. Because the leadership of Syria were all drunk, the force from Samaria

Understanding I Kings 171

routed the numerically superior Syrian forces. Benhadad escaped for his life.

20:22 God therefore warned Ahab of another impending Syrian attack. **And the prophet came to the king of Israel, and said unto him, Go, strengthen thyself, and mark, and see what thou doest: for at the return of the year the king of Syria will come up against thee.** It may be surmised that God helped Israel because they remained His people. He was not pleased with their sin, but the time for them to be removed from the land had not as yet arrived. Therefore, God providentially preserved them.

20:23-26 And the servants of the king of Syria said unto him, Their gods *are* gods of the hills; therefore they were stronger than we; but let us fight against them in the plain, and surely we shall be stronger than they. The Syrians came to the conclusion that Israel had prevailed because their God was that of the hills whence Samaria was. They reasoned therefore that if they could draw Israel into battle on the plain, they would prevail. They would soon learn to not so underestimate Jehovah God.

24 And do this thing, Take the kings away, every man out of his place, and put captains in their rooms: 25 And number thee an army, like the army that thou hast lost, horse for horse, and chariot for chariot: and we will fight against them in the plain, *and* surely we shall be stronger than they. And he hearkened unto their voice, and did so. They counseled Benhadad to reorganize another army with the same number of men, horses, and chariots as they had before. When they fought in the plain, they would surely prevail this time. Benhadad therefore agreed.

26 And it came to pass at the return of the year, that Benhadad numbered the Syrians, and went up to Aphek, to

fight against Israel. Aphek was in the Valley of Jezreel, a large flat valley in central Israel. It certainly had the characteristics of a plain.

20:27-28 The impending battle was thus arrayed. **And the children of Israel were numbered, and were all present, and went against them: and the children of Israel pitched before them like two little flocks of kids; but the Syrians filled the country.** It would seem that every one of Israel's original 7,000 men were present. However, compared to the powerful Syrian forces, they in comparison were like to little flocks of kid-goats.

However, **28 there came a man of God, and spake unto the king of Israel, and said, Thus saith the LORD, Because the Syrians have said, The LORD *is* God of the hills, but he *is* not God of the valleys, therefore will I deliver all this great multitude into thine hand, and ye shall know that I *am* the LORD**. God through an unnamed prophet informed Ahab of the foolhardy thinking of the Syrians. To prove His mighty power, God therefore informed Ahab that He would deliver the mighty Syrian forces to him. It would seem that Ahab needed to be reminded of God's power as much as the Syrians.

20:29-30 And they pitched one over against the other seven days. And *so* it was, that in the seventh day the battle was joined: and the children of Israel slew of the Syrians an hundred thousand footmen in one day. After eyeing each other for seven days, the battle was joined with Israel killing 100,000 Syrians. Clearly this was by God's power and not Israel's for they only had 7,000 men. God therefore glorified Himself before not only the Syrians, but apostate Israel as well. **30 But the rest fled to Aphek, into the city; and *there* a wall fell upon twenty and seven thousand of the men *that were* left. And Benhadad fled, and came into the city, into an inner chamber.** Things went from bad to worse for Benhadad.

His remaining forces in open rout fled into the city of Aphek only to have a wall of the city collapse upon 27,000 of what was left of his forces. He himself found a room in the city and thus hid.

20:31-34 And his servants said unto him, Behold now, we have heard that the kings of the house of Israel *are* merciful kings: let us, I pray thee, put sackcloth on our loins, and ropes upon our heads, and go out to the king of Israel: peradventure he will save thy life. 32 So they girded sackcloth on their loins, and *put* ropes on their heads, and came to the king of Israel, and said, Thy servant Benhadad saith, I pray thee, let me live. And he said, *Is* he yet alive? he *is* my brother.

Benhadad's servants persuaded him to prevail upon the mercy of Ahab. Therefore, Benhadad's servant presented themselves with the appearance of submission and humility and came to Ahab. Ahab was astonished to learn Benhadad was still alive. Apparently, he had an affinity to this pagan king as if he was a brother, notwithstanding his attacks against him.

33 Now the men did diligently observe whether *any thing would come* from him, and did hastily catch *it*: and they said, Thy brother Benhadad. Then he said, Go ye, bring him. Then Benhadad came forth to him; and he caused him to come up into the chariot. Benhadad's servants had determined to listen carefully to how Ahab responded. When he referred to Benhadad as a brother, they took that as a good sign. When Ahab directed them to bring him out, they thus went and brought Benhadad, who thus climbed up into Ahab's chariot.

34 And *Benhadad* said unto him, The cities, which my father took from thy father, I will restore; and thou shalt make streets for thee in Damascus, as my father made in Samaria. Then *said Ahab*, I will send thee away with this

covenant. **So he made a covenant with him, and sent him away.** Ahab now held the upper hand and Benhadad knew it. He therefore offered to restore unto Ahab the cities his father had taken from Omri, Ahab's father. He even offered to name streets in Damascus after Ahab. Ahab therefore agreed thereto and sent Benhadad on his way.

20:35-38 Meanwhile, other events were taking place. **And a certain man of the sons of the prophets said unto his neighbour in the word of the LORD, Smite me, I pray thee. And the man refused to smite him. 36 Then said he unto him, Because thou hast not obeyed the voice of the LORD, behold, as soon as thou art departed from me, a lion shall slay thee. And as soon as he was departed from him, a lion found him, and slew him.** A prophet of God was led to prepare an object lesson. He directed one of his neighbors to strike him. The man refused. The prophet therefore informed him that because of his disobedience to the leading of God's Spirit, that a lion would shortly kill him, which it did.

37 Then he found another man, and said, Smite me, I pray thee. And the man smote him, so that in smiting he wounded *him*. He ordered another neighbor to strike him. This time his other neighbor complied in some way causing injury to the prophet. **38 So the prophet departed, and waited for the king by the way, and disguised himself with ashes upon his face.**

20:39-40 This unnamed prophet therefore waited along the road for King Ahab. **And as the king passed by, he cried unto the king: and he said, Thy servant went out into the midst of the battle; and, behold, a man turned aside, and brought a man unto me, and said, Keep this man: if by any means he be missing, then shall thy life be for his life, or else thou shalt pay a talent of silver.** The prophet thus stopped the king as he passed by and proceeded to tell him an ominous parable. The story was not true, but was a metaphor of what had happened. The prophet therefore posed the story of being given charge of a prisoner by a superior officer in a battle. He was ordered to watch the man on pain of death or at least a heavy fine.

However, 40 **as thy servant was busy here and there, he was gone. And the king of Israel said unto him, So** *shall* **thy judgment** *be***; thyself hast decided** *it*. The prophet finished his parable by declaring that he got busy with other things and his prisoner escaped. Ahab, thinking this was a true story, told him that the agreed judgment would stand.

20:41-43 And he hasted, and took the ashes away from his face; and the king of Israel discerned him that he *was* **of the prophets. 42 And he said unto him, Thus saith the LORD, Because thou hast let go out of** *thy* **hand a man whom I appointed to utter destruction, therefore thy life shall go for his life, and thy people for his people**. The prophet swiftly removed his disguise and the king recognized him as one of the prophets. The prophet therefore informed Ahab that because he had allowed Benhadad to escape (whom God had appointed for destruction), judgment awaited Ahab. God would allow Benhadad to soon kill Ahab and defeat Israel. See I Kings 22:31-37.

43 **And the king of Israel went to his house heavy and displeased, and came to Samaria**. The prophet's announcement took the starch out of Ahab's sails. He may have thought that by his hand the Syrians had been routed. However, God made clear that for his sin in allowing Benhadad to escape, judgment was coming. Ahab therefore returned home in a funk. The word translated as **displeased** (זָעֵף *za'eph*) also has the thought of being angry.

* * * * *

Overview of I Kings 21: *The incident of Ahab and Naboth's vineyard is recorded. Elijah therefore appeared on the scene once again and announced God's judgment against Ahab. In hearing that, Ahab repented, temporarily postponing God's wrath.*

21:1-3 After the battle with Benhadad, Ahab returned home to more mundane things. **And it came to pass after these things,** *that* **Naboth the Jezreelite had a vineyard, which** *was* **in Jezreel, hard by the palace of Ahab king of Samaria.** It is noteworthy that Jezreel (or the valley thereof) was at least twenty miles as the crow flies from Samaria. It would appear therefore that Ahab had a secondary palace at Jezreel adjacent to Naboth's vineyard. The reference here to Samaria may refer to the nation of Israel (which it sometimes did) rather than the city so named.

Therefore, **2 Ahab spake unto Naboth, saying, Give me thy vineyard, that I may have it for a garden of herbs, because it** *is* **near unto my house: and I will give thee for it a better vineyard than it;** *or***, if it seem good to thee, I will give thee the worth of it in money.** Ahab wanted Naboth's land. He offered to swap land for it or even to buy it.

3 And Naboth said to Ahab, The LORD forbid it me, that I should give the inheritance of my fathers unto thee. Naboth refused to sell his land. In Leviticus 25:23, God forbad Israelites from selling their family inheritance. Out of regard to God's Word and perhaps for his own family, Naboth would not co-operate with Ahab.

21:4-6 Ahab was king, but he had been thwarted by one of his subjects. **And Ahab came into his house heavy and displeased because of the word which Naboth the Jezreelite had spoken to him: for he had said, I will not give thee the inheritance of my fathers. And he laid him down upon his**

bed, and turned away his face, and would eat no bread. Because he could not get his wish, Ahab went home, laid down, and pouted about the matter.

5 But Jezebel his wife came to him, and said unto him, Why is thy spirit so sad, that thou eatest no bread? 6 And he said unto her, Because I spake unto Naboth the Jezreelite, and said unto him, Give me thy vineyard for money; or else, if it please thee, I will give thee *another* **vineyard for it: and he answered, I will not give thee my vineyard.** When Jezebel, his wife, saw him sulking, she wanted to know why. He told her. Naboth would not cooperate with him in selling him his land.

21:7-10 Jezebel, the wicked woman that she was, saw no problem. **And Jezebel his wife said unto him, Dost thou now govern the kingdom of Israel? arise,** *and* **eat bread, and let thine heart be merry: I will give thee the vineyard of Naboth the Jezreelite.** She in effect asked him, "Aren't you the king? Get up and eat, and I will take care of this matter."

Therefore, Jezebel **8 wrote letters in Ahab's name, and sealed** *them* **with his seal, and sent the letters unto the elders and to the nobles that** *were* **in his city, dwelling with Naboth** She therefore hatched an evil scheme to eliminate Naboth Using the king's name and seal she wrote to the leaders of Jezreel.

9 And she wrote in the letters, saying, Proclaim a fast, and set Naboth on high among the people: 10 And set two men, sons of Belial, before him, to bear witness against him, saying, Thou didst blaspheme God and the king. And *then* **carry him out, and stone him, that he may die.** Her wicked conspiracy was simple. A feast would be appointed to honor Naboth, thus putting him in the public spotlight. However, two crooked fellows were to be bribed to then rise up and publicly accuse Naboth of blaspheming both God and the king. With those charges made public, Naboth was to be taken and killed.

21:11-13 The corrupt leaders of Jezreel did as directed by Jezebel. **And the men of his city,** *even* **the elders and the nobles who were the inhabitants in his city, did as Jezebel had sent unto them,** *and* **as it** *was* **written in the letters which she had sent unto them. 12 They proclaimed a fast, and set Naboth on high among the people. 13 And there came in two men, children of Belial, and sat before him: and the men of Belial witnessed against him,** *even* **against Naboth, in the presence of the people, saying, Naboth did blaspheme God and the king. Then they carried him forth out of the city, and stoned him with stones, that he died.**

Naboth was put in the public spotlight. Then, the crooked false witnesses made their damning allegations against Naboth whereupon he was summarily taken and executed.

21:14-16 Then they sent to Jezebel, saying, Naboth is stoned, and is dead. And it came to pass, when Jezebel heard that Naboth was stoned, and was dead, that Jezebel said to Ahab, Arise, take possession of the vineyard of Naboth the Jezreelite, which he refused to give thee for money: for Naboth is not alive, but dead.

When the evil deed was accomplished, word was sent to Jezebel informing her. She therefore told her miserable husband to go and seize the vineyard. That he did. **15 And it came to pass, when Ahab heard that Naboth was dead, that Ahab rose up to go down to the vineyard of Naboth the Jezreelite, to take possession of it.** However, what neither Ahab nor Jezebel had counted upon was that Another had witnessed this sordid event.

21:17-19 And the word of the LORD came to Elijah the Tishbite, saying, 18 Arise, go down to meet Ahab king of Israel, which *is* **in Samaria: behold,** *he is* **in the vineyard of Naboth, whither he is gone down to possess it.** God informed

Understanding I Kings

Elijah of what had happened and directed Elijah to go to Naboth's vineyard and confront Ahab there.

19 And thou shalt speak unto him, saying, Thus saith the LORD, Hast thou killed, and also taken possession? And thou shalt speak unto him, saying, Thus saith the LORD, In the place where dogs licked the blood of Naboth shall dogs lick thy blood, even thine. Moreover, God gave Elijah the precise message he was to deliver to Ahab. That message was blunt and foreboding. In the same place where dogs had licked up Naboth's blood would they also lick up Ahab's blood.

21:20-22 Elijah thus marched down to Naboth's vineyard and confronted the corrupt king. Upon his arrival, **Ahab said to Elijah, Hast thou found me, O mine enemy? And he answered, I have found *thee*: because thou hast sold thyself to work evil in the sight of the LORD.** It was Elijah who had ordered the rain to cease for three years. It was Elijah who had slain Ahab's prophets of Baal. Though there was an uneasy truce between the two, Ahab rightly discerned Elijah as his enemy. Elijah thus began his blistering message of judgement against Ahab. He let it be known that the impending judgment against him was because he had sold himself "to work evil in the sight of the LORD." Ahab had not only given himself to work evil, he had sold himself thereto.

Elijah thundered, **21 Behold, I will bring evil upon thee, and will take away thy posterity, and will cut off from Ahab him that pisseth against the wall, and him that is shut up and left in Israel.** God through the prophet announced that He was going to (1) remove Ahab's posterity. He would have no dynasty to follow him. Moreover, (2) He would slay every male of Ahab's lineage. (See comments for I Kings 14:10 regarding the phrase "pisseth against the wall.") The greater thought here is that God was about to destroy the house of Ahab, especially the males thereof.

22 And will make thine house like the house of Jeroboam the son of Nebat, and like the house of Baasha the son of Ahijah, for the provocation wherewith thou hast provoked *me* to anger, and made Israel to sin. Even as God had already destroyed the dynasty of Jeroboam and Baasha for their wickedness, now it was about to come upon Ahab and his descendants. See I Kings 15:29 and 16:11. A great deal of the provocation of Ahab was the abomination of his idolatry. See verse 26.

21:23-24 Moreover, **of Jezebel also spake the LORD, saying, The dogs shall eat Jezebel by the wall of Jezreel.** Ahab's wicked wife would face similar judgment. Before long, she would be killed and eaten by dogs beside the wall of Jezreel. The full judgment of God against Ahab is thus summarized. **24 Him that dieth of Ahab in the city the dogs shall eat; and him that dieth in the field shall the fowls of the air eat.** After the violent deaths which would befall the family of Ahab, no one would even bury their bodies. Wild dogs and scavenging birds would clean up their carnage. See also I Kings 14:11 and 16:4. For a Hebrew, there was no lower indignity than not to be buried at death.

21:25-26 The sacred historian pauses briefly to comment: **But there was none like unto Ahab, which did sell himself to work wickedness in the sight of the LORD, whom Jezebel his wife stirred up. 26 And he did very abominably in following idols, according to all *things* as did the Amorites, whom the LORD cast out before the children of Israel.** To this point in the history of Israel, there had been no couple more wicked than Ahab and Jezebel. The epitome thereof was their reintroduction of idolatry into Israel which the Amorites had practiced hundreds of years earlier. God had cast them out of the land for their abomination. Now Ahab and Jezebel had brought that same wickedness back.

21:27 Though Ahab had been wicked, to his credit, he had a vestige of a tender heart. **And it came to pass, when Ahab heard those words, that he rent his clothes, and put sackcloth upon his flesh, and fasted, and lay in sackcloth, and went softly.** Upon hearing of God's impending judgment, the man humbled himself openly and repented. He put on the outward symbols of humiliation. He prostrated himself before God. Moreover, he went about *softly* or humbled.

21:28-29 And the word of the LORD came to Elijah the Tishbite, saying, 29 Seest thou how Ahab humbleth himself before me? because he humbleth himself before me, I will not bring the evil in his days: *but* **in his son's days will I bring the evil upon his house.** An amazing truth is revealed here. God is moved by genuine repentance and a humbling of oneself. Though Ahab had been abominably wicked, God was moved by his repentance and remorse. The judgment was not eliminated, but it was postponed. Ahab's son would prove to be just as wicked as his father. Therefore, God would exact His wrath upon Jehoram, Ahab's son. See II Kings 9:25. Evident here is an illustration of Proverbs 28:13, which see.

* * * * *

Overview of I Kings 22: This final chapter of I Kings presents details of the final battle between Ahab and Syria, this time with the assistance of Jehoshaphat. Record is also made of Micaiah's prophecy against Ahab. In the ensuing battle, Ahab is killed. The focus then returns to Judah with record being made of the accession of Jehoshaphat as king thereof. Brief comments is made about Jehoshaphat's and Ahab's successors.

22:1-4 After the confrontation by Elijah the prophet, record is made of a lull in the war between Israel and Syria. **And they continued three years without war between Syria and Israel. 2 And it came to pass in the third year, that Jehoshaphat the king of Judah came down to the king of Israel.** Though there had been hostility between Judah and Israel since the split in the kingdom, it appears that the two kings were willing to seek some sort of truce. It may be that they both feared the common threat of Syria.

3 And the king of Israel said unto his servants, Know ye that Ramoth in Gilead *is* ours, and we *be* still, *and* take it not out of the hand of the king of Syria? Ramoth of Gilead was a town on the east side of the Jordan River which originally had belonged to Israel. In the preceding years, Syria had seized possession thereof and still held it. This was a bur under Ahab's saddle. He therefore conferred with his advisors about retaking Ramoth.

Because Jehoshaphat had arrived, Ahab **4 said unto Jehoshaphat, Wilt thou go with me to battle to Ramothgilead? And Jehoshaphat said to the king of Israel, I *am* as thou *art*, my people as thy people, my horses as thy horses**. Ahab asked Jehoshaphat if he would assist him in retaking Ramoth. To that, he placed at Ahab's disposal all of the military resources of Judah.

22:5 And Jehoshaphat said unto the king of Israel, Enquire, I pray thee, at the word of the LORD to day. Jehoshaphat was one of the more godly kings of Judah. However, his dalliance with Ahab was born of spiritual compromise. He had no business courting the favor of his apostate colleague to the north. To place a guise of propriety upon their budding alliance, Jehoshaphat therefore requested that they seek the mind of Jehovah in the matter.

22:6 Therefore, **the king of Israel gathered the prophets together, about four hundred men, and said unto them,**

Understanding I Kings

Shall I go against Ramothgilead to battle, or shall I forbear? And they said, Go up; for the Lord shall deliver *it* into the hand of the king. It is significant that the prophets of Ahab are not called prophets of Jehovah. They were false prophets, not unlike the 450 prophets of Baal slain several years earlier at Mount Carmel. When asked by Ahab if they should retake Syria, as 'yes men,' his prophets with one accord said, "go." It is noteworthy that the reference to **Lord** is not Jehovah, but 'Adonay.' The former is a proper name of God. The latter is a more generic term. They may not have been even referring to God Himself.

22:7-9 And Jehoshaphat said, *Is there* not here a prophet of the LORD besides, that we might enquire of him? 8 And the king of Israel said unto Jehoshaphat, *There is* yet one man, Micaiah the son of Imlah, by whom we may enquire of the LORD: but I hate him; for he doth not prophesy good concerning me, but evil. And Jehoshaphat said, Let not the king say so.

Jehoshaphat was not impressed with the prophets of Ahab. He wanted to hear from a prophet of Jehovah. He therefore pressed Ahab to that end. Ahab therefore grudgingly recalled a prophet still faithful to Jehovah by the name of Micaiah. However, Ahab noted that he hated this prophet of Jehovah because he never had anything good to say about him. It is possible that Micaiah was one and the same as the prophet of Jehovah mentioned in I Kings 20:13, 22, 35, and 38. To that Jehoshaphat said, "Let not the king say so." The idea is of a gentile rebuke to Ahab, "You really shouldn't say that." **9 Then the king of Israel called an officer, and said, Hasten *hither* Micaiah the son of Imlah.**

22:10-12 Meanwhile, **the king of Israel and Jehoshaphat the king of Judah sat each on his throne, having put on their**

robes, in a void place in the entrance of the gate of Samaria; and all the prophets prophesied before them. It was an ancient, middle-eastern custom for official business of state or city to be conducted in a public area near or at the gate of a city. There evidently was such a 'square' or 'courtyard' at Samaria. There, both kings set up official seats while the prophets of Ahab went through their incantations.

11 And Zedekiah the son of Chenaanah made him horns of iron: and he said, Thus saith the LORD**, With these shalt thou push the Syrians, until thou have consumed them.** One of Ahab's prophets was so bold as to claim to be prophesying in the name of Jehovah. He made horns of iron and proclaimed that with them Ahab would push back the Syrians to defeat. There might be a veiled reference here to Deuteronomy 33:17, which see.

His colleagues therefore all joined together with one consent. **12 And all the prophets prophesied so, saying, Go up to Ramothgilead, and prosper: for the L**ORD **shall deliver *it* into the king's hand.** Thus, the advice of Ahab's prophets was to attack Ramoth in Gilead. Though they normally had no respect to Jehovah, now for the benefit of Jehoshaphat in their midst, they began to invoke that sacred name. It was false piety at its worst. They preached what they perceived their royal audience wished to hear. Ahab wanted to hear of victory. Jehoshaphat wanted the blessing of Jehovah. No problem, the prophets of Ahab delivered whatever they wished.

22:13-14 And the messenger that was gone to call Micaiah spake unto him, saying, Behold now, the words of the prophets *declare* good unto the king with one mouth: let thy word, I pray thee, be like the word of one of them, and speak *that which is* good. While the prophets of Ahab were delivering the message he wished to hear, the messenger sent to fetch Micaiah thus informed him of the prevailing party line. He therefore directed Micaiah to pronounce the same flattering

Understanding I Kings

speech to the two assembled kings. **14 And Micaiah said, *As* the LORD liveth, what the LORD saith unto me, that will I speak**. Micaiah, to his credit, vowed by the name of Jehovah that he would speak only what God laid upon his heart.

22:15-16 So he came to the king. And the king said unto him, Micaiah, shall we go against Ramothgilead to battle, or shall we forbear? And he answered him, Go, and prosper: for the LORD shall deliver *it* into the hand of the king. It may be that Micaiah thought better and decided to tow the party line. Rather, it is more likely that he spoke before Ahab sarcastically and, in a fashion clearly not sincere, told them to proceed. **16 And the king said unto him, How many times shall I adjure thee that thou tell me nothing but *that which is* true in the name of the LORD?** Ahab thus admonished him to be truthful.

22:17-18 Micaiah therefore said, **I saw all Israel scattered upon the hills, as sheep that have not a shepherd: and the LORD said, These have no master: let them return every man to his house in peace**. The message of Micaiah was plain. Israel would be defeated. The army of Ahab would be as a flock of sheep scattered across the hills. They would be without a leader. Clearly implied is the death of Ahab. The prophet therefore indicated that the scattered army of Israel would slink back home.

To which **18 the king of Israel said unto Jehoshaphat, Did I not tell thee that he would prophesy no good concerning me, but evil?** In so many words, Ahab said to Jehoshaphat, "See! Didn't I tell you he would have nothing good to say about me?"

22:19-23 Micaiah was not finished. He continued, **Hear thou therefore the word of the LORD: I saw the LORD sitting**

on his throne, and all the host of heaven standing by him on his right hand and on his left. Micaiah therefore depicted a purported scene in heaven. (There is no indication that this actually took place.) In the midst was God Himself seated upon His throne with the angels of heaven on each side of Him.

20 **And the LORD said, Who shall persuade Ahab, that he may go up and fall at Ramothgilead? And one said on this manner, and another said on that manner.** 21 **And there came forth a spirit, and stood before the LORD, and said, I will persuade him.** It is not likely that this scene in heaven actually took place. Rather, Micaiah, perhaps at God's leading, made up this story to illustrate the point. It may be that he used as an illustration a situation of which Ahab was familiar—a council with his advisors. Thus, in this purported counsel in heaven, God asked who would go and persuade Ahab to go to Ramoth to his defeat. One angel stepped forward and so volunteered.

22 **And the LORD said unto him, Wherewith? And he said, I will go forth, and I will be a lying spirit in the mouth of all his prophets. And he said, Thou shalt persuade *him*, and prevail also: go forth, and do so.** 23 **Now therefore, behold, the LORD hath put a lying spirit in the mouth of all these thy prophets, and the LORD hath spoken evil concerning thee.** As this purported story continued, the Lord asked the angel how he intended to persuade Ahab to his defeat. The angel is to have answered that he would go and act as a lying spirit to the prophets of Ahab. By having them all say the same thing, he would thus persuade Ahab to go out to his death. Once again, it should not be supposed that this event actually took place in heaven. There no longer are any unholy angels left there and God would not tolerate deceit. Rather, Micaiah made up the story altogether. At the least, it was a strategy to which Ahab could relate and illustrated how his 'yes-man' prophets could easily be led astray by a lying spirit.

22:24-25 But Zedekiah the son of Chenaanah went near, and smote Micaiah on the cheek, and said, Which way went the Spirit of the LORD from me to speak unto thee? Zedekiah, Ahab's chief prophet, did not miss the implication. He was insulted and went and slapped Micaiah across the face asking sarcastically, how the Spirit of Jehovah had moved over to Micaiah from him. **25 And Micaiah said, Behold, thou shalt see in that day, when thou shalt go into an inner chamber to hide thyself.** To Zedekiah's sarcastic question, Micaiah told him, you will find out soon enough. In short order, he would hide in fear of capture.

22:26-28 And the king of Israel said, Take Micaiah, and carry him back unto Amon the governor of the city, and to Joash the king's son; And say, 27 Thus saith the king, Put this *fellow* in the prison, and feed him with bread of affliction and with water of affliction, until I come in peace. Ahab therefore ordered Micaiah to be consigned to the common prison of the city and provided a starvation diet. (Bread of affliction and water of affliction were essentially moldy bread and dirty water.) Ahab directed to so keep the prophet until he returned victorious.

To that **28 Micaiah said, If thou return at all in peace, the LORD hath not spoken by me. And he said, Hearken, O people, every one of you.** Micaiah's parting shot was pungent. If Ahab returned at all, God had not spoken by him. The implication is that the proof of his prophecy would be the state of Ahab after the battle. Micaiah had clearly foretold the death of Ahab. He thus ordered Israel to take note of what he spoke.

22:29-30 Thus, **the king of Israel and Jehoshaphat the king of Judah went up to Ramothgilead. 30 And the king of Israel said unto Jehoshaphat, I will disguise myself, and enter into the battle; but put thou on thy robes. And the king**

of Israel disguised himself, and went into the battle. The lack of leadership in Ahab is apparent. Knowing that the enemy might target him because he was king, he hatched the idea of going into battle incognito. He therefore convinced Jehoshaphat to wear his royal robes and thus appear as the king of Israel.

22:31-33 As anticipated by Ahab, **the king of Syria commanded his thirty and two captains that had rule over his chariots, saying, Fight neither with small nor great, save only with the king of Israel. 32 And it came to pass, when the captains of the chariots saw Jehoshaphat, that they said, Surely it *is* the king of Israel. And they turned aside to fight against him: and Jehoshaphat cried out.** The Syrian king directed his divisional officers to ignore the common foot soldiers and rather go for the king of Israel. Thus upon joining the battle, they spied Jehoshaphat dressed in the royal array of Ahab and supposed it was him. They therefore focused their attack against Jehoshaphat. Realizing what was happening, Jehoshaphat cried out. It may be that he cried out to let the Syrians know who he was. Or, it may be that he cried out to God for help. In the parallel account of this incident in II Chronicles 18:31, it is recorded that thereupon, God helped him.

Thus, **33 it came to pass, when the captains of the chariots perceived that it *was* not the king of Israel, that they turned back from pursuing him.** It was ordained by God for Jehoshaphat to live and for Ahab to die.

22:34-36 And a *certain* man drew a bow at a venture, and smote the king of Israel between the joints of the harness: wherefore he said unto the driver of his chariot, Turn thine hand, and carry me out of the host; for I am wounded. Implicit is that a soldier in the Syrian army drew his bow and shot it indiscriminately into the battle. The arrow not

Understanding I Kings

only found its way to Ahab, but pierced him at the joints of his armor. There can be little question that God so providentially directed that arrow to strike Ahab at such a small place—between the joints of his body armor. Ahab knew he was in trouble. He thus directed the driver of his chariot to retreat from the battle.

35 And the battle increased that day: and the king was stayed up in his chariot against the Syrians, and died at even: and the blood ran out of the wound into the midst of the chariot. The idea is that Ahab was propped up in his chariot the rest of that day, but died at sundown. Meanwhile, the blood from his wound ran down into his chariot. The stage for fulfilled prophecy was being set.

Realizing that their king was dead, word went out through the army of Israel to retreat. It turned into a rout. **36 And there went a proclamation throughout the host about the going down of the sun, saying, Every man to his city, and every man to his own country.** The proclamation may have been from Jehoshaphat. In any event, by sundown of that day, Israel was clearly defeated in the battle. The prophecy made by Micaiah in 22:17 was fulfilled in detail.

22:37-38 So the king died, and was brought to Samaria; and they buried the king in Samaria. The dead body of Ahab was returned to Samaria and there they buried him. **38 And *one* washed the chariot in the pool of Samaria; and the dogs licked up his blood; and they washed his armour; according unto the word of the LORD which he spake.** In bringing Ahab's chariot back to Samaria, someone took it upon himself to wash the blood out of his chariot. As he did so, neighborhood dogs came and licked up his blood. Thus was fulfilled in detail the prophecy made by Elijah against Ahab in I Kings 21:19. At the same place wherein Naboth's blood had been spilt and licked by dogs, so it happened to Ahab.

22:39-40 Summary mention is made of the reign of Ahab and the succession of the throne of Israel. **Now the rest of the acts of Ahab, and all that he did, and the ivory house which he made, and all the cities that he built, *are* they not written in the book of the chronicles of the kings of Israel? 40 So Ahab slept with his fathers; and Ahaziah his son reigned in his stead.** The chronicles of the kings of Israel are not likely the biblical book of I & II Chronicles for no mention is made of these details there. Reference is made of a **ivory house** which may mean it was trimmed with ivory. See also Amos 3:15. Ahaziah, the son of Ahab, thus became the next king of Israel.

22:41-42 For the first time since I Kings 15:24, the focus of the book returns to the affairs in Judah. There, brief mention was made of the accession of Jehoshaphat as king of Judah. More detail of this next king of Judah is thus provided. **And Jehoshaphat the son of Asa began to reign over Judah in the fourth year of Ahab king of Israel. 42 Jehoshaphat *was* thirty and five years old when he began to reign; and he reigned twenty and five years in Jerusalem. And his mother's name *was* Azubah the daughter of Shilhi.** Jehoshaphat would reign for twenty-five years, dying when he was about sixty. Mention is made here of his mother's name which is no where else mentioned.

22:43-44 The character of Jehoshaphat's reign is here summarized. (Far greater detail is provided in II Chronicles 17:1-20:31.) **And he walked in all the ways of Asa his father; he turned not aside from it, doing *that which was* right in the eyes of the LORD: nevertheless the high places were not taken away; *for* the people offered and burnt incense yet in the high places. 44 And Jehoshaphat made peace with the king of Israel.** In the main, Jehoshaphat was one of the godly and great kings of Judah. He is characterized as walking in the

Understanding I Kings

ways of Asa, his father. As noted in I Kings 15:11, Asa did that which was right in the eyes of the Lord even as had David. Thus, Jehoshaphat was placed in the same league as the godly kings which had gone on before him. He here is also noted as 'doing *that which was* right in the eyes of the LORD."

However, the weaknesses of Jehoshaphat are also noted. (1) He failed to stop the casual offering of incense to Jehovah upon irregular altars in various high places. God had directed that all formal worship of Him was to be at the Temple at Jerusalem. (2) He also compromised and joined into an alliance with Ahab, the wicked king to the north. It almost cost him his life. The latter affiliation was clearly that of spiritual compromise.

22:45-46 Additional details regarding the reign of Jehoshaphat are thus provided. **Now the rest of the acts of Jehoshaphat, and his might that he shewed, and how he warred, *are* they not written in the book of the chronicles of the kings of Judah?** Further information about Jehoshaphat is certainly found in the biblical book of II Chronicles. Whether this is the same as mentioned here is not clear. Other reference to "the chronicles of the kings of Judah" was made earlier which apparently does not appertain to the inspired account.

To Jehoshaphat's credit, **46 the remnant of the sodomites, which remained in the days of his father Asa, he took out of the land**. Though his father Asa had sought to exterminate sodomy from the land, he apparently had missed some. Therefore, Jehoshaphat threw out of Judah any other homosexuals he could find.

22:47-49 Further historical detail regarding Jehoshaphat's reign is noted. ***There was* then no king in Edom: a deputy *was* king. 48 Jehoshaphat made ships of Tharshish to go to Ophir for gold: but they went not; for the ships were broken**

at Eziongeber. Because there was no strong ruler in Edom (analogous to the southern portion of modern Jordan), Jehoshaphat built ships to sail to Ophir to bring back gold as had Solomon. These ships were evidently of the style to sail the Indian Ocean and were called ships of Tharshish. That idea is that they were built for the high seas. However, apparently not having the sailing skills of Hiram's sailors which Solomon had, Jehoshaphat's ships were wrecked on the rocks near the port of Eziongeber. The modern name is Elat which is at the head of the northeastward sound of the Red Sea.

Hearing of that, **49 then said Ahaziah the son of Ahab unto Jehoshaphat, Let my servants go with thy servants in the ships. But Jehoshaphat would not**. The new king of Israel to the north therefore requested to send some of his men, perhaps to help sail, or more likely to just reap the profits of the venture. However, to his credit, Jehoshaphat had evidently learned his lesson about cooperating with the apostate kingdom to the north. He thus refused Ahaziah's request.

22:50 The death and succession of Jehoshaphat is thus noted. **And Jehoshaphat slept with his fathers, and was buried with his fathers in the city of David his father: and Jehoram his son reigned in his stead**. Again the euphemism of death as 'sleeping with one's fathers' is used. His son Jehoram succeeded him as king. More detail regarding this new king is found in II Chronicles 21.

22:51-53 The focus of the book now turns back to happenings in the northern kingdom. **Ahaziah the son of Ahab began to reign over Israel in Samaria the seventeenth year of Jehoshaphat king of Judah, and reigned two years over Israel**. The son of Ahab would be little different than his father. The evil of his reign would be terminated after only two years of rule.

52 And he did evil in the sight of the LORD, and walked in the way of his father, and in the way of his mother, and in the way of Jeroboam the son of Nebat, who made Israel to sin: 53 For he served Baal, and worshipped him, and provoked to anger the LORD God of Israel, according to all that his father had done. Ahaziah was no different than Ahab, Jezebel, or even Jeroboam. Like his wicked forefathers, he served Baal. In so doing, he provoked Jehovah God to anger. God would soon terminate him and the house of his father. See II Kings 1.

THE SECOND BOOK OF THE
KINGS
COMMONLY CALLED
THE FOURTH BOOK OF THE KINGS

Introduction to II Kings: This next book of the Kings is also known as the fourth book of the Kings. The Jewish perspective is that I and II Samuel are the first two. The period covered parallels the ministries of Elijah, Elisha, Amos, Hosea, Obadiah, Joel, Isaiah, Micah, Nahum, Habakkuk, Zephaniah, and Jeremiah. The narrative picks up directly where it left off at the end of I Kings.

Overview of II Kings 1: This first chapter presents the confrontation between the messengers of Ahaziah and Elijah. It culminates in a showdown between the prophet and Ahaziah himself with Elijah delivering notice that the king would die.

1:1-2 Ahaziah, the son of Ahab, was the next king of the northern kingdom, Israel. The sacred text records, **Then Moab rebelled against Israel after the death of Ahab**. Moab was the region to the east and south of the main portion of Israel and is analogous to part of the modern state of Jordan. It had been under subjugation to Israel since the time of David. See II Samuel 8:2. Meanwhile, **2 Ahaziah fell down through a lattice in his upper chamber that *was* in Samaria, and was sick: and he sent messengers, and said unto them, Go, enquire of Baalzebub the god of Ekron whether I shall recover of this disease.** In some fashion, Ahaziah fell through a lattice, perhaps covering an upper story window. It may be that sickness prompted his fall or it may be that complications from his injuries produced infection and sickness thereafter. He therefore sent his servants to inquire of "Baalzebub the god of Ekron" whether he would recover. The name *Baalzebub* literally means 'lord of the flies' and was a Philistine idol.

1:3-4 However, **the angel of the LORD said to Elijah the Tishbite, Arise, go up to meet the messengers of the king of Samaria, and say unto them, *Is it* not because *there is* not a God in Israel, *that* ye go to enquire of Baalzebub the god of Ekron?** God through His angel directed Elijah to confront the messengers of Ahaziah on their way to Ekron. He was to challenge them as to why they were going to Ekron and its pagan god. Implied in the question is that God had been discharged from the northern kingdom. They had forsaken Jehovah God and now had to turn to a foreign, pagan idol for help.

Elijah did as directed and so confronted Ahaziah's messengers. In meeting them, Elijah said, **4 Now therefore thus saith the LORD, Thou shalt not come down from that bed on which thou art gone up, but shalt surely die. And Elijah departed.** Ahaziah's messengers never made it to Ekron. Elijah told them exactly what was going to happen. Ahaziah would not recover. He soon would die. He thus turned upon his heel and left.

1:5-6 The messengers therefore returned to Samaria. **And when the messengers turned back unto him, he said unto**

them, Why are ye now turned back? 6 And they said unto him, There came a man up to meet us, and said unto us, Go, turn again unto the king that sent you, and say unto him, Thus saith the LORD, *Is it* not because *there is* not a God in Israel, *that* thou sendest to enquire of Baalzebub the god of Ekron? therefore thou shalt not come down from that bed on which thou art gone up, but shalt surely die. Ahaziah interrogated his messengers as to why they had returned. They told him what had happened, understanding not however who it was that had confronted them. They, however, repeated exactly what Elijah had told them.

1:7-8 And he said unto them, What manner of man *was he* which came up to meet you, and told you these words? 8 And they answered him, *He was* an hairy man, and girt with a girdle of leather about his loins. And he said, It *is* Elijah the Tishbite. The reference to Elijah being hairy may refer to his beard and haircut. It may refer to body hair upon his arms and torso. It may also refer to him wearing an animal skin. In any event, after hearing this description, Ahaziah knew exactly who they had met. It was Elijah the prophet.

1:9-10 Then the king sent unto him a captain of fifty with his fifty. And he went up to him: and, behold, he sat on the top of an hill. And he spake unto him, Thou man of God, the king hath said, Come down. Ahaziah therefore sent a company of fifty soldiers to bring Elijah by force if necessary. The word translated as **sat** (ישׁב *yashab*) can also have the sense to 'dwell.' That may be the thought here. Elijah in any event was upon a hilltop when Ahaziah's men arrived. The captain of the men ordered him to come down by the king's decree. To that, Elijah replied, **10 If I *be* a man of God, then let fire come down from heaven, and consume thee and thy fifty. And there came down fire from heaven, and consumed him and his**

fifty. Whether the fire was a massive bolt of lightning or more conventional fire, in any event, Ahaziah's men were devoured on the spot.

1:11-12 It is not noted if or how Ahaziah was informed of the fate of his first force. It would seem however that there probably had been witnesses to the destruction of his men and word got back to him. Thus, **again also he sent unto him another captain of fifty with his fifty. And he answered and said unto him, O man of God, thus hath the king said, Come down quickly.** Another force was sent. It is noteworthy that in both instances, the captain addressed Elijah as a man of God. They knew who he was and Whom he represented. It is more than ironic that Ahaziah had discounted the God of heaven but his men knew better.

Again, 12 **Elijah answered and said unto them, If I** *be* **a man of God, let fire come down from heaven, and consume thee and thy fifty. And the fire of God came down from heaven, and consumed him and his fifty**. Though Ahaziah had rejected Jehovah God, he was receiving a clear lesson of God's power.

1:13-14 However, the wicked king remained stubborn in his defiance of God's message and man. **And he sent again a captain of the third fifty with his fifty. And the third captain of fifty went up, and came and fell on his knees before Elijah, and besought him, and said unto him, O man of God, I pray thee, let my life, and the life of these fifty thy servants, be precious in thy sight.** A third contingent was sent to arrest Elijah. However, this officer rather pled with Elijah to spare his life and those of his men. He clearly knew what happened to his comrades' in arms.

14 **Behold, there came fire down from heaven, and burnt up the two captains of the former fifties with their**

Understanding II Kings

fifties: therefore let my life now be precious in thy sight. He thus repeated his plea for mercy. To their credit, these common soldiers had the good sense to fear God and His messenger. That is more than the wicked and stubborn king of Israel did.

1:15-16 And the angel of the LORD said unto Elijah, Go down with him: be not afraid of him. And he arose, and went down with him unto the king. God thus directed His man this time to go to Ahaziah. Upon arriving before Ahaziah, Elijah said to him, **16 Thus saith the LORD, Forasmuch as thou hast sent messengers to enquire of Baalzebub the god of Ekron, *is it* not because *there is* no God in Israel to enquire of his word? therefore thou shalt not come down off that bed on which thou art gone up, but shalt surely die.**

The prophet confronted the king with his rejection of Jehovah God. It was not that God was not present in Israel. Rather, from the king on down, the nation had rejected Jehovah as God. Therefore, they were reduced to seeking help from a pagan idol in time of need. Moreover, Elijah delivered to Ahaziah, face to face, the news that he would soon die.

1:17-18 So he died according to the word of the LORD which Elijah had spoken. And Jehoram reigned in his stead in the second year of Jehoram the son of Jehoshaphat king of Judah; because he had no son. The implication is that Ahaziah died shortly after Elijah's verdict was delivered to him. Because he had no son, his brother, Jehoram ascended his throne. Ironically, in Judah, the new king there was also named Jehoram. The latter was the son of Jehoshaphat. See I Kings 22:50.

18 Now the rest of the acts of Ahaziah which he did, *are* they not written in the book of the chronicles of the kings of Israel? The chronicles of the kings of Israel were uninspired history books of the kings of the northern kingdom and are long lost.

Overview of II Kings 2: *This unusual chapter records the translation of Elijah to heaven and the beginning of the ministry of Elisha. Record is also made of the confusion of Elijah's young students at the departure of their master. Two miracles are noted performed at the hand of Elisha.*

2:1-2 And it came to pass, when the LORD would take up Elijah into heaven by a whirlwind, that Elijah went with Elisha from Gilgal. It seems that both Elijah and Elisha were aware of the imminent departure of Elijah. It also seems that Elijah had foreknowledge that his translation to heaven would be by a whirlwind. Whether this would be by a tornado or some lessor type of whirlwind is not clear. Tornadoes are primarily a North American phenomena. However, God could produce such wheresoever He desires. The setting at hand is at Gilgal, which is in the Jordan River valley, not far from Jericho.

2 And Elijah said unto Elisha, Tarry here, I pray thee; for the LORD hath sent me to Bethel. And Elisha said *unto him*, As the LORD liveth, and *as* thy soul liveth, I will not leave thee. So they went down to Bethel. Elijah instructed Elisha to stay at Gilgal while he went up into the highlands to Bethel as God had directed him. However, perceiving that God was about to take him to heaven, Elisha swore by Jehovah's name that he would not depart from Elijah. They thus both went up into the highlands and then descended into the shallow valley whence was Bethel.

2:3-4 Upon arriving at Bethel, **the sons of the prophets that *were* at Bethel came forth to Elisha, and said unto him, Knowest thou that the LORD will take away thy master from thy head to day? And he said, Yea, I know *it*; hold ye your peace**. Though Jeroboam had made Bethel an idolatrous city, it seems that Elijah may have also established a school of the prophets there to counteract the idolatry of the land. Of interest is that these young prophets also were aware that God was about to take Elijah to heaven. They thus accosted Elisha with the news, referring to the event as removing Elijah from Elisha's head. The implication is that Elijah was as a crown to Elisha.

Apparently, God had by revelation made known to this group of prophets what was about to happen to Elijah. Upon hearing this, Elisha essentially acknowledged he already knew it and told them to hush. The tone of his comments are not clear. He may have been quite sharp in rebuking them. Implied is that this was a sore spot for Elisha.

Therefore, 4 **Elijah said unto him, Elisha, tarry here, I pray thee; for the LORD hath sent me to Jericho. And he said,** *As* **the LORD liveth, and** *as* **thy soul liveth, I will not leave thee. So they came to Jericho.** Elijah therefore directed Elisha to stay at Jericho because the Lord had sent him down to Jericho. Once again, Elisha swore by the name of Jehovah that he would not leave him. He knew the time of Elijah's departure was at hand and he wanted to receive a double blessing of his spirit when that time came. What also seems clear is that Elijah seemed to be testing Elisha and his call to the ministry. It is evident that Elisha was determined to receive the blessing of God upon himself at Elijah's departure.

2:5 Upon arriving at Jericho, **the sons of the prophets that** *were* **at Jericho came to Elisha, and said unto him, Knowest thou that the LORD will take away thy master from thy head to day? And he answered, Yea, I know** *it***; hold ye your peace.** In fashion almost identical to what happened at Bethel, the prophets at Jericho informed Elisha of Elijah's imminent departure. In fashion similar to above, he rebuked them as well.

2:6 Again, Elijah sought to test Elisha. **And Elijah said unto him, Tarry, I pray thee, here; for the LORD hath sent**

me to Jordan. And he said, *As* the LORD liveth, and *as* thy soul liveth, I will not leave thee. And they two went on. This time, Elijah informed Elisha that he was heading to the Jordan River, several miles to the east. Again, Elisha refused to leave him.

2:7-8 Meanwhile, **fifty men of the sons of the prophets went, and stood to view afar off: and they two stood by Jordan.** It seems clear that the prophets of God in the region all knew that Elijah was about to be taken to heaven. Thus, fifty of them followed behind, hoping to catch a glimpse of Elijah's rapture.

8 **And Elijah took his mantle, and wrapped** *it* **together, and smote the waters, and they were divided hither and thither, so that they two went over on dry ground.** The mantle referenced was an outer garment such as a cloak. Elijah thus rolled it up and struck the waters of the Jordan River. They immediately divided before them and they both walked across on a completely dry river bed.

2:9-11 And it came to pass, when they were gone over, that Elijah said unto Elisha, Ask what I shall do for thee, before I be taken away from thee. And Elisha said, I pray thee, let a double portion of thy spirit be upon me. It seems that Elisha had passed the test as far as Elijah was concerned. He thus asked what Elisha wished prior to his departure. Elisha's request was for a double portion of the prophetic spirit upon him. This may be a reference to the Holy Spirit or it may simply refer to the gift of prophecy which Elijah obviously had.

In any event, Elijah said, 10 **Thou hast asked a hard thing:** *nevertheless*, **if thou see me** *when I am* **taken from thee, it shall be so unto thee; but if not, it shall not be** *so*. Elijah acknowledged that this was a difficult request. However, he informed Elisha that if he saw him taken up to heaven, his request would be granted. Implicit is that if Elisha was so privileged to see his translation that the Lord would so grant his request.

11 **And it came to pass, as they still went on, and talked, that, behold,** *there appeared* **a chariot of fire, and horses of fire, and parted them both asunder; and Elijah went up by a whirlwind into heaven.** As the two prophets walked along, God sent a chariot of fire drawn by horses of fire which took Elijah. In conjunction with that, Elijah was drawn up by a whirlwind. See comments about a whirlwind in 2:1. It may be that the whirlwind drew Elijah into the chariot and thus took him to heaven.

2:12-13 And Elisha saw *it***, and he cried, My father, my father, the chariot of Israel, and the horsemen thereof. And he saw him no more: and he took hold of his own clothes, and rent them in two pieces.** Though Elisha had longed to see the translation of his master Elijah, it seems that when he did, he was struck by his loss. It would seem that his cry, "My father, my father," was of Elijah. Though he was not his biological father, Elijah had been as a spiritual father to him. Some hold the view that Elisha's reference to "the chariot of Israel, and the horsemen thereof" is to the God of Israel and his defense thereof as by a chariot and horsemen of fire. The rending of his clothes seemed to be Elisha's public mourning over the loss of his mentor.

However, as Elijah was taken up, his mantle fell from him. Elisha 13 **took up also the mantle of Elijah that fell from him, and went back, and stood by the bank of Jordan.**

2:14-15 Upon arriving back at the banks of the Jordan River, Elisha **took the mantle of Elijah that fell from him, and smote the waters, and said, Where** *is* **the LORD God of Elijah? and when he also had smitten the waters, they parted hither and thither: and Elisha went over.** As his predecessor had done, Elisha thus smote the waters of the

Jordan, asking for the power of the God of Elijah. Just as God had done for Elijah, he did for Elisha. The river parted before him and he crossed to the other side. God clearly had placed his stamp of approval upon the ministry of Elisha.

15 And when the sons of the prophets which *were* to view at Jericho saw him, they said, The spirit of Elijah doth rest on Elisha. And they came to meet him, and bowed themselves to the ground before him. The fifty prophets watching from the west bank became aware of God's power upon Elisha and they therefore bowed before him. It is unclear if they saw Elijah's translation to heaven. But they certainly saw the parting of the river at Elisha's return.

2:16-18 However, it is apparent that the young prophets did not fully understand what had happened. **And they said unto him, Behold now, there be with thy servants fifty strong men; let them go, we pray thee, and seek thy master: lest peradventure the Spirit of the LORD hath taken him up, and cast him upon some mountain, or into some valley. And he said, Ye shall not send.** These young prophets, though aware that the Lord would take Elijah to heaven, thought that he would soon be deposited back, perhaps upon a mountain top or into some valley. The region around Jericho abounds with both. However, Elisha said forget it. He knew better.

17 And when they urged him till he was ashamed, he said, Send. They sent therefore fifty men; and they sought three days, but found him not. Notwithstanding his decision against searching for Elijah, the young prophets continued to urge him until he was embarrassed to say no. They evidently were quite persuasive. Therefore, he allowed them to search which they did for three days. However, their search proved futile. **18 And when they came again to him, (for he tarried at Jericho,) he said unto them, Did I not say unto you, Go not?**

2:19-22 While at Jericho, **the men of the city said unto Elisha, Behold, I pray thee, the situation of this city** *is* **pleasant, as my lord seeth: but the water** *is* **naught, and the ground barren**. Jericho is in the Jordan River valley not far from where the river empties into the Dead Sea. It is east of the coastal mountains and therefore typically semi-arid. It may be that water from the Dead Sea had seeped into the local ground water and the water therefore was bitter. The word translated as **naught** (רע *rah*) has the sense of 'bad.'

Elisha therefore said, **20 Bring me a new cruse, and put salt therein. And they brought** *it* **to him. 21 And he went forth unto the spring of the waters, and cast the salt in there, and said, Thus saith the** LORD**, I have healed these waters; there shall not be from thence any more death or barren** *land*. Speaking on behalf of the Lord, Elisha therefore pronounced the bitter water to be healed. From henceforth the land therefore would be productive. To this day, there is good water at Jericho. **22 So the waters were healed unto this day, according to the saying of Elisha which he spake**.

2:23-25 And he went up from thence unto Bethel: and as he was going up by the way, there came forth little children out of the city, and mocked him, and said unto him, Go up, thou bald head; go up, thou bald head. As Elisha ascended up into the highlands toward the city of Bethel, youngsters of the city came out and mocked him. They likely were young adolescents. It is evident that Elisha was bald. Their taunts likely referred to their hearing of the story of Elijah's translation to heaven. They therefore jeered at Elisha to do the same thing. The utter disrespect to this prophet and the God he represented is apparent.

24 And he turned back, and looked on them, and cursed them in the name of the LORD**. And there came forth two she bears out of the wood, and tare forty and two children**

of them. Quite evidently with God's permission, Elisha thus placed a curse upon these blasphemous youths in the name of Jehovah. Whereupon two sow bears came out of the woods and killed forty two of the insolent adolescents.

Meanwhile, Elisha **25 went from thence to mount Carmel, and from thence he returned to Samaria**. Clearly, he was not welcome at Bethel, so Elisha traveled westward to Mount Carmel and then eventually back to the area of Samaria.

* * * * *

***Overview of II Kings 3**: In this chapter, details of the reign of Jehoram, the son of Ahab, are presented. Record is made of Moab's rebellion against Israel. Elisha rebuked the alli-ance of Jehoshaphat with Jehoram, And then the chapter concludes with Elisha's promise of water and victory over Moab which came to pass.*

3:1-3 Now Jehoram the son of Ahab began to reign over Israel in Samaria the eighteenth year of Jehoshaphat king of Judah, and reigned twelve years. The focus shifts from the ministry of Elisha back to the politics of the northern kingdom. Jehoram, Ahab's son, had ascended his father's throne. **2 And he wrought evil in the sight of the LORD; but not like his father, and like his mother: for he put away the image of Baal that his father had made**. Though he was not a godly king by any stretch of the imagination, to his credit, he did get rid of his father's image of Baal. See I Kings 16:31-32. **3 Nevertheless he cleaved unto the sins of Jeroboam the son of Nebat, which made Israel to sin; he departed not therefrom**. Though departing from official Baal worship, Jehoram nevertheless still adhered to the golden calves which Jeroboam had erected.

3:4-5 And Mesha king of Moab was a sheepmaster, and rendered unto the king of Israel an hundred thousand lambs, and an hundred thousand rams, with the wool. 5 But it came to pass, when Ahab was dead, that the king of Moab rebelled against the king of Israel. Since the time of David, Moab had been in subjection to Israel, paying substantial annual tribute tax in sheep and wool. However, after the death of Ahab, Mesha saw an opportunity to revolt against young Jehoram. That he did and ceased paying tribute to the northern kingdom of Israel.

3:6-7 And king Jehoram went out of Samaria the same time, and numbered all Israel. The idea is that he took a census to determine his potential military resources. **7 And he went and sent to Jehoshaphat the king of Judah, saying, The king of Moab hath rebelled against me: wilt thou go with me against Moab to battle? And he said, I will go up: I *am* as thou *art*, my people as thy people, *and* my horses as thy horses.** One would think that Jehoshaphat had learned his lesson some years earlier when he entered into a alliance with Ahab against the Syrians. See I Kings 22. Nevertheless, Jehoshaphat joined together with Jehoram to war against their common enemy Moab.

3:8-9 Whereupon, Jehoram asked, **Which way shall we go up? And he answered, The way through the wilderness of Edom.** Jehoram sought advice of Jehoshaphat as to the best route for attack against Moab. Jehoshaphat therefore counseled that they attack Moab from Edom which was to the south. They thus would march down the west side of the Dead Sea and assault Moab by a surprise attack from the south.

9 So the king of Israel went, and the king of Judah, and the king of Edom: and they fetched a compass of seven days' journey: and there was no water for the host, and for

the cattle that followed them. The armies of Judah and Israel evidently joined together with the king of Edom for a joint attack against Moab. The region around the Dead Sea on either side is arid and mostly desert. They thus marched in a circuitous route (i.e., "fetched a compass") down around the Dead Sea and up the other side into Edom. During the seven-day march, they soon realized that they were out of water.

3:10-12 And the king of Israel said, Alas! that the LORD hath called these three kings together, to deliver them into the hand of Moab! Ironically, it was the king of Israel (Jehoram) who had instigated this whole campaign. Now it was he who complained the loudest. **11 But Jehoshaphat said, *Is there* not here a prophet of the LORD, that we may enquire of the LORD by him? And one of the king of Israel's servants answered and said, Here *is* Elisha the son of Shaphat, which poured water on the hands of Elijah.**

The whole scene is remarkably similar to the debacle recorded in I Kings 22 wherein Jehoshaphat asked the same question. See I Kings 22: 7. Of interest is that it was Jehoram, the king of the apostate north, which recommended Elisha to Jehoshaphat. **12 And Jehoshaphat said, The word of the LORD is with him. So the king of Israel and Jehoshaphat and the king of Edom went down to him.** Jehoshaphat certainly had heard of Elisha and knew he was a man of God. Therefore, both he and Jehoram went to see the prophet rather than the other way around. Evidently, Elisha was part of Jehoram's army. He may have been drafted, perhaps to serve as a 'chaplain.'

3:13-15 Upon being confronted by Jehoram, Elisha had nothing good to say to him. **And Elisha said unto the king of Israel, What have I to do with thee? get thee to the prophets of thy father, and to the prophets of thy mother. And the**

king of Israel said unto him, Nay: for the LORD hath called these three kings together, to deliver them into the hand of Moab. Elisha, knowing of the apostasy of Jehoram, told him to go and inquire of his own pagan Gods. His willingness to seek counsel from a prophet of Jehovah in time of crisis revealed his own spiritual bankruptcy.

Elisha therefore delivered bad news. He announced that the Lord had indeed called these three kings to be chastened by Moab. It seems that this initial pronouncement was made 'off the cuff' without consultation of the Lord. Elisha apparently was thus sharing his own sentiments in the matter. Though Jehoshaphat was basically a godly king, his willingness to compromise with first Ahab and now Jehoram put him in a place where he was rebuked by God. A lesson remains of spiritual compromise for expediency and God's displeasure therewith.

14 And Elisha said, *As* **the LORD of hosts liveth, before whom I stand, surely, were it not that I regard the presence of Jehoshaphat the king of Judah, I would not look toward thee, nor see thee.** Moreover, Elisha let Jehoram know that he would have had nothing to do with him whatsoever except that he had some respect for Jehoshaphat, king of Judah.

Therefore, he directed, **15 But now bring me a minstrel. And it came to pass, when the minstrel played, that the hand of the LORD came upon him.** It seems that some Old Testament prophets were stirred to prophesy when inspired by music. The word translated as **minstrel** (נגן *nagan*) essentially means a 'musician.' Thus, when such an one played before him, "the hand of the LORD came upon him."

3:16-17 Elisha thus directed, **Thus saith the LORD, Make this valley full of ditches. 17 For thus saith the LORD, Ye shall not see wind, neither shall ye see rain; yet that valley shall be filled with water, that ye may drink, both ye, and your cattle, and your beasts.** Though Elisha had initially predicted doom, now as God spoke through him, he rather had good news. First, God would miraculously provide water for the assembled armies. He directed them to dig ditches throughout the valley whence they were. Though there would be no rainstorm, nevertheless, they soon would have more than enough water.

3:18-19 And this is *but* a light thing in the sight of the LORD. Providing water for them was as nothing for the Lord. Furthermore, Elisha foretold that the Lord **will deliver the Moabites also into your hand. 19 And ye shall smite every fenced city, and every choice city, and shall fell every good tree, and stop all wells of water, and mar every good piece of land with stones.** Not only would God give them an overwhelming victory over the Moabites, Israel and Judah were to utterly destroy that wicked nation. They were to destroy every fortified city and cut down every substantial tree. They were to plug up every well they found and fill farm land with stones.

3:20 And it came to pass in the morning, when the meat offering was offered, that, behold, there came water by the way of Edom, and the country was filled with water. Apparently, even out in the battlefield, Jehoshaphat's men observed the morning sacrifice prescribed by the law. At that time, water flowed down from the highlands of Edom to the south. It may be that God had sent heavy rain there which ran off toward where the armies were encamped. Or, it may be that God simply caused a major spring of water to spring from the rock outcroppings in that direction. In any event, the valley whence they were soon was flowing with water and the ditches which had been dug were now filled with water.

3:21-23 Meanwhile, the Moabites became aware of the armies invading from the south. **And when all the Moabites**

heard that the kings were come up to fight against them, they gathered all that were able to put on armour, and upward, and stood in the border. 22 **And they rose up early in the morning, and the sun shone upon the water, and the Moabites saw the water on the other side *as* red as blood.**

The nation of Moab thus mobilized militarily and marched to the border with Edom. However, as they looked down into the valley whence were the invading armies, the water in the ditches looked red as blood to them. (Of interest is that the name *Edom* literally means red. It may be that God caused minerals in the water from Edom to cause reflected light to appear red.) The Moabites concluded, 23 **This *is* blood: the kings are surely slain, and they have smitten one another: now therefore, Moab, to the spoil.** They interpreted what they saw as blood from an internecine fight between the invading armies. They therefore ordered their forces to go down and loot the camps of their foes.

3:24-25 And when they came to the camp of Israel, the Israelites rose up and smote the Moabites, so that they fled before them: but they went forward smiting the Moabites, even in *their* country. The Moabites advanced to loot and not to fight. Their entire mind set was changed. They may also have laid aside their cumbersome armor to better loot the camps. However, Israel and its allies were waiting for them and attacked. The Moabites were turned to a total rout and were chased back into Moab.

25 **And they beat down the cities, and on every good piece of land cast every man his stone, and filled it; and they stopped all the wells of water, and felled all the good trees: only in Kirharaseth left they the stones thereof; howbeit the slingers went about *it*, and smote it.** As directed by God, they set about to destroy the land. Their only difficulty was at the chief city of Moab, **Kirharaseth**, for which they brought up

their combat engineers to break down the city walls to conquer it.

3:26-27 And when the king of Moab saw that the battle was too sore for him, he took with him seven hundred men that drew swords, to break through *even* unto the king of Edom: but they could not. Seeing that the battle was lost, the king of Moab with seven hundred of his men attempted a breakout against the forces of Edom thinking they would be easier to fight. However, they were thwarted even there. **27 Then he took his eldest son that should have reigned in his stead, and offered him *for* a burnt offering upon the wall. And there was great indignation against Israel: and they departed from him, and returned to *their own* land.** In desperation, the king of Moab offered his son upon the wall of the city, perhaps hoping to appease his pagan gods. Or, it may be that he hoped to evoke sympathy from his enemies. It seems that though utterly victorious, Israel and allies allowed the king of Moab to live. He in turn harbored great indignation against Israel. Israel, meanwhile, packed up and went home victorious.

* * * * *

Overview of II Kings 4: *The focus turns to the life of and ministry of Elisha. The first portion of the chapter presents Elisha and the miracle of the widow's oil, the miracle of a son for the great woman of Shunem, and Elisha's raising that son from the dead. The chapter also contains the account of the healing of the poisonous pottage at Gilgal and his miraculous feeding of one-hundred men.*

4:1-2 The focus now returns to Israel (the northern kingdom) and more domestic events. The location is not noted, but

Understanding II Kings 213

it evidently was somewhere in the northern kingdom. **Now there cried a certain woman of the wives of the sons of the prophets unto Elisha, saying, Thy servant my husband is dead; and thou knowest that thy servant did fear the LORD: and the creditor is come to take unto him my two sons to be bondmen.** The widow of the prophet is held by Jewish tradition to be the wife of Obadiah who had hid the fifty prophets in a cave in the time of Ahab. However, there is no scriptural basis for this. She came and complained to Elisha how that she could not pay her creditor. Moreover, the latter was seeking to take her two sons to be sold into bondage to pay her debt. She thence reminded Elisha how her husband had feared the Lord.

2 And Elisha said unto her, What shall I do for thee? tell me, what hast thou in the house? And she said, Thine handmaid hath not any thing in the house, save a pot of oil. Upon inquiring of her, Elisha was told that all she had in her house was a container of olive oil (cooking oil).

4:3-4 Then he said, Go, borrow thee vessels abroad of all thy neighbours, *even* **empty vessels; borrow not a few. 4 And when thou art come in, thou shalt shut the door upon thee and upon thy sons, and shalt pour out into all those vessels, and thou shalt set aside that which is full.** The prophet instructed her to borrow as many empty vessels as she could and then begin to pour the oil she had into them. She was to take her sons into the house, close the door, and then begin to pour out her oil, filling each vessel. The prophet thus placed a test of faith before the woman. She could have rejected his advice claiming it to be impossible. To her credit, she did not.

4:5-7 So she went from him, and shut the door upon her and upon her sons, who brought *the vessels* **to her; and she poured out. 6 And it came to pass, when the vessels were full, that she said unto her son, Bring me yet a vessel. And he said**

unto her, *There is* not a vessel more. And the oil stayed. 7 **Then she came and told the man of God. And he said, Go, sell the oil, and pay thy debt, and live thou and thy children of the rest**. As long as she had vessels to fill, there was adequate oil. Only when she ran out of containers into which to pour did the oil abate. Elisha therefore directed for her to go and sell the oil to pay her debt and then she would have enough left over to sell for a living. This surely was a miracle from God. It also is a lesson of faith and of God taking care of His people.

4:8 The focus now turns to the town of Shunem which is located on the north side of the Valley of Jezreel, on the edge of the region of Galilee. **And it fell on a day, that Elisha passed to Shunem, where** *was* **a great woman; and she constrained him to eat bread. And** *so* **it was,** *that* **as oft as he passed by, he turned in thither to eat bread**. Evidently, Elisha passed through Shunem from time to time. In that town was *a great woman* which likely refers to her wealth and reputation. She therefore urged him to stop for a meal when passing through, which the prophet thus did.

4:9-11 And she said unto her husband, Behold now, I perceive that this *is* **an holy man of God, which passeth by us continually. 10 Let us make a little chamber, I pray thee, on the wall; and let us set for him there a bed, and a table, and a stool, and a candlestick: and it shall be, when he cometh to us, that he shall turn in thither**.

The Shunammite woman therefore suggested to her husband that they build a *prophet's chamber* for Elisha to stay when passing through town. Moreover she proposed to fully furnish it for him. Thus, 11 **it fell on a day, that he came thither, and he turned into the chamber, and lay there**. Elisha took them up on their offer and used their guest chamber when passing through.

Understanding II Kings

4:12-14 Appreciating the kindness of this woman to him, Elisha **said to Gehazi his servant, Call this Shunammite. And when he had called her, she stood before him. 13 And he said unto him, Say now unto her, Behold, thou hast been careful for us with all this care; what *is* to be done for thee? wouldest thou be spoken for to the king, or to the captain of the host? And she answered, I dwell among mine own people.** Elisha therefore directed his servant Gehazi to inquire of the woman how he might return her kindness to her. He suggested recommending her to the king or other high officials. The woman however answered modestly to the effect that she was content as she was.

Elisha however was determined to do something for her. **14 And he said, What then *is* to be done for her? And Gehazi answered, Verily she hath no child, and her husband is old.** Gehazi reminded Elisha that this gracious woman had no children and her husband's was advanced in years.

4:15-17 Therefore, Elisha directed his servant to **Call her. And when he had called her, she stood in the door. 16 And he said, About this season, according to the time of life, thou shalt embrace a son. And she said, Nay, my lord, *thou* man of God, do not lie unto thine handmaid.** Upon being summoned to the prophet, the woman only came to the doorway of his room. However, Elisha announced to her that at about that time a year hence, she would hold in her arms her own son. The woman apparently was utterly flabbergasted and could only blurt out for him not to lie to her. Nevertheless, **17 the woman conceived, and bare a son at that season that Elisha had said unto her, according to the time of life.** Soon after, she conceived and, after a full-term pregnancy, bore a son.

4:18-21 And when the child was grown, it fell on a day, that he went out to his father to the reapers. 19 And he said

unto his father, My head, my head. And he said to a lad, Carry him to his mother.** There is no indication how old this boy became. However, some years later, he fell gravely ill one day, complaining about pain in his head, while helping his father with the harvest. The father thus sent him to his mother.

20 And when he had taken him, and brought him to his mother, he sat on her knees till noon, and *then* died. 21 And she went up, and laid him on the bed of the man of God, and shut *the door* upon him, and went out. The lad died on his mother's lap about noon that day whereupon she laid him on the bed in the prophet's chamber, shut the door, and left.

4:22-25 And she called unto her husband, and said, Send me, I pray thee, one of the young men, and one of the asses, that I may run to the man of God, and come again. 23 And he said, Wherefore wilt thou go to him to day? *it is* neither new moon, nor sabbath. And she said, *It shall be* well. The woman in her despair knew she must find Elisha. She thus asked her husband to prepare a donkey and a servant for her to go find him. He reminded her there was no special occasion for such a visit which was otherwise customary. She knew it, but prepared to go anyway.

24 Then she saddled an ass, and said to her servant, Drive, and go forward; slack not *thy* riding for me, except I bid thee. 25 So she went and came unto the man of God to mount Carmel. And it came to pass, when the man of God saw her afar off, that he said to Gehazi his servant, Behold, *yonder is* that Shunammite. The woman thus headed out across the Valley of Jezreel as fast as she could go on her donkey toward Mount Carmel whence was Elisha. From the heights, he saw her coming and noted it to his servant.

4:26-27 Elisha instructed Gehazi to **Run now, I pray thee, to meet her, and say unto her, *Is it* well with thee? *is it* well

Understanding II Kings 217

with thy husband? *is it* well with the child? And she answered, *It is* well. Upon being asked of her affairs, she modestly answered that she was well. The idea likely is that at least she at that moment was not in any danger.

However, **27 when she came to the man of God to the hill, she caught him by the feet: but Gehazi came near to thrust her away. And the man of God said, Let her alone; for her soul *is* vexed within her: and the LORD hath hid *it* from me, and hath not told me.** Upon meeting Elisha, the woman prostrated herself at his feet, taking hold of them. Gehazi sought to toss her away, but Elisha perceived her distress. He noted that God had not as yet revealed the trouble to him.

4:28-30 The woman therefore bitterly cried out, **Did I desire a son of my lord? did I not say, Do not deceive me?** She reminded Elisha that it was not her who had requested a son. And she also reminded him how she had directed him not to lie to her.

Elisha quickly perceived what had happened. **29 Then he said to Gehazi, Gird up thy loins, and take my staff in thine hand, and go thy way: if thou meet any man, salute him not; and if any salute thee, answer him not again: and lay my staff upon the face of the child.** He ordered Gehazi to go at top speed to where the child was and to stop for no one or nothing. Upon arriving, he was to place his staff upon the face of the child.

Undeterred, **30 the mother of the child said,** *As* **the LORD liveth, and** *as* **thy soul liveth, I will not leave thee. And he arose, and followed her.** The woman vowed she would not depart from Elisha evidently until he came to her son. Elisha likely sent Gehazi ahead because he was more swift of foot than the older prophet.

4:31-34 And Gehazi passed on before them, and laid the staff upon the face of the child; but *there was* neither voice,

nor hearing. Wherefore he went again to meet him, and told him, saying, The child is not awaked. Gehazi did as instructed, but to no avail. He thus went and met Elisha with his negative report.

32 And when Elisha was come into the house, behold, the child was dead, *and* laid upon his bed. 33 He went in therefore, and shut the door upon them twain, and prayed unto the LORD. 34 And he went up, and lay upon the child, and put his mouth upon his mouth, and his eyes upon his eyes, and his hands upon his hands: and he stretched himself upon the child; and the flesh of the child waxed warm.

Though possessing special power of God, it was not until Elisha prayed that God responded. A lesson remains to this day. He thus laid upon the child, pressing his body against the lifeless form of the boy. God answered the prayer of the prophet and the child's body was brought back to life, though apparently in a coma.

4:35-37 Then he returned, and walked in the house to and fro; and went up, and stretched himself upon him: and the child sneezed seven times, and the child opened his eyes. Meanwhile, Elisha went down into the main house and paced back and forth, evidently still in prayer, and thought about the boy. He then returned and prostrated himself upon the boy again and this time the child sneezed seven times and opened his eyes.

36 And he called Gehazi, and said, Call this Shunammite. So he called her. And when she was come in unto him, he said, Take up thy son. 37 Then she went in, and fell at his feet, and bowed herself to the ground, and took up her son, and went out. The boy was thus presented to his mother who took him to her quarters. However, before so doing, she fell at the feet of the prophet and then bowed before him in gratitude. God through Elisha had wrought a mighty miracle.

He had honored this virtuous woman and her godly faithfulness.

4:38-39 Thereafter, Elisha traveled to Gilgal which is in the Jordan River valley near Jericho. **And Elisha came again to Gilgal: and *there was* a dearth in the land; and the sons of the prophets *were* sitting before him: and he said unto his servant, Set on the great pot, and seethe pottage for the sons of the prophets.** At Gilgal, there evidently was a school for the sons of the prophets. The sacred text notes that there was a **dearth** (i.e., famine) in the land. Elisha therefore directed his servant (probably Gehazi) to prepare a meal of stew in the large cooking pot there.

39 And one went out into the field to gather herbs, and found a wild vine, and gathered thereof wild gourds his lap full, and came and shred *them* into the pot of pottage: for they knew *them* not. One of the sons of the prophets went out to find ingredients for the stew and found a wild vine with a type of gourds he did not recognize. Nevertheless, he returned and cut up the gourds and placed them into the pot.

4:40-41 So they poured out for the men to eat. And it came to pass, as they were eating of the pottage, that they cried out, and said, O *thou* man of God, *there is* death in the pot. And they could not eat *thereof*. When the stew was served, it quickly became apparent that the gourds placed in the pot were noxious. They feared they would be poisoned to death. They therefore cried out to Elisha in despair.

41 But he said, Then bring meal. And he cast *it* into the pot; and he said, Pour out for the people, that they may eat. And there was no harm in the pot. Elisha therefore asked for flour which he poured into the pot. He then directed that it be served to the sons of the prophets. Miraculously, the poison herbs were neutralized and the stew no longer was noxious.

4:42-44 Another miracle is thus noted. Once again, the greater context is of famine in the land. The implication is that the school for the sons of the prophets had nothing to provide for these young men. **And there came a man from Baalshalisha, and brought the man of God bread of the firstfruits, twenty loaves of barley, and full ears of corn in the husk thereof. And he said, Give unto the people, that they may eat.** A man showed up from *Baalshalisha* which is in Gilead. He came with the firstfruits of his harvest which amounted to twenty loaves of bread and unthreshed grain. It should be noted that a loaf of bread then likely was about the size of a large hamburger bun today. Elisha thus directed this food to be served to the people (i.e., the sons of the prophets).

43 And his servitor said, What, should I set this before an hundred men? He said again, Give the people, that they may eat: for thus saith the LORD, They shall eat, and shall leave *thereof*. Elisha's assistant rather claimed that this quantity of food could not feed one-hundred men. Nevertheless, Elijah directed him to serve them, noting that they would not leave hungry.

44 So he set *it* before them, and they did eat, and left *thereof*, according to the word of the LORD. Implied is that after all of the men ate, there was food left over even as God through the prophet had foretold.

* * * * *

Overview of II Kings 5: This next chapter presents the story of the healing of Naaman and the folly of Gehazi.

5:1 The focus of the sacred text now shifts to Syria. **Now Naaman, captain of the host of the king of Syria, was a great man with his master, and honourable, because by him the**

LORD **had given deliverance unto Syria: he was also a mighty man in valour,** *but he was* **a leper.** It is thought that Naaman was considered honorable in that it was he who had defeated Israel. Jewish tradition holds that it was he who had slain Ahab. However, the text makes it clear that he did so by God's providence. Moreover, he was the chief general of Syria.

5:2-4 God's providence is evident in the little maid mentioned next. **And the Syrians had gone out by companies, and had brought away captive out of the land of Israel a little maid; and she waited on Naaman's wife.** A marauding band of Syrians had snatched a little Hebrew girl out of Israel and sold her as a slave in Syria. This little girl became the maid of Naaman's wife.

It is evident that there was a pleasant relationship between this young maid and the family she served. 3 **And she said unto her mistress, Would God my lord** *were* **with the prophet that** *is* **in Samaria! for he would recover him of his leprosy.** 4 **And** *one* **went in, and told his lord, saying, Thus and thus said the maid that** *is* **of the land of Israel.** From the following, it is apparent that the king of Syria did not have a clue as to whence the real source of help lay.

5:5-6 And the king of Syria said, Go to, go, and I will send a letter unto the king of Israel. And he departed, and took with him ten talents of silver, and six thousand *pieces* **of gold, and ten changes of raiment.** 6 **And he brought the letter to the king of Israel, saying, Now when this letter is come unto thee, behold, I have** *therewith* **sent Naaman my servant to thee, that thou mayest recover him of his leprosy.** Either the king of Syria did not understand the matter or perhaps he simply dumped it into the lap of the king of Israel for him to deal with it. In any event, he sent a substantial sum of money to the king of Israel and even new clothing to effect the healing of Naaman.

5:7 And it came to pass, when the king of Israel had read the letter, that he rent his clothes, and said, *Am* I God, to kill and to make alive, that this man doth send unto me to recover a man of his leprosy? wherefore consider, I pray you, and see how he seeketh a quarrel against me. Jehoram, king of Israel, was exasperated. In frustration he rent his clothing, a middle-eastern symbol of bitter emotion. Moreover, he rightly asked if he were as God to heal the man. Rather, he suspicioned that Syria was trying to provoke a fight and make this an international incident.

5:8-9 And it was *so*, when Elisha the man of God had heard that the king of Israel had rent his clothes, that he sent to the king, saying, Wherefore hast thou rent thy clothes? let him come now to me, and he shall know that there is a prophet in Israel. Elisha saw the situation differently. He saw an opportunity to demonstrate the power of God and be a testimony for Him. Therefore, 9 **Naaman came with his horses and with his chariot, and stood at the door of the house of Elisha.** Implicit is pomp and pride as Naaman rode up to Elisha's house with his entourage.

5:10-12 Elisha did not even come out of his house. Rather, he sent a messenger out to the proud Syrian general. That in itself must have angered Naaman. **And Elisha sent a messenger unto him, saying, Go and wash in Jordan seven times, and thy flesh shall come again to thee, and thou shalt be clean.** Elisha's directive for Naaman was simple. Go wash in the a Jordan River seven times. We are not told where Elisha was living at the time. The last place mentioned was Gilgal in I Kings 4:38. It may be that Elisha was still there. If so, the Jordan River was nearby.

11 **But Naaman was wroth, and went away, and said, Behold, I thought, He will surely come out to me, and stand,**

and call on the name of the LORD his God, and strike his hand over the place, and recover the leper. Naaman was angered by this directive. He wanted Elisha to come out with pomp and circumstance and piously heal him. His pride was about to preclude his deliverance.

Moreover, he asked, 12 *Are* **not Abana and Pharpar, rivers of Damascus, better than all the waters of Israel? may I not wash in them, and be clean? So he turned and went away in a rage.** The Jordan River has historically been a muddy river. Naaman knew that. Furthermore, rivers to the north in Syria tended to be clean and clear. He thus turned on his heel and stomped away enraged.

5:13-14 However, the servants of Naaman had more sense than he. Moreover, they were not afflicted by pride as was their master. Thus, **his servants came near, and spake unto him, and said, My father,** *if* **the prophet had bid thee** *do some great thing,* **wouldest thou not have done** *it***? how much rather then, when he saith to thee, Wash, and be clean?** Their advice was simple. Why not do what the prophet has said?

Undoubtedly with reluctance, 14 **then went he down, and dipped himself seven times in Jordan, according to the saying of the man of God: and his flesh came again like unto the flesh of a little child, and he was clean.** To his astonishment and delight, upon the seventh time rising from the water, his leprosy was gone. In fact, his skin was as fair as that of a small child.

5:15-16 And he returned to the man of God, he and all his company, and came, and stood before him: and he said, Behold, now I know that *there is* **no God in all the earth, but in Israel: now therefore, I pray thee, take a blessing of thy servant.** Returning to Elisha, Naaman testified that only in Israel was the God of all the earth. It is significant that Naaman realized that Jehovah God was not only powerful, but was God of the entire earth. That likely had been the testimony of Israel through the years. It also may be that the little Hebrew maid back home had testified the same to him. But the gentile, pagan Syrians had rejected that truth. However, having witnessed the power of God in his own life, Naaman became a believer. He therefore urged Elisha to receive a monetary reward for his help.

16 But he said, *As* the LORD liveth, before whom I stand, I will receive none. And he urged him to take *it*; but he refused. Though Naaman pressed him, Elisha refused to take anything from him. Elisha even vowed such in the name of Jehovah.

5:17-19 And Naaman said, Shall there not then, I pray thee, be given to thy servant two mules' burden of earth? for thy servant will henceforth offer neither burnt offering nor sacrifice unto other gods, but unto the LORD. Naaman then requested that he be allowed to take with him as much dirt from Israel as two mules could carry. Implied is that when he returned to Syria that he would on that earth build an altar to Jehovah God. Moreover, he indicated that he would no longer offer sacrifices to any other gods. Jewish tradition holds that Naaman thus became a 'proselyte of righteousness.'

Naaman continued, **18 In this thing the LORD pardon thy servant, *that* when my master goeth into the house of Rimmon to worship there, and he leaneth on my hand, and I bow myself in the house of Rimmon: when I bow down myself in the house of Rimmon, the LORD pardon thy servant in this thing.** As an officer of the king of Syria, Naaman knew he would be expected to go into the temple of Rimmon, a pagan god of Syria. Moreover, he was expected to steady the king of Syria when he so entered to worship. Naaman therefore asked God's pardon for such duties which were beyond his control.

Elisha thus **19 said unto him, Go in peace. So he departed from him a little way.** Elisha did not put his blessing upon Naaman's involvement with Rimmon, but he did send him away in peace. Of note is that Naaman only went a short distance and then stopped.

5:20-21 But Gehazi, the servant of Elisha the man of God, said, Behold, my master hath spared Naaman this Syrian, in not receiving at his hands that which he brought: but, *as* the LORD liveth, I will run after him, and take somewhat of him. Gehazi, Elisha's servant, foolishly and greedily saw the opportunity for gain. **21 So Gehazi followed after Naaman. And when Naaman saw *him* running after him, he lighted down from the chariot to meet him, and said, *Is* all well?** In seeing him come, Naaman asked if everything was alright.

5:22-24 And he said, All *is* well. My master hath sent me, saying, Behold, even now there be come to me from mount Ephraim two young men of the sons of the prophets: give them, I pray thee, a talent of silver, and two changes of garments. Not only did Gehazi act in a mercenary fashion, he lied in Elisha's name. He also lied about two young prophets in need by asking money and clothing for them. **23 And Naaman said, Be content, take two talents. And he urged him, and bound two talents of silver in two bags, with two changes of garments, and laid *them* upon two of his servants; and they bare *them* before him.** Naaman in turn offered him two talents whereas Gehazi had only asked for one. Naaman even had two of his servants help carry it all for Gehazi. **24 And when he came to the tower, he took *them* from their hand, and bestowed *them* in the house: and he let the men go, and they departed.** The tower in question evidently was a fortified place noted here as a landmark.

5:25-27 Upon arriving back at Elisha's house, Gehazi **went in, and stood before his master. And Elisha said unto him, Whence** *comest thou,* **Gehazi? And he said, Thy servant went no whither.** Elisha therefore asked where he went. To this Gehazi lied again and said he went nowhere. His sin was finding him out. 26 **And he said unto him, Went not mine heart** *with thee,* **when the man turned again from his chariot to meet thee?** *Is it* **a time to receive money, and to receive garments, and oliveyards, and vineyards, and sheep, and oxen, and menservants, and maidservants?** God revealed to Elisha what Gehazi had done. He therefore confronted him with his sin. Elisha noted that his heart went with Gehazi when he went after Naaman. The idea is that Elisha knew what Gehazi had done. With the honor of Elisha, the testimony of Jehovah, and a new convert all on the line, it was no time for greed and dishonesty.

Therefore, Elisha announced, 27 **The leprosy therefore of Naaman shall cleave unto thee, and unto thy seed for ever. And he went out from his presence a leper** *as white* **as snow.** What came pass with Gehazi thereafter is unclear. However, he is again described as Elisha's servant in II Kings 8:4-5.

* * * * *

Overview of II Kings 6: Record of the ministry of Elisha continues with the incident of the axe head which did float, Elisha's revelation of Benhadad's military plans, and the incident of Elisha at Dothan. The chapter thence concludes with the invasion and siege of Samara by the Syrians and the pathetic deprivation which took place in Samaria. The chapter concludes with the confrontation of Jehoram's messenger with Elisha.

6:1-3 The scene evidently is still near Gilgal, not distant from the Jordan River. **And the sons of the prophets said unto**

Elisha, Behold now, the place where we dwell with thee is too strait for us. Implicit is that Elisha oversaw a school for the sons of the prophets. They had evidently outgrown their facilities and therefore brought the problem to Elisha.

Their suggestion was, **2 Let us go, we pray thee, unto Jordan, and take thence every man a beam, and let us make us a place there, where we may dwell. And he answered, Go ye.** Along the Jordan River were numerous trees (growing by the river.) The idea was for the young prophets to go and cut down trees and bring back timbers by which they could erect their proposed building. To this Elisha gave his blessing. **3 And one said, Be content, I pray thee, and go with thy servants. And he answered, I will go.** One of the young prophets urged Elisha to accompany them to which he also agreed.

6:4-7 So he went with them. And when they came to Jordan, they cut down wood. 5 But as one was felling a beam, the axe head fell into the water: and he cried, and said, Alas, master! for it was borrowed. Any borrowed tool is valuable. But it seems that wrought iron implements were expensive and not easy to replace. Hence, the young prophet was dismayed when the axe head fell into the river. **6 And the man of God said, Where fell it? And he shewed him the place. And he cut down a stick, and cast *it* in thither; and the iron did swim.** Upon hearing of the loss, Elisha asked about where the axe head fell in the river. Upon being shown where, he threw a stick in **and the iron did swim**. The word translated as **swim** (צוף *tsuwph*) essentially means to float. Elisha thus said, **7 Take *it* up to thee. And he put out his hand, and took it.** Though not major in character, this miracle demonstrates that God is willing to intervene and help His people in even the 'little' problems of life.

6:8-10 Meanwhile, **the king of Syria warred against Israel, and took counsel with his servants, saying, In such**

and such a place *shall be* my camp. Benhadad again went to war against Israel. In his privy council with his military advisors, he informed them where they would encamp. However, **9 the man of God sent unto the king of Israel, saying, Beware that thou pass not such a place; for thither the Syrians are come down.** God revealed to Elisha the plans of the Syrians who in turn warned Jehoram thereof. **10 And the king of Israel sent to the place which the man of God told him and warned him of, and saved himself there, not once nor twice.** Jehoram therefore sent spies to verify the Syrian incursion and thus avoided their ambush. This happened more than twice.

6:11-12 Therefore the heart of the king of Syria was sore troubled for this thing; and he called his servants, and said unto them, Will ye not shew me which of us *is* for the king of Israel? The king of Syria soon sensed his plans were being revealed to the Israelites. His conclusion was that one of his own men was informing Israel what was being planned. **12 And one of his servants said, None, my lord, O king: but Elisha, the prophet that *is* in Israel, telleth the king of Israel the words that thou speakest in thy bedchamber.** It evidently was common knowledge in Israel as to what was happening. Syrian intelligence therefore picked upon what Elisha was doing. This was therefore reported to Benhadad. They warned him that his most privy comments, made even in his own bedroom, were known to Elisha and thence relayed to Jehoram.

6:13-14 Benhadad of Syria therefore directed, **Go and spy where he *is*, that I may send and fetch him. And it was told him, saying, Behold, *he is* in Dothan. 14 Therefore sent he thither horses, and chariots, and a great host: and they came by night, and compassed the city about.** The Syrian king accordingly ordered a force to go and capture Elisha. The king was informed that Elisha dwelt in a little town called Dothan in north-central Israel. Thus, the Syrians came with a great force of cavalrymen, chariots, and infantry, surrounding the place by night.

6:15-17 And when the servant of the man of God was risen early, and gone forth, behold, an host compassed the city both with horses and chariots. And his servant said unto him, Alas, my master! how shall we do? It is not clear if the servant of Elisha here was still Gehazi. However, one is noted again as his servant in chapter 8. In any event, the servant of Elisha in rising early that next morning went out and saw their little town surrounded by a powerful army along the heights above. He fled back to Elisha and cried out, **Alas, my master! how shall we do?** The servant saw the problem from a human perspective and perceived no escape.

However, Elisha saw things from God's perspective. He thus answered, **16 Fear not: for they that *be* with us *are* more than they that *be* with them**. Humanly, there was Elijah, his servant, and the small number of men of the little town of Dothan. Upon the heights above and surrounding them was a division of the Syrian Army in full array. How could Elisha claim more with them than the Syrians? However, Elisha saw the matter from God's perspective.

17 And Elisha prayed, and said, LORD, I pray thee, open his eyes, that he may see. And the LORD opened the eyes of the young man; and he saw: and, behold, the mountain *was* full of horses and chariots of fire round about Elisha. In asking God to open his servants eyes, the young man saw the angelic armies of heaven poised above the Syrians with horses and chariots of fire. Elisha knew full well the power of God at his disposal. It was there all the time. Now his servant realized it as well.

6:18-20 And when they came down to him, Elisha prayed unto the LORD, and said, Smite this people, I pray thee, with blindness. And he smote them with blindness according to the word of Elisha. The Syrian force therefore moved out and came down into Dothan. Elisha therefore prayed and asked God to blind them all. That God did. **19 And Elisha said unto them, This *is* not the way, neither *is* this the city: follow me, and I will bring you to the man whom ye seek. But he led them to Samaria.** Blinded and helpless, Elisha therefore directed them to follow him and he would lead them to whom they were seeking. However, he marched them ten miles to Samaria.

20 And it came to pass, when they were come into Samaria, that Elisha said, LORD, open the eyes of these *men*, that they may see. And the LORD opened their eyes, and they saw; and, behold, *they were* in the midst of Samaria. Upon arriving in Samaria, Elisha prayed again for God to open their eyes which He did. To the astonishment of the Syrian army, they realized they were now in Samaria, the capital city of Israel, and before the king thereof.

6:21-23 And the king of Israel said unto Elisha, when he saw them, My father, shall I smite *them*? shall I smite *them*? It is apparent in realizing what had happened that the king of Israel was eager to fall upon his disadvantaged enemy. He thus twice asked permission of Elisha to attack them. Of note is Jehoram's reference to Elisha as *my father*. Implicit is his respect to him.

22 And he answered, Thou shalt not smite *them*: wouldest thou smite those whom thou hast taken captive with thy sword and with thy bow? set bread and water before them, that they may eat and drink, and go to their master. Elisha rather directed King Jehoram to feed his vanquished enemy and treat them humanely even as he would other prisoners of war. He then directed them to be released. **23 And he prepared great provision for them: and when they had eaten and drunk, he sent them away, and they went to their master. So the bands of Syria came no more into the land of Israel.** In being sent home humanely, the Syrians ceased from sending marauding bands into Israel to plunder their neighbor.

6:24-25 However, **it came to pass after this, that Benhadad king of Syria gathered all his host, and went up, and besieged Samaria.** Notwithstanding the kindness which Jehoram had shown to his forces, Benhadad now attacked Israel with his entire army. His animosity was still evident. His strategy this time was to starve them out by military siege.

25 And there was a great famine in Samaria: and, behold, they besieged it, until an ass's head was *sold* **for fourscore** *pieces* **of silver, and the fourth part of a cab of dove's dung for five** *pieces* **of silver.** The starvation in Samaria became so severe that a donkey's head sold for eighty pieces of silver and even bird manure was sold for fuel at inflated prices.

6:26-30 Meanwhile, **as the king of Israel was passing by upon the wall, there cried a woman unto him, saying, Help, my lord, O king. And he said, 27 If the LORD do not help thee, whence shall I help thee? out of the barnfloor, or out of the winepress?** People cried out to Jehoram for help. All he could do was protest that if God would not help them, what could he do?

The king then came upon a woman arguing with another. He asked further, **28 What aileth thee? And she answered, This woman said unto me, Give thy son, that we may eat him to day, and we will eat my son to morrow. 29 So we boiled my son, and did eat him: and I said unto her on the next day, Give thy son, that we may eat him: and she hath hid her son.** The desperate conditions in the city were evident.

Mothers near starvation and crazed with hunger had stooped so low as to eat their small children. Two such women had agreed to eat the one's son one day and the other's the next. However, in receiving some nourishment, albeit by cannibalism, the second woman then refused to share her son with the first.

30 And it came to pass, when the king heard the words of the woman, that he rent his clothes; and he passed by upon the wall, and the people looked, and, behold, *he had* sackcloth within upon his flesh. The king was revolted upon hearing this awful story. He therefore rent his royal garments and put on sackcloth to show his despair. He thus publicly displayed himself before his people. This proud wicked king of Israel had been finally humbled. God allowed this terrible situation to break the hard, proud heart of this backslidden king.

6:31 The king however, blamed Elisha for his troubles. **Then he said, God do so and more also to me, if the head of Elisha the son of Shaphat shall stand on him this day**. Blaming Elisha for the release of the Syrians and thus the siege of Samaria, Jehoram therefore vowed to cut off the head of Elisha before that day ended.

6:32-33 Meanwhile, **Elisha sat in his house, and the elders sat with him; and *the king* sent a man from before him: but ere the messenger came to him, he said to the elders, See ye how this son of a murderer hath sent to take away mine head? look, when the messenger cometh, shut the door, and hold him fast at the door: *is* not the sound of his master's feet behind him?**

The elders mentioned likely refer to the older prophets associated with Elisha. He referred to Jehoram as the son of a murderer because his mother Jezebel had ordered Naboth killed. See I Kings 21. Elisha thus informed his colleagues that Jehoram had sent to behead him. Elisha therefore ordered his colleagues to bar the door and detain Jehoram's henchman when he arrived. He knew that the king himself would not be far behind.

33 And while he yet talked with them, behold, the messenger came down unto him: and he said, Behold, this evil *is* of the LORD; what should I wait for the LORD any longer? Sure enough, the man from Jehoram arrived. Verse 2 of the next chapter implies that Jehoram showed up immediately thereafter. The **he** above very well may have been Jehoram himself speaking to Elisha. His word to the prophet was that this siege and famine was of God. Why should he therefore fight it any longer. Implicit is that Jehoram was ready to throw in the towel and surrender. He was unwilling to wait for God's deliverance. That would come the next day as the following chapter details.

* * * * *

***Overview of II Kings 7*:** *The incident of the four lepers entering the camp of the Syrians after God's miraculous deliverance is recorded.*

7:1-2 As the chapter begins, the context remains of the starvation in the city of Samaria because of the Syrian siege thereof. **Then Elisha said, Hear ye the word of the LORD; Thus saith the LORD, To morrow about this time *shall* a measure of fine flour *be sold* for a shekel, and two measures of barley for a shekel, in the gate of Samaria.** When conditions seemed utterly hopeless, Elisha announced a message from God. The next day, a measure of finely milled flour would cost only a shekel and two measures of barley would also cost the same. It is not clear how much a measure of either was nor how much worth was a shekel. However, what is clearly implied is that though there were hyper-inflated prices for food then, the next day, it would be selling for bargain prices. Significant is that this announcement was in the name of Jehovah God.

2 Then a lord on whose hand the king leaned answered the man of God, and said, Behold, *if* the LORD would make windows in heaven, might this thing be? And he said, Behold, thou shalt see *it* with thine eyes, but shalt not eat thereof. Upon hearing Elisha's announcement, one of Jehoram's close advisors not only doubted such abundance could happen the next day, even worse, he doubted if Jehovah Himself could bring it to pass. Elisha announced that the next day this fellow would see it for himself, but would not be allowed to partake thereof.

7:3-4 Meanwhile, **there were four leprous men at the entering in of the gate: and they said one to another, Why sit we here until we die?** According to Leviticus 13:46, lepers were to be forced to live outside the camp. Thus, four lepers of Samaria lived on the outside of the city wall during the Syrian siege. They there eked out a living the best they could. However, in seeing the dire straits in which they were in, they knew they had nothing to lose by leaving the city walls.

They reasoned therefore, **4 If we say, We will enter into the city, then the famine *is* in the city, and we shall die there: and if we sit still here, we die also. Now therefore come, and let us fall unto the host of the Syrians: if they save us alive, we shall live; and if they kill us, we shall but die**. Their options were bleak. Even if they could enter the city (which they could not), there was no food there. If they stayed put, they would die as well. Thus, they decided to go to the camp of the Syrians nearby. They faced no worse a fate there than awaited them where they were at. The Syrians might per chance spare them.

7:5-7 Thus, **they rose up in the twilight, to go unto the camp of the Syrians: and when they were come to the uttermost part of the camp of Syria, behold,** *there was* **no man there.** Upon arriving at the encampment of the Syrians at dusk that day, they found it deserted. The sacred text explains why. **6 For the Lord had made the host of the Syrians to hear a noise of chariots, and a noise of horses,** *even* **the noise of a great host: and they said one to another, Lo, the king of Israel hath hired against us the kings of the Hittites, and the kings of the Egyptians, to come upon us. 7 Wherefore they arose and fled in the twilight, and left their tents, and their horses, and their asses, even the camp as it** *was***, and fled for their life.**

That afternoon, God had caused the Syrian army to hear what sounded like the noise of a major military operation with the sound of chariots of war, horses snorting and whinnying, orders being barked, and the tramp of infantrymen. The Syrians thus concluded that Jehoram, king of Israel, had hired other nations as allies to fight against them. They therefore up and fled for their lives thinking they were vastly outnumbered.

7:8-9 Thus, **when these lepers came to the uttermost part of the camp, they went into one tent, and did eat and drink, and carried thence silver, and gold, and raiment, and went and hid** *it***; and came again, and entered into another tent, and carried thence** *also***, and went and hid** *it***.** In discovering this windfall, the four lepers ate all they wanted and then began to loot the abandoned tents of the Syrians of everything of value they could find.

However, **9 they said one to another, We do not well: this day** *is* **a day of good tidings, and we hold our peace: if we tarry till the morning light, some mischief will come upon us: now therefore come, that we may go and tell the king's household.** Their conscience pricked them. They soon remembered their brethren starving back in Samaria. They realized the good news they had. They realized if they held their peace, many of their brethren would perish. They also feared that something might happen to them before dawn. Therefore, they determined to tell their good tidings to the authorities for their desperate brethren in the city.

7:10-11 So they came and called unto the porter of the city: and they told them, saying, We came to the camp of the Syrians, and, behold, *there was* no man there, neither voice of man, but horses tied, and asses tied, and the tents as they *were*. 11 And he called the porters; and they told *it* to the king's house within. The four lepers thus rushed backed to the city and informed the gatekeeper of their discovery. The camp of the Syrians was intact, but the Syrians were gone. The gatekeeper thus informed the other watchmen who in turn notified the king.

7:12-15 And the king arose in the night, and said unto his servants, I will now shew you what the Syrians have done to us. They know that we *be* hungry; therefore are they gone out of the camp to hide themselves in the field, saying, When they come out of the city, we shall catch them alive, and get into the city. King Jehoram was immediately suspicious. He thought that the Syrians had set a trap for them.

However, **13 one of his servants answered and said, Let *some* take, I pray thee, five of the horses that remain, which are left in the city, (behold, they *are* as all the multitude of Israel that are left in it: behold, *I say*, they *are* even as all the multitude of the Israelites that are consumed:) and let us send and see.** One of Jehoram's men suggested that they send a party into the camp of the Syrians to verify the situation. It is noteworthy that there were not many horses left in Samaria which could be ridden. Such was the ravages of the siege.

Therefore, **14 they took therefore two chariot horses; and the king sent after the host of the Syrians, saying, Go and see. 15 And they went after them unto Jordan: and, lo, all the way *was* full of garments and vessels, which the Syrians had cast away in their haste. And the messengers returned, and told the king.** Jehoram thus sent two men on chariot horses and they followed the route of the Syrians all way to the Jordan River. They had left in such haste that they had dropped clothing and various vessels behind them as they fled.

7:16-17 And the people went out, and spoiled the tents of the Syrians. So a measure of fine flour was *sold* for a shekel, and two measures of barley for a shekel, according to the word of the LORD. Just as Elisha had prophesied on God's behalf the day before, that next day flour and barley were in such abundance, they sold for bargain prices. God had miraculously fulfilled His Word.

Moreover, **17 the king appointed the lord on whose hand he leaned to have the charge of the gate: and the people trode upon him in the gate, and he died, as the man of God had said, who spake when the king came down to him.** Not only did God fulfill His Word in providing food, but also the man which had openly doubted God's ability to do so died. God providentially judged such a fool. The eager crowds trampled him to death.

7:18-20 The sacred text reiterates the matter to drive home the point. **And it came to pass as the man of God had spoken to the king, saying, Two measures of barley for a shekel, and a measure of fine flour for a shekel, shall be to morrow about this time in the gate of Samaria: 19 And that lord answered the man of God, and said, Now, behold, *if* the LORD should make windows in heaven, might such a thing be? And he said, Behold, thou shalt see it with thine eyes, but**

shalt not eat thereof. 20 And so it fell out unto him: for the people trode upon him in the gate, and he died. The one who openly doubted if God had the ability to so deliver His people was thus providentially judged by God.

* * * * *

Overview of II Kings 8: The latter days of Elisha's prophetic ministry are noted. He foretells an impending seven-year famine for Israel. Through the reminder of Gehazi, the Shunamite woman's land is restored. Elisha predicts the new king in Syria in Hazael. Then the chapter shifts back to history in Judah under the reign of Jehoram and then Ahaziah.

8:1-2 Then spake Elisha unto the woman, whose son he had restored to life, saying, Arise, and go thou and thine household, and sojourn wheresoever thou canst sojourn: for the LORD hath called for a famine; and it shall also come upon the land seven years. The woman in question is the great woman of Shunem as noted in II Kings 4:8-17. Because of her faithfulness to Jehovah, God through the prophet warned her of an impending famine which would last for seven years. Elisha thus urged her to flee the nation. Accordingly, **2 the woman arose, and did after the saying of the man of God: and she went with her household, and sojourned in the land of the Philistines seven years.**

8:3 Thus, it came to pass at the seven years' end, that the woman returned out of the land of the Philistines: and she went forth to cry unto the king for her house and for her land. Evidently, during her absence, the land holdings of this woman had been appropriated by others in her absence. Thus, after the seven years were expired she returned to find others occupying her land. She thus appealed to the king for relief.

8:4-6 In the meantime, **the king talked with Gehazi the servant of the man of God, saying, Tell me, I pray thee, all the great things that Elisha hath done.** The last we read of Gehazi was at the end of chapter 5 wherein he had leprosy. Some years had obviously passed. Whether Gehazi was healed of his leprosy is not noted. However, the fact that he was an associate to the king would seem to so indicate. Furthermore, implicit is that he no longer was Elisha's servant. Therefore, the king was interested to know all about Elisha's miracles.

5 And it came to pass, as he was telling the king how he had restored a dead body to life, that, behold, the woman, whose son he had restored to life, cried to the king for her house and for her land. And Gehazi said, My lord, O king, this *is* the woman, and this *is* her son, whom Elisha restored to life. God providentially so ordained events that as Gehazi was telling the king about the Shunamite woman and how Elisha had raised her son from the dead, she appeared to appeal her cause. Gehazi thus announced her to the king.

6 And when the king asked the woman, she told him. So the king appointed unto her a certain officer, saying, Restore all that *was* hers, and all the fruits of the field since the day that she left the land, even until now. Upon hearing her appeal, the king directed one of his officers to not only restore her land to her, but also the crops she was denied in her absence.

8:7-8 Elisha however was elsewhere. **And Elisha came to Damascus; and Benhadad the king of Syria was sick; and it was told him, saying, The man of God is come hither.** Curious indeed is the arrival of Elisha, a prophet of Jehovah, in pagan Damascus. Benhadad, who had been an inveterate enemy to Israel was seriously sick. Elisha's arrival was thus made known to him. **8 And the king said unto Hazael, Take a present in thine hand, and go, meet the man of God, and enquire of the LORD by him, saying, Shall I recover of this disease?** Having had previous experience with Elisha, Benhadad knew he was a prophet of God and sent word for him to ask God if he would recover.

8:9-10 So Hazael went to meet him, and took a present with him, even of every good thing of Damascus, forty camels' burden, and came and stood before him, and said, Thy son Benhadad king of Syria hath sent me to thee, saying, Shall I recover of this disease? The respect which Benhadad had come to develop for Elisha is apparent. Even as a pagan gentile, he had learned firsthand of God's power upon him and through him. He therefore sent massive gifts and sent his lieutenant Hazael to meet Elisha. The king even humbled himself to the degree that he referred to himself as Elisha's son. That was tantamount to referring to him as his servant. King Benhadad therefore directed Hazael to ask the prophet if he would recover of his disease.

To that **10 Elisha said unto him, Go, say unto him, Thou mayest certainly recover: howbeit the LORD hath shewed me that he shall surely die.** Elisha's answer was enigmatic. He informed Hazael that the king would indeed recover of his disease. However, Elisha also informed him that Jehovah had revealed to him that he would soon die otherwise.

8:11-12 Upon so announcing this to Hazael, Elisha **settled his countenance stedfastly, until he was ashamed: and the man of God wept**. The thought is that Elisha refrained his facial expression until he was embarrassed and then he wept.

12 And Hazael said, Why weepeth my lord? And he answered, Because I know the evil that thou wilt do unto the

Understanding II Kings

children of Israel: their strong holds wilt thou set on fire, and their young men wilt thou slay with the sword, and wilt dash their children, and rip up their women with child. When Hazael inquired as to why Elisha wept, the prophet told him how he knew of the cruelty that Hazael would inflict someday upon Israel. Elisha knew that Hazel would someday be king of Syria and that he would attack Israel with cruelty. He thus wept in reflection thereupon.

8:13 Hazael was taken aback that Elisha would so accuse him. **And Hazael said, But what, *is* thy servant a dog, that he should do this great thing? And Elisha answered, The LORD hath shewed me that thou *shalt be* king over Syria.** Upon being confronted by Hazael's protest, Elisha thus informed him that he would someday be king of Syria. Though not noted as such, Elisha may have anointed Hazael king of Syria as foretold in I Kings 19:15.

8:14-15 So he departed from Elisha, and came to his master; who said to him, What said Elisha to thee? And he answered, He told me *that* thou shouldest surely recover. Upon returning to Benhadad, Hazael informed him how that Elisha said he would recover. However, he did not tell him all that Elisha had told him. **15 And it came to pass on the morrow, that he took a thick cloth, and dipped *it* in water, and spread *it* on his face, so that he died: and Hazael reigned in his stead.** Hazael's character is thus revealed. Upon learning that he would someday be king, he did not wait. The next day, he murdered the still sick Benhadad by suffocating him as noted in the text. He thus ascended the throne of Syria.

8:16-17 The focus of the book now turns to Judah. **And in the fifth year of Joram the son of Ahab king of Israel, Jehoshaphat *being* then king of Judah, Jehoram the son of**

Jehoshaphat king of Judah began to reign. **17 Thirty and two years old was he when he began to reign; and he reigned eight years in Jerusalem.**

It is thought by some that Jehoram, the son of Jehoshaphat, co-reigned with his father for the final two years of his reign. Collating II Kings 3:1 together with I Kings 22:42, it is apparent that Jehoram, son of Jehoshaphat, became joint-king with his father in the twenty-third year of Jehoshaphat. That latter reigned a total of twenty-five years. It should also be noted that *Joram*, son of Ahab, is also known as *Jehoram* as well. However, to prevent further confusion, *Jehoram* of the northern kingdom is at times referred to as *Joram*. As noted, Jehoram, king of Judah, reigned for eight years.

8:18-19 Sadly, Jehoram, king of Judah **walked in the way of the kings of Israel, as did the house of Ahab: for the daughter of Ahab was his wife: and he did evil in the sight of the LORD.** Because Jehoram married Ahab's daughter, the wicked influence of that lineage was strengthened in Judah. Accordingly, **he did evil in the sight of the LORD.**

19 Yet the LORD would not destroy Judah for David his servant's sake, as he promised him to give him alway a light, *and* to his children. Notwithstanding the sin that continued in Judah, God remained faithful to His promise to David. He always keeps His Word. See Psalm 132:11,17.

8:20-22 Though God would not destroy Judah because of His covenant with David, He nevertheless chastened them for their sin. **In his days Edom revolted from under the hand of Judah, and made a king over themselves.** Edom, a small country to the south and east of Judah, had been a tributary to Judah since the time of David. Now they revolted. At the very least, sin brings a removal of God's blessings. Jehoram (Joram) thus lost part of his empire because of his sin.

21 So Joram went over to Zair, and all the chariots with him: and he rose by night, and smote the Edomites which compassed him about, and the captains of the chariots: and the people fled into their tents. As noted above in comments for verses 16-17, the *Joram* mentioned is another name of *Jehoram* of Judah. He thus attacked Edom and initially prevailed.

22 Yet Edom revolted from under the hand of Judah unto this day. Then Libnah revolted at the same time. Though Joram (Jehoram) had initially subdued Edom, apparently as soon as Joram went home, they revolted again. Moreover, Libnah, another city toward the border of Philistia in the opposite direction, revolted at the same time. Implicit is that Joram did not have the resources to deal with both revolts. Things were not going well for Joram. He had lost God's blessing. In fact, it seems clear that God was chastening him for his sin.

8:23-24 And the rest of the acts of Joram, and all that he did, *are* they not written in the book of the chronicles of the kings of Judah? The chronicles mentioned here are probably in addition to those which are recorded in the II Chronicles 21.

24 And Joram slept with his fathers, and was buried with his fathers in the city of David: and Ahaziah his son reigned in his stead. With the death of Joram, his son, Ahaziah ascended the throne of Judah.

8:25-27 As will be noted, Ahaziah was a weak and wicked king like his father. **In the twelfth year of Joram the son of Ahab king of Israel did Ahaziah the son of Jehoram king of Judah begin to reign.** According to II Chronicles 21:17, Ahaziah was also called *Jehoahaz*, the youngest king of Jehoram (Joram). He is noted as beginning to reign in the twelfth year of Joram, king of the northern kingdom.

26 Two and twenty years old *was* **Ahaziah when he began to reign; and he reigned one year in Jerusalem. And his mother's name** *was* **Athaliah, the daughter of Omri king of Israel.** This young king reigned for only one year. II Chronicles 22:1-4 notes that the influence of his mother and the house of Ahab to the north were his counselors to his destruction. How he died is not noted, but implicit is that it was with God's providential permission.

II Chronicles 22:2 notes that Ahaziah began to reign at age forty two. John Gill explains the difference accordingly. "These forty two years are not the date of the age of Ahaziah, but of the reign of the family of Omri king of Israel."

Sadly, **27 he walked in the way of the house of Ahab, and did evil in the sight of the LORD, as** *did* **the house of Ahab: for he** *was* **the son in law of the house of Ahab.** Because of the influence of his mother Athaliah and the house of Ahab (son of Omri), he did evil before God. Family can be an influence for either good or evil. In this case, it was the latter.

8:28-29 And he went with Joram the son of Ahab to the war against Hazael king of Syria in Ramothgilead; and the Syrians wounded Joram. Ahaziah thus cooperated with Jehoram (Joram) king of Israel against the Syrians. **29 And king Joram went back to be healed in Jezreel of the wounds which the Syrians had given him at Ramah, when he fought against Hazael king of Syria. And Ahaziah the son of Jehoram king of Judah went down to see Joram the son of Ahab in Jezreel, because he was sick.** However, the coming of Ahaziah to Jezreel to visit Joram was his undoing. As will be noted in II Kings 9:27-28, Ahaziah got caught in an insurrection in the northern kingdom against Jehoram and was there killed as was Jehoram.

* * * * *

Understanding II Kings

Overview of II Kings 9: *The ninth chapter of II Kings presents the rise of Jehu as king over Israel and his bloody accession to power. He slew Jehoram the sitting king, and then also killed Ahaziah, king of Judah. The chapter concludes with Jehu ordering the death of Jezebel and her ignominious end.*

9:1-3 And Elisha the prophet called one of the children of the prophets, and said unto him, Gird up thy loins, and take this box of oil in thine hand, and go to Ramothgilead. The word translated as **children** (בן *ben*) is the common word for 'son.' Elisha thus directed one of the sons of the prophets to take a flask of anointing oil. **Ramothgilead** literally means the 'heights of Gilead' which accordingly would be somewhere in the highlands east of the Jordan River in the region of Gilead.

This young prophet was therefore directed by Elisha, **2 And when thou comest thither, look out there Jehu the son of Jehoshaphat the son of Nimshi, and go in, and make him arise up from among his brethren, and carry him to an inner chamber.** Upon arrival there, the young prophet was to find Jehu who was the same one whom Elijah was to have anointed king. It would seem that this was deferred because of the self-humbling of Ahab. Upon finding Jehu, the young prophet was therefore to take him into a private room.

3 Then take the box of oil, and pour *it* **on his head, and say, Thus saith the LORD, I have anointed thee king over Israel. Then open the door, and flee, and tarry not.** After so anointing Jehu as next king over Israel, the prophet was directed to immediately flee.

9:4-6 Accordingly, **the young man,** *even* **the young man the prophet, went to Ramothgilead. 5 And when he came, behold, the captains of the host** *were* **sitting; and he said, I have an errand to thee, O captain. And Jehu said, Unto which of all us? And he said, To thee, O captain.** At

Ramothgilead were gathered officers of the garrison assigned there. The young prophet announced that he had business with Jehu and thus took him aside as directed. **6 And he arose, and went into the house; and he poured the oil on his head, and said unto him, Thus saith the LORD God of Israel, I have anointed thee king over the people of the LORD, *even* over Israel.** In anointing Jehu, the young prophet announced on behalf of Jehovah God that Jehu would be the next king over Israel.

9:7-8 Continuing to deliver word from God, the young prophet declared to Jehu, **And thou shalt smite the house of Ahab thy master, that I may avenge the blood of my servants the prophets, and the blood of all the servants of the LORD, at the hand of Jezebel.** Jehu was thus ordered by God to exterminate the dynasty of Ahab. Ahab is referred to as his master through Jehoram his son. God made it clear that this judgment was in retribution for the those who had been slain by Jezebel. Indeed, vengeance is the Lord's. **8 For the whole house of Ahab shall perish: and I will cut off from Ahab him that pisseth against the wall, and him that is shut up and left in Israel.** The message to Jehu was that the entire dynasty of Ahab would be destroyed, especially all males thereof. See comments for I Kings 4:10 regarding the second phrase of verse 8.

9:9-10 The dynasty of Ahab was finished. God foretold, **And I will make the house of Ahab like the house of Jeroboam the son of Nebat, and like the house of Baasha the son of Ahijah.** Even as God had destroyed the dynasties of Jeroboam and Baasha for their wickedness, so the dynasty of Ahab was about to perish. Moreover, **10 the dogs shall eat Jezebel in the portion of Jezreel, and *there shall be* none to bury her. And he opened the door, and fled.** When Jezebel would

Understanding II Kings

be put to death, she would not be buried. Scavenging dogs would devour her carcase. Having thus made this devastating prophecy, the prophet threw open the door and fled.

9:11-13 After the prophet had uncewremoniously fled, **then Jehu came forth to the servants of his lord: and *one* said unto him, *Is* all well? wherefore came this mad *fellow* to thee? And he said unto them, Ye know the man, and his communication.** Other of Jehu's fellow officers, servants to Jehoram, inquired of the welfare of Jehu after the prophet had so abruptly fled. Of interest is that they considered the prophet to be a mad man. They therefore asked Jehu why the prophet had taken him aside. Evidently, the prophet had not spoken quietly and Jehu's colleagues heard what was said. Jehu therefore intimated that they knew what the prophet had announced.

12 **And they said, *It is* false; tell us now. And he said, Thus and thus spake he to me, saying, Thus saith the LORD, I have anointed thee king over Israel.** These officers of Jehoram were disbelieving at what they had overheard. They thus implored Jehu to tell them that it was not so. However, he could only repeat to them what the prophet had told him and had anointed him as the next king of Israel.

13 **Then they hasted, and took every man his garment, and put *it* under him on the top of the stairs, and blew with trumpets, saying, Jehu is king.** It is apparent that Jehu's fellow officers did not have a great amount of loyalty to Jehoram, the sitting king. Upon hearing of Jehu being anointed as new king, they immediately threw their allegiance to him and treated him as king.

9:14-15 Jehu and his fellow officers at Ramothgilead thus began to conspire to overthrow Jehoram. **So Jehu the son of Jehoshaphat the son of Nimshi conspired against Joram.** The name *Joram* is another name for *Jehoram*. **(Now Joram**

had kept Ramothgilead, he and all Israel, because of Hazael king of Syria. 15 But king Joram was returned to be healed in Jezreel of the wounds which the Syrians had given him, when he fought with Hazael king of Syria.)**

This parenthetic comment gives further background information. Jehoram (Joram) had left a garrison at Ramothgilead to defend that region from Syria and Hazael its king. In the recent war with Syria, Jehoram had been wounded in battle and was convalescing back at Jezreel, in central Israel. Thus, **Jehu said, If it be your minds,** *then* **let none go forth** *nor* **escape out of the city to go to tell** *it* **in Jezreel.** Jehu therefore consulted with his officers that no one be allowed to leave the city of Ramothgilead to leak word of his insurrection to Jehoram at Jezreel.

9:16-20 So Jehu rode in a chariot, and went to Jezreel; for Joram lay there. And Ahaziah king of Judah was come down to see Joram. Jehu therefore evidently set out with his co-conspirators for Jezreel by chariot, a distance of approximately twenty-five miles. 17 **And there stood a watchman on the tower in Jezreel, and he spied the company of Jehu as he came, and said, I see a company. And Joram said, Take an horseman, and send to meet them, and let him say,** *Is it* **peace?** Watchmen at Jezreel saw Jehu's company approaching. King Jehoram (Joram) therefore directed that a messenger be sent to meet them and inquire if they had hostile intentions.

18 **So there went one on horseback to meet him, and said, Thus saith the king,** *Is it* **peace? And Jehu said, What hast thou to do with peace? turn thee behind me. And the watchman told, saying, The messenger came to them, but he cometh not again.**

The messenger approached Jehu's party and asked if they came in peace. Jehu curtly asked him what he had to do with peace and directed him to fall in behind their party. The watch-

Understanding II Kings

man in Jezreel noted that their messenger did not return. **19 Then he sent out a second on horseback, which came to them, and said, Thus saith the king, Is it peace? And Jehu answered, What hast thou to do with peace? turn thee behind me.** A second emissary was dealt with the same way.

20 And the watchman told, saying, He came even unto them, and cometh not again: and the driving is like the driving of Jehu the son of Nimshi; for he driveth furiously. The watchman at Jezreel reported that this second emissary had not returned, falling in with the approaching company as well. He then made the comment that the driving of the chariot was like that of Jehu, "for he driveth furiously." Apparently, Jehu's reputation as a chariot driver preceded him. The word translated as **furiously** (שגעון *shig-gaw-yone'*) can also have the idea of 'madness.' Jehu was thus driving like a madman.

9:21-22 Though still recovering from earlier wounds, **Joram said, Make ready. And his chariot was made ready. And Joram king of Israel and Ahaziah king of Judah went out, each in his chariot, and they went out against Jehu, and met him in the portion of Naboth the Jezreelite.** As noted in 8:29, Ahaziah, king of Judah, was visiting Jehoram (Joram) at Jezreel. After having his chariot hastily readied, Jehoram (Joram) and Ahaziah thus rode out to meet Jehu. Ironically, the place they met was the land which had been owned by Naboth.

22 And it came to pass, when Joram saw Jehu, that he said, Is it peace, Jehu? And he answered, What peace, so long as the whoredoms of thy mother Jezebel and her witchcrafts *are so* many? Upon being asked if he came in peace, Jehu asked, "what peace?" He then threw back at Jehoram the sin of his mother, Jezebel. Mentioned were her numerous whoredoms and witchcrafts. The allusion likely is to the spiritual harlotry of Jezebel in introducing idolatry and Baal worship into Israel though she may have been physically immoral as well. However, there is no record of the latter. Moreover, she also was involved in the occult.

9:23-24 And Joram turned his hands, and fled, and said to Ahaziah, *There is* treachery, O Ahaziah. Jehoram (Joram) quickly perceived Jehu's intent and cried out treachery to his colleague, Ahaziah. **24 And Jehu drew a bow with his full strength, and smote Jehoram between his arms, and the arrow went out at his heart, and he sunk down in his chariot.** Implicit is that Jehoram turned around to flee. Whereupon, Jehu drew his bow back with all his strength and shot the king of Israel through the back with such force that the arrow came out at his heart in the front. He thus slumped over dead in his chariot.

9:25-26 Then said *Jehu* to Bidkar his captain, Take up, *and* cast him in the portion of the field of Naboth the Jezreelite: for remember how that, when I and thou rode together after Ahab his father, the LORD laid this burden upon him. Jehu therefore ordered one of his lieutenants to throw the body of Jehoram onto the former land of Naboth. He then reminded him how that they both evidently had earlier rode in formation behind Ahab when Elijah the prophet had foretold Ahab's death for having Naboth murdered. God's judgment at times is ironic.

Jehu continued reminding his lieutenant, Bidkar, what God through Elijah had prophesied. **26 Surely I have seen yesterday the blood of Naboth, and the blood of his sons, saith the LORD; and I will requite thee in this plat, saith the LORD. Now therefore take *and* cast him into the plat *of ground*, according to the word of the LORD.** The prophecy made by Elijah in I Kings 21:19 was thus fulfilled. Jehoram, Ahab's son, suffered the fate promised to his father both for his own sins as well as those of his father. Because Ahab had humbled himself

Understanding II Kings

and repented as noted in I Kings 21:29, the judgment fell upon his son, Jehoram, as was there promised.

9:27-29 The focus now turns to Ahaziah, king of Judah. By spiritual compromise, Ahaziah had placed himself at the wrong place at the wrong time. He had no business associating with the wicked Jehoram, king of apostate Israel. His folly therefore came upon him. **But when Ahaziah the king of Judah saw *this*, he fled by the way of the garden house. And Jehu followed after him, and said, Smite him also in the chariot. *And they did so* at the going up to Gur, which *is* by Ibleam. And he fled to Megiddo, and died there.** Ahaziah managed to escape—temporarily. However, Jehu caught up with him at Ibleam, about five miles south of Jezreel. He ordered Ahaziah attacked in his chariot. However, he managed to flee wounded to Megiddo, a distance of about another eight miles. However, there he died.

28 **And his servants carried him in a chariot to Jerusalem, and buried him in his sepulchre with his fathers in the city of David.** His servants thus carried their dead king back to Jerusalem where he was buried in the city of David, a section of eastern Jerusalem. Chronological details of the reign of Ahaziah are thus noted. 29 **And in the eleventh year of Joram the son of Ahab began Ahaziah to reign over Judah.** II Kings 8:25 notes Ahaziah's reign as beginning in the twelfth year of Joram. It may be that it was at the close of the eleventh year of Joram's reign, and the beginning of his twelfth. Or, it may be that he began to reign with his father in the eleventh year as here, and in the twelfth year as noted in II Kings 8:25 when his father was dead.

9:30-31 Meanwhile, Jehu headed back to Jezreel. **And when Jehu was come to Jezreel, Jezebel heard *of it*; and she painted her face, and tired her head, and looked out at a**

window. Jezebel knew the jig was up. She therefore made herself up. The idea of her painting her face refers to putting on makeup. The comment that she "tired her head" refers to having her hair made beautiful. She thus sought to beautify herself, perhaps to deflect judgment by seduction. When Jehu rode back into town, she thus presented herself through an upper window, perhaps to detract him with her physical charms. Others suggest that though an older woman by now, she simply wished to display her pride and haughty spirit.

31 **And as Jehu entered in at the gate, she said, *Had Zimri peace, who slew his master?*** No doubt having by now heard what had happened to her son Jehoram and Jehu's threats against her, she tried to deflect him by reminding Jehu what had happened to Zimri. In I Kings 16:10,18, Zimri had been killed for his insurrection against Elah, then king of Israel. Her protestation had no affect upon Jehu.

9:32-33 And he lifted up his face to the window, and said, Who *is* on my side? who? And there looked out to him two *or* three eunuchs. Upon hearing Jehu shout, **Who *is* on my side?**, several eunuchs appeared also at the window. These were castrated men who were servants to Jezebel. It was more than likely that she was never kind to them and treated them roughly. Moreover, they could read the swirling political winds. It was apparent that the rule of Jehoram and his wicked mother were over. They therefore were willing to switch their allegiance to Jehu.

33 **And he said, Throw her down. So they threw her down: and *some* of her blood was sprinkled on the wall, and on the horses: and he trode her under foot**. Upon being ordered by Jehu to throw Jezebel down, her servants did so. Whereupon, Jehu ran over her with his chariot and its team of horses thus killing her. Her blood was thus splattered upon the palace wall as well as upon his horses.

Understanding II Kings

9:34-35 Thereafter, Jehu, paused to eat. **And when he was come in, he did eat and drink, and said, Go, see now this cursed *woman*, and bury her: for she *is* a king's daughter.** After having supper, Jehu sent subordinates to check on the body of Jezebel and to bury her. Though she was a cursed woman as far as he was concerned, he thought her royal heritage deserved a decent burial.

35 **And they went to bury her: but they found no more of her than the skull, and the feet, and the palms of *her* hands.** Upon returning to her body, Jehu's men could find only her skull, feet and the palms of her hands. Everything else had been devoured by scavenging dogs. This is precisely what had been foretold by the prophet who had anointed Jehu. See 9:10.

9:36-37 Wherefore they came again, and told him. And he said, This *is* the word of the LORD, which he spake by his servant Elijah the Tishbite, saying, In the portion of Jezreel shall dogs eat the flesh of Jezebel. Not only had the young prophet foretold this end of Jezebel, so had Elijah in I Kings 21:23. Apparently, Elijah had made further comment not recorded in I Kings 21. However, Jehu had been present that day and had heard Elijah say, 37 **And the carcase of Jezebel shall be as dung upon the face of the field in the portion of Jezreel; *so* that they shall not say, This *is* Jezebel.** Elijah had also foretold how all that would be left of Jezebel would be little more than fertilizer in the portion of the field of Jezreel. Implied is that the field she schemed to steal from Naboth was so fertilized by her remains. However, there was so little left that no one could say, "this is Jezebel."

As an epilogue, it may well be noted that the mills of God's judgment grind slow, but they grind exceedingly fine. God may not send judgment for sin immediately. However, He will bring vengeance in His perfect time. When that judgment comes, it is terrible in its completion. The sins of Ahab and Jezebel over a period of forty years were not judged by God. Not only was this wicked woman summarily dealt with, but so also was her son.

* * * * *

Overview of II Kings 10*: The chapter presents the reign of Jehu over Israel including his execution of the rest of the dynasty of Ahab, the princes of Judah visiting in Israel, and followers of Baal. However, because of his general disregard to Jehovah, record is made how that God began to work against him.*

10:1-3 Jehu wasted no time in seeking out the sons of the Ahab and his dynasty. **And Ahab had seventy sons in Samaria. And Jehu wrote letters, and sent to Samaria, unto the rulers of Jezreel, to the elders, and to them that brought up Ahab's** *children***, saying, 2 Now as soon as this letter cometh to you, seeing your master's sons** *are* **with you, and** *there are* **with you chariots and horses, a fenced city also, and armour; 3 Look even out the best and meetest of your master's sons, and set** *him* **on his father's throne, and fight for your master's house.**

Jehu sent word to the rulers of Samaria regarding the descendants of Ahab and particularly to those who were over them. The intent of the letter dripped with sarcasm, taunting them to defend themselves. Thus, he challenged them to "fight for your master's house."

10:4-5 Jehu clearly intimidated the house of Ahab and that no doubt was his intent. **But they were exceedingly afraid, and said, Behold, two kings stood not before him: how then shall we stand? 5 And he that** *was* **over the house, and he that** *was* **over the city, the elders also, and the bringers up** *of the* *children*, **sent to Jehu, saying, We *are* thy servants, and will do all that thou shalt bid us; we will not make any king: do thou *that which is* good in thine eyes**. The descendants of Ahab "were exceedingly afraid." They correctly perceived they would not prevail against Jehu after he had personally eliminated two kings. They therefore submitted themselves to him.

10:6-8 Jehu therefore **wrote a letter the second time to them, saying, If ye *be* mine, and *if* ye will hearken unto my voice, take ye the heads of the men your master's sons, and come to me to Jezreel by to morrow this time. Now the king's sons, *being* seventy persons, *were* with the great men of the city, which brought them up**. Jehu wasted no time in demanding the literal heads of the descendants of Ahab. He ordered that those heads be delivered to him at Jezreel within twenty-four hours. Moreover, the descendants of Ahab were living with important families of Samaria.

7 And it came to pass, when the letter came to them, that they took the king's sons, and slew seventy persons, and put their heads in baskets, and sent him *them* to Jezreel. The prominent families of Samaria therefore promptly complied with Jehu's orders and sent the heads of the seventy sons of Ahab in baskets to Jezreel. **8 And there came a messenger, and told him, saying, They have brought the heads of the king's sons. And he said, Lay ye them in two heaps at the entering in of the gate until the morning**. With the arrival of the heads of the sons of Ahab, Jehu directed that they be piled in two heaps until the morning.

10:9-11 And it came to pass in the morning, that he went out, and stood, and said to all the people, Ye *be* righteous: behold, I conspired against my master, and slew him: but who slew all these? The next day, Jehu sarcastically and sanctimoniously announced to Jezreel that they were righteous. He had killed his master (Jehoram, Ahab's grandson). But he then with pious hypocrisy asked who killed all the sons of Ahab? Implicit is his intimation that he had nothing to do with it.

10 Know now that there shall fall unto the earth nothing of the word of the LORD, which the LORD spake concerning the house of Ahab: for the LORD hath done *that* which he spake by his servant Elijah. Though Jehu had caused these many deaths, he now put it into perspective. This was ultimately done at the direction of God through Elijah. Though Jehu was not a godly man, he did make a profound statement: "Know now that there shall fall unto the earth nothing of the word of the LORD." God always keeps His Word. Using the analogy of something falling to the ground and being lost, Jehu rightly noted that none of God's Word is ever dropped and forgotten. It always comes to pass. Implicit is the doctrine of preservation.

11 So Jehu slew all that remained of the house of Ahab in Jezreel, and all his great men, and his kinsfolks, and his priests, until he left him none remaining. Though foretold by Elijah in I Kings 21:21-26 sixteen or seventeen years earlier, the prophecy of the destruction of the house of Ahab was now complete. Their cup of iniquity was full. God's time for judgment had come. *All* which remained of the house of Ahab at Jezreel were destroyed.

10:12-14 And he arose and departed, and came to Samaria. *And* as he *was* at the shearing house in the way, 13 Jehu met with the brethren of Ahaziah king of Judah, and said, Who *are* ye? And they answered, We *are* the brethren of Ahaziah; and we go down to salute the children of the king and the children of the queen. Meanwhile, blood relatives of Ahaziah, the new king in Judah, were journeying to visit their royal counterparts in the northern kingdom. They evidently were unaware of the recent revolution in the north by

Jehu. Confronted by Jehu, they innocently revealed their identity. Jehu therefore ordered, **14 Take them alive. And they took them alive, and slew them at the pit of the shearing house,** *even* **two and forty men; neither left he any of them**. Jehu therefore ordered them slain at the pit (i.e., well) of the city. These evidently were from their grandmother's side and thus of the house of Ahab. Jehu therefore considered them part of his divine mandate to kill them as well. That he did—all forty two of them. See also II Chronicles 22:1,8.

10:15-16 And when he was departed thence, he lighted on Jehonadab the son of Rechab *coming* **to meet him: and he saluted him, and said to him, Is thine heart right, as my heart** *is* **with thy heart? And Jehonadab answered, It is. If it be, give** *me* **thine hand. And he gave** *him* **his hand; and he took him up to him into the chariot**.

Jehonadab the son of Rechab may have been a descendant of Jethro the Kenite, the father-in-law of Moses. Jeremiah 35:6-10 likely refers to this same family lineage. As Jehonadab met Jehu, the latter asked, "Is thine heart right, as my heart *is* with thy heart?" This was essentially asking, "Are you with me?" or, "Are you loyal to me and my cause?" Upon pledging to loyalty to Jehu, Jehonadab was thus invited to ride with Jehu in his chariot.

Jehu thus said, **16 Come with me, and see my zeal for the LORD. So they made him ride in his chariot**. Indeed, Jehu was zealous in effecting the charge given him by God to exterminate the house of Ahab. He accordingly took Jehonadab with him on his next mission in fulfilling his charge.

10:17-18 And when he came to Samaria, he slew all that remained unto Ahab in Samaria, till he had destroyed him, according to the saying of the LORD, which he spake to Elijah. Jehu had not only killed all he could find in Jezreel where Ahab had once lived, he also had slain even distant relatives in the brethren of Ahaziah, king of Judah. Now, he completed the task by killing all the relatives of Ahab which still lived in and about the city of Samaria. Though a harsh man, Jehu was in fact fulfilling God's promised judgment against the wicked dynasty of Ahab.

He now turned his attention to further apostasy in Israel. **18 And Jehu gathered all the people together, and said unto them, Ahab served Baal a little;** *but* **Jehu shall serve him much.** With deceptive sarcasm, Jehu hinted at his next target—Baal worship in Israel.

10:19-20 Now therefore call unto me all the prophets of Baal, all his servants, and all his priests; let none be wanting: for I have a great sacrifice *to do* **to Baal; whosoever shall be wanting, he shall not live. But Jehu did** *it* **in subtilty, to the intent that he might destroy the worshippers of Baal.** With subtlety, Jehu ordered *all* followers of Baal in the northern kingdom to assemble for a great sacrifice to be made to Baal. What he did not tell them was that *they* were going to be the sacrifice. Any follower of Baal who did not attend would be summarily killed. He thus gave added incentive for worshipers of Baal to attend this great convocation. However, Jehu clearly had a hidden agenda.

20 And Jehu said, Proclaim a solemn assembly for Baal. And they proclaimed *it*. A special holy day and convocation for Baal was thus proclaimed throughout the land.

10:21-23 And Jehu sent through all Israel: and all the worshippers of Baal came, so that there was not a man left that came not. And they came into the house of Baal; and the house of Baal was full from one end to another. Jehu therefore rounded up all worshipers of Baal from throughout the northern kingdom. They assembled to a man in what evi-

Understanding II Kings

dently was the temple of Baal at Samaria. Noteworthy is the comment that the house was packed out.

Then, 22 **he said unto him that** *was* **over the vestry, Bring forth vestments for all the worshippers of Baal. And he brought them forth vestments.** He thus ordered the special pagan vestments involved in Baal worship to be brought forth. These evidently were placed upon the worshipers of Baal not only as irony, but no doubt also to clearly identify their allegiance.

23 **And Jehu went, and Jehonadab the son of Rechab, into the house of Baal, and said unto the worshippers of Baal, Search, and look that there be here with you none of the servants of the LORD, but the worshippers of Baal only.** Jehu then made sure that there were no servants of Jehovah God in the crowd. All that were present were Baal worshipers.

10:24-25 Meanwhile, **when they went in to offer sacrifices and burnt offerings, Jehu appointed fourscore men without, and said,** *If* **any of the men whom I have brought into your hands escape,** *he that letteth him go***, his life** *shall be* **for the life of him.** Eighty men were ordered to kill *all* the followers of Baal. He further warned, if his men allowed any to escape, their life would be taken in return.

25 **And it came to pass, as soon as he had made an end of offering the burnt offering, that Jehu said to the guard and to the captains, Go in,** *and* **slay them; let none come forth. And they smote them with the edge of the sword; and the guard and the captains cast** *them* **out, and went to the city of the house of Baal.** Thus, the entirety of the worshipers of Baal were killed. Jehu then turned his attention to what evidently was an associated community called the city of the house of Baal. This perhaps may have been where the priests of Baal and their families lived.

10:26-28 And they brought forth the images out of the house of Baal, and burned them. 27 And they brake down the image of Baal, and brake down the house of Baal, and made it a draught house unto this day. 28 Thus Jehu destroyed Baal out of Israel. Not only were the followers of Baal exterminated, Jehu made sure that all images and physical reminders of Baal worship were obliterated from Israel. Where the temple of Baal had once stood, he made it into a city dump. To his credit, Jehu thus destroyed Baal worship out of the northern kingdom.

10:29 Notwithstanding the zeal of Jehu is exterminating the wicked house of Ahab and its pagan idolatrous Baal worship, **Howbeit *from* the sins of Jeroboam the son of Nebat, who made Israel to sin, Jehu departed not from after them, *to wit*, the golden calves that *were* in Bethel, and that *were* in Dan.** Jehu was an enigma. He claimed to be zealous for Jehovah God. However, he still followed in the sin of Jeroboam and allowed the golden calves in Bethel and Dan. His zeal for Jehovah was therefore not as true as he professed.

10:30-31 God commended Jehu for his obedience in fulfilling His commands. **And the LORD said unto Jehu, Because thou hast done well in executing *that which is* right in mine eyes, *and* hast done unto the house of Ahab according to all that *was* in mine heart, thy children of the fourth *generation* shall sit on the throne of Israel.** Because of his obedience and resultant uprightness, God promised to Jehu that his children would be allowed to succeed him for four generations.

31 But Jehu took no heed to walk in the law of the LORD God of Israel with all his heart: for he departed not from the sins of Jeroboam, which made Israel to sin. Notwithstanding, God's promise of a continuing royal lineage to Jehu, he ignored the Lord. Noteworthy is the comment of him not walking in the Law of the Lord *with all his heart*. His half-hearted dedication led to complete apostasy in the idolatry of Jeroboam and the golden calves.

10:32-33 Accordingly, **In those days the LORD began to cut Israel short: and Hazael smote them in all the coasts of Israel; 33 From Jordan eastward, all the land of Gilead, the Gadites, and the Reubenites, and the Manassites, from Aroer, which *is* by the river Arnon, even Gilead and Bashan.** Disobedience and ignoring of God's blessing inevitably leads to a loss of God's blessing and then His chastening. Because of Jehu's careless attitude toward God, the Lord allowed Hazael, king of Syria, to begin to attack Israel, especially from the north and east. This follows what Elisha had foretold in II Kings 8:12.

10:34-36 Final chronological details of the reign of Jehu are noted. **Now the rest of the acts of Jehu, and all that he did, and all his might, *are* they not written in the book of the chronicles of the kings of Israel?** The chronicles of the kings of Israel are not inspired and have apparently been lost to history. They are not the biblical books of Chronicles. **35 And Jehu slept with his fathers: and they buried him in Samaria. And Jehoahaz his son reigned in his stead. 36 And the time that Jehu reigned over Israel in Samaria *was* twenty and eight years**. After ruling the northern kingdom for twenty-eight years, Jehu's son, Jehoahaz, succeeded him upon his throne.

* * * * *

Overview of II Kings 11: *This next chapter of II Kings presents the dramatic establishment of Joash (also known as*

Jehoash) as king in Judah. There is also record of the revival brought about in Judah by Jehoiada the priest.

11:1-3 The focus of the book now returns to Judah and events there. The account hearkens back to II Kings 9:27*ff* where record is made of the death of Ahaziah, former king of the Judah. **And when Athaliah the mother of Ahaziah saw that her son was dead, she arose and destroyed all the seed royal.** According to II Kings 8:18 and 26, Athaliah was the daughter of Ahab, king of Israel, and thus the granddaughter of Omri. Accordingly, she was of the ungodly mindset of the northern kingdom. As noted in the text, she proceeded to destroy all others of royal descent so that she might seize the throne. What is even more grisly is that this "seed royal" likely were either the children or grandchildren of this wicked woman.

However, 2 **Jehosheba, the daughter of king Joram, sister of Ahaziah, took Joash the son of Ahaziah, and stole him from among the king's sons *which were* slain; and they hid him, *even* him and his nurse, in the bedchamber from Athaliah, so that he was not slain.** Jehosheba was Ahaziah's sister. The *bedchamber* mentioned literally was a 'chamber of beds' and likely was one of the chambers of the priests and Levites in the Temple, which adjoined it.

There, 3 **he was with her hid in the house of the LORD six years. And Athaliah did reign over the land.** As the arithmetic of the text will reveal, little Joash was evidently one year old when he was hidden by Jehosheba in the Temple. Six years later, when he was seven years old, he was revealed as king.

11:4 And the seventh year Jehoiada sent and fetched the rulers over hundreds, with the captains and the guard, and brought them to him into the house of the LORD, and made a covenant with them, and took an oath of them in the house of the LORD, and shewed them the king's son.

According to II Chronicles 22:11, Jehoiada was the husband of Jehosheba. When little Joash was seven years old, Jehoiada took action to establish the boy as king. He thus enlisted the support of the leadership of Judah seeking their loyalty. They in turn took an oath of secrecy whereupon he showed them the boy-king.

11:5-8 Jehoiada, the high priest therefore announced to these his plan of action. **And he commanded them, saying, This *is* the thing that ye shall do; A third part of you that enter in on the sabbath shall even be keepers of the watch of the king's house.** He assigned one third of the leadership of the Temple to serve as guards where the king was hidden on the coming Sabbath day.

6 And a third part *shall be* at the gate of Sur; and a third part at the gate behind the guard: so shall ye keep the watch of the house, that it be not broken down. The gate of Sur was thought to be an eastern gate to Jerusalem which probably entered directly into the Temple. One third of the Temple priests and Levites and their temple guard were placed there to secure that entrance. Finally, the other third would guard the rest of the Temple itself against Athaliah's party.

7 And two parts of all you that go forth on the sabbath, even they shall keep the watch of the house of the LORD about the king. The two parts mentioned likely were the courses of Levites coming on and going off duty on that Sabbath day. Those going off duty were not to go home, but stay put and assist in the looming confrontation.

Jehoiada's plan was this. **8 And ye shall compass the king round about, every man with his weapons in his hand: and he that cometh within the ranges, let him be slain: and be ye with the king as he goeth out and as he cometh in.** The assembled Levites, priests, and Temple police were to surround the young king with weapons drawn. The word translated as

ranges (שדרה *sederah*) simply means 'ranks.' Therefore, anyone who challenged their ranks was to be killed. They were to be the armed bodyguard and escort for the young king.

11:9-11 And the captains over the hundreds did according to all *things* that Jehoiada the priest commanded: and they took every man his men that were to come in on the sabbath, with them that should go out on the sabbath, and came to Jehoiada the priest. On the appointed Sabbath day, the Levites, priests, and Temple police did as directed by Jehoiada. The incoming course of Levites was pressed into their ranks and the outgoing course did not leave.

10 And to the captains over hundreds did the priest give king David' spears and shields, that *were* in the Temple of the LORD. 11 And the guard stood, every man with his weapons in his hand, round about the king, from the right corner of the Temple to the left corner of the Temple, *along* by the altar and the Temple. Apparently during the reign of David, weapons of war had been taken from enemies and dedicated to the Temple for its defense. Jehoiada therefore provided these arms to his followers. They in turn formed a line of defense from one end of the Temple to the other near the front of the Temple by the altar of sacrifice. A defensive perimeter was thus formed around young king Joash at the entrance of the Temple proper.

11:12 And he brought forth the king's son, and put the crown upon him, and *gave him* the testimony; and they made him king, and anointed him; and they clapped their hands, and said, God save the king. In the morning light, young Joash, son of Ahaziah the deceased king of Judah, was formally brought forth. In the Temple of God, Jehoiada, the high priest, placed the royal crown of Judah upon him and presented him with the *testimony*, that is the Book of the Law.

Understanding II Kings

Jehoiada then anointed him as king over Judah. Whereupon, the assembled force of Levites, Priests, and the Temple guard erupted in applause and they roared, "God save the king."

11:13-14 Meanwhile, **when Athaliah heard the noise of the guard *and* of the people, she came to the people into the Temple of the LORD.** Wicked Athaliah heard the roar of the crowd in the Temple. She therefore marched into the Temple to see what was going on. 14 **And when she looked, behold, the king stood by a pillar, as the manner *was*, and the princes and the trumpeters by the king, and all the people of the land rejoiced, and blew with trumpets: and Athaliah rent her clothes, and cried, Treason, Treason.**

Apparently, it was the custom in Judah, when the king entered the Temple, that he stood at a prescribed place by a pillar. It was the place of the king. As Athaliah marched in, the priests and Levites blew their trumpets as a royal fanfare to the king as the people cheered. Athaliah did not mistake what was going on. In surprise and no doubt consternation, she cried out, "Treason, Treason." Yet, she was the treasonous one.

11:15-16 But Jehoiada the priest commanded the captains of the hundreds, the officers of the host, and said unto them, Have her forth without the ranges: and him that followeth her kill with the sword. For the priest had said, Let her not be slain in the house of the LORD. Upon Jehoiada's orders, Athaliah was forcibly escorted out of the ranks by the Temple guards. Moreover, anyone who followed her was to be slain as well. However, it was the direction of Jehoiada that bloodshed not take place in the Temple itself.

Therefore, the Temple guard 16 **laid hands on her; and she went by the way by the which the horses came into the king's house: and there was she slain.** The wicked queen was hustled out of the Temple to a place near the palace where the horses entered, perhaps its stables, and there she was executed.

11:17-19 And Jehoiada made a covenant between the LORD and the king and the people, that they should be the LORD'S people; between the king also and the people. Upon ridding Judah of the wicked queen Athaliah, Jehoiada therefore reaffirmed a covenant between the king and the people that they should be Jehovah's people. The final phrase of the verse seems to indicate that the king for his part would rule the people according to the Law of God. Thus, after years of weak or no godly influence in the land, a king was re-established who would honor the Lord God.

Furthermore, **18 all the people of the land went into the house of Baal, and brake it down; his altars and his images brake they in pieces thoroughly, and slew Mattan the priest of Baal before the altars. And the priest appointed officers over the house of the LORD.** Evident is that Athaliah had built a temple for Baal in the heart of Jerusalem. Therefore, forces loyal to the new king destroyed this pagan temple and killed its chief priest, a fellow by the name of Mattan.

19 And he took the rulers over hundreds, and the captains, and the guard, and all the people of the land; and they brought down the king from the house of the LORD, and came by the way of the gate of the guard to the king's house. And he sat on the throne of the kings. After having purged the wicked influence of Athaliah and Baal worship from the land, Jehoiada therefore officially brought young Joash from the Temple (where he had lived) to the royal palace. There, he was placed upon the royal throne of Judah. He thus was established as king altogether.

11:20-21 The climatic events of the preceding chapter are thus summarily rehearsed. **And all the people of the land**

rejoiced, and the city was in quiet: and they slew Athaliah with the sword *beside* the king's house. The nation of Judah thus rejoiced in being relieved of the wicked oppression of Athaliah. Moreover, when she was executed as noted above, the city was quiet. No one rose up in her defense.

21 Seven years old *was* Jehoash when he began to reign. Though he is called *Jehoash* here, he is otherwise called Joash, both in the following chapter as well as in the account in II Chronicles.

* * * * *

Overview of II Kings 12: *This next chapter records the repair of the Temple of Jehovah under the reign of Joash. Record is then made of the incident of Joash and Hazael of the Syrians. The chapter then concludes with the ignoble end of Joash. The record in II Chronicles 24 presents the unseemly details of his final years.*

12:1-3 In the seventh year of Jehu Jehoash began to reign; and forty years reigned he in Jerusalem. And his mother's name *was* Zibiah of Beersheba. Further detail concerning young king Joash is noted. He reigned a total of forty years. His mother was originally from Beer Sheba.

2 And Jehoash did *that which was* right in the sight of the LORD all his days wherein Jehoiada the priest instructed him. Though Jehoiada the high priest was not his father; he had raised Joash from infancy. He had been mentor to the young king and for all practical purposes had been as a father to him. Significant is the statement that Joash did right in the sight of the Lord all the days of Jehoiada. However, in II Chronicles 24:17*ff*, record is made of his rapid spiritual declension after the death of Jehoiada.

Moreover, 3 **the high places were not taken away: the people still sacrificed and burnt incense in the high places**. God had clearly commanded in the Law that Israel was to sacrifice to Him only in the place which the Lord should choose. See Deuteronomy 12:14, 26. Other high places were an accommodation to the idolatry of the nations around them. They were a form of compromise which quickly led to idolatry altogether. Though Joash, in the main, did right during the tenure of Jehoiada, he never went to the trouble to eliminate the spurious high places around Judah.

12:4-5 The record now turns back to the early years of the reign of Joash. No doubt through the influence of Jehoiada, Jehoash said to the priests, **All the money of the dedicated things that is brought into the house of the LORD,** *even* **the money of every one that passeth** *the account***, the money that every man is set at,** *and* **all the money that cometh into any man's heart to bring into the house of the LORD,**
5 **Let the priests take** *it* **to them, every man of his acquaintance: and let them repair the breaches of the house, wheresoever any breach shall be found**. In short, Joash directed that funds coming into the Temple should be used to repair and restore the Temple complex. It evidently had fallen into disrepair during the reign of Athaliah and her predecessors.

12:6-8 But it was *so, that* **in the three and twentieth year of king Jehoash the priests had not repaired the breaches of the house**. After being on the throne for twenty-three years, the Temple had still not been repaired. It is not clear if the people were derelict in their giving or if the priests had converted the funds for their own use. The latter likely is the case which caused the people to lose confidence. The result was that the Temple saw little repair.

7 Then king Jehoash called for Jehoiada the priest, and the *other* priests, and said unto them, Why repair ye not the breaches of the house? now therefore receive no *more* money of your acquaintance, but deliver it for the breaches of the house. Finally, the king suspected what was going on and ordered the priests to stop receiving any monies from the Temple (which they otherwise were due). Rather, it all was to go to the repair of the Temple.

Being suspect of less than honorable conduct, **8 the priests consented to receive no *more* money of the people, neither to repair the breaches of the house.** They therefore stopped receiving these funds. However, neither did they repair the Temple.

12:9-10 But Jehoiada the priest took a chest, and bored a hole in the lid of it, and set it beside the altar, on the right side as one cometh into the house of the LORD: and the priests that kept the door put therein all the money *that was* brought into the house of the LORD. Rather than the normal channels for handling Temple monies, Jehoiada placed a chest beside the altar of sacrifice at the Temple for the express purpose for the repair of the Temple. All funds which were brought to the Temple were deposited therein at the order of the high priest.

10 And it was *so*, when they saw that *there was* much money in the chest, that the king's scribe and the high priest came up, and they put up in bags, and told the money that was found in the house of the LORD. Accordingly, the people gave generously for the repair of the Temple. Lest there be any question of propriety, Jehoiada brought the king's secretary to account the funds thus received.

12:11-12 And they gave the money, being told, into the hands of them that did the work, that had the oversight of

the house of the LORD: and they laid it out to the carpenters and builders, that wrought upon the house of the LORD, 12 And to masons, and hewers of stone, and to buy timber and hewed stone to repair the breaches of the house of the LORD, and for all that was laid out for the house to repair *it*. After being properly accounted, the monies were disbursed to the job superintendents who in turn paid the various craftsmen: carpenters, stone masons, and stone cutters. These therefore set about to effect the necessary repairs to the Temple.

12:13-14 Howbeit there were not made for the house of the LORD bowls of silver, snuffers, basons, trumpets, any vessels of gold, or vessels of silver, of the money *that was* brought into the house of the LORD: 14 But they gave that to the workmen, and repaired therewith the house of the LORD. Though the renovation of the Temple complex itself proceeded, at this point, nothing was done to upgrade the various instruments and utensils used for service. The worked focused only on structural repairs.

12:15-16 Moreover they reckoned not with the men, into whose hand they delivered the money to be bestowed on workmen: for they dealt faithfully. To the credit of the overseers of the renovation, they ordered themselves in such a fashion that they were completely trusted. As a testimony to the ages, "they dealt faithfully." Total honesty is a rare gem indeed.

Meanwhile, **16 the trespass money and sin money was not brought into the house of the LORD: it was the priests'.** As prescribed by the Law of Moses, monies brought to the Temple for trespass and sin offerings went to the priests for their living. This evidently was by those who lived a distance who brought monies to the Temple to purchase cattle for sacrifice. The remainder became the priests.

12:17-18 Then Hazael king of Syria went up, and fought against Gath, and took it: and Hazael set his face to go up to Jerusalem. The record in II Chronicles 24:23-24 makes clear that this event took place after the death of Jehoiada and the treacherous treatment Joash bestowed upon Jehoiada's son, Zechariah. Moreover, it was at this time that Joash allowed the nation to slide back into idolatry. See II Chronicles 24:17-19. Therefore, God began to chasten Judah. The invasion by Hazael of Syria clearly was at God's hand. Gath was to the west along the coast of the Mediterranean. The Syrians therefore essentially had Jerusalem at their mercy.

Therefore, 18 **Jehoash king of Judah took all the hallowed things that Jehoshaphat, and Jehoram, and Ahaziah, his fathers, kings of Judah, had dedicated, and his own hallowed things, and all the gold** *that was* **found in the treasures of the house of the LORD, and in the king's house, and sent** *it* **to Hazael king of Syria: and he went away from Jerusalem.**

In desperation, Joash raided the treasuries of the Temple and the palace to pay off Hazael. Having thus received such payola, Hazael retreated. Clearly, the hand of God was no longer upon Joash.

12:19 And the rest of the acts of Joash, and all that he did, *are* **they not written in the book of the chronicles of the kings of Judah?** This evidently is reference to II Chronicles 24:1-27.

12:20-21 And his servants arose, and made a conspiracy, and slew Joash in the house of Millo, which goeth down to Silla. 21 For Jozachar the son of Shimeath, and Jehozabad the son of Shomer, his servants, smote him, and he died; and they buried him with his fathers in the city of David: and Amaziah his son reigned in his stead. The account of II Chronicles 24:25-27 notes that the uprising against Joash was for his treachery against Zechariah, the son of Jehoiada. Though Joash had been a good king through the influence of Jehoiada the priest, thereafter, he quickly backslid. God's blessing was removed and it likely was at God's dispensation that Joash was ignobly removed from his throne. After his burial, his son, Amaziah ascended the throne.

* * * * *

Overview of II Kings 13: *This next chapter of II Kings presents the history of Jehoahaz over Israel followed by the reign of his son, Jehoash (or Joash). The events surrounding the death of Elisha are then recorded.*

13:1-3 The focus of the text now shifts from Judah back to Israel. The next king of the northern kingdom is referenced against the tenure of the king of Judah. **In the three and twentieth year of Joash the son of Ahaziah king of Judah Jehoahaz the son of Jehu began to reign over Israel in Samaria,** *and reigned* **seventeen years**.

Thus, in the twenty-third year of Joash, Jehoahaz, king of Judah, ascended the throne of Israel. As noted, he was the son of Jehu. This was the same year that Joash renovated the Temple in Jerusalem. See II Kings 12:6. John Gill makes these observations. "Whereas Joash began to reign in the seventh year of Jehu, and Jehu reigned but twenty eight years, II Kings 10:36 and II Kings 12:1, this could be but the twenty first of Joash; to reconcile which it must be observed, that it was at the beginning of the seventh year of Jehu that Joash began to reign, and at the beginning of the twenty third of Joash that Jehoahaz began to reign, as the Jewish commentators observe." As noted, there is no contradiction in biblical details.

Unfortunately, **Jehoahaz 2 did *that which was* evil in the sight of the LORD, and followed the sins of Jeroboam the son of Nebat, which made Israel to sin; he departed not therefrom.** The sins of Jeroboam were the golden calves placed at Bethel and Dan. Jehoahaz continued that abomination. Therefore, **3 the anger of the LORD was kindled against Israel, and he delivered them into the hand of Hazael king of Syria, and into the hand of Benhadad the son of Hazael, all *their* days.** God in mercy chastened his people to draw them back to Himself. In this case, it was through economic depression brought about by a hostile neighbor, Syria.

13:4 To his credit, **Jehoahaz besought the LORD, and the LORD hearkened unto him: for he saw the oppression of Israel, because the king of Syria oppressed them.** The Hebrew word translated as **oppression** (לחץ *lachats*) also has the idea of 'affliction' or 'pressure.' Because of the chastening of God through the Syrians, Jehoahaz for the first time in his life besought the Lord. Implicit is a repentant spirit and God in His mercy heard the prayer of Jehoahaz.

13:5-6 These next two verses are parenthetical as indicated. (**And the LORD gave Israel a saviour, so that they went out from under the hand of the Syrians: and the children of Israel dwelt in their tents, as beforetime. 6 Nevertheless they departed not from the sins of the house of Jeroboam, who made Israel sin, *but* walked therein: and there remained the grove also in Samaria.**) The word translated as **saviour** (ישע *yashà*) can also have the idea of a 'deliverer.' Though not explicitly noted, that deliverer is thought to be Jehoahaz' son, Jehoash, as noted in verse 25. Alternately, it may be some other unnamed individual. However, the greater context seems to imply that the deliverer was in fact Jehoash. God thus gave deliverance to His people and they dwelt in peace as in early times. Sadly, however, the northern kingdom still persisted in allowing the golden calves at Dan and Bethel as well as a pagan grove at Samaria.

13:7 The text thus returns to where its main thought left off from verse 4. **Neither did he leave of the people to Jehoahaz but fifty horsemen, and ten chariots, and ten thousand footmen; for the king of Syria had destroyed them, and had made them like the dust by threshing**. The thought is how the king of Syria, during his oppression of Israel, had left them with only fifty cavalrymen, ten chariots, and a meager army of 10,000 infantrymen. At God's allowance, Syria had virtually destroyed Israel leaving them like the dusty chaff of wheat threshing. See Psalm 1:4.

13:8-9 **Now the rest of the acts of Jehoahaz, and all that he did, and his might, *are* they not written in the book of the chronicles of the kings of Israel?** 9 **And Jehoahaz slept with his fathers; and they buried him in Samaria: and Joash his son reigned in his stead**. The reign of Jehoahaz over the northern kingdom is thus summarized noting that his son, Joash (or Jehoash) ascended the throne after his death.

13:10-11 The reign of Jehoash over the northern kingdom is thus tartly described. **In the thirty and seventh year of Joash king of Judah began Jehoash the son of Jehoahaz to reign over Israel in Samaria, *and reigned* sixteen years.** 11 **And he did *that which was* evil in the sight of the LORD; he departed not from all the sins of Jeroboam the son of Nebat, who made Israel sin: *but* he walked therein.**

Because the sitting king in Judah at this time was also named Joash, the sacred writer calls the king of Israel Jehoash though he also was known as Joash as well. Like his forefathers, he also refused to remove the golden calves, the sin of Jero-

Understanding II Kings

boam, from Israel. Like his predecessors, he too walked in that abomination.

13:12-13 The epitaph of Jehoash is thus noted. **And the rest of the acts of Joash, and all that he did, and his might wherewith he fought against Amaziah king of Judah, are they not written in the book of the chronicles of the kings of Israel?** Once again, the chronicles of the kings of Israel refer to uninspired history books lost to time. The mention of him fighting against Amaziah, king of Judah, will be described in the following chapter. 13 **And Joash slept with his fathers; and Jeroboam sat upon his throne: and Joash was buried in Samaria with the kings of Israel.** The *Joash* mentioned here is *Jehoash* of the northern kingdom. Upon his death, his son Jeroboam II, ascended the throne of the northern kingdom.

13:14 The narrative now returns to the life of Elisha and his last days. **Now Elisha was fallen sick of his sickness whereof he died. And Joash the king of Israel came down unto him, and wept over his face, and said, O my father, my father, the chariot of Israel, and the horsemen thereof.** In hearing of the mortal illness of Elisha, Joash, the king of Israel, came to him and wept. His reference to him as the father and the "chariot of Israel, and the horsemen thereof" hearkens back to the day when Elisha had witnessed Elijah's translation to heaven. Word of that no doubt had reached Joash. See II Kings 2:12. Though certainly not living for the Lord, Joash still perceived the spiritual blessing and power of God in His prophet. His death would be the loss of a national resource and Joash knew it.

13:15-17 As Elisha lay sick unto death, he said to Joash the king, And Elisha said unto him, **Take bow and arrows. And he took unto him bow and arrows. 16 And he said to the king of Israel, Put thine hand upon the bow. And he put his hand**

upon it: **and Elisha put his hands upon the king's hands. 17 And he said, Open the window eastward. And he opened** *it*. **Then Elisha said, Shoot. And he shot. And he said, The arrow of the LORD'S deliverance, and the arrow of deliverance from Syria: for thou shalt smite the Syrians in Aphek, till thou have consumed** *them*.

In a graphic object lesson, Elisha placed his hands upon those of Joash as he shot an arrow to the east as directed. He thus announced that by Jehovah, Israel would be delivered from the Syrian oppression as was noted in verse 4. The mention of Israel smiting the Syrian at Aphek very well may have the thought of Syria being smitten *as* at Aphek when Ahab routed the Syrians years earlier. The following context will support this thought. See I Kings 20:26-30. As will be noted at the end of this chapter, Israel under Joash (Jehoash) did defeat Syria three times. See I Kings 13:25.

13:18-19 Moreover, Elisha directed Joash to **take the arrows. And he took** *them*. **And he said unto the king of Israel, Smite upon the ground. And he smote thrice, and stayed. 19 And the man of God was wroth with him, and said, Thou shouldest have smitten five or six times; then hadst thou smitten Syria till thou hadst consumed** *it*: **whereas now thou shalt smite Syria** *but* **thrice.** The object lesson should have been clear to Joash from the preceding comments of Elisha. So when he was directed to smite the ground three times, he did just that. However, Elisha rebuked him for not doing more, indicating that he could have thus defeated Syrian to an even greater extent.

13:20-21 Thus, **Elisha died, and they buried him. And the bands of the Moabites invaded the land at the coming in of the year. 21 And it came to pass, as they were burying a man, that, behold, they spied a band** *of men*; **and they cast**

Understanding II Kings

the man into the sepulchre of Elisha: and when the man was let down, and touched the bones of Elisha, he revived, and stood up on his feet. Jewish tradition holds that Elisha was buried at Samaria, though some hold that he was buried at Mount Carmel with Elijah. In any event, record is made of God's miraculous work through Elisha even after he was dead. John Gill says that according to Jewish chronology, he died in the tenth year of Joash and he prophesied more than sixty years.

The raid of the Syrians was in the spring which was the beginning of the new year in the land of Israel. Though there is no scriptural record thereof, Jewish tradition claims that the man revived was Shallum the husband of Huldah the prophetess who purportedly lived many years thereafter.

13:22-25 The chapter is thus summarized in these several verses. **But Hazael king of Syria oppressed Israel all the days of Jehoahaz. 23 And the LORD was gracious unto them, and had compassion on them, and had respect unto them, because of his covenant with Abraham, Isaac, and Jacob, and would not destroy them, neither cast he them from his presence as yet.** Though God had allowed and even sent the Syrians to militarily and economically oppress Israel for their sin, nevertheless, He was gracious to them. In His compassion and faithfulness to His covenant to Abraham, Isaac, and Jacob, God did not allow Israel to be destroyed. He always keeps His Word. Israel suffered from their sin, but God preserved them nevertheless.

24 So Hazael king of Syria died; and Benhadad his son reigned in his stead. Israel's long antagonist thus went the way of all flesh. His son Benhadad ascended the throne who would also cause much trouble for God's people. Nevertheless, as prophesied, **25 Jehoash the son of Jehoahaz took again out of the hand of Benhadad the son of Hazael the cities, which he had taken out of the hand of Jehoahaz his father by war.**

Three times did Joash beat him, and recovered the cities of Israel. This was the fulfillment of the prophecy made in 13:5 as well as 13:17, and specifically 13:18. Though used as an instrument of chastening by God, the Syrians were thus eventually defeated by Israel at God's allowance.

* * * * *

Overview of II Kings 14: *The focus of the chapter shifts back to Judah and the reign of Amaziah along with his war with Jehoash of the northern kingdom. The end of the chapter then shifts back to the northern kingdom and the reign of Jeroboam II over Israel.*

14:1-2 The sacred writ now shifts its focus to the southern kingdom. **In the second year of Joash son of Jehoahaz king of Israel reigned Amaziah the son of Joash king of Judah. 2 He was twenty and five years old when he began to reign, and reigned twenty and nine years in Jerusalem. And his mother's name *was* Jehoaddan of Jerusalem**. At the age of twenty five, Amaziah ascended the throne of Judah and was king until he was fifty four. Nothing further is known of his mother, noted here as Jehoaddan.

14:3-4 His reign is thus described from God's perspective. **And he did *that which was* right in the sight of the LORD, yet not like David his father: he did according to all things as Joash his father did. 4 Howbeit the high places were not taken away: as yet the people did sacrifice and burnt incense on the high places.** To this king's credit, he basically did right before the Lord, though not to the degree of David his ancestor. To his demerit, Amaziah allowed the high places to remain in Judah contrary to the Law of Moses. Accordingly, the common people offered sacrifices and burned incense thereon rather than at the Temple as prescribed. See notes for I Kings 12:3. Of further interest is the word translated **right** (יָשָׁר *yasshar*). It is not the word used for *righteous* as a principle (צַדִּיק *tzaddiq*), but rather conveys the idea of doing right in practice. Amaziah did right practically, but righteousness evidently was not the governing principle of his life. The chronicle of him in II Chronicles 25:2, says that "he did *that which was right* in the sight of the LORD, but not with a perfect heart."

14:5-7 Accordingly, Amaziah sought vengeance against his enemies. **And it came to pass, as soon as the kingdom was confirmed in his hand, that he slew his servants which had slain the king his father.** His father, Joash (king of Judah), had killed Zechariah for preaching against his sin (II Chronicles 24:20-22). In turn, Joash in due season was murdered by his own servants in retaliation (II Chronicles 24:25-27). Upon establishing himself as king, Amaziah in turn killed those who had murdered his father. This may have been through a court of law, but illustrated is the vicious cycle of retaliation.

However, **6 the children of the murderers he slew not: according unto that which is written in the book of the law of Moses, wherein the LORD commanded, saying, The fathers shall not be put to death for the children, nor the children be put to death for the fathers; but every man shall be put to death for his own sin.** Quoted here is Deuteronomy 24:16. To his credit, Amaziah sought to observe God's Word in dealing with the guilty and their families.

Further record is made of the accomplishments of Amaziah. **7 He slew of Edom in the valley of salt ten thousand, and took Selah by war, and called the name of it Joktheel unto this day.** The valley of salt likely is the southern end of the dead sea. Indeed, there are salt deposits there to this day. He there defeated Edom which adjoins that area and killed ten-thousand soldiers thereof. The place noted as **Selah** is thought to have been an ancient name for Petra of Petraia. Further details of this campaign are found in II Chronicles 25:5-16.

14:8 In his campaign against Edom, Amaziah had hired 100,000 soldiers from Israel to assist him. However, because he bungled that arrangement, he provoked animosity with the northern kingdom. Flush from victory to the south, Amaziah therefore brashly **sent messengers to Jehoash, the son of Jehoahaz son of Jehu, king of Israel, saying, Come, let us look one another in the face.** In so many words, Amaziah challenged Jehoash of Israel to war.

14:9-10 Whereupon, Jehoash replied with a sardonic parable. **And Jehoash the king of Israel sent to Amaziah king of Judah, saying, The thistle that *was* in Lebanon sent to the cedar that *was* in Lebanon, saying, Give thy daughter to my son to wife: and there passed by a wild beast that *was* in Lebanon, and trode down the thistle.** Jehoash thus, via his parable, likened Amaziah to an annoying thistle plant which would eventually be crushed by a passing animal.

Lest, Amaziah should miss the point, Jehoash, made it clear to him. 10 **Thou hast indeed smitten Edom, and thine heart hath lifted thee up: glory *of this*, and tarry at home: for why shouldest thou meddle to *thy* hurt, that thou shouldest fall, *even* thou, and Judah with thee?** Jehoash reminded Amaziah that he was lifted up with pride from his victory over Edom. However, he would be bettered served than to pick a fight with his much larger neighbor to the north.

14:11-14 Foolishly, **Amaziah would not hear. Therefore Jehoash king of Israel went up; and he and Amaziah king of Judah looked one another in the face at Bethshemesh, which *belongeth* to Judah.** Bethshemesh was the place whence the stolen Ark of the Covenant was returned after its stay in Philistia. See I Samuel 6:9:12.

12 And Judah was put to the worse before Israel; and they fled every man to their tents. 13 And Jehoash king of Israel took Amaziah king of Judah, the son of Jehoash the son of Ahaziah, at Bethshemesh, and came to Jerusalem, and brake down the wall of Jerusalem from the gate of Ephraim unto the corner gate, four hundred cubits. 14 And he took all the gold and silver, and all the vessels that were found in the house of the LORD, and in the treasures of the king's house, and hostages, and returned to Samaria.

As noted, the northern kingdom utterly defeated Judah. Moreover, Jehoash destroyed a significant portion of the wall of Jerusalem and then looted the Temple. However, the record in II Chronicles 25:14-15 notes how that Amaziah bowed to the idols of Edom thus incurring the wrath of God against him. The narrative there makes it clear this is why God allowed Amaziah to be so miserably defeated.

14:15-16 The narrative briefly shifts to the northern kingdom again. **Now the rest of the acts of Jehoash which he did, and his might, and how he fought with Amaziah king of Judah, *are* they not written in the book of the chronicles of the kings of Israel? 16 And Jehoash slept with his fathers, and was buried in Samaria with the kings of Israel; and Jeroboam his son reigned in his stead.** This parallels the record made in I Kings 13:12-13.

14:17-20 The record now shifts back again briefly to the southern kingdom, Judah. **And Amaziah the son of Joash king of Judah lived after the death of Jehoash son of Jehoahaz king of Israel fifteen years. 18 And the rest of the acts of Amaziah, *are* they not written in the book of the**

chronicles of the kings of Judah? The chronicles of the kings of Judah may refer to other than the biblical book of Chronicles.

Amaziah had begun his reign by killing those who killed his father. It seems that it eventually came back upon him. **19 Now they made a conspiracy against him in Jerusalem: and he fled to Lachish; but they sent after him to Lachish, and slew him there. 20 And they brought him on horses: and he was buried at Jerusalem with his fathers in the city of David.** The record in II Chronicles 25:27 indicates that the demise of Amaziah was connected to his turning away from following the Lord. Lachish was an ancient fortified city south and west of Jerusalem. Though fleeing for his life, Amaziah came to his end there.

14:21-22 And all the people of Judah took Azariah, which *was* sixteen years old, and made him king instead of his father Amaziah. 22 He built Elath, and restored it to Judah, after that the king slept with his fathers. As is the case in II Kings, the reign of the next king is briefly summarized and then the focus turns to the other kingdom. That is the case here. Azariah is also called Uzziah in the next chapter as well as in II Chronicles 26. Elath was the port city at the tip of the northeast arm of the Red Sea. It today is known at Elat.

14:23-24 The focus shifts back to the northern kingdom, Israel. **In the fifteenth year of Amaziah the son of Joash king of Judah Jeroboam the son of Joash king of Israel began to reign in Samaria, *and reigned* forty and one years. 24 And he did *that which was* evil in the sight of the LORD: he departed not from all the sins of Jeroboam the son of Nebat, who made Israel to sin.** As noted in 14:15-16, Jeroboam II succeeded his father upon the throne. However, he was like his predecessors in continuing in the sins of Jeroboam—the golden calves in Dan and Bethel.

Understanding II Kings

14:25 More details of Jeroboam II's reign are thus noted. **He restored the coast of Israel from the entering of Hamath unto the sea of the plain, according to the word of the LORD God of Israel, which he spake by the hand of his servant Jonah, the son of Amittai, the prophet, which** *was* **of Gathhepher.**

Hamath was at the northern border of Israel. The *sea of the plain* is another name for the Dead Sea into which flows the Jordan River. The greater thought is that Jeroboam II was an able ruler restoring much territory to Israel. Of special interest is the mention of Jonah the prophet. The specific prophecy is not noted here nor in the book bearing his name. However, this is the first place in the Bible that Jonah is mentioned. In fact, this is the first mention of any of the later writing prophets (Samuel excluded).

14:26-27 For the LORD saw the affliction of Israel, *that it was* **very bitter: for** *there was* **not any shut up, nor any left, nor any helper for Israel. 27 And the LORD said not that he would blot out the name of Israel from under heaven: but he saved them by the hand of Jeroboam the son of Joash.** The tender mercies of God toward his people are again unveiled. Because of their backslidden condition, God had allowed the Syrians to chasten Israel. Notwithstanding, God in his mercy and compassion was gracious to His people. Though Jeroboam was not a godly man, it is implied that the rest of the nation did not share his evil heart.

God therefore allowed even a king such as Jeroboam II to deliver his people from the oppression they suffered. Though God had chastened them, his tender mercy still remained. Moreover, God kept His Word. He had repeatedly promised the patriarchs of Israel that He would fulfill His covenant to them in preserving the nation of Israel in perpetuity. God keeps His Word.

14:28-29 The reign of Jeroboam II is thus summarized. **Now the rest of the acts of Jeroboam, and all that he did, and his might, how he warred, and how he recovered Damascus, and Hamath,** *which belonged* **to Judah, for Israel, are they not written in the book of the chronicles of the kings of Israel?** 29 **And Jeroboam slept with his fathers,** *even* **with the kings of Israel; and Zachariah his son reigned in his stead.** During the reign of Jeroboam II, even Damascus was made subject to Israel even as it had been in the time of David. Once again, the chronicles of the kings of Israel are un-inspired historical books lost to time. After his death, the son of Jeroboam II, Zachariah ascended the throne of Israel.

* * * * *

Overview II Kings 15: The fifteenth chapter of II kings is chronological touching upon the reign of two kings of Judah and five kings of Israel.

15:1-4 The chapter begins with the focus in Judah. **In the twenty and seventh year of Jeroboam king of Israel began Azariah son of Amaziah king of Judah to reign.** 2 **Sixteen years old was he when he began to reign, and he reigned two and fifty years in Jerusalem. And his mother's name** *was* **Jecholiah of Jerusalem.** The Azariah named here is one and the same with Uzziah who is described in greater detail in II Chronicles 26.

In the broader scope found in II Chronicles, Uzziah 3 **did** *that which was* **right in the sight of the LORD, according to all that his father Amaziah had done;** 4 **Save that the high places were not removed: the people sacrificed and burnt incense still on the high places.** Azariah (Uzziah) like other kings of Judah never put a stop to the casual and indiscriminate

Understanding II Kings

sacrifice upon high places which was the root for greater idolatry.

15:5 Sadly, **the LORD smote the king, so that he was a leper unto the day of his death, and dwelt in a several house. And Jotham the king's son** *was* **over the house, judging the people of the land.** II Chronicles 26:16-21 presents the details of Uzziah's sin which was prompted by pride. God therefore smote him with leprosy. The word translated as **several** (חפשית *chophshuwth*) has the sense of a 'separate' house. His son, Jotham, therefore took care of the administrative details in his place.

15:6-7 And the rest of the acts of Azariah, and all that he did, *are* **they not written in the book of the chronicles of the kings of Judah? 7 So Azariah slept with his fathers; and they buried him with his fathers in the city of David: and Jotham his son reigned in his stead.** Upon the death of Azariah (Uzziah), Jotham his son ascended the throne of Judah.

15:8-9 The focus now shifts back to the northern kingdom, Israel. **In the thirty and eighth year of Azariah king of Judah did Zachariah the son of Jeroboam reign over Israel in Samaria six months. 9 And he did** *that which was* **evil in the sight of the LORD, as his fathers had done: he departed not from the sins of Jeroboam the son of Nebat, who made Israel to sin.** The reign of this next king of Israel was short lived which exemplifies the principle of Proverbs 28:2, which see. Moreover, he continued in the idolatry begun by Jeroboam many years before.

15:10-12 And Shallum the son of Jabesh conspired against him, and smote him before the people, and slew him, and reigned in his stead. 11 And the rest of the acts of

Zachariah, behold, they *are* written in the book of the chronicles of the kings of Israel.** Zachariah's tenure as king was short because Shallum not only conspired against him, but killed him. **12 This *was* the word of the LORD which he spake unto Jehu, saying, Thy sons shall sit on the throne of Israel unto the fourth *generation*. And so it came to pass.** As God had spoken to Jehu, four generations of his sons followed in his dynasty. Of greater significance is the final phrase "and so it came to pass." God's Word always comes to pass. Jehu had been promised four generations. That is exactly what came to pass.

15:13-15 However, things got even worse in Samaria, the capital of Israel. **Shallum the son of Jabesh began to reign in the nine and thirtieth year of Uzziah king of Judah; and he reigned a full month in Samaria. 14 For Menahem the son of Gadi went up from Tirzah, and came to Samaria, and smote Shallum the son of Jabesh in Samaria, and slew him, and reigned in his stead.** The instability and chaos which results from unrighteousness was manifesting itself in Israel. The principle of Proverbs 28:2 continued. Shallum managed to reign for a total of one month.

15 **And the rest of the acts of Shallum, and his conspiracy which he made, behold, they *are* written in the book of the chronicles of the kings of Israel.** Though no other details are provided, the conspiracy of Shallum evidently refers to his treachery in the death of Zachariah, his predecessor.

15:16-18 Then Menahem smote Tiphsah, and all that *were* therein, and the coasts thereof from Tirzah: because they opened not *to him*, therefore he smote *it; and* all the women therein that were with child he ripped up. The location of Tiphsah is not clear. However, it apparently was at the border with Syria. In any event, Menahem with barbarity killed the inhabitants thereof, including pregnant women whom he ripped open.

17 In the nine and thirtieth year of Azariah king of Judah began Menahem the son of Gadi to reign over Israel, *and reigned* ten years in Samaria. 18 And he did *that which was* evil in the sight of the LORD: he departed not all his days from the sins of Jeroboam the son of Nebat, who made Israel to sin. As did his forefathers, Menahem continued in the national abomination of the golden-calf worship begun by Jeroboam. Spiritual sin (idolatry) leaves the way open for other abominations such as the barbarity done by Menahem at Tiphsah. Menahem's reign lasted ten years.

15:19-20 God did not leave this wicked king unpunished, however. ***And* Pul the king of Assyria came against the land: and Menahem gave Pul a thousand talents of silver, that his hand might be with him to confirm the kingdom in his hand. 20 And Menahem exacted the money of Israel, *even* of all the mighty men of wealth, of each man fifty shekels of silver, to give to the king of Assyria. So the king of Assyria turned back, and stayed not there in the land.**

God allowed and may have even sent the Assyrians to attack Israel. In turn, Menahem paid Pul, king of Assyria, one-thousand talents of silver to back off. The sacred text notes this was to "confirm the kingdom in his hand." Evidently, the rule of Menahem was tenuous. He had seized the throne through treachery and the kingdom accordingly was not stable. Apparently, Menahem hoped that by paying off the Assyrians that his own reign would be prolonged. He thus extracted the monies from various wealthy men of his kingdom.

What one-thousand talents of silver would translate into modern money is difficult to say. However, a talent could be as much as one-hundred pounds, English weight. Therefore, one-thousand talents was a very substantial amount of silver. In being paid off, Pul, king of Assyria, backed off.

It is of interest that this is the first mention of the Assyrian empire in the Bible. Assyria was an empire which arose between the ninth and seventh centuries before Christ. Its territory, at least initially, would approximate the modern State of Iraq. The Assyrians for several centuries would dominate the Middle East as a 'super power,' ruling primarily from Nineveh.

15:21-22 And the rest of the acts of Menahem, and all that he did, *are* they not written in the book of the chronicles of the kings of Israel? 22 And Menahem slept with his fathers; and Pekahiah his son reigned in his stead. Thus, the reign of Menahem ended with his son Pekahiah succeeding him.

15:23-24 In the fiftieth year of Azariah king of Judah Pekahiah the son of Menahem began to reign over Israel in Samaria, *and reigned* two years. 24 And he did *that which was* evil in the sight of the LORD: he departed not from the sins of Jeroboam the son of Nebat, who made Israel to sin. The reign of Pekahiah was short. Details of his demise will be provided directly. Like his predecessors in the northern kingdom, Pekahiah continued the idolatrous abomination of the golden calves of Bethel and Dan, begun by Jeroboam.

15:25-26 But Pekah the son of Remaliah, a captain of his, conspired against him, and smote him in Samaria, in the palace of the king's house, with Argob and Arieh, and with him fifty men of the Gileadites: and he killed him, and reigned in his room. Principle and integrity were of little value in the northern kingdom. Thus, one of Pekahiah's officers conspired against him, killed him in his very palace, and usurped the throne. This arrogant new ruler was Pekah. The reign of

Understanding II Kings

Pekahiah is thus summarized. 26 **And the rest of the acts of Pekahiah, and all that he did, behold, they** *are* **written in the book of the chronicles of the kings of Israel.**

15:27-28 Sadly, the reign of Pekah was little different from his predecessors. **In the two and fiftieth year of Azariah king of Judah Pekah the son of Remaliah began to reign over Israel in Samaria,** *and reigned* **twenty years. 28 And he did** *that which was* **evil in the sight of the LORD: he departed not from the sins of Jeroboam the son of Nebat, who made Israel to sin.** Though ruling for twenty years, Pekah continued the idolatry characteristic of the northern kingdom in the golden calves.

15:29 In the days of Pekah king of Israel came Tiglathpileser king of Assyria, and took Ijon, and Abelbethmaachah, and Janoah, and Kedesh, and Hazor, and Gilead, and Galilee, all the land of Naphtali, and carried them captive to Assyria.

During the reign of Pekah, the next Assyrian ruler to the north and east, *Tiglathpileser*, began to expand his empire. He began to move southward from Syria and Lebanon into northern Israel. He thus captured much of the northern section of Israel including the territory of Naphtali, the region of Galilee, and Gilead to the east. The beginnings of the Assyrian captivity were under way. The long prophesied dispersion of Israel because of apostasy was about to begin. See Leviticus 26:32*ff* and Deuteronomy 28:58*ff*. Though the full Assyrian captivity against the northern kingdom was still about seven-teen years away, the specter of it was already looming.

15:30-31 And Hoshea the son of Elah made a conspiracy against Pekah the son of Remaliah, and smote him, and slew him, and reigned in his stead, in the twentieth year

of Jotham the son of Uzziah. **31 And the rest of the acts of Pekah, and all that he did, behold, they *are* written in the book of the chronicles of the kings of Israel.** Pekah had risen to power through treacherous conspiracy. He was to succumb to the same when one of his subordinates, Elah, led a conspiracy against him. Thus, Pekah passed into oblivion as an unjust king of Israel.

15:32-35 The focus of the sacred narrative now returns to the southern kingdom. **In the second year of Pekah the son of Remaliah king of Israel began Jotham the son of Uzziah king of Judah to reign. 33 Five and twenty years old was he when he began to reign, and he reigned sixteen years in Jerusalem. And his mother's name *was* Jerusha, the daughter of Zadok.** After the death of Uzziah at Jerusalem, his son Jotham ascended the throne.

34 And he did *that which was* right in the sight of the LORD: he did according to all that his father Uzziah had done. 35 Howbeit the high places were not removed: the people sacrificed and burned incense still in the high places. He built the higher gate of the house of the LORD. Though briefly noted here, Jotham was one of the righteous kings of Judah. II Chronicles 27:6 notes that "Jotham became mighty, because he prepared his ways before the LORD his God." Notwithstanding, he, like his father, failed to remove the high places from Judah. He also is remembered for notable renovations and improvements to the Temple and its main gate.

15:36-38 Now the rest of the acts of Jotham, and all that he did, *are* they not written in the book of the chronicles of the kings of Judah? Indeed, more details are recorded concerning the reign of Jotham in II Chronicles 27.

37 In those days the LORD began to send against Judah Rezin the king of Syria, and Pekah the son of Remaliah.

Understanding II Kings

Though Jotham was a relatively righteous king, the nation itself was becoming increasingly corrupt. See II Chronicles 27:2. The years of compromise were beginning to catch up with them. Thus God Himself sent Rezin, king of Syria, and Pekah, king of Israel, against the southern kingdom. It is in this context that the notable prophecy of Isaiah 7:1-17 takes place. The ministry of Isaiah was now also underway in Judah. See Isaiah 1:1.

38 And Jotham slept with his fathers, and was buried with his fathers in the city of David his father: and Ahaz his son reigned in his stead. With the death of Jotham, his son, Ahaz ascended the throne of Judah.

* * * * *

Overview of II Kings 16: This next chapter of II Kings keeps its focus completely in Judah and the reign of Ahaz. The time parallels that of Isaiah 7.

16:1-2 In the seventeenth year of Pekah the son of Remaliah Ahaz the son of Jotham king of Judah began to reign. 2 Twenty years old *was* **Ahaz when he began to reign, and reigned sixteen years in Jerusalem, and did not** *that which was* **right in the sight of the LORD his God, like David his father.** The focus of this chapter will be upon Ahaz, one of the most wicked kings of the southern kingdom. Noteworthy is the summary of his reign, he "did not *that which was* right in the sight of the LORD his God, like David his father." Though some of his predecessors had in fact done right before God, Ahaz did the opposite.

16:3-4 Specifically, Ahaz **walked in the way of the kings of Israel, yea, and made his son to pass through the fire, according to the abominations of the heathen, whom the**

LORD **cast out from before the children of Israel.** 4 **And he sacrificed and burnt incense in the high places, and on the hills, and under every green tree.**

The mention of him making his son pass through the fire refers to the abomination of Molech in which children were either sacrificed thereto, or at least passed through the angry flames of this despicable idol. This son may in fact have been Hezekiah. In Leviticus 18:21, God had specifically forbidden His people to do precisely what Ahaz did. He thus made himself abominable in God's eyes. Whereas his predecessors had allowed high places throughout the land, now Ahaz did the same. Implied however is that his sacrifices in such places were to idols. The phrase "under every green tree" was an euphemism of idolatrous practices of the heathen. Ahaz not only allowed but openly participated in such practices in Judah.

16:5-6 Then Rezin king of Syria and Pekah son of Remaliah king of Israel came up to Jerusalem to war: and they besieged Ahaz, but could not overcome *him***.** 6 **At that time Rezin king of Syria recovered Elath to Syria, and drave the Jews from Elath: and the Syrians came to Elath, and dwelt there unto this day**. The invasion and attack against Judah and Jerusalem at this time clearly was no coincidence. God used Syria and Israel to chastise Judah for its sin. Nevertheless, the allied forces of Rezin and Pekah could not subdue Jerusalem. The Syrians therefore moved on to the south and the Red-Sea port city of Elath (Elat in modern terms), seizing it from Judah. Of interest is that the word *Jews* appears for the first time in the Bible. It refers specifically to those pertaining to the tribe of Judah. Again, it is in this direct context that Isaiah 7:1-16 takes place.

16:7-8 Meanwhile, **Ahaz sent messengers to Tiglath-pileser king of Assyria, saying, I** *am* **thy servant and thy son:**

Understanding II Kings

come up, and save me out of the hand of the king of Syria, and out of the hand of the king of Israel, which rise up against me. Facing invasion and siege by Syria and Israel against Jerusalem, Ahaz offered himself as a vassal to the powerful Assyrians. In turn, he asked **Tiglathpileser king of Assyria** to intervene militarily on his behalf to deliver him. **8 And Ahaz took the silver and gold that was found in the house of the LORD, and in the treasures of the king's house, and sent *it for* a present to the king of Assyria.** Sadly, Ahaz raided the treasuries of the Temple as well as his own palace to make up a payoff for the Assyrians to intervene on his behalf. Noteworthy is that there was no prayer or seeking of God's help as Jehoshaphat had done in II Chronicles 20. Of course, Ahaz had turned his back on Jehovah God.

16:9 Seeing an opportunity to expand his empire, **the king of Assyria hearkened unto him: for the king of Assyria went up against Damascus, and took it, and carried *the people of it* captive to Kir, and slew Rezin.** In one fell swoop, the Assyrians added Syria to their domain. Moreover, Rezin, king of Syria was eliminated. This is exactly what Isaiah had prophesied in Isaiah 7:7-9.

16:10-11 And king Ahaz went to Damascus to meet Tiglathpileser king of Assyria, and saw an altar that *was* at Damascus: and king Ahaz sent to Urijah the priest the fashion of the altar, and the pattern of it, according to all the workmanship thereof. 11 And Urijah the priest built an altar according to all that king Ahaz had sent from Damascus: so Urijah the priest made *it* against king Ahaz came from Damascus. Ahaz thus went to Damascus to meet his new lord. While there, he saw an impressive pagan, idolatrous altar. He had a drawing made thereof and sent it back to Jerusalem for such an altar to be built there. Though a priest of

Jehovah, Urijah sadly used those plans to build such a pagan altar at Jerusalem. Implicit is that Urijah had constructed the pagan altar by the time Ahaz returned from Damascus.

16:12-14 And when the king was come from Damascus, the king saw the altar: and the king approached to the altar, and offered thereon. 13 And he burnt his burnt offering and his meat offering, and poured his drink offering, and sprinkled the blood of his peace offerings, upon the altar. 14 And he brought also the brasen altar, which *was* before the LORD, from the forefront of the house, from between the altar and the house of the LORD, and put it on the north side of the altar.

Implied is that Ahaz himself directly offered sacrifices upon this pagan altar. These offerings were likely a combination of pagan sacrifices merged in with those to Jehovah. Whereas the brazen altar built by Solomon had been at the eastern entry of the Temple (from its beginning as prescribed by God), Ahaz now moved it northward off into a corner. Now in entering the main gate to the Temple, his new pagan altar is what was first encountered.

16:15-16 And king Ahaz commanded Urijah the priest, saying, Upon the great altar burn the morning burnt offering, and the evening meat offering, and the king's burnt sacrifice, and his meat offering, with the burnt offering of all the people of the land, and their meat offering, and their drink offerings; and sprinkle upon it all the blood of the burnt offering, and all the blood of the sacrifice: and the brasen altar shall be for me to enquire *by*. 16 Thus did Urijah the priest, according to all that king Ahaz commanded.

Ahaz directed that the daily sacrifices in the morning and evening, along with all other sacrifices, were to be offered upon

Understanding II Kings

his new greater altar. Nevertheless, Ahaz still left the brazen altar off to the side as a standby for his own personal inquiry. Ironically, God never worked through the altar as an oracle. Yet, Ahaz cared little for how God worked. He had his new pagan altar from which to offer sacrifices and that is where the main activities of the Temple now took place.

16:17-18 Moreover, **king Ahaz cut off the borders of the bases, and removed the laver from off them; and took down the sea from off the brasen oxen that** *were* **under it, and put it upon a pavement of stones.** Gill writes, "In the Temple there were ten lavers for the priests to wash in, which are here meant the singular being put for the plural; and these had bases of brass, on which they were set; and about these bases were borders, which had on them figures of various creatures, lions, oxen, and cherubim; and these Ahaz cut off, either to deface them, in contempt of them, or to convert the brass to other uses, as he might also the bases themselves, since he removed the lavers from off of them." See 1Kings 7:27-30. Furthermore, Ahaz dismantled the brazen laver of the Temple, setting it upon the floor thereof. He may have intended to diminish its magnificence, or he may have had other plans for its brass.

18 **And the covert for the sabbath that they had built in the house, and the king's entry without, turned he from the house of the LORD for the king of Assyria.** Apparently, an open tent-like structure or covered walkway had been constructed at the Temple for the king's use upon the Sabbath day to shelter him from the elements. Now, Ahaz reoriented this esplanade toward the direction whence might come the king of Assyria, clearly in deference to him.

16:19-20 Now the rest of the acts of Ahaz which he did, *are* **they not written in the book of the chronicles of the kings of Judah?** 20 **And Ahaz slept with his fathers, and was**

buried with his fathers in the city of David: and Hezekiah his son reigned in his stead. Thus, the record of one of the most wicked kings of Judah is noted. Ironically, his son, Hezekiah, would become one of the truly godly kings of the southern kingdom.

* * * * *

Overview of II Kings 17: *This next chapter of II Kings is a climactic one. Though the next king of Israel (Hoshea) is briefly chronicled, it was during his reign that God sent the Assyrians which carried away captive the northern kingdom. Moreover, the text makes it exceedingly clear that the Assyrian captivity was because of the sin of Israel.*

17:1-2 In the twelfth year of Ahaz king of Judah began Hoshea the son of Elah to reign in Samaria over Israel nine years. 2 And he did *that which was* **evil in the sight of the LORD, but not as the kings of Israel that were before him.** The focus of the book changes for the last time to the affairs of Israel, the northern kingdom. Its last king, Hoshea, continued in the evil tradition of his predecessors. Though Hoshea was not as wicked as many before him, God had had enough. His judgment was about to fall upon Israel.

17:3-4 Against him came up Shalmaneser king of Assyria; and Hoshea became his servant, and gave him presents. As the Assyrian empire was flexing its imperialistic muscles across the Middle East, God not only allowed the Assyrians to invade Israel, but to subdue them. Moreover, the remainder of the chapter will make it clear that the Assyrian invasion was at God's hand. I Chronicles 5:26 speaks of *Tilgathpilneser*, king of Assyria, invading Israel. However, *Shal-*

maneser likely is the son of Tilgathpilneser. In any event, the Assyrian king forced Israel into vassal status, requiring payment of substantial tribute-taxes on a regular basis.

However, **4 the king of Assyria found conspiracy in Hoshea: for he had sent messengers to So king of Egypt, and brought no present to the king of Assyria, as *he had done* year by year: therefore the king of Assyria shut him up, and bound him in prison.** Hoshea, however, endeavored to make an alliance with Egypt to throw off the Assyrian yoke. Assyria evidently learned of this attempted conspiracy and they certainly became aware of the cessation of tribute monies flowing from Israel. The Assyrians therefore returned to Israel, arrested Hoshea, and threw him in prison. The latter may have taken place after the complete defeat of Israel as noted in the next two verses.

17:5-6 With almost understatement, the sacred text records, **then the king of Assyria came up throughout all the land, and went up to Samaria, and besieged it three years**. Though the Assyrians had had little trouble in overrunning Israel previously; evidently, this time, Hoshea and his forces withstood them by fortifying themselves in Samaria, their capital city.

After three years of siege, **6 in the ninth year of Hoshea the king of Assyria took Samaria, and carried Israel away into Assyria, and placed them in Halah and in Habor *by the river of Gozan*, and in the cities of the Medes**. The long foretold dispersion of Israel from their land had begun. Not only were the inhabitants of the city of Samaria deported, but all of the ten tribes of the remainder of the northern kingdom were as well. As early as Leviticus 26:32-39 and Deuteronomy 28:58-67, God had long warned His people that He would eventually remove them from their land if they turned their back on Him and followed idols.

The Assyrian captivity of the northern kingdom began in about 722 B.C. The places mentioned in Assyria where Israel was placed were "Halah and in Habor *by* the river of Gozan, and in the cities of the Medes." These were in the northern part of Assyria. In more modern terms, these areas would be northern Iraq and into central Iran.

17:7 The sacred text makes exceedingly clear why Israel was deported from their land. **For *so* it was, that the children of Israel had sinned against the LORD their God, which had brought them up out of the land of Egypt, from under the hand of Pharaoh king of Egypt, and had feared other gods**. God is longsuffering. He had put up with the sin of Israel for more than 250 years. He had sent prophets to warn them. He had mercifully delivered them from their enemies. He had given them provision in times of famine. Yet, Israel and its kings stubbornly rebelled against their God. The patience and longsuffering of God finally expired. He had had enough. As He had foretold in the Law of Moses, He took Israel out of their land.

The Assyrian captivity has never officially ended. Though Judah, the southern kingdom would go into captivity about 117 years later and return with God's blessing, the northern kingdom has never *officially* returned. To this day, the descendants of Jacob are called *Jews* after the tribe of Judah. Though individual Israelites from the ten northern tribes surely did and have returned to their land over the centuries, they have never come back as a whole. That evidently will not happen until the Day of the Lord. See further comments in verses 23, 34-35, and 41.

17:8-9 The sacred writer further enumerates the sins of Israel. They **walked in the statutes of the heathen, whom the LORD cast out from before the children of Israel, and of the kings of Israel, which they had made**. Israel degenerated into

Understanding II Kings

the idolatrous and immoral practices of the Canaanites which had inhabited the land before them. God had cast them out because of their sin. Now the same fate fell upon Israel. Moreover, Israel willingly followed after the sins of the kings of Israel, namely the golden calves set up at Bethel and Dan.

Moreover, 9 **the children of Israel did secretly** *those* **things that** *were* **not right against the LORD their God, and they built them high places in all their cities, from the tower of the watchmen to the fenced city**. Not only had Israel participated in the open idolatry of Jeroboam, they also secretly and privately practiced sin in their homes. This extended not only from the fortified major cities of the land but into the small towns as well. They built private high places for idolatrous practices throughout the land.

17:10-12 Specifically, **they set them up images and groves in every high hill, and under every green tree**. Throughout the land of Israel, the people of Jehovah had set up pagan idols atop every high hill (which are numerous across the land) and even under every green tree. This was the practice of the heathen round about and Israel willingly conformed themselves thereto. See also Jeremiah 3:6.

Moreover, 11 **there they burnt incense in all the high places, as** *did* **the heathen whom the LORD carried away before them; and wrought wicked things to provoke the LORD to anger**. Though the covenant-people of Jehovah, Israel had backslidden into such a degenerate state that there was little difference between them and the world about them. They accordingly provoked Jehovah God to anger.

Their sin is summarized as follows: 12 **For they served idols, whereof the LORD had said unto them, Ye shall not do this thing**. Israel had blatantly ignored the first two commandments as recorded in Exodus 20:3-5. The mills of God's judgment grind slow, but they grind exceedingly fine. Israel, perhaps, thought that they were getting away with their sin. But God dealt against them with righteous wrath in His perfect time.

17:13 Notwithstanding the sin of Israel, **the LORD testified against Israel, and against Judah, by all the prophets, *and by* all the seers, saying, Turn ye from your evil ways, and keep my commandments *and* my statutes, according to all the law which I commanded your fathers, and which I sent to you by my servants the prophets.** In mercy and longsuffering, God sent various prophets to warn Israel. Though their message may have been sharp, it was gracious in that God gave Israel ample warning of their sin. God then and to this day warns His people to **Turn ye from your evil ways, and keep my commandments *and* my statutes, according to all the law which I commanded your fathers, and which I sent to you by my servants the prophets.** Sadly, Israel refused to hearken.

17:14-15 Notwithstanding they would not hear, but hardened their necks, like to the neck of their fathers, that did not believe in the LORD their God. 15 And they rejected his statutes, and his covenant that he made with their fathers, and his testimonies which he testified against them; and they followed vanity, and became vain, and went after the heathen that *were* round about them, *concerning* whom the LORD had charged them, that they should not do like them.

The inspired penman elaborated further against the sin of Israel. (1) They refused to listen to the prophets sent by God. (2) They hardened their necks in stubbornness against the message of God and the God of the message. (3) They refused to trust Jehovah their God. (4) They rejected His commandments and the covenant God had made with their forefathers. (5) They rejected the warnings of the prophets against them. (6) They pursued after vanity. (7) They willingly conformed themselves to the world round about, notwithstanding the commandment of God to not be like them. Sadly, many a nominal Christian in this age is quite similar in nature to Israel then.

17:16-17 The sacred writer continues the litany of the sins of Israel. To compound the insult against their God, Israel **left all the commandments of the LORD their God, and made them molten images,** *even* **two calves, and made a grove, and worshipped all the host of heaven, and served Baal.** Not only did Israel accept the abomination of Jeroboam and his golden calves, they also became involved in astrology in worshiping various heavenly bodies. On top of that, they practiced the sexual immorality of the heathen in their pagan god named Baal.

Furthermore, 17 **they caused their sons and their daughters to pass through the fire, and used divination and enchantments, and sold themselves to do evil in the sight of the LORD, to provoke him to anger**. If all the wickedness thus far were not enough, Israel stooped to offering their small children to the pagan atrocity called Molech. They also dabbled in the occult to the degree that they prostituted themselves to do evil before God. Implied is that they not only sinned against God, but did so on purpose to defy and provoke the God of their fathers.

17:18-19 Therefore the LORD was very angry with Israel, and removed them out of his sight: there was none left but the tribe of Judah only. If Israel was intent in provoking the God of their fathers, they succeeded. God had had enough. He therefore threw Israel out its land leaving only the tribe of Judah. (It should be recalled that Judah also included the tribe of Benjamin.) **Also Judah kept not the commandments of the LORD their God, but walked in the statutes of Israel which**

they made. The sin of Judah was not initially as blatant as that of their northern brethren. Furthermore, there were times of revival in the southern kingdom. However, Judah as well had backslidden and little by little emulated the example of their wicked northern brethren.

17:20-21 The following four verses summarize the situation of Israel. Certainly included is the northern kingdom. And quite possibly, the coming Babylonian captivity of the southern kingdom may be in view as well. **And the LORD rejected all the seed of Israel, and afflicted them, and delivered them into the hand of spoilers, until he had cast them out of his sight.** The northern kingdom was deported as noted above. The southern kingdom would face the same fate approximately 117 years later. Specifically, God had 21 **rent Israel from the house of David; and they made Jeroboam the son of Nebat king: and Jeroboam drave Israel from following the LORD, and made them sin a great sin.** Because of the sins of Solomon and Rehoboam, God allowed the nation of Israel to split. Yet after the division, the northern kingdom willingly followed the sin of Jeroboam, who drove Israel even further away from Jehovah God.

17:22-23 For the children of Israel walked in all the sins of Jeroboam which he did; they departed not from them; 23 Until the LORD removed Israel out of his sight, as he had said by all his servants the prophets. So was Israel carried away out of their own land to Assyria unto this day. God's climactic and decisive action against Israel is thus summarized. For 250 years, Israel had defied Jehovah God with the idolatry of Jeroboam. Therefore, God threw them out of the land as He had forewarned He would do. God thus used the Assyrians as the instrument of His chastisement. The northern kingdom was therefore obliterated, never again to be officially restored.

Though those ten tribes have passed into oblivion, nevertheless, Revelation 7 makes clear that they are still exist scattered across the world. Many of them no doubt are already in Israel in preparation for the fulfillment of Revelation 7 and 14 in the 144,000.

17:24-25 The focus of the text now shifts away from the deported ten tribes to events which continued in the land in their absence. **And the king of Assyria brought *men* from Babylon, and from Cuthah, and from Ava, and from Hamath, and from Sepharvaim, and placed *them* in the cities of Samaria instead of the children of Israel: and they possessed Samaria, and dwelt in the cities thereof.** In deporting the ten tribes of Israel, the Assyrians replaced them with gentiles from around their empire. The name *Samaria* is here used as another name for the northern kingdom. Though there certainly was a city by that name, which in fact had been the capital city of the northern kingdom, Samaria also came to be a synonym of the northern kingdom. Israel no longer dwelt therein. Now it was called Samaria.

25 And *so* it was at the beginning of their dwelling there, *that* they feared not the LORD: therefore the LORD sent lions among them, which slew *some* of them. These pagan gentiles transplanted in the land came with no fear of Jehovah. Though the people of the covenant had been removed, the land remained the covenant land. It still was the holy land (and still is to this day). God therefore instilled the fear of the Lord in them by sending lions throughout the country. As will be clear in the following context, these new gentiles clearly realized the lions were a chastisement of Jehovah.

17:26 Wherefore they spake to the king of Assyria, saying, The nations which thou hast removed, and placed in the cities of Samaria, know not the manner of the God of the

land: therefore he hath sent lions among them, and, behold, they slay them, because they know not the manner of the God of the land. Word was sent back to Assyria ascribing the plague of lions to the God of the land. Indeed it was. They therefore determined to placate this unknown God.

17:27-28 Then the king of Assyria commanded, saying, Carry thither one of the priests whom ye brought from thence; and let them go and dwell there, and let him teach them the manner of the God of the land. 28 Then one of the priests whom they had carried away from Samaria came and dwelt in Bethel, and taught them how they should fear the LORD. A priest (apparently of the lineage of Aaron) was found in the captivity and sent back to Bethel to instruct the new inhabitants of the land in the ways of Jehovah.

17:29-31 Howbeit every nation made gods of their own, and put *them* in the houses of the high places which the Samaritans had made, every nation in their cities wherein they dwelt. The 'goyim' (the various gentile peoples imported into the land) brought their own forms of idolatry with them. Sadly, the deported Israelites had left behind numerous high places suitable for the continuation of pagan worship.

Specifically, **30 the men of Babylon made Succothbenoth, and the men of Cuth made Nergal, and the men of Hamath made Ashima.** The gentile transplants from Babylon made an idol to their deity *Succothbenoth*. The latter has impure overtones meaning the bedchamber of the daughter. Frequently, pagan deities practiced some sort of ritual prostitution as part of their abominable practices. This is implicit here. Likewise, the gentiles imported from *Cuth* made an idol to their pagan deity, *Nergal*. Likewise did the men of Hamath with their idol to *Ashima*.

Moreover, 31 **the Avites made Nibhaz and Tartak, and the Sepharvites burnt their children in fire to Adrammelech and Anammelech, the gods of Sepharvaim**. Other pagan deities are noted. However, the Sepharvites adopted a form of the pagan abomination of Molech in offering small children thereto.

17:32-33 The dismal spiritual conditions of the land are thus described. **So they feared the LORD, and made unto themselves of the lowest of them priests of the high places, which sacrificed for them in the houses of the high places**. As had Jeroboam, the lowest scoundrels of the land were made priests of the numerous pagan high places of the land. Nevertheless, they maintained a slight fear of Jehovah because of the fear of His chastisement upon them.

The sacred writer therefore summarizes the situation in that **33 they feared the LORD, and served their own gods, after the manner of the nations whom they carried away from thence**. Though a semblance of the fear of the Lord was maintained, these pagan priests continued with their own idols. Ironically, they were not different from Israel "after the manner of the nations whom they carried away from thence."

17:34-35 Unto this day they do after the former manners: they fear not the LORD, neither do they after their statutes, or after their ordinances, or after the law and commandment which the LORD commanded the children of Jacob, whom he named Israel; 35 With whom the LORD had made a covenant, and charged them, saying, Ye shall not fear other gods, nor bow yourselves to them, nor serve them, nor sacrifice to them.

The *they* likely refers to Israel even in their captivity (though some think it may refer to the colonies of transplanted gentiles in the land). If the former is the case (and the context lends itself thereto), the implication is that the ten northern tribes never repented of their sin or of their idolatry. If that be the case, the ten northern tribes simply assimilated into the gentile culture of the nations in which they were dispersed. They accordingly likely intermarried with gentiles to such a degree that they no longer exist as a distinct people.

Notwithstanding, there was a remnant of those ten northern tribes which migrated to the south. See II Chronicles 30:1, 5-11, 25-26. Though the ten tribes may be officially 'lost,' the evidence of II Chronicles 30 is that a remnant of each tribe migrated back to Judah before the Assyrian captivity to worship Jehovah God. There is absolutely no biblical or historical evidence that the 'ten lost tribes of Israel' migrated to England and populated the British Isles. To the contrary, the account of II Chronicles 30 indicates that God preserved a remnant of the ten northern tribes in their meager migration to Judah.

17:36-39 Further credence that the northern tribes are in view are in view here. **But the LORD, who brought you up out of the land of Egypt with great power and a stretched out arm, him shall ye fear, and him shall ye worship, and to him shall ye do sacrifice. 37 And the statutes, and the ordinances, and the law, and the commandment, which he wrote for you, ye shall observe to do for evermore; and ye shall not fear other gods. 38 And the covenant that I have made with you ye shall not forget; neither shall ye fear other gods. 39 But the LORD your God ye shall fear; and he shall deliver you out of the hand of all your enemies.** Summarized is the covenant which Jehovah God had made with Israel over the preceding centuries. The sacred writer made clear the basis of God's dealing with Israel even in their dispersion.

17:40 The sad comment is made, **howbeit they did not hearken, but they did after their former manner.** Though chastened by their God, Israel continued in their idolatry and sin in Assyria.

17:41 Thus ends one of the saddest chapters in the Bible. **So these nations feared the LORD, and served their graven images, both their children, and their children's children: as did their fathers, so do they unto this day.** The pagan gentile nations transplanted in the land feared Jehovah God more than Israel, though they continued to practice their idolatry. The mention *to this day* may refer all the way to the time of Ezra, the presumed author of the book.

Though not mentioned in the text here, other sources indicate that a remnant of Israelites were missed in the deportation and remained in the land. These evidently intermarried with the various gentile transplants into the land. The offspring of these became the genesis of what came to be known as the Samaritans in Jesus' day. They were partly Hebrew in their lineage as well as gentile. They formed a hybrid religion on Mount Gerizim which in some ways was similar to the Mosaic Law practiced at Jerusalem. However, it also had pagan influences from the gentile influence of this mixed race.

* * * * *

Overview of II Kings 18: With the demise of the northern kingdom, the focus of the remainder of the book shifts to the southern kingdom. Chapter 18 begins a three-chapter chronicle of the reign of Hezekiah. Record is made here of the invasion of Judah by Assyria under the leadership of Sennacherib.

18:1-3 As was noted above, the focus of the book of II Kings now shifts to Judah, the southern kingdom. This will continue to the end of the book. The sacred historian here turns his attention to the reign of Hezekiah. **Now it came to pass in the third year of Hoshea son of Elah king of Israel, *that* Hezekiah the son of Ahaz king of Judah began to reign.** The name *Hezekiah* literally means 'Jehovah is my strength.' Of the numerous kings throughout the history of Judah, Hezekiah surely was one of the great and godly kings thereof.

2 Twenty and five years old was he when he began to reign; and he reigned twenty and nine years in Jerusalem. His mother's name also *was* Abi, the daughter of Zachariah. However, the Holy Spirit saw fit to describe him as follows. **3 And he did *that which was* right in the sight of the LORD, according to all that David his father did.**

The life and reign of Hezekiah may be summarized with the brief characterization—he did right. Hezekiah, as all men, was a sinner. The implication of the text is not that he was sinless. Rather, practical righteousness characterized his person and his reign. The word translated as **right** in this context (ישר *yashar*) is the Hebrew word which refers to righteousness in a practical sense. Morever, the righteous character of Hezekiah was likened unto that of David, his royal ancestor. Though no passage of Scripture directly summarizes the life of David as doing that which was right *per se*, here, that appellation is indirectly ascribed to David.

18:4 Specifically, Hezekiah **removed the high places, and brake the images, and cut down the groves, and brake in pieces the brasen serpent that Moses had made: for unto those days the children of Israel did burn incense to it: and he called it Nehushtan**. Upon acceding the throne, Hezekiah lost no time in removing the high places of the land, braking up the idolatrous images thereof, and destroying the accompanying groves of trees around the idolatrous high places.

Mentioned for the first time in the Old Testament is the fact that the Israel had preserved the golden serpent made by Moses in the wilderness. However, by the time of Hezekiah, it had become an idol in itself, with backslidden Jews offering incense to it. Hezekiah's characterization of it as *Nehushtan* literally means 'a thing of brass.' The idea is that Hezekiah derisively so referred to it before destroying it. It was only brass. Yet, Jews were foolishly worshiping it.

18:5-7 The godly character of Hezekiah is further noted in that **he trusted in the LORD God of Israel; so that after him was none like him among all the kings of Judah, nor *any* that were before him**. Not only did Hezekiah do that which was right before God, he also trusted in Him. Moreover, that personal trust in Jehovah was unlike any other king of Judah—before or after. He not only was righteous of character, he lived by faith before God altogether. No other king in the history of Judah was so esteemed by God.

6 For he clave to the LORD, *and* departed not from following him, but kept his commandments, which the LORD commanded Moses. Further description of the godly character of Hezekiah is recorded. He additionally "clave to the LORD." The word translated as **clave** (דבק *dabaq*) has the idea of 'clinging.' Hezekiah sought to walk as close to the Lord as he could. Accordingly, he **departed not from following him**. He not only walked with the Lord, he walked in His ways. Furthermore, Hezekiah **kept his commandments**. This godly king was careful to obey God's Word in every way which he could.

His person and reign therefore could be summarized as being righteous, having complete trust in God, walking close to Him and with Him, and as altogether obedient to Him. Therefore, **7 the LORD was with him; *and* he prospered whithersoever he went forth: and he rebelled against the king of Assyria, and served him not**. Because of his righteous, godly character, God blessed Hezekiah and prospered him. (See also II Chronicles 31:21.) This evidently gave the king the courage needed to rebel against the oppression of Assyria under which Ahaz, his father, had placed Judah.

18:8 Record is also made of Hezekiah's victory over Philistia. **He smote the Philistines,** *even* **unto Gaza, and the borders thereof, from the tower of the watchmen to the fenced city.**

18:9-10 The historical record now shifts back to what happened to the northern kingdom. **And it came to pass in the fourth year of king Hezekiah, which** *was* **the seventh year of Hoshea son of Elah king of Israel,** *that* **Shalmaneser king of Assyria came up against Samaria, and besieged it. 10 And at the end of three years they took it:** *even* **in the sixth year of Hezekiah, that** *is* **the ninth year of Hoshea king of Israel, Samaria was taken.** The mention of Samaria refers not only to the city by that name, but also to the entire northern kingdom. Over the years, the name *Samaria* had come to be a synonym for the northern kingdom of Israel. Record is thus reiterated of the defeat of that northern kingdom of Israel.

18:11-12 And the king of Assyria did carry away Israel unto Assyria, and put them in Halah and in Habor *by* **the river of Gozan, and in the cities of the Medes.** The Assyrian captivity of the northern ten tribes of Israel is again recorded. Furthermore, the sacred writer makes clear the cause thereof. 12 **Because they obeyed not the voice of the LORD their God, but transgressed his covenant,** *and* **all that Moses the servant of the LORD commanded, and would not hear** *them*, **nor do** *them*. The distilled essence of why Israel was so judged by God is disobedience. They ignored God's Word and His will for them. Though God is longsuffering and was more than for-

Understanding II Kings

bearing to Israel, they pressed His mercy for too long. God had had enough. The northern kingdom ceased to exist. The basic reason was flagrant disobedience.

18:13 About eight years later, the Assyrians turned their attention against Judah which had rebelled against their suzerainty. **Now in the fourteenth year of king Hezekiah did Sennacherib king of Assyria come up against all the fenced cities of Judah, and took them.** The Assyrians bypassed Jerusalem and proceeded to attack and take the more weakly defended cities throughout Judah in preparation for a final siege against Jerusalem.

18:14-16 Realizing that **Hezekiah king of Judah sent to the king of Assyria to Lachish, saying, I have offended; return from me: that which thou puttest on me will I bear. And the king of Assyria appointed unto Hezekiah king of Judah three hundred talents of silver and thirty talents of gold.** Lachish (pronounced *laKEESH*) was a fortified city of Judah about twenty-eight miles southwest of Jerusalem (as the crow flies) in the Shephelah (hill country) of Judah. Sennacherib apparently was besieging this fortified hilltop city.

Hezekiah therefore in discouragement agreed to submit to Assyria and pay heavy tribute to them. The levy of 300 talents of silver and 30 talents of gold, though uncertain in modern terms, evidently was a significant amount.

Thus, **15 Hezekiah gave *him* all the silver that was found in the house of the LORD, and in the treasures of the king's house. 16 At that time did Hezekiah cut off *the gold from* the doors of the Temple of the LORD, and *from* the pillars which Hezekiah king of Judah had overlaid, and gave it to the king of Assyria.** Though a godly man, it is apparent at this juncture that Hezekiah did not seek God's help in this crisis as Jehoshaphat had done in a similar crisis in II Chronicles 20. Moreover,

Hezekiah, in his fear of Assyria, raided the Temple of its silver and gold to pay off the Assyrians.

18:17-18 The events which are described below closely follow Isaiah 36, which see. Sensing the weakness of Jerusalem, Sennacherib determined to now take it as well. He thus would have control of the entire land of Israel. **And the king of Assyria sent Tartan and Rabsaris and Rabshakeh from Lachish to king Hezekiah with a great host against Jerusalem. And they went up and came to Jerusalem. And when they were come up, they came and stood by the conduit of the upper pool, which *is* in the highway of the fuller's field.**

Sennacherib therefore sent armies under the leadership of three of his chief generals named *Tartan and Rabsaris and Rabshakeh.* It may be that the latter was the overall commander because he was the spokesman of the three. Sennacherib remained at Lachish, still besieging it. Reference is made to what today is called Hezekiah's tunnel, here called the conduit of the upper pool (in Jerusalem). This was a tunnel carved through a hillside of Jerusalem to furnish water during attack against the city. Though the Assyrian forces positioned themselves at the upper pool thereof, they evidently were unaware of the secret tunnel which channeled water into the city. In so surrounding the upper pool, they may have thought that they had seized control of the water supply to Jerusalem.

18 And when they had called to the king, there came out to them Eliakim the son of Hilkiah, which *was* over the household, and Shebna the scribe, and Joah the son of Asaph the recorder. The insolence and audacity of the Assyrian generals is apparent in placing themselves directly outside the wall of Jerusalem and demanding to speak to the king thereof. Rather than face such indignity, Hezekiah sent out officers of his cabinet to the wall of the city to hear the Assyrian demands.

Understanding II Kings

18:19-20 And Rabshakeh said unto them, Speak ye now to Hezekiah, Thus saith the great king, the king of Assyria, What confidence *is* this wherein thou trustest. The Assyrian general Rabshakeh clearly sought to intimidate his Jewish foe. He mocked the military strength of Jerusalem. **20 Thou sayest, (but *they are but* vain words,) *I have* counsel and strength for the war. Now on whom dost thou trust, that thou rebellest against me?**

18:21-22 Now, behold, thou trustest upon the staff of this bruised reed, *even* upon Egypt, on which if a man lean, it will go into his hand, and pierce it: so *is* Pharaoh king of Egypt unto all that trust on him. Hezekiah evidently had entered into a military alliance with Egypt for mutual aide. However, Rabshakeh mocked any help which might come from Egypt. He likened the Egyptians to a broken reed along the Nile River which if one leaned upon would put splinters into his hand. The Assyrian general therefore ridiculed any help which Hezekiah might receive from Egypt.

Furthermore, Rabshakeh continued, **22 But if ye say unto me, We trust in the LORD our God: *is* not that he, whose high places and whose altars Hezekiah hath taken away, and hath said to Judah and Jerusalem, Ye shall worship before this altar in Jerusalem?** Rabshakeh therefore sought to ridicule any reliance upon Jehovah God. However, he completely misunderstood what Hezekiah had done in removing the high places from Judah. He thought that was an affront to Jehovah when in fact, it was God's will.

18:23-25 Rabshakeh therefore ordered, **Now therefore, I pray thee, give pledges to my lord the king of Assyria, and I will deliver thee two thousand horses, if thou be able on thy part to set riders upon them.** The Assyrian general continued to mock and seek to intimidate Hezekiah. He first sought to receive a pledge from Hezekiah that he would submit himself to Sennacherib. Then he mockingly offered Hezekiah 2,000 horses to put his forces upon to ride and surrender to the king of Assyria. Moreover, he scoffed that Hezekiah probably did not have that many men who could handle a horse.

If Hezekiah was so weak (as Rabshakeh claimed), he asked, **24 How then wilt thou turn away the face of one captain of the least of my master's servants, and put thy trust on Egypt for chariots and for horsemen?** Rabshakeh further mocked Hezekiah by asking how his feeble forces (even with Egyptian intervention) could withstand even one regiment of the mighty Assyrian army.

Rabshakeh waxed even bolder in his effort to intimidate Hezekiah. **25 And am I now come up without the LORD against this land to destroy it? the LORD said unto me, Go up against this land, and destroy it.** He brazenly claimed to be coming against Judah with the permission and blessing of Jehovah, the God of Israel. Morever, he lied outright claiming that God had directed the Assyrians to attack and destroy Judah and Jerusalem. It is one thing to seek to intimidate, but it is another to blatantly lie in God's name.

18:26 Then said Eliakim and Shebna and Joah unto Rabshakeh, Speak, I pray thee, unto thy servants in the Syrian language; for we understand *it*: and speak not to us in the Jews' language, in the ears of the people that *are* on the wall. Rabshakeh evidently knew Hebrew and thus made his intimidating, mocking speech therein. Therefore, the Jewish officials upon the wall (Eliakim and Shebna and Joah) requested that he rather speak to them in the Syrian language. They clearly were concerned about the common people of the city being demoralized by the intimidating threats being made in their own language.

Understanding II Kings

18:27 Rabshakeh knew what he was doing. He was speaking in Hebrew precisely to attempt to demoralize the city. He thus retorted, **But Rabshakeh said unto them, Hath my master sent me to thy master, and to thee, to speak these words?** *hath he not sent me* **to the men which sit on the wall, that they may eat their own dung, and drink their own piss with you?** Rabshakeh therefore became even more intimidating by using the coarse threats of a siege. He intimated that Sennacherib had sent him to not only threaten Hezekiah, but his subordinates as well. He thus warned that they would soon be eating and drinking their own excrement as the starvation of a siege overcame them.

18:28-29 Then Rabshakeh stood and cried with a loud voice in the Jews' language, and spake, saying, Hear the word of the great king, the king of Assyria: 29 Thus saith the king, Let not Hezekiah deceive you: for he shall not be able to deliver you out of his hand. The Assyrian general pompously warned the inhabitants of Jerusalem that their king, Hezekiah, would not be able to deliver them from the Assyrians.

18:30-32 Rabshakeh continued, **Neither let Hezekiah make you trust in the LORD, saying, The LORD will surely deliver us, and this city shall not be delivered into the hand of the king of Assyria.** The arrogant Assyrian warned the inhabitants of Jerusalem to not trust Jehovah for deliverance. He intimated that even Jehovah could not deliver them from the might of the Assyrian army. In his insolence, Rabshakeh had just sown the seeds of his own destruction. To claim that even Jehovah could not defeat him was a sure-fire way to bring the wrath of the Lord down on them. That is exactly what would happen shortly thereafter.

The impudent Assyrian general therefore made the inhabitants of Jerusalem an offer. **31 Hearken not to Hezekiah: for**

thus saith the king of Assyria, Make *an agreement* with me by a present, and come out to me, and *then* eat ye every man of his own vine, and every one of his fig tree, and drink ye every one the waters of his cistern: 32 Until I come and take you away to a land like your own land, a land of corn and wine, a land of bread and vineyards, a land of oil olive and of honey, that ye may live, and not die: and hearken not unto Hezekiah, when he persuadeth you, saying, The LORD will deliver us.

No mercy was offered to Hezekiah, but Rabshakeh sought to incite surrender amongst the people of Jerusalem by offering them amnesty if they would capitulate. What he had in mind was to deport them to Assyria even as had been done to the northern ten tribes. He sought to entice their surrender by painting the description of their captivity in glowing terms. If they overthrew Hezekiah, they would be shown mercy by the Assyrians. If not, they would die. Rabshakeh therefore warned them not to listen to Hezekiah when he claimed that Jehovah God would deliver them.

18:33-35 The foolish Assyrian general then made another blasphemous blunder. He asked the people of Jerusalem, **Hath any of the gods of the nations delivered at all his land out of the hand of the king of Assyria?** This arrogant Assyrian therefore equated the Almighty God of Israel with the pagan deities of the surrounding nations. It was utter blasphemy.

Undeterred, he continued, **34 Where *are* the gods of Hamath, and of Arpad? where *are* the gods of Sepharvaim, Hena, and Ivah? have they delivered Samaria out of mine hand?** As the Assyrians had crushed neighboring countries, Rabshakeh impudently asked, where were the gods of those places? Could they deliver from the power of the mighty Assyrian army? Well, of course, those pagan idols had no power in any event. But, Rabshakeh had sealed his doom by implying the Jehovah God was no better than them. **35 Who *are***

Understanding II Kings

they among all the gods of the countries, that have delivered their country out of mine hand, that the LORD should deliver Jerusalem out of mine hand? He asked, if the pagan idols of the various nations which Assyria had conquered could not deliver from the power of Sennacherib, how could Jehovah deliver them? That was a big mistake to equate the power of Jehovah to the impotent gods of the pagan nations around. Rabshakeh had sealed his own fate by challenging Jehovah.

18:36-37 But the people held their peace, and answered him not a word: for the king's commandment was, saying, Answer him not. Hezekiah had wisely instructed his people to keep their mouths shut. They were not to reply to the taunts from below. They accordingly held their peace.

37 Then came Eliakim the son of Hilkiah, which *was* over the household, and Shebna the scribe, and Joah the son of Asaph the recorder, to Hezekiah with *their* clothes rent, and told him the words of Rabshakeh. The three officials sent by Hezekiah to listen to the taunts of Rabshakeh therefore returned to their king in despair with their clothes rent. They accordingly repeated to the king the ominous threats and derision which Rabshakeh had made. The next chapter will record Hezekiah's response to this grave threat.

* * * * *

Overview of II Kings 19: *II Kings 19 is essentially identical with Isaiah 37. The exception is the addition of verse 30 in Isaiah 37. The story is of the response of Hezekiah to the threats of Rabshakeh and the Assyrians followed by Hezekiah's prayer for deliverance. God answered his prayer through Isaiah the prophet. Divine deliverance was then effected as the angel of the Lord slew 185,000 Assyrians soldiers.*

19:1-2 The chapter opens with the response of Hezekiah to Rabshakeh's threat. **And it came to pass, when king Hezekiah heard *it*, that he rent his clothes, and covered him-self with sackcloth, and went into the house of the LORD.** Because of the blasphemy of the Assyrian general and because of the straits they were in, Hezekiah humbled himself before Jehovah God by ripping his clothing (a middle-eastern symbol of great distress) and putting on *sackcloth*. The latter was a coarse, rough material similar to a modern 'gunny' sack (or, seed bag). Not only was it uncomfortable, but it again was a symbol of great humiliation and distress.

The king thus 2 **sent Eliakim, which *was* over the household, and Shebna the scribe, and the elders of the priests, covered with sackcloth, to Isaiah the prophet the son of Amoz.** The king's cabinet, as it were—his top officials—were sent to the prophet Isaiah. This is the first reference to Isaiah in the Bible. Hezekiah therefore sought word from the Lord from the man of God for direction in this hour of crisis.

19:3-5 The officials sent by Hezekiah came to Isaiah and said, **Thus saith Hezekiah, This day *is* a day of trouble, and of rebuke, and of blasphemy: for the children are come to the birth, and *there is* not strength to bring forth.** As the very existence of the nation of Judah was at stake, indeed, it was a day of trouble, rebuke, and blasphemy against God. Hezekiah thence used the analogy of a pregnant woman in labor, but without strength to deliver the child. Implicit was death for both. The situation facing Judah truly was a crisis of life-and-death proportions.

The message from Hezekiah to Isaiah continued, 4 **It may be the LORD thy God will hear the words of Rabshakeh, whom the king of Assyria his master hath sent to reproach the living God, and will reprove the words which the LORD thy God hath heard: wherefore lift up *thy* prayer for the**

Understanding II Kings

remnant that is left. Hezekiah mused that perhaps Jehovah God would take note of what Rabshakeh had said and would rebuke him. Thus, Hezekiah directed Isaiah to "lift up *thy* prayer for the remnant that is left." The remnant spoken of undoubtedly was the two remaining tribes of Israel: Judah and Benjamin, which comprised the nation of Judah. Realizing the crisis they faced, Hezekiah knew their only help was through prayer. He thus sent word for Isaiah to pray. 5 **So the servants of king Hezekiah came to Isaiah.**

19:6-7 It appears that Isaiah wasted no time in replying to Hezekiah. It may be that he was waiting with an answer when they arrived. If so, it would be an illustration of Isaiah 65:24, which see. **And Isaiah said unto them, Thus shall ye say unto your master, Thus saith the LORD, Be not afraid of the words that thou hast heard, wherewith the servants of the king of Assyria have blasphemed me.** Appearing once again is the encouragement from God to be not afraid. God had heard the blasphemy and threats of the Assyrians.

He thus sent word via Isaiah, 7 **Behold, I will send a blast upon him, and he shall hear a rumour, and return to his own land; and I will cause him to fall by the sword in his own land.** Of interest is the word translated as **blast** (רוּחַ *ruwach*). It is the common Hebrew word for 'spirit.' It also is routinely translated as 'breath' or 'wind.' Though some commentators apply this to the coming victory over Assyria by God in verses 35-37, the context seems to indicate that God sent word, causing the king of Assyria to hear a rumor (or, a report) which distracted him from Judah. This in turn caused him to return home to tend to trouble there. Indeed, upon returning to Nineveh, Sennacherib was assassinated there.

19:8 Whether or not the message from God via Isaiah to Hezekiah regarding the Assyrians found its way to Rabshakeh is not clear. However, after delivering his threats to Hezekiah, the Assyrian general Rabshakeh departed. **So Rabshakeh returned, and found the king of Assyria warring against Libnah: for he had heard that he was departed from Lachish.** Lachish (pronounced *LaKEESH*)was a fortified city atop a hill in southwestern Judah. Sennacherib, king of Assyria, apparently could not prevail against it, or at least had moved on to attack another city in Judah about nine miles north called Libnah.

19:9-10 Meanwhile, as foretold by God through Isaiah, Sennacherib heard a foreboding rumor. **And he heard say concerning Tirhakah king of Ethiopia, He is come forth to make war with thee.** While fighting against Libnah, Sennacherib received a report that the king of Ethiopia named *Tirhakah* was on his way to attack him. **And when he heard *it*, he sent messengers to Hezekiah, saying, 10 Thus shall ye speak to Hezekiah king of Judah, saying, Let not thy God, in whom thou trustest, deceive thee, saying, Jerusalem shall not be given into the hand of the king of Assyria.**

Lest Hezekiah should think that God had delivered him as He said He would, Sennacherib sent a threatening letter back to him. In that letter, Sennacherib with blasphemy informed Hezekiah that Jehovah God in whom he trusted would not be able to deliver him. In short order, he (i.e., Sennacherib) would return to Jerusalem and destroy it.

19:11-13 With arrogance and haughtiness, Sennacherib warned Hezekiah, **Behold, thou hast heard what the kings of Assyria have done to all lands by destroying them utterly; and shalt thou be delivered?** Once again implying that Jehovah God was no different than the pagan idols of the region, Sennacherib taunted Hezekiah by asking, **12 Have the gods of the nations delivered them which my fathers have**

destroyed, *as* Gozan, and Haran, and Rezeph, and the children of Eden which *were* in Telassar? He listed various gentile cities and city-states of the region which Assyria had overrun. Had their gods delivered them? Furthermore, he taunted, **13 Where *is* the king of Hamath, and the king of Arphad, and the king of the city of Sepharvaim, Hena, and Ivah?** With insolence, Sennacherib asked Hezekiah what had happened to other kings of the regions which had resisted the might of Assyria.

19:14 Once again, Hezekiah was faced with a renewed threat from Assyria. Moreover, it seemed that Sennacherib was more intent than ever in making an example out of a nation so disdainful as Judah which had ignored his demands to surrender. **And Hezekiah received the letter from the hand of the messengers, and read it: and Hezekiah went up unto the house of the LORD, and spread it before the LORD.** This was no small threat. Hezekiah knew he had thumbed his nose at the most powerful king on the face of the earth of that day. He knew the Assyrians would return with vengeance against such an impudent rejection. Hezekiah knew he was in deep trouble. Therefore, he did the best thing he could do. After reading the threatening letter from Sennacherib, Hezekiah went into the Temple of God and spread the very letter out for Jehovah Himself to read.

19:15-19 Thus, Hezekiah did the only thing he could do. He prayed. **And Hezekiah prayed before the LORD, and said, O LORD God of Israel, which dwellest *between* the cherubims, thou art the God, *even* thou alone, of all the kingdoms of the earth; thou hast made heaven and earth.** Notice how his prayer of desperation began by praising God. He acknowledged God's sovereignty over all nations. Moreover, God was the very Creator of heaven and earth.

He thus implored God, **16 LORD, bow down thine ear, and hear: open, LORD, thine eyes, and see: and hear the words of Sennacherib, which hath sent him to reproach the living God.** Hezekiah pled with God to take note of what Sennacherib had said and written. This pagan king had in fact taunted and defied the living God. Hezekiah reminded God of that.

Furthermore, Hezekiah reminded God, **17 Of a truth, LORD, the kings of Assyria have destroyed the nations and their lands, 18 And have cast their gods into the fire: for they *were* no gods, but the work of men's hands, wood and stone: therefore they have destroyed them.** Hezekiah reminded God how that the Assyrians had conquered and destroyed other nations of the region. Moreover, they had destroyed the pagan idols of those same nations. (Implicit was that the testimony of Jehovah was at stake if He allowed the Assyrians to overrun Judah.)

Accordingly, Hezekiah implored God, **19 Now therefore, O LORD our God, I beseech thee, save thou us out of his hand, that all the kingdoms of the earth may know that thou *art* the LORD God, *even* thou only.** The king of Judah thus pled with God to deliver them. Furthermore in so doing, God would make clear to all other nations that He was God alone.

19:20 It once again appears that God wasted no time in answering Hezekiah's prayer. Once again, God answered through the prophet Isaiah. **Then Isaiah the son of Amoz sent to Hezekiah, saying, Thus saith the LORD God of Israel, *That* which thou hast prayed to me against Sennacherib king of Assyria I have heard.** God acknowledged that He had heard the prayer of Hezekiah in the Temple.

19:21-22 God thus sent to Hezekiah a 'copy' of a message evidently sent via Isaiah to Sennacherib. **This *is* the word that the LORD hath spoken concerning him; The virgin the**

daughter of Zion hath despised thee, *and* laughed thee to scorn; the daughter of Jerusalem hath shaken her head at thee. God sent word to Sennacherib that Jerusalem had in fact held his threats in contempt. The "virgin the daughter of Zion" likely refers to Jerusalem or perhaps to Judah itself. The Jews had in effect shaken their heads in contempt at the threats of the Assyrian king. God was now taunting him.

He thus asked, 22 **Whom hast thou reproached and blasphemed? and against whom hast thou exalted** *thy* **voice, and lifted up thine eyes on high?** *even* **against the Holy** *One* **of Israel**. God therefore made clear in His message to Sennacherib that this pagan king had in fact taunted and blasphemed the God of Israel. The Assyrians would soon find out with whom they were dealing.

19:23-24 God therefore reminded Sennacherib of his foolish threats. **By thy messengers thou hast reproached the Lord, and hast said, With the multitude of my chariots I am come up to the height of the mountains, to the sides of Lebanon, and will cut down the tall cedar trees thereof,** *and* **the choice fir trees thereof: and I will enter into the lodgings of his borders,** *and into* **the forest of his Carmel. 24 I have digged and drunk strange waters, and with the sole of my feet have I dried up all the rivers of besieged places**. God threw back into the face of Sennacherib the very threats he had made against Judah. They were braggadocios indeed.

19:25-26 God continued to remind Sennacherib of his taunts, **Hast thou not heard long ago** *how* **I have done it,** *and* **of ancient times that I have formed it? now have I brought it to pass, that thou shouldest be to lay waste fenced cities** *into* **ruinous heaps. 26 Therefore their inhabitants were of small power, they were dismayed and confounded; they were** *as* **the grass of the field, and** *as* **the green herb,** *as* **the**

grass on the housetops, and *as corn* blasted before it be grown up. Though Sennacherib made powerful boasts, God was about to deliver His *coup dé grace*.

19:27-28 God therefore delivered His own warning to Sennacherib. **But I know thy abode, and thy going out, and thy coming in, and thy rage against me**. God in effect said, "I know who you are and where you live." Additionally, God informed the Assyrian king that He was quite aware of his forays against other nations. Furthermore, God let this pompous king know that He was aware of his blasphemy against Him.

Therefore, God informed Sennacherib, **28 Because thy rage against me and thy tumult is come up into mine ears, therefore I will put my hook in thy nose, and my bridle in thy lips, and I will turn thee back by the way by which thou camest**. God reminded this arrogant pagan king of his blasphemous taunts and **tumult**. The latter word is translated from the Hebrew word(שַׁאֲנָן) *sha'anan* and in this context has the sense of 'arrogance.' Therefore God informed Sennacherib that he would put a hook in his nose and a bridle over his lips to shut his mouth and he thus would be turned back in the way he had come. In other words, God would ignominiously defeat him.

19:29-31 The focus of God's message through Isaiah now turns back to Hezekiah. **And this *shall be* a sign unto thee, Ye shall eat this year such things as grow of themselves, and in the second year that which springeth of the same; and in the third year sow ye, and reap, and plant vineyards, and eat the fruits thereof**. God informed Hezekiah that as a sign, he and Judah would eat whatever the land brought forth in the wake of the destructive Assyrian siege. In the next year, they would eat what grew up from those trampled crops. However, in the following season, they would be able to return to planting crops in the normal fashion. The implication is that God would deliver them. Though the Assyrians had devoured their crops by foraging them for themselves, Judah would find enough to live upon in what was left and a year and one-half later, they would enjoy the harvest of their own crops once again. It was a sign given by Jehovah to them.

Furthermore, God promised Hezekiah, **30 And the remnant that is escaped of the house of Judah shall yet again take root downward, and bear fruit upward**. Not only would the crops of Judah once again bear fruit, but also the remnant of the nation itself would again take root downward and bring forth fruit upward.

God promised further, **31 For out of Jerusalem shall go forth a remnant, and they that escape out of mount Zion: the zeal of the LORD *of hosts* shall do this**. God clearly promised that a remnant of his people would escape by His hand. The remnant spoken of here undoubtedly refers to the nation of Judah itself. God would preserve His people who had remained faithful to Him.

19:32-34 Regarding the impending Assyrian threat, God had further good news. **Therefore thus saith the LORD concerning the king of Assyria, He shall not come into this city, nor shoot an arrow there, nor come before it with shield, nor cast a bank against it**. The implication of the context is that Sennacherib and the Assyrian army were not far from Jerusalem. II Chronicles 32 implies the same. Hezekiah's fears were certainly real. But God promised him that the Assyrians would not enter the city. In fact, they would not even get close enough to shoot an arrow against it or undertake any other military operations against it.

33 By the way that he came, by the same shall he return, and shall not come into this city, saith the LORD. By the same route by which Sennacherib had approached Jerusalem would he return in defeat. God promised Hezekiah, **34 For I will**

defend this city, to save it, for mine own sake, and for my servant David's sake. For God's own purposes, He would defend Jerusalem. Furthermore, God would still keep His promise which He had made to David centuries earlier. Then, He had promised that He would maintain a posterity of David's seed upon the throne of Judah. God always keeps His Word.

19:35 In one of the most poignant verses in the entire Bible, the sacred writer records, **And it came to pass that night, that the angel of the LORD went out, and smote in the camp of the Assyrians an hundred fourscore and five thousand: and when they arose early in the morning, behold, they *were* all dead corpses**. By dawn's light, 185,000 Assyrian soldiers lay dead in their tents, slain by the angel of the Lord. The text in almost humorous fashion reads as if when the Assyrians arose, they were all dead. Rather the thought is that when the Jews arose the next morning, the main force of their enemies were dead. God had delivered His people. He had heard the blasphemy and taunts of Sennacherib and his subordinates. There was never any question as to what would happen. When one defies God to do something, be assured He will.

19:36-37 As foretold by God through Isaiah, the prophet, **So Sennacherib king of Assyria departed, and went and returned, and dwelt at Nineveh**. Implicit is that Sennacherib was not in the actual camp of his army which was slain by God. By the way route he had invaded Judah, he and what was left of his forces limped back to Nineveh.

37 **And it came to pass, as he was worshipping in the house of Nisroch his god, that Adrammelech and Sharezer his sons smote him with the sword: and they escaped into the land of Armenia. And Esarhaddon his son reigned in his stead**. While in a pagan Temple in Nineveh, the elder sons of Sennacherib murdered their own father. They thus fled to

Armenia for refuge. Thereafter, another son of Sennacherib, Esarhaddon, assumed rule over Assyria. As God had said in 19:7, Sennacherib came to an untimely end. God's Word always comes true.

* * * * *

Overview of II Kings 20: *This next chapter presents the final years of the reign of Hezekiah in Judah, his sickness, and God's deliverance. The chapter concludes with his folly in revealing the treasures of the palace to Babylonian visitors.*

20:1 In the months after the miraculous defeat of the Assyrian army, **in those days was Hezekiah sick unto death. And the prophet Isaiah the son of Amoz came to him, and said unto him, Thus saith the LORD, Set thine house in order; for thou shalt die, and not live.** Facing a critical illness, God sent word through the prophet for him to prepare for death.

20:2-3 Once again in facing a major crisis of life, Hezekiah turned to heaven for help. **Then he turned his face to the wall, and prayed unto the LORD, saying, 3 I beseech thee, O LORD, remember now how I have walked before thee in truth and with a perfect heart, and have done *that which is* good in thy sight. And Hezekiah wept sore.** The wall in question may have been the wall of the Temple adjacent to Hezekiah's palace. He thus poured out his heart to God in a fervent prayer. Once again, another great prayer is recorded for us. Hezekiah reminded God how over the course of his life that he had walked uprightly before God with complete dedication. (It should be noted that only a person who had actually so lived could make such a claim before God. It is clear that Hezekiah had so lived his life.) He thus broke down and wept before God.

20:4-5 Though God does not always answer prayer on the spot, in this case, here He so chose to do so. **And it came to pass, afore Isaiah was gone out into the middle court, that the word of the LORD came to him.** Before Isaiah had reached the door of the palace, God spoke unto him to return.

God thus directed Isaiah to 5 **turn again, and tell Hezekiah the captain of my people, Thus saith the LORD, the God of David thy father, I have heard thy prayer, I have seen thy tears: behold, I will heal thee: on the third day thou shalt go up unto the house of the LORD.** Isaiah was to return to Hezekiah with the news that God had heard his prayer and seen his tears. Recorded herein is clear evidence how the effectual fervent prayer of a righteous man moves God to act. Hezekiah was informed he would he would be healed and three days later would be able to go to the Temple to worship.

20:6-7 Moreover, God promised, **And I will add unto thy days fifteen years; and I will deliver thee and this city out of the hand of the king of Assyria; and I will defend this city for mine own sake, and for my servant David's sake.** Not only would God add fifteen years to the life of Hezekiah, He further promised to defend Jerusalem from any other attacks from Assyria.

Therefore, 7 **Isaiah said, Take a lump of figs. And they took and laid** *it* **on the boil, and he recovered**. We are now given insight into the illness of Hezekiah. The word translated as **boil** (שְׁחִין *shechiyn*) can refer to a boil, an inflamed spot, an inflammation, or an eruption. It is apparent that whatever sort this was, it was life threatening. It may have been a form of cancer. In any event, God directed Isaiah to take a lump of figs and lay it upon Hezekiah's boil.

The word translated as **recovered** (חָיָה *chayah*) most literally means to 'live' and in this context, 'alive.' God thus directly healed him.

Understanding II Kings

20:8-9 In II Kings 19:29, God had promised a sign to Hezekiah of His impending deliverance. Now, Hezekiah asked for a sign confirming God's promise. **And Hezekiah said unto Isaiah, What** *shall be* **the sign that the LORD will heal me, and that I shall go up into the house of the LORD the third day?** It may be that Hezekiah did not so much doubt God as he questioned the word of Isaiah. Shortly before, Isaiah had announced his death and now he announced his recovery. Hezekiah wanted confirmation of the word of *Isaiah*.

9 **And Isaiah said, This sign shalt thou have of the LORD, that the LORD will do the thing that he hath spoken: shall the shadow go forward ten degrees, or go back ten degrees?** The word translated as **degrees** (מעלה *ma*'alah) literally refers to 'steps' as in a stairway. It may be that in Jerusalem there was some sort of sundial device which utilized the steps of a stairway against a wall. Or, it also is possible that the degrees in question may have been on an actual sundial (though the term *sundial* is not in the text). Isaiah offered him the option of having the shadow of the sun go forward or backward ten degrees.

20:10-11 And Hezekiah answered, It is a light thing for the shadow to go down ten degrees: nay, but let the shadow return backward ten degrees. Hezekiah rightly noted that it was no big deal for the shadow of the sun to go down ten degrees. It did that every day. However, he directed the prophet that the shadow should go backward ten degrees. That would be a real miracle.

11 **And Isaiah the prophet cried unto the LORD: and he brought the shadow ten degrees backward, by which it had gone down in the dial of Ahaz**. Isaiah therefore besought God to move the shadow of the sun backward ten degrees and that is exactly what happened. Isaiah's account also so states this. See Isaiah 38:8. A powerful miracle was thus accomplished as a sign for Hezekiah.

20:12-13 At that time Berodachbaladan, the son of Baladan, king of Babylon, sent letters and a present unto Hezekiah: for he had heard that Hezekiah had been sick. Word of the illness of Hezekiah evidently reached the ears of the new king in Babylon. He thus sent letters of condolence and a gift to him. It should be noted that though Assyria had been the major 'super-power' in the Middle East, a new power was rising in Babylon. Though not as yet a menace to Judah, it would eventually overthrow Assyria and become the dominant power in the Middle East. Also implicit is that the letters and gifts were delivered by emissaries of the king of Babylon.

13 And Hezekiah hearkened unto them, and shewed them all the house of his precious things, the silver, and the gold, and the spices, and the precious ointment, and *all* the house of his armour, and all that was found in his treasures: there was nothing in his house, nor in all his dominion, that Hezekiah shewed them not. Hezekiah therefore foolishly revealed all of his riches as well as in his kingdom to his Babylonian guests. In so doing, he put the nation of Judah on a future target list for Babylonian conquest.

20:14-15 Then came Isaiah the prophet unto king Hezekiah, and said unto him, What said these men? and from whence came they unto thee? And Hezekiah said, They are come from a far country, *even* from Babylon. The following context will make it clear that Isaiah was sent by God to confront Hezekiah for his folly. The prophet thus came and brusquely interrogated Hezekiah as to who his guests had been.

The prophet thus demanded, **15 What have they seen in thine house? And Hezekiah answered, All *the things* that *are* in mine house have they seen: there is nothing among my treasures that I have not shewed them.** The king admitted that he had shown all that he had, perhaps thinking to impress his pagan guests.

20:16-18 The prophet thus rebuked Hezekiah for his foolishness. **And Isaiah said unto Hezekiah, Hear the word of the LORD.** 17 **Behold, the days come, that all that** *is* **in thine house, and that which thy fathers have laid up in store unto this day, shall be carried into Babylon: nothing shall be left, saith the LORD.** Hezekiah was bluntly told that *everything* in his palace and the entire wealth of Judah would someday be carried to Babylon. In trying to impress his guests, he had placed himself on their target list for conquest.

Furthermore, 18 **of thy sons that shall issue from thee, which thou shalt beget, shall they take away; and they shall be eunuchs in the palace of the king of Babylon.** Though more than one-hundred years would pass before this was accomplished, the descendants of Hezekiah and his royal dynasty would someday be servants and eunuchs in the court of Babylon. The sense of the word translated **eunuchs** (סריס *saw-reece*) is unclear. It may refer to men who have been castrated. However, the word also has the sense of being an official in a government. The latter certainly was true in the case of Daniel and his comrades. Whether or not they were neutered is not otherwise clear.

20:19 Then said Hezekiah unto Isaiah, Good *is* **the word of the LORD which thou hast spoken. And he said,** *Is it* **not** *good***, if peace and truth be in my days?** Hezekiah could only reply that God's Word was good. What else could he say? However, Isaiah replied to him, *Is it* **not** *good***, if peace and truth be in my days?** The thought may be, "Would not it be better if peace and truth were in my days?"

20:20-21 Thus, the completion of the reign of Hezekiah is noted. **And the rest of the acts of Hezekiah, and all his might, and how he made a pool, and a conduit, and brought water into the city,** *are* **they not written in the book of the**

chronicles of the kings of Judah? 21 **And Hezekiah slept with his fathers: and Manasseh his son reigned in his stead.** The book of the chronicles mentioned may be the biblical book of II Chronicles. Reference is also again made to the tunnel (conduit) which he made to bring water into Jerusalem for military purposes. That tunnel exists to this day. After the death of Hezekiah, his son Manasseh ascended the throne of Judah.

* * * * *

Overview of II Kings 21: The beginning of the end of the nation of Judah is at hand. In this chapter, the reigns of Manasseh and Amon over Judah are recorded. Both were wicked and incurred the wrath of God.

21:1-2 Though Hezekiah had been a godly king, his son Manasseh was not. **Manasseh *was* twelve years old when he began to reign, and reigned fifty and five years in Jerusalem. And his mother's name *was* Hephzibah.** Of interest is that the name *Hephzibah* means 'my delight is in her.' Unfortunately, the same would not be said of Manasseh. This young king, though reigning a long time, would incur the wrath of God against Judah. 2 **And he did *that which was* evil in the sight of the LORD, after the abominations of the heathen, whom the LORD cast out before the children of Israel.**

21:3-4 The sacred historian thus begins a litany of the wickedness of Manasseh. **For he built up again the high places which Hezekiah his father had destroyed; and he reared up altars for Baal, and made a grove, as did Ahab king of Israel; and worshipped all the host of heaven, and served them.** Though Hezekiah had removed pagan high places from Judah, Manasseh restored them. He restored pagan

Baal worship in Judah, growing a grove of trees thereto. He became involved in astrology in following the order of the stars. Furthermore, he blasphemed Jehovah God in that **4 he built altars in the house of the LORD, of which the LORD said, In Jerusalem will I put my name**. He was so brazen in his idolatry that he even erected pagan idols in the Temple of God, mocking God's choice of Jerusalem as the city of testimony to Him.

21:5-6 Moreover, **he built altars for all the host of heaven in the two courts of the house of the LORD**. Not only did he dabble with astrology, Manasseh even further desecrated the Temple by building altars to the sun, moon, and stars in the court of the priests and the court of the people.

If that were not enough, **6 he made his son pass through the fire, and observed times, and used enchantments, and dealt with familiar spirits and wizards**. He offered his own sons to the pagan abomination of Molech. He also became involved with black magic and the occult. The sacred writer therefore summarizes his wickedness by noting that **he wrought much wickedness in the sight of the LORD, to provoke *him* to anger**.

21:7-8 And he set a graven image of the grove that he had made in the house, of which the LORD said to David, and to Solomon his son, In this house, and in Jerusalem, which I have chosen out of all tribes of Israel, will I put my name for ever. The blasphemy of Manasseh reached its depth when he set up a pagan idol in the Temple of God at Jerusalem. The sacred writer thus quoted what God had said to David and Solomon regarding the Temple. See II Samuel 7:13 and I Kings 8:29. Manasseh had thereby desecrated the very Temple built to worship Jehovah God.

Continuing to quote what God had said about the Temple, the text continues, **8 Neither will I make the feet of Israel**

move any more out of the land which I gave their fathers. In placing His name at the Temple, God had promised to not remove Israel from their land. However, He reiterated the basic condition of that promise, **Only if they will observe to do according to all that I have commanded them, and according to all the law that my servant Moses commanded them**. That basic condition was obedience. See Isaiah 1:19.

21:9 Tragically, **they hearkened not: and Manasseh seduced them to do more evil than did the nations whom the LORD destroyed before the children of Israel**. The sad indictment against Israel is that "they hearkened not" to God. That is, they were disobedient to His Word. Furthermore, Manasseh enticed Israel to do even more evil than the pagan, gentile nations whom God had directed them to destroy (the Canaanites) centuries earlier.

21:10-12 And the LORD spake by his servants the prophets. During the final century of the existence of Judah, God clearly warned His people through prophets such as Isaiah, Joel, Nahum, and Habakkuk. The collective essence of message from God by the prophets during that time was **11 because Manasseh king of Judah hath done these abominations, *and* hath done wickedly above all that the Amorites did, which *were* before him, and hath made Judah also to sin with his idols**.

Because of the abominable idolatry of Manasseh which the people willingly accepted, God sent this word. **12 Therefore thus saith the LORD God of Israel, Behold, I *am* bringing *such* evil upon Jerusalem and Judah, that whosoever heareth of it, both his ears shall tingle**. God made a similar statement against Eli in I Samuel 3:11, which see. The wrath of God against Jerusalem and Judah via Manasseh was such that the ears of all who heard thereof would ring from the shock.

Understanding II Kings

21:13-14 Specifically, God warned, **And I will stretch over Jerusalem the line of Samaria, and the plummet of the house of Ahab: and I will wipe Jerusalem as** *a man* **wipeth a dish, wiping** *it***, and turning** *it* **upside down.**

Two analogies of the judgment of God are presented. First, God hearkened to the judgment which He had sent against the northern kingdom. The mention of a line and plummet is a reference to instruments of measurement. A line may refer to what today is called a 'tape-measure.' A plummet was an instrument for determining level (or vertical) such as a level and more likely a plum-bob. With poetic eloquence, God said with the same measure which He dealt with the northern ten tribes (i.e., Samaria) and Ahab, He would also deal with Judah and Jerusalem. The second analogy (better understood by women) was that he would wipe Jerusalem clean like one would wipe a dish and then turn it upside down to dry. God foretold His impending wrath against Jerusalem and Judah because of the sin of Manasseh.

Furthermore, God warned, **14 I will forsake the remnant of mine inheritance, and deliver them into the hand of their enemies; and they shall become a prey and a spoil to all their enemies.** Judah, the remnant of Israel, would be delivered to its enemies who would despoil the nation.

21:15 The reason for God's wrath was simple: **because they have done** *that which was* **evil in my sight, and have provoked me to anger, since the day their fathers came forth out of Egypt, even unto this day.** God recalled the rebellion and disobedience of Israel from the earliest days of the Exodus. Israel had rebelled against Him from day one. God had had enough.

21:16 Moreover Manasseh shed innocent blood very much, till he had filled Jerusalem from one end to another;

beside his sin wherewith he made Judah to sin, in doing *that which was* evil in the sight of the LORD. The innocent blood noted is not further described. However, one may conclude that Manasseh killed any and all who dared oppose his wickedness. Furthermore, he promoted the abomination of Molech in which innocent children perished in its despicable mouth. God had had it. Judah had cooked their goose. Clearly implied is that Jerusalem and Judah went along with the wickedness of Manasseh. See II Chronicles 33:10

21:17-18 The end of the reign of Manasseh is thus recorded. **Now the rest of the acts of Manasseh, and all that he did, and his sin that he sinned, *are* they not written in the book of the chronicles of the kings of Judah?** Further detail regarding the sin of Manasseh may be found in II Chronicles 33.

Thus, 18 **Manasseh slept with his fathers, and was buried in the garden of his own house, in the garden of Uzza: and Amon his son reigned in his stead.** At the age of sixty-seven, Manasseh died and was buried in his own private garden rather than where most of the kings were buried in the city of David. He was not considered worthy to occupy the same ground as those who had gone before him. His son, Amon, thus succeeded him.

21:19-20 Amon *was* **twenty and two years old when he began to reign, and he reigned two years in Jerusalem. And his mother's name *was* Meshullemeth, the daughter of Haruz of Jotbah.** Though a young king, Amon 20 **did *that which was* evil in the sight of the LORD, as his father Manasseh did.**

21:21-22 Specifically, Amon **walked in all the way that his father walked in, and served the idols that his father served, and worshipped them:** 22 **And he forsook the LORD**

God of his fathers, and walked not in the way of the LORD. Manasseh's young son did exactly as had his father. He was an idolater who forsook Jehovah God of his forefathers. Accordingly, he "walked not in the way of the LORD." Though his grandfather Hezekiah had risen above the wickedness of his father Ahaz to become a godly king, Amon ignored any inclination in that direction and continued on in the wickedness of his father Manasseh.

21:23-24 His arrogant rule was such that his own servants did him in. **And the servants of Amon conspired against him, and slew the king in his own house.** Not unlike Zimri in the northern kingdom, Amon's servants could not stomach his arrogance. However, 24 **the people of the land slew all them that had conspired against king Amon; and the people of the land made Josiah his son king in his stead.** Even the people of the land were fed up with the wickedness and power grabs going on in Jerusalem. Therefore, they killed the conspirators against Amon and installed his son, Josiah, as king.

21:25-26 Now the rest of the acts of Amon which he did, *are* they not written in the book of the chronicles of the kings of Judah? Further details of the short reign of Amon may be found in II Chronicles 33:21-25. 26 **And he was buried in his sepulchre in the garden of Uzza: and Josiah his son reigned in his stead.** Amon was evidently buried in the same place as his father, Manasseh—the garden of Uzza.

* * * * *

Overview of II Kings 22: Notwithstanding the wickedness of his father and grandfather before him, Josiah turned out to be one of the greatest and godly kings of Judah. Through his rule, a great revival broke out in the land. Recorded in this chapter is the discovery of the Law of God and the staying of God's judgment against Judah because of the righteousness of king Josiah.

22:1 Josiah *was* eight years old when he began to reign, and he reigned thirty and one years in Jerusalem. And his mother's name *was* Jedidah, the daughter of Adaiah of Boscath. As a little boy of eight, Josiah ascended to the throne of Israel. His reign would be cut short by his ill-advised expedition against the Egyptians noted in the next chapter. His mother is noted who evidently was a wife of Amon. Nothing more is known of her. The morality (or lack thereof) of his father is apparent in that he was only sixteen years old when he fathered Josiah by Jedidah.

22:2 Notwithstanding that, Josiah **did *that which was* right in the sight of the LORD, and walked in all the way of David his father, and turned not aside to the right hand or to the left.**

It is apparent that young Josiah had godly influence throughout his youth. Whether that was through his mother or others is not recorded. His godly character is summarized in that (1) he did that which was right, (2) he walked in the way of David his forefather, and (3) he did not deviate in the least from so ordering his life. He focused his life in the center of God's will and Word and departed not therefrom.

22:3 And it came to pass in the eighteenth year of king Josiah, *that* the king sent Shaphan the son of Azaliah, the son of Meshullam, the scribe, to the house of the LORD. When Josiah was twenty-six years old, he sent Shaphan, his secretary of state, to the Temple which had fallen into disrepair after more than a half-century of disregard by Manasseh and Amon.

22:4-6 The instructions to Shaphan were to **go up to Hilkiah the high priest, that he may sum the silver which is brought into the house of the LORD, which the keepers of the door have gathered of the people.** Shaphan was to direct the high priest (Hilkiah) to count and account of the funds which had been received at the Temple from the people of Judah.

5 And let them deliver it into the hand of the doers of the work, that have the oversight of the house of the LORD. The treasurers of the Temple were then to present these funds to contractors for the repair of the Temple.

And let them give it to the doers of the work which *is* in the house of the LORD, to repair the breaches of the house, 6 Unto carpenters, and builders, and masons, and to buy timber and hewn stone to repair the house. It is apparent that the Temple had fallen into disrepair. Josiah therefore directed that immediate steps be taken in hiring contractors to begin repairs thereon.

22:7 Because of the urgency of the need and the reputation of those hired, **there was no reckoning made with them of the money that was delivered into their hand, because they dealt faithfully.** The integrity of the contractors and the nature of the work was such that they trusted them in their disbursement of funds. They clearly were faithful men—men of integrity and honor.

22:8-10 As the work progressed in the renovation of the Temple, **Hilkiah the high priest said unto Shaphan the scribe, I have found the book of the law in the house of the LORD. And Hilkiah gave the book to Shaphan, and he read it.** It is apparent that the Word of God had fallen into disuse. Though not lost, it was no longer read. Evidently, Shaphan, the king's secretary, had never read it before because he immediately sat down to read thereof.

9 And Shaphan the scribe came to the king, and brought the king word again, and said, Thy servants have gathered the money that was found in the house, and have delivered it into the hand of them that do the work, that have the oversight of the house of the LORD. The king's secretary thus reported back to the king regarding the progress of the Temple restoration project. Almost as an afterthought, he also reported to Josiah that 10 **Hilkiah the priest hath delivered me a book. And Shaphan read it before the king.**

22:11 And it came to pass, when the king had heard the words of the book of the law, that he rent his clothes. In his notes for this section, C. I. Scofield commented "*By the law is the knowledge of sin.*" As Josiah heard the Law of God, likely from Leviticus or Deuteronomy, he was convicted of the sin of the nation and of his forefathers. He thus ripped his royal clothing as a demonstration of his despair and sorrow. It is apparent that even godly Josiah had not heretofore been directly exposed to the Word of God.

22:12-13 Therefore, **the king commanded Hilkiah the priest, and Ahikam the son of Shaphan, and Achbor the son of Michaiah, and Shaphan the scribe, and Asahiah a servant of the king's, saying, 13 Go ye, enquire of the LORD for me, and for the people, and for all Judah, concerning the words of this book that is found: for great *is* the wrath of the LORD that is kindled against us, because our fathers have not hearkened unto the words of this book, to do according unto all that which is written concerning us.**

Upon hearing the ominous warnings of God in Deuteronomy (or perhaps Leviticus) against Israel if they forsook God's Law, Josiah therefore sent a delegation of high officials to enquire of the Lord regarding Judah. He realized, for the first time in his life, the impending wrath of God against his king-

Understanding II Kings

dom. He knew full well how his forefathers had utterly disregarded God's Word. Now, he had heard from God's Word what God promised for such sin. In Deuteronomy 28, God made it very clear that His people would be removed from their land. Josiah was all too aware of what had happened to the northern ten tribes. He now realized that same fate faced his kingdom.

22:14 So Hilkiah the priest, and Ahikam, and Achbor, and Shaphan, and Asahiah, went unto Huldah the prophetess, the wife of Shallum the son of Tikvah, the son of Harhas, keeper of the wardrobe; (now she dwelt in Jerusalem in the college;) and they communed with her. The fact that the royal delegation went to a female prophet indicates there was no other prophet or priest in the land which had any power with God. Apparently, Huldah was the only such godly person in the realm. The word translated **college** (משנה *mishneh*) is uncertain. In any event, the royal delegation turned to Huldah for word from God.

22:15-17 God had a message for Judah and Josiah. It was not what they wanted to hear. **And she said unto them, Thus saith the LORD God of Israel, Tell the man that sent you to me.** Huldah clearly spoke on behalf of God with the declaration, "*Thus saith the LORD.*" She had a message from God to be delivered to the king.

That message was, **16 Thus saith the LORD, Behold, I will bring evil upon this place, and upon the inhabitants thereof, even all the words of the book which the king of Judah hath read.** It may be that Josiah had read Leviticus 26:14-45 or Deuteronomy 28:15-68. There, God warned of the curses He would bring against the Lord for disobedience to His Word.

Specifically and on behalf of God, Huldah warned it was **17 because they have forsaken me, and have burned incense unto other gods, that they might provoke me to anger with** all the works of their hands; therefore my wrath shall be kindled against this place, and shall not be quenched. Judah had forsaken their God by turning to other idolatrous gods, provoking Him to anger. Therefore, His wrath was impending against Jerusalem. Moreover, nothing they could do would prevent God's wrath from falling upon them.

22:18-20 However, Huldah offered this reprieve for Josiah. **But to the king of Judah which sent you to enquire of the LORD, thus shall ye say to him, Thus saith the LORD God of Israel, *As touching* the words which thou hast heard**. God however was well aware of the godly character of Josiah and his attempts to restore righteousness to the kingdom.

Therefore, God informed the young king, **19 because thine heart was tender, and thou hast humbled thyself before the LORD, when thou heardest what I spake against this place, and against the inhabitants thereof, that they should become a desolation and a curse, and hast rent thy clothes, and wept before me; I also have heard *thee*, saith the LORD**. God noticed how that (1) Josiah had a tender heart and (2) how he had humbled himself before God. Because (3) of his godly sorrow over the sin of his kingdom, God informed Josiah that He had heard his prayer.

God therefore informed Josiah, **20 Behold therefore, I will gather thee unto thy fathers, and thou shalt be gathered into thy grave in peace; and thine eyes shall not see all the evil which I will bring upon this place. And they brought the king word again**.

The wrath of God would not be turned away from Judah. However, because of the righteous heart, humility, and godly sorrow of Josiah, God promised that His wrath would not come in Josiah's lifetime. It would be postponed. Though Josiah would die an untimely death, it would not be connected with God's wrath against Judah. His righteous spirit had deferred the

Understanding II Kings

judgment of God. It would still come, but not in Josiah's lifetime.

* * * * *

Overview of II Kings 23: *After hearing the words of the book of the Law, Josiah then read God's Word to the assembled nation and made a covenant before them to serve the Lord. The chapter then lists the reformations and purging of idolatry from the land by Josiah. Record is also made of the re-insti-ution of the Passover in Judah by Josiah. His untimely death is recorded followed by brief account of his ungodly successors in Jehoahaz and Jehoiakim.*

23:1-2 After hearing the reading of the Law of Moses by Huldah, **the king sent, and they gathered unto him all the elders of Judah and of Jerusalem. 2 And the king went up into the house of the LORD, and all the men of Judah and all the inhabitants of Jerusalem with him, and the priests, and the prophets, and all the people, both small and great: and he read in their ears all the words of the book of the covenant which was found in the house of the LORD.** Josiah thus assembled the entire leadership as well as all of the men of Jerusalem and Judah to the Temple where he, himself, read to them "the words of the book of the covenant." Precisely which portions of the Law were read is not sure. But it likely may have been from Exodus 24 as well as portions of Deuteronomy warning of God's chastening upon Israel if they forsook Him.

23:3 Moreover, **the king stood by a pillar, and made a covenant before the LORD, to walk after the LORD, and to keep his commandments and his testimonies and his statutes with all *their* heart and all *their* soul, to perform the**

words of this covenant that were written in this book. And all the people stood to the covenant.

It may be that Josiah stood upon the brazen scaffold which Solomon had made for official appearances at the Temple. See II Kings 11:14. In any event, he there publicly recommitted himself to a covenant with the Lord (1) to walk after the Lord, (2) to obey His commandments, testimonies and statutes (i.e., all the laws of God, moral, civil, and ceremonial). Implicit in the text is that the king made this covenant with God on behalf of the nation that they as well would obey all of God's word "with all *their* heart and all *their* soul." Furthermore, the king determined before his people (3) to perform the words of the covenant written in God's Word. Evidently, in standing to the covenant, the men of Judah publicly agreed thereto.

23:4 Josiah lost no time in proceeding to purge idolatry from Judah. **And the king commanded Hilkiah the high priest, and the priests of the second order, and the keepers of the door, to bring forth out of the Temple of the LORD all the vessels that were made for Baal, and for the grove, and for all the host of heaven: and he burned them without Jerusalem in the fields of Kidron, and carried the ashes of them unto Bethel.**

Josiah thus ordered those in authority at the Temple to rid the Temple of anything which pertained to Baal, their groves, and worship of the heavens. The "priests of the second order" likely refers to the second course of priests which were on duty when ordered to cleanse the Temple. The "keepers of the door" were Levites. Thus, all priests and Levites on duty at the Temple were ordered to throw out anything which was idolatrous.

Not only were there items pertaining to Baal worship, but also the idol of the grove for Ashtoreth. There also were items pertaining to worship of the heavens. All of these Josiah ordered burned in the Kidron valley just east of and below the Temple.

Understanding II Kings

The ashes thereof were then carried to Bethel (in what had been the northern kingdom). This was where Jeroboam had first erected a golden calf centuries earlier. In so sending the ashes there, Josiah showed contempt of that place and his detestation of the idolatry there.

23:5-7 Moreover, Josiah **put down the idolatrous priests, whom the kings of Judah had ordained to burn incense in the high places in the cities of Judah, and in the places round about Jerusalem; them also that burned incense unto Baal, to the sun, and to the moon, and to the planets, and to all the host of heaven.** Josiah thus removed the priests of the idolatrous places in Jerusalem and throughout Judah.

6 **And he brought out the grove from the house of the LORD, without Jerusalem, unto the brook Kidron, and burned it at the brook Kidron, and stamped *it* small to powder, and cast the powder thereof upon the graves of the children of the people.** The context lends itself to the idea that the *grove* in the house of the Lord was rather a carved one, as some think the image of the grove, possibly of Ashtoreth itself. This Josiah had burned at the Kidron brook in the deep valley just east and beneath the Temple mount. He then ordered the ashes thereof ground into powder and cast them upon the graves of those who had worshiped these idols. See II Chronicles 34:3-4.

Furthermore, 7 **Josiah brake down the houses of the sodomites, that *were* by the house of the LORD, where the women wove hangings for the grove.** In the midst of the apostasy which had overtaken Jerusalem, homosexuality had also come out of the closet to openness. The association between apostasy and such immorality is not a coincidence. The reference may be to a house of homosexual prostitution or at the least homosexual activity. Also, trappings for idolatrous worship were manufactured at this same place. Josiah destroyed it all.

23:8-9 Josiah also **brought all the priests out of the cities of Judah, and defiled the high places where the priests had burned incense, from Geba to Beersheba, and brake down the high places of the gates that *were* in the entering in of the gate of Joshua the governor of the city, which *were* on a man's left hand at the gate of the city.**

The king then ordered all the priests from their homes throughout Judah to defile the high places scattered across the realm. This may have been accomplished by placing dead carcases upon the high places across the land. Geba and Beersheba were the northern and southern extremities of Judah respectively. There evidently were also high places at one of the very gates of Jerusalem on the left-hand side. Josiah destroyed these as well. The mention of Joshua, governor of the city, evidently refers to a chief magistrate or 'mayor' of the city.

9 Nevertheless the priests of the high places came not up to the altar of the LORD in Jerusalem, but they did eat of the unleavened bread among their brethren. This apparently refers to priests of Jehovah who had compromised their ministry by offering sacrifices upon spurious high places around the kingdom. They were thus no longer allowed to come to the official altar of Jehovah at Jerusalem. However, they were permitted to partake of the holy things with the priests, such as the meal offerings made of unleavened flour. Josiah was thorough in purging sin and compromise from his kingdom.

23:10 Furthermore, **Josiah defiled Topheth, which *is* in the valley of the children of Hinnom, that no man might make his son or his daughter to pass through the fire to Molech**. The valley of Hinnom (also known as Gehenna in the New Testament) was immediately to the south of the ancient city of Jerusalem. For centuries, there had been a city dump which through spontaneous combustion was continuously on fire. There also was located the image of Molech, the pagan idol

Understanding II Kings 347

to which infant children were made to pass through its flames. Josiah thus destroyed this abomination.

23:11-12 The purging of wickedness form Judah by Josiah was relentless and thorough. **And he took away the horses that the kings of Judah had given to the sun, at the entering in of the house of the LORD, by the chamber of Nathanmelech the chamberlain, which *was* in the suburbs, and burned the chariots of the sun with fire.** Though some think these were real horses, the context lends itself to the view that they were statues thereof (graven images) which had been dedicated by earlier kings of Judah to the worship of the sun. There also were chariots for these pagan idols to sun worship nearby which Josiah also destroyed.

Also, 12 **the altars that *were* on the top of the upper chamber of Ahaz, which the kings of Judah had made, and the altars which Manasseh had made in the two courts of the house of the LORD, did the king beat down, and brake *them* down from thence, and cast the dust of them into the brook Kidron.** Earlier kings of Judah evidently had erected pagan, idolatrous altars upon the roof of the royal palace which Ahaz had built. The apostate king Manasseh also had erected pagan altars in the outer courts of the Temple. Josiah there had them violently thrown down, broken up, and ground into powder. He once again cast the dust thereof into the brook Kidron.

23:13-14 Josiah was relentless in purging all vestiges of idolatry from Jerusalem. **And the high places that *were* before Jerusalem, which *were* on the right hand of the mount of corruption, which Solomon the king of Israel had builded for Ashtoreth the abomination of the Zidonians, and for Chemosh the abomination of the Moabites, and for Milcom the abomination of the children of Ammon, did the king defile.** What is astounding is that some of these corrupt high places had existed since the time of Solomon approximately 375 years earlier. The mount of corruption is thought to be the Mount of Olives immediately east of Jerusalem. Evidently, along the way to the Jerusalem from the Mount of Olives were pagan high places built to Ashtoreth, Chemosh, and Milcom, the idolatrous abominations of neighboring pagan nations. Josiah proceeded to destroy each of these.

He thus 14 **brake in pieces the images, and cut down the groves, and filled their places with the bones of men**. Not only did Josiah utterly destroy these places, he also desecrated them by placing the bones of dead men thereon rendering them unfit to ever be used for any kind of worship.

23:15 Having utterly purged the idolatry scattered throughout Judah, Josiah now turned his attention to the apostasy of the now defunct northern kingdom. Israel (the northern kingdom). The latter had been deported from their land for almost one-hundred years. The Assyrian influence there had waned. Therefore, **the altar that *was* at Bethel, *and* the high place which Jeroboam the son of Nebat, who made Israel to sin, had made, both that altar and the high place he brake down, and burned the high place, *and* stamped *it* small to powder, and burned the grove**. Though not in Judah as such, Josiah traveled north to Bethel and utterly destroyed what originally had been one of the high places for the golden calves erected by Jeroboam I centuries earlier.

23:16-18 While at Bethel, **as Josiah turned himself, he spied the sepulchres that *were* there in the mount, and sent, and took the bones out of the sepulchres, and burned *them* upon the altar, and polluted it, according to the word of the LORD which the man of God proclaimed, who proclaimed these words**. Josiah saw tombs near mount Bethel. He thus ordered them opened and the bones of those buried therein were to be burned and their ashes spread upon the idolatrous altar of Bethel thus desecrating it. These likely were the graves of the priests and other worshipers of the golden calves. About 350 years earlier, a man of God from Judah had foretold the day when Josiah would burn the bones of the priests of the golden calves upon their own altar. See I Kings 13:1-3. That prophecy found its fulfillment here. Josiah, no doubt was aware thereof.

However, as Josiah continued to look about Bethel, he said, **17 What title *is* that that I see? And the men of the city told him, *It is* the sepulchre of the man of God, which came from Judah, and proclaimed these things that thou hast done against the altar of Bethel.** Upon a grave marker, Josiah read an inscription which caught his attention. He therefore inquired of the local population about it. They in turn informed him that it was the grave of the man of God from Judah who had prophesied (350 years earlier) what Josiah did that day.

18 And he said, Let him alone; let no man move his bones. So they let his bones alone, with the bones of the prophet that came out of Samaria. Josiah ordered that the grave of this prophet not be disturbed. Reference is also made to the compromising prophet of Samaria who had directed that his own body be buried with the prophet of Judah. It should be noted that tombs of Israel down through the centuries were not caskets in the ground as is common in America. Rather, they were crypts in which the bones of the deceased were placed after their flesh had decomposed in a preliminary grave.

23:19-20 Josiah continued his campaign of exterminating idolatry out of not only Judah but also the largely empty land of Israel to the north. **And all the houses also of the high places that *were* in the cities of Samaria, which the kings of Israel had made to provoke *the* LORD to anger, Josiah took away, and did to them according to all the acts that he had done in Bethel.** He purged the land of the northern kingdom even as he had Judah. Furthermore, **20 he slew all the priests of the high places that *were* there upon the altars, and burned men's bones upon them, and returned to Jerusalem**. Josiah rounded up all remaining priests of these idolatrous shrines and killed them. Wherever he found idolatrous altars, even in the defunct northern kingdom, he desecrated them by burning dead men's bones upon them. Having accomplished to the best of his knowledge his campaign to exterminate idolatry from the whole of Israel, Josiah returned to Jerusalem.

23:21-23 Upon his return to Jerusalem, **the king commanded all the people, saying, Keep the passover unto the LORD your God, as *it is* written in the book of this covenant**. It is apparent that the observance of the Passover in Judah had faded into oblivion. Josiah therefore ordered that it be observed once again as commanded in the book of Exodus.

Moreover, **22 surely there was not holden such a passover from the days of the judges that judged Israel, nor in all the days of the kings of Israel, nor of the kings of Judah**. Throughout the centuries in which Israel had occupied their land, no Passover had been celebrated to the degree which Josiah ordered. What is remarkable is that his observance of the Passover exceeded anything which had ever been done from the time of Joshua including the reigns of David, Solomon, Jehoshaphat, Hezekiah, or any other king of Judah. Josiah was determined to honor the Lord His God as had no other king before him. That he did. It was **23 in the eighteenth year of king Josiah, *wherein* this passover was holden to the LORD in Jerusalem**. In having some years to comprehend the importance of the sacred character of Passover, Josiah ordered this major observance. For further details see II Chronicles 35:1-19.

23:24 Throughout his reign, as Josiah became aware of further ungodliness in his kingdom he rooted it out. **Moreover the**

workers with **familiar spirits, and the wizards, and the images, and the idols, and all the abominations that were spied in the land of Judah and in Jerusalem, did Josiah put away, that he might perform the words of the law which were written in the book that Hilkiah the priest found in the house of the LORD.** Not only did Josiah purge idolatry from the land, he also got rid of anyone involved with occult activities. Noteworthy is the association implied here between idolatry and the occult. Even more significant was the determination of Josiah to obey the written Word of God in every detail. Whatever he read in the Word of God, Josiah set out to obey in the uttermost.

23:25 The sacred historian under the inspiration of the Holy Spirit thus notes, **And like unto him was there no king before him, that turned to the LORD with all his heart, and with all his soul, and with all his might, according to all the law of Moses; neither after him arose there *any* like him**. In the history of either Judah or Israel, there was no king, before or after, which turned to the Lord with (1) all his heart, (2) all his soul, and (3) all his might as did Josiah. He obeyed the Law of God in its every detail to the utmost of his ability. What is even more significant is that sacred writ thus places Josiah on a higher plane spiritually than even King David. He truly was one of the great kings of Judah (and certainly greater than any king of Israel).

23:26-27 Sadly, the sin of Judah had accumulated to such a degree in his predecessors that even the righteousness of Josiah could not stay the wrath of God against Judah. **Notwithstanding the LORD turned not from the fierceness of his great wrath, wherewith his anger was kindled against Judah, because of all the provocations that Manasseh had provoked him withal.** 27 **And the LORD said, I will remove**

Judah also out of my sight, as I have removed Israel, and will cast off this city Jerusalem which I have chosen, and the house of which I said, My name shall be there.

The sin of Manasseh, Josiah's grandfather, was such that God had had it with Judah. The righteousness of Josiah only delayed that judgment. It would not come in Josiah's lifetime as God had promised him. See II Kings 22:19-20. Just beneath the surface is the truth that God always keeps His Word. He promised in Leviticus 26 and Deuteronomy 28 that if His people departed from Him, He eventually would remove them from their land. But God also promised Josiah it would not come in his lifetime. God kept both His written Word as well as His spoken Word. He always keeps His Word.

23:28-30 Perhaps in foolishness or perhaps in God's providential timing—likely both, Josiah placed himself in a situation in which he died an untimely death. **Now the rest of the acts of Josiah, and all that he did, *are* they not written in the book of the chronicles of the kings of Judah?** Further details of the reign of Josiah may be found in II Chronicles 34-35.

29 In his days Pharaohnechoh king of Egypt went up against the king of Assyria to the river Euphrates: and king Josiah went against him; and he slew him at Megiddo, when he had seen him. International politics so conspired that Egypt went to war against Assyria to the north and east. The Egyptian army, led by "Pharaohnechoh king of Egypt" marched through Judah without the permission of Josiah. The king of Judah therefore imprudently marched out to do battle with the discourteous Egyptians at Megiddo.

The Egyptians, though encroaching upon the kingdom of Judah had no fight with Josiah and they let him know that. See II Chronicles 35:20-27. However, Josiah persisted. Thus, in one of the great battlefields of history, the valley of Jezreel beneath

Understanding II Kings

mount Megiddo, Josiah was slain in battle by Egyptian forces. It may have been imprudence on the part of Josiah. It may have been the providential timing of God for greater fulfillment of the divine calendar. Likely, it was a combination of both. God allowed Josiah to foolishly confront the Egyptians to his death. Thus, at about the age of thirty-nine, this great king slept with his fathers.

30 And his servants carried him in a chariot dead from Megiddo, and brought him to Jerusalem, and buried him in his own sepulchre. And the people of the land took Jehoahaz the son of Josiah, and anointed him, and made him king in his father's stead. After burying their king, the men of Judah placed his son, Jehoahaz, upon the throne of Judah. Sadly, the son of this great king did not follow in his father's footsteps.

23:31-33 Jehoahaz *was* twenty and three years old when he began to reign; and he reigned three months in Jerusalem. And his mother's name *was* Hamutal, the daughter of Jeremiah of Libnah. The mother of Jehoahaz is noted as that of Jeremiah of Libnah. Though the time frame here is contemporaneous with Jeremiah the prophet, the latter was from the town of Anathoth in Benjamin. (See Jeremiah 1:1-2.) Libnah was in southwestern Judah. There likely is no relation therefore to the prophet Jeremiah.

This young king reigned for only three months. **32 And he did *that which was* evil in the sight of the LORD, according to all that his fathers had done.** Several things are amazing. (1) As a young man and in reigning only three months, God already noted him as evil. (2) Though the son of one of the greatest and godliest kings of Judah, he did not follow in the character of his father. One reason may have been a less-than dedicated mother who influenced him. (3) This young king reverted back to the wickedness of his forefathers.

Accordingly, God allowed **Pharaohnechoh put him in bands at Riblah in the land of Hamath, that he might not reign in Jerusalem; and put the land to a tribute of an hundred talents of silver, and a talent of gold.** Riblah in Hamath was in Syria. What Jehoahaz was doing there after being king for only three months is not noted. One thing is for sure. He did not belong there. (It might be inferred that this young king foolishly set out to avenge the death of his father. However, the text is silent at this point.) The Egyptian king therefore deposed him as king and imposed a tribute tax upon Judah of one-hundred talents of silver and a talent of gold. This may have been an annual tax.

23:34 And Pharaohnechoh made Eliakim the son of Josiah king in the room of Josiah his father, and turned his name to Jehoiakim, and took Jehoahaz away: and he came to Egypt, and died there. After deposing Jehoahaz from the throne of Judah, the Egyptians placed his brother Eliakim on the throne and renamed him Jehoiakim. The name *Eliakim* means "God raises" or "God sets up." The name *Jehoiakim* means "Jehovah raises up." Precisely why Pharaohnechoh changed his name is unclear other than perhaps to assert who was in charge, forcing the young king of Judah to even change his name.

23:35-37 And Jehoiakim gave the silver and the gold to Pharaoh; but he taxed the land to give the money according to the commandment of Pharaoh: he exacted the silver and the gold of the people of the land, of every one according to his taxation, to give *it* unto Pharaohnechoh. To pay the heavy tribute money to Egypt, Jehoiakim taxed the people of Judah. He thus paid the Egyptians.

36 Jehoiakim *was* twenty and five years old when he began to reign; and he reigned eleven years in Jerusalem. And his mother's name *was* Zebudah, the daughter of

Understanding II Kings

Pedaiah of Rumah. 37 And he did *that which was* **evil in the sight of the LORD, according to all that his fathers had done.** Evidently two years older than his brother Jehoahaz, Jehoiakim ascended the throne of Judah and reigned for eleven years. Notwithstanding the fact that he had the same godly father as his brother in Josiah, this young king did evil before God as his forefathers had done. The fate of Judah was thus sealed.

* * * * *

Overview of II Kings 24: The beginning of the end of the southern kingdom is at hand. The Babylonians imposed sovereignty over Judah under Jehoiakim. Notwithstanding, King Jehoiakim did wickedly before God. After his death, the first of the Babylonian deportations began with King Jehoiachin being deported. The chapter concludes with Zedekiah his son rebelling against the Babylonians.

24:1 In his days Nebuchadnezzar king of Babylon came up, and Jehoiakim became his servant three years: then he turned and rebelled against him. During the reign of Jehoiakim, son of Josiah, the Babylonians invaded Judah and defeated it. Jehoiakim was allowed to remain as king on the condition that he be in subjection to the Babylonians and obey their edicts. The Babylonian ruler was *Nebuchadnezzar*. According to Daniel 1:1-2, this was the time when Daniel and his companions were deported to Babylon. The date was 606 B.C. However, after agreeing to Babylonian sovereignty, Jehoiakim rebelled three years later.

24:2-4 Lest there be any question as to God's role in all of this, the sacred historian notes, **And the LORD sent against him bands of the Chaldees, and bands of the Syrians, and**

bands of the Moabites, and bands of the children of Ammon, and sent them against Judah to destroy it, according to the word of the LORD, which he spake by his servants the prophets. Notice that it was the Lord who sent various hostile nations against Judah (including Babylon) to *destroy* it. Moreover, this impending destruction had been clearly foretold by prophets such as Isaiah, Jeremiah, Zephaniah, and Huldah the prophetess.

Lest there be any question as to God's position in this matter, the sacred writer reiterates, 3 **Surely at the commandment of the LORD came *this* upon Judah, to remove *them* out of his sight, for the sins of Manasseh, according to all that he did**. The sins of Manasseh, his idolatry and godlessness, had taken place almost one-hundred years earlier. Notwithstanding, the judgment of God was delayed because of the righteousness of Josiah. But it fell upon Judah nevertheless. The Babylonian captivity was God's judgment upon his sinful people. Not only was God's judgment because of the idolatry of Manasseh, it was 4 **also for the innocent blood that he shed: for he filled Jerusalem with innocent blood; which the LORD would not pardon**. The modern abomination of abortion with its shedding of innocent blood certainly is a parallel to the sins of Manasseh. The judgment of God will fall against it sooner or later.

24:5-6 Now the rest of the acts of Jehoiakim, and all that he did, *are* they not written in the book of the chronicles of the kings of Judah? 6 So Jehoiakim slept with his fathers: and Jehoiachin his son reigned in his stead. With the demise of Jehoiakim, his son Jehoiachin assumed the throne of Judah. Further details regarding both of their reigns is found in II Chronicles 36.

24:7 An additional historical note is added. **And the king of Egypt came not again any more out of his land: for the**

Understanding II Kings 357

king of Babylon had taken from the river of Egypt unto the river Euphrates all that pertained to the king of Egypt. Though the Egyptians had imposed a tax upon Judah during the reign of Jehoahaz, Jehoiakim's brother, Babylon had extended its influence to the border of Egypt and the Egyptians chose not to challenge it. The river of Egypt likely is the Nile River, or possibly a smaller streambed coming from the Sinai region between Judah and Egypt.

24:8-9 Summary of the reign of Jehoiachin is thus noted. **Jehoiachin *was* eighteen years old when he began to reign, and he reigned in Jerusalem three months. And his mother's name *was* Nehushta, the daughter of Elnathan of Jerusalem. 9 And he did *that which was* evil in the sight of the LORD, according to all that his father had done.** John Gill makes this comment regarding a supposed discrepancy of Scripture. "In II Chronicles 36:9 he is said to be but eight years old; which may be reconciled by observing, that he might be made and declared king by his father, in the first year of his reign, who reigned eleven years, so that he was eight years old when he began to reign with him, and eighteen when he began to reign alone." This young king, in any event, is remembered having done that which was evil before God even as his father had done. His mother's name *Nehushta* literally means 'brass.' Implicit is that she may have been brazen in her ways.

24:10-11 The judgment of God against Judah was not finished. **At that time the servants of Nebuchadnezzar king of Babylon came up against Jerusalem, and the city was besieged. 11 And Nebuchadnezzar king of Babylon came against the city, and his servants did besiege it.** Approximately eight years after the initial incursion by Babylon against Judah, Nebuchadnezzar, king of Babylon, (in about 597 B.C.) returned against Jerusalem. The Jews resisted and the Babylonians proceeded to besiege the city. Precisely how long the siege lasted is not noted. However, it apparently was not long.

24:12-13 Jehoiachin soon surrendered. **And Jehoiachin the king of Judah went out to the king of Babylon, he, and his mother, and his servants, and his princes, and his officers: and the king of Babylon took him in the eighth year of his reign.** In the eighth year of Nebuchadnezzar's reign, he captured Jerusalem—*again*—and took captive Jehoiachin along with his royal family and all his royal administration.

Furthermore, the king of Babylon 13 **carried out thence all the treasures of the house of the LORD, and the treasures of the king's house, and cut in pieces all the vessels of gold which Solomon king of Israel had made in the Temple of the LORD, as the LORD had said.** The Babylonians proceeded to loot the Temple of God, the king's palace, and even the sacred gold vessels for worship at the Temple. They all were carried back to Babylon. Mention of those golden and silver vessels is made again in Daniel 5:2-3. Not only did Nebuchadnezzar conquer Jerusalem, he essentially depleted the Temple of all its treasuries and vessels for service.

24:14-16 Moreover, **he carried away all Jerusalem, and all the princes, and all the mighty men of valour, *even* ten thousand captives, and all the craftsmen and smiths: none remained, save the poorest sort of the people of the land.** The second deportation of Judah to Babylon was thus executed. Again, this was in about 597 B.C. Anyone of rank, position, or skill in Judah was deported to Babylon. It evidently was at this time when Ezekiel was taken to Babylon as well.

15 **And he carried away Jehoiachin to Babylon, and the king's mother, and the king's wives, and his officers, and the mighty of the land, *those* carried he into captivity from**

Understanding II Kings

Jerusalem to Babylon. Most all of the royal family and other nobles of Judah were also deported to Babylon as captives.

16 **And all the men of might,** *even* **seven thousand, and craftsmen and smiths a thousand, all** *that were* **strong** *and* **apt for war, even them the king of Babylon brought captive to Babylon.** Along with the nobility and royal family, all men of any military significance were also deported to Babylon. These evidently totaled 10,000 as noted in verse 14.

24:17 And the king of Babylon made Mattaniah his father's brother king in his stead, and changed his name to Zedekiah. Mattaniah was another son of Josiah as noted in I Chronicles 3:15. He was uncle to Jehoiachin who had been just deposed by the Babylonians. The name given him by the Babylonians, *Zedekiah*, means 'Jehovah is righteous.' There undoubtedly is irony and possibly sarcasm in the name. The Babylonians likely knew that Jehovah, God of Judah, was using them to chastise His people. Jeremiah the prophet had made that clear. They thus renamed this last hapless king of Judah with a reminder of Jehovah's judgment upon Judah.

24:18-19 Zedekiah *was* **twenty and one years old when he began to reign, and he reigned eleven years in Jerusalem. And his mother's name** *was* **Hamutal, the daughter of Jeremiah of Libnah.** As per II Kings 23:31, it is apparent that Zedekiah was a full brother to Jehoahaz. See notes thereto regarding his mother being the daughter of Jeremiah. This was not the prophet Jeremiah. Sadly, 19 **Zedekiah did** *that which was* **evil in the sight of the LORD, according to all that Jehoiakim had done.**

24:20 For through the anger of the LORD it came to pass in Jerusalem and Judah, until he had cast them out from his presence, that Zedekiah rebelled against the king of

Babylon. Further details regarding the evil of Zedekiah are recorded in II Chronicles 36:10-13 and Jeremiah 52:1-3. He hardened himself against God and humbled not himself before Jeremiah the prophet. God's anger against Judah in general and Zedekiah in particular was about to come to its climax. God therefore providentially led Zedekiah to rebel against the Babylonians which soon brought the fury of their wrath down upon him. God thus used Nebuchadnezzar, king of Babylon, to effect His righteous wrath against His rebellious sinful people.

* * * * *

Overview of II Kings 25: *The final judgment of God against Judah is unleashed. The Babylonians returned in fury and utterly destroyed Jerusalem. They enslaved its rebel king Zedekiah. They destroyed the Temple of God. The third and final phase of the Babylonian captivity was effected. Details of the continuing political instability of those who remained in Judah are noted along with kindness being shown to Jehoiachin, former king of Judah.*

25:1-2 Precise dating is given for the final return of the Babylonians against rebellious Jerusalem. **And it came to pass in the ninth year of his reign, in the tenth month, in the tenth** *day* **of the month,** *that* **Nebuchadnezzar king of Babylon came, he, and all his host, against Jerusalem, and pitched against it; and they built forts against it round about. 2 And the city was besieged unto the eleventh year of king Zedekiah**. The ninth year refers to that of Zedekiah's reign. The actual date is about 588 B.C. with the siege being broken in 586 B.C. During that interval of the siege, the Babylonians erected siege forts against the city, allowing no one to leave or enter the city. Their plan was simple. They would starve the city into submission. (The account in verse 1-7 is identical to that of Jeremiah 52:4-11).

25:3-4 That is exactly what happened. **And on the ninth day of the *fourth* month the famine prevailed in the city, and there was no bread for the people of the land. 4 And the city was broken up, and all the men of war *fled* by night by the way of the gate between two walls, which *is* by the king's garden: (now the Chaldees *were* against the city round about:) and *the king* went the way toward the plain.** With starvation facing the city, the Babylonians broke into the weakened city. However, the remaining forces of the city fled by night through an obscure gate. Furthermore, Zedekiah, as a coward, fled by night as well and headed toward the plains of Jordan by Jericho. He never got away.

25:5-7 And the army of the Chaldees pursued after the king, and overtook him in the plains of Jericho: and all his army were scattered from him. The reference to the Chaldees is another name of the Babylonians which were located in the greater region of the Chaldees. The Babylonians thus caught up to Zedekiah in the vicinity of Jericho in the Jordan River valley. His army scattered and the king was captured. **6 So they took the king, and brought him up to the king of Babylon to Riblah; and they gave judgment upon him.** Nebuchadnezzar himself had not been personally involved in the siege of Jerusalem, having delegated that to subordinate officers. He was presently at Riblah, a town in the land of Hamath, on the great road between Babylon and Palestine. There, the Babylonian forces brought Zedekiah for judgment.

7 And they slew the sons of Zedekiah before his eyes, and put out the eyes of Zedekiah, and bound him with fetters of brass, and carried him to Babylon. Nebuchadnezzar had earlier extended mercy to Zedekiah in placing him upon the throne of Judah as his vassal. Zedekiah had completely broken that trust in his rebellion against Babylon. Clearly, Nebuchadnezzar had no more patience or kindness to him. He ordered Zedekiah's sons murdered before his eyes. He then put out the eyes of this wicked Jewish king so that the last visual memory he ever had was seeing his sons killed before him.

Though royalty, Nebuchadnezzar ordered this rebellious subordinate bound with brass fetters as a common criminal and sent to Babylon. The house of David was truncated. That removal of the descendants of David remains to this day. Only when the greatest Son of David returns will the throne of David be restored.

25:8-10 And in the fifth month, on the seventh *day* of the month, which *is* the nineteenth year of king Nebuchadnezzar king of Babylon, came Nebuzaradan, captain of the guard, a servant of the king of Babylon, unto Jerusalem. The final fall of Jerusalem is noted with precise detail. The nineteenth year of Nebuchadnezzar is in about 586 B.C. Thus, the third and final assault against Jerusalem came after twenty years of Babylonian chastisement against Judah, having begun in 606 B.C.

9 And he burnt the house of the LORD, and the king's house, and all the houses of Jerusalem, and every great *man's* house burnt he with fire. 10 And all the army of the Chaldees, that *were with* the captain of the guard, brake down the walls of Jerusalem round about. The Babylonians had had enough of rebellious Judah. Nebuchadnezzar ordered the Temple of God destroyed along with the royal palace. He proceeded to burn the entire city and then tore down the walls thereof. When Nebuchadnezzar was done, nothing was left of Jerusalem. He had totally destroyed the city. Judah (and Israel) as a free *independent* state ceased to exist and remained so until 1948 when Israel was reconstituted in the land as a nation.

25:11-12 Now the rest of the people *that were* left in the city, and the fugitives that fell away to the king of Babylon, with the remnant of the multitude, did Nebuzaradan the captain of the guard carry away. 12 But the captain of the guard left of the poor of the land *to be* vinedressers and husbandmen. The third and final phase of the Babylonian captivity was accomplished. Virtually everyone living at Jerusalem was deported to Babylon. Any one of any significance in Judah was deported as well. It was Babylonian policy to mingled captured peoples in distant portions of their empire to mitigate against any further uprising. It also made the empire more homogenized and easier to rule. Seeing however the value of the vineyards of Judah, the Babylonians left the lower class of the nation behind to tend these as a cash crop for Babylon.

25:13-17 Before departing, the Babylonians proceeded to strip and loot anything of value from the destruction of Jerusalem. **And the pillars of brass that *were* in the house of the LORD, and the bases, and the brasen sea that *was* in the house of the LORD, did the Chaldees break in pieces, and carried the brass of them to Babylon. 14 And the pots, and the shovels, and the snuffers, and the spoons, and all the vessels of brass wherewith they ministered, took they away.** All of the brass of the Temple was stripped and broken up for shipment back to Babylon.

This included **15 the firepans, and the bowls, *and* such things as *were* of gold, *in* gold, and of silver, *in* silver, the captain of the guard took away. 16 The two pillars, one sea, and the bases which Solomon had made for the house of the LORD; the brass of all these vessels was without weight. 17 The height of the one pillar *was* eighteen cubits, and the chapiter upon it *was* brass: and the height of the chapiter three cubits; and the wreathen work, and pomegranates upon the chapiter round about, all of brass: and like unto** these had the second pillar with wreathen work. Nothing of value was left. All of the metal work of the Temple from whatever golden vessels remained to all of the brass work was stripped and shipped back to Babylon. They left Jerusalem totally desolate. Jeremiah lamented the desolation thereof in Lamentations 3-4.

25:18-21 And the captain of the guard took Seraiah the chief priest, and Zephaniah the second priest, and the three keepers of the door: 19 And out of the city he took an officer that was set over the men of war, and five men of them that were in the king's presence, which were found in the city, and the principal scribe of the host, which mustered the people of the land, and threescore men of the people of the land *that were* **found in the city: 20 And Nebu-zaradan captain of the guard took these, and brought them to the king of Babylon to Riblah.**

All remaining religious, military, and civil leaders were rounded up and marched to Riblah where Nebuchadnezzar's regional headquarters were located. There, **21 the king of Babylon smote them, and slew them at Riblah in the land of Hamath.**

With stunning understatement, the sacred text records, **So Judah was carried away out of their land.** Israel as a *nation* was no longer. The northern kingdom had been deported by the Assyrians approximately 136 years earlier. Now, the southern kingdom ceased to exist as well. God had removed His people from their land as He had warned in Deuteronomy 28 as well as through later prophets.

25:22-24 And *as for* **the people that remained in the land of Judah, whom Nebuchadnezzar king of Babylon had left, even over them he made Gedaliah the son of Ahikam, the son of Shaphan, ruler.** Some Jews were left in the land to dress the vineyards for the Babylonians. Having utterly intimicated them, Nebuchadnezzar thus appointed Gedaliah to be regional governor over them. He evidently was willing to pledge allegiance to Nebuchadnezzar in return for this privilege. Precisely who Gedaliah was is not certain. However, his lineage as noted clearly was not of the line and lineage of David.

23 And when all the captains of the armies, they and their men, heard that the king of Babylon had made Gedaliah governor, there came to Gedaliah to Mizpah, even Ishmael the son of Nethaniah, and Johanan the son of Careah, and Seraiah the son of Tanhumeth the Netophathite, and Jaazaniah the son of a Maachathite, they and their men. 24 And Gedaliah sware to them, and to their men, and said unto them, Fear not to be the servants of the Chaldees: dwell in the land, and serve the king of Babylon; and it shall be well with you.

Evidently, some of the Jewish forces which had fled before the Babylonians now returned from hiding to meet with Gedaliah. Loyal now to Nebuchadnezzar, Gedaliah urged to them submit to Babylonian authority and live in the land. He assured them that all would be well for them in so doing. This portion closely parallels the ministry of Jeremiah the prophet. See Jeremiah 40.

25:25-26 Notwithstanding, **it came to pass in the seventh month, that Ishmael the son of Nethaniah, the son of Elishama, of the seed royal, came, and ten men with him, and smote Gedaliah, that he died, and the Jews and the Chaldees that were with him at Mizpah.** In the seventh month of that year, one named *Ishmael* who was of royal descent took ten men with him and killed Gedaliah along with the Jews and Babylonians with him. They undoubtedly considered him a traitor.

26 And all the people, both small and great, and the captains of the armies, arose, and came to Egypt: for they

were afraid of the Chaldees. Seeing what Ishmael had done and fearing retribution from the Babylonians, the remnant of Jews left in the land fled to Egypt. Here read Jeremiah 41-43.

25:27-30 Meanwhile, in Babylon, **it came to pass in the seven and thirtieth year of the captivity of Jehoiachin king of Judah, in the twelfth month, on the seven and twentieth** *day* **of the month,** *that* **Evilmerodach king of Babylon in the year that he began to reign did lift up the head of Jehoiachin king of Judah out of prison.**
Nebuchadnezzar had died. His son **Evilmerodach** ascended the throne of Babylon. (The name *Evilmerodach* means the man or soldier of Merodach, a pagan god of Babylon.) Some think him to be the same as Belshazzar. Perhaps Jehoiachin had truly repented and God in mercy put it in the heart of the new Babylonian ruler to show kindness to him. It also may be that Daniel, who by now was in a position of rank in Babylon, influenced Belshazzar to show mercy to this wretched Jewish king. However, Jewish tradition holds that Belshazzar had been imprisoned for a time by his father Nebuchadnezzar and got to know Jehoiachin in prison. Upon ascending the throne, Belshazzar therefore showed kindness to him.

28 And he spake kindly to him, and set his throne above the throne of the kings that *were* **with him in Babylon; 29 And changed his prison garments: and he did eat bread continually before him all the days of his life. 30 And his allowance** *was* **a continual allowance given him of the king, a daily rate for every day, all the days of his life.** Jehoiachin was thus promoted to a place befitting his royal lineage in Babylon. He there prospered to the end of his life. God was merciful to him. Thus, the book of the Kings abruptly ends. The last living king of Judah was a vassal in a gentile nation. Israel and Judah would remain so generally until 1948 though a remnant of Judah would return under Ezra and Nehemiah.

THE FIRST BOOK OF THE
CHRONICLES

Introduction: *The two books of Chronicles are considered one book in the Jewish Bible. The Christian Bible has divided the Chronicles into two books. As Old Testament history books, the focus is particularly upon the nation of Judah and its kings. The Chronicles likely were written during the Babylonian captivity in Babylon, though the text does not include specific date makers. However, the end of II Chronicles looks not only to the end of the Jewish monarchy in I Chronicles 36:21, but also into the reign of Cyrus, king of Persia. It is thought by some that Ezra therefore may have been the inspired chronicler. Jewish traditions supports this view.*

I Chronicles has essentially three parts. The first section (1:1 - 9:44) is a listing of genealogies, including the lineage of Christ. The second section (10:1 - 12:40) is a brief overview of the reign of Saul. Section three (13:1 - 29:30) is an overview of the reign of David unto his death.

Overview of I Chronicles 1: *In the first section of the book, genealogies of the human race from Adam to Abraham are presented in verses 1-27. Then, the descendants of Abraham are presented in verses 28-54. Though other lineages are presented, the greater lineage is that of Christ. That will become apparent in the following chapters. I Chronicles 1 gives an overview of the godly line stemming from Adam to Jacob. The* *end of the chapter presents also the lineage of Esau and his descendent, including kings of Edom (which is modern Jordan).*

1:1-7 Adam, Sheth, Enosh, 2 Kenan, Mahalaleel, Jered, 3 Henoch, Methuselah, Lamech, 4 Noah, Shem, Ham, and Japheth. The lineage presented clearly is the godly lineage of Adam, culminating in Noah. The *Sheth* here is the Seth of Genesis 4. He became the channel of the godly line after Abel was murdered.

1:5-7 The sons of Japheth; Gomer, and Magog, and Madai, and Javan, and Tubal, and Meshech, and Tiras. 6 And the sons of Gomer; Ashchenaz, and Riphath, and Togarmah. 7 And the sons of Javan; Elishah, and Tarshish, Kittim, and Dodanim. The sacred chronicler thence presents the lineage of the sons of Japheth.

1:8-16 The sons of Ham; Cush, and Mizraim, Put, and Canaan. 9 And the sons of Cush; Seba, and Havilah, and Sabta, and Raamah, and Sabtecha. And the sons of Raamah; Sheba, and Dedan. 10 And Cush begat Nimrod: he began to be mighty upon the earth. 11 And Mizraim begat Ludim, and Anamim, and Lehabim, and Naphtuhim, 12 And Pathrusim, and Casluhim, (of whom came the Philistines,) and Caphthorim.

13 And Canaan begat Zidon his firstborn, and Heth, 14 The Jebusite also, and the Amorite, and the Girgashite, 15 And the Hivite, and the Arkite, and the Sinite, 16 And the Arvadite, and the Zemarite, and the Hamathite. The lineage of Ham is presented. It is interesting to take note of the lineage thereof. It included Canaan and in verse 12, the Philistines, Jebusites, and Amorites to name a few. All of these were later enemies of God's people. It is noteworthy how an ungodly ancestor in Ham produced a long-lasting legacy of

Understanding I Chronicles 369

ungodliness through Canaan and his descendants. The legacy of Ham continues to this day in the system commonly called the *world*.

1:17-23 The sons of Shem; Elam, and Asshur, and Arphaxad, and Lud, and Aram, and Uz, and Hul, and Gether, and Meshech. 18 And Arphaxad begat Shelah, and Shelah begat Eber. 19 And unto Eber were born two sons: the name of the one *was* Peleg; because in his days the earth was divided: and his brother's name *was* Joktan. 20 And Joktan begat Almodad, and Sheleph, and Hazarmaveth, and Jerah, 21 Hadoram also, and Uzal, and Diklah, 22 And Ebal, and Abimael, and Sheba, 23 And Ophir, and Havilah, and Jo-bab. All these *were* the sons of Joktan.

The lineage of Shem is here presented. One of the sons of Shem was Uz which probably gave the name to the land in which Job later lived. Also, the descendants of Shem were those peoples who migrated to the east. Elam later became known as Persia. Asshur later became the Assyrians. Most oriental peoples are descended from Shem.

1:24-27 Shem, Arphaxad, Shelah, 25 Eber, Peleg, Reu, 26 Serug, Nahor, Terah, 27 Abram; the same *is* Abraham. The lineage of Shem is presented. It is noteworthy that Abraham descended from Shem.

1:28-31 The sons of Abraham; Isaac, and Ishmael. 29 These *are* their generations: The firstborn of Ishmael, Nebaioth; then Kedar, and Adbeel, and Mibsam, 30 Mishma, and Dumah, Massa, Hadad, and Tema, 31 Jetur, Naphish, and Kedemah. These are the sons of Ishmael. As noted in the last line, the lineage of Ishmael is here set forth.

1:32-33 Now the sons of Keturah, Abraham's concubine: she bare Zimran, and Jokshan, and Medan, and

Midian, and Ishbak, and Shuah. And the sons of Jokshan; Sheba, and Dedan. 33 And the sons of Midian; Ephah, and Epher, and Henoch, and Abida, and Eldaah. All these *are* the sons of Keturah.** The lineage of Abraham through Keturah is presented. She bore six sons to Abraham as noted. In Genesis 25:1, Keturah is called the wife of Abraham. Here she is called his concubine. However, inasmuch as Sarah was already dead when Abraham *took* Keturah, she undoubtedly was his wife. However, the sacred writer may have referred to her as a concubine so as not to elevate her or her sons to the same status as that of Sarah and Isaac.

1:34 And Abraham begat Isaac. The sons of Isaac; Esau and Israel. Abraham, however, only had one son of promise and that was Isaac. The sacred chronicler seemingly follows a pattern of presenting the lessor of posterity first and then placing the godly line and specifically the line of the Messiah last. Isaac accordingly was noted only after Ishmael and the sons of Keturah were mentioned.

1:35-42 The sons of Esau; Eliphaz, Reuel, and Jeush, and Jaalam, and Korah. 36 The sons of Eliphaz; Teman, and Omar, Zephi, and Gatam, Kenaz, and Timna, and Amalek. 37 The sons of Reuel; Nahath, Zerah, Shammah, and Mizzah. 38 And the sons of Seir; Lotan, and Shobal, and Zibeon, and Anah, and Dishon, and Ezer, and Dishan. 39 And the sons of Lotan; Hori, and Homam: and Timna *was* Lotan's sister.

40 The sons of Shobal; Alian, and Manahath, and Ebal, Shephi, and Onam. And the sons of Zibeon; Aiah, and Anah. 41 The sons of Anah; Dishon. And the sons of Dishon; Amram, and Eshban, and Ithran, and Cheran. 42 The sons of Ezer; Bilhan, and Zavan, *and* Jakan. The sons of Dishan; Uz, and Aran.

Before focusing upon the godly lineage of Abraham through Isaac, the sacred writer first presents the lineage of Abraham through Esau. Esau had five sons: Eliphaz, Reuel, and Jeush, and Jaalam, and Korah.

1:43-50 Now these *are* the kings that reigned in the land of Edom before *any* king reigned over the children of Israel; Bela the son of Beor: and the name of his city *was* Dinhabah. 44 And when Bela was dead, Jobab the son of Zerah of Bozrah reigned in his stead. 45 And when Jobab was dead, Husham of the land of the Temanites reigned in his stead. 46 And when Husham was dead, Hadad the son of Bedad, which smote Midian in the field of Moab, reigned in his stead: and the name of his city *was* Avith.

47 And when Hadad was dead, Samlah of Masrekah reigned in his stead. 48 And when Samlah was dead, Shaul of Rehoboth by the river reigned in his stead. 49 And when Shaul was dead, Baalhanan the son of Achbor reigned in his stead. 50 And when Baalhanan was dead, Hadad reigned in his stead: and the name of his city *was* Pai; and his wife's name *was* Mehetabel, the daughter of Matred, the daughter of Mezahab. Listed are kings in Edom, the land of Esau, before any king was anointed in Israel. Eight kings of Edom are listed from the first, evidently up until the time of the writing of Chronicles.

1:51-54 Hadad died also. And the dukes of Edom were; duke Timnah, duke Aliah, duke Jetheth, 52 Duke Aholibamah, duke Elah, duke Pinon, 53 Duke Kenaz, duke Teman, duke Mibzar, 54 Duke Magdiel, duke Iram. These *are* the dukes of Edom. Eleven dukes or 'princes' of Edom are also listed.

* * * * *

Overview of I Chronicles 2: *I Chronicles 2 briefly lists the sons of Israel and then proceeds to follow various branches of the lineage of Judah. The chapter then narrows its focus to the heritage of David in Jesse and then the lineage of Caleb—all sons of Judah.*

2:1-2 These *are* the sons of Israel; Reuben, Simeon, Levi, and Judah, Issachar, and Zebulun, 2 Dan, Joseph, and Benjamin, Naphtali, Gad, and Asher. In chapter 1:34, the two sons of Isaac, Esau and Israel (i.e., Jacob) are listed. Now the sacred chronicle lists the sons of Israel. (Noteworthy is that only the male descendants are herein recorded.) Again, the genealogy narrows its focus to the godly line and the greater lineage of the Messiah. Accordingly, the twelve sons of Jacob are herein recorded.

2:3-12 The sons of Judah; Er, and Onan, and Shelah: *which* three were born unto him of the daughter of Shua the Canaanitess. And Er, the firstborn of Judah, was evil in the sight of the LORD; and he slew him. 4 And Tamar his daughter in law bare him Pharez and Zerah. All the sons of Judah *were* five. 5 The sons of Pharez; Hezron, and Hamul. 6 And the sons of Zerah; Zimri, and Ethan, and Heman, and Calcol, and Dara: five of them in all.

7 And the sons of Carmi; Achar, the troubler of Israel, who transgressed in the thing accursed. 8 And the sons of Ethan; Azariah. 9 The sons also of Hezron, that were born unto him; Jerahmeel, and Ram, and Chelubai. 10 And Ram begat Amminadab; and Amminadab begat Nahshon, prince of the children of Judah; 11 And Nahshon begat Salma, and Salma begat Boaz, 12 And Boaz begat Obed, and Obed begat Jesse.

The sacred chronicle now narrows its focus even more, following the lineage of Judah all the way to Jesse.

Understanding I Chronicles

Notice also that in verse 3 the cryptic statement is made of how Er "was evil in the sight of the LORD; and he slew him." The lineage of Judah to and through Jesse is not only the lineage of the royal line of Israel, but also that of the Messiah. Judah had five sons. Of interest is that the royal line and that of the Messiah flowed through Pharez which was the illegitimate son of Tamar. In verse 7, **Achar** is a reference to Achan in Joshua 7. He came to be known as "the troubler of Israel." In verse 12, record also is made of Boaz who begat Obed, the husband of Ruth in the Book of Ruth.

2:13-17 And Jesse begat his firstborn Eliab, and Abinadab the second, and Shimma the third, 14 Nethaneel the fourth, Raddai the fifth, 15 Ozem the sixth, David the seventh: 16 Whose sisters *were* **Zeruiah, and Abigail. And the sons of Zeruiah; Abishai, and Joab, and Asahel, three. 17 And Abigail bare Amasa: and the father of Amasa** *was* **Jether the Ishmeelite.**

The sacred chronicle narrows its focus even more to the family of Jesse and David in particular. Jesse had seven sons of which David was the youngest. See I Samuel 16 for further details. David also had two sisters named Zeruiah and Abigail. These women were the mothers of David's well-known nephews, Abishai, Joab, Asahel, and Amasa.

2:18-20 And Caleb the son of Hezron begat *children* **of Azubah** *his* **wife, and of Jerioth: her sons** *are* **these; Jesher, and Shobab, and Ardon. 19 And when Azubah was dead, Caleb took unto him Ephrath, which bare him Hur. 20 And Hur begat Uri, and Uri begat Bezaleel.**

The focus of the sacred chronicle shifts away from the lineage of David. Caleb, however, was certainly a godly man. It was he, along with Joshua, who by faith believed that with God's help, Israel could conquer the land promised to them.

Accordingly, it was only Joshua and Caleb of that generation who were allowed by God into the promised land.

2:21-24 And afterward Hezron went in to the daughter of Machir the father of Gilead, whom he married when he *was* threescore years old; and she bare him Segub. 22 And Segub begat Jair, who had three and twenty cities in the land of Gilead. 23 And he took Geshur, and Aram, with the towns of Jair, from them, with Kenath, and the towns thereof, *even* threescore cities. All these *belonged to* the sons of Machir the father of Gilead. 24 And after that Hezron was dead in Calebephratah, then Abiah Hezron's wife bare him Ashur the father of Tekoa.

Further details of the greater family of Caleb are recorded. Hezron was Caleb's father. In the course of events, he married "the daughter of Machir the father of Gilead" whose descendants populated twenty-three towns in Gilead, east of the Jordan River. Jewish traditions holds that he enticed a virgin, the daughter of Machir which suggesting he committed fornication with her, though afterward marrying her. Her name is not mentioned. Gilead was not part of the tribal territory of Judah, however, a branch thereof settled there. It was from this branch of Judah that Barzillai, the Gileadite and friend of David, gave aid to him when fleeing from Absalom. See II Samuel 17:26-29.

2:25-33 And the sons of Jerahmeel the firstborn of Hezron were, Ram the firstborn, and Bunah, and Oren, and Ozem, *and* Ahijah. 26 Jerahmeel had also another wife, whose name *was* Atarah; she *was* the mother of Onam. 27 And the sons of Ram the firstborn of Jerahmeel were, Maaz, and Jamin, and Eker.

28 And the sons of Onam were, Shammai, and Jada. And the sons of Shammai; Nadab, and Abishur. 29 And the

name of the wife of Abishur *was* Abihail, and she bare him Ahban, and Molid. 30 And the sons of Nadab; Seled, and Appaim: but Seled died without children. 31 And the sons of Appaim; Ishi. And the sons of Ishi; Sheshan. And the children of Sheshan; Ahlai.

32 And the sons of Jada the brother of Shammai; Jether, and Jonathan: and Jether died without children. 33 And the sons of Jonathan; Peleth, and Zaza. These were the sons of Jerahmeel. Another branch of the tribe of Judah is recorded, presenting the lineage of Jerameel, the brother of Caleb, and son of Hezron, his father.

2:34-41 Now Sheshan had no sons, but daughters. And Sheshan had a servant, an Egyptian, whose name *was* Jarha. 35 And Sheshan gave his daughter to Jarha his servant to wife; and she bare him Attai.

36 And Attai begat Nathan, and Nathan begat Zabad, 37 And Zabad begat Ephlal, and Ephlal begat Obed, 38 And Obed begat Jehu, and Jehu begat Azariah, 39 And Azariah begat Helez, and Helez begat Eleasah, 40 And Eleasah begat Sisamai, and Sisamai begat Shallum, 41 And Shallum begat Jekamiah, and Jekamiah begat Elishama. Sheshan was descended from Jerahmeel, the brother of Caleb and of the tribe of Judah. Details of this lineage are here recorded.

2:42-49 Now the sons of Caleb the brother of Jerahmeel *were*, Mesha his firstborn, which was the father of Ziph; and the sons of Mareshah the father of Hebron. 43 And the sons of Hebron; Korah, and Tappuah, and Rekem, and Shema. 44 And Shema begat Raham, the father of Jorkoam: and Rekem begat Shammai.

45 And the son of Shammai *was* Maon: and Maon *was* the father of Bethzur. 46 And Ephah, Caleb's concubine, bare Haran, and Moza, and Gazez: and Haran begat Gazez.

47 And the sons of Jahdai; Regem, and Jotham, and Geshan, and Pelet, and Ephah, and Shaaph. **48** Maachah, Caleb's concubine, bare Sheber, and Tirhanah. **49** She bare also Shaaph the father of Madmannah, Sheva the father of Machbenah, and the father of Gibea: and the daughter of Caleb *was* Achsah. Further details of the descendants of Caleb are presented. These are sons and their descendants of a third wife named Azubah after Ephrath, his second wife, died.

2:50-55 These were the sons of Caleb the son of Hur, the firstborn of Ephratah; Shobal the father of Kirjathjearim, 51 Salma the father of Bethlehem, Hareph the father of Bethgader. 52 And Shobal the father of Kirjathjearim had sons; Haroeh, *and* half of the Manahethites. 53 And the families of Kirjathjearim; the Ithrites, and the Puhites, and the Shumathites, and the Mishraites; of them came the Zareathites, and the Eshtaulites.

54 The sons of Salma; Bethlehem, and the Netophathites, Ataroth, the house of Joab, and half of the Manahethites, the Zorites. 55 And the families of the scribes which dwelt at Jabez; the Tirathites, the Shimeathites, *and* Suchathites. These *are* the Kenites that came of Hemath, the father of the house of Rechab.

This lineage evidently is of *another* Caleb, the grandson of Caleb the son of Hezron. He was the son of Hur, the firstborn of his wife Ephratah. See I Chronicles 2:19. Notice familiar biblical names and places associated with this branch of the tribe of Judah—the descendants of Caleb senior: Ephratah, Bethlehem, and Kirjathjearim. Also included in this lineage of Judah was a family of scribes, descended of Jethro the father of Moses.

Though technically not of the tribe of Judah, they are included here in a *de facto* sense. These also were whence the Rechabites descended. See Jeremiah 35:2. Details are thus pre-

Understanding I Chronicles 377

sented of various branches of the tribe of Judah, particularly those families of note.

* * * * *

Overview of I Chronicles 3: I Chronicles 3 presents the lineage of David and his succeeding royal dynasty up to the Babylonian captivity and then beyond to the beginning of the restoration. David had many children of his multiple wives. However, the royal lineage flowed from Solomon. The book of II Chronicles will detail the lives and reigns of each of the royal descendants of David to the Babylonian captivity.

3:1-9 Now these were the sons of David, which were born unto him in Hebron; the firstborn Amnon, of Ahinoam the Jezreelitess; the second Daniel, of Abigail the Carmelitess: 2 The third, Absalom the son of Maachah the daughter of Talmai king of Geshur: the fourth, Adonijah the son of Haggith: 3 The fifth, Shephatiah of Abital: the sixth, Ithream by Eglah his wife.

4 *These* six were born unto him in Hebron; and there he reigned seven years and six months: and in Jerusalem he reigned thirty and three years. 5 And these were born unto him in Jerusalem; Shimea, and Shobab, and Nathan, and Solomon, four, of Bathshua the daughter of Ammiel: 6 Ibhar also, and Elishama, and Eliphelet, 7 And Nogah, and Nepheg, and Japhia, 8 And Elishama, and Eliada, and Eliphelet, nine. 9 *These were* all the sons of David, beside the sons of the concubines, and Tamar their sister.

Record of David's descendants and his reign are summarized here. His family lineage is organized around the several venues of tenure as king. In Hebron where David ruled over Judah for seven and one-half years, six sons were born to David of six separate wives. (Again, polygamy was tolerated in the Old Testament as a social custom, but *never* has been God's perfect will. One of the ill effects of David's polygamous family was that his wives essentially raised the children with not a great deal of influence from their father. Accordingly, David reaped bitter results from his children in his later years.)

Upon becoming king over all of Israel, David fathered thirteen other sons in Jerusalem from a number of other wives, including Solomon by Bathsheba (i.e., Bathshua). The sacred chronicle lists four sons by Bathsheba and nine other sons by other unnamed wives. David had other unspecified sons of his concubines (i.e., harem) of which he had at least ten. See II Samuel 15:16 and II Samuel 20:3. Tamar was not the sister of the sons of the concubines, but of his other sons and specifically was the full sister of Absalom. See II Samuel 13:1-39.

3:10-16 And Solomon's son *was* Rehoboam, Abia his son, Asa his son, Jehoshaphat his son, 11 Joram his son, Ahaziah his son, Joash his son, 12 Amaziah his son, Azariah his son, Jotham his son, 13 Ahaz his son, Hezekiah his son, Manasseh his son, 14 Amon his son, Josiah his son. 15 And the sons of Josiah *were*, the firstborn Johanan, the second Jehoiakim, the third Zedekiah, the fourth Shallum. 16 And the sons of Jehoiakim: Jeconiah his son, Zedekiah his son.

The royal dynasty of David, to its divinely appointed hiatus in Zedekiah, is here recorded. Nineteen kings descended from David and then reigned over Israel and then Judah until the Babylonian captivity. At the end of this lineage, Jehoiakim, son of Josiah, reigned followed by Jehoiakim, his son Jeconiah (i.e., Jehoiachin), and Zedekiah son of Jehoiakim. With Zedekiah, the royal dynasty of David has been put on hold until the final and greatest Son of David will sit upon the throne—Jesus Christ the Righteous.

Understanding I Chronicles

3:17-24 And the sons of Jeconiah; Assir, Salathiel his son, 18 Malchiram also, and Pedaiah, and Shenazar, Jecamiah, Hoshama, and Nedabiah. 19 And the sons of Pedaiah *were*, Zerubbabel, and Shimei: and the sons of Zerubbabel; Meshullam, and Hananiah, and Shelomith their sister: 20 And Hashubah, and Ohel, and Berechiah, and Hasadiah, Jushabhesed, five.

21 And the sons of Hananiah; Pelatiah, and Jesaiah: the sons of Rephaiah, the sons of Arnan, the sons of Obadiah, the sons of Shechaniah. 22 And the sons of Shechaniah; Shemaiah: and the sons of Shemaiah; Hattush, and Igeal, and Bariah, and Neariah, and Shaphat, six. 23 And the sons of Neariah; Elioenai, and Hezekiah, and Azrikam, three. 24 And the sons of Elioenai *were*, Hodaiah, and Eliashib, and Pelaiah, and Akkub, and Johanan, and Dalaiah, and Anani, seven.

The descendants of Jehoiachin are thus recorded. In the final tumultuous years of the kingdom of Judah, Jehoiakim died apparently in captivity. See II Kings 24:1-4 and II Chronicles 36:5-6. Zedekiah was killed by Nebuchadnezzar. Only Jehoiachin survived in captivity in Babylon and went on to have children. See I Kings 25:27*ff.* Hence, his descendants are here listed. Though pronounced childless by Jeremiah in Jeremiah 22:30, the thought there is that he had no descendants to follow him upon the throne.

Of interest is that there are apparently nine generations after Jeconiah listed here. This implies that someone other than Ezra, the presumed author of Chronicles, added these names to the listing. Nevertheless, whoever the sacred editor was, the text remains inspired. Some have sought to link this lineage with that of Matthew 1, noting the name Zerubbabel in both (I Chronicles 3:19 and Matthew 1:12-13). However, other than that similarity, the two lineages are not the same.

* * * * *

Overview of I Chronicles 4: *This next chapter continues following the lineage of Judah through Caleb, Ashur, and Shelah. Then, the chapter gives an overview of the lineage of Simeon, another one of the sons of Israel.*

4:1-4 The sons of Judah; Pharez, Hezron, and Carmi, and Hur, and Shobal. 2 And Reaiah the son of Shobal begat Jahath; and Jahath begat Ahumai, and Lahad. These *are* **the families of the Zorathites. 3 And these** *were of* **the father of Etam; Jezreel, and Ishma, and Idbash: and the name of their sister** *was* **Hazelelponi: 4 And Penuel the father of Gedor, and Ezer the father of Hushah. These** *are* **the sons of Hur, the firstborn of Ephratah, the father of Bethlehem.**

The posterity of Judah by Caleb, the son of Hur, is further recorded. Record is also made of the descendants of Shobal, the son of Judah. Of interest is that Hur, the son of Judah, was the father of Ephratah, the father of Bethlehem whence David was born.

4:5-8 And Ashur the father of Tekoa had two wives, Helah and Naarah. 6 And Naarah bare him Ahuzam, and Hepher, and Temeni, and Haahashtari. These *were* **the sons of Naarah. 7 And the sons of Helah** *were***, Zereth, and Jezoar, and Ethnan. 8 And Coz begat Anub, and Zobebah, and the families of Aharhel the son of Harum.** Another branch of the posterity of Judah is noted in Ashur, son of Hezron, son of Judah. One of his sons was named Tekoa which went on to become a village in the territory of Judah whence other Old Testament events transpired. See II Samuel 14:1-9, II Chronicles 20:20*ff*, Jeremiah 6:1*ff*, and Amos1:1.

4:9-10 And Jabez was more honourable than his brethren: and his mother called his name Jabez, saying, Because I bare him with sorrow. 10 And Jabez called on the

God of Israel, saying, Oh that thou wouldest bless me indeed, and enlarge my coast, and that thine hand might be with me, and that thou wouldest keep *me* from evil, that it may not grieve me! And God granted him that which he requested.

Part of the lineage of Judah through Caleb was Jabez. Not a great deal is known about him, but he has been long remembered for his evident faith and willingness to come before God's throne of grace and make request as recorded in verse 10. The name *Jabez* (יַעְבֵּץ *Ya'bets*) literally means 'sorrow.' Why his mother so named him is unclear. She may have gone through very hard labor or perhaps other sad events, perhaps the death of her husband.

However, the faith of Jabez is apparent. In simple faith and fervent prayer, this otherwise unknown man of Judah cried out to God and besought Him to grant (1) blessing, (2) greater territory, (3) divine help, (4) protection from evil (i.e., trouble) lest he suffer hurt. As God perceived his heart of faith, his sincere request, and the clear fervency of Jabez's prayer, God granted his fourfold request. Undoubtedly, God will honor similar prayer of similar heart condition to this day.

4:11-20 And Chelub the brother of Shuah begat Mehir, which *was* the father of Eshton. 12 And Eshton begat Bethrapha, and Paseah, and Tehinnah the father of Irnahash. These *are* the men of Rechah. 13 And the sons of Kenaz; Othniel, and Seraiah: and the sons of Othniel; Hathath. 14 And Meonothai begat Ophrah: and Seraiah begat Joab, the father of the valley of Charashim; for they were craftsmen.

15 **And the sons of Caleb the son of Jephunneh; Iru, Elah, and Naam: and the sons of Elah, even Kenaz. 16 And the sons of Jehaleleel; Ziph, and Ziphah, Tiria, and Asareel. 17 And the sons of Ezra *were*, Jether, and Mered, and Epher,**

and Jalon: and she bare Miriam, and Shammai, and Ishbah the father of Eshtemoa.

18 **And his wife Jehudijah bare Jered the father of Gedor, and Heber the father of Socho, and Jekuthiel the father of Zanoah. And these** *are* **the sons of Bithiah the daughter of Pharaoh, which Mered took.** 19 **And the sons of** *his* **wife Hodiah the sister of Naham, the father of Keilah the Garmite, and Eshtemoa the Maachathite.** 20 **And the sons of Shimon** *were***, Amnon, and Rinnah, Benhanan, and Tilon. And the sons of Ishi** *were***, Zoheth, and Benzoheth.**

John Gill commented, "If Shuah is the same with Hushah, I Chronicles 4:4, then Chelub was the son of Ezer "which *was* the father of Eshton." Hence, further posterity of the greater lineage of Caleb is recorded.

4:21-23 The sons of Shelah the son of Judah *were***, Er the father of Lecah, and Laadah the father of Mareshah, and the families of the house of them that wrought fine linen, of the house of Ashbea,** 22 **And Jokim, and the men of Chozeba, and Joash, and Saraph, who had the dominion in Moab, and Jashubilehem. And** *these are* **ancient things.** 23 **These** *were* **the potters, and those that dwelt among plants and hedges: there they dwelt with the king for his work.**

The posterity of Shelah, the youngest son of Judah, is recorded. These became craftsman employed in making fine linen. The Targum adds: "for the garments of kings and priests or for the curtains of the tabernacle."

The mention of "ancient things" literally is "ancient words" and likely has the sense that ancient Jewish tradition was the source of this information. Others of this lineage were employed as potters and in planting gardens and orchards (with their incumbent hedge-fences). Their work was of such quality that they were employed by the king for his purposes.

Understanding I Chronicles 383

4:24-38 The sons of Simeon *were*, Nemuel, and Jamin, Jarib, Zerah, *and* Shaul: 25 Shallum his son, Mibsam his son, Mishma his son. 26 And the sons of Mishma; Hamuel his son, Zacchur his son, Shimei his son. 27 And Shimei had sixteen sons and six daughters; but his brethren had not many children, neither did all their family multiply, like to the children of Judah.

28 And they dwelt at Beersheba, and Moladah, and Hazarshual, 29 And at Bilhah, and at Ezem, and at Tolad, 30 And at Bethuel, and at Hormah, and at Ziklag, 31 And at Bethmarcaboth, and Hazarsusim, and at Bethbirei, and at Shaaraim. These *were* their cities unto the reign of David. 32 And their villages *were*, Etam, and Ain, Rimmon, and Tochen, and Ashan, five cities: 33 And all their villages that *were* round about the same cities, unto Baal. These *were* their habitations, and their genealogy.

34 And Meshobab, and Jamlech, and Joshah the son of Amaziah, 35 And Joel, and Jehu the son of Josibiah, the son of Seraiah, the son of Asiel, 36 And Elioenai, and Jaakobah, and Jeshohaiah, and Asaiah, and Adiel, and Jesimiel, and Benaiah, 37 And Ziza the son of Shiphi, the son of Allon, the son of Jedaiah, the son of Shimri, the son of Shemaiah; 38 These mentioned by *their* names *were* princes in their families: and the house of their fathers increased greatly.

Though the genealogy thus far has been of Judah, the sacred chronicle now turns to the tribe of Simeon. It may be that Simeon is addressed next rather than Reuben (the firstborn) because some of its inheritance lay in the tribe of Judah. Also, some of the towns and villages of the tribe of Simeon are also recorded. The various names recorded here "*were* princes in their families: and the house of their fathers increased greatly."

4:39-43 And they went to the entrance of Gedor, *even* unto the east side of the valley, to seek pasture for their flocks. 40 **And they found fat pasture and good, and the land** *was* **wide, and quiet, and peaceable; for** *they* **of Ham had dwelt there of old.** 41 **And these written by name came in the days of Hezekiah king of Judah, and smote their tents, and the habitations that were found there, and destroyed them utterly unto this day, and dwelt in their rooms: because** *there was* **pasture there for their flocks.**

42 **And** *some* **of them,** *even* **of the sons of Simeon, five hundred men, went to mount Seir, having for their captains Pelatiah, and Neariah, and Rephaiah, and Uzziel, the sons of Ishi.** 43 **And they smote the rest of the Amalekites that were escaped, and dwelt there unto this day.**

A segment of the tribe of Simeon attempted to settle elsewhere—on the east of the valley of Gedor. Though not of certain location, some modern Jewish archaeologists think that Gedor was in region of Gilead, east of the Jordan River. (The context to follow however might indicate that there was a Gedor elsewhere, likely to the south of the traditional territory of Judah.) They dislocated the gentiles living there during the time of Hezekiah. In the course of time, 500 men (and presumably their families) moved to the region of Mount Seir. There certainly was such a place south of the Dead Sea. There also was a Mount Seir on the border between Judah and Benjamin. However, the comment that "they smote the rest of the Amal-ekites that were escaped" seems to indicate that this branch of Simeon actually settled south of the Dead Sea. Four captains or leaders of this splinter of Simeon are noted.

* * * * *

Overview of I Chronicles 5: *I Chronicles 5 gives an overview of the lineage of Reuben, Gad, and half of the descendants of Manasseh.*

Understanding I Chronicles 385

5:1-2 Now the sons of Reuben the firstborn of Israel, (for he *was* the firstborn; but, forasmuch as he defiled his father's bed, his birthright was given unto the sons of Joseph the son of Israel: and the genealogy is not to be reckoned after the birthright. 2 For Judah prevailed above his brethren, and of him *came* the chief ruler; but the birthright *was* Joseph's:)

The first genealogy of the chapter begins with the posterity of Reuben. Though the firstborn of Jacob, the birthright (i.e., the greater share of the inheritance) passed to the sons of Joseph. However, because Reuben had violated the sanctity of his father's bed by committing adultery with Bilhah, Jacob's surrogate wife, he thus lost the privilege of the birthright. See Genesis 35:22. Jacob passed over Reuben when issuing his benediction to his twelve sons in Genesis 49:3-4.

Though Reuben's sin did not remove his sonship, it certainly caused him to lose reward which otherwise would have been his. Such is true for Christians to this hour. In the New Testament, both Jesus and John spoke of rewards in heaven and the potential loss thereof because of sin. See Mark 9:41 and II John 8. Because of Reuben's sin, the privilege of the birthright was assigned to Joseph's sons. Though Judah would become the tribe whence the royal dynasty of Israel would develop, the birthright (i.e., special inheritance blessings) passed to the descendants of Joseph. Indeed, the two tribes of Joseph, together, were larger than any other one tribe of Israel.

5:3-8 The sons, *I say*, of Reuben the firstborn of Israel *were*, Hanoch, and Pallu, Hezron, and Carmi. 4 The sons of Joel; Shemaiah his son, Gog his son, Shimei his son, 5 Micah his son, Reaia his son, Baal his son, 6 Beerah his son, whom Tilgathpilneser king of Assyria carried away *captive*: he *was* prince of the Reubenites. 7 And his brethren by their families, when the genealogy of their generations was

reckoned, *were* the chief, Jeiel, and Zechariah, 8 **And Bela the son of Azaz, the son of Shema, the son of Joel, who dwelt in Aroer, even unto Nebo and Baalmeon.**

With intended irony, Reuben is again noted as the "firstborn of Israel," but he clearly did not receive the reward of the birthright he could have received. Sin is always destructive. Reuben had four sons as noted. The *Joel* mentioned in verse 4 likely was the son of Hanoch, Reuben's firstborn, since the descendants of him were the princes of the tribe. The posterity of Reuben is thus listed.

5:9-10 And eastward he inhabited unto the entering in of the wilderness from the river Euphrates: because their cattle were multiplied in the land of Gilead. 10 And in the days of Saul they made war with the Hagarites, who fell by their hand: and they dwelt in their tents throughout all the east *land* of Gilead. The *he* of verse 9 refers either to either Bela (mentioned in verse 8,) or the tribe of Reuben. The latter is more likely. It is likely that the reference to the river Euphrates refers to a different river than the one in Babylon. It probably was the river "Phrat" which was in Moab, on the east side of the Jordan. This was the territory whence Reuben occupied. During the time of Saul, the tribe of Reuben expanded their territory by conquering the Hagarites when Saul defeated the Ammonites. See I Samuel 11:1-14. Reuben thus also occupied portions of Gilead, all of which are east of the Jordan River.

5:11-17 And the children of Gad dwelt over against them, in the land of Bashan unto Salchah: 12 Joel the chief, and Shapham the next, and Jaanai, and Shaphat in Bashan. 13 And their brethren of the house of their fathers *were*, Michael, and Meshullam, and Sheba, and Jorai, and Jachan, and Zia, and Heber, seven. 14 These *are* the children of Abihail the son of Huri, the son of Jaroah, the son of

Gilead, the son of Michael, the son of Jeshishai, the son of Jahdo, the son of Buz; 15 Ahi the son of Abdiel, the son of Guni, chief of the house of their fathers. 16 And they dwelt in Gilead in Bashan, and in her towns, and in all the suburbs of Sharon, upon their borders. 17 All these were reckoned by genealogies in the days of Jotham king of Judah, and in the days of Jeroboam king of Israel.

The posterity of the tribe of Gad is here recorded. Like the tribe of Reuben, their inherited lands were east of the Jordan River in Bashan, just north of the possessions of Reuben. Though not specifically noted as such, Gad evidently had four sons which are here noted as Joel the chief and his three brothers: Shapham, Jaanai, and Shaphat. Other prominent men of Gad are also listed. They again lived in Bashan and Gilead to the east of the Jordan River. Apparently, during the reign of Jotham, king of Judah, and at a different time by Jeroboam, king of Israel, a census had been taken of the families of Reuben, Gad, and half Manasseh.

5:18-22 The sons of Reuben, and the Gadites, and half the tribe of Manasseh, of valiant men, men able to bear buckler and sword, and to shoot with bow, and skilful in war, *were* **four and forty thousand seven hundred and threescore, that went out to the war. 19 And they made war with the Hagarites, with Jetur, and Nephish, and Nodab. 20 And they were helped against them, and the Hagarites were delivered into their hand, and all that** *were* **with them: for they cried to God in the battle, and he was intreated of them; because they put their trust in him. 21 And they took away their cattle; of their camels fifty thousand, and of sheep two hundred and fifty thousand, and of asses two thousand, and of men an hundred thousand. 22 For there fell down many slain, because the war** *was* **of God. And they dwelt in their steads until the captivity.**

A summary of the battles won by the tribes of Reuben, Gad, and half Manasseh is recorded here. These two and one-half tribes fielded armed forces totaling 44,760 men. Over the years, they went to war against the Hagarites as also noted in 5:10. These evidently were descended of Ishmael, the son of Hagar. In the battle, this army of Israel was helped against the Hagarites either by other forces of greater Israel, or, perhaps and more likely, by the Lord Himself. The sacred chronicle records how they cried out to God for help and God heard their prayer "because they put their trust in him."

Once again, the clear principle is illustrated that God responds to those who, in true faith toward Him, seek His help. See Hebrews 11:33. God gave these tribes a clear victory and great spoils of war thereafter. For those who proclaim a loving God would never sanction war, take note of the phrase, "For there fell down many slain, because the war *was* of God." These tribes therefore dwelt in their expanded territory, taken from the Hagarites, until the time of the Assyrian captivity.

5:23-24 And the children of the half tribe of Manasseh dwelt in the land: they increased from Bashan unto Baalhermon and Senir, and unto mount Hermon. 24 And these *were* the heads of the house of their fathers, even Epher, and Ishi, and Eliel, and Azriel, and Jeremiah, and Hodaviah, and Jahdiel, mighty men of valour, famous men, *and* heads of the house of their fathers.

The half tribe of Manasseh, living east of Jordan, thus upon the defeat of the Hagarites, expanded their territories northward all the way to Mount Hermon. The latter is north by northeast from the Sea of Galilee by about thirty-five miles. The principal men of that portion of Manasseh are thus listed for the record. Thus, when these several tribes, by faith, sought God's help in battle against ungodly occupants of the land promised to them, God gave them a major victory and they in turn greatly expanded their territories. "Blessed *are* all they that put their trust in him" (Psalm 2:12).

5:25-26 And they transgressed against the God of their fathers, and went a whoring after the gods of the people of the land, whom God destroyed before them. 26 And the God of Israel stirred up the spirit of Pul king of Assyria, and the spirit of Tilgathpilneser king of Assyria, and he carried them away, even the Reubenites, and the Gadites, and the half tribe of Manasseh, and brought them unto Halah, and Habor, and Hara, and to the river Gozan, unto this day.

Notwithstanding the great victories wrought by faith, these tribes by and by backslid and fell into sin. "They transgressed against the God of their fathers, and went a whoring after the gods of the people of the land, whom God destroyed before them." The temptation to be like the world and emulate their pagan religious practices proved to be an enticement to which many in Israel would succumb. As a result, as God had long promised, He chastened them.

The sin was idolatry and a transgression of the first three of the Ten Commandments. To become unfaithful to God is like one becoming unfaithful to a spouse. The latter is physical adultery, the former spiritual adultery. Both are egregious sins. Notice the chastisement which God brought upon them for their spiritual adultery. It was God Himself who stirred up Pul, king of Assyria, in the times of Menahem, king of Israel. See II Kings 15:19-20. Israel still refused to learn their lesson. Therefore, God sent Tilgathpilneser king of the Assyrians in the times of Pekah, king of Israel, to invade the land and make war against it. See II Kings 15:29. The ten northern tribes were ultimately all deported from their land and remained in captivity even until the time of the writing of Chronicles, presumably by Ezra.

* * * * *

Overview of I Chronicles 6: *I Chronicles 6 presents an overview of the lineage of Levi, the priesthood, and their related cities.*

6:1-3 The sons of Levi; Gershon, Kohath, and Merari. 2 And the sons of Kohath; Amram, Izhar, and Hebron, and Uzziel. 3 And the children of Amram; Aaron, and Moses, and Miriam. The sons also of Aaron; Nadab, and Abihu, Eleazar, and Ithamar. The posterity of Levi is herein recorded. Aaron had seven sons. Nadab and Abihu died when God killed them as recorded in Leviticus 10. The sons Gershon, Kohath, and Merari became the heads of the three respective lineages of the Levites. The lineage of the Old Testament priests descended from Aaron is thus presented. Aaron was the grandson of Kohath, son of Levi. Eleazar succeeded Aaron and commenced the proper lineage of the Aaronic priesthood.

6:4-15 Eleazar begat Phinehas, Phinehas begat Abishua, 5 And Abishua begat Bukki, and Bukki begat Uzzi, 6 And Uzzi begat Zerahiah, and Zerahiah begat Meraioth, 7 Meraioth begat Amariah, and Amariah begat Ahitub, 8 And Ahitub begat Zadok, and Zadok begat Ahimaaz, 9 And Ahimaaz begat Azariah, and Azariah begat Johanan, 10 And Johanan begat Azariah, (he *it is* that executed the priest's office in the temple that Solomon built in Jerusalem:) 11 And Azariah begat Amariah, and Amariah begat Ahitub, 12 And Ahitub begat Zadok, and Zadok begat Shallum, 13 And Shallum begat Hilkiah, and Hilkiah begat Azariah, 14 And Azariah begat Seraiah, and Seraiah begat Jehozadak, 15 And Jehozadak went *into captivity*, when the LORD **carried away Judah and Jerusalem by the hand of Nebuchadnezzar.**

The lineage of the Aaronic priesthood from Eleazar unto the time of the Babylonian captivity is here recorded. In the time of Uzzi, the priesthood was transferred to the family of Ithamar, of which Eli was the first high priest. It then continued to the times of Solomon, when it was restored to Zadok, of the line of Eleazar.

6:16 The sons of Levi; Gershom, Kohath, and Merari. The three divisions of the Levites are introduced and will be delineated below.

6:17-30 And these *be* the names of the sons of Gershom; Libni, and Shimei. 18 And the sons of Kohath *were*, Amram, and Izhar, and Hebron, and Uzziel. 19 The sons of Merari; Mahli, and Mushi. And these *are* the families of the Levites according to their fathers. The immediate sons of the three sons of Levi are listed. **20 Of Gershom; Libni his son, Jahath his son, Zimmah his son, 21 Joah his son, Iddo his son, Zerah his son, Jeaterai his son. 22 The sons of Kohath; Amminadab his son, Korah his son, Assir his son, 23 Elkanah his son, and Ebiasaph his son, and Assir his son, 24 Tahath his son, Uriel his son, Uzziah his son, and Shaul his son. 25 And the sons of Elkanah; Amasai, and Ahimoth. 26 *As for* Elkanah: the sons of Elkanah; Zophai his son, and Nahath his son, 27 Eliab his son, Jeroham his son, Elkanah his son. 28 And the sons of Samuel; the firstborn Vashni, and Abiah. 29 The sons of Merari; Mahli, Libni his son, Shimei his son, Uzza his son, 30 Shimea his son, Haggiah his son, Asaiah his son.** Further descendants of the sons of Levi are thus listed.

6:31-32 And these *are they* whom David set over the service of song in the house of the LORD, after that the ark had rest. 32 And they ministered before the dwelling place of the tabernacle of the congregation with singing, until Solomon had built the house of the LORD in Jerusalem: and

then **they waited on their office according to their order.** Listed below are the musicians of the Tabernacle and later the Temple. All were Levites. It was David who so ordered them. After the Temple was built, the Levites listed below then rotated on a specific schedule as ordered by David in I Chronicles 25.

6:33-48 And these *are* they that waited with their children. Of the sons of the Kohathites: Heman a singer, the son of Joel, the son of Shemuel, 34 The son of Elkanah, the son of Jeroham, the son of Eliel, the son of Toah, 35 The son of Zuph, the son of Elkanah, the son of Mahath, the son of Amasai, 36 The son of Elkanah, the son of Joel, the son of Azariah, the son of Zephaniah, 37 The son of Tahath, the son of Assir, the son of Ebiasaph, the son of Korah,

38 The son of Izhar, the son of Kohath, the son of Levi, the son of Israel. 39 And his brother Asaph, who stood on his right hand, *even* Asaph the son of Berachiah, the son of Shimea, 40 The son of Michael, the son of Baaseiah, the son of Malchiah, 41 The son of Ethni, the son of Zerah, the son of Adaiah, 42 The son of Ethan, the son of Zimmah, the son of Shimei, 43 The son of Jahath, the son of Gershom, the son of Levi.

44 And their brethren the sons of Merari *stood* on the left hand: Ethan the son of Kishi, the son of Abdi, the son of Malluch, 45 The son of Hashabiah, the son of Amaziah, the son of Hilkiah, 46 The son of Amzi, the son of Bani, the son of Shamer, 47 The son of Mahli, the son of Mushi, the son of Merari, the son of Levi. 48 Their brethren also the Levites *were* appointed unto all manner of service of the tabernacle of the house of God.

Thus listed are Temple musicians, all of the lineage of Kohath, whence also was the priestly line of Aaron. Of note is **Elkanah** in verse 34. This quite likely was the father of **Samuel**. His son, noted as *Shemuel*, is another pronunciation for

Understanding I Chronicles 393

Samuel. It thus is clear that Samuel was a Levite of the lineage of Kohath, whence also sprang the priestly line. He is here listed as one of the early musicians of the Tabernacle. In verses 33, 39 and 44, we read of the early Temple musicians referred to in the Psalms: **Heman**, **Asaph**, and **Ethan**. These all were descended from Kohath from whence the priestly line also descended.

6:49-53 But Aaron and his sons offered upon the altar of the burnt offering, and on the altar of incense, *and were appointed* for all the work of the *place* most holy, and to make an atonement for Israel, according to all that Moses the servant of God had commanded. 50 And these *are* the sons of Aaron; Eleazar his son, Phinehas his son, Abishua his son, 51 Bukki his son, Uzzi his son, Zerahiah his son, 52 Meraioth his son, Amariah his son, Ahitub his son, 53 Zadok his son, Ahimaaz his son.

The lineage of Levi now shifts again to that of Aaron, the work of the priests, and the priestly line. Specifically, they were "to make an atonement for Israel, according to all that Moses the servant of God had commanded." The lineage of Aaron through Eleazar is again noted to Ahimaaz.

6:54-81 A detailed listing of the towns and villages of the Levites and priests is here listed. Some cities of note are Hebron (verse 55), Debir (verse 58), Beth-shemesh (verse 59), and Anathoth (verse 60). The sons of Kohath were assigned ten cities by lot in verse 61. The sons of Gerhon were assigned thirteen cities in verse 62. And the sons of Merari were assigned twelve cities in verse 63.

Cities of refuge are also listed. Some of the more familiar names listed are: Shechem (verse 67), Beth-horon (verse 68), Golan (verse 71), Kirjathaim (verse 76), Ramoth (verse 80), Mahanaim (verse 80), and Heshbon (verse 81).

Overview of I Chronicles 7: *I Chronicles 7 presents overviews of the lineage of Issachar, Benjamin, Naphtali, Ephraim and Asher. In verse 27, Joshua is noted of the tribe of Ephraim.*

7:1-5 Now the sons of Issachar *were*, Tola, and Puah, Jashub, and Shimron, four. 2 And the sons of Tola; Uzzi, and Rephaiah, and Jeriel, and Jahmai, and Jibsam, and Shemuel, heads of their father's house, *to wit*, of Tola: *they were* valiant men of might in their generations; whose number *was* in the days of David two and twenty thousand and six hundred. 3 And the sons of Uzzi; Izrahiah: and the sons of Izrahiah; Michael, and Obadiah, and Joel, Ishiah, five: all of them chief men.

4 And with them, by their generations, after the house of their fathers, *were* bands of soldiers for war, six and thirty thousand *men*: for they had many wives and sons. 5 And their brethren among all the families of Issachar *were* valiant men of might, reckoned in all by their genealogies fourscore and seven thousand.

The posterity of Issachar is presented. Issachar fathered four sons, Tola, Puah, Jashub, and Shimron. At a time not defined, there were 87,000 men fit for battle from the tribe of Issachar.

7:6-12 *The sons* of Benjamin; Bela, and Becher, and Jediael, three. 7 And the sons of Bela; Ezbon, and Uzzi, and Uzziel, and Jerimoth, and Iri, five; heads of the house of *their* fathers, mighty men of valour; and were reckoned by their genealogies twenty and two thousand and thirty and four. 8 And the sons of Becher; Zemira, and Joash, and Eliezer, and Elioenai, and Omri, and Jerimoth, and Abiah, and Anathoth, and Alameth. All these *are* the sons of Becher. 9 And the number of them, after their genealogy by

their generations, heads of the house of their fathers, mighty men of valour, *was* twenty thousand and two hundred.

10 **The sons also of Jediael; Bilhan: and the sons of Bilhan; Jeush, and Benjamin, and Ehud, and Chenaanah, and Zethan, and Tharshish, and Ahishahar.** 11 **All these the sons of Jediael, by the heads of their fathers, mighty men of valour, *were* seventeen thousand and two hundred *soldiers*, fit to go out for war *and* battle.** 12 **Shuppim also, and Huppim, the children of Ir, *and* Hushim, the sons of Aher.**

The posterity of the tribe of Benjamin is here recorded. Benjamin had five sons, though only Bela, Becher, and Jediael are mentioned here. See I Chronicles 8:1-2. Notice the familiar modern name of *Uzzi* as coming from the tribe of Benjamin. Though not totaled in the text, the men fit for battle descended from the three sons of Benjamin totaled 59,434.

7:13 The sons of Naphtali; Jahziel, and Guni, and Jezer, and Shallum, the sons of Bilhah. Four sons were born to Naphtali: Jahziel, Guni, Jezer, and Shallum. Why further details regarding the posterity of Naphtali were not recorded is not clear.

7:14-19 The sons of Manasseh; Ashriel, whom she bare: (*but* his concubine the Aramitess bare Machir the father of Gilead: 15 **And Machir took to wife *the sister* of Huppim and Shuppim, whose sister's name *was* Maachah;) and the name of the second *was* Zelophehad: and Zelophehad had daughters.**

16 **And Maachah the wife of Machir bare a son, and she called his name Peresh; and the name of his brother *was* Sheresh; and his sons *were* Ulam and Rakem.** 17 **And the sons of Ulam; Bedan. These *were* the sons of Gilead, the son of Machir, the son of Manasseh.** 18 **And his sister Ham-**

moleketh bare Ishod, and Abiezer, and Mahalah. 19 And the sons of Shemida were, Ahian, and Shechem, and Likhi, and Aniam.

The posterity of Manasseh is described. The sacred chronicle begins by distinguishing between the sons of Manasseh's wife versus those of his concubine. Those by his wife were Ashriel and Zelophehad. The son of his concubine was Machir the father of Gilead. Further record is made of the daughters of Zelophehad in Numbers 26:33; 27:1; 36:11; and Joshua 17:3. It appears that the primary male descent of Manasseh was through Machir. Though not noted here, Ashriel also had children as briefly noted in Numbers 26:31. Why they are not listed here is unclear.

7:20-27 And the sons of Ephraim; Shuthelah, and Bered his son, and Tahath his son, and Eladah his son, and Tahath his son, 21 And Zabad his son, and Shuthelah his son, and Ezer, and Elead, whom the men of Gath *that were* born in *that* land slew, because they came down to take away their cattle. 22 And Ephraim their father mourned many days, and his brethren came to comfort him. 23 And when he went in to his wife, she conceived, and bare a son, and he called his name Beriah, because it went evil with his house.

24 (And his daughter *was* Sherah, who built Bethhoron the nether, and the upper, and Uzzensherah.) 25 And Rephah *was* his son, also Resheph, and Telah his son, and Tahan his son, 26 Laadan his son, Ammihud his son, Elishama his son, 27 Non his son, Jehoshua his son.

Though a number of generations of Ephraim are here listed, it appears that he only had three sons: Shuthelah, Zabad, and Beriah. (Some think that Rephah was also a son of Ephraim rather than a son of Beriah.) Evidently, Zabad and his three sons were slain by men of Gath. The sorrow prompted Ephraim to be intimate with his wife who in turn conceived Beriah. The thought in verse 24 is that he went in to his wife because evil had befallen his house in the death of Zabad and his sons. Ephraim also had a daughter by the name of Sherah who built both upper and lower Bethhoron. Perhaps the greatest de-scendant of Ephraim was Jehoshua or more commonly known as *Joshua the son of Nun.*

7:28-29 And their possessions and habitations *were,* **Bethel and the towns thereof, and eastward Naaran, and westward Gezer, with the towns thereof; Shechem also and the towns thereof, unto Gaza and the towns thereof: 29 And by the borders of the children of Manasseh, Bethshean and her towns, Taanach and her towns, Megiddo and her towns, Dor and her towns. In these dwelt the children of Joseph the son of Israel.** Towns taken by Ephraim and by Manasseh are listed. Notable were the towns of Bethel, Shechem and Gaza, of Ephraim. Notable towns of Manasseh were Bethshean and Megiddo, among others.

7:30-40 The sons of Asher; Imnah, and Isuah, and Ishuai, and Beriah, and Serah their sister. 31 And the sons of Beriah; Heber, and Malchiel, who *is* **the father of Birzavith. 32 And Heber begat Japhlet, and Shomer, and Hotham, and Shua their sister. 33 And the sons of Japhlet; Pasach, and Bimhal, and Ashvath. These** *are* **the children of Japhlet. 34 And the sons of Shamer; Ahi, and Rohgah, Jehubbah, and Aram. 35 And the sons of his brother Helem; Zophah, and Imna, and Shelesh, and Amal.**

36 The sons of Zophah; Suah, and Harnepher, and Shual, and Beri, and Imrah, 37 Bezer, and Hod, and Shamma, and Shilshah, and Ithran, and Beera. 38 And the sons of Jether; Jephunneh, and Pispah, and Ara. 39 And the sons of Ulla; Arah, and Haniel, and Rezia. 40 All these *were* the children of Asher, heads of *their* father's house, choice *and* mighty men of valour, chief of the princes. And the number throughout the genealogy of them that were apt to the war *and* to battle *was* twenty and six thousand men.

The posterity of Asher is here recorded. Asher had four sons and one daughter: Imnah, Isuah, Ishuai, Beriah, and Serah their sister. At the time of the counting, Asher had 26,000 men for battle.

* * * * *

Overview of I Chronicles 8*: I Chronicles 8 gives more detail of the descendants of Benjamin, particularly of the stock of Saul and Jonathon.*

8:1-32 Further details of the posterity of Benjamin are recorded, including two sons not mentioned in 6:6*ff*—Nohah and Rapha. Family record of other principal men of the tribe of Benjamin are also here recorded. The tribe of Benjamin shared a border with Judah across the northern section of the city of Jerusalem. Hence, in verses 28-32, the chief men of Benjamin dwelling at Jerusalem are noted.

8:33-40 And Ner begat Kish, and Kish begat Saul, and Saul begat Jonathan, and Malchishua, and Abinadab, and Eshbaal. 34 And the son of Jonathan *was* **Meribbaal; and Meribbaal begat Micah. 35 And the sons of Micah** *were*, **Pithon, and Melech, and Tarea, and Ahaz. 36 And Ahaz begat Jehoadah; and Jehoadah begat Alemeth, and Azmaveth, and Zimri; and Zimri begat Moza, 37 And Moza begat Binea: Rapha** *was* **his son, Eleasah his son, Azel his son: 38 And Azel had six sons, whose names** *are* **these, Azrikam, Bocheru, and Ishmael, and Sheariah, and Obadiah, and Hanan. All these** *were* **the sons of Azel. 39 And**

Understanding I Chronicles

the sons of Eshek his brother *were*, Ulam his firstborn, Jehush the second, and Eliphelet the third. 40 And the sons of Ulam were mighty men of valour, archers, and had many sons, and sons' sons, an hundred and fifty. All these *are* of the sons of Benjamin.

The lineage of Benjamin now focuses upon the lineage of Saul—both his heritage and his posterity. It is likely that Ner, grandfather of Saul, had another name. In I Samuel 9:1, the sacred text reads, "Now there was a man of Benjamin, whose name *was* Kish, the son of Abiel." Evidently, Abiel and Ner were one and the same. Likewise, Abinadab was the same as Ishui (see 1Samuel 14:49). Esh-baal likely was Ish-bosheth. Meribbaal is the same as Mephibosheth. See II Samuel 4:4 and 9:6 .

From verse 34 onward is the posterity of Jonathon, Saul's son. Noted in verse 35 is Ahaz which is not in the text in 9:41. In verse 36, Jehoadah is called Jara in 9:42. In verse 37, Rapha is called Rephaiah in 9:43. Also, Elasah in verse 37 is called Eleasah in verse 43. A later descendant of Saul named Ulam had many sons and 150 grandsons who all were valiant warriors. These all were significant descendants of Benjamin.

* * * * *

Overview of I Chronicles 9: I Chronicles 9 finishes the main genealogies of the book with other miscellaneous lists. Included are the lists of the first families to actually take possession of the land following the conquest. And, an interesting people mentioned later in Nehemiah, the Nethinims, are also mentioned in verses 14 - 25. These mysterious people were servants to the Levites.

9:1 So all Israel were reckoned by genealogies; and, behold, they *were* written in the book of the kings of Israel

and Judah, *who* were carried away to Babylon for their transgression. From the beginning of the Hebrew nation, public records were kept containing a registration of the name of every individual as well as the tribe and family to which he belonged. The "book of the kings of Israel and Judah" does not refer to a biblical book, but rather to civil records maintained by Hebrew authorities of the respective kingdoms of Israel. The history of Old Testament Israel is tersely summarized in the comment, "*who* were carried away to Babylon for their transgression." The following lists were those who eventually returned from Babylon under Ezra and perhaps Nehemiah.

9:2-9 Now the first inhabitants that *dwelt* in their possessions in their cities *were*, the Israelites, the priests, Levites, and the Nethinims. 3 And in Jerusalem dwelt of the children of Judah, and of the children of Benjamin, and of the children of Ephraim, and Manasseh; 4 Uthai the son of Ammihud, the son of Omri, the son of Imri, the son of Bani, of the children of Pharez the son of Judah. 5 And of the Shilonites; Asaiah the firstborn, and his sons. 6 And of the sons of Zerah; Jeuel, and their brethren, six hundred and ninety.

7 And of the sons of Benjamin; Sallu the son of Meshullam, the son of Hodaviah, the son of Hasenuah, 8 And Ibneiah the son of Jeroham, and Elah the son of Uzzi, the son of Michri, and Meshullam the son of Shephathiah, the son of Reuel, the son of Ibnijah; 9 And their brethren, according to their generations, nine hundred and fifty and six. All these men *were* chief of the fathers in the house of their fathers.

Verse 2 essentially summrizes the initial Jews who returned from the Babylonian captivity. They were (1) Israelites, (2) priests, (3) Levites, and (4) Nethinims. The first mention of the Nethinims in the Bible is here made. These were servants of the Levites and priests. It is thought that they were the descendants of the Gibeonites who had made the covenant with Joshua under false pretenses. See Joshua 9:27.

Jerusalem became the home of returning Jews and Benjamites. (1) These were the tribes predominantly represented in the Babylonian captivity. And, (2) both of these tribes claimed Jerusalem. The territory of Benjamin included the northern area of the city of Jerusalem. But also members of the tribes of Ephraim and Manasseh also returned in the captiv-ity. These undoubtedly were Israelites along with other tribes which had fled to Judah when Jeroboam I had introduced idolatry into the northern kingdom. Others had fled to Judah when Samaria was taken or when Assyria was about to overrun the north. Families of these groups are mentioned in verse 4 and 5. The *Shilonites* refers to former inhabitants of Shiloh. Specific families of returning Benjamites are noted in verses 7-9. From Benjamin returned a total of 956 men who were leaders of the tribe.

9:10-13 And of the priests; Jedaiah, and Jehoiarib, and Jachin, 11 And Azariah the son of Hilkiah, the son of Meshullam, the son of Zadok, the son of Meraioth, the son of Ahitub, the ruler of the house of God; 12 And Adaiah the son of Jeroham, the son of Pashur, the son of Malchijah, and Maasiai the son of Adiel, the son of Jahzerah, the son of Meshullam, the son of Meshillemith, the son of Immer; 13 And their brethren, heads of the house of their fathers, a thousand and seven hundred and threescore; very able men for the work of the service of the house of God.

Priests returning from the exile are listed. One-thousand-seven-hundred-sixty priests returned from Babylon. They are here called "very able men for the work of the service of the house of God." The thought is that they were strong both of body and mind for the daunting task of the reconstituting of the

Temple and its sacrifices. Names of interest in this list are: the son of Hilkiah (the latter likely was Jeremiah's father); the son of Zadok; and the son of Pashur (the latter who so persecuted Jeremiah.)

9:14-16 And of the Levites; Shemaiah the son of Hasshub, the son of Azrikam, the son of Hashabiah, of the sons of Merari; 15 And Bakbakkar, Heresh, and Galal, and Mattaniah the son of Micah, the son of Zichri, the son of Asaph; 16 And Obadiah the son of Shemaiah, the son of Galal, the son of Jeduthun, and Berechiah the son of Asa, the son of Elkanah, that dwelt in the villages of the Netophathites. The sacred chronicler now begins a lengthy section, listing the Levites who returned from exile. Those listed here are not mentioned in the specific tasks soon to be delineated and therefore may be assumed to have been chief Levites.

9:17-22 And the porters *were*, Shallum, and Akkub, and Talmon, and Ahiman, and their brethren: Shallum *was* the chief; 18 Who hitherto *waited* in the king's gate eastward: they *were* porters in the companies of the children of Levi. 19 And Shallum the son of Kore, the son of Ebiasaph, the son of Korah, and his brethren, of the house of his father, the Korahites, *were* over the work of the service, keepers of the gates of the tabernacle: and their fathers, *being* over the host of the LORD, *were* keepers of the entry.

20 And Phinehas the son of Eleazar was the ruler over them in time past, *and* the LORD *was* with him. 21 *And* Zechariah the son of Meshelemiah *was* porter of the door of the tabernacle of the congregation. 22 All these *which were* chosen to be porters in the gates *were* two hundred and twelve. These were reckoned by their genealogy in their

Understanding I Chronicles

villages, whom David and Samuel the seer did ordain in their set office.

A list of returning Levites who were porters of the Temple is presented. A porter was a gatekeeper and in a real sense, guards of the Temple. Only those duly qualified could enter the Temple, especially the internal courts reserved for ceremonially clean Jewish men. The *Phinehas* mentioned originally was the priest in charge of the porters of the Tabernacle. Those Levites who returned from exile as porters were numbered as 212.

9:23-25 So they and their children *had* the oversight of the gates of the house of the LORD, *namely*, the house of the tabernacle, by wards. 24 In four quarters were the porters, toward the east, west, north, and south. 25 And their brethren, *which were* in their villages, *were* to come after seven days from time to time with them. The Levites mentioned above were thence committed the charge of being porters in the rebuilt Temple of Ezra. The schedule of 'courses' of Levites and priests was on duty one week at time. They then returned to their home and village until the next time their 'course' was scheduled for service.

9:26-34 For these Levites, the four chief porters, were in *their* set office, and were over the chambers and treasuries of the house of God. 27 And they lodged round about the house of God, because the charge *was* upon them, and the opening thereof every morning *pertained* to them. 28 And *certain* of them had the charge of the ministering vessels, that they should bring them in and out by tale. 29 *Some* of them also *were* appointed to oversee the vessels, and all the instruments of the sanctuary, and the fine flour, and the wine, and the oil, and the frankincense, and the spices. 30 And *some* of the sons of the priests made the ointment of the spices. 31 And Mattithiah, *one* of the Levites, who *was* the

firstborn of Shallum the Korahite, had the set office over the things that were made in the pans. 32 And *other* of their brethren, of the sons of the Kohathites, *were* over the shewbread, to prepare *it* every sabbath. 33 And these *are* the singers, chief of the fathers of the Levites, *who remaining* in the chambers *were* free: for they were employed in *that* work day and night. 34 These chief fathers of the Levites *were* chief throughout their generations; these dwelt at Jerusalem.

Specific Levites were assigned specific duties such as the opening of the Temple each day, oversight of the various appurtenant chambers (i.e., halls), oversight of the treasuries, oversight of the ministering vessels, oversight of the ingredients for sacred offerings, and oversight of the sacred elements such as the shewbread etc. Those with oversight actually lived either on site or immediately adjacent to the Temple. Moreover, the Temple musicians lived free in special chambers of the Temple complex. Their ministries went day and night.

9:35-44 And in Gibeon dwelt the father of Gibeon, Jehiel, whose wife's name *was* Maachah: 36 And his firstborn son Abdon, then Zur, and Kish, and Baal, and Ner, and Nadab, 37 And Gedor, and Ahio, and Zechariah, and Mikloth. 38 And Mikloth begat Shimeam. And they also dwelt with their brethren at Jerusalem, over against their brethren. 39 And Ner begat Kish; and Kish begat Saul; and Saul begat Jonathan, and Malchishua, and Abinadab, and Eshbaal. 40 And the son of Jonathan *was* Meribbaal: and Meribbaal begat Micah.

41 And the sons of Micah *were*, Pithon, and Melech, and Tahrea, *and Ahaz*. 42 And Ahaz begat Jarah; and Jarah begat Alemeth, and Azmaveth, and Zimri; and Zimri begat Moza; 43 And Moza begat Binea; and Rephaiah his son, Eleasah his son, Azel his son. 44 And Azel had six sons, whose

names *are* these, Azrikam, Bocheru, and Ishmael, and Sheariah, and Obadiah, and Hanan: these *were* the sons of Azel.

Further details of the heritage and posterity of Saul and the tribe of Benjamin are presented. The list parallels that of I Chronicles 8:33-40. There are anomalies between the two lists, but see comments for I Chronicles 8:33-40 for reconciliation thereof.

* * * * *

Overview of I Chronicles 10: *The mid-section of I Chronicles begins an overview of the final days of Saul's reign and of the first part of David's reign. Chapter 10 present only the briefest comment on the life and reign of Saul. Here the details parallel I Samuel 31.*

10:1-3 Now the Philistines fought against Israel; and the men of Israel fled from before the Philistines, and fell down slain in mount Gilboa. 2 And the Philistines followed hard after Saul, and after his sons; and the Philistines slew Jonathan, and Abinadab, and Malchishua, the sons of Saul. 3 And the battle went sore against Saul, and the archers hit him, and he was wounded of the archers.

The narrative here closely parallels that of I Samuel 31. The greater scene is the final battle of Saul and his bitter death. Variance of details between here and I Samuel 31 are not conflicting but rather complementary to each other. Collating the two accounts together provides full details of the event.

10:4-7 Then said Saul to his armourbearer, Draw thy sword, and thrust me through therewith; lest these uncircumcised come and abuse me. But his armourbearer

would not; for he was sore afraid. So Saul took a sword, and fell upon it. 5 And when his armourbearer saw that Saul was dead, he fell likewise on the sword, and died. 6 So Saul died, and his three sons, and all his house died together. 7 And when all the men of Israel that *were* in the valley saw that they fled, and that Saul and his sons were dead, then they forsook their cities, and fled: and the Philistines came and dwelt in them.**

The thought is virtually identical with I Samuel 31. See comments thereto.

10:8-10 And it came to pass on the morrow, when the Philistines came to strip the slain, that they found Saul and his sons fallen in mount Gilboa. 9 And when they had stripped him, they took his head, and his armour, and sent into the land of the Philistines round about, to carry tidings unto their idols, and to the people. 10 And they put his armour in the house of their gods, and fastened his head in the temple of Dagon. Again, the information her is almost identical to that of I Samuel 31. The one significant detail of note is that the Philistines fastened Saul's head in the temple of Dagon—while the trunk or headless corpse of his body was affixed to the wall of Beth-shan. See I Samuel 31:10.

10:11-12 And when all Jabeshgilead heard all that the Philistines had done to Saul, 12 They arose, all the valiant men, and took away the body of Saul, and the bodies of his sons, and brought them to Jabesh, and buried their bones under the oak in Jabesh, and fasted seven days. Again, see comments for I Samuel 10:11-12. Again, slight difference in details are complementary and not conflicting.

10:13-14 So Saul died for his transgression which he committed against the LORD, *even* against the word of the

Understanding I Chronicles

LORD, which he kept not, and also for asking *counsel* of *one that had* a familiar spirit, to enquire *of it*; 14 And enquired not of the LORD: therefore he slew him, and turned the kingdom unto David the son of Jesse.

Verses 13-14 list why God allowed Saul's premature death. In a word, it was because of his *disobedience*. Unto whom much is given, much is required. Three specific charges are made again Saul. (1) He kept not the word of the Lord. (2) He sought counsel of one having a familiar spirit. And, (3) he enquired not of the Lord. The latter two were direct disobedience to the Word of God. This was not only a lack of faith but also an indication of His backslidden spiritual condition. Because of the serious nature of Saul's sin, God killed him. That may sound severe—it was. God takes sin by those in leadership seriously. He therefore turned the kingdom of Israel over to David.

* * * * *

Overview of I Chronicles 11: *This chapter presents an overview of the initial reign of David. The following chapters will go back and present some of the intervening details. The Chronicle's account pass over the fact that David was king of Judah for seven years in Hebron. This chapter picks up the chronology when the leaders of the other eleven tribes asked him to become king over all of Israel. Shortly thereafter, David took the city of Jerusalem militarily which had never been totally conquered from the Jebusites since the time of Joshua. From that time onward, the basic capital city of Israel has been Jerusalem, also known as Mount Zion. The remainder of this chapter presents a listing of David's 'mighty men.'*

11:1-3 Then all Israel gathered themselves to David unto Hebron, saying, Behold, we *are* thy bone and thy flesh.

2 And moreover in time past, even when Saul was king, thou *wast* he that leddest out and broughtest in Israel: and the LORD thy God said unto thee, Thou shalt feed my people Israel, and thou shalt be ruler over my people Israel. 3 Therefore came all the elders of Israel to the king to Hebron; and David made a covenant with them in Hebron before the LORD; and they anointed David king over Israel, according to the word of the LORD by Samuel. The section here closely parallels that of II Samuel 5:1-3. See comments thereto.

11:4-6 And David and all Israel went to Jerusalem, which *is* Jebus; where the Jebusites *were*, the inhabitants of the land. 5 And the inhabitants of Jebus said to David, Thou shalt not come hither. Nevertheless David took the castle of Zion, which *is* the city of David. 6 And David said, Whosoever smiteth the Jebusites first shall be chief and captain. So Joab the son of Zeruiah went first up, and was chief.

Upon acceding to the throne of all of Israel, David made it an early priority to conquer Jerusalem completely. Its ancient name had been *Jebus* which literally meant a 'threshing place.' Though Judah had occupied the lower elevations of the city; the Jebusites were smug, thinking their fortifications of the heights of Jerusalem were impregnable. They therefore taunted David saying in effect, "You will never make it up here." See comments for II Samuel 5:6-12 for greater details.

In the vicinity of the city of David in east Jerusalem is a deep shaft down to a subterranean water source. The ancient Jebusites had so dug the shaft to provide water during times of military assault. David was aware of this and offered the reward of leadership for any of his men who would so ascend that dark shaft up the mountain. In recent times, an archaeologist by the name of Warren discovered this shaft and it today is known as

'Warren's Shaft.' The Jebusites thought they were secure in their stronghold of Zion, thinking their water supply and shaft were unknown to David. He rather surreptitiously sent men up it who then attacked the city from within. Joab, David's nephew, was the first to enter the upper city of Jerusalem, known also as the castle of Zion. He therefore and thereafter became the chief of staff of David's army.

11:7-9 And David dwelt in the castle; therefore they called it the city of David. 8 And he built the city round about, even from Millo round about: and Joab repaired the rest of the city. 9 So David waxed greater and greater: for the LORD of hosts *was* with him.

The section of east Jerusalem, particularly the heights thereof, came to be known as the city of David. Fortifications between the lower city and the upper were called Millo. The city thus began to be built to the north and west. One of Joab's first projects was oversight of the repair and reconstruction of the city of Jerusalem. Because God was with David and he was in the center of God's will, God blessed him greatly. Accordingly, David became greater and greater. The blessing of the Lord is good and a rare commodity never to be allowed to be lost.

11:10-11 These also *are* the chief of the mighty men whom David had, who strengthened themselves with him in his kingdom, *and* with all Israel, to make him king, according to the word of the LORD concerning Israel. 11 And this *is* the number of the mighty men whom David had; Jashobeam, an Hachmonite, the chief of the captains: he lifted up his spear against three hundred slain *by him* at one time.

From here to the end of the chapter is a listing of David's chief men—men who had helped him win his battles and who had assisted him to the throne. The first thereof was a man named "*Jashobeam*, an Hachmonite, the chief of the captains." Apparently in one (otherwise not described) battle, he had slain 300 enemy soldiers with his spear.

11:12-14 And after him *was* Eleazar the son of Dodo, the Ahohite, who *was one* of the three mighties. 13 He was with David at Pasdammim, and there the Philistines were gathered together to battle, where was a parcel of ground full of barley; and the people fled from before the Philistines. 14 And they set themselves in the midst of *that* parcel, and delivered it, and slew the Philistines; and the LORD saved *them* by a great deliverance.

The next mighty man of David was a man named "*Eleazar* the son of Dodo, the Ahohite." The event in question was when David was a fugitive in the wilderness. The Philistines had attacked Israel at Pasdammim and overran the local populace. David, with the assistance of Eleazar, routed the Philistines and won the battle. See II Samuel 23:9-12 and comments thereto for further details. The sacred chronicler also makes clear that the ultimate victory was from God.

11:15-19 Now three of the thirty captains went down to the rock to David, into the cave of Adullam; and the host of the Philistines encamped in the valley of Rephaim. 16 And David *was* then in the hold, and the Philistines' garrison *was* then at Bethlehem. 17 And David longed, and said, Oh that one would give me drink of the water of the well of Bethlehem, that *is* at the gate!

18 And the three brake through the host of the Philistines, and drew water out of the well of Bethlehem, that *was* by the gate, and took *it*, and brought *it* to David: but David would not drink *of* it, but poured it out to the LORD, 19 And said, My God forbid it me, that I should do this thing: shall I drink the blood of these men that have put their lives

Understanding I Chronicles

in jeopardy? for with *the jeopardy of* their lives they brought it. Therefore he would not drink it. These things did these three mightiest.

David evidently also had thirty captains or lieutenant officers in his army. Three of these took forces against the Philistines when they invaded Israel and encamped at Rephaim. See II Samuel 5:18*ff* and I Chronicles 14:9*ff*. The rock of David and the cave Adullam evidently was the 'hold' or 'stronghold' of David. The word translated as **hold** (מצודה *matsuwdah*) also refers to what later came to be known as *Masada*. However, because the hold is here described in connection of cave of Adullam which likely was near Engedi, the 'hold' here and Masada, likely are not the same, though they certainly are in the same area. On that occasion, David longed for water from the well at his hometown of Bethlehem.

The three captains of David's forces, without the knowledge of David therefore fought their way into Bethlehem, drew water from the well thereof, and brought it to David. He however would not drink of it because his loyal lieutenants had endangered their lives in procuring it. The **three mightiest** evidently were Jashobeam (verse 11), Eleazar (verse 12), and Abishai (verse 20).

11:20-21 And Abishai the brother of Joab, he was chief of the three: for lifting up his spear against three hundred, he slew *them*, and had a name among the three. 21 Of the three, he was more honourable than the two; for he was their captain: howbeit he attained not to the *first* three.

Abishai was the brother of Joab and David's nephew. He was therefore appointed chief of the three captains of David's mighty men. He thus was the chief field commander of David's armies under Joab. In one battle, Abishai had also killed 300 enemies combatants. Therefore, of all of David's captains, Abishai was the highest rank under Joab.

11:22-25 **Benaiah the son of Jehoiada, the son of a valiant man of Kabzeel, who had done many acts; he slew two lionlike men of Moab: also he went down and slew a lion in a pit in a snowy day.** 23 **And he slew an Egyptian, a man of** *great* **stature, five cubits high; and in the Egyptian's hand** *was* **a spear like a weaver's beam; and he went down to him with a staff, and plucked the spear out of the Egyptian's hand, and slew him with his own spear.** 24 **These** *things* **did Benaiah the son of Jehoiada, and had the name among the three mighties.** 25 **Behold, he was honourable among the thirty, but attained not to the** *first* **three: and David set him over his guard.**

Another of David's mighty men is described by the name of "Benaiah the son of Jehoiada, the son of a valiant man of Kabzeel." Over his career as a military man, he had (1) killed a lion single-handedly during the winter. The lion likely was a mountain-lion type of wildcat. Nevertheless, such a victory was quite a feat. (2) He also killed an Egyptian who was more than seven and one-half feet tall. The latter carried a spear like a two by four. Benaiah plucked that massive spear from the giant's hand and killed him with it. Benaiah thus had a reputation amongst David's mighty men and was considered as honorable amongst the thirty captains. However, he was not as highly reputed as the first three. David therefore assigned him to be over the Cherethites and Pelethites that composed the bodyguard, always in attendance on the king. The latter would be comparable to the secret service and their protection of an American president.

11:26-47 Listed are the rest of David's mighty men. Asahel the brother of Joab Asahel was their chief. More than forty other mighty men are described.

* * * * *

Understanding I Chronicles 413

Overview of I Chronicles 12: *This chapter reverts back into an earlier period of David's life when he fled from Saul and went to Ziklag in the land of the Philistines in verses 1-22. The remainder of the chapter lists those who later joined forces with David and ultimately placed him on the throne after Saul's death in verses 23-40.*

12:1-7 Now these *are* they that came to David to Ziklag, while he yet kept himself close because of Saul the son of Kish: and they *were* among the mighty men, helpers of the war. 2 *They were* armed with bows, and could use both the right hand and the left in *hurling* stones and *shooting* arrows out of a bow, *even* of Saul's brethren of Benjamin. 3 The chief *was* Ahiezer, then Joash, the sons of Shemaah the Gibeathite; and Jeziel, and Pelet, the sons of Azmaveth; and Berachah, and Jehu the Antothite, 4 And Ismaiah the Gibeonite, a mighty man among the thirty, and over the thirty; and Jeremiah, and Jahaziel, and Johanan, and Josabad the Gederathite, 5 Eluzai, and Jerimoth, and Bealiah, and Shemariah, and Shephatiah the Haruphite, 6 Elkanah, and Jesiah, and Azareel, and Joezer, and Jashobeam, the Korhites, 7 And Joelah, and Zebadiah, the sons of Jeroham of Gedor.

The sacred chronicler now presents records of the men who assembled to David while he was in Ziklag. The time was when David had fled from Saul to Philistia and the Philistine king of Ziklag gave him refuge. Some of these are noted as David's earliest mighty men. See also I Samuel 22:2. The text makes clear that all of these men either were or became skilled marksmen with bow or sling. Some of these men were even of the tribe of Benjamin, whence sprang Saul.

Chief of these men of the early days of David's ascent to power was a man named *Ahiezer*. Towns from whence these men came certainly included some from Benjamin, including

Gibeah, Anathoth, and Gibeon. At least one of these men, Ismaiah the Gibeonite, went on to become one of David's mighty men and a captain over the *thirty*. The latter referring to the thirty captains in the previous chapter.

12:8-15 And of the Gadites there separated themselves unto David into the hold to the wilderness men of might, *and* **men of war** *fit* **for the battle, that could handle shield and buckler, whose faces** *were like* **the faces of lions, and** *were* **as swift as the roes upon the mountains; 9 Ezer the first, Obadiah the second, Eliab the third, 10 Mishmannah the fourth, Jeremiah the fifth, 11 Attai the sixth, Eliel the seventh, 12 Johanan the eighth, Elzabad the ninth, 13 Jeremiah the tenth, Machbanai the eleventh.**

14 These *were* **of the sons of Gad, captains of the host: one of the least** *was* **over an hundred, and the greatest over a thousand. 15 These** *are* **they that went over Jordan in the first month, when it had overflown all his banks; and they put to flight all** *them* **of the valleys,** *both* **toward the east, and toward the west.**

Mention is made of men of the tribe of Gad who specifically deserted from Saul and cast their lot with David while he hid in the *hold* of the wilderness. See comments for I Chronicles 11:15-19 for the latter. These men were also skilled in use of weapons and were physically fit. Eleven are named and all were *captains* or leaders. What is remarkable is that these men chose to cross the Jordan River during spring flooding (the first month being Nisan which is the beginning of Spring). They had to fight their way through forces loyal to Saul on both sides of the river (east and west) to make their way to where David was.

12:16-18 And there came of the children of Benjamin and Judah to the hold unto David. 17 And David went out to

meet them, and answered and said unto them, If ye be come peaceably unto me to help me, mine heart shall be knit unto you: but if *ye be come* to betray me to mine enemies, seeing *there is* no wrong in mine hands, the God of our fathers look *thereon*, and rebuke *it*. 18 **Then the spirit came upon Amasai,** *who was* **chief of the captains,** *and he said*, **Thine** *are we*, **David, and on thy side, thou son of Jesse: peace, peace** *be* **unto thee, and peace** *be* **to thine helpers; for thy God helpeth thee. Then David received them, and made them captains of the band.**

In addition to the men of Benjamin who defected to David in verse 2, another band of Benjamites made their way to the hold whence David was encamped. Upon meeting them, David very well may have been suspicious. He told them that if they came in peace that his heart would be united with theirs. However, if they came to betray him, God would be their judge. In an Old Testament reference to the work of the Holy Spirit, "the spirit came upon Amasai, *who was* chief of the captains."

The word translated as **came upon** (לבשׁ *labash*) literally means to 'clothe.' Amasai was *clothed* with the Spirit of God when he replied to David. In New Testament terminology, he was *filled* with the Spirit. In other words, God's Spirit directed what he had to say to David. Amasai made clear to David that they came in submission to him. He ascribed peace to David and presented themselves as his servants. David therefore received them and made them officers over his band of men.

12:19-22 And there fell *some* **of Manasseh to David, when he came with the Philistines against Saul to battle: but they helped them not: for the lords of the Philistines upon advisement sent him away, saying, He will fall to his master Saul to** *the jeopardy of* **our heads. 20 As he went to Ziklag, there fell to him of Manasseh, Adnah, and Jozabad, and Jediael, and Michael, and Jozabad, and Elihu, and Zilthai,**

captains of the thousands that *were* of Manasseh. 21 **And they helped David against the band *of the rovers*: for they *were* all mighty men of valour, and were captains in the host.** 22 **For at *that* time day by day there came to David to help him, until *it was* a great host, like the host of God.**

In the months in which David was in the vicinity of Ziklag, men from Manasseh joined with him. Though the Philistines would not allow David and his men to join with them in battle against Saul, nevertheless, David's band continued to grow. Apparent was the unpopularity of Saul in his own realm. These volunteers were military men with leadership ability. These David placed over his ragtag band of displaced followers. Moreover, they proved to be of great help to David when he pursued the Amalekites (i.e., the band of rovers) who had raided his camp. Men continued to so defect from Saul to David on a daily basis that David's *ad hoc* army began to be a great army (i.e., host). Reference to the **host of God** may refer to the official army of Israel, led by Saul. Some think it refers to the armies of heaven. However, the former is more likely. That being the case, the army of David began to rival the army of Saul in number and strength.

12:23 -37 The defections to David from the armies of Saul became an landslide. And these *are* the numbers of the bands *that were* ready armed to the war, *and* came to David to Hebron, to turn the kingdom of Saul to him, according to the word of the LORD. 24 **The children of Judah that bare shield and spear *were* six thousand and eight hundred, ready armed to the war.** 25 **Of the children of Simeon, mighty men of valour for the war, seven thousand and one hundred.** 26 **Of the children of Levi four thousand and six hundred.**

27 **And Jehoiada *was* the leader of the Aaronites, and with him *were* three thousand and seven hundred;** 28 **And**

Zadok, a young man mighty of valour, and of his father's house twenty and two captains. 29 And of the children of Benjamin, the kindred of Saul, three thousand: for hitherto the greatest part of them had kept the ward of the house of Saul. 30 And of the children of Ephraim twenty thousand and eight hundred, mighty men of valour, famous throughout the house of their fathers. 31 And of the half tribe of Manasseh eighteen thousand, which were expressed by name, to come and make David king.

32 And of the children of Issachar, *which were men* that had understanding of the times, to know what Israel ought to do; the heads of them *were* two hundred; and all their brethren *were* at their commandment. 33 Of Zebulun, such as went forth to battle, expert in war, with all instruments of war, fifty thousand, which could keep rank: *they were* not of double heart. 34 And of Naphtali a thousand captains, and with them with shield and spear thirty and seven thousand. 35 And of the Danites expert in war twenty and eight thousand and six hundred.

36 And of Asher, such as went forth to battle, expert in war, forty thousand. 37 And on the other side of Jordan, of the Reubenites, and the Gadites, and of the half tribe of Manasseh, with all manner of instruments of war for the battle, an hundred and twenty thousand.

Military men from throughout Israel defected from Saul's army to that of David while he was still in Hebron. They came "ready armed," that is, they were armed and ready to fight. Moreover, they were ready to overturn Saul's reign and give it to David. See II Samuel 5:1*ff.*

Of the various tribes, military men from these came to David: 6,800 from Judah; 7,100 from Simeon; 4,600 from Levi; 3,700 Aaronites (i.e., priests) along with 22 priestly captains; 3,000 bodyguards of Saul from Benjamin; 2,800 soliders from Ephraim; 18,000 men from the western half of Manasseh who came expressly to make David king; 200 leaders from Issachar who had the allegiance of the rest of their entire tribe; 50,000 expert soldiers from Zebulun (the latter were militarily disciplined and were totally loyal to David); 1,000 military officers from Naphtali who led 37,000 shield and spear men; 28,600 battle veterans from Dan; 40,000 veteran soldiers from Asher; 120,000 soldiers from the tribes east of the Jordan. This totals 326,522 soldiers, not including the entire armed forces of Isaachar who were loyal to David. David thus had an army at his disposal of approximately 350,000 men while he was still in Hebron. The days of the house of Saul certainly were numbered.

12:38-40 All these men of war, that could keep rank, came with a perfect heart to Hebron, to make David king over all Israel: and all the rest also of Israel *were* of one heart to make David king. 39 And there they were with David three days, eating and drinking: for their brethren had prepared for them. 40 Moreover they that were nigh them, *even* unto Issachar and Zebulun and Naphtali, brought bread on asses, and on camels, and on mules, and on oxen, *and* meat, meal, cakes of figs, and bunches of raisins, and wine, and oil, and oxen, and sheep abundantly: for *there was* joy in Israel.

The time of this event likely parallels that of II Samuel 5. The nation united behind David after the death of Saul and the murder of Ish-bosheth. They came for a three-day inaugural convention to anoint David king of the entire nation of Israel. Those tribes which were in closer proximity to Hebron brought voluminous foodstuffs for the celebration of their new king. Thus God exalted David as ruler over His people.

* * * * *

Understanding I Chronicles

Overview of I Chronicles 13: *This next chapter presents some of David's first acts as king over all of Israel. Because of his love for the Lord, he sought to honor Him by bringing the ark of the covenant to Jerusalem. It had been taken by the Philistines earlier and God had forced its release. Since, it had resided at Kirjath-jearim, a village on the border of Judah and Benjamin.*

13:1-4 And David consulted with the captains of thousands and hundreds, *and* with every leader. 2 And David said unto all the congregation of Israel, If *it seem* good unto you, and *that it be* of the LORD our God, let us send abroad unto our brethren every where, *that are* left in all the land of Israel, and with them *also* to the priests and Levites *which are* in their cities *and* suburbs, that they may gather themselves unto us: 3 And let us bring again the ark of our God to us: for we enquired not at it in the days of Saul. 4 And all the congregation said that they would do so: for the thing was right in the eyes of all the people.

The events of this chapter parallel the record of II Samuel 6. Tragically, David allowed the ark to be transported in an unscriptural way. God's clear instruction in Numbers was that only the Levites were to carry the ark and then with staves upon their shoulders. When a certain Jew by the name of Uzza "put forth his hand to hold the ark" when it was in peril of falling, God struck him dead. The ark of the covenant was a tangible form of the holiness of God. God struck Uzza because he, as a sinful man, had approached God's earthly holy presence. Though God is merciful, His holiness is absolute with deadly consequences. To his credit, David desired to do a good thing. However, he did it the wrong way.

13:5-8 So David gathered all Israel together, from Shihor of Egypt even unto the entering of Hemath, to bring

the ark of God from Kirjathjearim. 6 And David went up, and all Israel, to Baalah, *that is*, to Kirjathjearim, which *belonged* to Judah, to bring up thence the ark of God the LORD, that dwelleth *between* the cherubims, whose name is called *on it*.

7 And they carried the ark of God in a new cart out of the house of Abinadab: and Uzza and Ahio drave the cart. 8 And David and all Israel played before God with all *their* might, and with singing, and with harps, and with psalteries, and with timbrels, and with cymbals, and with trumpets.

In preparation to move the ark of God to Jerusalem, David gathered the entire nation: from the border of Egypt on the southwest to the border of Syria to the northeast. With great pomp and ceremony, David had the ark placed upon a new ox cart (no doubt suitably decorated). The parade therefore began its procession from the house of Abinadab of Kirjathjearim (i.e., the village of forests) toward Jerusalem. Two Jews named Uzza and Ahio drove the ark (no doubt, walking alongside thereof as they urged the oxen on). David had a marching band in the procession which played "before God with all *their* might." What a spectacle this procession must have been. There was only one thing wrong. David was doing something contrary to the specific instructions of Scripture.

13:9-12 And when they came unto the threshingfloor of Chidon, Uzza put forth his hand to hold the ark; for the oxen stumbled. 10 And the anger of the LORD was kindled against Uzza, and he smote him, because he put his hand to the ark: and there he died before God. 11 And David was displeased, because the LORD had made a breach upon Uzza: wherefore that place is called Perezuzza to this day. 12 And David was afraid of God that day, saying, How shall I bring the ark of God *home* to me?

As the procession made its way along, one of the oxen stumbled by the threshingfloor of Chidon. Uzza, therefore, reached out to grab the ark with his bare hands lest it fall off the cart. There on the spot, God killed Uzza. That place therefore was named *Perezuzza* (breach of Uzza) even until the time of the writing of Chronicles. The word translated **afraid** (ירא *yare*) can also be translated as 'feared.' That likely is the sense at hand. David was puzzled at how the ark should be transported to Jerusalem. Clearly, he was rusty in his memory of the details of moving the ark as described in the Law.

13:13-14 So David brought not the ark *home* to himself to the city of David, but carried it aside into the house of Obededom the Gittite. 14 And the ark of God remained with the family of Obededom in his house three months. And the LORD blessed the house of Obededom, and all that he had.

The ark was apparently properly moved into the house of one named Obededom which evidently was near at hand. Though not noted here, Obededom was a Levite for he was later appointed to be doorkeeper of the Temple at Jerusalem. He is called a Gittite either because he had lived in Gath for some time or rather because he was of Gathrimmon, a city of the Levites. See Joshua 21:24.

The ark remained in his house for three months. However, as long as the ark was in the home of Obededom, God visibly blessed this man and his family. Apparently, the blessing of God brought affluence because it quickly became known to others.

* * * * *

Overview of I Chronicles 14: *This next chapter recounts the full establishment of David's reign. His royal neighbor to* *the north, Hiram, king of Tyre, honored David by providing him materials and craftsmen to build a palace for David.*

14:1-2 Now Hiram king of Tyre sent messengers to David, and timber of cedars, with masons and carpenters, to build him an house. 2 And David perceived that the LORD had confirmed him king over Israel, for his kingdom was lifted up on high, because of his people Israel.

It is clear that David early on established a friendly relationship with Hiram, king of Tyre, to the north. Hiram sent cedar lumber, along with stone masons and carpenters to help David build a palace at Jerusalem. Meanwhile, David realized that God had established him as king over the entire nation of Israel.

The blessing of God is apparent. His ascent to power had clearly been by God's providential help. David had the united political support of his nation and the kingdom was prospering. David thus perceived God's hand upon him.

14:3-7 And David took more wives at Jerusalem: and David begat more sons and daughters. 4 Now these *are* the names of *his* children which he had in Jerusalem; Shammua, and Shobab, Nathan, and Solomon, 5 And Ibhar, and Elishua, and Elpalet, 6 And Nogah, and Nepheg, and Japhia, 7 And Elishama, and Beeliada, and Eliphalet.

As the reign of David prospered, he added more wives to himself. Polygamy was tolerated in the Old Testament, but it never has been God's perfect will. Moreover, David reaped a bitter harvest in his children in later years. Some of that was a direct result of his domestic arrangement. Listed here are thirteen children born to David at Jerusalem. See also I Chronicles 3:9 and II Samuel 5:14-16. In the latter list, the names of Eliphalet and Nogah do not occur and Beeliada appears to be the same as Eliada.

14:8-9 And when the Philistines heard that David was anointed king over all Israel, all the Philistines went up to seek David. And David heard *of it*, and went out against them. 9 And the Philistines came and spread themselves in the valley of Rephaim. The event recorded here parallels that of II Samuel 5:17*ff.* Word reached Philistia of David becoming king over all of Israel. In reaction thereto, the Philistine nation determined to test David's mettle and invaded Israel with the intent of war. The valley of Rephaim opens to the southwest only about five miles from Jerusalem. There they encamped. David therefore led his army out to confront them.

14:10-12 And David enquired of God, saying, Shall I go up against the Philistines? and wilt thou deliver them into mine hand? And the LORD said unto him, Go up; for I will deliver them into thine hand. 11 So they came up to Baalperazim; and David smote them there. Then David said, God hath broken in upon mine enemies by mine hand like the breaking forth of waters: therefore they called the name of that place Baalperazim. 12 And when they had left their gods there, David gave a commandment, and they were burned with fire.

In an hour of crisis when the answer seemed obvious, David first sought God's face in the matter. He likely availed himself of the Urim and Thummin available for the leadership of Israel. In New Testament terminology, we would say that he prayed about the matter. Simply, he asked God what he should do. David clearly had not leaned upon his own understanding. Though it would seem obvious that he ought to fight against invaders, before he moved militarily, he first sought God's counsel. God made it clear to him to proceed, promising victory. The place, Baalperazim, was only about two miles to the southwest of Jerusalem. It is clear that the Philistines had made a deep incursion into Israel. The word *Baalperazim* literally means 'lord of the breach' or 'lord of the break.' Implicit is that God allowed David to break through the Philistine lines like a great flood of water. The Philistines were routed to such a degree that they left behind their idols. These David directed his forces to burn on the spot.

14:13-16 And the Philistines yet again spread themselves abroad in the valley. 14 Therefore David enquired again of God; and God said unto him, Go not up after them; turn away from them, and come upon them over against the mulberry trees. 15 And it shall be, when thou shalt hear a sound of going in the tops of the mulberry trees, *that* then thou shalt go out to battle: for God is gone forth before thee to smite the host of the Philistines. 16 David therefore did as God commanded him: and they smote the host of the Philistines from Gibeon even to Gazer.

One would think that the Philistines had learned their lesson. But not long thereafter, they invaded Israel once again, returning to the valley of Rephaim to the southwest of Jerusalem. It may be that they thought that they had a better strategy. Josephus records that they returned with an army three times larger than before. In any event, they thought that this time they would prevail over David. Once again, David sought God's guidance for the crisis at hand.

This time God gave David different instructions. The natural human response would be to go out and defeat them like the last time. However, David had the godly wisdom to seek God's face again. It may be that he sensed the Philistines had something new up their sleeve. Or, it simply may be that he received intelligence reports indicating they had returned with overwhelming military force. In any event, God instructed him to circle behind them to a grove of mulberry trees. In classic military tactic, David outflanked the Philistine forces. In lying in wait behind the mulberry woods, David was to wait for the sound of the wind rustling in the tops of the trees. God directed him to then attack through the woods and to the rear of the Philistines, upon hearing the wind.

It may be that the Philistines became impatient in waiting for David to come out to battle and began to move against Jerusalem. Not anticipating an attack from the rear, God directed David to do precisely so when they least expected it. Accordingly, "David did so, as the LORD had commanded him; and smote the Philistines from Geba until thou come to Gazer. The Philistines fled to the north and then the west with David in hot pursuit through Geba (Gibeah) all the way to Gazer." The latter was the beginning of the coastal plain whence the Philistines came.

In verses 10 and 14 we read that "David enquired of God." As David came to critical decisions in his life, he sought God's counsel and guidance. What is clear is that David was a man who lived by faith, seeking God's will and guidance in the day-to-day decisions of life. See Psalm 32:8 and Proverbs 3:5-6. In verse 16, we read that "David therefore did as God commanded him." Another insight into David's life was that he was obedient to God's will and leading. That placed him even more in the focus of God's blessing.

14:17 And the fame of David went out into all lands; and the LORD brought the fear of him upon all nations. Reputation of David thus spread across the world of that day. Because David was in the center of His will, God caused neighboring nations which otherwise might have been belligerent to fear David and his power. Peace thus prevailed for Israel.

* * * * *

Overview of I Chronicles 15: This next chapter recounts how David finally brought the ark to Jerusalem the right way. He enlisted the services of the Levites as prescribed in the Law of Moses.

15:1-3 And *David* made him houses in the city of David, and prepared a place for the ark of God, and pitched for it a tent. 2 Then David said, None ought to carry the ark of God but the Levites: for them hath the LORD chosen to carry the ark of God, and to minister unto him for ever. 3 And David gathered all Israel together to Jerusalem, to bring up the ark of the LORD unto his place, which he had prepared for it.

Evidently some years had passed since the initial attempt to bring the ark of the covenant to Jerusalem. David in the meantime had built palaces at Jerusalem for his growing family. David also had been refreshed from the Law how that only Levites were to carry the ark with staves upon their shoulders. See Numbers 4:5, 15; 7:9; and 10:17. David therefore organized another festive procession to bring the ark to his capital city, this time doing it the right way. Meanwhile, he had prepared a special place (tent) for it.

15:4-10 And David assembled the children of Aaron, and the Levites: 5 Of the sons of Kohath; Uriel the chief, and his brethren an hundred and twenty: 6 Of the sons of Merari; Asaiah the chief, and his brethren two hundred and twenty:

7 Of the sons of Gershom; Joel the chief, and his brethren an hundred and thirty: 8 Of the sons of Elizaphan; Shemaiah the chief, and his brethren two hundred: 9 Of the sons of Hebron; Eliel the chief, and his brethren fourscore: 10 Of the sons of Uzziel; Amminadab the chief, and his brethren an hundred and twelve.

David therefore assembled the leading priests and Levites of the land. Of the three divisions of the Levites, the Kohathites sent 120 men; the Merarites sent 220 men; and the Gershomites sent 130 men. Elizaphan was a grandson of Kohath whose clan sent 200 Levites. Hebron was also descended of Kohath and his clan sent 80 Levites. Uzziel was another descendant of Kohath and his clan sent 112 Levites. Thus a total of 862 Levites were sent to assist in the transportation of the ark.

15:11-13 And David called for Zadok and Abiathar the priests, and for the Levites, for Uriel, Asaiah, and Joel, Shemaiah, and Eliel, and Amminadab, 12 And said unto them, Ye *are* **the chief of the fathers of the Levites: sanctify yourselves,** *both* **ye and your brethren, that ye may bring up the ark of the LORD God of Israel unto** *the place that* **I have prepared for it. 13 For because ye** *did it* **not at the first, the LORD our God made a breach upon us, for that we sought him not after the due order.**

Zadok and Abiathar represented the two lineages of the sons of Aaron—Eleazar and Ithamar. Uriel, Asaiah, and Joel, Shemaiah, and Eliel, and Amminadab were the chief Levites. David therefore ordered them to make themselves ceremonially clean—sanctify yourselves. David was determined to properly bring the ark to Jerusalem this time. He had learned his lesson in doing it man's way the first time. Now, he would do it God's way. They had not done it "after the due order" the first time. Of interest is that the word translated as **due order** (מִשְׁפָּט *mishpat*) is most commonly rendered as 'judgment.' It also has the sense of 'right.' Essentially, David confessed he did not do it right the first time.

15:14-15 So the priests and the Levites sanctified themselves to bring up the ark of the LORD God of Israel. 15 And the children of the Levites bare the ark of God upon their

shoulders with the staves thereon, as Moses commanded according to the word of the LORD. Thus, the priests and Levites made the necessary preparations so that they all were ceremonially clean (i.e., sanctified) for the task at hand. They therefore properly transported the ark of the covenant upon their shoulders "with the staves thereon, as Moses com-manded according to the word of the LORD." See Exodus 25:14 and Numbers 7:9.

15:16-24 And David spake to the chief of the Levites to appoint their brethren *to be* **the singers with instruments of musick, psalteries and harps and cymbals, sounding, by lifting up the voice with joy. 17 So the Levites appointed Heman the son of Joel; and of his brethren, Asaph the son of Berechiah; and of the sons of Merari their brethren, Ethan the son of Kushaiah; 18 And with them their brethren of the second** *degree***, Zechariah, Ben, and Jaaziel, and Shemiramoth, and Jehiel, and Unni, Eliab, and Benaiah, and Maaseiah, and Mattithiah, and Elipheleh, and Mikneiah, and Obededom, and Jeiel, the porters.**

19 So the singers, Heman, Asaph, and Ethan, *were appointed* **to sound with cymbals of brass; 20 And Zechariah, and Aziel, and Shemiramoth, and Jehiel, and Unni, and Eliab, and Maaseiah, and Benaiah, with psalteries on Alamoth; 21 And Mattithiah, and Elipheleh, and Mikneiah, and Obededom, and Jeiel, and Azaziah, with harps on the Sheminith to excel. 22 And Chenaniah, chief of the Levites,** *was* **for song: he instructed about the song, because he** *was* **skilful. 23 And Berechiah and Elkanah** *were* **doorkeepers for the ark. 24 And Shebaniah, and Jehoshaphat, and Nethaneel, and Amasai, and Zechariah, and Benaiah, and Eliezer, the priests, did blow with the trumpets before the ark of God: and Obededom and Jehiah** *were* **doorkeepers for the ark.**

Understanding I Chronicles 429

Meanwhile, David had directed that Levitical musicians be prepared to play and sing joyfully as the ark was moved. Essentially, David prepared a marching orchestra along with marching choirs who accompanied and escorted the ark, making a joyful sound unto the Lord as they ascended to Jerusalem. In verses 16-19, mention is made again of biblical musicians Asaph, Heman and Ethan. Each of these were of the tribe of Levi and each were responsible for developing some of the Psalms. It is apparent that Obededom was also a Levite for he thereafter became a doorkeeper at the tent of the ark. Thus, with great pomp and ceremony, the ark of the covenant was properly delivered to Jerusalem.

15:25-28 So David, and the elders of Israel, and the captains over thousands, went to bring up the ark of the covenant of the LORD out of the house of Obededom with joy. 26 And it came to pass, when God helped the Levites that bare the ark of the covenant of the LORD, that they offered seven bullocks and seven rams. 27 And David *was* clothed with a robe of fine linen, and all the Levites that bare the ark, and the singers, and Chenaniah the master of the song with the singers: David also *had* upon him an ephod of linen. 28 Thus all Israel brought up the ark of the covenant of the LORD with shouting, and with sound of the cornet, and with trumpets, and with cymbals, making a noise with psalteries and harps.

What a great procession it must have been! David, the elders of the nation, and officers over thousands of his forces followed the priests and Levites, along with the Levitical orchestra and choirs. Moreover, God helped the Levites which bare the ark. He likely helped them physically and that no other procedural errors were committed. Therefore David offered special sacrifices on the spot of "seven bullocks and seven rams." David was dressed in the finest of linen robe as were the

Levites and all the official procession. David also wore a linen ephod over his robe. The latter was a shoulder-garment over his robe, like a vest. It was worn by the priests, but was not so peculiar to them as to be forbidden others. (See 1Samuel 2:18 and 22:18.) Thus, with the airs of a triumphal procession, the ark of the covenant was taken to Jerusalem with great music, cheering, and throngs of people.

15:29 And it came to pass, *as* the ark of the covenant of the LORD came to the city of David, that Michal the daughter of Saul looking out at a window saw king David dancing and playing: and she despised him in her heart. Verse 29 speaks of how David in his joy of bringing the ark back to Jerusalem was **dancing**.

The word so translated (רקד *raqad*) has the sense of skipping or jumping for joy. It has no relationship to the idea of modern dancing. As David 'danced' and played a harp, wearing an ephod, his wife Michal was disgusted with him and despised him. The thought likely was that Michal thought that David had demeaned himself as king by skipping and learping for joy while wearing what she considered to be a garment (i.e., an ephod) below his dignity as king. Pride of life is apparent in her heart and would become an obstacle in their marriage.

* * * * *

Overview of I Chronicles 16*: This next chapter presents the celebration and festivities which followed as the ark of the covenant was properly brought to Jerusalem and set in its place. In the course of events, David appointed additional Levites to sing and have a ministry of music before the ark. The first Temple choir director Asaph was also duly appointed.*

Understanding I Chronicles

16:1-3 So they brought the ark of God, and set it in the midst of the tent that David had pitched for it: and they offered burnt sacrifices and peace offerings before God. 2 And when David had made an end of offering the burnt offerings and the peace offerings, he blessed the people in the name of the LORD. 3 And he dealt to every one of Israel, both man and woman, to every one a loaf of bread, and a good piece of flesh, and a flagon *of wine*.

David had prepared a special tent in Jerusalem for the ark and there it was placed. He then offered more sweet savor sacrifices for praise and thanksgiving. Finally, he blessed his people in God's name. Truly, it was a time of great rejoicing and blessing. David thus presented his people with a feast before they returned to their homes. The words **flagon *of wine*** (אשישה '*ashiyshah*) are thought to have been a raisin cake used in sacrificial feasts. Of course it was made of dried grapes. It should not be thought that David sent his people home with containers of alcoholic beverages.

16:4-6 And he appointed *certain* of the Levites to minister before the ark of the LORD, and to record, and to thank and praise the LORD God of Israel: 5 Asaph the chief, and next to him Zechariah, Jeiel, and Shemiramoth, and Jehiel, and Mattithiah, and Eliab, and Benaiah, and Obededom: and Jeiel with psalteries and with harps; but Asaph made a sound with cymbals; 6 Benaiah also and Jahaziel the priests with trumpets continually before the ark of the covenant of God.

Upon situating the ark in a special tabernacle at Jerusalem, David appointed various Levites to be ministers before the ark. Their ministries were primarily musical. The word translated as **record** (זכר *zakar*) means to "make remembrance." These essentially wrote down praises to God. In more modern terms, they were sacred song writers. Others were musicians who played or sang the music. But the focus and purpose of the music was "to thank and praise the LORD God of Israel." The purpose of sacred music is *always* to praise God and not entertain the listener. Various musical instruments are thus noted, including **psalteries** which were a stringed type of instrument, **harps** which are self-explanatory, **cymbals** which were a type of percussion instrument, and **trumpets**. The word so translated (הַצֹצְרָה *chatsotsarah*) is not the traditional 'shofar,' but a brass type of 'trumpet.' Clearly implied is that there was sacred music being played and sang before the ark of God continually. He was the audience, not human ears.

16:7 Then on that day David delivered first *this psalm* to thank the LORD into the hand of Asaph and his brethren. On the day the ark was officially seated in the special tent erected for it at Jerusalem, David presented the following psalm of thanksgiving and praise to Asaph the choir director. The psalm to follow closely parallels that of Psalm 105.

16:8-12 The psalm begins with a lengthy list of imperatives directing God's people to thank and praise the Lord. **Give thanks unto the LORD; call upon his name: make known his deeds among the people**. A profound triad of spiritual orders are here: (1) thanks, (2) prayer, and (3) witnessing. God's people were commanded to do so then. The charge remains to this day.

9 Sing unto him, sing psalms unto him: talk ye of all his wondrous works. The focus of Christian music is made clear. We are to sing unto *Him*. Entertainment or even blessing for human ears is not in view. Not only are we charged to sing unto *Him*, but we also are directed to talk about the wonderful things God has done.

10 Glory ye in his holy name: let the heart of them rejoice that seek the LORD. Moreover, we are charged to glory

Understanding I Chronicles 433

in *His* holy name. Our problem often is that our focus is all too earthly. As we turn our focus toward heaven and He who dwells therein, there is great cause to rejoice. Simple indeed is the psychology of God's Word.

We thus are directed to 11 **seek the LORD, and his strength: seek his face evermore**. In seeking the Lord and His face comes strength to the seeker. The practical outworking of seeking His face certainly is found in prayer. We need to pray more, not less.

This introductory list of imperatives concludes by commanding us to 12 **remember his marvellous works that he hath done; his wonders, and the judgments of his mouth**. How we need to refresh our memory of the wondrous works which God has done. That in large measure comes from continually going to His Word. That, more than anything else, will keep our memory fresh of God's works.

16:13-14 This introductory section of the psalm ends by noting who is to so seek the Lord. **O ye seed of Abraham his servant, ye children of Jacob his chosen**. Though we as gentile Christians are not the physical seed of Abraham, we certainly are his seed spiritually in Christ. Paul wrote, "And if ye *be* Christ's, then are ye Abraham's seed, and heirs according to the promise" (Galatians 3:29).

Yet, the focus remains on Him to whom we are to praise. 14 **He *is* the LORD our God: his judgments *are* in all the earth**. The latter thought might be how that the judgments of God were throughout the *land* of Israel. (The Hebrew word *eretz* is commonly translated as either *earth* or *land*.) In David's day, certainly the judgments of Jehovah were known throughout the land of Israel. In the Millennium, they will be throughout the entire world. However, David may have had in mind the invisible things of Him from the creation—the line gone out through all the world of general revelation as described in Psalm 19.

16:15-17 Be ye mindful always of his covenant; the word *which* he commanded to a thousand generations. God always keeps His Word—in this case the covenant He made with Abraham. Moreover, He never forgets His promises. In Deuteronomy 7:9, Moses reminded us that He "keepeth covenant and mercy with them that love him and keep his commandments to a thousand generations." A generation is typically thought of as lasting about thirty years. A thousand generations would therefore be 30,000 years. Undoubtedly, however, the greater thought is how that God keeps His Word forever. A thousand generations clearly is a poetic metaphor for eternity. God never breaks His promises!

16 ***Even of the covenant*** **which he made with Abraham, and his oath unto Isaac; 17 And confirmed the same unto Jacob for a law, *and* to Israel *for* an everlasting covenant.** The covenant made by God to Abraham is noted specifically. (See Genesis 12:1-3, 17:1-8 and 22:16-18.) That same covenant was confirmed to both Isaac and Jacob. (See Genesis 26:3 and 28:13-14.) It remains an everlasting covenant. The land which God promised to Abraham is still there. God has promised it to the seed of Isaac and Jacob—the Jewish nation.

16:18-20 Saying, Unto thee will I give the land of Canaan, the lot of your inheritance. Lest there be any question unto whom Palestine belongs, God made clear that He promised it to the descendants of Jacob which is Israel today. The covenant which God made to Abraham suddenly becomes the focal point of modern current events, for the struggle in the Middle East remains over who has the right to the land in Israel.

God promised it to Abraham, Isaac, and Jacob **19 when they were *but* a few men in number; yea, very few, and**

Understanding I Chronicles 435

strangers in it. And *when* they went from one nation to another, from *one* kingdom to another people. That covenant has never been abrogated. To the contrary, it is an everlasting covenant! Though the nation of Israel was only a small number of people when God made that covenant, the promise still stands.

16:21-22 He suffered no man to do them wrong: yea, he reproved kings for their sakes, 22 *Saying,* **Touch not mine anointed, and do my prophets no harm.**Therefore David recalled how that God "suffered no man to do them wrong: yea, he reproved kings for their sakes." When Abraham and his descendants walked in obedience to God, God providentially protected them. He thwarted kings such as Pharaoh of Egypt and Abimelech of Gerar. God takes care of His people when they walk before Him in obedience and faith.

Moreover, God warned, "Touch not mine anointed, and do my prophets no harm." God certainly warned Abimelech regarding Abraham in Genesis 20:6-7. He likewise intervened to protect Moses and Aaron when rebels rose up against them in the camp. See Numbers 12:7 and 16:1 *ff*. God takes care of His servants when they are doing His will. That principle remains to this day.

16:23-26 Sing unto the LORD, all the earth; shew forth from day to day his salvation. 24 Declare his glory among the heathen; his marvellous works among all nations. 25 For great *is* **the LORD, and greatly to be praised: he also** *is* **to be feared above all gods. 26 For all the gods of the people** *are* **idols: but the LORD made the heavens.**

The psalmist therefore ordered God's people to sing unto the Lord. Once again, the purpose of sacred (i.e., Christian) music is to sing to the *Lord*. He is the audience and not ourselves. Sacred music is for the purpose of glorifying God and not entertaining or 'reaching' others. Notice the injunction for God's people to (1) "shew forth from day to day his salvation." If that were true for Old Testament saints, how much more is it true today? God's people have always been under an obligation to tell others of God's wonderful salvation. We also are directed to (2) "declare his glory among the heathen."

The word translated as **heathen** (גוי *goy* or גוים *goyim* plural) refers to gentiles. More broadly it had the sense of the *ungodly* or in terms of today, the *world*. We have longed been charged by God to declare His glory to the world around us. It is part of the greater injunction to witness. Specifically, Israel was charged to declare "his marvellous works among all nations." Whether creation or redemption, His works are wondrous.

The psalmist thus sets forth other reasons to sing unto the Lord and witness of Him: (1) He is great and therefore greatly to be praised. (2) "He also *is* to be feared above all gods." In a world full of idols and false gods of that day, truly Jehovah God was greater than all and to be feared. He has surely shown His fearsome power over the ages. (3) The puny gods of the nations were inanimate, impotent pieces of wood, metal, or stone. However, Jehovah God created the universe, including the heavens above!

16:27-30 Glory and honour *are* in his presence; strength and gladness *are* in his place. 28 Give unto the LORD, ye kindreds of the people, give unto the LORD glory and strength. 29 Give unto the LORD the glory *due* unto his name: bring an offering, and come before him: worship the LORD in the beauty of holiness. 30 Fear before him, all the earth: the world also shall be stable, that it be not moved.

The initial thought is that glory and majesty are before Him. He is glory personified. He is the epitome of majesty. Moreover, "strength and gladness *are* in his place." Before the throne

Understanding I Chronicles

of God is the wellspring of all strength and joy. He is the source of joy and joy characterizes the atmosphere about His throne. (The immediate context likely was the joy {i.e., gladness}) before the ark when it was brought to Jerusalem. However, the ark was merely a tiny microcosm of the glory of heaven above.)

Therefore, David charged his people to (1) "Give unto the LORD the glory *due* unto his name." God's people to this day have an obligation to glorify God's name. It is not an option. (Moreover, for the Old Testament saints, they were directed to bring an offering to the Tabernacle—likely a sweet-savor offering.) (2) To this day, we are enjoined to "worship the LORD in the beauty of holiness." The word translated as **worship** (שׁחה *shachah*) literally means to 'to bow down' or 'prostrate oneself.' Implicit is utter submission and reverence. Moreover, notice that there is genuine beauty in true holiness. Additionally, there is genuine holiness associated with true beauty.

We therefore are under orders from on high to worship God in holiness— it is beautiful to God. (3) God's people are also directed to "fear before him." In fact, the entire earth is under orders to fear God. Touched upon is the greater truth of the fear of the Lord. It is not an option. Sadly, many a man will come to fear God the hard way. Either God in mercy may have to do something drastic to get one's attention. Or, if at no other time, men will be confronted with the fear of God when they someday stand before Him. Far better is it to fear Him now and order our lives accordingly. Because of the mercy of God, the earth is stable. God has given us a stable planet on which to live. We therefore ought to praise Him for that as well.

16:31-33 Therefore the entire creation is enjoined to praise Him. **Let the heavens rejoice, and let the earth be glad; 32 let the sea roar, and the fulness thereof. Let the field be joyful, and all that *is* therein: 33 then shall all the trees of the wood sing out at the presence of the LORD, because he cometh to**

judge the earth. All creation is called upon to rejoice before the Lord. The reason is that He is coming to judge the earth and His judgment will be in righteousness and in truth. In that day, righteousness and truth will prevail.

16:34-36 O give thanks unto the LORD; for *he is* good; for his mercy *endureth* for ever. 35 And say ye, Save us, O God of our salvation, and gather us together, and deliver us from the heathen, that we may give thanks to thy holy name, *and* glory in thy praise. 36 Blessed *be* the LORD God of Israel for ever and ever. And all the people said, Amen, and praised the LORD.

As repeated in Psalm 106, 107, 118, and 136; we as God's people are under an eternal injunction to give thanks unto the Lord. The reason is as simple as it is profound: He is good! Moreover, "His mercy *endureth* for ever." David also directed God's people to say, "Save us, O God of our salvation." Implicit therein is the essence of salvation—calling upon God in simple faith for His salvation. In the immediate context, the thought likely was a prayer for deliverance from gentile (i.e., heathen) enemies. As God delivered His people, they would have even further cause to "give thanks to thy holy name, *and* glory in thy praise."

David therefore concluded his psalm of praise and thanksgiving with the great benediction: "Blessed *be* the LORD God of Israel for ever and ever." That truth remains to this day. Moreover, as New Testament Christians, we can add, blessed be the Lord God of *our* salvation for ever and ever. Upon David's eloquent and profound benediction, "all the people said, Amen, and praised the LORD."

The word *Amen* is not translated but transliterated from the Hebrew word אָמֵן. It is a word which has gone around the world in many languages. As in the New Testament, it means 'verily,' 'truly,' or, 'so be it.'

Understanding I Chronicles

16:37-40 So he left there before the ark of the covenant of the LORD Asaph and his brethren, to minister before the ark continually, as every day's work required: 38 And Obededom with their brethren, threescore and eight; Obededom also the son of Jeduthun and Hosah *to be* porters: 39 And Zadok the priest, and his brethren the priests, before the tabernacle of the LORD in the high place that *was* at Gibeon, 40 To offer burnt offerings unto the LORD upon the altar of the burnt offering continually morning and evening, and *to do* according to all that is written in the law of the LORD, which he commanded Israel.

The ark of the covenant now rested in Jerusalem. It seems that David had constructed a special tent for it and its resting place was not in the original Tabernacle which was still located at Gibeon. See verse 39. However, David also appointed Levites to "minister before the ark continually, as every day's work required." They evidently ministered daily with songs of praise. The director thereof was Asaph over other Levitical musicians. No sacrifices were offered there nor incense burnt, because the altars were not there. Nevertheless, the ark became a specific place in Jerusalem whence David could offer prayer to heaven and worship God.

Obededom, along with sixty-eight other Levites, also served before the ark as porters or gatekeepers. "Obededom also the son of Jeduthun" has the sense Obededom, even the son of Jeduthun. There were not two Obedeoms. Both named here were one and the same person. Hosah also became a chief porter.

Meanwhile at Gibeon, which was about seven miles northwest of Jerusalem in the territory of Benjamin, remained the original Tabernacle of God. There, Zadok along with other priests continued to offer sacrifices and burnt-offerings "unto the LORD upon the altar of the burnt offering continually morning and evening, and *to do* according to all that is written in the law of the LORD, which he commanded Israel." Thus, not distant from Jerusalem the Levitical system of sacrifices continued at Gibeon. The ark of the covenant, however, was now located in Jerusalem.

16:41-43 And with them Heman and Jeduthun, and the rest that were chosen, who were expressed by name, to give thanks to the LORD, because his mercy *endureth* for ever; 42 And with them Heman and Jeduthun with trumpets and cymbals for those that should make a sound, and with musical instruments of God. And the sons of Jeduthun *were* porters. 43 And all the people departed every man to his house: and David returned to bless his house.

Other Levites such as Heman and Jeduthun, along with others, were chosen to regularly thank the Lord "because his mercy *endureth* for ever." Both Heman and Jeduthun were musicians at the Tabernacle at Gibeon. The sons of Jeduthun were porters or gatekeepers at the Tabernacle in those days. Thus, after having described the joy of moving the ark to Jerusalem and briefly describing the Tabernacle at Gibeon, the sacred chronicler records how that all the people departed every man to his house: and David returned to bless his house." II Samuel 6:20 adds an additional postscript to this joyous time. Unfortunately, it was not joyous for David.

* * * * *

Overview of Chapter 17: *This next chapter presents the Davidic covenant and its content. David desired to build a permanent house (i.e., temple) for the Lord at Jerusalem. Rather, God sent word to David that He would build David an house. There is a slight play on words here. David's intent was to build a physical house for God. But God's intention was to*

Understanding I Chronicles

build a posterity or dynasty from David. Of course, the apex of David's lineage would be none other than Jesus Christ. The Davidic covenant outlined how God would providentially preserve David's seed as the royal line of Israel in perpetuity. The ultimate fulfillment of this covenant would be in the Messiah. This chapter closely parallels that of II Samuel 7.

17:1-2 Now it came to pass, as David sat in his house, that David said to Nathan the prophet, Lo, I dwell in an house of cedars, but the ark of the covenant of the LORD remaineth under curtains. 2 Then Nathan said unto David, Do all that *is* in thine heart; for God *is* with thee.

The time is evidently not long after David had moved the ark to Jerusalem. On a given day, David sat in his palace talking to Nathan the prophet. He mused how that he lived in a palace constructed and finished with cedar, but the ark of the covenant was still in a tent. Implicit, though not stated here, was desire to build a permanent Temple for God. Nathan, clearly speaking 'off the top of his head' told David to go ahead and do it, for God would be with him. However, as the following text will reveal, that is not what God would allow.

17:3-6 And it came to pass the same night, that the word of God came to Nathan, saying, 4 Go and tell David my servant, Thus saith the LORD, Thou shalt not build me an house to dwell in: 5 For I have not dwelt in an house since the day that I brought up Israel unto this day; but have gone from tent to tent, and from *one* tabernacle *to another*. 6 Wheresoever I have walked with all Israel, spake I a word to any of the judges of Israel, whom I commanded to feed my people, saying, Why have ye not built me an house of cedars?

Though Nathan had casually told David to proceed with his plans, God that night told Nathan that He had others plans.

Nathan was to go to David the next day and inform him on behalf of God that he was not to build a Temple. Moreover, God had never asked His people to build Him a temple made of cedar. In fact, God's earthly presence had dwelt in tabernacles (i.e., tents) throughout the years.

17:7-9 Now therefore thus shalt thou say unto my servant David, Thus saith the LORD of hosts, I took thee from the sheepcote, *even* from following the sheep, that thou shouldest be ruler over my people Israel: 8 And I have been with thee whithersoever thou hast walked, and have cut off all thine enemies from before thee, and have made thee a name like the name of the great men that *are* in the earth. 9 Also I will ordain a place for my people Israel, and will plant them, and they shall dwell in their place, and shall be moved no more; neither shall the children of wickedness waste them any more, as at the beginning.

Nathan was to remind David how that God had taken him from the **sheepcote** (i.e., the place where shepherds lived). The thought is of very humble and rustic origins. As a young man, David had followed his father's sheep as they moved from place to place to graze. Yet, from those most humble of origins, God had raised David to be king of His people Israel. Moreover, God had been with David throughout his life. He had helped David defeat his enemies whether the Philistines, Saul, or other hostile nations.

David had become the greatest king on the earth of that day. God additionally promised to David that Israel as a nation would dwell permanently in the land which God had given to them. At least during the reign of David, their enemies would no longer harass them as had happened in earlier centuries. In short, God had blessed David and promised to continue to do so. The stage was thus set for the profound promise about to be given.

17:10-15 And since the time that I commanded judges *to be* **over my people Israel. Moreover I will subdue all thine enemies. Furthermore I tell thee that the LORD will build thee an house. 11 And it shall come to pass, when thy days be expired that thou must go** *to be* **with thy fathers, that I will raise up thy seed after thee, which shall be of thy sons; and I will establish his kingdom.** God had helped His people since the time of the judges. He promised to continue to do so.

However, God had a proposition to offer David. Rather than David building Him a house, God promised to build a house for David. There clearly is a play on words and God intended it so. Whereas David had proposed to build a physical and literal house for God; God intended to build a great posterity—a house in the sense of a dynasty. God promised to David that his sons would sit upon his throne in perpetuity. God Himself would establish their kingdom.

He shall build me an house, and I will stablish his throne for ever. 13 I will be his father, and he shall be my son: and I will not take my mercy away from him, as I took *it* **from** *him* **that was before thee: 14 But I will settle him in mine house and in my kingdom for ever: and his throne shall be established for evermore.**

The son of David which who would succeed him (i.e., Solomon) would build the physical Temple which David envisioned. Moreover, God promised to established the throne of Solomon forever. The ultimate fulfillment of that promise is still pending and will be fulfilled when Jesus Christ returns in power and glory to rule and reign from Jerusalem forever. God promised that he would not remove Solomon from the throne as He had done to Saul. In short, God promised to establish an everlasting dynasty through David and his son (Solomon).

According to all these words, and according to all this vision, so did Nathan speak unto David. Nathan thus delivered to David what ever since has come to be known as the Davidic Covenant.

17:16-18 The text from here to the end of the chapter closely parallels that of II Samuel 7:18-29. David thus in obvious humility cried out to God, **Who *am* I, O LORD God?** and what *is* my house, that thou hast brought me hitherto? David realized how unremarkable he was as a sinner before God. Moreover, he was well aware of the humble origins of his family lineage at Bethlehem. How God could so exalt him was only by His grace.

He continued, **17 And yet this was a small thing in thy eyes, O LORD God; for thou hast *also* spoken of thy servant's house for a great while to come**. Furthermore, the exaltation which God had bestowed upon David was a small thing in comparison to the promise He had made for David's posterity. Notice how David (as king) referred to himself as God's servant. He continued, **and hast regarded me according to the estate of a man of high degree, O LORD God** The question was rhetorical. David knew this was not the way that men operated. Only a merciful sovereign God would exalt one so inferior as he to such blessing and promise. It was truly a tribute to the grace of God.

David could only say, **18 What can David *speak* more to thee for the honour of thy servant? for thou knowest thy servant**. The humility of David is thus apparent.

17:19-20 O LORD, for thy servant's sake, and according to thine own heart, hast thou done all this greatness, in making known all *these* great things. 20 O LORD, *there is* none like thee, neither *is there any* God beside thee, according to all that we have heard with our ears. Notice how that David referred to himself as God's servant. Though king, he realized how insignificant he was. Moreover, he, even

Understanding I Chronicles

as king, remained God's servant. David could therefore only praise God for His greatness. No other could do as God had done.

17:21-22 And what one nation in the earth *is* like thy people Israel, whom God went to redeem *to be* his own people, to make thee a name of greatness and terribleness, by driving out nations from before thy people, whom thou hast redeemed out of Egypt? 22 For thy people Israel didst thou make thine own people for ever; and thou, LORD, becamest their God.

David momentarily turned his attention to his own nation. They were God's people. God had not intervened and redeemed any other nation. Yet, it was ultimately to glorify and magnify God's name. The word translated as **terribleness** (יראֹ *yare´*) is the common Hebrew word for 'fear.' In part, God dealt powerfully on behalf of Israel to not only magnify His name but to instill the fear of the Lord for all involved.

17:23-25 Therefore now, LORD, let the thing that thou hast spoken concerning thy servant and concerning his house be established for ever, and do as thou hast said. 24 Let it even be established, that thy name may be magnified for ever, saying, The LORD of hosts *is* the God of Israel, *even* a God to Israel: and *let* the house of David thy servant *be* established before thee. 25 For thou, O my God, hast told thy servant that thou wilt build him an house: therefore thy servant hath found *in his heart* to pray before thee.

David therefore invoked God to do what He had said. He implored God to in fact establish his house so that God's name might be magnified. Notice that it was not for any selfish purpose on David's part. Rather, he invoked God to fulfill His Word that He might be "magnified for ever." Moreover, it would be forever clear that Jehovah God was the God of Israel.

David therefore asked God to build the dynasty He had promised. God had promised it to him. Therefore, David had thus prayed before God.

17:26-27 And now, LORD, thou art God, and hast promised this goodness unto thy servant: 27 Now therefore let it please thee to bless the house of thy servant, that it may be before thee for ever: for thou blessest, O LORD, and *it shall be* blessed for ever. David thus concluded his prayer of thanks and praise to God for the covenant which God had made with him. He then ended his magnificent prayer with a plea for God to bless him and his house. His reference to his house clearly was not his physical dwelling place, but rather his posterity which would come after him.

* * * * *

Overview of I Chronicles 18: *The eighteenth chapter presents God's providential and protective blessing upon David. The blessing of God has tangible and highly desirable affects. Here, David was helped to one military victory after another.*

18:1-5 Now after this it came to pass, that David smote the Philistines, and subdued them, and took Gath and her towns out of the hand of the Philistines. 2 And he smote Moab; and the Moabites became David's servants, *and* brought gifts. 3 And David smote Hadarezer king of Zobah unto Hamath, as he went to stablish his dominion by the river Euphrates.

4 And David took from him a thousand chariots, and seven thousand horsemen, and twenty thousand footmen: David also houghed all the chariot *horses*, but reserved of

Understanding I Chronicles

them an hundred chariots. 5 And when the Syrians of Damascus came to help Hadarezer king of Zobah, David slew of the Syrians two and twenty thousand men.

David's kingdom was now reaching its zenith. God enabled him to completely subdue the Philistines to his west. He then defeated Moab to his east. Moreover, the Moabites became ser-vants to David. David then defeated the Syrians to the northeast (Zobah and Hadarezer) all the way to the Euphrates River. Moreover, David seized 1,000 chariots, 7,000 cavalry, and 20,000 infantrymen from the several Syrian kings. David there-fore houghed or cut the hamstring tendons of the rest of the chariot horses of these kings and left them only 100 chariots. When the Syrians of Damascus came to the aid of Hadarezer king of Zobah, David killed 22,000 of them.

18:6 Then David put *garrisons* in Syriadamascus; and the Syrians became David's servants, *and* brought gifts. Thus the LORD preserved David whithersoever he went. The kingdom of David thus became solidified all the way into Syria, including Damascus. The latter therefore submitted themselves to David's rule. Notice here and in verses 13, the statement, "Thus the LORD preserved David whithersoever he went." David experienced first hand the blessing of Psalm 5:12. God clearly blessed his reign.

18:7-8 And David took the shields of gold that were on the servants of Hadarezer, and brought them to Jerusalem. 8 Likewise from Tibhath, and from Chun, cities of Hadarezer, brought David very much brass, wherewith Solomon made the brasen sea, and the pillars, and the vessels of brass.

The chief servants of Hadarezer heretofore had carried shields of gold. David thus took them to Jerusalem. From other cities of Syria, David brought vast amounts of brass. Solomon would later utilize this for the production of the brass implements of the coming Temple.

18:9-11 Now when Tou king of Hamath heard how David had smitten all the host of Hadarezer king of Zobah; 10 He sent Hadoram his son to king David, to enquire of his welfare, and to congratulate him, because he had fought against Hadarezer, and smitten him; (for Hadarezer had war with Tou;) and *with him* all manner of vessels of gold and silver and brass.

Hamath was another small kingdom to the north and east of Israel in what today is called Syria. When the king thereof, Tou, heard of David's victories, he sent his son as an ambassador to David. He no doubt hoped by diplomacy to avoid conquest by David. The text reveals that "Hadarezer had war with Tou" and Tou no doubt was happy that David had defeated Hadarezer. Tou's son thus brought substantial 'peace offerings' of gold, silver, and brass to David.

Them also king David dedicated unto the LORD, with the silver and the gold that he brought from all *these* nations; from Edom, and from Moab, and from the children of Ammon, and from the Philistines, and from Amalek. As gold, silver, and brass poured in to David, both by conquest and as peace offerings, David dedicated it all the Lord. He kept none of it for himself. It all would undoubtedly be used in the construction of the coming Temple. Not only did gold, silver, and brass come from the kingdoms of Syria, but also from Edom, Moab, and Ammon to the east, the Philistines to the west, and the Amalekites to the south.

18:12-13 Moreover Abishai the son of Zeruiah slew of the Edomites in the valley of salt eighteen thousand. 13 And he put garrisons in Edom; and all the Edomites became David's servants. Thus the LORD preserved David

whithersoever he went. Abishai was one of David's chief military lieutenants and he defeated the Edomites to the southeast, killing 18,000 of them in the process. Edom thus became part of David's empire. In modern geographical terms, the empire of David extend from Egypt to the southwest, to Iraq and the Euphrates River to the northeast, to Saudi Arabia to the southeast, and to Lebanon to the north who were friendly to David. Indeed, God preserved him wherever he went.

18:14-17 So David reigned over all Israel, and executed judgment and justice among all his people. 15 And Joab the son of Zeruiah *was* **over the host; and Jehoshaphat the son of Ahilud, recorder. 16 And Zadok the son of Ahitub, and Abimelech the son of Abiathar,** *were* **the priests; and Shavsha was scribe; 17 And Benaiah the son of Jehoiada** *was* **over the Cherethites and the Pelethites; and the sons of David** *were* **chief about the king.**

David therefore reigned over much of the Middle East as king of Israel. His rule was characterized by *judgment and justice*—justice and righteousness. God indeed blesses righteousness. Listed are his principal officers: Joab as general officer of the Army; Jehoshaphat as secretary of state; Zadok as and Abimelech high priests, Shavsha as chief scribe, Benaiah was chief of the palace guard (the Cherethites and the Pelethites); and David's sons were head over various other departments of the government.

* * * * *

Overview of I Chronicles 19: The nineteenth chapter parallels II Samuel 10. David had reached the pinnacle of his life and career. His tremendous fall was at hand. War developed with the Ammonites and Syrians. The ancient Ammonites are the forerunners of the city of Ammon in Jordan today. David continued to roll, but a fall was coming.

19:1-5 Now it came to pass after this, that Nahash the king of the children of Ammon died, and his son reigned in his stead. 2 And David said, I will shew kindness unto Hanun the son of Nahash, because his father shewed kindness to me. And David sent messengers to comfort him concerning his father. So the servants of David came into the land of the children of Ammon to Hanun, to comfort him.

3 But the princes of the children of Ammon said to Hanun, Thinkest thou that David doth honour thy father, that he hath sent comforters unto thee? are not his servants come unto thee for to search, and to overthrow, and to spy out the land? 4 Wherefore Hanun took David's servants, and shaved them, and cut off their garments in the midst hard by their buttocks, and sent them away.

One of the great blunders of diplomatic history is herein recorded. Nahash, though conquered by David, had become an ally to him. When he died, his son Hanun ascended his throne. David therefore determined to send ambassadors to greet the new king and share official condolences to him on the death of his father. However, rather than receive these ambassadors as guests, they were treated as spies. Hanun therefore ordered half their beards to be shaved (see II Samuel 10:4) and their robes cut off just below the waist. Not only had foolish Hanun committed a major *faux pas* politically, he had the stupidity to offend the most powerful ruler on the earth of that day.

Then there went *certain*, and told David how the men were served. And he sent to meet them: for the men were greatly ashamed. And the king said, Tarry at Jericho until your beards be grown, and *then* return. News reached David how Hanun had utterly humiliated his ambassadors. David therefore directed them to reside in Jericho, which was in Israel proper when returning from Ammon. There, their beards could regrow.

19:6-7 And when the children of Ammon saw that they had made themselves odious to David, Hanun and the children of Ammon sent a thousand talents of silver to hire them chariots and horsemen out of Mesopotamia, and out of Syriamaachah, and out of Zobah. 7 So they hired thirty and two thousand chariots, and the king of Maachah and his people; who came and pitched before Medeba. And the children of Ammon gathered themselves together from their cities, and came to battle.

When the Ammonites realized their stupidity and the inevitable consequences thereof, they quickly solicited mercenary soldiers from Mesopotamia (lower Iraq in modern terms) and Zobah, a small kingdom northeast of Damascus. 32,000 mercenary chariots were hired who encamped in Medeba of Moab to the north. They thus joined with the forces of Ammon.

19:8-13 And when David heard *of it*, he sent Joab, and all the host of the mighty men. 9 And the children of Ammon came out, and put the battle in array before the gate of the city: and the kings that were come *were* by themselves in the field. 10 Now when Joab saw that the battle was set against him before and behind, he chose out of all the choice of Israel, and put *them* in array against the Syrians. 11 And the rest of the people he delivered unto the hand of Abishai his brother, and they set *themselves* in array against the children of Ammon. 12 And he said, If the Syrians be too strong for me, then thou shalt help me: but if the children of Ammon be too strong for thee, then I will help thee.

Joab, David's nephew, remained his chief commander. David thus sent Joab with an army against Ammon. In seeing the army of Israel advancing upon them, the Ammonites placed their own forces outside the city gate in defense thereof. However, they deployed their mercenary forces apart in the nearby countryside. The reason is not clear. It may be that they did not trust these mercenaries or it may be that they planned to ambush Joab's army from the flanks or from behind. The following account lends credence to the latter. Intimated is that upon joining action with the Ammonites in front of their city, they were attacked from behind by the mercenary forces (collectively called the Syrians). In realizing the predicament he was in, Joab determined to send his best units against the Syrians. His strategy likely was to defeat them first and then deal with the Ammonites later.

To his lieutenant commander, Abishai his brother, Joab directed the rest of his forces against the Ammonites. Joab further shared his battle plans with his brother. And, their plan was simple. Where help was needed most, they would assist the other. Thus, a flexible strategy was developed to react to the battle as it developed.

Joab concluded his strategy session with Abishai with this exhortation. 13 **Be of good courage, and let us behave ourselves valiantly for our people, and for the cities of our God: and let the LORD do** *that which is* **good in his sight**. Joab thus sent Abishai out with the charge to be courageous and strong. Their people, their nation, and the testimony of their God was at stake. Moreover, he entrusted the battle to the Lord: "and the LORD do that which seemeth him good." He thus committed the battle to God.

19:14-16 So Joab and the people that *were* with him drew nigh before the Syrians unto the battle; and they fled before him. 15 And when the children of Ammon saw that the Syrians were fled, they likewise fled before Abishai his brother, and entered into the city. Then Joab came to Jerusalem. 16 And when the Syrians saw that they were put

Understanding I Chronicles

to the worse before Israel, they sent messengers, and drew forth the Syrians that *were* beyond the river: and Shophach the captain of the host of Hadarezer *went* before them.

The battle turned into a rout for the Israelites. Joab ferociously attacked against the Syrians who promptly fled. They apparently had received payment for their services in advance. They thus grabbed the money and ran. They had shown up but they were not about to be killed by Joab. However, when the Ammonite forces saw the Syrians being routed, they retreated into their city. Implied is that Joab thus surrounded it and prepared for a siege. Meanwhile, Joab himself returned to Jerusalem, undoubtedly to report the situation to David. Though routed in the initial battle, it appears that the Syrians regrouped perhaps in a more defensible position.

Meanwhile, word of their defeat had evidently reached home. Therefore, Hadadezer, one of the kings of the region of Syria, sent reenforcements. The Jewish historian Josephus claims that Hadarezer sent a force of 80,000 men under the command of Shobach. They marched southward to a place called Helam which was somewhere in Gilead to the north of Ammon. (This is all in present day Jordan.)

19:17-19 And it was told David; and he gathered all Israel, and passed over Jordan, and came upon them, and set *the battle* in array against them. So when David had put the battle in array against the Syrians, they fought with him. 18 But the Syrians fled before Israel; and David slew of the Syrians seven thousand *men which fought in* chariots, and forty thousand footmen, and killed Shophach the captain of the host.

19 And when the servants of Hadarezer saw that they were put to the worse before Israel, they made peace with David, and became his servants: neither would the Syrians help the children of Ammon any more.

When David learned of this new threat, his attention was diverted from Ammon. Whether or not a siege force was left there is not clear. David thus mobilized his national reserves and marched out against the combined forces of Syria. It seems apparent that David personally commanded his forces. (This is in distinct contrast to him tarrying at Jerusalem as noted in the next chapter.) The battle was joined at Helam and there David utterly defeated the Syrian forces. Of those who escaped the sword, they fled in a rout. Seven-thousand chariot men of the Syrians were destroyed. Also, 40,000 cavalry of Syria were slain. Their commander, Shobach was also killed in the battle.

Some have assumed there is a discrepancy between the account in II Samuel 10:18 and here. In the account of Samuel, seven-hundred chariots were destroyed while here is noted the men which fought in chariots. Evidently, the Syrians had large 'battle-wagon' type of chariots which could hold ten men each. The two accounts complement each other and do not contradict.

The several lessor kings mentioned earlier in the chapter realized that they were beaten. Also noted is that they were under the lordship of Hadarezer (Hadadezer). However, the Syrians had learned a lesson. Though they were not friends of Israel, they would never again give military aid to Ammon. The battle with the Syrians was over for the time being, but the score with Ammon had not been fully settled. That battle would resume as noted in the next chapter. It also was at this time when the infamous sin in David's life took place.

* * * * *

Overview of I Chronicles 20: *The account to follow parallels that of II Samuel 11. However, here the sacred chronicler provides details only of the military outcome of battle and says nothing about David's adultery with Bathsheba.*

Also, another war with Philistia is recorded. After David's great sin, things began to go wrong for Israel.

20:1-3 And it came to pass, that after the year was expired, at the time that kings go out *to battle*, Joab led forth the power of the army, and wasted the country of the children of Ammon, and came and besieged Rabbah. But David tarried at Jerusalem. And Joab smote Rabbah, and destroyed it. 2 And David took the crown of their king from off his head, and found it to weigh a talent of gold, and *there were* precious stones in it; and it was set upon David's head: and he brought also exceeding much spoil out of the city. 3 And he brought out the people that *were* in it, and cut *them* with saws, and with harrows of iron, and with axes. Even so dealt David with all the cities of the children of Ammon. And David and all the people returned to Jerusalem.

The account here parallels that of II Samuel 11. The war with Ammon was not over. It was customary in middle-eastern wars in ancient times to call a 'cease-fire' during the winter. David and his forces evidently put the war against Ammon on hold over the winter. Moreover, the Hebrew year ended at the end of February; hence, the comment about how "after the year was expired." As spring was blossoming, David again sent military units under Joab, his chief general, back into battle. It is noted that they first destroyed the main forces of the Ammonites in battle and then proceeded to besiege the city of Rabbah which was a chief city of the region of Ammon.

However, for reasons untold, David stayed in Jerusalem rather than lead his forces into battle. It would prove to be his undoing. Rather than abounding in the work of the Lord, he took a break. Christians doing the same today often get into trouble as well. When David should have been at the forefront of the battle as commander-in-chief, he "tarried at Jerusalem." He thus became easy prey for sin when he failed to do as he ought.

Afer the debacle of Bathsheba and its tragic aftermath, David therefore personally led the final battle against Rabbah and captured it. It has been suggested that this event took place shortly after Uriah's death and while Bathsheba was still in mourning. Record is made of him taking as the spoil of war the magnificent crown of the king of Rabbah. Moreover, David and his men captured a large spoil of war from Rabbah. It should be recalled that this war was started when the Ammonites humiliated David's ambassadors as recorded in 19:1-3.

Some have suggested that the description above was of David torturing his captives after winning the victory over them. However, it rather likely refers to David forcing the Ammonites into servitude as common laborers who sawed lumber, did field work (**harrows of iron**), cut trees (**axes of iron**), and made bricks, etc. That seems more in character with David than cruel torture of his enemies. He thus returned to Jerusalem victorious. But more trouble was brewing.

19:4-8 And it came to pass after this, that there arose war at Gezer with the Philistines; at which time Sibbechai the Hushathite slew Sippai, *that was* **of the children of the giant: and they were subdued. 5 And there was war again with the Philistines; and Elhanan the son of Jair slew Lahmi the brother of Goliath the Gittite, whose spear staff** *was* **like a weaver's beam.**

6 And yet again there was war at Gath, where was a man of *great* **stature, whose fingers and toes** *were* **four and twenty, six** *on each hand***, and six** *on each foot***: and he also was the son of the giant. 7 But when he defied Israel, Jonathan the son of Shimea David's brother slew him. 8 These were born unto the giant in Gath; and they fell by the hand of David, and by the hand of his servants.**

Notice there were ongoing wars after David's great sin. God's hand of blessing was being withheld from David. Sin

Understanding I Chronicles

does have consequences. The war described here is thought to be the same as in II Samuel 21:18*ff*. Philistine forces invaded Israel and attacked Gezer of the tribal region of Ephraim. In that battle "Sibbechai the Hushathite slew Sippai, *that was* of the children of the giant: and they were subdued." Another battle erupted with Philistia "and Elhanan the son of Jair slew Lahmi the bro-ther of Goliath the Gittite, whose spear staff *was* like a weaver's beam."

Similar account is found in II Samuel 21:19. A weaver's beam would be analogous to a '2 x 4.' Still more warfare erupted with Philistia at Gath, "where was a man of *great* stature, whose fingers and toes *were* four and twenty, six *on each hand*, and six *on each foot*: and he also was the son of the giant."It seems that the family of Goliath was determined to avenge their father's death at the hand of David, though years earlier. This time another son, a giant himself with six fingers on each hand and six toes on each foot, defied Israel to fight him. This time David's nephew Shimea dispatched him. Though large in size, the giants of Philistia were no match for the fierce warriors of Israel. David's men, one by one, killed them.

* * * * *

Overview of I Chronicles 21: *Details of David's census of the nation in his latter years are her provided. (This parallels II Samuel 24.) The problem here was not finding out how many people lived in Israel. Rather, it was for military purposes. David wanted to know how many soldiers he could depend upon if need arose. The sin here was relying on human resources rather than upon his God.*

21:1-2 And Satan stood up against Israel, and provoked David to number Israel. 2 And David said to Joab and to the

rulers of the people, Go, number Israel from Beersheba even to Dan; and bring the number of them to me, that I may know *it*.

The account of David's numbering of Israel will prove to be disastrous. However, the instigator of it all is revealed here: "Satan stood up against Israel, and provoked David to number Israel." Though tempted by David during a time of a lack of faith, it ultimately turned to good in that the site of the future Temple was selected and procured. David's military strength depended upon the size of his armed forces. David therefore directed Joab to conduct a military census to determine his available pool of reserves. Rather than trust God for help, David turned to human resources. As recorded in the preceding chapter, 'brush fire' wars had been popping up with which David had to contend. In a backslidden condition and lack of faith, he ordered the military census.

Joab, the chief of staff of David's army was ordered to take the census from Beer-sheba in the extreme south to Dan in the extreme north. David wanted to know how many men were in his national reserve for military purposes.

21:3-5 And Joab answered, The LORD make his people an hundred times so many more as they *be*: but, my lord the king, *are* they not all my lord's servants? why then doth my lord require this thing? why will he be a cause of trespass to Israel? 4 Nevertheless the king's word prevailed against Joab. Wherefore Joab departed, and went throughout all Israel, and came to Jerusalem. 5 And Joab gave the sum of the number of the people unto David. And all *they of* Israel were a thousand thousand and an hundred thousand men that drew sword: and Judah *was* four hundred threescore and ten thousand men that drew sword.

Though Joab at times had been of questionable loyalty, he here had the good sense to question David's decision. He perceived David's orders to have originated in the flesh and resulted from a lack of faith in God. Notwithstanding Joab's protests to the contrary, David's order stood. Joab accordingly accomplished the military census of Israel. As with the modern Israeli army, all young adult men of Israel then were part of the national military reserves. Joab thus counted 1.1 million men in the northern ten tribes and in Judah he counted 470,000 men able to fight. This evidently was over and above the 300,000 men in David's standing army. See I Chronicles 27:1-9. Why Judah constituted approximately 43 percent of the national reserves is not clear other than perhaps God had blessed that tribe because of David.

21:6-7 But Levi and Benjamin counted he not among them: for the king's word was abominable to Joab. 7 And God was displeased with this thing; therefore he smote Israel.

Notwithstanding the king's order, Joab refused to count the tribe of Levi or Benjamin. It is unclear as to why he passed over Benjamin. It may be that they were included with the disproportional number of Judah, inasmuch as Benjamin had essentially merged with Judah for all practical purposes.

However, even more ominous than Joab's displeasure with the census was that God was displeased. He therefore 'smote' Israel. II Samuel 24:1 gives further insight into the situation. There, the text records, "And again the anger of the LORD was kindled against Israel, and he moved David against them to say, Go, number Israel and Judah." Implicit is that God had become angry over the growing sin and backslidden condition of greater Israel. Implied is that because he was angry with the nation as a whole, he allowed the devil to so provoke David to order the census. God therefore proceeded to chasten Israel. Apparent is that the greater nation had backslidden from God from David on down.

21:8 And David said unto God, I have sinned greatly, because I have done this thing: but now, I beseech thee, do away the iniquity of thy servant; for I have done very foolishly. Smitten by a convicted conscience, David confessed to God, "I have sinned greatly, because I have done this thing." He therefore besought the Lord to take away his sin. He freely admitted to God that he had done very foolishly.

21:9-13 And the LORD spake unto Gad, David's seer, saying, 10 Go and tell David, saying, Thus saith the LORD, I offer thee three *things*: choose thee one of them, that I may do *it* unto thee. 11 So Gad came to David, and said unto him, Thus saith the LORD, Choose thee 12 Either three years' famine; or three months to be destroyed before thy foes, while that the sword of thine enemies overtaketh *thee*; or else three days the sword of the LORD, even the pestilence, in the land, and the angel of the LORD destroying throughout all the coasts of Israel.

Now therefore advise thyself what word I shall bring again to him that sent me. 13 And David said unto Gad, I am in a great strait: let me fall now into the hand of the LORD; for very great *are* his mercies: but let me not fall into the hand of man.

God sent a prophet by the name of Gad to confront David. Not much is known about Gad. But it seems that he was a prophet during the time of David and appears to have joined David when he was in the hold. He reappeared here in connection with the punishment for taking the census. He also assisted in the arrangements for the musical service of the Temple.

God through the prophet offered David three options for punishment: (1) three years of famine; (2) three months being defeated in battle; or (3) three days of pestilence by a death angel moving across the land. David was directed to chose which. David deferred to chose any, allowing the Lord to so choose.

21:14-17 So the LORD sent pestilence upon Israel: and there fell of Israel seventy thousand men. 15 And God sent an angel unto Jerusalem to destroy it: and as he was destroying, the LORD beheld, and he repented him of the evil, and said to the angel that destroyed, It is enough, stay now thine hand. And the angel of the LORD stood by the threshingfloor of Ornan the Jebusite. 16 And David lifted up his eyes, and saw the angel of the LORD stand between the earth and the heaven, having a drawn sword in his hand stretched out over Jerusalem. Then David and the elders *of Israel, who were* clothed in sackcloth, fell upon their faces. 17 And David said unto God, *Is it* not I *that* commanded the people to be numbered? even I it is that have sinned and done evil indeed; but *as for* these sheep, what have they done? let thine hand, I pray thee, O LORD my God, be on me, and on my father's house; but not on thy people, that they should be plagued.

God therefore sent a pestilence of death across Israel for three days. In that plague, 70,000 men in Israel died. When the death angel began to sweep across Jerusalem, God stayed him. The holy wrath of God had been appeased and His mercy prevailed. Notice how that God **repented** of the trouble (i.e., evil) caused by the death angel. When the angel was stopped, he did so "by the threshingfloor of Ornan the Jebusite." Ornan, evidently was a Jebusite still living at Jerusalem. II Samuel 24:23 refers to him as a king. He may have descended from the last king of the Jebusites and likely was the leader of whatever small group of descendants of them that still lived in the area.

God evidently also allowed David to see the otherwise unseen angel of death standing over Jerusalem with sword outstretched. Other leaders of Israel were allowed to see the same thing. They therefore humbled themselves before God in sackcloth and fell on their faces before Him. David further confessed his sin, being convicted in his heart of the error of his ways. He therefore besought God to be merciful to His people and rather implored God to judge him and his family for his own sin. Again, II Samuel 24:1 clearly implies that God judged Israel not only because of David's sin, but also for the sin of the nation as a whole.

24:18-23 Then the angel of the LORD commanded Gad to say to David, that David should go up, and set up an altar unto the LORD in the threshingfloor of Ornan the Jebusite. 19 And David went up at the saying of Gad, which he spake in the name of the LORD. 20 And Ornan turned back, and saw the angel; and his four sons with him hid themselves. Now Ornan was threshing wheat. 21 And as David came to Ornan, Ornan looked and saw David, and went out of the threshingfloor, and bowed himself to David with *his* face to the ground.

22 Then David said to Ornan, Grant me the place of *this* threshingfloor, that I may build an altar therein unto the LORD: thou shalt grant it me for the full price: that the plague may be stayed from the people. 23 And Ornan said unto David, Take *it* to thee, and let my lord the king do *that which is* good in his eyes: lo, I give *thee* the oxen *also* for burnt offerings, and the threshing instruments for wood, and the wheat for the meat offering; I give it all.

The angel of God therefore instructed the prophet Gad to direct David to erect an altar on the site of the threshingfloor of Ornan the Jebusite. David therefore proceeded to Ornan's threshingfloor whence the latter was threshing wheat. (Ornan evidently was in the grain business.) In seeing the king coming, Ornan bowed. David therefore requested to purchase Ornan's threshing floor atop Mount Moriah. David offered the full market value of the land. Ornan declined to take payment for the land. Rather, he proposed to give it all to David. In fact, he said, "Lo, I give *thee* the oxen *also* for burnt offerings, and the threshing instruments for wood, and the wheat for the meat offering; I give it all." In short, Ornan offered to give all to God. Would to God that Christians to this day have such a surrendered heart as Ornan the Jebusite.

21:24-27 And king David said to Ornan, Nay; but I will verily buy it for the full price: for I will not take *that* which *is* thine for the LORD, nor offer burnt offerings without cost. 25 So David gave to Ornan for the place six hundred shekels of gold by weight. 26 And David built there an altar unto the LORD, and offered burnt offerings and peace offerings, and called upon the LORD; and he answered him from heaven by fire upon the altar of burnt offering. 27 And the LORD commanded the angel; and he put up his sword again into the sheath thereof.

David refused to take Ornan's land for nothing. Rather, he insisted on paying full price to Ornan. He therefore paid Ornan 600 shekels of gold. (The account in II Samuel 24:24 mentions fifty shekels for the *oxen*, but not for the land.) David thereupon built an altar to God and offered both burnt and peace offerings (sweet savor offerings). He also prayed to God, likely for mercy. God therefore answered from heaven by sending fire onto the altar. Moreover, God ordered the death angel to desist from further chastisement of Israel.

24:28-30 At that time when David saw that the LORD had answered him in the threshingfloor of Ornan the Jebusite, then he sacrificed there. 29 For the tabernacle of the LORD, which Moses made in the wilderness, and the altar of the burnt offering, *were* at that season in the high place at Gibeon. 30 But David could not go before it to

enquire of God: for he was afraid because of the sword of the angel of the LORD.

In seeing the fire fall from heaven upon the altar of sacrifice built there, David thence proceeded to offer sacrifice to God. Note is made how that the Tabernacle still remained at Gibeon, about seven miles northwest of Jerusalem in the territory of Benjamin. In the preceding judgment, David had been terrified to venture out of Jerusalem to Gibeon and the Tabernacle. He thence offered sacrifices to God upon the altar built upon the threshingfloor of Ornan. As the next chapter will note, this would be the site of the future Temple of God. It also evidently was the same site upon which Abraham had offered Isaac.

* * * * *

Overview of I Chronicles 22: This chapter details how David in his old age began preparation for the coming Temple construction. Though God would not allow David to actually construct the Temple, nevertheless, "David prepared abundantly before his death."

22:1 Then David said, This *is* the house of the LORD God, and this *is* the altar of the burnt offering for Israel. David perceived that the spot whence he stood was the site of the coming Temple. It was atop Mount Moriah, which David no doubt knew was where Abraham had prepared to offer Isaac centuries earlier. Indeed, Solomon would build the Temple of God upon that very site some years later.

22:2-5 And David commanded to gather together the strangers that *were* in the land of Israel; and he set masons to hew wrought stones to build the house of God. 3 And David prepared iron in abundance for the nails for the

doors of the gates, and for the joinings; and brass in abundance without weight; 4 Also cedar trees in abundance: for the Zidonians and they of Tyre brought much cedar wood to David. 5 And David said, Solomon my son *is* young and tender, and the house *that is* to be builded for the LORD *must be* exceeding magnifical, of fame and of glory throughout all countries: I will *therefore* now make preparation for it. So David prepared abundantly before his death.

Though God would not allow David to actually build the Temple, nevertheless, he began preparations thereof in earnest. Strangers (i.e., foreigners) living in Israel were gathered to assist in preparatory work, including stone cutters and masons. These began to prepare the massive stone work off-site. The rounded top of Mount Moriah would be built up around the edges thereof to make a massive platform upon which to erect the Temple itself. Some of that stonework exists to this day.

Meanwhile, David made other preparations in collecting vital materials for the Temple construction: iron in abundance for nails and hardware, brass in vast quantities, and cedar timber from Lebanon. David knew that his son Solomon was young and inexperienced. He also knew that the Temple to be built would be "exceeding magnifical, of fame and of glory throughout all countries." Therefore, David prepared materials in abundance for the coming massive Temple construction project.

22:6–10 Then he called for Solomon his son, and charged him to build an house for the LORD God of Israel. David therefore called Solomon before him and straitly directed him to build the Temple once he ascended the throne.

And David said to Solomon, My son, as for me, it was in my mind to build an house unto the name of the LORD my God: 8 But the word of the LORD came to me, saying, Thou hast shed blood abundantly, and hast made great wars:

thou shalt not build an house unto my name, because thou hast shed much blood upon the earth in my sight. David explained his desire to build a vast, magnificent Temple for God; but God would not allow him to do so. David had been a warrior his entire adult life. He had shed much blood in killing many a foe. God therefore would not allow him to be the builder of the Temple.

9 Behold, a son shall be born to thee, who shall be a man of rest; and I will give him rest from all his enemies round about: for his name shall be Solomon, and I will give peace and quietness unto Israel in his days. 10 He shall build an house for my name; and he shall be my son, and I *will be* his father; and I will establish the throne of his kingdom over Israel for ever.

David explained that God had foretold to him that his son who would be a man of peace and that He would give him peace from his enemies. Moreover, David told Solomon how that God had named him (i.e., Solomon) by name. He it was who would become the builder of the Temple. In so doing, God promised that He would establish the throne of David and Solomon over Israel for ever. Though that dynasty was abrogated after Zedekiah, it is only a temporary interruption. It will be renewed again when Jesus Christ returns and assumes the throne of David.

22:11-13 Now, my son, the LORD be with thee; and prosper thou, and build the house of the LORD thy God, as he hath said of thee. David therefore invoked God's blessing upon Solomon and straitly charged him to build the Temple as directed by God.

12 Only the LORD give thee wisdom and understanding, and give thee charge concerning Israel, that thou mayest keep the law of the LORD thy God. David therefore also invoked God to grant wisdom and understanding to Solomon as

Understanding I Chronicles

he assumed command of the nation of Israel. Specifically, David so prayed that Solomon would "keep the law of the LORD thy God." The bottom line was obedience. David besought God to give Solomon wisdom so that he would obey God's Word. Solomon did so for about the first half of his reign. Sadly, he then forgot the Word of God and slid into a dismal tailspin spiritually.

13 Then shalt thou prosper, if thou takest heed to fulfil the statutes and judgments which the LORD charged Moses with concerning Israel: be strong, and of good courage; dread not, nor be dismayed.

Notwithstanding, David told Solomon that if he would obey God's Word, that "then shalt thou prosper." The greater principle is that God blesses those who on purpose and as a matter of principle obey Him. This is particularly so for those in leadership. If Solomon would carefully obey God's Word, God would prosper and bless him. Again, the condition for such prospering is set forth: "if thou takest heed to fulfil the statutes and judgments which the LORD charged Moses with concerning Israel." The same principle remains for New Testament Christians to this hour. God blesses obedience to His Word. He also has, He always will. See Revelation 1:3, 22:7,14.

David therefore exhorted his son to "be strong, and of good courage; dread not, nor be dismayed." The thought was to be strong of spirit and encouraged; not worrying or anxious. God would assist Solomon as he was obedient.

22:14-16 Now, behold, in my trouble I have prepared for the house of the LORD an hundred thousand talents of gold, and a thousand thousand talents of silver; and of brass and iron without weight; for it is in abundance: timber also and stone have I prepared; and thou mayest add thereto.

David therefore informed his son how that with considerable difficulty (i.e., trouble), he had made preparations for the construction of the Temple. He had over the years accumulated 100,000 talents of gold. The amount thereof in modern terms is uncertain. However, it has been estimated that 100,000 talents of gold would approximate 6,000 tons of gold. That very well could translate into one billion dollars in modern money.

Moreover, David had accumulated one million talents of silver. The latter certainly would be more than one billion dollars in modern terms. Furthermore, the stores of brass and iron accumulated for the coming Temple project were so immense, they were not even accounted. In addition, vast quantities of timber and stone stock had been accumulated and stored. David informed Solomon that he could add thereto as he so desired.

15 Moreover *there are* workmen with thee in abundance, hewers and workers of stone and timber, and all manner of cunning men for every manner of work. In addition, David had assembled an army of skilled craftsmen for the coming work: stone masons, carpenters, and all necessary trades and craftsmen.

16 Of the gold, the silver, and the brass, and the iron, *there is* no number. Arise *therefore*, and be doing, and the LORD be with thee. Of the necessary materiel for the coming Temple building program, there was no accounting of the necessary materials. Implied is that there was more than enough to do the job. David, therefore, ordered Solomon to get on with it. It very may be that even before Solomon officially became king that he began to familiarize himself with blueprints and make preliminary organizational plans.

22:17-19 David also commanded all the princes of Israel to help Solomon his son, *saying*, 18 *Is* not the LORD your God with you? and hath he *not* given you rest on every side? for he hath given the inhabitants of the land into mine hand; and the land is subdued before the LORD, and before

his people. David also ordered his subordinates to assist Solomon in every way. He reminded them that God had helped them heretofore and given them peace.

19 Now set your heart and your soul to seek the LORD your God; arise therefore, and build ye the sanctuary of the LORD God, to bring the ark of the covenant of the LORD, and the holy vessels of God, into the house that is to be built to the name of the LORD. David therefore ordered Solomon to begin the necessary preparations for the upcoming Temple construction. Upon completion, he was to bring the ark of the covenant along with the sacred vessels of service into the Temple for worship of God. It would appear that this charge to Solomon was made some time before David transferred the throne to him. It no doubt was obvious to all that Solomon was the heir apparent. That fact therefore provides insight into the wickedness of Adonijah when he tried to wrest the crown to himself prior to David's death.

* * * * *

Overview of I Chronicles 23: Upon Solomon's coronation, the chapter presents a listing of the three main families of the Levites: the sons of Gershon, the sons of Kohath, an the sons of Merari. They were formally assigned to the service of the Temple and to assist the sons of Aaron. Notice also their charge in verse 30 "to stand every morning to thank and praise the LORD, and likewise at even." There is a lesson there for our personal devotional life even today.

23:1 So when David was old and full of days, he made Solomon his son king over Israel. See I Kings 1:33-40 and I Chronicles 28:4-5. Solomon thus acceded the throne of his father David.

23:2-6 And he gathered together all the princes of Israel, with the priests and the Levites. One of the first acts of Solomon as king was to assemble the leaders of the nation: princes, priests, and Levites. This quite apparently was to finalize plans for the commencement of work upon the new Temple.

3 Now the Levites were numbered from the age of thirty years and upward: and their number by their polls, man by man, was thirty and eight thousand. 4 Of which, twenty and four thousand *were* to set forward the work of the house of the LORD; and six thousand *were* officers and judges. Levites were enumerated for service once they became thirty years of age. Solomon therefore learned that there were 38,000 Levites in the realm available for service. 24,000 of these were to (by courses or shifts) **set forward** the work of the Temple.

The word so translated (נצח *natsach*) in this context has the sense to 'oversee.' Though the Levites were under the supervision of the priests, they themselves were over the Nethinims who were their servants. Another 6,000 Levites were appointed as "officers and judges." These were administrators or foremen of Levites. Those as judges were appointed to act as civil magistrates for the people to hear disputes.

5 Moreover four thousand *were* porters; and four thousand praised the LORD with the instruments which I made, *said David*, to praise *therewith*. 4,000 Levites were assigned to be porters or gatekeepers of the coming Temple. These essentially became the Temple police, guarding against entrance by unclean Jews or unqualified gentiles. Another 4,000 Levites were assigned to be permanent Temple musicians who wrote, played, and sang sacred music to Jehovah God.

6 And David divided them into courses among the sons of Levi, *namely*, Gershon, Kohath, and Merari. David therefore organized the 38,000 Levites into courses (i.e., shifts). The primary divisions were made along the three family lines of the

Understanding I Chronicles

sons of Levi; The priests were organized into twenty-four orders according to 24:5*ff.* The Levites were as well. Thus, one-twenty-fourth of these Levites were on duty at any one time for seven days at time. See I Chronicles 9:25. Thus, on any given week, there were about 1,600 Levites on duty at the Temple. Their courses thus cycled about twice a year—one week on duty, twenty-three weeks off. The Levites thence returned to their villages and crops.

23:7-11 Of the Gershonites *were*, Laadan, and Shimei. 8 The sons of Laadan; the chief *was* Jehiel, and Zetham, and Joel, three. 9 The sons of Shimei; Shelomith, and Haziel, and Haran, three. These *were* the chief of the fathers of Laadan. 10 And the sons of Shimei *were*, Jahath, Zina, and Jeush, and Beriah. These four *were* the sons of Shimei. 11 And Jahath was the chief, and Zizah the second: but Jeush and Beriah had not many sons; therefore they were in one reckoning, according to *their* father's house. The principal elders of the descendants of Gershon are here noted. These likely were the administrators over their section of Levites when they were scheduled for service.

23:12-20 The sons of Kohath; Amram, Izhar, Hebron, and Uzziel, four. 13 The sons of Amram; Aaron and Moses: and Aaron was separated, that he should sanctify the most holy things, he and his sons for ever, to burn incense before the LORD, to minister unto him, and to bless in his name for ever. 14 Now *concerning* Moses the man of God, his sons were named of the tribe of Levi. 15 The sons of Moses *were*, Gershom, and Eliezer.

Before listing the principal elders of the Kohathites, the sacred chronicler presents the lineage of Moses and Aaron, both Kohathites. Both were sons of Amram. God had specifically separated Aaron and his sons unto His service. Of interest is the listing of the two sons of Moses, Gershom, and Eliezer. Not since Moses sent them away with the mother in Exodus 18:3 have they been mentioned. Though as Kenites (and Levites), they likely were later assimilated back into the nation of Israel. There is no other record of them elsewhere in the Bible.

16 Of the sons of Gershom, Shebuel *was* the chief. 17 And the sons of Eliezer *were*, Rehabiah the chief. And Eliezer had none other sons; but the sons of Rehabiah were very many. 18 Of the sons of Izhar; Shelomith the chief. 19 Of the sons of Hebron; Jeriah the first, Amariah the second, Jahaziel the third, and Jekameam the fourth. 20 Of the sons of Uzziel; Micah the first, and Jesiah the second. Of interest is that the descendants of Kohath through Amram are listed through Moses' two sons, Gershom and Eliezer. Then, the elders of the Levites of David's day, descended from Kohath—Izhar, Hebron, and Uzziel—are here listed. These likely were the administrators over the Levites descended from Kohath in the coming Temple.

23:21-23 The sons of Merari; Mahli, and Mushi. The sons of Mahli; Eleazar, and Kish. 22 And Eleazar died, and had no sons, but daughters: and their brethren the sons of Kish took them. 23 The sons of Mushi; Mahli, and Eder, and Jeremoth, three. The elders of the Levitical line of Merari are here noted. These likely also became the administrators of their brethren descended from Merari in the coming Temple.

23:24-26 These *were* the sons of Levi after the house of their fathers; *even* the chief of the fathers, as they were counted by number of names by their polls, that did the work for the service of the house of the LORD, from the age of twenty years and upward. Further enumeration of Levites from twenty years and upward are noted. Evidently, Levites between the ages of twenty and thirty served as 'apprentice'

Levites at the Temple, learning the skills of their given ministry. They also did the more manual and menial tasks associated with their order of service. Apparently, at age thirty, they thence became full-fledged Levites.

25 For David said, The LORD God of Israel hath given rest unto his people, that they may dwell in Jerusalem for ever: 26 And also unto the Levites; they shall no *more* carry the tabernacle, nor any vessels of it for the service thereof. David reasoned that because God had given rest and peace to His people at Jerusalem, the older Levites should no longer bare the manual-labor tasks of the Temple. And indeed, much of the ministry of the Levites required much physical work. Those chores would now fall to the young apprentice Levites (and the Nethinims).

23:27-32 For by the last words of David the Levites *were* numbered from twenty years old and above: 28 Because their office *was* to wait on the sons of Aaron for the service of the house of the LORD, in the courts, and in the chambers, and in the purifying of all holy things, and the work of the service of the house of God. Recorded is that one of the last commandments of David prior to his death was the inclusion of Levites from twenty years and older into the Levitical ministry. It was their overall task to assist the priests in their official service at the Temple.

29 Both for the shewbread, and for the fine flour for meat offering, and for the unleavened cakes, and for *that which is baked in* the pan, and for that which is fried, and for all manner of measure and size; 30 And to stand every morning to thank and praise the LORD, and likewise at even; 31 And to offer all burnt sacrifices unto the LORD in the sabbaths, in the new moons, and on the set feasts, by number, according to the order commanded unto them, continually before the LORD: 32 And that they should keep

the charge of the tabernacle of the congregation, and the charge of the holy *place*, and the charge of the sons of Aaron their brethren, in the service of the house of the LORD.

The specific tasks in which the Levites were to assist the priests are listed. These ranged from the baking of the shewbread, to the Levitical choir each morning, to assisting the priests with the various sacrifices, especially on high holy days when there was a high volume of sacrifices brought. Furthermore, the Levites were assigned the duty of overseeing and guarding all the sacred precincts of the Temple, the safekeeping of the priests, and all other work necessary for the proper functioning of the Temple. The duties of the Levites were thus codified by David before his death.

* * * * *

Overview of I Chronicles 24: This next chapter details how the three divisions of the tribe of Levi were organized into 24 orders. Though the Scripture here is not explicit, Jewish custom held that each of these orders would take their turn serving at the Temple for one week at a time twice a year. See comments for I Chronicles 9:25.

24:1-4Now *these are* the divisions of the sons of Aaron. The sons of Aaron; Nadab, and Abihu, Eleazar, and Ithamar. 2 But Nadab and Abihu died before their father, and had no children: therefore Eleazar and Ithamar executed the priest's office. The sons of Aaron are listed, along with the two who died for usurping their office—Nadab and Abihu. The priestly lineage therefore descended through Eleazar and Ithamar who over the years executed the office of priest.

3 And David distributed them, both Zadok of the sons of Eleazar, and Ahimelech of the sons of Ithamar, according

Understanding I Chronicles 475

to their offices in their service. Before his death, David therefore organized the descendants of Eleazar and Ithamar as priestly 'shifts.' The descendant of Eleazar in that day was Zadok. The parallel descendant of Ithamar was Ahimelech. Each had specific oversights assigned to them

4 And there were more chief men found of the sons of Eleazar than of the sons of Ithamar; and *thus* were they divided. Among the sons of Eleazar *there were* sixteen chief men of the house of *their* fathers, and eight among the sons of Ithamar according to the house of their fathers.

By the end of David's reign, the descendants of Eleazar outnumbered those of Ithamar by a margin of two to one. Therefore, David assigned sixteen heads of Eleazar as principal priests and eight heads of the descendants of Ithamar as principal priests. There thus were ordered twenty-four divisions or shifts of priests. The clear implication is that they served for one week and then went home for twenty-three weeks. They thus were away from their home and crops for only one week at a time. See comments for I Chronicles 9:23.

24:5-19 Thus were they divided by lot, one sort with another; for the governors of the sanctuary, and governors *of the house* of God, were of the sons of Eleazar, and of the sons of Ithamar. David ordered that the several areas of priestly oversight to be assigned by lot. Some were thus assigned oversight of the holy of holies. Others were assigned oversight of the greater Temple structure itself.

6 And Shemaiah the son of Nethaneel the scribe, *one* of the Levites, wrote them before the king, and the princes, and Zadok the priest, and Ahimelech the son of Abiathar, and *before* the chief of the fathers of the priests and Levites: one principal household being taken for Eleazar, and *one* taken for Ithamar. Shemaiah, a Levitical scribe, was therefore ordered to write the names of the twenty-four priestly heads for the assignments by lot (i.e., drawing). The names were thus drawn out of the 'hat' and they were assigned their course (i.e., shift) accordingly.

Now the first lot came forth to Jehoiarib, the second to Jedaiah, 8 The third to Harim, the fourth to Seorim, 9 The fifth to Malchijah, the sixth to Mijamin, 10 The seventh to Hakkoz, the eighth to Abijah, 11 The ninth to Jeshua, the tenth to Shecaniah, 12 The eleventh to Eliashib, the twelfth to Jakim, 13 The thirteenth to Huppah, the fourteenth to Jeshebeab, 14 The fifteenth to Bilgah, the sixteenth to Immer, 15 The seventeenth to Hezir, the eighteenth to Aphses, 16 The nineteenth to Pethahiah, the twentieth to Jehezekel, 17 The one and twentieth to Jachin, the two and twentieth to Gamul, 18 The three and twentieth to Delaiah, the four and twentieth to Maaziah. The twenty-four orders of priests were thus assigned by lot (i.e., by drawing). Each order or course (i.e., shift) would be on duty for one week and then off for the next twenty-three weeks.

24:19 These *were* the orderings of them in their service to come into the house of the LORD, according to their manner, under Aaron their father, as the LORD God of Israel had commanded him. The priestly orders were therefore established by David. The word translated as **according to their manner** (מִשְׁפָּט mishpat) is most frequently rendered as 'judgment' but here has the thought of 'proper order.' They all were descended from Aaron and served as priests "as the LORD God of Israel had commanded him."

24:20-25 And the rest of the sons of Levi *were these*: Of the sons of Amram; Shubael: of the sons of Shubael; Jehdeiah. 21 Concerning Rehabiah: of the sons of Rehabiah, the first *was* Isshiah. 22 Of the Izharites; Shelomoth: of the sons of Shelomoth; Jahath. 23 And the sons *of Hebron*;

Jeriah *the first,* Amariah the second, Jahaziel the third, Jekameam the fourth. 24 *Of* the sons of Uzziel; Michah: of the sons of Michah; Shamir. 25 The brother of Michah *was* Isshiah: of the sons of Isshiah; Zechariah.

The rest of the principal descendants of Levi through Kohath and then Amram are here recorded. These were the other chief Kohathites at the end of David's reign. These are in distinction to the sons of Kohath through Moses' son as recorded in 23:12-20.

24:26-31 The sons of Merari *were* **Mahli and Mushi: the sons of Jaaziah; Beno.** 27 **The sons of Merari by Jaaziah; Beno, and Shoham, and Zaccur, and Ibri.** 28 **Of Mahli** *came* **Eleazar, who had no sons.** 29 **Concerning Kish: the son of Kish** *was* **Jerahmeel.** Other principal Levitical descendants of Merari at the end of David's reign are noted. These are in addition to those listed in 23:21-23.

31 **These likewise cast lots over against their brethren the sons of Aaron in the presence of David the king, and Zadok, and Ahimelech, and the chief of the fathers of the priests and Levites, even the principal fathers over against their younger brethren.** As the priests above had been assigned their specific courses (i.e., shifts) by lot (i.e., drawings), thus the Levites were likely organized in to twenty-four orders (i.e., shifts) in the presence of David and the two priestly lineages: Zadok and Ahimelech. Thus in a public setting before the leaders of the nation, the Levites were organized and assigned their lots without regard to rank or age.

* * * * *

Overview of I Chronicles 25: *This next chapter details how the descendants of the three main musicians of the Temple,*

Asaph, Heman and Jeduthun, were ordered. Again, they were organized into twenty-four orders for service at the Temple. Evident is that the service of God's house was orderly and organized.

25:1-5 Moreover David and the captains of the host separated to the service of the sons of Asaph, and of Heman, and of Jeduthun, who should prophesy with harps, with psalteries, and with cymbals: and the number of the workmen according to their service was. Before his death, David organized the permanent musicians of the coming Temple. The "captains of the host" in this context likely refers to the principal leaders of the Levites and priests. David likely consulted with them as to who the most gifted musicians in their ranks were. Three families were chosen (i.e., set apart) for this special ministry: "the sons of Asaph, and of Heman, and of Jeduthun." Their ministry would be to **prophesy** musically. Implied is that they would be led by the Spirit of God in writing, playing, and singing the music impressed upon them. They thus in very real sense were 'Spirit-filled' musicians. There were not only Levitical choirs at the Temple, but orchestras as well. The text below will specify these 'workmen.' The latter thought is that of the working musicians.

2 Of the sons of Asaph; Zaccur, and Joseph, and Nethaniah, and Asarelah, the sons of Asaph under the hands of Asaph, which prophesied according to the order of the king. The sons of Asaph, as noted, evidently formed or led the Levitical choirs for they "prophesied according to the order of the king." Implicit is that the sons of Asaph wrote and sang the sacred hymns and psalms of the Temple.

3 Of Jeduthun: the sons of Jeduthun; Gedaliah, and Zeri, and Jeshaiah, Hashabiah, and Mattithiah, six, under the hands of their father Jeduthun, who prophesied with a harp, to give thanks and to praise the LORD. The sons of

Jeduthun apparently were more instrumental musicians. Again, their ministry was of prophecy of praise to the Lord. Implied is that even these instrumental musicians were Spirit filled and Spirit led. Their music was specifically to praise the Lord. Never in Scripture was sacred music designed to entertain or even 'bless' the human ear. Its focus was always to Him who dwells above.

4 Of Heman: the sons of Heman; Bukkiah, Mattaniah, Uzziel, Shebuel, and Jerimoth, Hananiah, Hanani, Eliathah, Giddalti, and Romamtiezer, Joshbekashah, Mallothi, Hothir, *and* **Mahazioth: 5 All these** *were* **the sons of Heman the king's seer in the words of God, to lift up the horn. And God gave to Heman fourteen sons and three daughters.**

The musicians under the leadership of Heman are noted. Heman is also described as "the king's seer in the words of God, to lift up the horn." Heman evidently was also an instrumental musician. As the **seer** (or, overseer), Heman may have been the chief of the musicians, or at least of the instrumental musicians. Of interest is the record of Heman having not only fourteen sons, but also three daughters. What is remarkable about is that record of daughters are usually not mentioned in Levitical lineages.

25:6-7 All these *were* **under the hands of their father for song** *in* **the house of the LORD, with cymbals, psalteries, and harps, for the service of the house of God, according to the king's order to Asaph, Jeduthun, and Heman.** The list to follow in verses 8-31 are the sons of the three principal Temple musicians: Asaph, Jeduthun, and Heman. Their ministry was exclusively "for song *in* the house of the LORD." They were appointed by David specifically to provide sacred music, both in word and in melody at the Temple. The three principal instruments (or classes of instruments) used at the Temple are again noted as "cymbals, psalteries, and harps." Cymbals were percussive while the other two were stringed instruments. They, in short, were the basis of a sacred orchestra at the Temple.

7 So the number of them, with their brethren that were instructed in the songs of the LORD, *even* all that were cunning, was two hundred fourscore and eight. 288 musicians were thus organized. As will be noted below, there were twenty-four orders (i.e., shifts) of twelve lead musicians each. Thus, in each course (i.e., shift), twelve lead Levitical musicians would be on duty for a week and then go home for the next twenty-three weeks before returning to duty again.

According to I Chronicles 23:5, a total of 4,000 Levites were assigned as musicians. The greater thought evidently is that there were twenty-four orders of lead musicians who in turn directed or worked with the other 4,000. No doubt, the other 4,000 Levitical musicians also were divided into twenty-four orders so that on any given week (or shift), there were more than 166 Levitical musicians on duty, not including the twelve lead musicians listed below. These formed the Temple orchestras and choirs on a daily basis.

25:8 And they cast lots, ward against *ward*, as well the small as the great, the teacher as the scholar. As with the priests and general Levites, lots were cast to determine the order, sequence, and composition of the courses (i.e., shifts). Apparently, each of the twenty-four family heads of these musicians were placed into a 'hat' and names were then drawn out, thus assigning each family to their specific order. Thus, no favoritism was made for the well-known musician or the apprentice musician, teacher or student (i.e., scholar).

25:9-31 The twenty-four orders of Levitical lead musicians are thus listed according to the order their names were drawn.

Understanding I Chronicles

These then became the standing musicians for the Temple once it opened for services. In each 'order' were twelve lead musicians. They thus rotated on and off duty, one week at a time. In a given year, each order would serve two one-week tours of duty.

* * * * *

Overview of I Chronicles 26: This next chapter provides details and further organization and order of the Levites, particularly in regard to the porters (gatekeepers of the Temple).

26:1-5 Concerning the divisions of the porters: Of the Korhites *was* Meshelemiah the son of Kore, of the sons of Asaph. 2 And the sons of Meshelemiah *were*, Zechariah the firstborn, Jediael the second, Zebadiah the third, Jathniel the fourth, 3 Elam the fifth, Jehohanan the sixth, Elioenai the seventh. 4 Moreover the sons of Obededom *were*, Shemaiah the firstborn, Jehozabad the second, Joah the third, and Sacar the fourth, and Nethaneel the fifth, 5 Ammiel the sixth, Issachar the seventh, Peulthai the eighth: for God blessed him.

The organization of the porters of the coming Temple is presented. Porters were the gatekeepers and guards of the Temple complex. They later would become the Temple police in Jesus' day. There were several divisions of the porters. Listed here are the sons of Korah, the son of Levi. Notice the final phrase of verse 5 "for God blessed him." The reference is to Obed-edom, noted in verse 4. God gave him seven sons. His housing of the ark prior to its delivery to Jerusalem focused the blessing of God upon his family.

26:6-9 Also unto Shemaiah his son were sons born, that ruled throughout the house of their father: for they *were*

mighty men of valour. 7 **The sons of Shemaiah; Othni, and Rephael, and Obed, Elzabad, whose brethren** *were* **strong men, Elihu, and Semachiah.** 8 **All these of the sons of Obededom: they and their sons and their brethren, able men for strength for the service,** *were* **threescore and two of Obededom.** 9 **And Meshelemiah had sons and brethren, strong men, eighteen**. Further descendants of Korah through Shemaiah are listed with the porters of the coming Temple. Even more descendants of Obed-edom are listed—62 to be exact. Indeed, God richly blessed this righteous men.

26:10-12 Also Hosah, of the children of Merari, had sons; Simri the chief, (for *though* **he was not the firstborn, yet his father made him the chief;)** 11 **Hilkiah the second, Tebaliah the third, Zechariah the fourth: all the sons and brethren of Hosah** *were* **thirteen.** 12 **Among these** *were* **the divisions of the porters,** *even* **among the chief men,** *having* **wards one against another, to minister in the house of the LORD**. A final division of porters descended from Hosah of the sons of Merari are listed. Listed are only the "chief men" or chief porters, for according to I Chronicles 23:5, a total of 4,000 Levites were porters at the Temple. Each division had sections (i.e., wards) assigned for their watch. That is, each division had its own section of gates of the Temple to police.

26:13-19 And they cast lots, as well the small as the great, according to the house of their fathers, for every gate. Though no doubt this is not precisely how they did it, the idea of casting of lots would be analogous to drawing names out a hat. The greater thought is how that the various assignments of duties was by lot (i.e., drawing names out of a 'hat'). Neither important Levites or obscure had any advantage.

14 **And the lot eastward fell to Shelemiah. Then for Zechariah his son, a wise counsellor, they cast lots; and his**

lot came out northward. 15 To Obededom southward; and to his sons the house of Asuppim. 16 To Shuppim and Hosah *the lot came forth* westward, with the gate Shallecheth, by the causeway of the going up, ward against ward. 17 Eastward *were* six Levites, northward four a day, southward four a day, and toward Asuppim two *and* two. 18 At Parbar westward, four at the causeway, *and* two at Parbar. 19 These *are* the divisions of the porters among the sons of Kore, and among the sons of Merari.

Listed here were the working assignments of the various divisions of the porters of the Temple. Notice how that one Levite named Zechariah had a son renowned as "a wise counsellor." In summary, the porters of the soon-to-come Temple were from the descendants of Korah and Merari.

26:20-24 And of the Levites, Ahijah *was* over the treasures of the house of God, and over the treasures of the dedicated things. A listing is now made of Levites who were assigned to work in the treasury of the Temple. They might be likened more to trustees of a financial corporation. They kept track of the monies and assets of the Temple.

21 *As concerning* **the sons of Laadan; the sons of the Gershonite Laadan, chief fathers,** *even* **of Laadan the Gershonite,** *were* **Jehieli. 22 The sons of Jehieli; Zetham, and Joel his brother,** *which were* **over the treasures of the house of the LORD. 23 Of the Amramites,** *and* **the Izharites, the Hebronites,** *and* **the Uzzielites: 24 And Shebuel the son of Gershom, the son of Moses,** *was* **ruler of the treasures.** Though most of the names are obscure, noteworthy is how that "Shebuel the son of Gershom, the son of Moses, *was* ruler of the treasures." Thus, a descendant of Moses would the first chief-treasurer of the Temple.

26:25-28 And his brethren by Eliezer; Rehabiah his son, and Jeshaiah his son, and Joram his son, and Zichri his

son, and Shelomith his son. **26 Which Shelomith and his brethren *were* over all the treasures of the dedicated things, which David the king, and the chief fathers, the captains over thousands and hundreds, and the captains of the host, had dedicated. 27 Out of the spoils won in battles did they dedicate to maintain the house of the LORD.** Also other descendants of Moses were assistant treasurers at the Temple. They had specific charge over "the dedicated things, which David the king, and the chief fathers, the captains over thousands and hundreds, and the captains of the host, had dedicated." The latter refers to valuables taken in battle by David which were then dedicated to the Lord and stored in the treasuries at Jerusalem and elsewhere. See I Chronicles 18:7-11.

28 And all that Samuel the seer, and Saul the son of Kish, and Abner the son of Ner, and Joab the son of Zeruiah, had dedicated; *and* **whosoever had dedicated** *any thing, it was* **under the hand of Shelomith, and of his brethren.** The treasury of God also included assets placed there by Samuel, Saul, Abner, and Joab over the years. All which was dedicated—donated or given to God—was placed in the treasury of God. These treasures would be used as a major part of the "building fund" when the time came to build the Temple. This section of the treasury was under the oversight of "Shelomith, and of his brethren."

26:29-30 Of the Izharites, Chenaniah and his sons *were* for the outward business over Israel, for officers and judges. 30 *And* **of the Hebronites, Hashabiah and his brethren, men of valour, a thousand and seven hundred,** *were* **officers among them of Israel on this side Jordan westward in all the business of the LORD, and in the service of the king.**

Izhar was the grandson of Levi through Kohath. To his descendants were assigned oversight of financial affairs pertain-

Understanding I Chronicles

ing to the Tabernacle and then the Temple which were outside of Jerusalem. Hebron was another grandson of Levi. Of his lineage were 1,700 officers and judges assigned duties in the outlaying districts of the land west of the Jordan River. They oversaw business dealings of the Temple and of the king in these outlying districts.

26:31-32 Among the Hebronites *was* Jerijah the chief, *even* among the Hebronites, according to the generations of his fathers. In the fortieth year of the reign of David they were sought for, and there were found among them mighty men of valour at Jazer of Gilead. Also of the Hebronites, Jerijah was chief thereof. In David's final year as king, other portions of this lineage were located on the east side of the Jordan River at Jazer of Gilead.

32 And his brethren, men of valour, *were* two thousand and seven hundred chief fathers, whom king David made rulers over the Reubenites, the Gadites, and the half tribe of Manasseh, for every matter pertaining to God, and affairs of the king. Of this group of business officers of the realm were 2,700 from the tribes east of the Jordan River: "the Reubenites, the Gadites, and the half tribe of Manasseh." These were faithful and loyal Levites who took care of Temple business and that of the king in the eastern part of the kingdom.

* * * * *

***Overview of I Chronicles 27**: In this chapter, a further administrative organization of the kingdom of Israel is detailed. Rotating military leadership was organized for each month of the year. The end of the chapter gives further details of the governmental structure of Israel in David's final years.*

27:1 Now the children of Israel after their number, *to wit*, the chief fathers and captains of thousands and hundreds, and their officers that served the king in any matter of the courses, which came in and went out month by month throughout all the months of the year, of every course *were* twenty and four thousand. In this chapter is a description of the structure of David's militia system. As today in the modern Israeli army, all adult men are members of the military in their young adult years. Thereafter, they are in the reserves until at least middle age. During David's time, there was a standing militia of 24,000 soldiers which rotated on duty each month of the year. There therefore were twelve different courses or divisions thereof.

27:2-15 The twelve separate divisions of monthly rotation are delineated here. Most were military men who were otherwise obscure. However, in verses 5-6, Benaiah is listed who was one of David's 30 mighty men.

2:16-22 Furthermore over the tribes of Israel: the ruler of the Reubenites *was* Eliezer the son of Zichri: of the Simeonites, Shephatiah the son of Maachah: 17 Of the Levites, Hashabiah the son of Kemuel: of the Aaronites, Zadok: 18 Of Judah, Elihu, *one* of the brethren of David: of Issachar, Omri the son of Michael: 19 Of Zebulun, Ishmaiah the son of Obadiah: of Naphtali, Jerimoth the son of Azriel: 20 Of the children of Ephraim, Hoshea the son of Azaziah: of the half tribe of Manasseh, Joel the son of Pedaiah: 21 Of the half *tribe* of Manasseh in Gilead, Iddo the son of Zechariah: of Benjamin, Jaasiel the son of Abner: 22 Of Dan, Azareel the son of Jeroham. These *were* the princes of the tribes of Israel.

Listed here were the twelve rulers, also known as "princes of the tribes of Israel." These would be analogous to governors

Understanding I Chronicles 487

of states in the American political system. They are called both rulers (verse 16) and princes (verse 22). Of interest is the word translated as **prince** (שַׂר *sar*). It the etymological root for *ruler* in other languages such as *Czar* in Russian or *Caesar* in Latin.

27:23-24 But David took not the number of them from twenty years old and under: because the LORD had said he would increase Israel like to the stars of the heavens. 24 Joab the son of Zeruiah began to number, but he finished not, because there fell wrath for it against Israel; neither was the number put in the account of the chronicles of king David. The incident of David's census, described in II Samuel 24 and I Chronicles 21, is here briefly mentioned again. Joab's incomplete census was therefore not recorded in the official "account of the chronicles of king David."

27:25-32 And over the king's treasures *was* Azmaveth the son of Adiel: and over the storehouses in the fields, in the cities, and in the villages, and in the castles, *was* Jehonathan the son of Uzziah: 26 And over them that did the work of the field for tillage of the ground *was* Ezri the son of Chelub: 27 And over the vineyards *was* Shimei the Ramathite: over the increase of the vineyards for the wine cellars *was* Zabdi the Shiphmite: 28 And over the olive trees and the sycomore trees that *were* in the low plains *was* Baalhanan the Gederite: and over the cellars of oil *was* Joash:

29 And over the herds that fed in Sharon *was* Shitrai the Sharonite: and over the herds *that were* in the valleys *was* Shaphat the son of Adlai: 30 Over the camels also *was* Obil the Ishmaelite: and over the asses *was* Jehdeiah the Meronothite: 31 And over the flocks *was* Jaziz the Hagerite. All these *were* the rulers of the substance which *was* king David's. 32 Also Jonathan David's uncle was a counsellor, a wise man, and a scribe: and Jehiel the son of Hachmoni *was*

with the king's sons: 33 **And Ahithophel** *was* **the king's counsellor: and Hushai the Archite** *was* **the king's companion:** 34 **And after Ahithophel** *was* **Jehoiada the son of Benaiah, and Abiathar: and the general of the king's army** *was* **Joab.**

Other administrative officers of David's kingdom are here listed. Listed are his treasurer (which is in distinction to the Levitical treasurers of the Temple as noted in 26:20-28); his secretary of storehouses; his secretary of land use; his secretary of vineyards; his secretary of vineyard production; his secretary of olive and sycamore trees; his secretary of olive oil production; and his several secretaries of livestock. Clearly implied is that David was the ultimate owner of these vast resources as noted in verse 31. Then, special counselors to the king are listed, including Ahithophel (who later turned coat) and Hushai the Archite. The general officer of the army was Joab.

* * * * *

Overview of I Chronicles 28: This next to the last chapter finds David presenting his son Solomon to the leadership of the nation as their next king. Also David presents a charge to his son, about to ascend the throne.

28:1 And David assembled all the princes of Israel, the princes of the tribes, and the captains of the companies that ministered to the king by course, and the captains over the thousands, and captains over the hundreds, and the stewards over all the substance and possession of the king, and of his sons, with the officers, and with the mighty men, and with all the valiant men, unto Jerusalem. The scene is the last days of David's reign, evidently not long after when he became ill as recorded in II Kings 1. In those final days of his

Understanding I Chronicles

reign, after his illness, David assembled the officers and leadership of the nation, both military and civilian for a solemn convocation.

28:2-5 Then David the king stood up upon his feet, and said, Hear me, my brethren, and my people: *As for me,* **I** *had* **in mine heart to build an house of rest for the ark of the covenant of the LORD, and for the footstool of our God, and had made ready for the building.** David began his valedictory speech by reminding his subordinates of his long desire to build a permanent Temple. He had thus been long making preparations toward that end.

3 But God said unto me, Thou shalt not build an house for my name, because thou *hast been* **a man of war, and hast shed blood.** David also reminded his assembled leaders that God had prohibited him from the actual construction of the coming Temple because he had been a warrior who had shed much blood.

4 Howbeit the LORD God of Israel chose me before all the house of my father to be king over Israel for ever: for he hath chosen Judah *to be* **the ruler; and of the house of Judah, the house of my father; and among the sons of my father he liked me to make** *me* **king over all Israel.** Notwithstanding the prohibition of building the Temple, David reminded his men that God had clearly chosen him to be king.

And of all my sons, (for the LORD hath given me many sons,) he hath chosen Solomon my son to sit upon the throne of the kingdom of the LORD over Israel. Moreover, David announced to the assembled leadership of the nation that God had chosen Solomon to be the next king over Israel. This event evidently took place after the failed attempt of Adonijah to seize the throne. See I Chronicles 29:22.

28:6-7 And he said unto me, Solomon thy son, he shall build my house and my courts: for I have chosen him *to be*

my son, and I will be his father. 7 Moreover I will establish his kingdom for ever, if he be constant to do my commandments and my judgments, as at this day.

David therefore announced to his assembled subordinates that God had directed for Solomon to build the Temple. God had already told David that He had chosen Solomon to be his son (i.e., king) and He would be as a Father to him. God already had promised the kingdom to Solomon forever, *if* he was faithful in obeying the commandments and laws (i.e., judgments) of God. Thus, the stage was set for Solomon's accession to the throne of his father David.

28:8-10 Now therefore in the sight of all Israel the congregation of the LORD, and in the audience of our God, keep and seek for all the commandments of the LORD your God: that ye may possess this good land, and leave *it* for an inheritance for your children after you for ever. David therefore turned to Solomon, who obviously was present. He issued him an injunction to obey and seek the commandments of the Lord his God. In turn, God would give him rule of the good land of Israel. Moreover, his sons would likewise inherit the rule thereof for ever. Sadly, Solomon eventually forgot that charge when he became rich and powerful.

9 And thou, Solomon my son, know thou the God of thy father, and serve him with a perfect heart and with a willing mind: for the LORD searcheth all hearts, and understandeth all the imaginations of the thoughts: if thou seek him, he will be found of thee; but if thou forsake him, he will cast thee off for ever. David further charged Solomon to (1) "know thou the God of thy father." The charge was more than to just know about the Lord, but to know Him intimately—to really know Him. David also charged Solomon to (2) "serve him with a perfect heart and with a willing mind." The word translated as **perfect** (שלם *shalem*) has the sense of 'complete.' David in effect directed Solomon to serve the Lord will all his heart and with a willing mind. See Psalm 119:2,10. David spoke from experience for he had so served the Lord his entire life.

David further warned Solomon that "the LORD searcheth all hearts, and understandeth all the imaginations of the thoughts." God knows the thoughts and intents of the heart. He knows our motives. He knows our innermost thoughts. And, he knew the heart of Solomon as well. David additionally warned Solomon (publicly yet) that "if thou seek him, he will be found of thee; but if thou forsake him, he will cast thee off for ever." If Solomon would seek the Lord his God throughout his reign as king, God would be with him and bless him. If he forsook the Lord, God would turn his blessing from him. That God did when Solomon turned to other God as recorded in I Kings 11:9, 14, 23, 25, 26. When Solomon forsook the Lord, things started to become rough for him. The blessing of God turned to the chastening of God.

11 Take heed now; for the LORD hath chosen thee to build an house for the sanctuary: be strong, and do *it*. David thus admonished Solomon (publicly). God had chosen him to build the Temple. David therefore urged him to be strong (of spirit and mind) and to do it—to not procrastinate.

28:11-13 Then David gave to Solomon his son the pattern of the porch, and of the houses thereof, and of the treasuries thereof, and of the upper chambers thereof, and of the inner parlours thereof, and of the place of the mercy seat, 12 And the pattern of all that he had by the spirit, of the courts of the house of the LORD, and of all the chambers round about, of the treasuries of the house of God, and of the treasuries of the dedicated things: 13 Also for the courses of the priests and the Levites, and for all the work of the service of the house of the LORD, and for all the vessels of service in the house of the LORD.

In the meeting of the leaders of Israel with David and Solomon, David therefore gave to Solomon the plans for the upcoming Temple from its outer porches to the holy of holies. Verse 12 makes it clear that the Spirit of God revealed to David the precise plans of the entire Temple including the organization of he courses (i.e., shifts) of the priests and Levites. It was ordained by God and revealed by God's Spirit to David. Clearly, David was sensitive to the leading of the Holy Spirit and recorded all that God revealed to him.

28:14-18 *He gave* **of gold by weight for** *things* **of gold, for all instruments of all manner of service;** *silver also* **for all instruments of silver by weight, for all instruments of every kind of service: 15 Even the weight for the candlesticks of gold, and for their lamps of gold, by weight for every candlestick, and for the lamps thereof: and for the candlesticks of silver by weight,** *both* **for the candlestick, and** *also* **for the lamps thereof, according to the use of every candlestick.**

The Spirit of God also specified to David the precise amount of gold or silver for the various implements of service in the Temple. Specifically, David was informed by God of the precise plans and the amount of gold which should be used for the candlesticks (מנורה *menora*h) of gold as well as the candlesticks of silver.

15 Even the weight for the candlesticks of gold, and for their lamps of gold, by weight for every candlestick, and for the lamps thereof: and for the candlesticks of silver by weight, *both* **for the candlestick, and** *also* **for the lamps thereof, according to the use of every candlestick.** Not only were the precise specifications for the primary menorah of the Temple given, but also the other ten candlesticks (*menorahs*) which were to be placed in the Temple. See I Kings 7:49.

Understanding I Chronicles

16 And by weight *he gave* gold for the tables of shewbread, for every table; and *likewise* silver for the tables of silver. The precise amount of gold to be used for the tables of shewbread was specified by God to David as well as the silver for lesser tables of the Temple.

17 Also pure gold for the fleshhooks, and the bowls, and the cups: and for the golden basons *he gave gold* by weight for every bason; and *likewise silver* by weight for every bason of silver. God also specified to David the precise plans and amounts of gold and silver to be used in the various implements and utensils used for sacrifice at the Temple.

18 And for the altar of incense refined gold by weight; and gold for the pattern of the chariot of the cherubims, that spread out *their wings*, and covered the ark of the covenant of the LORD. Precise specifications including the amount of gold to be used in the altar of incense were revealed by God to David as well as the golden cherubims whose wings were outstretched above the ark of the covenant.

28:19 All *this, said David*, the LORD made me understand in writing by *his* hand upon me, *even* all the works of this pattern. David here made a most amazing revelation. The precise plans of the Temple were actually delivered to him in writing, having been written by God Himself—the entire "works of this pattern." Lest one should question the precedent for this, it should be remembered that the initial giving of the Law was "written with the finger of God." In ways not described, God delivered to David the written plans for the Temple with precise specifications included.

28:20-21 And David said to Solomon his son, Be strong and of good courage, and do *it*: fear not, nor be dismayed: for the LORD God, *even* my God, *will be* with thee; he will not fail thee, nor forsake thee, until thou hast finished all the

work for the service of the house of the LORD. David therefore urged Solomon to get on with the work. David urged him to be strong of spirit and encouraged of mind. Above all, he was to simply do it. Moreover, he counseled Solomon to not be frightened of the impending task or be dismayed. The reason for such courage was that "the LORD God, *even* my God, *will be* with thee; he will not fail thee, nor forsake thee, until thou hast finished all the work for the service of the house of the LORD." God would be with him and strengthen him until the massive task of the building of the Temple be complete.

And, behold, the courses of the priests and the Levites, ***even they shall be with thee*** **for all the service of the house of God: and** ***there shall be*** **with thee for all manner of workmanship every willing skilful man, for any manner of service: also the princes and all the people** *will be* **wholly at thy commandment**. David also encouraged Solomon in that the various courses of priests and Levites would be there to assist him in the accomplishing of the massive task ahead. In addition, the princes (i.e., governors) of the various tribes would also be there for assistance. In short, not only would Solomon have the help of God for the task ahead, but also the leadership of the nation.

* * * * *

Overview of I Chronicles 29: The final chapter of I Chronicles presents David's charge to the nation, his prayer of thanksgiving and request of help from God, Solomon's accession to the throne, and David's death.

29:1 Furthermore David the king said unto all the congregation, Solomon my son, whom alone God hath chosen, *is yet* **young and tender, and the work** *is* **great: for**

the palace *is* not for man, but for the LORD God. In the preceding chapter, David had addressed the leaders of the nation along with Solomon. Here, David continued his speech to them. The focus now, however, is the responsibility of the nation to their new king. David once again made clear to the leadership that God had chosen Solomon to succeed him on the throne. Notwithstanding, Solomon was a young man and tender, compared to a veteran king such as David. A great task lay ahead—the construction of the Temple. Furthermore, David reminded the leaders of the nation that "the palace *is* not for man, but for the LORD God."

29:2-5 Now I have prepared with all my might for the house of my God the gold for *things to be made* of gold, and the silver for *things* of silver, and the brass for *things* of brass, the iron for *things* of iron, and wood for *things* of wood; onyx stones, and *stones* to be set, glistering stones, and of divers colours, and all manner of precious stones, and marble stones in abundance.

Notice David's statement: "I have prepared with all might for the house of my God." There remains a powerful lesson therein for us today. In David's later years, his focus had been upon preparations for the Temple his son would build. Rather than accrue vast wealth to himself, David had placed his wealth into the treasury of God for the coming Temple. Accordingly, he had stored up gold, silver, brass, iron, special woods, and all manner of gemstones, as well as marble (i.e., alabaster) for the coming construction.

3 Moreover, because I have set my affection to the house of my God, I have of mine own proper good, of gold and silver, *which* I have given to the house of my God, over and above all that I have prepared for the holy house. Because the Temple project was dear to his heart, David had given of his own wealth for "the house of my God, over and above all that I have prepared for the holy house." Not only had he collected resources in general for the coming Temple, but he had used his own monies thereto.

4 *Even* three thousand talents of gold, of the gold of Ophir, and seven thousand talents of refined silver, to overlay the walls of the houses *withal*. David had given of his own personal funds, 3,000 talents of gold. The gold of Ophir was considered the finest in the world of that day. He also had given 7,000 talents of his own highly refined silver "to overlay the walls of the houses *withal*."

5 The gold for *things* of gold, and the silver for *things* of silver, and for all manner of work *to be made* by the hands of artificers. And who *then* is willing to consecrate his service this day unto the LORD? David had thus given of his own funds toward the construction of the Temple. He therefore challenged the assembled leadership of the nation to likewise give. "And who *then* is willing to consecrate his service this day unto the LORD?" That is, who of you is willing to likewise give for God's work as I have?

29:6-9 Then the chief of the fathers and princes of the tribes of Israel, and the captains of thousands and of hundreds, with the rulers of the king's work, offered willingly. David had led by example. He had given generously of his own personal funds for the Temple building project. Accordingly, the leaders of the nation also "offered willingly.

7 And gave for the service of the house of God of gold five thousand talents and ten thousand drams, and of silver ten thousand talents, and of brass eighteen thousand talents, and one hundred thousand talents of iron. The leaders of the nation therefore rose to the occasion and pledged 5,000 talents of gold, 10,000 talents of silver, 18,000 talents of brass, and 100,000 talents of iron.

Understanding I Chronicles

8 And they with whom *precious* stones were found gave *them* to the treasure of the house of the LORD, by the hand of Jehiel the Gershonite. Those with precious gemstones also presented them to the treasury to Jehiel the Gershonite; who, with his sons, had charge of the Temple treasury. See I Chronicles 26:21-22.

Then the people rejoiced, for that they offered willingly, because with perfect heart they offered willingly to the LORD: and David the king also rejoiced with great joy. In verse 9 is a powerful lesson of stewardship. When God's people give willingly and with a perfect (i.e., total) heart to God's work, there is rejoicing. As the representatives of the nation likewise gave as David had given, they rejoiced. There truly is joy in giving. It is more blessed to give than to receive. They had offered willingly. The word translated as **perfect** (שלם *shalem*) has the sense of 'complete' or 'total.' They had given with all their hearts. In turn, David rejoiced with them with great joy. When God's people rise and give with all their heart, there is joy. Miserliness and stinginess only bring sourness of spirit. Generosity brings joy.

29:10-12 Wherefore David blessed the LORD before all the congregation: and David said, Blessed *be* thou, LORD God of Israel our father, for ever and ever. 11 Thine, O LORD, *is* the greatness, and the power, and the glory, and the victory, and the majesty: for all *that is* in the heaven and in the earth *is thine*; thine *is* the kingdom, O LORD, and thou art exalted as head above all. 12 Both riches and honour come of thee, and thou reignest over all; and in thine hand *is* power and might; and in thine hand *it is* to make great, and to give strength unto all.

David therefore rose to bless (i.e., praise) the Lord before the assembled congregation of the leaders of the nation (28:1). As the nation as a whole gave, David therefore praised Jehovah

God. Notice the manifold praise of David to God. (1) To Him belongs greatness, power, glory, victory, and majesty. The entire universe belongs to him. See Psalm 24:1. (2) The kingdom of God (and of Israel) are His. He is exalted above all. (3) He is the source of riches and honor and He is king over all. (4) In His hand are power and might and (5) in His hand is the ability to make great and give strength to all.

29:13 Now therefore, our God, we thank thee, and praise thy glorious name. Accordingly, David thanked His heavenly Father and praised His glorious name. He gloried in his God.

29:14-15 But who *am* I, and what *is* my people, that we should be able to offer so willingly after this sort? for all things *come* of thee, and of thine own have we given thee. In the midst of his paean of praise, David paused to reflect upon the insignificance of himself and his nation. David was indeed humble and humbled before Almighty God. He was humbled that his people would rise and give so substantially and willingly to God. He freely acknowledged that "every good gift and every perfect gift is from above, and cometh down from the Father of lights, with whom is no variableness, neither shadow of turning" (James 1:17).

15 For we *are* strangers before thee, and sojourners, as *were* all our fathers: our days on the earth *are* as a shadow, and *there is* none abiding. David freely acknowledged that "they were strangers and pilgrims on the earth" (Hebrews 11:13). He realized how that life was like a shadow (i.e., fleeting). See James 4:14.

29:16 O LORD our God, all this store that we have prepared to build thee an house for thine holy name *cometh* of thine hand, and *is* all thine own. Though David and the people had given substantially for the construction of the Temple, David realized that it ultimately came from God Himself, for all is His. He therefore further praised Him.

29:17-19 I know also, my God, that thou triest the heart, and hast pleasure in uprightness. As for me, in the uprightness of mine heart I have willingly offered all these things: and now have I seen with joy thy people, which are present here, to offer willingly unto thee. David acknowledged that God indeed evaluates the human heart. See Psalm 66:10. Moreover, God is pleased with uprightness of heart. Indeed, God loves righteousness. See Psalm 5:12, 11:7, 33:5, 45:7, 146:8, and Hebrews 1:9. David therefore confessed that in the uprightness (i.e., integrity) of his heart, he had willingly given to God the funds for the Temple. He also rejoiced in seeing the joy of his own people as they in turn gave as well.

O LORD God of Abraham, Isaac, and of Israel, our fathers, keep this for ever in the imagination of the thoughts of the heart of thy people, and prepare their heart unto thee. David therefore besought God to keep this willing spirit in the hearts of his people and to continue to cause them to prepare their hearts unto Him.

And give unto Solomon my son a perfect heart, to keep thy commandments, thy testimonies, and thy statutes, and to do all *these things*, and to build the palace, *for* the which I have made provision. David therefore besought the Lord to also give Solomon a "perfect heart, to keep thy commandments, thy testimonies, and thy statutes." Again, the word translated as **perfect** (שלם *shalem*) has the sense of 'total' or 'complete.' In other words, David besought God to give Solomon a heart totally dedicated to obey His Word in every detail. Specifically, it was David's prayer to God that He would give Solomon a completely dedicated heart "to build the palace, *for* the which I have made provision." He here refers to the coming Temple as a 'palace.'

29:20-22 And David said to all the congregation, Now bless the LORD your God. And all the congregation blessed the LORD God of their fathers, and bowed down their heads, and worshipped the LORD, and the king. David therefore directed the assembled congregation of the leaders of the nation to bow and bless the Lord and worship Him. That they did.

21 And they sacrificed sacrifices unto the LORD, and offered burnt offerings unto the LORD, on the morrow after that day, *even* a thousand bullocks, a thousand rams, *and* a thousand lambs, with their drink offerings, and sacrifices in abundance for all Israel. The leaders of the nation therefore arose the next day and offered 1,000 bullocks, 1,000 rams, 1,000 lambs, along with drink offerings and numerous other sacrifices to God.

22 And did eat and drink before the LORD on that day with great gladness. And they made Solomon the son of David king the second time, and anointed *him* unto the LORD *to be* the chief governor, and Zadok *to be* priest. Thus, a great celebration was made as plans for the Temple were finalized and the people had given toward its construction. That day, they also formally and publicly re-anointed Solomon as king (the second time). David had already done so at the incident with Adonijah. See I Kings 1:39. Zadok was also anointed to be high priest.

29:23-25 Then Solomon sat on the throne of the LORD as king instead of David his father, and prospered; and all Israel obeyed him. 24 And all the princes, and the mighty men, and all the sons likewise of king David, submitted themselves unto Solomon the king. Solomon thence ascended the throne of David his father as the next king of Israel. Notice that he 'prospered.' God blessed him. And the nation followed his leadership. The various leaders and prominent men of the nation also submitted themselves to him as king.

25 And the LORD magnified Solomon exceedingly in the sight of all Israel, and bestowed upon him *such* **royal majesty as had not been on any king before him in Israel.** God thus magnified Solomon in the sight of his people and gave him royal majesty more than any king had ever had in Israel.

29:26-28 Thus David the son of Jesse reigned over all Israel. 27 And the time that he reigned over Israel *was* **forty years; seven years reigned he in Hebron, and thirty and three** *years* **reigned he in Jerusalem. 28 And he died in a good old age, full of days, riches, and honour: and Solomon his son reigned in his stead.**

The reign of David is thus summarized. He reigned for forty years: seven years over Judah in Hebron and thirty-three years over the entire nation from Jerusalem. Though the sin of Bathsheba would forever mar his legacy, nevertheless, David "died in a good old age, full of days, riches, and honour: and Solomon his son reigned in his stead."

29:29-30 Now the acts of David the king, first and last, behold, they *are* **written in the book of Samuel the seer, and in the book of Nathan the prophet, and in the book of Gad the seer, 30 With all his reign and his might, and the times that went over him, and over Israel, and over all the kingdoms of the countries**. The record of David's life and reign as king were recorded in the books of Samuel. It is thought that II Samuel was written by Nathan the prophet and also by Gad the prophet. Record of his rule and his might during those years are thus recorded in the books mentioned above—not only over Israel, but other nations brought into submission by David during his reign. Thus ends the book of I Chronicles.

THE SECOND BOOK OF THE
CHRONICLES

Introduction to II Chronicles: *The book of II Chronicles continues the history begun in I Chronicles. It differs from the history of the book of the Kings in that once the divided kingdom came to pass, the history follows only the line of the kings of Judah. The entire book is thus a succession of biographical overviews of the various kings of Judah, beginning with Solomon. The presumed author is Ezra, though there is no direct textual statement thereof. But Jewish tradition does support this view.*

The first nine chapters deal with the life and reign of Solomon. The remainder presents biographical sketches of varying length of the other kings who followed him to the time of the Babylonian captivity. An ominous sub-theme underlies throughout the book, revealing the developing apostasy not only of the kings of Judah but also of the people as well. Notable bright lights in the gathering spiritual darkness were the revivals brought forth under the leadership of Asa, Jehoshaphat, Hezekiah, and Josiah.

The events portrayed in II Chronicles cover a period of 427 years according to the dating of Bishop Ussher. All of the major prophets (Isaiah, Jeremiah, and Ezekiel) wrote during this time. Also, all of the pre-exile minor prophets wrote their prophecies during this period as well.

Overview of II Chronicles 1: II Chronicles 1 presents the initial years of Solomon's reign. There is apparent godly humility in his rule. God's blessing upon him and his realm is thus evident.

1:1 And Solomon the son of David was strengthened in his kingdom, and the LORD his God *was* with him, and magnified him exceedingly. The initial reign of Solomon is thus described. Notice how that Solomon "was strengthened in his kingdom, and the LORD his God was with him, and magnified him exceedingly." As God had promised in Psalm 112:2, "the generation of the upright shall be blessed." God will bless the children of righteous parents. There is a profound lesson there for us even today.

1:2-6 Then Solomon spake unto all Israel, to the captains of thousands and of hundreds, and to the judges, and to every governor in all Israel, the chief of the fathers. Early in the reign of Solomon, he ordered the leadership of the nation, "the captains of thousands and of hundreds, and to the judges, and to every governor in all Israel, the chief of the fathers," to assemble as a great congregation before him.

So Solomon, and all the congregation with him, went to the high place that *was* at Gibeon; for there was the tabernacle of the congregation of God, which Moses the servant of the LORD had made in the wilderness. During the reign of Saul, the Tabernacle had been placed at Gibeon which was a town in the tribal territory of Benjamin, about 7 miles (as the crow flies) north and west of Jerusalem. Solomon there ordered the congregation of the leadership of the nation to assemble.

But the ark of God had David brought up from Kirjathjearim to *the place which* David had prepared for it: for he had pitched a tent for it at Jerusalem. The sacred

Understanding II Chronicles

chronicler recounts how that the ark of the covenant had been taken from the village of Kirjathjearim (whence it was returned to by the Philistines) to Jerusalem by David. There, David had erected a special tent for it.

Moreover the brasen altar, that Bezaleel the son of Uri, the son of Hur, had made, he put before the tabernacle of the LORD: and Solomon and the congregation sought unto it. Either David or, more likely, Solomon had reestablished the brazen altar at the Tabernacle. Solomon and the assembled leadership of the nation therefore came to that altar.

And Solomon went up thither to the brasen altar before the LORD, which *was* at the tabernacle of the congregation, and offered a thousand burnt offerings upon it. Solomon there offered one-thousand burnt offerings upon the brazen altar at Gibeon. What is evident is the tremendous devotion and worship of the LORD God of his fathers. Solomon thus got his reign off on the right foot. He publicly and in royal fashion offered a massive sacrifice to God.

1:7–10 In that night did God appear unto Solomon, and said unto him, Ask what I shall give thee. After offering the 1,000 sacrifices to God, that very night, God appeared to Solomon and directed him to ask whatever he wished from Him.

8 And Solomon said unto God, Thou hast shewed great mercy unto David my father, and hast made me to reign in his stead. 9 Now, O LORD God, let thy promise unto David my father be established: for thou hast made me king over a people like the dust of the earth in multitude.

Notice the humble spirit of Solomon's prayer. Solomon acknowledged to God the great mercy which He had shown to David his father. God no doubt had shown mercy to David in general, but he certainly did when he spared David's life in the matter of Bathsheba and Uriah. Bathsheba was Solomon's mother and he no doubt was aware of how God in mercy had spared his father. He further ascribed mercy to God in allowing him to reign in his father's stead. Solomon therefore besought God to fulfill His promise to David in establishing him on the throne over Israel. He clearly implied that he needed God's help in ruling such a substantial nation.

Give me now wisdom and knowledge, that I may go out and come in before this people: for who can judge this thy people, *that is so* **great?** Rather than ask for wealth, power, or fame; Solomon asked God for wisdom to properly rule and judge God's people. His humility is evident. He knew he needed the help of God to rule justly as king. There is a profound irony in Solomon's prayer. Not only did he ask God for wisdom to properly rule his people, the request itself was the epitome of wisdom. As Solomon later wrote in Proverbs 4:5,7, wisdom indeed is the principal thing and in all our getting we should seek wisdom.

1:11-12 And God said to Solomon, Because this was in thine heart, and thou hast not asked riches, wealth, or honour, nor the life of thine enemies, neither yet hast asked long life; but hast asked wisdom and knowledge for thyself, that thou mayest judge my people, over whom I have made thee king. In replying to Solomon's request, God took note that he had not asked for "riches, wealth, or honour, nor the life of thine enemies." Neither had he asked for "long life," all selfish requests. Rather, God took note that Solomon had asked for "wisdom and knowledge for thyself, that thou mayest judge my people, over whom I have made thee king."

Therefore, God granted Solomon his request. 12 **Wisdom and knowledge** *is* **granted unto thee; and I will give thee riches, and wealth, and honour, such as none of the kings have had that** *have been* **before thee, neither shall there any after thee have the like.** God commended Solomon for such an unselfish request. The thought clearly is a fore-view of James

Understanding II Chronicles 507

1:5. Because of the selflessness of Solomon's request, God in fact promised that he would give to him "riches, and wealth, and honour, such as none of the kings have had that *have been before thee*, neither shall there any after thee have the like." Indeed, God granted Solomon wisdom and wealth such as no other king has ever had. In his early years, he surely was a type of Christ in His millennial reign. However, later in life, as Solomon began to indulge the lusts of his flesh, the wisdom which God had originally given to him evaporated and Solomon began a long slide into sin, trouble, and despair.

1:13 Then Solomon came *from his journey* to the high place that *was* at Gibeon to Jerusalem, from before the tabernacle of the congregation, and reigned over Israel. Solomon thus returned the short distance from Gibeon (about seven miles as the crow flies) to Jerusalem and began his reign over Israel.

1:14-17 And Solomon gathered chariots and horsemen: and he had a thousand and four hundred chariots, and twelve thousand horsemen, which he placed in the chariot cities, and with the king at Jerusalem. As Solomon began to accumulate wealth and even greater power, he began to build a powerful standing army. He initially had 1,400 chariots and 12,000 horsemen (i.e., cavalry men) which he stationed in special garrisons around the nation and at Jerusalem.

15 **And the king made silver and gold at Jerusalem *as plenteous* as stones, and cedar trees made he as the sycomore trees that *are* in the vale for abundance.** Solomon began to beautify Jerusalem with gold and silver ornamentation of buildings. Jerusalem became a city of massive and visible wealth. Gold and silver was multiplied to such a degree that it seemed to be as ubiquitous as the innumerable stones of Jerusalem. (Jerusalem has always been a city which proliferated in

stonework. It remains that way to this day.) Yet, Solomon caused gold and silver to be overlaid all over the city of Jerusalem, even on the facades of buildings. Moreover, cedar trees became the tree of choice and were planted all over Jerusalem. In ancient times, cedar trees were highly valued over more common and indigenous trees such as sycamore trees which grew wild throughout the land. Jerusalem thus became a city of great beauty and visible wealth.

16 And Solomon had horses brought out of Egypt, and linen yarn: the king's merchants received the linen yarn at a price. Solomon bought (and brought) horses and fine linen from Egypt. Solomon paid the going market rate for these. However, even this early in his reign, Solomon was flirting with one of the prohibitions God had made for kings of Israel in Deuteronomy 17:6, "But he shall not multiply horses to himself, nor cause the people to return to Egypt." Solomon not only began to in fact multiply to himself horse, but he went to Egypt to procure them along with other valued merchandise from Egypt.

17 And they fetched up, and brought forth out of Egypt a chariot for six hundred *shekels* of silver, and an horse for an hundred and fifty: and so brought they out *horses* for all the kings of the Hittites, and for the kings of Syria, by their means. It is not clear if Solomon's purchase of a chariot in Egypt for 600 shekels of silver was a bargain or the opposite. What is clear however is that Solomon in fact bought horses from Egypt, coming close to violating the injunction of Deuteronomy 17:6. Moreover, he also purchased horses from the Hittites and Syrians. (A branch of the Hittites, when expelled from Palestine, had settled north of Lebanon where they had land contiguous to Syria.) On the one hand, the wealth and power of Solomon were evident as he began to amass herds of horses from around the region. On the other hand, he clearly was living on the edge of ignoring God's clear commands for a

Understanding II Chronicles

king of Israel. The seeds of Solomon's downfall already were being sown.

* * * * *

Overview of II Chronicles 2: *The essence of II Chronicles 2 is the preparation of Solomon to build the Temple at Jerusalem. (It should be noted that to this point, God's appointed place had been the Tabernacle, and until now, it had never been at Jerusalem.) It should also be noted there was meticulous planning and preparation before work began upon the house of God. There is indeed a lesson for church building programs to this day.*

2:1-4 And Solomon determined to build an house for the name of the LORD, and an house for his kingdom. Solomon thus announced his intention to move forward with the building the Temple at Jerusalem. Thereafter, he also planned his own palace.

2 And Solomon told out threescore and ten thousand men to bear burdens, and fourscore thousand to hew in the mountain, and three thousand and six hundred to oversee them. Solomon therefore appointed 70,000 men as common laborers, 80,000 men as stone cutters in the mountains, and 3,600 men as foremen and supervisors. (The word translated as **told** { ספר caphar} among other things has the sense to 'count' or to 'number.' The latter seems to the thought here.)

It should be noted that these numbers probably also include provisions for his own palace which was built after the Temple. Moreover, the Temple was seven years in building, but his own palace was thirteen years in building according to I Kings 6-7. This very well may be an indication of the beginning of the spiritual decline of Solomon. It seems thereafter the focus of his reign shifted from glorifying the Lord to aggrandizing his own throne.

3 And Solomon sent to Huram the king of Tyre, saying, As thou didst deal with David my father, and didst send him cedars to build him an house to dwell therein, *even so deal with me*. David had had a good working relationship with Hiram (here called Huram), king of Tyre in Lebanon. Solomon therefore sought to continue that relationship.

4 Behold, I build an house to the name of the LORD my God, to dedicate *it* to him, *and* to burn before him sweet incense, and for the continual shewbread, and for the burnt offerings morning and evening, on the sabbaths, and on the new moons, and on the solemn feasts of the LORD our God. This *is an ordinance* for ever to Israel. Solomon therefore announced to Hiram his intent to build a major Temple to Jehovah God at Jerusalem. It would become the locus of all sacrifices to Jehovah for Israel.'

2:5-6 And the house which I build *is* great: for great *is* our God above all gods. The Temple Solomon was about to build would be great for "great *is* our God above all gods." The Temple of Herod, which may have been inferior to the one Solomon built, covered more than thirty acres. Great indeed would be the Temple.

But who is able to build him an house, seeing the heaven and heaven of heavens cannot contain him? who *am* I then, that I should build him an house, save only to burn sacrifice before him? In pondering the greatness of God Almighty, Solomon reflected, "But who is able to build him an house, seeing the heaven and heaven of heavens cannot contain him?" In considering that, Solomon again showed the humility of his early years. He wondered, "who *am* I then, that I should build him an house, save only to burn sacrifice before him?" Solomon knew that Jehovah God was omnipresent. He filled universe. There-

Understanding II Chronicles 511

fore, the Temple he would build could only be a station whence sacrifices might be offered.

2:7-10 Send me now therefore a man cunning to work in gold, and in silver, and in brass, and in iron, and in purple, and crimson, and blue, and that can skill to grave with the cunning men that *are* **with me in Judah and in Jerusalem, whom David my father did provide.** Solomon therefore first requested of Hiram that he send a master artisan who was skilled as a smith in precious metals as well as brass and iron. He wanted a man who knew how to skillfully apply dyes such as purple, crimson, and blue. He must be able to engrave with skill. Solomon already had some such craftsmen, but he sought even more 'professional' help from Hiram. The latter evidently had become the master 'contractor' for the Middle East of that day. Solomon sought the most highly qualified 'professional' in the world to supervise the work on the magnificent Temple he was about to build.

8 Send me also cedar trees, fir trees, and algum trees, out of Lebanon: for I know that thy servants can skill to cut timber in Lebanon; and, behold, my servants *shall be* **with thy servants.** Solomon also requisitioned the finest of saw lumber from Lebanon such as cedar, fir, and algum trees. Some think the latter were actually cypress trees. Lebanon was a region of deep forests and many a professional 'lumber jack' was available there. Solomon there requested assistance from these, offering to send his own people to assist in the work. It should not be thought that Solomon asked Hiram to donate these materials. Solomon no doubt paid the going rate to purchase finest materials and hire the best workmen as noted in verse 10

9 Even to prepare me timber in abundance: for the house which I am about to build *shall be* **wonderful great.** Thus, Solomon ordered the vast amounts of timbers need for the structural work of the Temple. It would be a massive project and he need "timber in abundance." Such timber would be used for (1) scaffolding and temporary framing, (2) structural members for roofs and upper floors, and (3) for finishing work.

10 And, behold, I will give to thy servants, the hewers that cut timber, twenty thousand measures of beaten wheat, and twenty thousand measures of barley, and twenty thousand baths of wine, and twenty thousand baths of oil. Solomon agreed to pay Hiram's people 20,000 measures of floor, 20,000 measures of barley (perhaps for their draft animals), 20,000 baths of wine for drinking (likely nonalcoholic), and 20,000 baths of (olive) oil for cooking.

The word translated as **measure** (כֹּר *kor*) likely refers to dry measure, approximating 6.25 bushels. Thus, 20,000 measures approximates 125,000 bushels of grain. The word translated as **bath** (בַּת *bath*) refers to a liquid measure of about ten gallons. Thus, 20,000 baths would approximate 200,000 of product.

Some have supposed a discrepancy between the figures given here and that in I Kings 5:11 which describes the same basic situation. However, there is no inconsistency between that passage and this. The yearly supplies of wine and oil, mentioned in I Kings were intended for Hiram's court in return for the cedars sent him. The quantities of grain, wine, and oil specified here were for the workmen in the field in Lebanon.

2:11-12 Then Huram the king of Tyre answered in writing, which he sent to Solomon, Because the LORD hath loved his people, he hath made thee king over them. Hiram no doubt was being both diplomatic as well as wise. Solomon had the military power to seize what he wished from Hiram. But the wisdom and integrity of Solomon are thus evident in seeking to purchase from Hiram what he needed.

Understanding II Chronicles

Huram said moreover, Blessed *be* the LORD God of Israel, that made heaven and earth, who hath given to David the king a wise son, endued with prudence and understanding, that might build an house for the LORD, and an house for his kingdom. Though Hiram as king of Tyre was a gentile and likely had pagan tendencies, nevertheless, he clearly had a respect and reverence for Jehovah God. He therefore blessed the name of Jehovah and ascribed Him as Creator of heaven and earth. He also gave deference to Solomon and praised David his father.

2:13-14 And now I have sent a cunning man, endued with understanding, of Huram my father's. 14 The son of a woman of the daughters of Dan, and his father *was* a man of Tyre, skilful to work in gold, and in silver, in brass, in iron, in stone, and in timber, in purple, in blue, and in fine linen, and in crimson; also to grave any manner of graving, and to find out every device which shall be put to him, with thy cunning men, and with the cunning men of my lord David thy father. In response to David's request for a skilled artisan to supervise the final finishing of the Temple, Hiram had good news. Implied is that master-builder/architectural superintendent he was sending was also named Hiram who actually was a Danite. He was the man for which Solomon was looking.

2:15-16 Now therefore the wheat, and the barley, the oil, and the wine, which my lord hath spoken of, let him send unto his servants:16 And we will cut wood out of Lebanon, as much as thou shalt need: and we will bring it to thee in floats by sea to Joppa; and thou shalt carry it up to Jerusalem. Though Solomon had offered to pay for the materiel and labor from Hiram, Hiram sent word to Solomon that they would cut as much wood as needed and send it free of charge. They in turn would float it in great rafts down the coast of the Mediterranean to Joppa. Solomon then would be responsible for the overland cartage thereof to Jerusalem.

2:17-18 And Solomon numbered all the strangers that *were* in the land of Israel, after the numbering wherewith David his father had numbered them; and they were found an hundred and fifty thousand and three thousand and six hundred. Solomon therefore counted all the foreign men in Israel and learned that there were 153,600 in the country. It has been suggested that these were the remnants of the Amorites, Hittites, Perizzites, and Jebusites who no longer were idolaters, but rather 'proselytes of the gates.' That is, they had submitted to Judaism, though not of the stock of Israel.

18 And he set threescore and ten thousand of them *to be* bearers of burdens, and fourscore thousand *to be* hewers in the mountain, and three thousand and six hundred overseers to set the people a work. Solomon therefore 'drafted' 70,000 of these men to be common laborers in the coming work. The other 80,000 were drafted to be **hewers**. The word so translated (חצב *chatsab*) can refer to cutting of wood, but the greater etymology thereof refers to quarrying of stone. Evidently, these latter were impressed into stone quarrying for the Temple project. The remaining 3,600 foreigners were drafted to be supervisors of this work.

* * * * *

Overview of II Chronicles 3: *Details of the beginning of the actual construction of the Temple in Jerusalem are herein presented.*

3:1-2 Then Solomon began to build the house of the LORD at Jerusalem in mount Moriah, where *the LORD*

appeared unto David his father, in the place that David had prepared in the threshingfloor of Ornan the Jebusite. After all the preparations made by both David and Solomon, the work on the Temple finally began. The site was atop Mount Moriah, located in the northeast quadrant of Jerusalem. Two other major biblical events had taken place on that site: (1) the offering of Isaac by Abraham in Genesis 22 and (2) the incident of the death angel and Ornan's threshingfloor near the end of David's reign in I Chronicles 21.

And he began to build in the second *day* of the second month, in the fourth year of his reign. In the spring of the year (probably about May) of Solomon's fourth year on the throne, work on the Temple commenced. It would continue for the next seven years.

3:3-4 Now these *are the things wherein* Solomon was instructed for the building of the house of God. The length by cubits after the first measure *was* threescore cubits, and the breadth twenty cubits. 4 And the porch that *was* in the front *of the house*, the length *of it was* according to the breadth of the house, twenty cubits, and the height *was* an hundred and twenty: and he overlaid it within with pure gold.

The basic dimensions of the Temple structure proper are here listed. A cubit approximated 1.5 feet and therefore the structure of the holy place proper was approximately ninety feet long and thirty feet wide. Noteworthy is the comment "*wherein* Solomon was instructed." As noted in I Chronicles 28:11*ff,* God had given specific plans and blueprints to David of the details of the Temple. David in turn passed these on to Solomon as noted here. In front of the structure of the holy place proper was a porch which extended thirty feet wide to the front. However, this porch was 180 feet high, towering above the rest of the structure. It was overlaid with pure gold.

3:5-9 Further architectural details are presented for the Temple. The exact plans thereof had been revealed by God to David prior to his death. (See I Chronicles 28:11-18.) It otherwise approximated the general plan and layout of the Tabernacle. Hebrews 9:23-24 indicate that the earthly Temple prescribed by God was actually patterned after the true Temple of God in heaven. **5 And the greater house he cieled with fir tree, which he overlaid with fine gold, and set thereon palm trees and chains.** The interior of the primary structure of the holy place (i.e., the greater house) was paneled with fir and then overlaid with the highly refined gold. This paneling was first carved with palm trees connected with chains. All of this was then overlaid with gold.

6 And he garnished the house with precious stones for beauty: and the gold *was* gold of Parvaim. The structure, likely its interior, had precious stones set into the architecture for added beauty and ornamentation. The source of the gold was from Parvaim, probably located in Arabia, and which was renowned for its quality of gold production.

7 He overlaid also the house, the beams, the posts, and the walls thereof, and the doors thereof, with gold; and graved cherubims on the walls. All of the interior of the main Temple structure was overlaid with gold. Moreover, there also were carved cherubims on the walls thereof. These also were overlaid with gold.

8 And he made the most holy house, the length whereof *was* according to the breadth of the house, twenty cubits, and the breadth thereof twenty cubits: and he overlaid it with fine gold, *amounting* to six hundred talents. The "most holy house" refers to the holy of holies which was a room thirty feet square in dimensions. The text here details that the overlayment of refined gold was 600 talents. In modern usage, that would approximate at least 300 million dollars just for the gold overlay.

Understanding II Chronicles

9 And the weight of the nails *was* **fifty shekels of gold. And he overlaid the upper chambers with gold.** In modern technology, a nail is a most common device. However, in ancient times such metallic fasteners were 'high tech.' The greater point is that the very hardware of the Temple was gold or at least gold plated. The upper chambers likely refers to the ceilings of the main Temple structure. Thus, the interior thereof was all of gold.

3:10-13 And in the most holy house he made two cherubims of image work, and overlaid them with gold. In the interior of the holy of holies were the massive cherubims which were overlaid with gold. These were two statues of the real angelic creatures which are before the throne of God in heaven. In as much as they were overlaid with gold, indicates the base material was something else—likely a type of wood which was carefully carved.

11 And the wings of the cherubims *were* **twenty cubits long: one wing** *of the one cherub was* **five cubits, reaching to the wall of the house: and the other wing** *was likewise* **five cubits, reaching to the wing of the other cherub. 12 And** *one* **wing of the other cherub** *was* **five cubits, reaching to the wall of the house: and the other wing** *was* **five cubits** *also***, joining to the wing of the other cherub.** Each cherubim(s) (the *im* is the suffix for plural in Hebrew) had two wings outstretched. The outer wing of each stretched out 7.5 feet to the exterior wall while the inner wings each stretched out toward each other for a total of 15 feet. Thus, the wingspan of each cherub was 15 feet. The inner wings of the two cherubim(s) thus touched each other, arching over the place where the ark of the covenant would sit and where the Shekinah glory of God would reside.

The wings of these cherubims spread themselves forth twenty cubits: and they stood on their feet, and their faces

***were* inward**. The golden cherubim(s) thus stood facing each other with their massive wings outstretched over the place where the mercy seat and the Shekinah of God would rest. Their beauty undoubtedly was exceeded only by their holy sternness.

3:14 And he made the vail *of* blue, and purple, and crimson, and fine linen, and wrought cherubims thereon. Solomon himself did not actually perform the construction and fabrication of the Temple. However, it was at his command and direction that the Temple was built. Accordingly, he ordered a special veil of blue, purple, and of crimson, made of the finest of linen. On this were woven images of cherubim(s). This, of course, was the veil which separated between the holy place and the holy of holies. It no doubt was massive in its weight as well as exquisite in its beauty.

3:15-17 Also he made before the house two pillars of thirty and five cubits high, and the chapiter that *was* on the top of each of them *was* five cubits. In front of the Temple structure proper and as part of the porch, Solomon erected two massive brass pillars. They are here described as being a total of forty cubits tall (sixty feet). Some have presumed a contradiction between details here and in I Kings 7:15. See comments thereto for resolution of presumed conflict. There actually is none at all. The mention of *chapiters* refers to the 'capitals' atop the pillars.

16 And he made chains, *as* in the oracle, and put *them* on the heads of the pillars; and made an hundred pomegranates, and put *them* on the chains. There were golden chains across the veil. See I Kings 6:21-22. However, here mention is also made of ornamental chains being stretched between the top of the pillars on the exterior of the Temple. Hung from this ornamental chain were one-hundred carved pomegranates. The material of the pillars according to I Kings

7 was brass. It may be assumed that the chain and pomegranates were brass as well.

17 And he reared up the pillars before the temple, one on the right hand, and the other on the left; and called the name of that on the right hand Jachin, and the name of that on the left Boaz. Solomon therefore named the two massive pillars at the front of the main Temple structure. The one on the right he named *Jachin* which means 'established' or 'he shall establish (it).' The pillar on the left was named *Boaz* which means 'strength' or 'in it is strength.' Thus, the Temple was established in its strength by God.

* * * * *

Overview of II Chronicles 4: *Chapter 4 presents the record of the construction and further architectural details of the Temple. It should be noted that the Temple which Ezra re-built five-hundred years later was much more modest than the Solomonic temple. The various accessory items associated with the Temple are described in this chapter including the brazen altar, the molten sea, the lavers, the candlesticks and all the miscellaneous utensils necessary for the proper operation of the Temple.*

4:1-5 Moreover he made an altar of brass, twenty cubits the length thereof, and twenty cubits the breadth thereof, and ten cubits the height thereof. 2 Also he made a molten sea of ten cubits from brim to brim, round in compass, and five cubits the height thereof; and a line of thirty cubits did compass it round about.

3 And under it *was* the similitude of oxen, which did compass it round about: ten in a cubit, compassing the sea round about. Two rows of oxen *were* cast, when it was cast.

4 It stood upon twelve oxen, three looking toward the north, and three looking toward the west, and three looking toward the south, and three looking toward the east: and the sea *was set* **above upon them, and all their hinder parts** *were* **inward. 5 And the thickness of it** *was* **an handbreadth, and the brim of it like the work of the brim of a cup, with flowers of lilies;** *and* **it received and held three thousand baths.**

The brazen altar is here described. Notice its size in verse one: twenty cubits square and ten cubits high. (That is 30 feet square and 15 feet high.) The **molten sea** literally means the "cast basin." It was cast of brass. We are told that it was 10 cubits (15 feet) in diameter and held 3,000 baths or about 30,000 gallons of water. This evidently provided the necessary water supply for the various cleansings and washing of the Temple ser-vice. It rested upon twelve brass oxen which formed its base. The 'sea' (i.e., laver) was mounted atop twelve brass oxen. See comments for I Kings 7:23 for further details.

4:6-8 Other pieces of utilitarian furniture are described. Some were placed in the courtyard of the priests where they did the actual work of preparing sacrifices to be offered upon the brazen altar. **6 He made also ten lavers, and put five on the right hand, and five on the left, to wash in them: such things as they offered for the burnt offering they washed in them; but the sea** *was* **for the priests to wash in.** The various animals for sacrifice were washed in the ten lavers in the courtyard of the priests. Presumably, the water for these lavers was drawn from the molten sea. See comments for I Kings 7:38 for further details.

7 And he made ten candlesticks of gold according to their form, and set *them* **in the temple, five on the right hand, and five on the left.** Ten candlesticks (i.e., menorahs) were made of gold and placed in the holy place with five lining the right wall and five lining the left wall. These gave light in the interior of the holy place.

8 He made also ten tables, and placed *them* in the temple, five on the right side, and five on the left. And he made an hundred basons of gold. The ten tables likely refer to tables for the preparation of sacrifices. Five were on the north side of the altar and five on the south side thereof. For use at these tables were one-hundred basins made of gold. The material of the tables is not noted, but presumed to be of either brass or gold. Brass is more likely.

4:9-10 Furthermore he made the court of the priests, and the great court, and doors for the court, and overlaid the doors of them with brass. 10 And he set the sea on the right side of the east end, over against the south. The exterior doors for the courtyard of the priests were made of brass. The large sea (laver) was placed off center to the right when facing the front (east) of the Temple. It was toward the front of the courtyard of the priests when facing the east.

4:11-17 And Huram made the pots, and the shovels, and the basons. And Huram finished the work that he was to make for king Solomon for the house of God. The master craftsmen Hiram, sent from Tyre, crafted the various utensils of the Temple. They were made either of gold or brass. He finished every portion of the designs given to Him from Solomon which ultimately came from God.

12 *To wit*, the two pillars, and the pommels, and the chapiters *which were* on the top of the two pillars, and the two wreaths to cover the two pommels of the chapiters which *were* on the top of the pillars; 13 And four hundred pomegranates on the two wreaths; two rows of pomegranates on each wreath, to cover the two pommels of the chapiters which *were* upon the pillars. Hiram supervised every detail, especially of the craft work of the Temple, including the brass pillars and all the associated intricate carving of them. Pommels were the bowl shaped portion of the capitals of the pillars of the Temple. These all were carved with ornamental pomegranates and wreaths. See comments for I Kings 7:16*ff* for greater details.

14 He made also bases, and lavers made he upon the bases; 15 One sea, and twelve oxen under it. Hiram supervised the fabrication of the bases for the pillars, the lavers and their bases, the molten sea with the twelve brass oxen under it.

16 The pots also, and the shovels, and the fleshhooks, and all their instruments, did Huram his father make to king Solomon for the house of the LORD of bright brass. All utensils of the Temple not made of gold were otherwise made of highly polished brass (i.e., shiny brass) for the Temple.

17 In the plain of Jordan did the king cast them, in the clay ground between Succoth and Zeredathah. The smelting for all the precious metals for the Temple was done in the plains of the Jordan River valley. Succoth was on the east side thereof. The location of Zeredathah is unknown. Thus, none of the dirty, smelly work of smelting was done on site of the Temple, but far away. All these items, especially the molten sea had to be transported up through the mountains to Jerusalem. The engineering and logistics thereof must have been marvels of that day.

4:18-22 Thus Solomon made all these vessels in great abundance: for the weight of the brass could not be found out. The items mentioned above were made of solid brass. The amount thereof was so great that no attempt was made to determine the quantity thereof.

19 And Solomon made all the vessels that *were for* **the house of God, the golden altar also, and the tables whereon the shewbread** *was set*; **20 Moreover the candlesticks with their lamps, that they should burn after the manner before**

the oracle, of pure gold; 21 **And the flowers, and the lamps, and the tongs,** *made he of* **gold,** *and* **that perfect gold.** 22 **And the snuffers, and the basons, and the spoons, and the censers,** *of* **pure gold: and the entry of the house, the inner doors thereof for the most holy** *place***, and the doors of the house of the temple,** *were of* **gold.**

Solomon specified that the sacred vessels of the Temple be all made of solid gold including the altar of incense, the candlesticks with their ornamentation, the tongs for the altar of incense as well. The attendant hardware for the candlesticks, the snuffers, were gold. The working utensils: basins, spoons, and censers were all of gold. Even the interior doors of the holy of holies were of gold. These evidently were behind the veil and allowed access to the most holy place.

In conclusion, the magnificence and wealth of the Temple was astounding. It was built of the materials which do not easily corrode or decay. It was a testimony to the greatness of the God whose earthly presence would thereafter dwell.

* * * * *

Overview of II Chronicles 5*: The life and reign of Solomon continue. In chapter 5, the completion, furnishing, and Divine entry of the Temple are recorded.*

5:1 Thus all the work that Solomon made for the house of the LORD was finished: and Solomon brought in *all* the things that David his father had dedicated; and the silver, and the gold, and all the instruments, put he among the treasures of the house of God. Solomon thus completed the Temple. (I Kings 6:38 and 7:1 make a salient point relative to the completion of the Temple. There it is noted that Solomon spent seven years completing the Temple, but thirteen years completing his own house. There is a foreshadow of the priorities in his life which would later be his downfall.) Solomon therefore carefully placed all the appropriate furniture and utensil of the Temple in their proper places. Extra vessels (i.e., instruments) of gold and silver were stored in the treasury of the Temple.

5:2-3 Then Solomon assembled the elders of Israel, and all the heads of the tribes, the chief of the fathers of the children of Israel, unto Jerusalem, to bring up the ark of the covenant of the LORD out of the city of David, which *is* Zion. 3 Wherefore all the men of Israel assembled themselves unto the king in the feast which *was* in the seventh month. Upon the completion and furnishing of the Temple, Solomon summoned the entire leadership of the nation to Jerusalem, including the heads of the tribes and all elders of the nation. They would thus formally deliver the ark of the covenant from the special tent David had erected for it upon Mount Zion, not far from Mount Moriah. The seventh month of the year is autumn and would approximate October whence were the feasts of Atonement and Tabernacles.

5:4-9 And all the elders of Israel came; and the Levites took up the ark. 5 And they brought up the ark, and the tabernacle of the congregation, and all the holy vessels that *were* in the tabernacle, these did the priests *and* the Levites bring up. The leaders of the nation with the specific services of the Levites therefore brought the ark from Mount Zion across and over to the newly finished Temple. The tabernacle of the congregation likely refers to the special tent David had made for the ark and not the full formal Tabernacle which presumably was still at Gibeon. However, it may be that the Tabernacle had actually been moved to Jerusalem in the meantime, though there is no record thereof. Rather, the thought likely is that the holy vessels were moved *and* the old Tabernacle was finally taken down and moved to Jerusalem. There, all the working utensils thereof were transferred to the Temple, or at least to its treasury-storerooms.

6 Also king Solomon, and all the congregation of Israel that were assembled unto him before the ark, sacrificed sheep and oxen, which could not be told nor numbered for multitude. 7 And the priests brought in the ark of the covenant of the LORD unto his place, to the oracle of the house, into the most holy *place, even* **under the wings of the cherubims.** What a majestic procession it must have been! King Solomon along with the dignitaries of the nation with the priests of God and the Levites, all in procession, thus marched across town with the ark of the covenant upon the shoulders of the Levites. Before actually placing the ark in its final resting place in the new holy of holies, Solomon and the leaders of the nation offered innumerable sacrifices of sheep and oxen to God. Then, the priests moved the ark into the holy of holies in the Temple—the oracle thereof, under the golden wings of the cherubim(s).

8 For the cherubims spread forth *their* **wings over the place of the ark, and the cherubims covered the ark and the staves thereof above. 9 And they drew out the staves** *of the ark,* **that the ends of the staves were seen from the ark before the oracle; but they were not seen without. And there it is unto this day**. The cherubim(s) of the holy of holies were made of carved wood and overlaid with gold and thus were inanimate. However, what is clearly implied is that when the ark of the covenant was situated in its proper place in the holy of holies that the golden cherubim(s) actually moved their wings and stretched them forth over the ark and its attendant carrying staves. The priests therefore carefully removed the staves out of the holy of holies (i.e., the oracle) and left them therein, but not visible beyond the veil. There the ark sat in perpetuity.

5:10 *There was* **nothing in the ark save the two tables which Moses put** *therein* **at Horeb, when the** LORD **made** *a covenant* **with the children of Israel, when they came out of Egypt.** All that was *in* the ark were the tables of stone which contained the Ten Commandments. Hebrews 9:4 indicates that at some other time other sacred items (Aaron's rod that budded, a golden pot manna, and a golden censer) were also located in the holy of holies, but not in the ark. When or where these items disappeared is not recorded in Scripture.

5:11-12 And it came to pass, when the priests were come out of the holy *place***: (for all the priests** *that were* **present were sanctified,** *and* **did not** *then* **wait by course: 12 Also the Levites** *which were* **the singers, all of them of Asaph, of Heman, of Jeduthun, with their sons and their brethren,** *being* **arrayed in white linen, having cymbals and psalteries and harps, stood at the east end of the altar, and with them an hundred and twenty priests sounding with trumpets:).**

What a spectacular sight it must have been. On that day, *all* the priests of God were present at the Temple and not just the course (i.e., shift) which might otherwise have been scheduled. Moreover, most, maybe all Levites also were present—no doubt all in their dress 'uniforms.'

Furthermore, the Temple choirs under the direction of Asaph, Heman, and Jeduthun, with their sons and their brethren, along with the Temple orchestra were present—all arrayed in their finest dress white 'uniforms.' They sang to God as the orchestra accompanied them. These all stood at the east end of the brazen altar—that is by the front gate. The word translated as **trumpets** (הצצרהים *chatsotserahim*) refers to (silver) trumpets and not the common shofar (i.e., rams horn). Thus, a fanfare by 120 priests likely sounded as the ark was placed in the Temple. The sights and sounds must have been awesome—almost heavenly.

Understanding II Chronicles

5:13-14 It came even to pass, as the trumpeters and singers *were* as one, to make one sound to be heard in praising and thanking the LORD; and when they lifted up *their* voice with the trumpets and cymbals and instruments of musick, and praised the LORD, *saying,* **For** *he is* **good; for his mercy** *endureth* **for ever: that** *then* **the house was filled with a cloud,** *even* **the house of the LORD.**

The Levitical choirs, accompanied by the Temple orchestra and trumpet fanfare all reached a great crescendo of praise and thanksgiving to God, praising him that He is good and that His mercy endureth forever. At that moment, "the house was filled with a cloud, *even* the house of the LORD." The Shekinah glory thus descended and filled the house. (It should be noted that the term *Shekinah glory* does not appear in the Bible. However, it is the traditional Jewish term used to de-scribe the glory of the presence of God at the Tabernacle and Temple of God.) The 'holy smoke' here evidently was a precursor to the full arrival of the glory of God recorded in 7:2.

14 So that the priests could not stand to minister by reason of the cloud: for the glory of the LORD had filled the house of God. The intensity of the cloud of God's presence (i.e., the Shekinah glory) was so overpowering that the priests could not remain in the Temple. Furthermore, the "the glory of the LORD had filled the house of God." Thus, the earthly presence of God Almighty assumed residence in the Temple at Jerusalem. The Temple was now officially ready for worship.

* * * * *

Overview of II Chronicles 6: *This next chapter describes Solomon's sermon in verses 1-11 and his prayer of dedication of the new Temple at Jerusalem verses 12-42.*

6:1-3 Then said Solomon, The LORD hath said that he would dwell in the thick darkness. 2 But I have built an house of habitation for thee, and a place for thy dwelling for ever. 3 And the king turned his face, and blessed the whole congregation of Israel: and all the congregation of Israel stood.

Solomon's sermon of dedication, perhaps in abbreviated form here, was before the entire nation of Israel which had congregated at Jerusalem for this momentous event. Solomon acknowledged the omnipresence of God (i.e., Him dwelling in thick darkness). Nevertheless, he had built an "house of habitation" for Himself. In reality, the Temple was a place for formal worship of God on earth. The full congregation of Israel then stood in respect to the God of the Temple as Solomon began the service of dedication.

6:4-6 And he said, Blessed *be* the LORD God of Israel, who hath with his hands fulfilled *that* which he spake with his mouth to my father David, saying. Notice how that Solomon blessed the Lord for the work which He had wrought through him. God specifically had kept His Word which He had promised to David regarding the completion of the Temple and the fulfillment of the Davidic Covenant.

5 Since the day that I brought forth my people out of the land of Egypt I chose no city among all the tribes of Israel to build an house in, that my name might be there; neither chose I any man to be a ruler over my people Israel: 6 But I have chosen Jerusalem, that my name might be there; and have chosen David to be over my people Israel. Solomon therefore acknowledged that God had not chosen any other city for His official dwelling other than Jerusalem. Moreover, God had chosen David as His chosen king. Implicit therefore is Solomon's thanks to God.

6:7-9 Now it was in the heart of David my father to build an house for the name of the LORD God of Israel. Solomon also acknowledged how that David had desired to build a formal Temple for God.

8 But the LORD said to David my father, Forasmuch as it was in thine heart to build an house for my name, thou didst well in that it was in thine heart: 9 Notwithstanding thou shalt not build the house; but thy son which shall come forth out of thy loins, he shall build the house for my name. The king continued to remind all present how that God would not allow David to build the Temple, but God had promised that David's son would be allowed to do so.

6:10-11 The LORD therefore hath performed his word that he hath spoken: for I am risen up in the room of David my father, and am set on the throne of Israel, as the LORD promised, and have built the house for the name of the LORD God of Israel. Solomon made clear that the completion of the Temple was a direct fulfillment of God's promise to David. For he, as David's son, not only had succeeded his father, but he had in fact now completed the Temple. Notice in verse 10 where Solomon noted that God "hath performed his word that he hath spoken." God always keeps His word.

11 And in it have I put the ark, wherein *is* the covenant of the LORD, that he made with the children of Israel. Moreover, Solomon had just officially placed the ark of the covenant of God in the holy of holies—the covenant which God had made with Israel long ago. Thus, the introductory comments for Solomon's prayer of dedication were made.

6:12-13 And he stood before the altar of the LORD in the presence of all the congregation of Israel, and spread forth his hands. Solomon therefore stood before the brazen altar of the Temple with outstretched hands before the assembled leadership of the nation.

13 For Solomon had made a brasen scaffold, of five cubits long, and five cubits broad, and three cubits high, and had set it in the midst of the court: and upon it he stood, and kneeled down upon his knees before all the congregation of Israel, and spread forth his hands toward heaven. Solomon had a brass platform built which was 4.5 feet high. From thence he first stood and then kneeled down before the entire congregation and "spread forth his hands toward heaven."

6:14-15 And said, O LORD God of Israel, *there is* no God like thee in the heaven, nor in the earth; which keepest covenant, and *shewest* mercy unto thy servants, that walk before thee with all their hearts. Solomon thus began his official prayer of dedication of the Temple by praising Jehovah God. There surely is none like Him, anywhere in the universe. He keeps His word and is merciful, especially to those who walk before Him "with all their hearts." That principle is as true today as it was then.

15 Thou which hast kept with thy servant David my father that which thou hast promised him; and spakest with thy mouth, and hast fulfilled *it* with thine hand, as *it is* this day. Solomon thus publicly praised God for fulfilling His Word. God had promised to David that his son would be allowed to build the Temple. That is exactly what had happened. God always keeps His Word!

6:16-17 Now therefore, O LORD God of Israel, keep with thy servant David my father that which thou hast promised him, saying, There shall not fail thee a man in my sight to sit upon the throne of Israel; yet so that thy children take heed to their way to walk in my law, as thou hast

walked before me. Solomon therefore besought God to fulfill the Davidic Covenant which He had promised to David that "there shall not fail thee a man in my sight to sit upon the throne of Israel." The one condition for the fulfillment of the Davidic Covenant was obedience. However, the party to be obedient was the king. Solomon here warned Israel to be obedient to God's Law.

17 **Now then, O LORD God of Israel, let thy word be verified, which thou hast spoken unto thy servant David.** Solomon therefore implored God to altogether fulfill the Davidic Covenant to his descendants.

6:18-21 But will God in very deed dwell with men on the earth? behold, heaven and the heaven of heavens cannot contain thee; how much less this house which I have built! Solomon again acknowledged the omnipresence and universality of God. He thus asked if God could dwell on the earth. The question was rhetorical and Solomon knew the an-swer thereof. If the universe could not contain the Almighty God, how could the meager Temple do so which Solomon had built.

19 **Have respect therefore to the prayer of thy servant, and to his supplication, O LORD my God, to hearken unto the cry and the prayer which thy servant prayeth before thee.** Solomon therefore besought the Lord pay heed to his prayer and hear that which he was about to pray. Notice again how that the powerful king Solomon referred to himself as God's servant. Not only was there genuine humility on his part, he fully realized how insignificant he was before God. See Psalm 8:3-9.

20 **That thine eyes may be open upon this house day and night, upon the place whereof thou hast said that thou wouldest put thy name there; to hearken unto the prayer which thy servant prayeth toward this place.** Solomon

therefore urged that God would pay heed day and night to prayer from the Temple or of prayer made toward it.

21 **Hearken therefore unto the supplications of thy servant, and of thy people Israel, which they shall make toward this place: hear thou from thy dwelling place,** *even* **from heaven; and when thou hearest, forgive.** Solomon thus concluded the introduction to his formal prayer of dedication by asking God to hear his prayer and those of his people as they would pray either at or toward the Temple. Inasmuch as the earthly presence of God dwelt therein, Israel could therefore pray toward the Temple from wherever they might be. However, Solomon acknowledged the true dwelling place of God was in heaven. But as God's people would pray toward the Temple, he invoked God to hear from above and forgive them.

6:22-23 Solomon thus begins a lengthy series of *if/then* requests to God, pertaining to situations in which Israel might pray toward the Temple. **If a man sin against his neighbour, and an oath be laid upon him to make him swear, and the oath come before thine altar in this house; 23 Then hear thou from heaven, and do, and judge thy servants, by requiting the wicked, by recompensing his way upon his own head; and by justifying the righteous, by giving him according to his righteousness.** If a man sinned against his neighbor and the cause was brought before the altar for adjudication (by Levites), Solomon therefore besought that then God would direct righteous judgment to be rendered.

6:24-25 And if thy people Israel be put to the worse before the enemy, because they have sinned against thee; and shall return and confess thy name, and pray and make supplication before thee in this house; 25 Then hear thou from the heavens, and forgive the sin of thy people Israel, and bring them again unto the land which thou gavest to

them and to their fathers. If Israel lost a war because of their own sin, and if they confessed their sin before God; then Solomon besought God to hear their prayer, forgive their sin, and restore them to their land. That certainly happened over the years as Israel would be chastened by God in battle, only to eventually repent and seek God's face.

6:26-27 When the heaven is shut up, and there is no rain, because they have sinned against thee; *yet* if they pray toward this place, and confess thy name, and turn from their sin, when thou dost afflict them; 27 Then hear thou from heaven, and forgive the sin of thy servants, and of thy people Israel, when thou hast taught them the good way, wherein they should walk; and send rain upon thy land, which thou hast given unto thy people for an inheritance. When God chastened the land by stopping the rain because of their sin; and they prayed to God at the Temple, confessing their sin; Solomon therefore besought God to "hear thou from heaven." Then, he besought the Lord to forgive them, instruct them in the way they should go, and send rain once again.

6:28-31 If there be dearth in the land, if there be pestilence, if there be blasting, or mildew, locusts, or caterpillers; if their enemies besiege them in the cities of their land; whatsoever sore or whatsoever sickness *there be*: 29 *Then* what prayer *or* what supplication soever shall be made of any man, or of all thy people Israel, when every one shall know his own sore and his own grief, and shall spread forth his hands in this house. If God sent plagues against Israel because of their sin; Solomon then besought God to hear their prayer when they repented.

30 Then hear thou from heaven thy dwelling place, and forgive, and render unto every man according unto all his ways, whose heart thou knowest; (for thou only knowest the

hearts of the children of men:) 31 **That they may fear thee, to walk in thy ways, so long as they live in the land which thou gavest unto our fathers**. Moreover, as Israel prayed for forgiveness, Solomon also implored God to forgive, for He knew their hearts. Solomon then paused to noted that God "only knowest the hearts of the children of men." The devil does not know what is in our hearts. Only God does. Solomon also besought God to hear and forgive the prayer of his people "that they may fear thee, to walk in thy ways, so long as they live in the land which thou gavest unto our fathers."

6:32-33 Moreover concerning the stranger, which is not of thy people Israel, but is come from a far country for thy great name's sake, and thy mighty hand, and thy stretched out arm; if they come and pray in this house; 33 Then hear thou from the heavens, *even* from thy dwelling place, and do according to all that the stranger calleth to thee for; that all people of the earth may know thy name, and fear thee, as *doth* thy people Israel, and may know that this house which I have built is called by thy name. Solomon further prayed for gentiles who would come to the Temple from afar to pray that God would hear their prayer that all nations would come to fear the Lord even as Israel. It was Solomon's desire that the whole world would know that the Temple was for the name of Jehovah.

6:34-35 If thy people go out to war against their enemies by the way that thou shalt send them, and they pray unto thee toward this city which thou hast chosen, and the house which I have built for thy name; 35 Then hear thou from the heavens their prayer and their supplication, and maintain their cause. When Israel went out to war against enemies and if they prayed to God at the Temple for help, Solomon therefore implored God to hear from heaven and help them and maintain their cause in the battle.

Understanding II Chronicles 535

6:36-39 If they sin against thee, (for *there is* no man which sinneth not,) and thou be angry with them, and deliver them over before *their* enemies, and they carry them away captives unto a land far off or near; 37 Yet *if* they bethink themselves in the land whither they are carried captive, and turn and pray unto thee in the land of their captivity, saying, We have sinned, we have done amiss, and have dealt wickedly. If Israel so sinned (as all men do) to the degree that God dispersed them out their land and if they in their captivity prayed to God, confessing their sin and in repentance, then Solomon urged,

If they return to thee with all their heart and with all their soul in the land of their captivity, whither they have carried them captives, and pray toward their land, which thou gavest unto their fathers, and *toward* the city which thou hast chosen, and toward the house which I have built for thy name: 39 Then hear thou from the heavens, *even* from thy dwelling place, their prayer and their supplications, and maintain their cause, and forgive thy people which have sinned against thee. If in their captivity, if Israel would repent, confess their sin, and pray to God in His Temple for help; then Solomon besought God to hear their prayer, help them, and forgive their sin. Daniel certainly did so. See Daniel 6:10.

6:40-42 Now, my God, let, I beseech thee, thine eyes be open, and *let* thine ears *be* attent unto the prayer *that is made* in this place. 41 Now therefore arise, O LORD God, into thy resting place, thou, and the ark of thy strength: let thy priests, O LORD God, be clothed with salvation, and let thy saints rejoice in goodness. 42 O LORD God, turn not away the face of thine anointed: remember the mercies of David thy servant. Solomon therefore concluded his dedicatory prayer by beseeching God to take heed to these proceedings and his prayer. He besought God to arise and place His earthly presence upon the ark of the covenant in the holy of holies. He ended his prayer by asking that the priests of God be clothed with God's salvation and God's people rejoice in God's goodness. The benediction to the prayer was for God to not turn away from His anointed (i.e., the King) and to remember the mercies which God had shown and promised to David.

* * * * *

Overview of II Chronicles 7: *This next chapter reveals Jehovah God's acceptance of the Temple which Solomon had built and his prayer of dedication. God not only manifested forth Himself in fiery glory, He appeared directly to Solomon by night and gave further specific instruction to him.*

7:1-3 Now when Solomon had made an end of praying, the fire came down from heaven, and consumed the burnt offering and the sacrifices; and the glory of the LORD filled the house. Notice how that the fire of God fell after Solomon had prayed. Though this undoubtedly was a unique event in the course of spiritual history, nevertheless, there is illustration here. When God's people pray and humble themselves before Him, the power and presence of God often falls in a perceptible way. Again, we read that the "glory of the LORD filled the house." The sacrifices upon the brazen altar were thus consumed. The precursor thereof had taken place in 5:13-14 as 'holy smoke' had filled the Temple upon the delivery of the ark to the holy of holies.

2 And the priests could not enter into the house of the LORD, because the glory of the LORD had filled the LORD'S house. The full presence of the Shekinah glory thence filled the Temple. See comments thereto in 5:13-14. Even the priests

Understanding II Chronicles 537

could not enter the holy place as the Shekinah glory of God descended.

3 And when all the children of Israel saw how the fire came down, and the glory of the LORD upon the house, they bowed themselves with their faces to the ground upon the pavement, and worshipped, and praised the LORD, *saying*, For *he is* good; for his mercy *endureth* for ever. As the assembled nation of Israel saw the glory of God fall as fire, they bowed and worshiped God, crying out, "For *he is* good; for his mercy *endureth* for ever."

7:4-7 Then the king and all the people offered sacrifices before the LORD. 5 And king Solomon offered a sacrifice of twenty and two thousand oxen, and an hundred and twenty thousand sheep: so the king and all the people dedicated the house of God. Notice also the magnitude of sacrifices which Solomon offered upon the brazen altar in dedicating it. 22,000 thousand oxen and 120,000 sheep were offered as sacrifices to God. And yet none of those sacrifices could wash away one sin. Only the shed blood of the coming Lamb of God could so cleanse the human race of its sin.

6 And the priests waited on their offices: the Levites also with instruments of musick of the LORD, which David the king had made to praise the LORD, because his mercy *endureth* for ever, when David praised by their ministry; and the priests sounded trumpets before them, and all Israel stood. The Temple now swung into full operation. The priests began to offer regular sacrifices for the people. The Levites began to praise God with their orchestras and choirs. The Temple was now fully operational. The Levites thus praised God and the priests heralded worship by trumpet.

7 Moreover Solomon hallowed the middle of the court that *was* before the house of the LORD: for there he offered burnt offerings, and the fat of the peace offerings, because

the brasen altar which Solomon had made was not able to receive the burnt offerings, and the meat offerings, and the fat. Solomon made a special dispensation and sanctified the middle court or outer courtyard of the Temple for sacrifice. So many sacrifices were being offered that more space was needed.

7:8-11 Also at the same time Solomon kept the feast seven days, and all Israel with him, a very great congregation, from the entering in of Hamath unto the river of Egypt. The time of the dedication of the Temple was at the time of the Feast of Tabernacles which lasted for eight days. In fact, the entire nation so observed the feast from one end to another.

9 And in the eighth day they made a solemn assembly: for they kept the dedication of the altar seven days, and the feast seven days. On the eighth and final day of the feast, Solomon convened a special assembly at the Temple for the final sacrifices of the Feast of Tabernacles.

10 And on the three and twentieth day of the seventh month he sent the people away into their tents, glad and merry in heart for the goodness that the LORD had shewed unto David, and to Solomon, and to Israel his people. Thus, on the 23rd day of the seventh month of the year—after the Feast of Tabernacles was complete—Solomon sent the nation home. There thus was rejoicing throughout the land for the goodness God had shown to the king and the people.

11 Thus Solomon finished the house of the LORD, and the king's house: and all that came into Solomon's heart to make in the house of the LORD, and in his own house, he prosperously effected. The Temple construction project and its inauguration into service was thus complete. Moreover, God had helped and prospered the task.

7:12-14 And the LORD appeared to Solomon by night, and said unto him, I have heard thy prayer, and have

chosen this place to myself for an house of sacrifice. As an epilogue to all that had taken place, God appeared to Solomon during the night shortly thereafter. He told Solomon that He had heard his prayer and had chosen the Temple as the place for formal worship.

Yet, **if I shut up heaven that there be no rain, or if I command the locusts to devour the land, or if I send pestilence among my people**. Notwithstanding the festivities of recent days with the inauguration of the Temple, if God chose to chasten Israel by withholding rain or sending plagues against the land, He promised,

14 **If my people, which are called by my name, shall humble themselves, and pray, and seek my face, and turn from their wicked ways; then will I hear from heaven, and will forgive their sin, and will heal their land**. The great outline for godly blessing is here pronounced. The focus is of God's people, specifically Israel. Four elements are noted. *If* God's people would (1) humble themselves, (2) pray, (3) seek God's face, (4) turn from their sin; *then* God promised to (a) hear their prayer, (b) forgive their sin, (c) and heal their land. The latter refers to sending rain and restraining plagues. The promise was made specifically to Israel. However, the principles surely apply by extension to any people or church of this age.

7:15-16 Now mine eyes shall be open, and mine ears attent unto the prayer *that is made* **in this place.** 16 **For now have I chosen and sanctified this house, that my name may be there for ever: and mine eyes and mine heart shall be there perpetually**. God therefore promised to Solomon that He thus would take heed to the prayers coming from the Temple. God had chosen that place and set the Temple apart as a testimony to His name forever. He therefore promised that His heart would be there in perpetuity.

7:17-20 **And as for thee, if thou wilt walk before me, as David thy father walked, and do according to all that I have commanded thee, and shalt observe my statutes and my judgments; 18 Then will I stablish the throne of thy kingdom, according as I have covenanted with David thy father, saying, There shall not fail thee a man** *to be* **ruler in Israel.** God therefore promised Solomon that if he would walk before Him as David had walked, in complete obedience and dedication that then God would establish his throne and his dynasty after him. God could not be more clear in that promise.

19 But if ye turn away, and forsake my statutes and my commandments, which I have set before you, and shall go and serve other gods, and worship them; 20 Then will I pluck them up by the roots out of my land which I have given them; and this house, which I have sanctified for my name, will I cast out of my sight, and will make it *to be* **a proverb and a byword among all nations.**

However, if Solomon turned away from God's commandments, particularly in pursuing idolatry; God vowed that He would remove the Davidic dynasty from their land and the Temple would be destroyed. Israel and the Temple would become a taunt and a scoffing to all nations. Tragically, that is precisely what happened. Later kings of Israel, beginning with Solomon dabbled with idolatry and eventually God removed the nation and destroyed their Temple. The rest of II Chronicles will detail that sad story.

7:21-22 And this house, which is high, shall be an astonishment to every one that passeth by it; so that he shall say, Why hath the LORD done thus unto this land, and unto this house? 22 And it shall be answered, Because they forsook the LORD God of their fathers, which brought them forth out of the land of Egypt, and laid hold on other gods, and worshipped them, and served them: therefore hath he

brought all this evil upon them. When Israel departed from their God, God would utterly destroy their magnificent Temple. That happened by not only the Babylonians but also by the Romans. When Israel turned their back on their God, they would suffered His holy wrath. They had entered into a covenant with Him, not unlike a marriage vow. When they violated that covenant, God justly turned His righteous anger against them.

* * * * *

Introduction to II Chronicles 8: *The next two chapters of II Chronicles present an overview of the life and reign of Solomon. I Kings gives additional details. Several general comments may be made concerning his life and reign.*

(1) During the first part of his reign, he walked with God and sought Him with all his heart. Accordingly God blessed him. God also blessed Solomon for David his father's sake. It was during this portion of his reign he was inspired of the Holy Spirit to pen Proverbs and the Song of Solomon. During these years, Israel grew in size geographically and power to a position it never has had since. For a period of time during Solomon's reign, Israel was the dominant nation of the earth and nations acquiesced to its leadership. Israel during this time became a type of the Millennium. Wealth, peace, and prosperity prevailed.

(2) Yet with Solomon's vast wealth and power came spiritual declension. According to I Kings 11, he multiplied to himself a vast number of wives and concubines indicating an immense appetite for sensuality. Many of them were pagans and turned him away from his devotion to Jehovah God. If wealth and power corrupt, Solomon was no exception. He backslid away from God and though immensely wealthy and

powerful, his latter years were miserable and far from God. During this time he authored Ecclesiastes. As penned there, he wrote, *"I have seen all the works that are done under the sun; and, behold, all is vanity and vexation of spirit"* (Ecclesiastes 1:14). And, *"Vanity of vanities, saith the Preacher, vanity of vanities; all is vanity"* (Ecclesiastes 1:2).

Solomon had anything any man could ever desire. He had wealth until it meant nothing. He was the most powerful man in the world of his day. He had 1,000 of the world's most beautiful women available for his sexual desires at any time and he could have had more if he wanted. Yet he was miserable. In his final years, he was a troubled man, chastened of God. He learned late in life the spiritual is far more important than material or sensual; that the heavenly is more important than the earthly.

Overview of II Chronicles 8: *This next chapter reflects the initial years of Solomon. There was a great expansion of Israel in the Middle East. Israel in that day ruled the known world from the Euphrates River to the northeast to the Nile River on the southwest. Never before or since has Israel had such dominion. It will not again have such until Jesus Christ sits upon his throne in Jerusalem.*

8:1-3 And it came to pass at the end of twenty years, wherein Solomon had built the house of the LORD, and his own house, 2 That the cities which Huram had restored to Solomon, Solomon built them, and caused the children of Israel to dwell there. 3 And Solomon went to Hamathzobah, and prevailed against it.

The building of the Temple took seven years. However, Solomon spent another thirteen years building his palace. See I kings 6:38 and 7:1. Indicative of his backsliding to come is the fact that he spent almost twice as much time on building his own house as he did the Temple. True, David had made many of the preparations for the Temple, but Solomon's materialistic streak began to show through. Hiram had given back to Solomon cities, likely in the region of Dan, which had once belonged to Israel. But Hiram was displeased with them so he gave them back. Solomon therefore had Israelites settle there and reoccupy them. See I Kings 9:12. Meanwhile, Solomon attacked a city named *Hamathzobah*. That likely is another name for Hamath and was in Syria.

8:4-6 And he built Tadmor in the wilderness, and all the store cities, which he built in Hamath. Solomon began to expand his empire to the northeast. Hamath and Tadmor both were cities located in what today is called Syria—and they were deep into Syria.

5 Also he built Bethhoron the upper, and Bethhoron the nether, fenced cities, with walls, gates, and bars. Bethhoron (upper and lower) were towns in central Israel, about twelve miles to the northwest of Jerusalem. These apparently were cities with military significance and Solomon fortified them.

6 And Baalath, and all the store cities that Solomon had, and all the chariot cities, and the cities of the horsemen, and all that Solomon desired to build in Jerusalem, and in Lebanon, and throughout all the land of his dominion. Solomon built other cities for defensive purposes such as Baalath where military materiel were stored. He garrisoned cavalry and chariot bases throughout the land and all across his dominion. He thus strengthened the national defense of his empire.

8:7-10 *As for* **all the people** *that were* **left of the Hittites, and the Amorites, and the Perizzites, and the Hivites, and the Jebusites, which** *were* **not of Israel, 8** *But* **of their children, who were left after them in the land, whom the children of Israel consumed not, them did Solomon make to**

pay tribute until this day. Even in the day of Solomon, remnants of the ancient Canaanite tribes: the Hittites, Amorites, Perizzites, Hivites, and Jebusites were scattered across the land. These, Solomon heavily taxed and drafted as servants.

9 But of the children of Israel did Solomon make no servants for his work; but they *were* men of war, and chief of his captains, and captains of his chariots and horsemen. However, Solomon did not force Israelites into servitude. Rather, they became soldiers and officers in his vast armed forces.

10 And these *were* the chief of king Solomon's officers, *even* two hundred and fifty, that bare rule over the people. Solomon also appointed 250 regional administrators across his empire.

8:11 And Solomon brought up the daughter of Pharaoh out of the city of David unto the house that he had built for her: for he said, My wife shall not dwell in the house of David king of Israel, because *the places are* holy, whereunto the ark of the LORD hath come. Solomon initially married an Egyptian princess. However, he assigned her a temporary abode in the city of David in Jerusalem until a suitable palace for her could be erected. While that palace was in progress, Solomon himself lodged in the palace of David, but he did not allow her to occupy it because he felt that she being a gentile, there would have been an impropriety in her living near to the Temple.

8:12-13 Then Solomon offered burnt offerings unto the LORD on the altar of the LORD, which he had built before the porch, 13 Even after a certain rate every day, offering according to the commandment of Moses, on the sabbaths, and on the new moons, and on the solemn feasts, three times in the year, *even* in the feast of unleavened bread, and in the

Understanding II Chronicles 545

feast of weeks, and in the feast of tabernacles. Solomon also proceeded to offer sacrifices to God every day, morning and evening, and on special holy days as prescribed in the Law of Moses.

8:14–15 And he appointed, according to the order of David his father, the courses of the priests to their service, and the Levites to their charges, to praise and minister before the priests, as the duty of every day required: the porters also by their courses at every gate: for so had David the man of God commanded. 15 And they departed not from the commandment of the king unto the priests and Levites concerning any matter, or concerning the treasures. Solomon therefore also instituted the prescribed courses (i.e., shifts) of Levites and priests which David had organized before his death. These faithfully fulfilled their ministries before Solomon.

16 Now all the work of Solomon was prepared unto the day of the foundation of the house of the LORD, and until it was finished. *So* **the house of the LORD was perfected.** Thus, all the associated ministries of the Temple were fully implemented.

8:17-18 Then went Solomon to Eziongeber, and to Eloth, at the sea side in the land of Edom. 18 And Huram sent him by the hands of his servants ships, and servants that had knowledge of the sea; and they went with the servants of Solomon to Ophir, and took thence four hundred and fifty talents of gold, and brought *them* **to king Solomon.** Thereafter, Solomon established a presence at Eloth (Elat in modern terms at the head of the gulf of Aqaba). Adjacent thereto was also Eziongeber. There, Solomon built a naval port. Hiram sent sailors from Lebanon who were experienced seamen. These sailed to Ophir (thought to be in southern Arabia) and brought back large amounts of gold for Solomon.

* * * * *

Overview of II Chronicles 9: *This next chapter is typical of the latter years of Solomon's reign. There is no mention of service to God. Rather what is emphasized is Solomon's wealth, splendor and his accomplishments. The visit of the queen of Sheba in recorded in verses 1-12 and Solomon's riches and his death are described in verses 13-31.*

9:1-4 And when the queen of Sheba heard of the fame of Solomon, she came to prove Solomon with hard questions at Jerusalem, with a very great company, and camels that bare spices, and gold in abundance, and precious stones: and when she was come to Solomon, she communed with him of all that was in her heart.

The account of the visit of the queen of Sheba is here recorded. Sheba likely was Ethiopia on the horn of Africa. Ethiopians to this day claim the queen of Sheba. Moreover, Ethiopian tradition holds that Solomon and the queen had a liaison, producing a son. The latter allegedly is the ancestor of many modern Ethiopians. However, there is absolutely no scriptural record thereof. The queen thus came with a impressive entourage and retinue. The recorded purpose of her visit was "to prove Solomon with hard questions at Jerusalem." This woman had heard of the wisdom and wealth of Solomon and came to test his wisdom with difficult questions.

2 And Solomon told her all her questions: and there was nothing hid from Solomon which he told her not. Solomon thus was candid with the queen and answered her questions directly. He withheld no secrets from her.

3 And when the queen of Sheba had seen the wisdom of Solomon, and the house that he had built, 4 And the meat of his table, and the sitting of his servants, and the attendance of his ministers, and their apparel; his cupbearers also, and their apparel; and his ascent by which he went up into the house of the LORD; there was no more spirit in her. When the queen of Sheba had witnessed Solomon's wealth, his wisdom, the demeanor of his servants, his exquisite clothing, even the apparel of his cupbearers, and the special 'skywalk' which had been built from his palace to the Temple, she was flabbergasted. Any pretense of pomp and ceremonial on her part was completely deflated. In comparison to the regal airs of Solomon, this queen was as nothing.

9:5-8 And she said to the king, *It was* a true report which I heard in mine own land of thine acts, and of thy wisdom: 6 Howbeit I believed not their words, until I came, and mine eyes had seen *it*: and, behold, the one half of the greatness of thy wisdom was not told me: *for* thou exceedest the fame that I heard. The reports of Solomon's wealth, wisdom, and splendor had reached the queen in Sheba. However, she had doubted them. But in seeing with her own eyes his royal splendor and hearing with her own ears his wisdom, she could only confess that the half had not been told her. What she saw perhaps was a foreshadow of conditions someday in the millennium.

7 Happy *are* thy men, and happy *are* these thy servants, which stand continually before thee, and hear thy wisdom. She declared, "Happy are thy men, and happy are these thy servants, which stand continually before thee, and hear thy wisdom." Solomon's fame as a wise man had thus spread across the known world.

The queen thus rose to praise Jehovah God. **8 Blessed be the LORD thy God, which delighted in thee to set thee on his**

throne, *to be* king for the LORD thy God: because thy God loved Israel, to establish them for ever, therefore made he thee king over them, to do judgment and justice. This gentile queen realized that all which Solomon possessed had come from Jehovah God.

9:9-12 And she gave the king an hundred and twenty talents of gold, and of spices great abundance, and precious stones: neither was there any such spice as the queen of Sheba gave king Solomon. Varying weights have been assigned to 'talents' over the years. The value of modern gold varies as well. However, the gold given by the queen to Solomon could range from 75 million dollars to as much as 150 million dollars. This excludes other gifts of value as noted. She truly paid homage to the one who in her day was a type of the Christ. In the Millennium, nations likewise will pay homage to the King of kings, ruling from Jerusalem.

10 And the servants also of Huram, and the servants of Solomon, which brought gold from Ophir, brought algum trees and precious stones. 11 And the king made *of* the algum trees terraces to the house of the LORD, and to the king's palace, and harps and psalteries for singers: and there were none such seen before in the land of Judah. The precise sense of algum trees is uncertain. However, they evidently were highly valued spice trees or perhaps were highly ornamental. In any event, Hiram's servants also brought such unique and valuable trees to Solomon who had them planted in the terraces of the Temple complex. Also, expensive harps and psalteries were imported for the Temple musicians. Never before had such exquisite trappings been witnessed in Judah.

12 And king Solomon gave to the queen of Sheba all her desire, whatsoever she asked, beside *that* which she had brought unto the king. So she turned, and went away to her own land, she and her servants. In turn for the queen's generosity, Solomon gave to her whatever she wanted. Whatever she asked, she was given. Thus, this unusual visit by the queen of Sheba ended and she returned home with her servants.

9:13-16 Now the weight of gold that came to Solomon in one year was six hundred and threescore and six talents of gold. Again, talents have varied in weight over the centuries and gold prices certainly have varied. However, the annual income of gold alone to Solomon could range from 350 million dollars to one billion dollars. He truly was a billionaire in his day.

14 Beside *that which* **chapmen and merchants brought. And all the kings of Arabia and governors of the country brought gold and silver to Solomon.** The amount above was over and above what businesses and merchants paid in taxes and fees. Moreover, the rulers of Arabia also paid substantial amounts of tribute to Solomon each year. Additionally, Solomon paid no taxes.

15 And king Solomon made two hundred targets *of* **beaten gold: six hundred** *shekels* **of beaten gold went to one target. 16 And three hundred shields** *made he of* **beaten gold: three hundred** *shekels* **of gold went to one shield. And the king put them in the house of the forest of Lebanon.** With some of his gold, Solomon made 200 ceremonial shields of wrought gold. Each shield contained 600 shekels of gold. He also made 300 smaller shields of wrought gold. (The word translated as **shield** {מָגֵן *magen*} refers to a 'buckler' which was a smaller shield strapped to the forearm.) These contained 300 shekels of gold. These Solomon hung as decorations in his summer palace in the mountain forests of Lebanon.

9:17-19 Moreover the king made a great throne of ivory, and overlaid it with pure gold. 18 And *there were* **six steps to the throne, with a footstool of gold,** *which were* **fastened to the throne, and stays on each side of the sitting**

place, and two lions standing by the stays: 19 **And twelve lions stood there on the one side and on the other upon the six steps. There was not the like made in any kingdom.**

Solomon had constructed an exquisite and massive throne of ivory which was overlaid with pure gold. Six steps led to the seat of the throne. Before the seat itself was a footstool of gold. On each side of the six steps leading up to the top of the throne were golden lions. No king on earth ever had a throne such as did Solomon.

9:20-21 And all the drinking vessels of king Solomon *were of* **gold, and all the vessels of the house of the forest of Lebanon** *were of* **pure gold: none** *were of* **silver; it was** *not* **any thing accounted of in the days of Solomon. 21 For the king's ships went to Tarshish with the servants of Huram: every three years once came the ships of Tarshish bringing gold, and silver, ivory, and apes, and peacocks.**

Verse 20 notes how even the common vessels of day-to-day life in Solomon's palace were of pure gold. Even silver was not considered worth accounting. Furthermore, Hiram's sailors traveled to Tarshish each year. Precisely where this city was is not clear. Some have thought that it a city of the Phoenicians in a distant part of the Mediterranean Sea perhaps in Cyprus or Spain. Others have speculated that it a was city somewhere near and accessible to the Red Sea to which ships constructed at Ezion-geber (on the Gulf of Elat on the Red Sea) sailed. In any event, they brought back "gold, and silver, ivory, and apes, and peacocks." Solomon thus received not only gold and silver from his far-flung reaches, but also exotic creatures as well.

9:22-24 And king Solomon passed all the kings of the earth in riches and wisdom. 23 And all the kings of the earth sought the presence of Solomon, to hear his wisdom, that God had put in his heart. 24 And they brought every man his

Understanding II Chronicles

present, vessels of silver, and vessels of gold, and raiment, harness, and spices, horses, and mules, a rate year by year. Solomon thus surpassed all the kings of the earth for power, splendor, riches, and wisdom. They rather therefore sought audiences with him to pay homage, hear his wisdom, and stay on his good side. Accordingly, they brought substantial amounts to tribute to Solomon each year. Truly, Solomon in these years was a forerunner of Jesus Christ upon His throne someday in the Millennium.

9:25-28 And Solomon had four thousand stalls for horses and chariots, and twelve thousand horsemen; whom he bestowed in the chariot cities, and with the king at Jerusalem. Solomon accrued to himself a considerable herd of horses. Though used primarily for military purposes, he was in violation of the restrictions which God had placed upon kings of Israel in Deuteronomy 17:16. The prohibition there was that a king of Israel "not multiply horses to himself." These horses were placed in chariot and cavalry garrisons around the nation, beginning at Jerusalem.

26 And he reigned over all the kings from the river even unto the land of the Philistines, and to the border of Egypt. The extent of Solomon's empire stretched from the Euphrates River to the northeast in modern Iraq, to the land of the Philistines to the west, to the border of Egypt to the southwest. Moreover, Solomon also dominated the regions to the south and east from Moab to Arabia

27 And the king made silver in Jerusalem as stones, and cedar trees made he as the sycomore trees that *are* in the low plains in abundance. 28 And they brought unto Solomon horses out of Egypt, and out of all lands. Not only did Solomon prosper, but it spilled over to his people. Prosperity reigned through Israel. Silver was as common as stones (which there are aplenty in Israel). Cedar trees were the tree of choice for the wealthy because of their fragrance, lumber, and beauty. However, cedar trees proliferated throughout the entire nation during his reign. To that degree, the reign of Solomon was a foreshadow of the great peace and prosperity which will prevail when Jesus reigns. Nevertheless, the sacred chronicler made mention of the inroads of spiritual compromise and disobedience which would unravel and undo the greatness of Solomon. In direct violation of Deuteronomy 17:16, Solomon imported many horses from Egypt and elsewhere.

9:29-31 Now the rest of the acts of Solomon, first and last, *are* they not written in the book of Nathan the prophet, and in the prophecy of Ahijah the Shilonite, and in the visions of Iddo the seer against Jeroboam the son of Nebat? 30 And Solomon reigned in Jerusalem over all Israel forty years. 31 And Solomon slept with his fathers, and he was buried in the city of David his father: and Rehoboam his son reigned in his stead.

Some have suggested that the prophecy of Nathan the prophet refers to the book of II Samuel. However, there is no record of Solomon's reign there. Others have suggested that the authors mentioned above were the inspired authors of I and II Kings. Likely, they are non-inspired history books, lost to time. The reign of Solomon lasted for forty years. When he died, he was buried "in the city of David." The latter was a section in east Jerusalem, first developed by David and where many of the kings of Judah were buried. The following text will detail the life of Rehoboam, Solomon's successor.

Epilogue: Deuteronomy 17:16-20 set forth divine instructions for the future kings of Israel. Sadly, Solomon in his latter years violated them all. God in Deuteronomy specified how the king of Israel was not to multiply to himself horses. Solomon did. (Horses were a visible symbol of military might.

Understanding II Chronicles 553

They indicated a reliance upon human power rather than upon God's deliverance.) Moreover, a king of Israel was not to multiply to himself wives. Solomon did. Nor was the king to greatly multiply to himself gold and silver. Solomon did. Noting how Solomon violated God's clear guidelines for a king, it is likely he did not daily spend time in God's Word as also was prescribed in Deuteronomy 17:18-20.

The lesson of Solomon in part is how God's blessing went to his head, causing him to turn to earthly pleasure and forget his God. His latter years as a result were miserable. Though he died materially rich, he died an unhappy, unfulfilled, miserable, backslidden man. People to this day name their sons, David. Rarely is a baby boy ever named Solomon (except by Jews).

* * * * *

Overview of II Chronicles 10: *This next chapter presents the accession to power of Rehoboam, Solomon's son. He was the arrogant son of Solomon who precipitated the split of the nation. His life is a curious mix of being an agent of God's will, yet arrogant. That arrogance brought God's chastisement upon Israel. Yet in the final analysis, Rehoboam humbled himself before God. God, in turn, restored a measure of blessing. There is a curious use by God of Rehoboam's arrogance and stupidity to effect His greater will. That was the division of Israel as chastisement for the apostasy which developed during Solomon's latter years.*

I Kings 11:31-40 details how God intended to chasten Solomon and his realm for their departure from the LORD *their God. God's plan was to give ten tribes to Jeroboam to rule, leaving only two tribes to the house of David. There is a clear lesson of how God will, in His perfect time, chasten His people for their sin. All of the glory and splendor of the era of Solomon* faded away after his death. The reason is simple. God removed His hand of blessing from Israel and in fact chastened them. Moreover, another lesson is how that the sins of the fathers often profoundly influence the lives of their children as well as others.

10:1-19 This chapter, with a few verbal alterations, is the same as in I Kings 12:1-19. See comments thereto for this chapter.

* * * * *

Overview of II Chronicles 11: *This next chapter presents further details of the initial hostility between the two divisions of Israel. The divided kingdom, as it is generally known, was a strange affair. The northern ten tribes were allowed their independence in God's providence to chasten Jerusalem, Rehoboam ,and the national pride for their spiritual apostasy.*

However, from the first, the northern ten tribes (Israel) were even more spiritually apostate. They became idolaters and Baal worshipers almost immediately. Even more curious, Jeroboam had been allowed to be king by God's direct providence. Yet, he became the leader of the spiritual apostasy of his realm, introducing the most base forms of idolatry and Baal worship.

Judah, on the other hand, though led by an amazingly foolish and arrogant king, in some measure remained true to God. They at least retained the prescribed Temple worship of Jehovah God according to the Law of Moses. Throughout their history, though there were good and bad times spiritually, on the whole, Judah remained generally true to her God.

Subdivisions of chapter 11 are: (1) Rehoboam forbidden to war against Israel in verses 1-12; (2) the priests and Levites of

Understanding II Chronicles

the northern kingdom find refuge in Judah in verses 13-17; and (3) the posterity of Rehoboam is listed in verses 18-23.

11:1-4 And when Rehoboam was come to Jerusalem, he gathered of the house of Judah and Benjamin an hundred and fourscore thousand chosen *men*, which were warriors, to fight against Israel, that he might bring the kingdom again to Rehoboam. Upon the rebellion of Jeroboam and the ten northern tribes, Rehoboam returned to Jerusalem and called up the army reserve of Judah in the amount of 180,000 men. By now Benjamin was essentially a *de facto* part of the tribe of Judah.

2 But the word of the LORD came to Shemaiah the man of God, saying, 3 Speak unto Rehoboam the son of Solomon, king of Judah, and to all Israel in Judah and Benjamin, saying, 4 Thus saith the LORD, Ye shall not go up, nor fight against your brethren: return every man to his house: for this thing is done of me. And they obeyed the words of the LORD, and returned from going against Jeroboam.

Notwithstanding Rehoboam's determination to chastize the northern tribes, God sent a prophet by the name of Shemaiah to Rehoboam and informed him on behalf of God to not fight with the northern tribes. Evidently, Shemaiah also made this clear to the assembled army of Rehoboam. Upon hearing the pronouncement of the prophet, they all packed up and went home. Notice God's comment, "this thing is done of me." The division of the kingdom was God's plan as part of his chastisement upon Rehoboam and Solomon for their sin. God thus intervened and stopped Rehoboam's attempt to re-unify the kingdom.

11:5-12 And Rehoboam dwelt in Jerusalem, and built cities for defence in Judah. Though restrained from war against the north by God, Rehoboam set out to militarize his kingdom. He thus fortified various cities across Judah against possible attack.

6 He built even Bethlehem, and Etam, and Tekoa, 7 And Bethzur, and Shoco, and Adullam, 8 And Gath, and Mareshah, and Ziph, 9 And Adoraim, and Lachish, and Azekah, 10 And Zorah, and Aijalon, and Hebron, which *are* in Judah and in Benjamin fenced cities. These various cities across Judah were all transformed into military installations, fortified against attack from Jeroboam or any other foe. Noteworthy is how the tone of Israel had changed. During the latter years of David and throughout the years of Solomon, peace had been the character of those decades. Now under Rehoboam and Jeroboam, impending war was the tenor of the times. The blessing of God had been removed from God's people because of their sin.

11 And he fortified the strong holds, and put captains in them, and store of victual, and of oil and wine. 12 And in every several city *he put* shields and spears, and made them exceeding strong, having Judah and Benjamin on his side. The cities mentioned above, and others, were made into military strongholds and supplied with necessary supplies and armaments. Again, the nation was on a war footing. Contrast that to the peace of David's later years and the reign of Solomon.

11:13-17 And the priests and the Levites that *were* in all Israel resorted to him out of all their coasts. 14 For the Levites left their suburbs and their possession, and came to Judah and Jerusalem: for Jeroboam and his sons had cast them off from executing the priest's office unto the LORD.

Verses 13-17 are of interest in that they detail how the Levites and priests from throughout the northern ten tribes fled to the southern kingdom. Jeroboam had "cast them off from executing the priest's office unto the LORD."

In the north, Jeroboam had 15 **ordained him priests for the high places, and for the devils, and for the calves which he had made.** Because of the blatant idolatry and utter rejection of the observance of the Mosaic law in the north, these godly priests and Levites fled to where they were welcome. Moreover, the reference to Jeroboam setting up high places and calves is a reference to Baal worship. Also note how these are referred to as **devils** or demons. Baal worship was not only worship of demonic gods, but also involved base sexual practices as well.

16 **And after them out of all the tribes of Israel such as set their hearts to seek the LORD God of Israel came to Jerusalem, to sacrifice unto the LORD God of their fathers.** Notice further how that godly individuals from "all the tribes of Israel" fled the north and moved to Jerusalem and environs. Not only does this bespeak their spiritual character, it also lays to rest the proposition that there were ever ten *lost* tribes. Godly representatives of *every* tribe of Israel migrated to Judah. Judah became representative of *all* twelve tribes of Israel. This demolishes the theology of British Israelism and the Worldwide Church of God. They begin with the premise there indeed were ten lost tribes of which Britain and America are today the descendants.

17 **So they strengthened the kingdom of Judah, and made Rehoboam the son of Solomon strong, three years: for three years they walked in the way of David and Solomon.** These godly refuges from the north thus strengthened Judah. Their influx helped to solidify Rehoboam as king, especially in the crucial first three years of his reign. These refugees from the north added a tone of godliness to the southern kingdom, but alas, it was to last for only about three years. Thereafter, Judah, from the king on down, "forsook the law of the LORD, and all Israel with him" (II Chronicles 12:1).

11:18-21 And Rehoboam took him Mahalath the daughter of Jerimoth the son of David to wife, *and* Abihail the daughter of Eliab the son of Jesse; 19 Which bare him children; Jeush, and Shamariah, and Zaham. 20 And after her he took Maachah the daughter of Absalom; which bare him Abijah, and Attai, and Ziza, and Shelomith. 21 And Rehoboam loved Maachah the daughter of Absalom above all his wives and his concubines: (for he took eighteen wives, and threescore concubines; and begat twenty and eight sons, and threescore daughters.)

The immediately family and posterity of Rehoboam are listed. Though he certainly did not multiply to himself wives as his father had, Rehoboam nevertheless was a polygamist. Here, four of his wives are named and their sons are noted. However, Rehoboam had a total of eighteen wives and sixty concubines (i.e., a harem) who bore him twenty-eight sons and sixty daughters.

11:22-23 And Rehoboam made Abijah the son of Maachah the chief, *to be* ruler among his brethren: for *he thought* to make him king. Rehoboam promoted his son Abijah (a son of his favorite wife) as the chief prince above his brothers. Rehoboam intended for Abijah to succeed him on throne and that he did. See 13:1.

23 And he dealt wisely, and dispersed of all his children throughout all the countries of Judah and Benjamin, unto every fenced city: and he gave them victual in abundance. And he desired many wives. Though not a godly man, Rehoboam was shrewd in placing his various children in the outlying areas of Judah and Benjamin, especially the fortified cities. They thus maintained a royal presence in these crucial places and helped solidify his reign. These also received 'royal' provisions across the land. They thus formed a loyal network across the nation. His character is summarized in the last phrase,

"And he desired many wives." The word translated as **wives** (נשים *nashiym*) can also simply mean 'women.' That seems to fit the general character of Rehoboam. Though he had a total of seventy-eight wives and concubines, he was always on the prowl for other women. Thus, the sensual immoral character of this man is further revealed. He also walked in direct disregard of God's rules for kings of Israel recorded in Deuteronomy 17:14-20.

* * * * *

Overview of II Chronicles 12: *This chapter gives an overview of Rehoboam's reign and that when he ignored God, God chastened him. However, when he humbled himself before God, things went better.*

12:1 And it came to pass, when Rehoboam had established the kingdom, and had strengthened himself, he forsook the law of the LORD, and all Israel with him. Notice when Rehoboam had established himself as king that "he forsook the law of the LORD, and all Israel with him." It is significant it does not say, he forsook the Lord. Rather he forsook the *Law* of the LORD. Trouble comes in the Christian life when God's people forsake His Word. Notice also that when the leader did so, the people followed suit. This is a strong lesson for husbands, parents, and anyone else in a position of leadership.

12:2-4 And it came to pass, *that* **in the fifth year of king Rehoboam Shishak king of Egypt came up against Jerusalem, because they had transgressed against the LORD, 3 With twelve hundred chariots, and threescore thousand horsemen: and the people** *were* **without number**

560   *Understanding II Chronicles*

that came with him out of Egypt; the Lubims, the Sukkiims, and the Ethiopians. 4 And he took the fenced cities which *pertained* to Judah, and came to Jerusalem.

Notice in verse 2, cause and effect. In verse 1, Rehoboam forsook the law of the Lord. In verse 2, he was invaded by Shishak, king of the Egyptians, and roundly defeated. The reason is made clear: "because they had transgressed against the LORD." Here is a clear illustration that God will chasten his people when they transgress. That principle remains to this day. See Hebrews 12:5-11. Egypt came with overwhelming force and not only overran Jerusalem, but also "the fenced cities which *pertained* to Judah." The defeat of Judah clearly was God's chastening. Specifically, they (1) had forsaken God's Word and (2) therefore transgressed against the Lord.

12:5-6 Then came Shemaiah the prophet to Rehoboam, and *to* the princes of Judah, that were gathered together to Jerusalem because of Shishak, and said unto them, Thus saith the LORD, Ye have forsaken me, and therefore have I also left you in the hand of Shishak. God again sent the prophet Shemaiah. He informed the nation, it was because they had forsaken their God that God had allowed them to be defeated by Shishak. Whereupon, from the King on down, Judah humbled themselves before God.

12:7-8 And when the LORD saw that they humbled themselves, the word of the LORD came to Shemaiah, saying, They have humbled themselves; *therefore* I will not destroy them, but I will grant them some deliverance; and my wrath shall not be poured out upon Jerusalem by the hand of Shishak. 8 Nevertheless they shall be his servants; that they may know my service, and the service of the kingdoms of the countries. God often is moved to mercy when sinners humble themselves before Him. Rather than utterly

Understanding II Chronicles   561

destroying Rehoboam and Judah, God only chastened them. There still were severe consequences for their sin, but at least, they were not destroyed. Judah was thus forced to become a vassal state to Egypt.

12:9-10 So Shishak king of Egypt came up against Jerusalem, and took away the treasures of the house of the LORD, and the treasures of the king's house; he took all: he carried away also the shields of gold which Solomon had made. 10 Instead of which king Rehoboam made shields of brass, and committed *them* to the hands of the chief of the guard, that kept the entrance of the king's house.

God nevertheless allowed Shishak, king of Egypt, to take away *all* of the treasure of the house of the LORD. (There has been much speculation in recent years about whatever happened to the ark of the covenant. To this time, Jerusalem had not been sacked. In as much as Shishak took *all* of the treasures of the house of the Lord and in as much as the ark was overlaid with solid gold, it may well be inferred, some have suggested that it disappeared at this time. However, in II Chronicles 35:3, the ark is again mentioned, though not in the holy of holies. But it seems that it actually was never removed from Jerusalem until the time the Babylonians destroyed the Temple.)

Moreover, the shields of gold which Solomon had made were taken as well. In their place, Rehoboam was forced to replace them with inferior shields made of brass. Sin always leaves one with second best or worse. God's way is always best. Sin always brings loss. It is the root of all poverty.

12:11-12 And when the king entered into the house of the LORD, the guard came and fetched them, and brought them again into the guard chamber. Evidently, the custom was that when the king made the short journey from his palace to the Temple complex, the palace guard would escort him in regal array, carrying the gold shields of Solomon. However, now the latter were gone. Now, even the brass shields were hidden away and had to be tediously gotten out for the ceremonial march to the Temple.

12 **And when he humbled himself, the wrath of the LORD turned from him, that he would not destroy *him* altogether: and also in Judah things went well.** However, when Rehoboam finally humbled himself before God after being humbled by God's chastening, God's anger turned away from him. It was only after Rehoboam humbled himself that things in Judah began to get better. Repentance and humbling before God are requisites for God's restored blessing. Rehoboam learned that the hard way.

12:13-14 So king Rehoboam strengthened himself in Jerusalem, and reigned: for Rehoboam *was* one and forty years old when he began to reign, and he reigned seventeen years in Jerusalem, the city which the LORD had chosen out of all the tribes of Israel, to put his name there. And his mother's name *was* Naamah an Ammonitess. Details of Rehoboam's reign are listed. He was forty-one years old when he acceded the throne. He reigned seventeen years thereon. His mother was Naamah, an Ammonitess—she originally was from Ammon. Notwithstanding, the sin of Judah, the sacred chronicler notes that Jerusalem was the "the city which the LORD had chosen out of all the tribes of Israel, to put his name there."

14 **And he did evil, because he prepared not his heart to seek the LORD.** Verse 14 summarizes the life of Rehoboam. In the main, "he did evil because he prepared not his heart to seek the LORD." Yet, "when he humbled himself, the wrath of the LORD turned from him . . . and also in Judah things went well." A lesson remains to this day. Two timeless spiritual principles are clearly illustrated here. When one does not prepare his heart to seek the LORD, evil eventually appears. Yet on the other

Understanding II Chronicles 563

hand, when one will humble himself before God, God is merciful and is pleased therewith.

12:15-16 Now the acts of Rehoboam, first and last, *are* they not written in the book of Shemaiah the prophet, and of Iddo the seer concerning genealogies? And *there were* wars between Rehoboam and Jeroboam continually. 16 And Rehoboam slept with his fathers, and was buried in the city of David: and Abijah his son reigned in his stead.

The books of Shemaiah and Iddo and their genealogies quite apparently are uninspired and have been to lost to history. Another comment of note is that "*there were* wars between Rehoboam and Jeroboam continually." Jeroboam never was right with God and for most of the reign of Rehoboam, he was not right with God either. Consequently, there was nothing but trouble. Being out of God's will removes the blessing of God.

Using a favored euphemism for death, the sacred chronicler records that " Rehoboam slept with his fathers, and was buried in the city of David." The city of David, again, was that section of east Jerusalem wherein David had first built his palace and where the royal cemetery of the Davidic dynasty was located. Upon the death of Rehoboam, Abijah, his favored son and his choice of succession, acceded the throne.

* * * * *

Overview of II Chronicles 13: *This chapter presents the life and reign of Abijah, the son of Rehoboam. A parallel passage is found in I Kings 15. Abijah is referred to as Abijam in I Kings. He reigned for only three years and nothing is mentioned concerning his decease. The account of him in II Chronicles 13 presents the better side of this king. I Kings 15:3 records how "he walked in all the sins of his father, which he had done before him: and his heart was not perfect with the Lord his God, as the heart of David his father." The reign of Abijah became typical of the years of the divided kingdom. There were constant wars between the north and the south. The north was religiously apostate from the start, while Judah in the south remained in a somewhat right relationship with God.*

13:1-2 Now in the eighteenth year of king Jeroboam began Abijah to reign over Judah. 2 He reigned three years in Jerusalem. His mother's name also *was* Michaiah the daughter of Uriel of Gibeah. And there was war between Abijah and Jeroboam

While Jeroboam continued to reign in the northern kingdom (Israel), Abijah ascended the throne in Judah. No reason is given for the relative shortness of his reign (three years). His mother is noted as " Michaiah the daughter of Uriel of Gibeah." At least, she was an Israelite. Notice the end of verse 2, "And there was war between Abijah and Jeroboam." God's blessing had been removed from both houses of Israel and there was nothing but trouble in the meanwhile.

13:3 And Abijah set the battle in array with an army of valiant men of war, *even* four hundred thousand chosen men: Jeroboam also set the battle in array against him with eight hundred thousand chosen men, *being* mighty men of valour. Notice the troop strength of each respective kingdom. Abijah went out to battle with an army of 400,000 men. "Jeroboam also set the battle in array against him with eight hundred thousand chosen men." Several comments are thus in order. (1) What is obvious is that Jeroboam entered the war with twice as many soldiers as Abijah. All things being equal, Jeroboam should have crushed Judah. (2) It should also be noted that it was the custom of the day for virtually all adult males between the ages of 21 and 50 to be part of the infantry. They truly were citizen armies. Accordingly, the armies were neither highly trained nor highly armed.

13:4-5 And Abijah stood up upon mount Zemaraim, which *is* in mount Ephraim, and said, Hear me, thou Jeroboam, and all Israel; 5 Ought ye not to know that the LORD God of Israel gave the kingdom over Israel to David for ever, *even* to him and to his sons by a covenant of salt? Before the impending battle, Abijah stood atop Mount Ephraim and cried out for the army of Jeroboam to hear. He reminded Jeroboam and the northern army that "God gave the kingdom over Israel to David for ever . . . and to his sons." Undoubtedly, the significance of that statement was not lost upon Jeroboam. Abijah was a direct descendant of David (great-grandson). Jeroboam was not of the lineage of David in any way.

Moreover, God had promised this to David "by a covenant of salt." This in general is a reference to the Davidic Covenant. Specifically, a "covenant of salt" was a metaphor of a lasting covenant. Salt was considered the basic food preservative of the time. It preserved from corruption and putrefaction. Hence, a covenant of salt was one which was considered long lasting or perpetual.

13:6-8 Yet Jeroboam the son of Nebat, the servant of Solomon the son of David, is risen up, and hath rebelled against his lord. Abijah rehearsed how Jeroboam in the northern kingdom had rebelled against the duly anointed kings of Judah to the point of going to war against them.

And there are gathered unto him vain men, the children of Belial, and have strengthened themselves against Rehoboam the son of Solomon, when Rehoboam was young and tenderhearted, and could not withstand them. Notice that Abijah accused the northern Israelites of being "children of Belial." The sense of the word *Belial* is of wickedness or worthlessness. In its proper sense, it is an allusion to the wicked one, Satan. Abijah also accused Jeroboam of taking advantage of Rehoboam when he was a young king and still inexperienced.

And now ye think to withstand the kingdom of the LORD in the hand of the sons of David; and ye *be* a great multitude, and *there are* with you golden calves, which Jeroboam made you for gods. Abijah thus accused Jeroboam and his army of withstanding Jehovah's king. Notice also that the army of the northern kingdom had brought with them their new gods. These were the golden calves which Jeroboam had made upon his accession to power in the north. Israel, the northern kingdom, had degenerated into the most base form of idolatry. Calf worship was closely related to Baal worship.

13:9 Have ye not cast out the priests of the LORD, the sons of Aaron, and the Levites, and have made you priests after the manner of the nations of *other* lands? so that whosoever cometh to consecrate himself with a young bullock and seven rams, *the same* may be a priest of *them that are* no gods. Furthermore, Jeroboam had cast out the duly anointed priests of God and the Levites from his borders. These had fled as refugees to Judah. See I Chronicles 11:14-17. In turn, Jeroboam had allowed anybody who wanted to be a priest to do so, provided they came up with "a young bullock and seven rams." Abijah thus justly accused Jeroboam of casting off the Aaronic priesthood and substituting a mongrel one in its place.

13:10-11 But as for us, the LORD *is* our God, and we have not forsaken him; and the priests, which minister unto the LORD, *are* the sons of Aaron, and the Levites *wait* upon *their* business: 11 And they burn unto the LORD every morning and every evening burnt sacrifices and sweet incense: the shewbread also *set they in order* upon the pure table; and

the candlestick of gold with the lamps thereof, to burn every evening: for we keep the charge of the LORD our God; but ye have forsaken him.** Abijah (perhaps a bit self-righteously) reminded Jeroboam that Jehovah was still their God, and "we have not forsaken him." He mentioned Jehovah (i.e., the LORD) four times in this short section. Judah still maintained the scripturally ordered priestly service. Judah still continued to keep the charge of the Lord their God (although in form only). Israel in the north indeed had forsaken him altogether.

13:12 And, behold, God himself *is* with us for *our* captain, and his priests with sounding trumpets to cry alarm against you. O children of Israel, fight ye not against the LORD God of your fathers; for ye shall not prosper. What is significant is that Judah looked to Jehovah God for their deliverance. Abijah thus uttered profound wisdom: "fight ye not against the LORD God of your fathers; for ye shall not prosper." That admonition remains to this day. People at times fight God in their lives. But they never prosper in so doing. Jeroboam was going to war not only against Judah, but against the God of Judah. Though not altogether a godly king, at least Abijah was right in framing the coming battle in terms of who was on the Lord's side.

13:13-14 But Jeroboam caused an ambushment to come about behind them: so they were before Judah, and the ambushment *was* behind them. 14 And when Judah looked back, behold, the battle *was* before and behind: and they cried unto the LORD, and the priests sounded with the trumpets. Here the sermon of Abijah abruptly stopped and the battle was joined. Jeroboam swung troops around Abijah's flank, circling in behind him. Abijah found himself in the impossible position of being surrounded by a superior force before and behind. Jeroboam held a double advantage. First, he had twice as many troops. Second, he managed to flank around, surrounding Abijah. To any observer, Abijah was beaten before the battle began.

Rather, when Judah saw the predicament they were in, "they cried unto the LORD." In the midst of the crisis, they turned to their God for deliverance. This is a classic example of faith in action. Faith is turning to God for help. It is trusting Him in time of need. Notice also that "the priests sounded with the trumpets." Abijah and Judah turned to God for help, trusting Him to deliver them.

13:15-17 Then the men of Judah gave a shout: and as the men of Judah shouted, it came to pass, that God smote Jeroboam and all Israel before Abijah and Judah. 16 And the children of Israel fled before Judah: and God delivered them into their hand. 17 And Abijah and his people slew them with a great slaughter: so there fell down slain of Israel five hundred thousand chosen men.

In turning to God for help, "then the men of Judah gave a shout." The probable shout was one of praise to Jehovah, their God. As they turned to and trusted the God of heaven, "it came to pass, that God smote Jeroboam and all Israel before Abijah and Judah." Faith moves God to action. Here the faith was the simple crying out to God for deliverance. Prayer is the most basic vehicle of faith. It verbalizes and crystalizes what is in the heart. Israel, the northern kingdom, was crippled. 500,000 men were slain in the battle. God thus gave Judah a great victory. They held the high ground morally and spiritually and they trusted God for His help. Indeed, "blessed *is* the man *that* trusteth in him" (Psalm 34:8).

13:18-20 Thus the children of Israel were brought under at that time, and the children of Judah prevailed, because they relied upon the LORD God of their fathers.

Rebellious Israel was defeated and Judah prevailed. One of the clearest illustrations of faith is herein described: "they relied upon the LORD God." The word translated as **relied** (שָׁעַן *sha'an*) has the sense to 'to lean on' or to 'trust on.' That is a classical definition of faith. Faith in God is reliance upon God. Judah had done exactly that and God wrought a wonderful salvation for them. God thus worked. He severely chastened his backslidden people in the northern kingdom. He also delivered Judah who (1) had held the scriptural position and (2) had trusted God to deliver them.

19 And Abijah pursued after Jeroboam, and took cities from him, Bethel with the towns thereof, and Jeshanah with the towns thereof, and Ephrain with the towns thereof. Not only was Judah delivered from the superior forces of Jeroboam, but God then allowed Judah to go on the offensive and conquer towns along the border of Judah, including Bethel, Jeshanah, and Ephraim with their associated villages. The blessing of God is further evident.

20 Neither did Jeroboam recover strength again in the days of Abijah: and the LORD struck him, and he died. Furthermore, Jeroboam's defeat, in effect challenging God's anointed with his blasphemy, was the beginning of the end of his reign. God therefore "struck him, and he died." The mills of God grind slow, but they grind exceedingly fine. God had tolerated the blasphemy of Jeroboam for a long time, perhaps even giving him space to repent. However, His judgment eventually fell with terrible finality.

13:21-22 But Abijah waxed mighty, and married fourteen wives, and begat twenty and two sons, and sixteen daughters. 22 And the rest of the acts of Abijah, and his ways, and his sayings, *are* written in the story of the prophet Iddo. Abijah, like his predecessors, ignored God's injunction against a king of Israel multiplying wives to themselves. He married fourteen women and had a total of eighteen children. The writing of the prophet Iddo mentioned here was an uninspired record of a prophet of the northern kingdom of the time.

* * * * *

Overview of II Chronicles 14: *The next king of Judah was Asa who reigned for forty-one years. Though in his latter years his failure was in not trusting the Lord altogether. Yet in the main, he was one of the great kings of Judah. The account in I Kings 15 summarized him as being "perfect with the LORD his God, as the heart of David his father." And, "Asa did that which was right in the eyes of the LORD" (I Kings 15:11), and 'Asa's heart was perfect with the LORD all his days" (I Kings 15:14).*

II Chronicles 14 recounts the early years of Asa's reign. It was characterized by ridding Judah of lingering idolatry and false gods. Additionally, Asa turned to the Lord for deliverance in a time of crisis and God delivered Judah.

14:1-2 So Abijah slept with his fathers, and they buried him in the city of David: and Asa his son reigned in his stead. In his days the land was quiet ten years. As is the case in much of II Chronicles, the next chapter details the death of the preceding king. Abijah in due season died and was buried in the royal cemetery in east Jerusalem, called the city of David. He was succeeded by Asa, one of the godly kings of Judah. Accordingly, notice how that "In his days the land was quiet ten years." The latter thought is that there was no war during that time. The blessing of God comes in various ways—in this case of peace.

2 **And Asa did** *that which was* **good and right in the eyes of the LORD his God**. Though not sinless, Asa's character was summarized by God as righteous. As will be the case with many of the kings of Judah, God summarized their character as doing

Understanding II Chronicles

either right or not right before Him. The righteousness of Asa very well may be the cause which produced the effect described in verse 1—"In his days the land was quiet ten years." As one pleases God in his living, God in turn sends specific blessing.

14:3-5 For he took away the altars of the strange *gods*, and the high places, and brake down the images, and cut down the groves. Asa sought to rid Judah of idolatry. The mention of the "high places, images and groves" all are references to Baal-type of worship. This form of pagan idolatry built their places of worship atop hills within groves of trees. There, not only idolatry was exercised, but often base sexual practices were performed, hoping to stimulate pagan gods to send fertility to land, beasts, and people. Asa to his credit, sought to exterminated this from Judah.

4 And commanded Judah to seek the LORD God of their fathers, and to do the law and the commandment. Not only did Asa Himself seek to honor the Lord, he *commanded* his nation to do the same. They were commanded to "seek the LORD God of their fathers." Asa also ordered his people to obey God's Law and commandments.

5 Also he took away out of all the cities of Judah the high places and the images: and the kingdom was quiet before him. Asa also sought to purge the *ad hoc* and *de facto* high places of Judah. These were unofficial places where Jews offered sacrifices to Jehovah. These in turn quickly degenerated into places of idolatry. Asa therefore sought to eliminate all pagan idols from his land. Accordingly, "the kingdom was quiet before him." God honors obedience to His Word. Because Asa sought to honor the Lord in obedience and true righteousness, God honored him with peace (i.e., no war or uprisings).

14:6-8 And he built fenced cities in Judah: for the land had rest, and he had no war in those years; because the

LORD had given him rest. Because of the peace (i.e., rest) in the land, Asa took advantage thereof and built fortified cities throughout his kingdom for future defense.

7 Therefore he said unto Judah, Let us build these cities, and make about *them* walls, and towers, gates, and bars, *while* the land *is* yet before us; because we have sought the LORD our God, we have sought *him*, and he hath given us rest on every side. So they built and prospered. Asa therefore went ahead with his planned defense installations while there was peace at hand. Moreover, he attributed the peace and prosperity in the land because they had sought the Lord their God. Because they had sought Him, God had given peace and tranquility in the land. Therefore, they built and prospered. Evident was the blessing of God upon His people. There was godly leadership who led the nation in the path of obedience and righteousness before God. God in turn prospered them.

8 And Asa had an army *of men* that bare targets and spears, out of Judah three hundred thousand; and out of Benjamin, that bare shields and drew bows, two hundred and fourscore thousand: all these *were* mighty men of valour. The army of Asa included 300,000 men of Judah and 280,000 men of Benjamin. The latter tribe had become a *de facto* part of Judah by this point in Jewish history. Notice how that the army of Judah was primarily men who bore targets (i.e., large shields) and spears. The army of Benjamin was comprised primarily of archers who carried small shields (i.e., bucklers). They might be categorized as heavy and light infantry respectively.

14:9-10 And there came out against them Zerah the Ethiopian with an host of a thousand thousand, and three hundred chariots; and came unto Mareshah. 10 Then Asa went out against him, and they set the battle in array in the valley of Zephathah at Mareshah. Notwithstanding God's

Understanding II Chronicles

blessing, He also allows times of testing in the lives of His servants. Asa was no exception. In verses 9-15 is the account of how God allowed the Ethiopians to attack Judah. A massive army from Ethiopia in north Africa, led by Zerah, marched up the coastal plain into the Shephelah (hill) country of Judah. The "valley of Zephathah at Mareshah" was about 15 miles west of Hebron, in southwestern Judah. The Ethiopians fielded an army of one million infantrymen, accompanied by 300 chariots, likely for their officers.

14:11-15 And Asa cried unto the LORD his God, and said, LORD, *it is* nothing with thee to help, whether with many, or with them that have no power: help us, O LORD our God; for we rest on thee, and in thy name we go against this multitude. O LORD, thou *art* our God; let not man prevail against thee.

In facing a force almost twice as large as his (over one million compared to 580,000) Asa had no recourse but to turn to God. The only place he could turn for help was up. He therefore prayed eloquently to God for deliverance. Asa clearly placed his trust in God for deliverance. "help us, O LORD our God; for we rest on thee, and in thy name we go against this multitude. O LORD, thou *art* our God; let not man prevail against thee." As with Abijah, he relied on the Lord God of his fathers. The truth is, Asa in simple faith trusted God for deliverance and God did exactly that. Verses 12 through 15 recount God's deliverance. Turning to the Lord and trusting Him in time of need is pleasing to Him.

12 So the LORD smote the Ethiopians before Asa, and before Judah; and the Ethiopians fled. God honored Asa for his obedience, righteousness, and faith. In turn, He gave Asa a great victory over the Ethiopians.

13 And Asa and the people that *were* with him pursued them unto Gerar: and the Ethiopians were overthrown,

that they could not recover themselves; for they were destroyed before the LORD, and before his host; and they carried away very much spoil. Not only did the army of Asa defeat the massive Ethiopian army, they pursued after them. Gerar is in southwestern Palestine more than twenty miles from the site of the initial battle at Mareshah. The retreat of the Ethiopians turned into an utter rout. They fled in panic back toward Egypt, whence they had come. The Ethiopian army was in fact "destroyed before the LORD, and before his host." Judah therefore was able to loot the campsites of the Ethiopians and carry away much spoils of war.

14 And they smote all the cities round about Gerar; for the fear of the LORD came upon them: and they spoiled all the cities; for there was exceeding much spoil in them. Gerar actually was in Philistia and was not far from Gaza. Asa and his army thus attacked and capture the Philistine towns near Gerar, "for the fear of the LORD came upon them." The army of Judah therefore plundered these Philistine towns and took a great amount of spoils from them.

15 They smote also the tents of cattle, and carried away sheep and camels in abundance, and returned to Jerusalem. Philistines tending their livestock were killed by the army of Judah who in turn took their livestock as the spoils of war. Thus, the attack of the Ethiopians, though a test, turned into a great victory. Judah returned from the battle with great spoils of war, richer than when they had begun. God thus blessed them because of their faith in Him.

* * * * *

Overview of II Chronicles 15: *The essence of II Chronicles 15 is how that God sent a prophet to Asa to admonish him and the people of Judah to remain faithful to their God. Asa paid*

Understanding II Chronicles

heed and continued to purge Judah of idolatry and renew the covenant with his God.

15:1-7 And the Spirit of God came upon Azariah the son of Oded: 2 And he went out to meet Asa, and said unto him, Hear ye me, Asa, and all Judah and Benjamin; The LORD *is* with you, while ye be with him; and if ye seek him, he will be found of you; but if ye forsake him, he will forsake you. Upon returning from the great victory over the Ethiopians and Philistines, God sent a prophet out to meet Asa by the name of "Azariah the son of Oded." Little or nothing is known about this prophet. However, he confronted Asa with a message from God. The essence of that message was honor the Lord and He will honor you. Forsake him, and he will forsake you.

3 Now for a long season Israel *hath been* without the true God, and without a teaching priest, and without law. 4 But when they in their trouble did turn unto the LORD God of Israel, and sought him, he was found of them. The prophet used the northern kingdom as a salient illustration. For a long time, since the earliest days of Jeroboam, they had been without the true God, true priests of God, and without the Law of God. However, when even they in trouble did turn to God and sought him, he was found of them to help them.

5 And in those times *there was* no peace to him that went out, nor to him that came in, but great vexations *were* upon all the inhabitants of the countries. 6 And nation was destroyed of nation, and city of city: for God did vex them with all adversity. When Israel turned away from their God, there was no safety or stability in their land. Things went from bad to worse. When God's hand of blessing is removed, things do not go well. They get even worse when God turns against a nation.

7 Be ye strong therefore, and let not your hands be weak: for your work shall be rewarded. God through the prophet therefore encouraged Asa to be not be discouraged, but to be strong of spirit, mind, and resolve. His work of reform and righteousness would be rewarded. That truth remains to this day. Oded delivered a message from God for them to continue the course they were on. They were to keep serving Jehovah God and honor him.

15:8-9 And when Asa heard these words, and the prophecy of Oded the prophet, he took courage, and put away the abominable idols out of all the land of Judah and Benjamin, and out of the cities which he had taken from mount Ephraim, and renewed the altar of the LORD, that *was* before the porch of the LORD.

Verse 8 therefore recounts how that Asa was encouraged to continue his eradication of idolatry and pagan worship still remaining in his realm. It is clear that idolatry had infested Judah and Benjamin from the time of Solomon onward. Asa purged this all from the land. The altar before the porch of the LORD refers to the brazen altar which was before the massive ornamental pillars of the front portal to the Temple structure proper. In other words, he renewed the prescribed Levitical sacrifices of the covenant.

9 And he gathered all Judah and Benjamin, and the strangers with them out of Ephraim and Manasseh, and out of Simeon: for they fell to him out of Israel in abundance, when they saw that the LORD his God *was* with him. Notice also in verse 9 that members of various tribes in the northern kingdom (including Ephraim, Manasseh, and Simeon) continued to emigrate to Judah as they "saw that the LORD his God was with him." Again, this neutralizes the premise of British Israelism that the ten northern tribes were lost in the dispersion. The fact is, godly members of each of the ten tribes migrated to Judah to continue to scripturally worship Jehovah God. Asa welcomed these and large numbers of them moved to

Understanding II Chronicles

Judah. The reference to strangers is not to gentiles, but to these emigres from the north.

15:10-15 So they gathered themselves together at Jerusalem in the third month, in the fifteenth year of the reign of Asa. 11 And they offered unto the LORD the same time, of the spoil *which* they had brought, seven hundred oxen and seven thousand sheep. These many refugees from the northern kingdom assembled in the third month of the Jewish year which is the time of Pentecost. They offered at that time 700 oxen and 7,000 sheep.

12 And they entered into a covenant to seek the LORD God of their fathers with all their heart and with all their soul; 13 That whosoever would not seek the LORD God of Israel should be put to death, whether small or great, whether man or woman. Asa and Judah along with their spiritual brethren from the northern kingdom thus entered into a "covenant to seek the LORD God of their fathers with all their heart and with all their soul." This was essentially a renewal or rededication of the covenant God had made with the nation at Sinai. Notice further that this rededication was with all their heart and all their soul. It was sincere, profound, and deep. They were determined to return to the Lord their God. Moreover, they further vowed that whoever would not so seek the Lord, should be executed—whether "small or great, whether man or woman." They meant business with God!

14 And they sware unto the LORD with a loud voice, and with shouting, and with trumpets, and with cornets. 15 And all Judah rejoiced at the oath: for they had sworn with all their heart, and sought him with their whole desire; and he was found of them: and the LORD gave them rest round about. The vows of rededication and revival were made openly "with a loud voice, and with shouting" and they heralded it with trumpet fanfares. (Of interest is that the word translated as

trumpets {חצצרהימ *chatsotserahim*} refers to a bugle or metallic trumpet while the word translated as **cornets** {שופרימ *shopharim*} refers to the rams' horns.) All Judah, both native and recent emigres, rejoiced. They had sworn with all their hearts to God and determined to seek Him again with all of their will. God thus was found of them. Notice the consequent result, "And the LORD gave them rest round about." God sent the blessing of peace.

15:16-17 And also *concerning* Maachah the mother of Asa the king, he removed her from *being* queen, because she had made an idol in a grove: and Asa cut down her idol, and stamped *it*, and burnt *it* at the brook Kidron. The spiritual mettle and courage of Asa are found in verse 16 when he removed his own mother from being the queen of the land "because she had made an idol in a grove: and Asa cut down her idol, and stamped it, and burnt it at the brook Kidron." Asa was a man of integrity and of principle. He had the moral courage to deal against even his own mother for her flagrant sin. The brook Kidron flowed through the valley to the immediate east of Jerusalem between the Temple Mount and the Mount of Olives. He thus showed his uttered disgust and disdain for his mother's idol.

17 **But the high places were not taken away out of Israel: nevertheless the heart of Asa was perfect all his days**. High places in this context likely refer to unofficial *ad hoc* places for sacrifice on hilltops scattered throughout Judah. They likely had been used to offer unofficial sacrifices to Jehovah and some had degenerated into idolatry as well. Asa, however, chose not to remove them.

Though Asa battled idolatry throughout his reign, "nevertheless the heart of Asa was perfect all his days." The sense of the word translated as **perfect** (שלמ *shalem*) is 'complete' or 'total.' The idea is that his heart was total toward the Lord. Or put another way, his heart was totally dedicated to the Lord all his days.

15:18-19 And he brought into the house of God the things that his father had dedicated, and that he himself had dedicated, silver, and gold, and vessels. 19 And there was no *more* war unto the five and thirtieth year of the reign of Asa. Asa dedicated to the Temple things which Abijah had taken from Jeroboam which, though dedicated, had not hitherto been represented. He also likely deposited the booty taken from the Ethiopians. Notice again how that God preserved the peace in the land during the reign of Asa. It surely is more than coincidence that Asa sought to honor the Lord and remove sin, seeking the Lord with a perfect heart, and the fact there was not war in the land for thirty-five years. God honors those who honor him.

* * * * *

Overview of II Chronicles 16: *This next chapter recounts the final six years of Asa's reign. Sadly, through the preceding years of peace and prosperity, he evidently came to trust his own resources rather than the Lord. God knowing this allowed war once again to come upon him. Rather than turn to the Lord for deliverance as he had in the past, Asa decided to take things into his own hands and handled things himself. The remainder of his life unfortunately was one of war and sickness.*

16:1-6 In the six and thirtieth year of the reign of Asa Baasha king of Israel came up against Judah, and built Ramah, to the intent that he might let none go out or come in to Asa king of Judah.

Notice that the king of the northern kingdom, Baasha, attacked Judah. The time is noted as the 36th year of the reign of Asa. However, I Kings 15:33 indicates that Baasha died in the 27th year of Asa. Jamieson, Fausett, and Brown comment, "this date (is) to be calculated from the separation of the kingdoms, and coincident with the sixteenth year of Asa's reign. This mode of reckoning was, in all likelihood, generally followed in the book of the kings of Judah and Israel, the public annals of the time (II Chronicles 16:11), the source from which the inspired historian drew his account." For more detailed explanation of this anomaly, see Floyd Jones *Chronology of the Old Testament*. Page 144.

Baasha thus fortified his border against Judah by building a fortress at Ramah (called *Ramallah* in modern Israel). Ramah was actually a part of Benjamin, but Baasha took it anyway and built a fortified border crossing point between the northern kingdom and Judah. He evidently hoped to stop the bleeding of emigres from the north to Judah.

2 **Then Asa brought out silver and gold out of the treasures of the house of the LORD and of the king's house, and sent to Benhadad king of Syria, that dwelt at Damascus, saying,** 3 *There is* **a league between me and thee, as** *there was* **between my father and thy father: behold, I have sent thee silver and gold; go, break thy league with Baasha king of Israel, that he may depart from me**.

Asa's reaction to this was to ask the pagan king of Syria, Benhadad, to come and help him in the war. There evidently was still a treaty in force between Abijah (Asa's father) and Benhadad—sort of mutual aide pact. Moreover, Asa took money from the treasury of the Temple to pay Benhadad. Benhadad proceeded to attack Israel from the north which diverted Baasha's attention from Judah. The upshot of the matter was that Asa's plan worked and Baasha left him alone. However, the spiritual condition of Asa is clearly revealed.

Rather than trust God, he sought human help and ungodly help at that. Morever, the same Asa which had dedicated funds to the Temple years earlier now raided those same funds to hire mercenary soldiers.

4 And Benhadad hearkened unto king Asa, and sent the captains of his armies against the cities of Israel; and they smote Ijon, and Dan, and Abelmaim, and all the store cities of Naphtali. 5 And it came to pass, when Baasha heard *it*, **that he left off building of Ramah, and let his work cease.** Asa's strategy was simple. If Benhadad would attack in the north, Baasha would be distracted and turn his attention to the north rather his southern border with Judah. That is exactly what happened. Benhadad attacked towns of the northern kingdom in the far north: "Ijon, and Dan, and Abelmaim, and all the store cities of Naphtali." These all were towns north of the Sea of Galilee in far northern Israel, not far from Damascus. When Baasha heard thereof, he immediately ceased building further fortifications at Ramah (in the far south and on the border with Judah).

6 Then Asa the king took all Judah; and they carried away the stones of Ramah, and the timber thereof, wherewith Baasha was building; and he built therewith Geba and Mizpah. Asa's plan had worked (in the flesh). He therefore led his forces to the border town of Ramah and tore down the fortifications which Baasha had made. Asa in turn used these materials to fortify defenses in the towns of Geba and Mizpah, which also were border towns with the northern kingdom.

16:7-9 And at that time Hanani the seer came to Asa king of Judah, and said unto him, Because thou hast relied on the king of Syria, and not relied on the LORD thy God, therefore is the host of the king of Syria escaped out of thine hand. However, God was not pleased with Asa's actions. Notice in verse 7 that God sent a **seer** (i.e., a prophet) named

Hanani who rebuked Asa. He told Asa, "because thou hast relied on the king of Syria, and not relied on the LORD thy God, therefore is the host of the king of Syria escaped out of thine hand." Asa could have defeated a potential enemy in Syria. Rather, he had made a decision in the flesh and certainly not of faith. He thus missed a potential victory. Asa rather sought to pacify and compromise with the godless pagan king of Syria.

8 Were not the Ethiopians and the Lubims a huge host, with very many chariots and horsemen? yet, because thou didst rely on the LORD, he delivered them into thine hand. God (through the prophet) reminded Asa of years earlier when the Ethiopians invaded with a huge army. Asa had relied on the LORD in that day, and God had "delivered them into thine hand." See 14:9*ff.* Asa's error was in trusting his own devices rather than the Lord. God was not pleased.

9 For the eyes of the LORD run to and fro throughout the whole earth, to shew himself strong in the behalf of *them* **whose heart** *is* **perfect toward him. Herein thou hast done foolishly: therefore from henceforth thou shalt have wars.** God thus reminded Asa, "for the eyes of the LORD run to and fro throughout the whole earth, to show himself strong in the behalf of them whose heart is perfect toward him." God is always in search of those who will trust Him completely. However, Asa had sinned in relying upon his own resources rather than his God. God thus told him, "Herein thou hast done foolishly: therefore from henceforth thou shalt have wars." Asa clearly had slidden back from the faith, godliness, and total dedication which characterized his early years. Blessing and prosperity evidently had caused his heart to focus elsewhere rather on his God.

16:10 Then Asa was wroth with the seer, and put him in a prison house; for *he was* **in a rage with him because of this** *thing***. And Asa oppressed** *some* **of the people the same time.**

Asa was enraged at the message the prophet delivered from God. How dare a fundamental Baptist preacher so insult the king? Asa therefore had Hanani thrown in prison. Evidently, the more godly 'conservatives' of the land were also upset with the king. He therefore brought oppression on them as well, perhaps by fines, imprisonments, or taxes.

16:11-12 And, behold, the acts of Asa, first and last, lo, they *are* written in the book of the kings of Judah and Israel. The record mentioned here may in fact be the Book of I Kings.

12 And Asa in the thirty and ninth year of his reign was diseased in his feet, until his disease *was* exceeding *great*: yet in his disease he sought not to the LORD, but to the physicians. After thirty-nine years on the throne, the health of Asa began to fail. Some have speculated whether the disease in his feet was gout. Maybe it was the results of diabetes. "Yet in his disease he sought not to the LORD, but to the physicians." The thought is not that it is wrong to go to the doctor. The *physicians* so mentioned likely were more magicians from Egypt or Babylon. The point is that rather seeking God's help, Asa turned to the world's crowd. The greater point is that he ignored God and sought help from the underworld.

16:13-14 And Asa slept with his fathers, and died in the one and fortieth year of his reign. This king reigned for almost forty-one years. He who had been a great king ended on a pathetic note. Early in his reign, he had sought the Lord, was spiritually courageous, had wrought a great revival in Judah, and had lived by faith. Yet in his final years, there was stubbornness, reliance upon self rather than the Lord, and a lack of faith. In his last two years he contracted a foot disease. Rather than seeking the Lord for help, he stubbornly turned to the occult physicians of the day. His error was that he turned to them and trusted them rather than his God. He thus died after forty-one years of rule, a shadow of the man he once had been spiritually.

14 And they buried him in his own sepulchres, which he had made for himself in the city of David, and laid him in the bed which was filled with sweet odours and divers kinds *of spices* prepared by the apothecaries' art: and they made a very great burning for him. Prior to his death, Asa had built an elaborate mausoleum for himself in the city of David, the royal cemetery of the kings of Judah. A royal public funeral was held in his honor. The great burning likely was that of incense. The Jews did not practice cremation, viewing it as pagan.

* * * * *

Overview of II Chronicles 17: *The sacred chronicle now comes to the life and times of Jehoshaphat, the fourth king of Judah. In the history of Judah, Jehoshaphat was one of the four great kings and reigned approximately twenty-five years in Jerusalem. In the main, Jehoshaphat was a godly king. Yet, he succumbed to spiritual compromise which got him into deep trouble and in the end was his undoing. That compromise was cooperating with his apostate colleagues in the northern kingdom. II Chronicles 17 presents the initial years of Jehoshaphat's reign. During this time, God blessed him for his efforts to maintain godliness and the way of Jehovah God in his kingdom.*

17:1-2 And Jehoshaphat his son reigned in his stead, and strengthened himself against Israel. 2 And he placed forces in all the fenced cities of Judah, and set garrisons in the land of Judah, and in the cities of Ephraim, which Asa his father had taken. Upon the death of Asa, Jehoshaphat his son acceded the throne of Judah. Evident were tense relations with Israel to the north. Jehoshaphat thus placed military garrisons in the fenced cities of Judah. The latter refers to cities with formidable walls for military defense. He also continued to occupy the cities of southern Ephraim which Asa had taken. These likely were the towns of Geba and Mizpah mentioned in 16:6

17:3-5 Notice how that 3 **the LORD was with Jehoshaphat, because he walked in the first ways of his father David, and sought not unto Baalim**. The term *Baalim* is a transliteration of the Hebrew word and represents the plural of Baal. Jehoshaphat did not pursue the Baal's which were the popular idolatrous religious fad of the time.

But rather, he 4 **sought to the LORD God of his father, and walked in his commandments, and not after the doings of Israel.** Israel, the northern kingdom, had been spiritually apostate from the beginning. Jehoshaphat would have nothing to do with their apostasy—at least in his early years.

Notice the cause and effect relationship set forth. Because Jehoshaphat walked in the way of the Lord, sought Him, and walked in His commandments; God 5 **therefore stablished the kingdom in his hand; and all Judah brought to Jehoshaphat presents; and he had riches and honour in abundance**. Jehoshaphat would blossom into one of the godly kings of Judah. His people sensed that and honored him therein. God also clearly blessed him for his godly obedience to the covenant. As a result, Jehoshaphat "had riches and honour in abundance." God blesses righteousness!

17:6-9 And his heart was lifted up in the ways of the LORD: moreover he took away the high places and groves out of Judah. Here was a king whose "heart was lifted up in the ways of the LORD." Jehoshaphat exalted in the Lord. The ways of God were a priority of life for him. He sought first the kingdom of God and His righteousness. Jehoshaphat's heart thus exalted in God's ways. Accordingly, " he took away the high places and groves out of Judah." High places had long dotted the hilltops of Judah. They initially had been used as unofficial *ad hoc* places of sacrifice to Jehovah which were specifically prohibited in the Law. However, they eventually degenerated into places of Baal worship and other forms of idolatry. Jehoshaphat thus outlawed such in Judah and removed them all.

7 Also in the third year of his reign he sent to his princes, *even* to Benhail, and to Obadiah, and to Zechariah, and to Nethaneel, and to Michaiah, to teach in the cities of Judah. 8 And with them *he sent* Levites, *even* Shemaiah, and Nethaniah, and Zebadiah, and Asahel, and Shemiramoth, and Jehonathan, and Adonijah, and Tobijah, and Tobadonijah, Levites; and with them Elishama and Jehoram, priests. When Jehoshaphat had been king for less than two years, he organized a contingent of princes of Judah along with Levites and priests as named above. These were to teach the things of Jehovah God in the outlying towns of Judah.

9 And they taught in Judah, and *had* the book of the law of the LORD with them, and went about throughout all the cities of Judah, and taught the people. This small army of Bible teachers went from town to town in Judah, teaching the things of God from "the book of the law of the LORD with them." Jehoshaphat thus saw to it that the people of his realm were directly taught the Word of God. As a result, the following text will record that God blessed this king and his kingdom.

17:10-13 And the fear of the LORD fell upon all the kingdoms of the lands that *were* round about Judah, so that they made no war against Jehoshaphat. God clearly blessed Jehoshaphat and Judah because of the restored level of godliness and obedience to God instilled across his realm. God therefore caused other nations of the region to fear Jehoshaphat and Judah. Accordingly, they "made no war against Jehoshaphat." There indeed is a reward for the righteous (Psalm 58:11). God does bless the righteous (Psalm 5:12).

11 Also *some* of the Philistines brought Jehoshaphat presents, and tribute silver; and the Arabians brought him flocks, seven thousand and seven hundred rams, and seven thousand and seven hundred he goats. Even the long-standing, inveterate enemies of Judah, the Philistines, brought tribute money and gifts to Jehoshaphat. Arabian neighbors to the southeast, usually suspicious of Israel, presented Jehoshaphat with 7,700 rams and 7,700 he goats. God blessed this young king for his godliness.

12 And Jehoshaphat waxed great exceedingly; and he built in Judah castles, and cities of store. God therefore magnified Jehoshaphat and he became the greatest king in either kingdom of Israel since Solomon. He built castles (i.e., fortified military installations) and logistical bases throughout his kingdom for support should war come.

13 And he had much business in the cities of Judah: and the men of war, mighty men of valour, *were* in Jerusalem. The high places and groves referred to are a reference to places for Baal worship. As Jehoshaphat became aware of this abomination in his realm, he removed it. God not only prospered Jehoshaphat politically and militarily, he also blessed him personally. "He had much business in the cities of Judah." God honored him in His business dealings. As noted in the text below, God also gave Jehoshaphat brilliant military men for the defense of the nation.

17:14-18 And these *are* the numbers of them according to the house of their fathers: Of Judah, the captains of thousands; Adnah the chief, and with him mighty men of valour three hundred thousand. Jehoshaphat's chief general commanded a force of 300,000 men.

15 And next to him *was* Jehohanan the captain, and with him two hundred and fourscore thousand. Another general commanded 280,000 men.

16 And next him *was* Amasiah the son of Zichri, who willingly offered himself unto the LORD; and with him two hundred thousand mighty men of valour. Another general named Amasiah is described as having "willingly offered himself unto the LORD." He commanded a division of 200,000 men.

17 And of Benjamin; Eliada a mighty man of valour, and with him armed men with bow and shield two hundred thousand. From the Benjamin portion of Judah, Eliada commanded a division of archers numbering 200,000.

18 And next him *was* Jehozabad, and with him an hundred and fourscore thousand ready prepared for the war. Jehozabad evidently was another general from Benjamin who commanded a division of 180,000 soldiers who were active duty. The other forces evidently were ready-reserve units such as the modern army of Israel. Together, these various military divisions totaled an army of 1,160,000 men.

Notice also how Jehoshaphat's armed forces were increased. During the reign of his grandfather Abijah, the armies of Judah numbered 400,000 (13:3). Now, as God prospered the realm, Jehoshaphat armies had increased to 1,160,000 men. God honors those who honor him.

17:19 These waited on the king, beside *those* whom the king put in the fenced cities throughout all Judah. This vast army mentioned above served Jehoshaphat besides military units which were garrisoned in the walled cities of defense around the kingdom.

* * * * *

Understanding II Chronicles 589

Overview of II Chronicles 18: This next chapter reveals the weakness and compromise into which Jehoshaphat got himself. It seems that when God has blessed men who honor him, they at times forget who it was who so helped them. Here, Jehoshaphat foolishly joined forces with Ahab, one of the worst kings of the northern kingdom of Israel. In so doing he almost lost his life.

18:1-3 Now Jehoshaphat had riches and honour in abundance, and joined affinity with Ahab. 2 And after *certain* years he went down to Ahab to Samaria. And Ahab killed sheep and oxen for him in abundance, and for the people that *he had* with him, and persuaded him to go up *with him* to Ramothgilead. 3 And Ahab king of Israel said unto Jehoshaphat king of Judah, Wilt thou go with me to Ramothgilead? And he answered him, I *am* as thou *art*, and my people as thy people; and *we will be* with thee in the war.

Jehoshaphat evidently did not understand the principle of separation. He thus began to associate with Ahab, king of the north. Accordingly, Jehoshaphat journeyed to the Samaria where Ahab wined and dined him. Ahab therefore invited him to go to war with him against Syria at a place called Ramothgilead east of the Jordan River. (The name Ramoth-gilead literally the heights of Gilead or 'Gilead Heights.') Jehoshaphat immediately agreed in principle to go along.

18:4 And Jehoshaphat said unto the king of Israel, Enquire, I pray thee, at the word of the LORD to day. Jehoshaphat therefore urged Ahab to "enquire . . . at the word of the LORD to day." After he had made a foolish decision, he then piously (in effect) announced, "Maybe we had better pray about it."

18:5-8 Therefore the king of Israel gathered together of prophets four hundred men, and said unto them, Shall we

go to Ramothgilead to battle, or shall I forbear? And they said, Go up; for God will deliver *it* into the king's hand. 6 But Jehoshaphat said, *Is there* not here a prophet of the LORD besides, that we might enquire of him? 7 And the king of Israel said unto Jehoshaphat, *There is* yet one man, by whom we may enquire of the LORD: but I hate him; for he never prophesied good unto me, but always evil: the same *is* Micaiah the son of Imla. And Jehoshaphat said, Let not the king say so. 8 And the king of Israel called for one *of his* officers, and said, Fetch quickly Micaiah the son of Imla.

Verses 5-27 tell the bizarre story how Ahab gathered 400 of his apostate prophets who told him to "go for it." However, Jehoshaphat requested a prophet of Jehovah. Ahab said there was still one of them around but he hated him; "for he never prophesied good unto me, but always evil; the same is Micaiah."

18:9-11 And the king of Israel and Jehoshaphat king of Judah sat either of them on his throne, clothed in *their* robes, and they sat in a void place at the entering in of the gate of Samaria; and all the prophets prophesied before them. 10 And Zedekiah the son of Chenaanah had made him horns of iron, and said, Thus saith the LORD, With these thou shalt push Syria until they be consumed. 11 And all the prophets prophesied so, saying, Go up to Ramothgilead, and prosper: for the LORD shall deliver *it* into the hand of the king.

Thereupon, Ahab had all of his apostate prophets once again prophecy before him and they once again told him to go for it. They claimed God would deliver Syria into the king's hand.

18:12-15 And the messenger that went to call Micaiah spake to him, saying, Behold, the words of the prophets *declare* good to the king with one assent; let thy word

therefore, I pray thee, be like one of theirs, and speak thou good. 13 And Micaiah said, *As* the LORD liveth, even what my God saith, that will I speak. 14 And when he was come to the king, the king said unto him, Micaiah, shall we go to Ramothgilead to battle, or shall I forbear? And he said, Go ye up, and prosper, and they shall be delivered into your hand. 15 And the king said to him, How many times shall I adjure thee that thou say nothing but the truth to me in the name of the LORD?

Then Ahab and Jehoshaphat sought what Micaiah the prophet of Jehovah would say. Micaiah, knowing that all the other prophets had foretold success in the battle, did as well. (Evidently, being forthright was not one his virtues.) Ahab, sensing that Micaiah was being a 'yes' man admonished him to really tell him the truth.

18:16-27 Then he said, I did see all Israel scattered upon the mountains, as sheep that have no shepherd: and the LORD said, These have no master; let them return *therefore* every man to his house in peace. 17 And the king of Israel said to Jehoshaphat, Did I not tell thee *that* he would not prophesy good unto me, but evil? Whereupon, Micaiah said, "I did see all Israel scattered upon the mountains, as sheep that have no shepherd." In other words, in the coming battle, Ahab would be killed.

18 Again he said, Therefore hear the word of the LORD; I saw the LORD sitting upon his throne, and all the host of heaven standing on his right hand and *on* his left. 19 And the LORD said, Who shall entice Ahab king of Israel, that he may go up and fall at Ramothgilead? And one spake saying after this manner, and another saying after that manner. 20 Then there came out a spirit, and stood before the LORD, and said, I will entice him. And the LORD said unto him, Wherewith? 21 And he said, I will go out, and be a lying

spirit in the mouth of all his prophets. And *the* LORD said, Thou shalt entice *him*, and thou shalt also prevail: go out, and do *even* so. 22 **Now therefore, behold, the LORD hath put a lying spirit in the mouth of these thy prophets, and the LORD hath spoken evil against thee.**

It is not likely that this scene in heaven actually took place. Rather, Micaiah, perhaps at God' s leading, made up this story to illustrate the point. It may be that he used as an illustration a situation of which Ahab was familiar—a council with his advisors. Thus, in this purported counsel in heaven, God asked who would go and persuade Ahab to go to Ramoth to his defeat. One angel stepped forward and so volunteered. As this purported story continued, the Lord asked the angel how he intended to persuade Ahab to his defeat. The angel is to have answered that he would go and act as a lying spirit to the prophets of Ahab. By having them all say the same thing, he would thus persuade Ahab to go out to his death.

Once again, it should not be supposed that this event actually took place in heaven. There no longer are any unholy angels left there and God would not tolerate deceit. Rather, Micaiah made up the story altogether. At the least, it was a strategy to which Ahab could relate and illustrated how his 'yes-man' prophets could easily be led astray by a lying spirit.

23 Then Zedekiah the son of Chenaanah came near, and smote Micaiah upon the cheek, and said, Which way went the Spirit of the LORD from me to speak unto thee? 24 And Micaiah said, Behold, thou shalt see on that day when thou shalt go into an inner chamber to hide thyself. 2

5 Then the king of Israel said, Take ye Micaiah, and carry him back to Amon the governor of the city, and to Joash the king's son; 26 And say, Thus saith the king, Put this *fellow* in the prison, and feed him with bread of affliction and with water of affliction, until I return in peace. 27 And Micaiah said, If thou certainly return in peace, *then*

Understanding II Chronicles

hath not the LORD spoken by me. And he said, Hearken, all ye people

There resulted a heated confrontation between Micaiah and the lead prophet of Ahab named Zedekiah. The upshot was Ahab ordered Micaiah to prison for his candid prophecy. Micaiah's parting shot to Ahab was "If thou certainly return in peace, then hath not the LORD spoken by me." As the battle turned out, Micaiah was vindicated.

18:28-34 So the king of Israel and Jehoshaphat the king of Judah went up to Ramothgilead. 29 And the king of Israel said unto Jehoshaphat, I will disguise myself, and will go to the battle; but put thou on thy robes. So the king of Israel disguised himself; and they went to the battle. 30 Now the king of Syria had commanded the captains of the chariots that *were* with him, saying, Fight ye not with small or great, save only with the king of Israel. 31 And it came to pass, when the captains of the chariots saw Jehoshaphat, that they said, It *is* the king of Israel. Therefore they compassed about him to fight: but Jehoshaphat cried out, and the LORD helped him; and God moved them *to depart* from him.

32 For it came to pass, that, when the captains of the chariots perceived that it was not the king of Israel, they turned back again from pursuing him. 33 And a *certain* man drew a bow at a venture, and smote the king of Israel between the joints of the harness: therefore he said to his chariot man, Turn thine hand, that thou mayest carry me out of the host; for I am wounded. 34 And the battle increased that day: howbeit the king of Israel stayed *himself* up in *his* chariot against the Syrians until the even: and about the time of the sun going down he died.

The lack of leadership in Ahab remains apparent. Knowing that the enemy might target him because he was king, he hatched the idea of going into battle incognito. He therefore convinced Jehoshaphat to wear his royal robes and thus appear as the king of Israel. Foolish Jehoshaphat still went into battle with Ahab. Ahab thus disguised himself but encouraged Jehoshaphat to go forth in his royal robes. Jehoshaphat was gullible enough to do so.

The Syrian king directed his divisional officers to ignore the common foot soldiers and rather go for the king of Israel. Thus upon joining the battle, they spied Jehoshaphat dressed in the royal array of Ahab and supposed it was him. They therefore focused their attack against Jehoshaphat. Realizing what was happening, Jehoshaphat cried out. It may be that he cried out to let the Syrians know who he was. Or, it may be that he cried out to God for help. It was only by God's providential care, he was not killed in the battle.

Implicit is that a soldier in the Syrian army drew his bow and shot it indiscriminately into the battle. The arrow not only found its way to Ahab, but pierced him at the joints of his armor. There can be little question that God so providentially directed that arrow to strike Ahab at such a small place—between the joints of his body armor. Ahab knew he was in trouble. He thus directed the driver of his chariot to retreat from the battle. The idea is that Ahab was propped up in his chariot the rest of that day, but died at sundown. Meanwhile, the blood from his wound ran down into his chariot. The stage for fulfilled prophecy was being set.

Realizing that their king was dead, word went out through the army of Israel to retreat. It turned into a rout. By sundown of that day, Israel was clearly defeated in the battle. The prophecy made by Micaiah was fulfilled in detail.

* * * * *

Understanding II Chronicles

Overview of II Chronicles 19*: This next chapter records how that God rebuked Jehoshaphat for his compromise. A sadder and chastened man, Jehoshaphat returned to strengthening the worship of Jehovah God in his kingdom and establishing a sound judicial system in the land.*

19:1-3 And Jehoshaphat the king of Judah returned to his house in peace to Jerusalem. 2 And Jehu the son of Hanani the seer went out to meet him, and said to king Jehoshaphat, Shouldest thou help the ungodly, and love them that hate the LORD? therefore *is* wrath upon thee from before the LORD.

God sent a prophet named Jehu to rebuke Jehoshaphat. Notice that God through the prophet confronted him, to wit: "Shouldest thou help the ungodly, and love them that hate the LORD? therefore is wrath upon thee from before the LORD." Yet in verse 3 God remembered Jehoshaphat's faithfulness otherwise. The wrath spoken of probably came in chapter 20. Jehoshaphat had no business having fellowship with Ahab. The latter was an apostate. They may have been colleagues in that both were kings over God's people. Jehu called Ahab ungodly and Jehoshaphat certainly knew that as well. By compromising the principle of separation, Jehoshaphat entered into a cooperative 'ministry' which God clearly did not endorse. Preachers to this day do the same when they join in cooperative ministries with compromisers and liberals. God is not pleased with them either.

3 Nevertheless there are good things found in thee, in that thou hast taken away the groves out of the land, and hast prepared thine heart to seek God. Notwithstanding the rebuke from God through the prophet, God still acknowledged the good which Jehoshaphat had done in exterminating groves wherein idolatry took place across the land. He moreover had prepared his heart to seek God. For these, God commended him.

19:4-7 And Jehoshaphat dwelt at Jerusalem: and he went out again through the people from Beersheba to mount Ephraim, and brought them back unto the LORD God of their fathers.

Like he had done earlier in his tenure as king, Jehoshaphat saw to it that the Word of God was taught directly to his people across the land. Earlier, he had sent others to teach. Now, he himself evidently went across his kingdom teaching the Word of God "from Beersheba to mount Ephraim." The latter thought is from one end of the kingdom to the other.

Beersheba was in the far south and Ephraim was the northern border of Judah. In so doing, Jehoshaphat brought his nation "back unto the LORD God of their fathers." Two things are evident: (1) even Judah was prone to quickly backslide from God and (2) Jehoshaphat was willing to do whatever was necessary to turn them back to God. Indeed, he was one of the great and godly kings of Judah.

5 And he set judges in the land throughout all the fenced cities of Judah, city by city, 6 And said to the judges, Take heed what ye do: for ye judge not for man, but for the LORD, who *is* with you in the judgment. 7 Wherefore now let the fear of the LORD be upon you; take heed and do *it*: for *there is* no iniquity with the LORD our God, nor respect of persons, nor taking of gifts.

Jehoshaphat also appointed a special judiciary of judges in all the important outlying cities of Judah who were to sit in judgment over day-to-day disputes of the people. However, he straitly warned them that they were not to judge as men, but on behalf of the Lord. In so doing, God would help them make right decisions. He therefore admonished them to sit as judges in the fear of the Lord. He further reminded them that God was just. He did not respect persons and He would not take bribes. So these judges were to do the same.

Understanding II Chronicles

19:8-11 Moreover in Jerusalem did Jehoshaphat set of the Levites, and *of* the priests, and of the chief of the fathers of Israel, for the judgment of the LORD, and for controversies, when they returned to Jerusalem. 9 And he charged them, saying, Thus shall ye do in the fear of the LORD, faithfully, and with a perfect heart.

10 And what cause soever shall come to you of your brethren that dwell in their cities, between blood and blood, between law and commandment, statutes and judgments, ye shall even warn them that they trespass not against the LORD, and *so* wrath come upon you, and upon your brethren: this do, and ye shall not trespass. 11 And, behold, Amariah the chief priest *is* over you in all matters of the LORD; and Zebadiah the son of Ishmael, the ruler of the house of Judah, for all the king's matters: also the Levites *shall be* officers before you. Deal courageously, and the LORD shall be with the good.

In similar fashion to the judges he appointed across the land, Jehoshaphat also appointed Levites, priests, and elders of the land in Jerusalem to hear controversies of the people when they were in Jerusalem. This likely was an appellate court. These as well were admonished to so judge in the "in the fear of the LORD, faithfully, and with a perfect heart." These judges were also to straitly warn those coming before them lest they "trespass not against the LORD, and *so* wrath come upon you, and upon your brethren." Jehoshaphat also appointed 'chief justices.' For disputes pertaining to things of God, Amariah the chief priest was appointed. Zebadiah was appointed as a chief justice for things pertaining to the house of Judah and for other civil matters. Levites would also serve as officers of the court. Therefore, Jehoshaphat charged his newly appointed judiciary to "Deal courageously, and the LORD shall be with the good." As these judges had the courage to make just decisions, God would be those who did good.

Overview of II Chronicles 20: *Record is here made how that God allowed Jehoshaphat to be invaded by a massive army from Ammon and Moab. This may have been God's means of chastening Jehoshaphat for his earlier compromise. However, Jehoshaphat, to his credit, sought the LORD in the greatest crisis of his life and God miraculously delivered Judah.*

20:1-2 It came to pass after this also, *that* **the children of Moab, and the children of Ammon, and with them** *other* **beside the Ammonites, came against Jehoshaphat to battle. 2 Then there came some that told Jehoshaphat, saying, There cometh a great multitude against thee from beyond the sea on this side Syria; and, behold, they** *be* **in Hazazontamar, which** *is* **Engedi.**

Sometime after the debacle of Jehoshaphat's alliance with Ahab, a coalition of armies from Moab, Ammon, and Mount Seir of that region invaded Judah. (Moab and Ammon, in modern terms, is the state of Jordan.) Reports thus reached Jehoshaphat how that a large invasion force had crossed the narrows of the Dead Sea and marched as far north as Engedi on the west shore of the Dead Sea. (This very well may be the chastening wrath of God foretold in 19:2 for Jehoshaphat's compromise with Ahab.)

20:3-4 As Jehoshaphat was invaded from the east (verses 1-2), he **feared, and set himself to seek the LORD, and proclaimed a fast throughout all Judah. 4 And Judah gathered themselves together, to ask help of the LORD even out of all the cities of Judah they came to seek the LORD.** Jehoshaphat therefore proclaimed a season of fasting throughout Judah to seek God's help. Because of this godly king's efforts, the entire nation assembled at the Temple at Jerusalem for prayer.

20:5-13 In verses 5-12 is recorded the eloquent and fervent prayer of Jehoshaphat. **And Jehoshaphat stood in the congregation of Judah and Jerusalem, in the house of the LORD, before the new court, 6 And said, O LORD God of our fathers, *art* not thou God in heaven? and rulest *not* thou over all the kingdoms of the heathen? and in thine hand *is there not* power and might, so that none is able to withstand thee? 7 *Art* not thou our God, *who* didst drive out the inhabitants of this land before thy people Israel, and gavest it to the seed of Abraham thy friend for ever?**

Jehoshaphat therefore stood in the court of the Temple and publicly cried out to God for help. He began his eloquent, fervent prayer by reminding God of who He is—the Almighty God of heaven. He further reminded God how that He had heretofore driven out the heathen nations which had previously occupied the land, giving it to Abraham's seed. (Notice also how Abraham is once again referred to as the friend of God in verse 7.)

8 And they dwelt therein, and have built thee a sanctuary therein for thy name, saying, 9 If, *when* evil cometh upon us, *as* the sword, judgment, or pestilence, or famine, we stand before this house, and in thy presence, (for thy name *is* in this house,) and cry unto thee in our affliction, then thou wilt hear and help. Jehoshaphat continued his prayer by reminding God that when the Temple was built that God had promised help if in trouble. Specifically, God had promised that if His people would prayer either in the Temple or toward it in time of crisis that He would hear and help. See II Chronicles 6:19*ff.*

10 And now, behold, the children of Ammon and Moab and mount Seir, whom thou wouldest not let Israel invade, when they came out of the land of Egypt, but they turned from them, and destroyed them not; 11 Behold, *I say, how* they reward us, to come to cast us out of thy possession,

which thou hast given us to inherit. Jehoshaphat therefore reminded God that the Ammonites and Moabites had invaded his nation. Moreover, he reminded God how when Israel had marched through that region after the exodus that they did not molest them. Therefore, Jehoshaphat reminded God how these kingdoms now treated Judah these many years later.

12 O our God, wilt thou not judge them? for we have no might against this great company that cometh against us; neither know we what to do: but our eyes *are* upon thee. With powerful eloquence, Jehoshaphat therefore invoked God to judge the Moabites and Ammonites with defeat. With profound faith, he pled before God that Judah had "no might against this great company that cometh against us."

He continued, "neither know we what to do: but our eyes *are* upon thee." There can be no clearer illustration of fervent prayer or of simple faith. Jehoshaphat had no recourse but to look up. He did not have a solution for the crisis before him. He could only look to God for help. That he did. Clearly evident was a total dependance upon the God of heaven to deliver them. That is faith! God to this day is moved when His people seek His deliverance in simple faith.

13 And all Judah stood before the LORD, with their little ones, their wives, and their children. Jehoshaphat's prayer was public. The entire nation of Judah, including wives and children, were assembled as Jehoshaphat publicly cried out to God for help. Moreover, Jehoshaphat's prayer was on solid scriptural ground. He was in fulfillment of the condition for answer prayer given in II Chronicles 6. Therefore, God was honor-bound to answer. That He did.

20:14-19 Then upon Jahaziel the son of Zechariah, the son of Benaiah, the son of Jeiel, the son of Mattaniah, a Levite of the sons of Asaph, came the Spirit of the LORD in the midst of the congregation. In the assembled congregation of Judah at the Temple was a Levite of the sons of Asaph named Jahaziel. On Him "came the Spirit of the LORD in the midst of the congregation." The Spirit coming on one in the Old Testament is analogous to if not synonymous with the filling of the Holy Spirit in the New Testament. What this Levite was about to say was through the agency of the direction and power of the Holy Spirit.

15 And he said, Hearken ye, all Judah, and ye inhabitants of Jerusalem, and thou king Jehoshaphat, Thus saith the LORD unto you, Be not afraid nor dismayed by reason of this great multitude; for the battle *is* not yours, but God's. This Spirit-filled Levite turned prophet announced to all present including the king. His pronouncement was from God—"Thus saith the LORD unto you." His message was simple. Do not be afraid or dismayed by the massive invading army from the east: "for the battle *is* not yours, but God's." What a wonderful perception! The coming battle really was not theirs but God's. God would fight against their enemies and defeat them.

16 To morrow go ye down against them: behold, they come up by the cliff of Ziz; and ye shall find them at the end of the brook, before the wilderness of Jeruel. 17 Ye shall not *need* to fight in this *battle*: set yourselves, stand ye *still*, and see the salvation of the LORD with you, O Judah and Jerusalem: fear not, nor be dismayed; to morrow go out against them: for the LORD *will be* with you.

Jahaziel informed Jehoshaphat that tomorrow they were to go out to meet the invaders from the east. Meanwhile, the Moabites and company had pushed north westward toward Jerusalem, up through the ascent of Ziz. The latter was a cut or pass through the mountainous country from Engedi. The Moabites and allies had thus pushed as far as "the brook, before the wilderness of Jeruel." There, Judah would find the Moabite army. However, Jahaziel informed them that they would not need to fight. Rather, he directed Judah to "set yourselves, stand ye *still*, and see the salvation of the LORD with you, O Judah and Jerusalem." He further counseled Judah to "fear not, nor be dismayed; to morrow go out against them: for the LORD *will be* with you." In ways not yet announced, Jahaziel foretold how that the next day God would be with Judah in the looming battle against Moab and company.

18 And Jehoshaphat bowed his head with *his* face to the ground: and all Judah and the inhabitants of Jerusalem fell before the LORD, worshipping the LORD. 19 And the Levites, of the children of the Kohathites, and of the children of the Korhites, stood up to praise the LORD God of Israel with a loud voice on high. Upon hearing such encouragement, Jehoshaphat and the assembled congregation of Judah therefore fell on their faces before God and worshiped Him. In addition, the Temple choirs of the Levites rose to sing praise to God with all their might.

20:20-25 And they rose early in the morning, and went forth into the wilderness of Tekoa: and as they went forth, Jehoshaphat stood and said, Hear me, O Judah, and ye inhabitants of Jerusalem; Believe in the LORD your God, so shall ye be established; believe his prophets, so shall ye prosper. Next morning at the crack of dawn, Jehoshaphat led the nation of Judah into the wilderness of Tekoa which was southeast of Jerusalem and about nine miles southeast of Bethlehem. The countryside was rugged. But as they marched, Jehoshaphat announced to his people, "Believe in the LORD your God, so shall ye be established; believe his prophets, so shall ye prosper." As they trusted in their God and His Word through His prophets, they would prevail and prosper. That truth remains to this day.

21 And when he had consulted with the people, he appointed singers unto the LORD, and that should praise

the beauty of holiness, as they went out before the army, and to say, Praise the LORD; for his mercy *endureth* for ever. Jehoshaphat therefore consulted with the people and appointed a choir even there, approaching the field of battle. That choir was to praise the beauty of God's holiness and to sing, "Praise the LORD; for his mercy *endureth* for ever." They may in fact have sung Psalm 96 and 136. These psalms set forth the two fold message noted above.

22 And when they began to sing and to praise, the LORD set ambushments against the children of Ammon, Moab, and mount Seir, which were come against Judah; and they were smitten. What a strange battle scene was at hand. Rather than sending out an army against the Moabites, Judah sent choirs singing praise to God at the scene. As they did, "the LORD set ambushments against the children of Ammon, Moab, and Mount Seir." As the coalition forces of Ammon, Moab, and Mount Seir headed into the hill country of Judah, God caused them to begin to ambush each other "and they were smitten."

23 For the children of Ammon and Moab stood up against the inhabitants of mount Seir, utterly to slay and destroy *them*: and when they had made an end of the inhabitants of Seir, every one helped to destroy another. As the armies of these several kingdoms marched against Judah, the Ammonites and Moabites turned on the forces of Mount Seir. God clearly caused the forces of Mount Seir to somehow or other provoke their erstwhile allies and they turned against them. After slaughtering the forces from Mount Seir, then the Moabites and Ammonites began to fight amongst themselves to the degree that managed to destroy each other. When they were done, these three supposed allies had all killed each other.

24 And when Judah came toward the watch tower in the wilderness, they looked unto the multitude, and, behold, they *were* dead bodies fallen to the earth, and none escaped. When Jehoshaphat and his people finally arrived on the scene, no doubt later in the day, they came to a watch tower (or perhaps a lookout point) above the wilderness of Tekoa below. All they could see was a sea of dead bodies before them.

25 And when Jehoshaphat and his people came to take away the spoil of them, they found among them in abundance both riches with the dead bodies, and precious jewels, which they stripped off for themselves, more than they could carry away: and they were three days in gathering of the spoil, it was so much. Therefore, Jehoshaphat and his people stripped the dead of valuables, money, and jewelry to the degree they could not carry it all. In fact, they spent three days looting the battlefield of spoils, there was so much. Evidently, the enemies of Judah had gone to battle with their finest clothes, jewelry, and weapons, thinking to impress their foes. Jehoshaphat and company took it home with them.

20:26-30 And on the fourth day they assembled themselves in the valley of Berachah; for there they blessed the LORD: therefore the name of the same place was called, The valley of Berachah, unto this day. On the fourth day after the slaughter, Judah assembled themselves in "the valley of Berachah." The latter was still in the wilderness of Tekoa and literally means 'the valley of blessing.' Indeed, God had blessed Judah on that spot.

27 Then they returned, every man of Judah and Jerusalem, and Jehoshaphat in the forefront of them, to go again to Jerusalem with joy; for the LORD had made them to rejoice over their enemies. 28 And they came to Jerusalem with psalteries and harps and trumpets unto the house of the LORD. Jehoshaphat thus led a triumphant return to Jerusalem. They accordingly came to Jerusalem and the Temple with songs of joy accompanied by a Levitical marching band.

29 And the fear of God was on all the kingdoms of *those* **countries, when they had heard that the LORD fought against the enemies of Israel. 30 So the realm of Jehoshaphat was quiet: for his God gave him rest round about.** Not only did God give Jehoshaphat and Judah a great victory, but God also caused other nations of the region to fear Him. They heard how that God had miraculously intervened on behalf of Judah and Jehoshaphat. Therefore, the realm of Jehoshaphat was quiet from invasions or attacks because God gave them peace. In-deed, a major blessing of God is peace with others. He so blessed Jehoshaphat for His godliness, faith, and righteousness.

20:31-34 And Jehoshaphat reigned over Judah: *he was* **thirty and five years old when he began to reign, and he reigned twenty and five years in Jerusalem. And his mother's name** *was* **Azubah the daughter of Shilhi. 32 And he walked in the way of Asa his father, and departed not from it, doing** *that which was* **right in the sight of the LORD.**

The reign of Jehoshaphat is here summarized. He acceded the throne at the age of thirty five and reigned for twenty-five years. Significant is the epitaph, "And he walked in the way of Asa his father, and departed not from it, doing *that which was* right in the sight of the LORD." Even as Asa had primarily done that which was right before the Lord (14:2), so did Jehoshaphat. Though erring in the matter of Ahab, in the main, Jehoshaphat "departed not from it, doing *that which was* right in the sight of the LORD." Indeed, God will bless the righteous (Psalm 5:12). Because of Jehoshaphat's righteousness, God richly blessed him.

33 Howbeit the high places were not taken away: for as yet the people had not prepared their hearts unto the God of their fathers. Though a godly and righteous king, Jehoshaphat failed to remove the high places from the hilltops across Judah. Though he had eradicated idol worship (17:6), he allowed the hilltop places of worship to remain. These were used to worship Jehovah, but were in violation of the command to worship only at the Temple (Deuteronomy 12:5-7). Though Jehoshaphat had made concerted efforts to teach and train his people in the ways of the Lord over the years, nevertheless, they failed to completely prepare their hearts unto God. Because of their spiritual lackadaisicalness, they failed to seek and serve Him wholly and according to his will in offering sacrifices to Him only at Jerusalem as the Law required. Thus, when a strong godly king such as Jehoshaphat passed the scene, Judah easily slid back into idolatry and other sins.

34 Now the rest of the acts of Jehoshaphat, first and last, behold, they *are* written in the book of Jehu the son of Hanani, who *is* mentioned in the book of the kings of Israel. Further details of Jehoshaphat's reign were recorded in the uninspired chronicle of "Jehu the son of Hanani." He is also mentioned in I Kings 16:1, 7 and II Chronicles 19:2.

20:35-37 And after this did Jehoshaphat king of Judah join himself with Ahaziah king of Israel, who did very wickedly: 36 And he joined himself with him to make ships to go to Tarshish: and they made the ships in Eziongeber. It would seem that for all his good, Jehoshaphat simply would not refrain himself from compromise with the ungodly kings of the northern kingdom. Perhaps, he had a 'professional colleague' view of them and that they were of the same 'fraternity' of kings. Notwithstanding his severe reprimand by God through the prophet Jehu in 19:2, Jehoshaphat again entered in an alliance with "Ahaziah king of Israel, who did very wickedly." Ahaziah walked in the ways of Ahab his father and of Jezebel his mother and of Jeroboam the son of Nebat. See I Kings 22:52. Jehoshaphat no doubt was aware of this.

Nevertheless, he entered into a business partnership and thus was unequally yoked together with Ahaziah. They proposed to build ships at Eziongeber (Elat in modern terms) on the gulf of Elat of the Red Sea. In turn, they planned to send their ships to Tarshish for lucrative business prospects.

37 Then Eliezer the son of Dodavah of Mareshah prophesied against Jehoshaphat, saying, Because thou hast joined thyself with Ahaziah, the LORD hath broken thy works. And the ships were broken, that they were not able to go to Tarshish. In the meantime, God sent another prophet by the name of Eliezer to Jehoshaphat who confronted him for his error. The prophet informed Jehoshaphat, "Because thou hast joined thyself with Ahaziah, the LORD hath broken thy works." Because Jehoshaphat had entered into a business partnership with Ahaziah, God would wreck his plan. God thus sent a storm or some other naval mishap which caused the ships of Jehoshaphat and Ahaziah to be wrecked. Their plan was thus thwarted. The otherwise godly life and reign of Jehoshaphat here ends on this dismal note. God never blesses compromise with apostates. That principle remains to this day.

* * * * *

Overview of II Chronicles 21: Chapters 21 and 22 of II Chronicles detail two of the worst kings of Judah—Jehoram and Ahaziah. Both did evil in the eyes of the Lord and both were dealt with severely by God. II Chronicles 21 presents the ignoble reign of Jehoram, Jehoshaphat's son. His reign lasted eight years during which God smote him with an incurable disease and he died.

21:1-4 Now Jehoshaphat slept with his fathers, and was buried with his fathers in the city of David. And Jehoram his son reigned in his stead. Upon the death of Jehoshaphat, Jehoram, his son acceded the throne of Judah.

2 And he had brethren the sons of Jehoshaphat, Azariah, and Jehiel, and Zechariah, and Azariah, and Michael, and Shephatiah: all these *were* **the sons of Jehoshaphat king of Israel. 3 And their father gave them great gifts of silver, and of gold, and of precious things, with fenced cities in Judah: but the kingdom gave he to Jehoram; because he** *was* **the firstborn. 4 Now when Jehoram was risen up to the kingdom of his father, he strengthened himself, and slew all his brethren with the sword, and** *divers* **also of the princes of Israel.**

Notice how that Jehoram was one of seven brothers. Jehoshaphat, their father, had given to each of them a handsome inheritance of money and authority. However, once Jehoram the first born was established as king, he killed all his brothers. He thus ended any possible rivalry from them.

21:5-7 Jehoram *was* **thirty and two years old when he began to reign, and he reigned eight years in Jerusalem.** This wicked and ruthless king ascended the throne when he was thirty-two years old and reigned until he was forty.

6 And he walked in the way of the kings of Israel, like as did the house of Ahab: for he had the daughter of Ahab to wife: and he wrought that which was evil in the eyes of the LORD. Israel, the northern kingdom, had been apostate from its beginning. Ahab was one of the worst kings of the north spiritually. Marrying his daughter only provided further wrong influence. Thus, Jehoram set his course of forsaking the Lord.

7 Howbeit the LORD would not destroy the house of David, because of the covenant that he had made with David, and as he promised to give a light to him and to his sons for ever. The only thing which prevented God from destroying Jehoram immediately was the covenant which He had made with David, his forefather. God had promised David a royal dynasty in perpetuity. The phrase "to give a light to him and to his sons for ever" refers to the Davidic Covenant and God's promise to maintain the line of David forever.

In one respect, there is a picture of salvation and God's blessing thereafter. Though Jehoram was relatively secure in his position as king because of the covenant God made with David, there was no guarantee of God's blessing. To the contrary, God severely chastened Jehoram for his ungodliness.

21:8-10 In his days the Edomites revolted from under the dominion of Judah, and made themselves a king. Edom was a nation which had been subjugated by David and down to the time of Jehoshaphat was governed by a tributary ruler. They had been part of the invasion of Judah against Jehoshaphat. See the preceding chapter. But now, they revolted against rule by Judah. Things were not going well for Jehoram.

9 Then Jehoram went forth with his princes, and all his chariots with him: and he rose up by night, and smote the Edomites which compassed him in, and the captains of the chariots. Jehoram therefore was forced to try and subjugate Edom. In this first attempt, Jehoram succeeded. However, as will be evident below, Edom succeeded in revolting against Judah and Judah's suzerainty over them.

10 So the Edomites revolted from under the hand of Judah unto this day. The same time *also* did Libnah revolt from under his hand; because he had forsaken the LORD God of his fathers. Not only did Edom succeed in revolting from Judah, but also the area of Libnah, thought to be to the south of Judah, also revolted. Clearly implied is that Jehoram was impotent to prevent either from seceding. The reason for his trouble and loss of influence is made clear: "because he had forsaken the LORD God of his fathers." God's blessing was removed from Jehoram and Judah. Rather, God had begun to chasten him for his sin.

21:11-15 Moreover he made high places in the mountains of Judah, and caused the inhabitants of Jerusalem to commit fornication, and compelled Judah *thereto*.

Whereas the high places in Judah had been used for sacrifice to Jehovah during the reign of Jehoshaphat, now Jehoram converted them to places of idolatry—likely Baal worship. In referring to Judah committing fornication, there is a clear double thought. Baal worship was spiritual adultery as God's people were unfaithful to their God. However, Baal worship was a pagan form of fertility rites in which sex acts were performed at the high places with the thought of (sexually) arousing Baal to send fertility to the land. Thus, those involved in Baal worship engaged in 'religious' prostitution as part of the abominable rites.

Therefore, both spiritual as well as physical adultery took place at the high places for Baal worship. The notion of going to a high place was so they presumably would be closer to their god. The practice of sex acts were intended to so arouse and stimulate their god Baal, so he would send fertility to their land, their wives, and their livestock

12 And there came a writing to him from Elijah the prophet, saying, Thus saith the LORD God of David thy father, Because thou hast not walked in the ways of Jehoshaphat thy father, nor in the ways of Asa king of Judah, 13 But hast walked in the way of the kings of Israel, and hast made Judah and the inhabitants of Jerusalem to go a whoring, like to the whoredoms of the house of Ahab, and also hast slain thy brethren of thy father's house, *which were* better than thyself.

God therefore sent a written message from Elijah to Jehoram. This is the first and only place in Chronicles were mention is made of Elijah the prophet. The message from God thus confronted Jehoram and his sin. Jehoram had forsaken the

Understanding II Chronicles 611

ways of Jehoshaphat his father and Asa his grandfather. Rather, Jehoram had gone the way of the kings of the northern kingdom Israel. In so doing, he made Judah and Jerusalem to "to go a whoring, like to the whoredoms of the house of Ahab." As noted in the comments for verse 11, the whoring of Judah was both spiritual and physical in Baal worship. Furthermore, God confronted Jehoram for the murder of his six brothers, all of whom God said were better than Jehoram.

14 Behold, with a great plague will the LORD smite thy people, and thy children, and thy wives, and all thy goods: 15 And thou *shalt have* great sickness by disease of thy bowels, until thy bowels fall out by reason of the sickness day by day.

The letter from Elijah therefore informed Jehoram that God was about to send calamities upon his immediate family, including his wives, children, and all their goods. His country would be ravaged, his capital taken, his palace plundered, his wives carried off, and all his children slain except the youngest. As for Jehoram himself, God was about to send an incurable disease of painful dysentery in which it seemed as if his very bowels would fall out. Inasmuch as he had no bowels of compassion for his murdered brothers, his own bowels would be ravaged with disease.

21:16-20 Moreover the LORD stirred up against Jehoram the spirit of the Philistines, and of the Arabians, that *were* near the Ethiopians: 17 And they came up into Judah, and brake into it, and carried away all the substance that was found in the king's house, and his sons also, and his wives; so that there was never a son left him, save Jehoahaz, the youngest of his sons. In the course of events soon to follow, God allowed Philistines and Arabian Ethiopians (the latter living in the southern part of the Arabian peninsula) to plunder Judah and Jerusalem. They robbed Jehoram's palace, took his wives, and killed all but one of his sons, Jehoahaz his youngest. The prophecy made by Elijah from God was coming to pass.

18 And after all this the LORD smote him in his bowels with an incurable disease. 19 And it came to pass, that in process of time, after the end of two years, his bowels fell out by reason of his sickness: so he died of sore diseases. And his people made no burning for him, like the burning of his fathers. The precise disease which God smote Jehoram with is not clear, but it is generally thought to have been a bloody dysentery. John Gill notes the possibility of "an 'hernia,' or rupture; others, the falling of the 'anus,' or a fistula in it; others, the colic, or iliac passion"—all of which sounds terrible. Upon his death, the people of Judah did not burn incense in respect to him. In other words, Jehoram was not given a regular funeral.

20 Thirty and two years old was he when he began to reign, and he reigned in Jerusalem eight years, and departed without being desired. Howbeit they buried him in the city of David, but not in the sepulchres of the kings. After reining for eight years, Jehoram died and "departed without being desired." Nobody missed him when he was gone. What a sad commentary upon the life of an apostate ruler. He was therefore buried, but not in the royal cemetery reserved for the kings of Judah in the city of David in east Jerusalem.

* * * * *

***Overview of II Chronicles 22:** This chapter presents the brief reign of Ahaziah. (He also used the names of Jehoahaz and Azariah.) He reigned one year and was killed. He, like Jehoram his father, did wickedly.*

22:1-4 And the inhabitants of Jerusalem made Ahaziah his youngest son king in his stead: for the band of men that

came with the Arabians to the camp had slain all the eldest. So Ahaziah the son of Jehoram king of Judah reigned. 2 Forty and two years old *was* Ahaziah when he began to reign, and he reigned one year in Jerusalem. His mother's name also *was* Athaliah the daughter of Omri.** After the chastening raid by the Philistines and Arabians (20:16-17) in which all but Jehoahaz, youngest son of Jehoram was slain, Jehoahaz, (here called Ahaziah) was made king of Judah. The instability of this wicked king is found in the shortness of his reign—one year. He was the son of the wicked Athaliah, the daughter of Omri.

3 He also walked in the ways of the house of Ahab: for his mother was his counsellor to do wickedly. Notice how Ahaziah walked in the ways of the house of Ahab. He, like his father was an ungodly king. Moreover it was his own mother who was his counsellor to do wickedly. (Recall that his mother was Ahab's daughter, the wicked king of the north.) What a sad commentary that a mother was the chief influence of wrong in this man's life.

Consequently, verse 4 records that **4 he did evil in the sight of the LORD like the house of Ahab: for they were his counsellors after the death of his father to his destruction.** What a pathetic comment that family and friends could be one's counselors to destruction. The reason was simple. They had rejected the Word of God and were therefore ensnared in the bottomless morass of human wisdom. Modern liberalism is much the same. They, as well, have rejected the Word of God and have sought to replace it with all of their bright ideas. The decadence of the culture which is destroying the land is a testimony to their folly.

22:7 He walked also after their counsel, and went with Jehoram the son of Ahab king of Israel to war against Hazael king of Syria at Ramothgilead: and the Syrians

smote Joram. Ahaziah walked according to the godless and corrupt philosophy of the Israel, the northern kingdom. The sitting king in the north at this time was also named Jehoram. He, like his father Ahab, decided to try to go to war against Syria at Ramothgilead (the heights of Gilead). And, like his father, Jehoram was also soundly defeated at Ramothgilead.

6 And he returned to be healed in Jezreel because of the wounds which were given him at Ramah, when he fought with Hazael king of Syria. And Azariah the son of Jehoram king of Judah went down to see Jehoram the son of Ahab at Jezreel, because he was sick. Jehoram was taken wounded back to Jezreel to heal. Here Ahaziah is also called Azariah (also Jehoahaz). The severally named king therefore journeyed north to Jezreel to visit Jehoram.

7 And the destruction of Ahaziah was of God by coming to Joram: for when he was come, he went out with Jehoram against Jehu the son of Nimshi, whom the LORD had anointed to cut off the house of Ahab. Yet, God providentially had plans for the death of wicked Ahaziah. Upon arriving, Ahaziah walked into an erupting *coup d' etat* by Jehu against Jehoram and the house of Ahab. See I Kings 10:12-14.

22:8-9 And it came to pass, that, when Jehu was executing judgment upon the house of Ahab, and found the princes of Judah, and the sons of the brethren of Ahaziah, that ministered to Ahaziah, he slew them. Princes of Judah had also traveled north to Samaria. When Jehu discovered these compromising princes of Judah in Samaria (who were the brothers of Ahaziah), he killed all of them. See II Kings 10:12-14.

9 And he sought Ahaziah: and they caught him, (for he was hid in Samaria,) and brought him to Jehu: and when they had slain him, they buried him: Because, said they, he *is* the son of Jehoshaphat, who sought the LORD with all his

heart. **So the house of Ahaziah had no power to keep still the kingdom.** Upon also finding Ahaziah in Samaria, Jehu killed him as well. For Ahaziah, at least, he was afforded a decent burial—something not given to Jehoram. Ahaziah was given a proper burial because he was the grandson of Jehoshaphat, the godly king of Judah. However, Ahaziah was also the grandson of Omri through his mother Athaliah. Thus, the reign of Ahaziah was short lived and he perished in the way.

22:10-12 But when Athaliah the mother of Ahaziah saw that her son was dead, she arose and destroyed all the seed royal of the house of Judah. When word reached Jerusalem of what had happened at Samaria, the queen mother, Athaliah the mother of Ahaziah, promptly proceeded to kill the rest of the royal family of the house of Judah and set herself up as queen. (Recall that she was Omri's daughter.)

11 But Jehoshabeath, the daughter of the king, took Joash the son of Ahaziah, and stole him from among the king's sons that were slain, and put him and his nurse in a bedchamber. So Jehoshabeath, the daughter of king Jehoram, the wife of Jehoiada the priest, (for she was the sister of Ahaziah,) hid him from Athaliah, so that she slew him not. Witnessing this wicked carnage at Jerusalem was Jehoshabeath who was Ahaziah's sister (and daughter of Jehoram). She was the wife of Jehoiada the high priest. Realizing that there was an infant son of Ahaziah, Jehoshabeath, as his aunt, snatched the infant and his nurse and hid them in an apartment in the Temple. Not only was the child hidden, but Athaliah apparently did not even know it.

12 And he was with them hid in the house of God six years: and Athaliah reigned over the land. Little Joash was therefore hidden in the Temple for six years while his wicked grandmother reigned over the land. The latter apparently was oblivious to the fact that the true heir to the throne was secretly being raised in the Temple.

* * * * *

Overview of II Chronicles 23: *Chapters 23-24 detail the life and reign of Joash, the next king of Judah. It is a fascinating story of political intrigue and justified treason. The mentor and patron of Joash was the high priest Jehoiada. Throughout the life time of Jehoiada, Joash did right before God. However, upon the death of Jehoiada, Joash sadly turned away from the Lord and even betrayed the goodness of Jehoiada to him. The end of Joash was an ignoble time of military defeat and ultimately assassination.*

II Chronicles 23 presents the account of the unusual accession to power of king Joash. Briefly, recall that Joash as an infant had been hid by his aunt Jehoshabeath (the wife of the high priest Jehoiada) from the wicked Athaliah. She had usurped the throne when king Ahaziah was killed. (She also had murdered all of the other sons of Ahaziah to clear the throne for herself.)

23:1-3 And in the seventh year Jehoiada strengthened himself, and took the captains of hundreds, Azariah the son of Jeroham, and Ishmael the son of Jehohanan, and Azariah the son of Obed, and Maaseiah the son of Adaiah, and Elishaphat the son of Zichri, into covenant with him. 2 And they went about in Judah, and gathered the Levites out of all the cities of Judah, and the chief of the fathers of Israel, and they came to Jerusalem. After Joash had been hidden for six years, Jehoiada the high priest organized a *coup d' etat* against Athaliah. He found willing co-conspirators in the military leaders of the realm, as well as the Levites and other leaders of Judah.

3 And all the congregation made a covenant with the king in the house of God. And he said unto them, Behold, the king's son shall reign, as the LORD hath said of the sons of David. The congregation noted was not of the entire nation, but of the assembled priests, leaders, and Levites noted above. Jehoiada thus announced to them that the time had come for the rightful king of Judah to be placed upon the throne. They had no loyalty to the wicked Athaliah.

23:4-7 Jehoiada announced his plan to his assembled co-conspirators. **This *is* the thing that ye shall do; A third part of you entering on the sabbath, of the priests and of the Levites, *shall be* porters of the doors; 5 And a third part *shall be* at the king's house; and a third part at the gate of the foundation: and all the people *shall be* in the courts of the house of the LORD.** A third of the priests and Levites headed by those mentioned above would guard the gates of the Temple on the appointed Sabbath day. Another third would be sent to guard the king's empty palace. A final third would guard the lower gates to the Temple. Assembled in the outer courtyard of the Temple would be those of Judah loyal to God and His king.

6 But let none come into the house of the LORD, save the priests, and they that minister of the Levites; they shall go in, for they *are* holy: but all the people shall keep the watch of the LORD. 7 And the Levites shall compass the king round about, every man with his weapons in his hand; and whosoever *else* cometh into the house, he shall be put to death: but be ye with the king when he cometh in, and when he goeth out.

On the appointed Sabbath day, the assembled priests and Levites were to allow no one into the Temple proper except Levites and priests. The greater congregation loyal to God would by their very number be a guard in the outer court of the Temple. At the appointed time, designated Levites would surround the young king with weapons drawn and escort him to his place. Anyone entering the Temple to disrupt the proceedings was to be taken and killed. The assigned Levites would serve as a bodyguard for the king as he was revealed to the nation.

23:8-11 So the Levites and all Judah did according to all things that Jehoiada the priest had commanded, and took every man his men that were to come in on the sabbath, with them that were to go *out* on the sabbath: for Jehoiada the priest dismissed not the courses. 9 Moreover Jehoiada the priest delivered to the captains of hundreds spears, and bucklers, and shields, that *had been* king David's, which *were* in the house of God.

On the appointed Sabbath day, the designated Levites did as ordered. Meanwhile, Jehoiada the high priest had ordered that the course (i.e., shift) of priests and Levites on duty not go home and that those coming on duty assemble also. He then armed the priests and Levites with weapons which had long been stored at the Temple since the time of David.

10 And he set all the people, every man having his weapon in his hand, from the right side of the temple to the left side of the temple, along by the altar and the temple, by the king round about. 11 Then they brought out the king's son, and put upon him the crown, and *gave him* the testimony, and made him king. And Jehoiada and his sons anointed him, and said, God save the king.

Jehoiada therefore lined up his force of Levites from one side of the Temple to the other—all with weapons drawn. Before that phalanx of armed officers, "they brought out the king's son, and put upon him the crown, and *gave him* the testimony, and made him king." Little Joash, though only seven

Understanding II Chronicles 619

years old, was made king of Judah. He was duly crowned and given a copy of the Word of God. They then officially anointed him as king of Judah and cried out, "God save the king." The latter has the thought of 'God preserve the king.' There then undoubtedly erupted a roar of cheering and applause.

23:12-13 Now when Athaliah heard the noise of the people running and praising the king, she came to the people into the house of the LORD: 13 And she looked, and, behold, the king stood at his pillar at the entering in, and the princes and the trumpets by the king: and all the people of the land rejoiced, and sounded with trumpets, also the singers with instruments of musick, and such as taught to sing praise. Then Athaliah rent her clothes, and said, Treason, Treason.

Athaliah heard the commotion and roar of the crowds. She saw people running to the Temple and praising the king. She therefore marched over to the Temple from her own palace and saw little Joash, standing at the place in the Temple reserved for the king of Judah. Meanwhile, the Temple musicians were singing praise to God accompanied by the Temple orchestra. In sizing up the situation, Athaliah ripped her garment and shrieked, "Treason, Treason."

23:14-15 Then Jehoiada the priest brought out the captains of hundreds that were set over the host, and said unto them, Have her forth of the ranges: and whoso followeth her, let him be slain with the sword. For the priest said, Slay her not in the house of the LORD.

In seeing Athaliah's appearance and disruption, Jehoiada ordered his armed forces to seize her. Upon Jehoiada's orders, Athaliah was forcibly escorted out of the ranks by the Temple guards. Moreover, anyone who followed her was to be slain as well. However, it was the direction of Jehoiada that bloodshed not take place in the Temple itself. The wicked queen was hustled out of the Temple to a place near the palace where the horses entered, perhaps its stables, and there she was executed.

23:16-21 A great revival broke out in Judah. **And Jehoiada made a covenant between him, and between all the people, and between the king, that they should be the LORD'S people. 17 Then all the people went to the house of Baal, and brake it down, and brake his altars and his images in pieces, and slew Mattan the priest of Baal before the altars.** With the death of the wicked Athaliah and the anointing of a new king over Judah, Jehoiada made a covenant between himself, the nation at large, and the king "that they should be the LORD'S people." All clearly agreed thereto. Whereupon they proceeded forth from the Temple of God and "went to the house of Baal, and brake it down, and brake his altars and his images in pieces, and slew Mattan the priest of Baal before the altars." Under Jehoiada's influence, the presence of Baal worship at Jerusalem was exterminated.

18 Also Jehoiada appointed the offices of the house of the LORD by the hand of the priests the Levites, whom David had distributed in the house of the LORD, to offer the burnt offerings of the LORD, as *it is* **written in the law of Moses, with rejoicing and with singing,** *as it was ordained* **by David. 19 And he set the porters at the gates of the house of the LORD, that none** *which was* **unclean in any thing should enter in.** Jehoiada therefore re-instituted the full ministry and organization of the Temple as David had prescribed prior to his death. To the best of his ability, the Temple and worship of Jehovah was reconstituted as God intended it upon the opening the Temple not long after the death of David.

20 And he took the captains of hundreds, and the nobles, and the governors of the people, and all the people of the land, and brought down the king from the house of the

LORD: **and they came through the high gate into the king's house, and set the king upon the throne of the kingdom.** The assembled officers of the nation described earlier in this chapter thereupon escorted young king Joash to the official palace of the king at Jerusalem. They crossed the bridge between the Temple Mount to the official palace of the king and there set Joash upon his throne. (Of course, at this point, Jehoiada was the clear influence and power behind the throne.)

21 And all the people of the land rejoiced: and the city was quiet, after that they had slain Athaliah with the sword. Upon the execution of Athaliah, the entire nation rejoiced. Moreover, there was no further political upheaval in Jerusalem. All was quiet.

* * * * *

Overview of II Chronicles 24: This next chapter presents the details of the actual reign of Joash. (It is unique that he became king at seven years of age and then reigned forty years.) The key verse describing his reign is found in verse 2. "And Joash did that which was right in the sight of the LORD all the days of Jehoiada the priest." There is here a classic illustration of how spiritual leadership makes a definite difference in one's life. As long as Joash was under the "preaching" of Jehoiada, "he did that which was right in the sight of the LORD." As will soon be demonstrated, when that influence was taken away, Joash departed from God.

24:1-2 Joash *was* **seven years old when he began to reign, and he reigned forty years in Jerusalem. His mother's name also** *was* **Zibiah of Beersheba. 2 And Joash did** *that which was* **right in the sight of the** LORD **all the days of Jehoiada the priest. 3 And Jehoiada took for him two wives;**

and he begat sons and daughters. Summary details of the reign of Joash are noted. He reigned until he was forty-seven years old. Other details of his mother and family are noted. However, what is particularly significant is the comment, "And Joash did *that which was* right in the sight of the LORD all the days of Jehoiada the priest." As long as Joash was under the influence of a godly and spiritual 'pastor,' he did right. Though the relationship of Joash and Jehoiada the high priest was unique, the broader principle remains. When one is under the preaching and influence of a man of God, he will tend to do right. That is true to this day. Sadly, when Jehoiada passed the scene, Joash turned to his own devices which were his undoing.

24:4-7 And it came to pass after this, *that* Joash was minded to repair the house of the LORD. 5 And he gathered together the priests and the Levites, and said to them, Go out unto the cities of Judah, and gather of all Israel money to repair the house of your God from year to year, and see that ye hasten the matter. Howbeit the Levites hastened *it* not.

Verses 4 and following describes how Joash (no doubt from the influence of Jehoiada) determined to repair the Temple which had fallen into disrepair during the years of Athaliah. He sent Levites throughout the land to urgently gather funds for the restoration. However, the Levites were careless and unfaithful in the task. The spiritual condition of the Levites was thus evident.

6 And the king called for Jehoiada the chief, and said unto him, Why hast thou not required of the Levites to bring in out of Judah and out of Jerusalem the collection, *according to the commandment* of Moses the servant of the LORD, and of the congregation of Israel, for the tabernacle of witness? 7 For the sons of Athaliah, that wicked woman, had broken up the house of God; and also all the dedicated

things of the house of the LORD did they bestow upon Baalim.

Joash therefore called in Jehoiada and asked him why he had not required the Levites to go throughout the land to collect the half-shekel offering which had been prescribed by Moses for the upkeep of the Tabernacle and Temple. Surely that would be a source of revenue. The sacred chronicler notes that during the reign of Athaliah, the Temple had been neglected and even had its treasures taken and used in the temple of Baal.

24:8-10 And at the king's commandment they made a chest, and set it without at the gate of the house of the LORD. 9 And they made a proclamation through Judah and Jerusalem, to bring in to the LORD the collection *that* Moses the servant of God *laid* upon Israel in the wilderness. 10 And all the princes and all the people rejoiced, and brought in, and cast into the chest, until they had made an end. Joash therefore ordered a special chest be placed before the Temple so that all Israel entering therein could give for the restoration of the Temple. The people of the land from the leaders on down therefore rose to the occasion and placed funds in the special chest until it was full each day.

24:11-14 Now it came to pass, that at what time the chest was brought unto the king's office by the hand of the Levites, and when they saw that *there was* much money, the king's scribe and the high priest's officer came and emptied the chest, and took it, and carried it to his place again. Thus they did day by day, and gathered money in abundance. Levites therefore brought the chest to the king's 'office' or care. The funds poured in and the king's officers brought the chest back and forth day by day.

12 And the king and Jehoiada gave it to such as did the work of the service of the house of the LORD, and hired

masons and carpenters to repair the house of the LORD, and also such as wrought iron and brass to mend the house of the LORD. 13 So the workmen wrought, and the work was perfected by them, and they set the house of God in his state, and strengthened it.** Rather than the Levites taking oversight of the work, the king and Jehoiada took charge of the renovation work of the Temple. They therefore hired skilled craftsmen for the repairs of the Temple and paid them from the funds collected. The Temple was thus repaired and restored to a semblance of its former glory.

14 And when they had finished *it*, they brought the rest of the money before the king and Jehoiada, whereof were made vessels for the house of the LORD, *even* vessels to minister, and to offer *withal*, and spoons, and vessels of gold and silver. And they offered burnt offerings in the house of the LORD continually all the days of Jehoiada. So much money was collected that they were able to replace and refurbish the sacred vessels and utensils of gold and silver at the Temple. Proper sacrifices to God were thus offered to God throughout the tenure of Jehoiada.

24:15-19 But Jehoiada waxed old, and was full of days when he died; an hundred and thirty years old *was he* when he died. 16 And they buried him in the city of David among the kings, because he had done good in Israel, both toward God, and toward his house. Verses 15-19 presents the spiritual declension and apostasy which quickly fell over the land upon the death of Jehoiada. (It is noteworthy that Jehoiada was buried among the kings of Judah "because he had done good in Israel, both toward God, and toward his house."

17 Now after the death of Jehoiada came the princes of Judah, and made obeisance to the king. Then the king hearkened unto them. 18 And they left the house of the LORD God of their fathers, and served groves and idols: and

wrath came upon Judah and Jerusalem for this their trespass. 19 Yet he sent prophets to them, to bring them again unto the LORD; and they testified against them: but they would not give ear. Tragically, the princes of Judah quickly returned to serving the groves and idols (Baal worship). God therefore sent both wrath against Judah and prophets to warn them. These unnamed prophets sought to see Judah returned to their God and they so testified to them. "But they would not give ear." They thus set themselves up for severe chastening by God in the days ahead.

24:20-22 And the Spirit of God came upon Zechariah the son of Jehoiada the priest, which stood above the people, and said unto them, Thus saith God, Why transgress ye the commandments of the LORD, that ye cannot prosper? because ye have forsaken the LORD, he hath also forsaken you. 21 And they conspired against him, and stoned him with stones at the commandment of the king in the court of the house of the LORD.

After Jehoiada's death, his son Zechariah was filled with the Holy Spirit to preach against the growing apostasy in the land. He was pointed and direct in calling their sin sin. "Why transgress ye the commandments of the LORD, that ye cannot prosper? because ye have forsaken the LORD, he hath also forsaken you." But the greatest travesty was that Joash the king quickly forgot the good Jehoiada had done personally for him. Whereupon the princes and lieutenants of Joash proceeded to stone Zechariah (Jehoiada's son) to death. What clearly is implied is that the death of Zechariah was certainly with Joash's knowledge and allowance.

The wretched summary of Joash is made in verse 22. **Thus Joash the king remembered not the kindness which Jehoiada his father had done to him, but slew his son. And when he died, he said, The LORD look upon it, and require** *it*. There is unbelievable arrogance and stupidity in the last phrase of verse 22. In effect Joash said, "Let God take note and do something about it." He did. The text to follow documents that. God judged the unsurpassed ingratitude of Joash.

24:23-24 And it came to pass at the end of the year, *that* the host of Syria came up against him: and they came to Judah and Jerusalem, and destroyed all the princes of the people from among the people, and sent all the spoil of them unto the king of Damascus. 24 For the army of the Syrians came with a small company of men, and the LORD delivered a very great host into their hand, because they had forsaken the LORD God of their fathers. So they executed judgment against Joash.

God sent the Syrian army against Judah and destroyed the godless princes of the land, looting Jerusalem and Judah. Curiously, the Syrians came with a small force and defeated a much larger army of Judah, "because they had forsaken the LORD God of their fathers. So they executed judgement against Joash." God indeed had looked upon the apostasy and sin of Joash and required it. He did something about Joash's sin and travesty of justice in the matter of Zechariah, Jehoiada's son.

24:25-27 And when they were departed from him, (for they left him in great diseases,) his own servants conspired against him for the blood of the sons of Jehoiada the priest, and slew him on his bed, and he died: and they buried him in the city of David, but they buried him not in the sepulchres of the kings.

26 And these are they that conspired against him; Zabad the son of Shimeath an Ammonitess, and Jehozabad the son of Shimrith a Moabitess. 27 Now *concerning* his sons, and the greatness of the burdens *laid* upon him, and the repairing of the house of God, behold, they *are* written in the

Understanding II Chronicles

story of the book of the kings. And Amaziah his son reigned in his stead.

The bitter and wretched end of Joash is recorded in verses 25-27. After his thrashing at the hands of the Syrians, he was stricken with great diseases. Moreover, his own servants conspired against him "and slew him on his bed, and he died." Though he was king, they would not bury him among the kings of Judah. He who had begun as a great king before God ended on an ignominious and miserable note. The moral of the life of Joash is that God blesses righteousness and judges unrighteousness. Joash's sin was unforgivable in allowing idolatry back into Judah along with his treatment of Jehoiada's son. God dealt severely with him as a result.

* * * * *

Overview of II Chronicles 25*: This next chapter presents the half-hearted godliness of Amaziah. He became king at age twenty five and reigned twenty-nine years. He was, for the most part, a mediocre king spiritually who trusted his own judgement rather than God's. He, like others, succumbed to the popular fad of idolatry and thus brought God's judgment upon himself. God chastened him militarily and his end was ignominious.*

25:1-4 Amaziah *was* twenty and five years old *when* he began to reign, and he reigned twenty and nine years in Jerusalem. And his mother's name *was* Jehoaddan of Jerusalem. 2 And he did *that which was* right in the sight of the LORD, but not with a perfect heart. Amaziah, the son of Joash, ascended his father's throne at age twenty five and reigned until he was fifty-four years old. Verse 2 well describes the spiritual mediocrity of Amaziah: "He did that which was right in the sight of the LORD, but not with a perfect heart." The word translated as **perfect** (שלם *shalem*) has the sense of 'complete' or 'total.' In other words, Amaziah's doing right was less than whole-hearted. His dedication was half-hearted. He did right half-way. This sadly well described his tenure as king.

3 Now it came to pass, when the kingdom was established to him, that he slew his servants that had killed the king his father. 4 But he slew not their children, but *did* as *it is* written in the law in the book of Moses, where the LORD commanded, saying, The fathers shall not die for the children, neither shall the children die for the fathers, but every man shall die for his own sin. In chapter 24, it is recorded that his father Joash had been slain by his own servants. Upon accession to the throne, Amaziah promptly had those servants killed. However, he piously avoided slaying their children in accordance with the Law of God.

25:5-8 Moreover Amaziah gathered Judah together, and made them captains over thousands, and captains over hundreds, according to the houses of *their* fathers, throughout all Judah and Benjamin: and he numbered them from twenty years old and above, and found them three hundred thousand choice *men, able* to go forth to war, that could handle spear and shield. 6 He hired also an hundred thousand mighty men of valour out of Israel for an hundred talents of silver.

Verses 5-16 describes the debacle of Amaziah's military campaign against Edom. He took a census of all men of military age (twenty and upward) and found he had 300,000 men at his disposal. For good measure, he also hired 100,000 mercenary soldiers from the northern kingdom, Israel, for 100 talents of silver.

7 But there came a man of God to him, saying, O king, let not the army of Israel go with thee; for the LORD *is* not with Israel, *to wit, with* all the children of Ephraim. 8 But if

thou wilt go, do *it*, be strong for the battle: God shall make thee fall before the enemy: for God hath power to help, and to cast down.** However, God sent a prophet and told Amaziah to not use the army from Israel "for the LORD is not with Israel." The prophet further told him to go ahead and go against Edom (modern day Jordan). The phrase "God shall make thee fall before the enemy" could also be translated "God shall make thee fall *against* the enemy." In other words, go in God's strength and He will give you the victory. "For God hath power to help, and to cast down." That truth remains to this day. God is able to help His people as they trust Him.

9 And Amaziah said to the man of God, But what shall we do for the hundred talents which I have given to the army of Israel? And the man of God answered, The LORD is able to give thee much more than this. 10 Then Amaziah separated them, *to wit*, the army that was come to him out of Ephraim, to go home again: wherefore their anger was greatly kindled against Judah, and they returned home in great anger. Amaziah complained that he had already paid the army of Israel. The prophet rather told him, "The LORD is able to give thee much more than this." The resources of our God are infinite. Whereupon, Amaziah sent the northern army home. However, they went in great anger and as they went, they pillaged and looted towns in Judah, killing 3,000 people in the process.

11 And Amaziah strengthened himself, and led forth his people, and went to the valley of salt, and smote of the children of Seir ten thousand. 12 And *other* ten thousand *left* alive did the children of Judah carry away captive, and brought them unto the top of the rock, and cast them down from the top of the rock, that they all were broken in pieces. 13 But the soldiers of the army which Amaziah sent back, that they should not go with him to battle, fell upon the cities

of Judah, from Samaria even unto Bethhoron, and smote three thousand of them, and took much spoil.

Amaziah proceeded to battle against the Edomites (called **Seir** in verse 11). Seir was a mountain in Edom and was synonymous with Edom. As promised, God delivered the Edomites into the hand of Amaziah. Ten thousand Edomites were killed in the battle and Amaziah cruelly executed another ten thousand of them in verse 12. Meanwhile, the dismissed mercenary soldiers from the north rampaged through towns in Judah, including Bethhoron, killing 3,000 Jews and looting their villages.

14 Now it came to pass, after that Amaziah was come from the slaughter of the Edomites, that he brought the gods of the children of Seir, and set them up *to be* his gods, and bowed down himself before them, and burned incense unto them. 15 Wherefore the anger of the LORD was kindled against Amaziah, and he sent unto him a prophet, which said unto him, Why hast thou sought after the gods of the people, which could not deliver their own people out of thine hand?

16 And it came to pass, as he talked with him, that *the king* said unto him, Art thou made of the king's counsel? forbear; why shouldest thou be smitten? Then the prophet forbare, and said, I know that God hath determined to destroy thee, because thou hast done this, and hast not hearkened unto my counsel.

Verse 14 details how Amaziah "brought the gods of the children of Seir, and set them up to be his gods, and bowed down himself before them and burned incense unto them." It was the fashionable and popular thing of the day to have multiple idols. Amaziah tragically went along with the fad of the day to his destruction. He foolishly violated the first of the Ten Commandments. This coming debacle was the result of Amaziah's failure to seek the Lord's counsel about the whole matter in the first place. He set off to do his own plans and the whole thing backfired in his face.

Notice in verse 15 how that "the anger of the LORD was kindled against Amaziah." God takes note of the sin of His people. God sent a prophet who condemned what Amaziah had done. Amaziah was not happy too hear what the prophet of God had to say and warned him to be careful or he would be smitten (verse 16). The prophet backed off, but told Amaziah that God would destroy him for his sin and for ignoring His counsel through the prophet.

25:17-24 Then Amaziah king of Judah took advice, and sent to Joash, the son of Jehoahaz, the son of Jehu, king of Israel, saying, Come, let us see one another in the face. 18 And Joash king of Israel sent to Amaziah king of Judah, saying, The thistle that *was* in Lebanon sent to the cedar that *was* in Lebanon, saying, Give thy daughter to my son to wife: and there passed by a wild beast that *was* in Lebanon, and trode down the thistle. 19 Thou sayest, Lo, thou hast smitten the Edomites; and thine heart lifteth thee up to boast: abide now at home; why shouldest thou meddle to *thine* hurt, that thou shouldest fall, *even* thou, and Judah with thee?

Verses 17-24 describes how Amaziah in pride foolishly challenged the northern kingdom to war. Because he had accomplished a degree of victory over Edom, it apparently went to his head and now he thought he could whip Israel to the north. Pride often leads to foolish decisions. Joash, king of Israel, sent back a sarcastic little parable to Amaziah. "The thistle that *was* in Lebanon sent to the cedar that *was* in Lebanon, saying, Give thy daughter to my son to wife: and there passed by a wild beast that *was* in Lebanon, and trode down the thistle." Joash likened himself to a cedar and Amaziah to a thistle. If the foolish little thistle was not careful, it would get stepped on by a large creature. Joash, the king of Israel of the time, basically told Amaziah to buzz off lest he get his nose bloodied. He therefore warned Amaziah to not meddle with him lest he be wounded and killed.

But Amaziah would not hear; for it came of God, that he might deliver them into the hand of their *enemies***, because they sought after the gods of Edom.** 21 **So Joash the king of Israel went up; and they saw one another in the face,** *both* **he and Amaziah king of Judah, at Bethshemesh, which** *belongeth* **to Judah.** 22 **And Judah was put to the worse before Israel, and they fled every man to his tent.** God allowed Israel to thrash Judah. The reason is clear: "because they sought after the gods of Edom." In the battle which ensued, conditions were such that Joash, king of Israel, was able to look Amaziah in the face at the town of Bethshemesh. There the battle was engaged and Judah was beaten by Israel.

23 **And Joash the king of Israel took Amaziah king of Judah, the son of Joash, the son of Jehoahaz, at Bethshemesh, and brought him to Jerusalem, and brake down the wall of Jerusalem from the gate of Ephraim to the corner gate, four hundred cubits.** 24 **And** *he took* **all the gold and the silver, and all the vessels that were found in the house of God with Obededom, and the treasures of the king's house, the hostages also, and returned to Samaria.**

Moreover, Israel pursued all the way back to Jerusalem, a distance of about twenty miles. In pursuing, they looted the city, knocking down a sizable portion of the its wall. Joash also proceeded to rob the Temple of its gold and silver and the sacred vessels for service along with the treasury of the Temple. He then turned around and went back to Samaria. What is clear is that this all came to pass because Amaziah had brought home the idols of Edom and would not listen to God's warning. That was the cause. Their military thrashing was the effect. God does chasten His people for their sin.

25:25-28 And Amaziah the son of Joash king of Judah lived after the death of Joash son of Jehoahaz king of Israel fifteen years. 26 Now the rest of the acts of Amaziah, first and last, behold, *are* they not written in the book of the kings of Judah and Israel? 27 Now after the time that Amaziah did turn away from following the LORD they made a conspiracy against him in Jerusalem; and he fled to Lachish: but they sent to Lachish after him, and slew him there. 28 And they brought him upon horses, and buried him with his fathers in the city of Judah.

Though Amaziah outlived his nemesis Joash by fifteen years, he came to an ignoble end. After his decision to turn away from the Lord "they made a conspiracy against him in Jerusalem; and he fled to Lachish: but they sent to Lachish after him, and slew him there." Like his father, Amaziah was assassinated by his own people for his folly. Lachish was a major city of Judah about thirty miles southwest of Jerusalem. Perhaps in fleeing there, he thought he could escape retribution. However, like the thistle in Joash's parable, he there was eliminated. His body was thus brought back to Jerusalem in the city of David—the royal cemetery.

In summary, Amaziah was a man who in pride made crucial decisions and never sought God's counsel in the matter. After a modicum of success, he, with inflated ego, bit off more than he could chew. That coupled with his violation of the first commandment pertaining to idolatry brought God's judgment against him. He died as a lackluster example of spiritual mediocrity. Half-hearted service of God often leads to disaster.

* * * * *

Overview of II Chronicles 26: *In this chapter is the life of Uzziah, the 9th king of Judah. He became king at the age of* sixteen and reigned fifty-two years. His life seems to have been in two sections. The first appears to be years of godliness. The latter half was that of disobedience to God and of God's chastening upon him. In II Kings 14, he is referred to as Azariah.

26:1-3 Then all the people of Judah took Uzziah, who was sixteen years old, and made him king in the room of his father Amaziah. 2 He built Eloth, and restored it to Judah, after that the king slept with his fathers. 3 Sixteen years old was Uzziah when he began to reign, and he reigned fifty and two years in Jerusalem. His mother's name also was Jecoliah of Jerusalem.

The reign of Uzziah is here summarized. In II Kings, he is referred to as Azariah. He became king when he was sixteen years old when his father was killed at Lachish. One of the major accomplishments of his reign was the building of Eloth (a.k.a, Elath or Elat) which was a port city on the Gulf of Elat on the Red Sea. It thus restored to Judah a seaport on the Red Sea and points beyond. Reigning for fifty-two years, he died at the age of seventy eight.

26:4-5 And he did *that which was* right in the sight of the LORD, according to all that his father Amaziah did. 5 And he sought God in the days of Zechariah, who had understanding in the visions of God: and as long as he sought the LORD, God made him to prosper.

Notice how in the early years of his reign he was characterized as doing "that which was right in the sight of the LORD, according to all that his father Amaziah did." Amaziah his father was characterized as doing right but not with a perfect heart (II Chronicles 25:2). That pretty well describes the life of Uzziah asa well. Like Joash his grandfather, he was positively influenced by a prophet or priest named Zechariah. This certainly is not the prophet who wrote the Book of Zechariah, nor is it the one slain by Joash in chapter 24. He, however, may have been the son of that prior Zechariah. More likely, he was the Zechariah mentioned Isaiah 8:2. In any event, Uzziah "sought God in the days of Zechariah." Moreover, "as long as he sought the LORD, God made him to prosper." That principle remains true to this day. See I Samuel 2:30. God honors those who honor him.

26:6-10 And he went forth and warred against the Philistines, and brake down the wall of Gath, and the wall of Jabneh, and the wall of Ashdod, and built cities about Ashdod, and among the Philistines. 7 And God helped him against the Philistines, and against the Arabians that dwelt in Gurbaal, and the Mehunims. The blessing and prospering of God are recorded in victories over the Philistines, long enemies of Israel. Notice specifically that "God helped him against the Philistines, and against the Arabians that dwelt in Gurbaal, and the Mehunims." The latter two peoples are unknown, but likely were to the south and east of Judah. The blessing of God often has very tangible results.

8 And the Ammonites gave gifts to Uzziah: and his name spread abroad *even* to the entering in of Egypt; for he strengthened *himself* exceedingly. To the east, the Ammonites sent tribute tax to Uzziah. His fame and reputation spread to Egypt in the opposite direction. The blessing of God is once again evidenced in that "he strengthened *himself* exceedingly." Uzziah became a powerful, successful, and renowned king. When God prospers one, it manifests itself in very tangible ways.

**9 Moreover Uzziah built towers in Jerusalem at the corner gate, and at the valley gate, and at the turning *of the wall*, and fortified them. 10 Also he built towers in the desert, and digged many wells: for he had much cattle, both in the low country, and in the plains: husbandmen *also*, and vine dressers in the mountains, and in Carmel: for he loved husbandry. Uzziah made major improvements and fortifications to Jerusalem and across his kingdom. He became personally wealthy having business interests throughout the nation. He accordingly had farms, 'ranches,' and vineyards throughout Judah, "for he loved husbandry."

26:11-15 Moreover Uzziah had an host of fighting men, that went out to war by bands, according to the number of their account by the hand of Jeiel the scribe and Maaseiah the ruler, under the hand of Hananiah, *one* of the king's captains. 12 The whole number of the chief of the fathers of the mighty men of valour *were* two thousand and six hundred. 13 And under their hand *was* an army, three hundred thousand and seven thousand and five hundred, that made war with mighty power, to help the king against the enemy.

Not only did Uzziah prosper politically and personally, but God also blessed him militarily. He had an army of 307,500 men led by 2,600 officers. They evidently were a formidable military force.

14 And Uzziah prepared for them throughout all the host shields, and spears, and helmets, and habergeons, and bows, and slings *to cast* stones. 15 And he made in Jerusalem engines, invented by cunning men, to be on the towers and upon the bulwarks, to shoot arrows and great stones withal. And his name spread far abroad; for he was marvellously helped, till he was strong. Uzziah also armed his army with the finest and latest of military technology. Habergeons refer to body army. His forces had full helmets and breastplates along with advanced hand weapons. Furthermore, he installed war "machines" atop the fortifications of Jerusalem. These evidently were catapult machines, crossbows, and other advanced military equipment.

Understanding II Chronicles

The first part of the reign of Uzziah is thus summarized, "for he was marvellously helped, till he was strong." God placed extraordinary blessings upon King Uzziah until he was a powerful and strong king. Sadly, he forgot whence his blessings flowed.

26:16 But when he was strong, his heart was lifted up to *his* destruction: for he transgressed against the LORD his God, and went into the temple of the LORD to burn incense upon the altar of incense

Verses 16 to the end of the chapter detail his pride, arrogance and God's subsequent chastisement. Some of the major pitfalls of success and power are pride, arrogance and forgetting how one achieved high position. Sadly, when Uzziah became strong, "his heart was lifted up to his destruction: for he transgressed against the LORD his God, and went into the temple of the LORD to burn incense upon the altar of incense." In his pride, Uzziah usurped the exclusive office of the priesthood. Exodus 30:7-8 and other places make it clear that only Aaron and his sons were to serve in the Temple. Uzziah arrogantly ignored that provision and usurped it to himself.

26:17-18 And Azariah the priest went in after him, and with him fourscore priests of the LORD, *that were* valiant men: 18 And they withstood Uzziah the king, and said unto him, *It appertaineth* not unto thee, Uzziah, to burn incense unto the LORD, but to the priests the sons of Aaron, that are consecrated to burn incense: go out of the sanctuary; for thou hast trespassed; neither *shall it be* for thine honour from the LORD God.

The chief priest Azariah thus confronted Uzziah along with eighty Levites and warned him not to proceed. Uzziah arrogantly brushed them aside. Yet God could not be brushed aside.

26:19-21 Then Uzziah was wroth, and *had* **a censer in his hand to burn incense: and while he was wroth with the priests, the leprosy even rose up in his forehead before the priests in the house of the LORD, from beside the incense altar. 20 And Azariah the chief priest, and all the priests, looked upon him, and, behold, he** *was* **leprous in his forehead, and they thrust him out from thence; yea, himself hasted also to go out, because the LORD had smitten him. 21 And Uzziah the king was a leper unto the day of his death, and dwelt in a several house,** *being* **a leper; for he was cut off from the house of the LORD: and Jotham his son** *was* **over the king's house, judging the people of the land.**

At that very hour God struck Uzziah with leprosy. Notice in verse 20, it is made clear that "the LORD had smitten him." He remained a leper to his death. The reference to Uzziah dwelling "in a several house" has the sense of a "separate" house. He essentially was quarantined the rest of his life. His son Jotham thus assumed rule over the nation, likely doing so before his father's death.

26:22-23 Now the rest of the acts of Uzziah, first and last, did Isaiah the prophet, the son of Amoz, write. 23 So Uzziah slept with his fathers, and they buried him with his fathers in the field of the burial which *belonged* **to the kings; for they said, He** *is* **a leper: and Jotham his son reigned in his stead.** The history of Uzziah written by Isaiah the prophet does not refer to the Book of Isaiah, but to other ancillary writings of Isaiah. Uzziah died the year in which Isaiah received his famous vision of Isaiah 6. See Isaiah 6:1. He was buried adjacent to the royal cemetery of the kings of Judah, but not actually in the same because he was a leper. Jotham then fully acceded the throne of Judah upon his father's death.

* * * * *

Understanding II Chronicles

Overview of II Chronicles 27: *This next chapter gives a brief summary of the life of Jotham, son of Uzziah. He began to reign at age of 25. He too is described as having done that which was right in the sight of the Lord. He reigned sixteen years. Fortunately, he learned from his father's sin. "He entered not in to the temple of the LORD." Sadly, however, "the people did yet corruptly."*

27:1-2 Jotham *was* twenty and five years old when he began to reign, and he reigned sixteen years in Jerusalem. His mother's name also *was* Jerushah, the daughter of Zadok. Another king of Judah is described. Interestingly, there is no criticism of this king. His mother evidently was descended of Zadok the priest and undoubtedly had an influence upon him for the good.

2 And he did *that which was* right in the sight of the LORD, according to all that his father Uzziah did: howbeit he entered not into the temple of the LORD. And the people did yet corruptly. Jotham is characterized as having done that which was right. So often God characterized kings of Judah or Israel simply as they did right or they did not that which was right. It is profoundly simple. The self-discipline to do what is right is the essence of godly character. To that degree, Uzziah was like his father. However, Jotham did not have the arrogance to usurp the office of the priest as did his father. The corruption of the people of the land evidently was their sacrifice and burning of incense upon unauthorized high places of the land according to II Kings 15:35.

27:3-6 He built the high gate of the house of the LORD, and on the wall of Ophel he built much. 4 Moreover he built cities in the mountains of Judah, and in the forests he built castles and towers. Some of the accomplishments of Jotham are noted, including building a new and high gate to the Temple;

improvements on the wall of the Ophel, a ridge on the southeastern slope of the Temple mount lying between the Kidron and Tyropoeon valleys and called the lower city; and military fortifications across the hills and forest of Judah.

5 He fought also with the king of the Ammonites, and prevailed against them. And the children of Ammon gave him the same year an hundred talents of silver, and ten thousand measures of wheat, and ten thousand of barley. So much did the children of Ammon pay unto him, both the second year, and the third.

A war developed with Ammon to the east (analogous with modern Ammon, Jordan) and Jotham prevailed. Thereafter, the Ammonites paid tribute to him in the amount of 100 talents of silver, 10,000 measures of wheat and 10,000 measures of barley. (A **measure** in Hebrew weight was a *kor* {כר} and approximated 6.25 bushels each.) This continued for only three years, for reasons not specified. The greater point is that Jotham enjoyed victory as God's blessing was upon him.

6 So Jotham became mighty, because he prepared his ways before the LORD his God. God clearly blessed Jotham. The king's life and reign was characterized as doing that which was right in the sight of the Lord. According to Psalm 5:12, God blessed him. He thus became mighty "because he prepared his ways before the LORD his God." For an overview of preparing one's heart before the LORD or the lack thereof, see II Chronicles 12:14, 19:3, 20:33, 30:19, and Ezra 7:10. His life was thus ordered by God's Word.

27:7-9 Now the rest of the acts of Jotham, and all his wars, and his ways, lo, they *are* written in the book of the kings of Israel and Judah. The books of the kings of Israel and Judah likely are not the canonical books of Kings, but evidently other non-inspired chronicles. Interesting it would be to read of his ways and his acts which the Holy Spirit has characterized as righteous and in preparation before the Lord.

8 He was five and twenty years old when he began to reign, and reigned sixteen years in Jerusalem. 9 And Jotham slept with his fathers, and they buried him in the city of David: and Ahaz his son reigned in his stead. How and why Jotham, a king blessed of God, died at age forty one is not recorded. However, he, like most of his royal ancestors, was buried in the royal cemetery of the city of David in east Jerusalem. His son Ahaz succeeded him on the throne. Sadly, he would not have the righteous character of his father.

* * * * *

Overview of II Chronicles 28: *In II Chronicles 28 is the account of Ahaz the eleventh king of Judah. Without a question, he was one of the worst kings thereof. His reign could be summarized in verses 1, 5, and 19. "He did not that which was right in the sight of the* LORD *. . . Wherefore the* LORD *his God delivered him in the hand of the king of Syria; and they smote him . . . For the* LORD *brought Judah low because of Ahaz king of Israel; for he made Judah naked, and transgressed sore against the* LORD*." Here was a king who blatantly violated God's Word. The record shows how God dealt with him.*

28:1-4 Ahaz *was* twenty years old when he began to reign, and he reigned sixteen years in Jerusalem: but he did not *that which was* right in the sight of the LORD**, like David his father.** Ahaz was characterized by the Holy Spirit as one who "did not that which was right in the sight of the LORD.
2 For he walked in the ways of the kings of Israel, and made also molten images for Baalim. 3 Moreover he burnt incense in the valley of the son of Hinnom, and burnt his

children in the fire, after the abominations of the heathen whom the LORD had cast out before the children of Israel. 4 He sacrificed also and burnt incense in the high places, and on the hills, and under every green tree**.

(1) Not only did Ahaz emulate the kings of Israel to the north, he made images for Baalim. This was a direct violation of the first two of the Ten Commandments. It also was the most base and degenerate form of idolatry. Baal worship involved ritual prostitution and other perverse sex acts, seeking to arouse the demonic god Baal. (2) Ahaz sacrificed some of his children in the valley of Hinnom, "after the abominations of the heathen whom the LORD had cast out before the children of Israel." Though what he practiced was not abortion, in principle it was quite similar. (3) The reference to sacrifice and burnt incense on the hills and under every green tree is another allusion to his blatant idolatry.

28:5-8 Wherefore the LORD his God delivered him into the hand of the king of Syria; and they smote him, and carried away a great multitude of them captives, and brought *them* to Damascus. And he was also delivered into the hand of the king of Israel, who smote him with a great slaughter. Notice how God directly sent judgement for his wickedness. First the Syrians chastised him militarily who took captive "a great multitude of them captives, and brought *them* to Damascus." Then God allowed the northern kingdom of Israel to chastize him militarily "with a great slaughter."

6 For Pekah the son of Remaliah slew in Judah an hundred and twenty thousand in one day, *which were* all valiant men; because they had forsaken the LORD God of their fathers. 7 And Zichri, a mighty man of Ephraim, slew Maaseiah the king's son, and Azrikam the governor of the house, and Elkanah *that was* next to the king. 8 And the children of Israel carried away captive of their brethren

two hundred thousand, women, sons, and daughters, and took also away much spoil from them, and brought the spoil to Samaria. The events described here are those referred to in Isaiah 7:1-9. It is in this direct context that the great prophecy of the virgin birth of Jesus Christ is made. The events herein are directly contemporaneous with Isaiah the prophet. The end of verse 6 makes it clear that these calamities came "because they had forsaken the LORD God of their fathers." In the war described above, Ahaz's son was killed, the chief of staff of his palace was killed, and the king's personal assistant was killed as well.

Moreover, when that war was over, Israel to the north took 200,000 women and children captive after the battle and proceeded to make them prisoners of war, likely to sell them into slavery. They also plundered Judah and Jerusalem, taking the spoils thereof back with them to Samaria. Judah had gone from experiencing the blessing of God under Jotham and Uzziah to the chastening of God under Ahaz. Profound is the difference.

28:9-15 But a prophet of the LORD was there, whose name *was* Oded: and he went out before the host that came to Samaria, and said unto them, Behold, because the LORD God of your fathers was wroth with Judah, he hath delivered them into your hand, and ye have slain them in a rage *that* reacheth up unto heaven. 10 And now ye purpose to keep under the children of Judah and Jerusalem for bondmen and bondwomen unto you: *but are there* not with you, even with you, sins against the LORD your God?

Meanwhile, God sent a prophet named Oded out to meet the victorious forces of the northern kingdom, returning from their triumph over Judah. This clearly is a different Oded than the one mentioned in II Chronicles 15:1,8. The prophet here warned that God had been angry with Judah and delivered them to the northern kingdom for chastisement. However, the latter had exceeded their bounds and ruthlessly slaughtered their brethren to the south. That outrage had reached to heaven and God was angered therewith. Israel had also taken 200,000 Jews captive as bondmen and bondwomen. However, God, through the prophet warned, that Israel was guilty of sins before God as well. They best take heed.

11 Now hear me therefore, and deliver the captives again, which ye have taken captive of your brethren: for the fierce wrath of the LORD *is* upon you. The prophet therefore (on behalf of God) ordered Israel to release their Jewish captives lest God's wrath fall upon them.

12 Then certain of the heads of the children of Ephraim, Azariah the son of Johanan, Berechiah the son of Meshillemoth, and Jehizkiah the son of Shallum, and Amasa the son of Hadlai, stood up against them that came from the war, 13 And said unto them, Ye shall not bring in the captives hither: for whereas we have offended against the LORD *already*, ye intend to add *more* to our sins and to our trespass: for our trespass is great, and *there is* fierce wrath against Israel. Upon learning of all that happened, leaders of the northern kingdom ordered their military men to release their Jewish captives. They knew they had overstepped their bounds and had offended Jehovah God. They knew that God was angered over the excesses of their army.

14 So the armed men left the captives and the spoil before the princes and all the congregation. 15 And the men which were expressed by name rose up, and took the captives, and with the spoil clothed all that were naked among them, and arrayed them, and shod them, and gave them to eat and to drink, and anointed them, and carried all the feeble of them upon asses, and brought them to Jericho, the city of palm trees, to their brethren: then they returned to Samaria.

The armed forces from the northern kingdom therefore released their Jewish captives before the civil leaders of the kingdom. Those named in verse 12 therefore took custody of the prisoners of war and clothed those needing clothing from the spoils of war, fed them, tended to their wounds, and helped the weak and crippled, placing them upon donkeys. They thus led them to Jericho near the Jordan River. To this day, Jericho is called the city of palm trees. The Jewish prisoners of war were therefore released and allowed to return home. That in itself was still some considerable distance.

Though the northern kingdom had exceeded God's intentions of chastising Judah, nevertheless, Judah was brought low for their sin of idolatry and departure from God. It all fell at the feet of Ahaz who so allowed the wickedness and even led them in the same.

28:16–19 At that time did king Ahaz send unto the kings of Assyria to help him. 17 For again the Edomites had come and smitten Judah, and carried away captives. 18 The Philistines also had invaded the cities of the low country, and of the south of Judah, and had taken Bethshemesh, and Ajalon, and Gederoth, and Shocho with the villages thereof, and Timnah with the villages thereof, Gimzo also and the villages thereof: and they dwelt there. 19 For the LORD brought Judah low because of Ahaz king of Israel; for he made Judah naked, and transgressed sore against the LORD.

Things got worse for Ahaz. He would not learn his lesson. Verse 16 and following describe how the Edomites to the east and the Philistines to the west were harassing Judah. On every side, there was trouble. Lest there be any question in the matter, it was God who was so chastening Ahaz and Judah, "For the LORD brought Judah low because of Ahaz king of Israel; for he made Judah naked, and transgressed sore against the LORD."

The word translated as **naked** (פָּרַע *para* in the Hiphil construct which it here is) has the sense to 'loose restraints.' Ahaz loosed the godly restraints against idolatry and morality across his land. In so doing, he transgressed sore against the Lord.

28:20-22 And Tilgathpilneser king of Assyria came unto him, and distressed him, but strengthened him not. 21 For Ahaz took away a portion *out* of the house of the LORD, and *out* of the house of the king, and of the princes, and gave *it* unto the king of Assyria: but he helped him not. 22 And in the time of his distress did he trespass yet more against the LORD: this *is that* king Ahaz.

In the midst of all his trouble, Ahaz sent to Tilgath-pilneser king of Assyria and asked for military assistance. In fact, he took funds from the Temple as well as from the leaders of the nation and sent it as payment to Tilgath-pilneser. Ahaz sinned against God even more. Notwithstanding have received payment from Ahaz, Tilgath-pilneser sent no help to Ahaz.

28:23-25 For he sacrificed unto the gods of Damascus, which smote him: and he said, Because the gods of the kings of Syria help them, *therefore* will I sacrifice to them, that they may help me. But they were the ruin of him, and of all Israel.

24 And Ahaz gathered together the vessels of the house of God, and cut in pieces the vessels of the house of God, and shut up the doors of the house of the LORD, and he made him altars in every corner of Jerusalem. 25 And in every several city of Judah he made high places to burn incense unto other gods, and provoked to anger the LORD God of his fathers.

Ahaz, far from God, therefore thought he could get help from the gods of Damascus. Therefore, he sacrificed to them. His twisted thinking was that if the gods of Damascus helped

Understanding II Chronicles 647

the Syrians, maybe if he sacrificed to them also, they would help him. This only added to the impending end coming upon him.

Demented Ahaz then removed the gold and silver vessels from the Temple (probably melting them down) and converted them to his own personal use. He then boarded up the doors of the Temple and closed it. In its place, he "he made him altars in every corner of Jerusalem." Moreover, he caused idolatry to proliferate across Judah and encouraged his nation to burn incense to other gods. In so doing, he "provoked to anger the LORD God of his fathers."

28:26-27 Now the rest of his acts and of all his ways, first and last, behold, they *are* written in the book of the kings of Judah and Israel. 27 And Ahaz slept with his fathers, and they buried him in the city, *even* in Jerusalem: but they brought him not into the sepulchres of the kings of Israel: and Hezekiah his son reigned in his stead. The abominable actions of this wicked king were also recorded in other non-inspired chronicles of Judah and Israel. When he died, he was buried in Jerusalem, but not in the royal cemetery of the kings of David. Even the people of Judah realized how wicked this king had been. His son Hezekiah thus inherited the mess of his father and succeeded him upon the throne of Judah.

* * * * *

Overview of II Chronicles 29: The reign of Hezekiah is here introduced.. Though he was the son of one of the worst kings of Judah, nevertheless he became one of its truly great kings. In fact, apart from King David, Hezekiah may have been the greatest king to grace the kingdom of Israel or Judah. Though there had been great apostasy during the reign of his father (Ahaz), through Hezekiah's leadership, a great revival swept the land. In fact, II Chronicles 30:26 says there was not such spiritual joy in the land since the early years of Solomon. II Chronicles 29 describes how Hezekiah in his first year as king immediately began to restore the Temple and its prescribed worship. He ascended the throne when he was twenty-five years old and reigned twenty-nine years.

29:1-2 Hezekiah began to reign *when he was* five and twenty years old, and he reigned nine and twenty years in Jerusalem. And his mother's name *was* Abijah, the daughter of Zechariah. One of the truly great kings of Judah thus sprang from one of the worst. Hezekiah was a great and godly king. He reigned from the time he was twenty-five years old until he was fifty four. Why he died at a relatively young age is not noted in Scripture. His mother's name, which in II Kings 18:2 appears in an abridged form, is fully given here. The key to the profound difference between himself and Ahaz his father likely lies in the training received from his mother and perhaps the influence of a godly priest in his early days.

2 And he did *that which was* right in the sight of the LORD, according to all that David his father had done. The character of this great king is summarized in a word, "he did *that which was* right." All his actions, accomplishments, statements, and motives were reduced to the simple equation: "he did *that which was* right." The simplicity thereof is exceeded only by its profundity. Accordingly, his life and reign were parallel and very similar to "all that David his father had done."

29:3-7 He in the first year of his reign, in the first month, opened the doors of the house of the LORD, and repaired them. 4 And he brought in the priests and the Levites, and gathered them together into the east street. After being king for less than one year, Hezekiah reopened the Temple and repaired its gates which had been desecrated by his father. He forthwith reinstated the Aaronic priesthood and the Levites to their proper service. He thus assembled them in the main courtyard of the Temple which is on the east side thereof.

5 And said unto them, Hear me, ye Levites, sanctify now yourselves, and sanctify the house of the LORD God of your fathers, and carry forth the filthiness out of the holy *place*. 6 For our fathers have trespassed, and done *that which was* evil in the eyes of the LORD our God, and have forsaken him, and have turned away their faces from the habitation of the LORD, and turned *their* backs.

Hezekiah therefore directed the Levites to first make themselves ceremonially clean (i.e., sanctify yourselves) and then to cleanse the Temple. The filthiness mentioned likely refers to idols or trappings of idolatry which had been brought into the Temple by Ahaz. Without a question, many in Judah had turned away from the Jehovah God and had forsaken him in the preceding years. They in fact had turned their backs on God.

7 Also they have shut up the doors of the porch, and put out the lamps, and have not burned incense nor offered burnt offerings in the holy *place* unto the God of Israel. Hezekiah reminded the assembled Levites how that during the reign of Ahaz, the Temple had been shut up, the menorahs therein were darkened, and there were no sacrifices made to the God of Israel.

29:8-11 Wherefore the wrath of the LORD was upon Judah and Jerusalem, and he hath delivered them to trouble, to astonishment, and to hissing, as ye see with your eyes. 9 For, lo, our fathers have fallen by the sword, and our sons and our daughters and our wives *are* in captivity for this. Because of the apostasy and wickedness of idolatry allowed in Judah, God's wrath had been poured out upon them in the endless warfare during the reign of Ahaz. Many in Judah had died in the battles and many family members had been taken into captivity as a result. The reference to **astonishment and hissing** basically means desolation and the reflexive sound one makes when seeing an astounding sight. In our culture, one might reflexively whistle and say "Oh, my goodness," upon seeing something truly astounding such as a bad accident or the devastation from a terrible storm. The point is that after God had dealt with His people, others saw it and so reacted.

10 Now *it is* in mine heart to make a covenant with the LORD God of Israel, that his fierce wrath may turn away from us. Hezekiah therefore announced that he had purposed in his heart to renew the covenant with God as Asa and Jehoiada had done. For Hezekiah, even at this early stage of his reign, feared the wrath of God. Clearly, his actions were motivated in part by the fear of the Lord.

11 My sons, be not now negligent: for the LORD hath chosen you to stand before him, to serve him, and that ye should minister unto him, and burn incense. The king therefore admonished the assembled Levites to not be negligent in restoring the rightful service to God at the Temple. He reminded them how that God had chosen them for the ministry. It was not only a duty, it was a privilege.

29:12-16 Then the Levites arose, Mahath the son of Amasai, and Joel the son of Azariah, of the sons of the Kohathites: and of the sons of Merari, Kish the son of Abdi, and Azariah the son of Jehalelel: and of the Gershonites; Joah the son of Zimmah, and Eden the son of Joah: 13 And of the sons of Elizaphan; Shimri, and Jeiel: and of the sons of Asaph; Zechariah, and Mattaniah: 14 And of the sons of Heman; Jehiel, and Shimei: and of the sons of Jeduthun; Shemaiah, and Uzziel. 15 And they gathered their brethren, and sanctified themselves, and came, according to the commandment of the king, by the words of the LORD, to cleanse the house of the LORD. 16 And the priests went into

the inner part of the house of the LORD, to cleanse *it*, and brought out all the uncleanness that they found in the temple of the LORD into the court of the house of the LORD. And the Levites took *it*, to carry *it* out abroad into the brook Kidron.

Listed above are leaders of the Levites who mobilized their brethren to cleanse the Temple and prepare it for service to God. Likewise, Aaronic priests went into the interior of the Temple proper and removed all abominable vestiges of previous idolatry. They deposited the paraphernalia thereof in the outer courtyard of the Temple. Whereupon the Levites took the idolatrous filth and dumped it in the Kidron brook, just to the east of the Temple. It presumably was washed away with the next rain.

29:17-19 Now they began on the first *day* of the first month to sanctify, and on the eighth day of the month came they to the porch of the LORD: so they sanctified the house of the LORD in eight days; and in the sixteenth day of the first month they made an end. 18 Then they went in to Hezekiah the king, and said, We have cleansed all the house of the LORD, and the altar of burnt offering, with all the vessels thereof, and the shewbread table, with all the vessels thereof. 19 Moreover all the vessels, which king Ahaz in his reign did cast away in his transgression, have we prepared and sanctified, and, behold, they *are* before the altar of the LORD.

The Temple cleansing project began on the first day of Nisan (i.e., approximately April). In one week, the Temple proper had been purged of all vestiges of idolatry out to the porch thereof. By the sixteenth of the month, they had cleansed the Temple altogether, including the courtyard thereof. They thereupon notified Hezekiah that the cleansing of the Temple was thus accomplished. Furthermore, the necessary vessels for service which had been discarded by Ahaz had been found, repaired, cleansed and were now ready for service at the brazen altar of the Temple.

29:20-24 Then Hezekiah the king rose early, and gathered the rulers of the city, and went up to the house of the LORD. Early the next day, Hezekiah assembled the leaders of Jerusalem and entered the Temple. He wasted no time honoring the Lord.

21 And they brought seven bullocks, and seven rams, and seven lambs, and seven he goats, for a sin offering for the kingdom, and for the sanctuary, and for Judah. And he commanded the priests the sons of Aaron to offer *them* on the altar of the LORD. 22 So they killed the bullocks, and the priests received the blood, and sprinkled *it* on the altar: likewise, when they had killed the rams, they sprinkled the blood upon the altar: they killed also the lambs, and they sprinkled the blood upon the altar. 23 And they brought forth the he goats *for* the sin offering before the king and the congregation; and they laid their hands upon them: 24 And the priests killed them, and they made reconciliation with their blood upon the altar, to make an atonement for all Israel: for the king commanded *that* the burnt offering and the sin offering *should be made* for all Israel.

Hezekiah therefore ordered the priests to offer seven bullocks (i.e., steers), seven lambs, and seven goats for a sin offering to God on behalf of the nation. They therefore carefully executed these sin offerings to make reconciliation before God on behalf of the sinful nation. Moreover, burnt offerings and sin offerings for all of Israel were made that day. In each case, the shed blood of the sacrificed animals was sprinkled upon the altar. Thus, the sins of Israel were atoned for that day.

29:25-30 And he set the Levites in the house of the LORD with cymbals, with psalteries, and with harps, according to

the commandment of David, and of Gad the king's seer, and Nathan the prophet: for *so was* the commandment of the LORD by his prophets. 26 And the Levites stood with the instruments of David, and the priests with the trumpets. Hezekiah also restored the Temple choirs and orchestras which David had ordered long before.

26 **And the Levites stood with the instruments of David, and the priests with the trumpets. 27 And Hezekiah commanded to offer the burnt offering upon the altar. And when the burnt offering began, the song of the LORD began *also* with the trumpets, and with the instruments *ordained* by David king of Israel. 28 And all the congregation worshipped, and the singers sang, and the trumpeters sounded:** *and* **all** *this continued* **until the burnt offering was finished. 29 And when they had made an end of offering, the king and all that were present with him bowed themselves, and worshipped.**

After the sin offerings for reconciliation and atonement had been made, Hezekiah ordered a special (sweet savor and thus voluntary) burnt offering be made for praise and thanksgiving to God. At that same time, the Levitical orchestra accompanied the Temple choir and they sang praise to God, along with trumpet fanfares to God. All of this continued until the burnt offering was completed. Thereupon, the king and all present bowed themselves in worship to God.

30 **Moreover Hezekiah the king and the princes commanded the Levites to sing praise unto the LORD with the words of David, and of Asaph the seer. And they sang praises with gladness, and they bowed their heads and worshipped.** Hezekiah also commanded all leaders and Levites present to sing praises to God from psalms written by David and Asaph. They thus sang praise to God "with gladness, and they bowed their heads and worshipped."

29:31-36 Then Hezekiah answered and said, Now ye have consecrated yourselves unto the LORD, come near and bring sacrifices and thank offerings into the house of the LORD. And the congregation brought in sacrifices and thank offerings; and as many as were of a free heart burnt offerings. 32 **And the number of the burnt offerings, which the congregation brought, was threescore and ten bullocks, an hundred rams,** *and* **two hundred lambs: all these** *were* **for a burnt offering to the LORD.** 33 **And the consecrated things** *were* **six hundred oxen and three thousand sheep.**

Thereupon, the Temple was opened for public worship and sacrifices by the nation at large. In the sacrifices to follow upon the reopening of the Temple that day, 70 bullocks (i.e., steers), 100 rams, and 200 lambs were offered as burnt offerings. The 600 oxen and 3,000 sheep as "consecrated things" likely refers to animals dedicated for peace offerings by their owners.

34 **But the priests were too few, so that they could not flay all the burnt offerings: wherefore their brethren the Levites did help them, till the work was ended, and until the** *other* **priests had sanctified themselves: for the Levites** *were* **more upright in heart to sanctify themselves than the priests.** Unfortunately, there were not enough priests properly cleansed ceremonially for service (i.e., sanctified) to handle all the sacrifices that day. Therefore, Levites were pressed into service in assisting the priests on duty until such time as other priests could properly be cleansed for service. Of interest is the note the Levites were more upright in heart in their dedication to the ministry than many of the priests. The latter quite apparently had been careless in getting ready for service.

35 **And also the burnt offerings** *were* **in abundance, with the fat of the peace offerings, and the drink offerings for** *every* **burnt offering. So the service of the house of the LORD was set in order.** 36 **And Hezekiah rejoiced, and all the people, that God had prepared the people: for the thing was**

done **suddenly**. Thus in the first month of his reign as king, Hezekiah not only reopened the Temple, but did so in a godly fashion. Not only were the sin offerings and burnt offerings offered, but also numerous peace offerings as well. He along with his people rejoiced that God had so prepared the people to worship Jehovah as they had done. There surely had not been much advance notice thereof inasmuch as it was early in Hezekiah's reign. Nevertheless, the tone of Hezekiah's reign was thus established.

* * * * *

Overview of II Chronicles 30*: This next chapter describes how after the Temple was reopened in the first month of the year, Hezekiah wasted no time in sending word through both Judah and Israel announcing the restoration of the Passover observance. Because the Passover was to be kept in the first month and that time had already passed, he announced it would be kept in the second month of the year (roughly the month of May). As the entire nation of Judah and portions of Israel responded, a great revival swept through the land such as was not seen since the time of Solomon when he first dedicated the Temple.*

30:1-5 And Hezekiah sent to all Israel and Judah, and wrote letters also to Ephraim and Manasseh, that they should come to the house of the LORD at Jerusalem, to keep the passover unto the LORD God of Israel. 2 For the king had taken counsel, and his princes, and all the congregation in Jerusalem, to keep the passover in the second month. 3 For they could not keep it at that time, because the priests had not sanctified themselves sufficiently, neither had the people gathered themselves together to Jerusalem.

Inasmuch as the Temple had been sanctified and reopened well into the first month of the year, the Passover could not be held at its normal time—the fifteenth day of the first month. Therefore, Hezekiah sought counsel of the leaders of the nation to conduct the Passover in the second month of the year. Furthermore, not enough priests had properly sanctified themselves nor had notice been sent out to the people. Therefore, they agreed to observe Passover in the second month of the year. Therefore, Hezekiah sent letters to *all* Israel, not just Judah, inviting them to come to Jerusalem to observe the Passover.

British Israelism and the Worldwide Church of God teach the ten northern tribes were lost, became later resident of the British Isles, and found refuge on the shores of North America. However, their entire premise is unraveled when note is taken that representatives from all Israel in some degree responded.

4 And the thing pleased the king and all the congregation. 5 So they established a decree to make proclamation throughout all Israel, from Beersheba even to Dan, that they should come to keep the passover unto the LORD God of Israel at Jerusalem: for they had not done *it* of a long *time in such sort* as it was written. The entire nation of Israel from Beersheba in the far south to Dan in the far north were therefore invited to come to Jerusalem to observe the Passover " for they had not done *it* of a long *time in such sort* as it was written." It is sure that the northern kingdom had not observed Passover in a long time. Sadly, even Judah had been derelict thereto in recent years.

30:6-9 So the posts went with the letters from the king and his princes throughout all Israel and Judah, and according to the commandment of the king, saying, Ye children of Israel, turn again unto the LORD God of Abraham, Isaac, and Israel, and he will return to the remnant of you, that are escaped out of the hand of the kings

of Assyria. 7 **And be not ye like your fathers, and like your brethren, which trespassed against the LORD God of their fathers, *who* therefore gave them up to desolation, as ye see.**

Messengers (literally runners) were sent across the entire nation of Israel, including the northern kingdom. No record is made how Hoshea, king of the north, reacted to Hezekiah's invitation. In the letters sent, Hezekiah urged all Israel, including the northern kingdom, to "turn again unto the LORD God of Abraham, Isaac, and Israel, and he will return to the remnant of you, that are escaped out of the hand of the kings of Assyria." God indeed will return to His people as they turn to Him. See James 4:8. God had already begun to chasten the northern kingdom by Assyria. See II Kings 15:19, 29. Some in Israel had already been taken captive by Assyria. (Hezekiah's letters were sent out about four years before the final captivity of Israel by Assyrian in 722 B.C.) Hezekiah also admonished his brethren in the north to "be not ye like your fathers, and like your brethren, which trespassed against the LORD God of their fathers, *who* therefore gave them up to desolation, as ye see."

8 **Now be ye not stiffnecked, as your fathers *were*, *but* yield yourselves unto the LORD, and enter into his sanctuary, which he hath sanctified for ever: and serve the LORD your God, that the fierceness of his wrath may turn away from you. 9 For if ye turn again unto the LORD, your brethren and your children *shall find* compassion before them that lead them captive, so that they shall come again into this land: for the LORD your God *is* gracious and merciful, and will not turn away *his* face from you, if ye return unto him.**

Hezekiah further admonished his brethren in the north to humble themselves before Jehovah their God and come to the Temple and serve Him lest He chasten them in anger. He further reminded them of the compassion and mercy of God for those who turn to him in repentance.

30:10-11 So the posts passed from city to city through the country of Ephraim and Manasseh even unto Zebulun: but they laughed them to scorn, and mocked them. 11 Nevertheless divers of Asher and Manasseh and of Zebulun humbled themselves, and came to Jerusalem. Reference to Ephraim and Manasseh is another generic term for the northern kingdom. The messengers of Hezekiah therefore passed throughout the northern kingdom only to be laughed to scorn and mocked in many places. Notwithstanding that, men from "Asher and Manasseh and of Zebulun humbled themselves, and came to Jerusalem."

30:12-14 Also in Judah the hand of God was to give them one heart to do the commandment of the king and of the princes, by the word of the LORD. 13 And there assembled at Jerusalem much people to keep the feast of unleavened bread in the second month, a very great congregation. 14 And they arose and took away the altars that *were* in Jerusalem, and all the altars for incense took they away, and cast *them* into the brook Kidron.

In Judah, the nation arose with one heart to observe the Passover because God had so given them a heart to do so. Therefore, a great congregation assembled at Jerusalem to observe Passover and the feast of Unleavened Bread in the second month of the year (about May). At that time, there also was a grassroots movement to purge Jerusalem of all idolatrous altars scattered across the city. They were thrown out into what amounted to the sewer of the city, the brook Kidron on the east side of town.

30:15-20 Then they killed the passover on the fourteenth *day* of the second month: and the priests and the Levites were ashamed, and sanctified themselves, and brought in the burnt offerings into the house of the LORD.

16 And they stood in their place after their manner, according to the law of Moses the man of God: the priests sprinkled the blood, *which they received* of the hand of the Levites.

The Passover was thus observed on the 14th day of the second month. However, many priests and Levites were ashamed of themselves for being so careless and negligent in not properly sanctifying themselves (i.e., cleansing themselves ceremonially) in contrast to the willingness and eagerness of the people. Those who did performed their service at the Temple did so according to the Law of Moses.

For *there were* many in the congregation that were not sanctified: therefore the Levites had the charge of the killing of the passovers for every one *that was* not clean, to sanctify *them* unto the LORD. Many who assembled at Jerusalem were not ceremonially clean. Therefore, many Levites were occupied with killing Passover lambs for those not clean to properly sanctify them.

18 For a multitude of the people, *even* many of Ephraim, and Manasseh, Issachar, and Zebulun, had not cleansed themselves, yet did they eat the passover otherwise than it was written. But Hezekiah prayed for them, saying, The good LORD pardon every one 19 *That* prepareth his heart to seek God, the LORD God of his fathers, though *he be* not cleansed according to the purification of the sanctuary.

Many of the pilgrims from the northern tribes were not properly cleansed, but were still at the Passover in violation of what was written in the Torah. Therefore, Hezekiah interceded for them asking God to "pardon every one *that* prepareth his heart to seek God, the LORD God of his fathers, though *he be* not *cleansed* according to the purification of the sanctuary."

20 And the LORD hearkened to Hezekiah, and healed the people. God therefore heard Hezekiah's prayer and pardoned them. God usually is more interested in the condition of the heart than the technicalities of outward service. These many had come to Jerusalem with an open and repentant heart. God therefore was merciful to them.

30:21-22 And the children of Israel that were present at Jerusalem kept the feast of unleavened bread seven days with great gladness: and the Levites and the priests praised the LORD day by day, *singing* with loud instruments unto the LORD. 22 And Hezekiah spake comfortably unto all the Levites that taught the good knowledge of the LORD: and they did eat throughout the feast seven days, offering peace offerings, and making confession to the LORD God of their fathers.

The Passover was thus observed at Jerusalem along with the Feast of Unleavened Bread. Accordingly, there was great joy and praise to God each day thereof. The king also (literally) spoke "to the heart" of the Levites and priests evidently to encourage them. It was these who specially instructed the many Jews who had become illiterate in the prescribed form of worship of Jehovah. All assembled therefore observed the Passover and feast of Unleavened Bread with many peace offerings and confessing their sins before God. It truly was a time of great revival.

30:23-27 And the whole assembly took counsel to keep other seven days: and they kept *other* seven days with gladness. 24 For Hezekiah king of Judah did give to the congregation a thousand bullocks and seven thousand sheep; and the princes gave to the congregation a thousand bullocks and ten thousand sheep: and a great number of priests sanctified themselves.

Hezekiah had personally given to the Temple 1,000 bullocks (steers) and 7,000 sheep for burnt offerings. Furthermore, the princes of the nation had also given 1,000 more

Understanding II Chronicles

bullocks and 10,000 sheep to be likewise offered. There was not time to offer them all during eight days of the combined holy days. Therefore, the assembled people, from the north along with those of Judah, agreed to observe another seven days. They all gladly agreed. Moreover, by now a great number of priests had properly sanctified themselves for service.

25 And all the congregation of Judah, with the priests and the Levites, and all the congregation that came out of Israel, and the strangers that came out of the land of Israel, and that dwelt in Judah, rejoiced. 26 So there was great joy in Jerusalem: for since the time of Solomon the son of David king of Israel *there was* not the like in Jerusalem.

The vast assembled congregation of Judah, priests, Levites, and representatives of the northern kingdom along with proselytes living in Judah rejoiced. The rejoicing in Jerusalem was greater than anytime since Solomon had originally dedicated the Temple.

27 Then the priests the Levites arose and blessed the people: and their voice was heard, and their prayer came up to his holy dwelling place, *even* unto heaven. At the conclusion of the two week observance of holy days, the priests and Levites arose at the Temple and blessed the people before they returned to their homes. Moreover, their benediction and prayer was heard all the way to heaven where God took special heed. Whether there was some special visible manifestation of God's approval is not recorded. However, the Holy Spirit clearly so revealed the same to the inspired chronicler.

* * * * *

Overview of II Chronicles 31: *This next chapter describes the results of the revival in Judah.*

31:1 Now when all this was finished, all Israel that were present went out to the cities of Judah, and brake the images in pieces, and cut down the groves, and threw down the high places and the altars out of all Judah and Benjamin, in Ephraim also and Manasseh, until they had utterly destroyed them all. Then all the children of Israel returned, every man to his possession, into their own cities. Notice that the entire nation, both in the Judah and the north, proceeded to destroy the idols of the land. When revival comes, wickedness is done away with.

31:2-6 And Hezekiah appointed the courses of the priests and the Levites after their courses, every man according to his service, the priests and Levites for burnt offerings and for peace offerings, to minister, and to give thanks, and to praise in the gates of the tents of the LORD. 3 *He appointed* also the king's portion of his substance for the burnt offerings, *to wit*, for the morning and evening burnt offerings, and the burnt offerings for the sabbaths, and for the new moons, and for the set feasts, as *it is* written in the law of the LORD.

After the reopening of the Temple and the magnificent observance of Passover, Hezekiah re-instituted the prescribed courses (i.e., shifts) of the Levites. He also re-instituted the king's regular burnt offerings each morning and evening as well as other prescribed offerings and holy days.

4 Moreover he commanded the people that dwelt in Jerusalem to give the portion of the priests and the Levites, that they might be encouraged in the law of the LORD. 5 And as soon as the commandment came abroad, the children of Israel brought in abundance the firstfruits of corn, wine, and oil, and honey, and of all the increase of the field; and the tithe of all *things* brought they in abundantly. Hezekiah also decreed the people of Jerusalem to give the priests and

Levites their rightful tithes of the firstfruits of the land. Realizing the needs of these servants of God, Hezekiah sought to encourage them in their work. As soon as this decree was issued, greater Israel rose to the occasion "and the tithe of all *things* brought they in abundantly" along with the prescribed firstfruits of the land.

6 And *concerning* the children of Israel and Judah, that dwelt in the cities of Judah, they also brought in the tithe of oxen and sheep, and the tithe of holy things which were consecrated unto the LORD their God, and laid *them* by heaps. Not only did the residents of Jerusalem willingly bring their tithes, but the rest of the nation did so as well, including those who belonged to the northern tribes. The thought is that they so gave heap upon heaps (i.e., heaps and heaps).

31:7-10 In the third month they began to lay the foundation of the heaps, and finished *them* in the seventh month. 8 And when Hezekiah and the princes came and saw the heaps, they blessed the LORD, and his people Israel. In the third month of the year (just a month after the massive Passover recorded in the previous chapter), the foundation for a storehouse near the Temple was laid for the heaps of firstfruits and tithes being brought thereto. Both Hezekiah and his princes therefore blessed the Lord and the people for their generosity and obedience to God.

9 Then Hezekiah questioned with the priests and the Levites concerning the heaps. 10 And Azariah the chief priest of the house of Zadok answered him, and said, Since *the people* began to bring the offerings into the house of the LORD, we have had enough to eat, and have left plenty: for the LORD hath blessed his people; and that which is left *is* this great store. When Hezekiah inquired of the priests and Levites about the huge piles of offerings, the high priest replied, "Since *the people* began to bring the offerings into the house of the LORD, we have had enough to eat, and have left plenty: for the LORD hath blessed his people; and that which is left *is* this great store." (Azariah was the high priest of the family of Eleazar of the line of Zadok, who was made high priest in Solomon's time, when Abiathar was thrust out.) Indeed, when God's people tithe, there is more than enough for the work of God. Tithing has always been God's way for God's work to be financed.

31:11-19 Then Hezekiah commanded to prepare chambers in the house of the LORD; and they prepared *them*, 12 And brought in the offerings and the tithes and the dedicated *things* faithfully: over which Cononiah the Levite *was* ruler, and Shimei his brother *was* the next. The chambers mentioned likely refer to the storehouse which was built adjacent to the Temple for the storage of the firstfruits and tithes of God's people. The people therefore rose up and "brought in the offerings and the tithes and the dedicated *things* faithfully." The chief treasurer thereof was a Levite named Cononiah with his brother Shimei as first assistant.

13 And Jehiel, and Azaziah, and Nahath, and Asahel, and Jerimoth, and Jozabad, and Eliel, and Ismachiah, and Mahath, and Benaiah, *were* overseers under the hand of Cononiah and Shimei his brother, at the commandment of Hezekiah the king, and Azariah the ruler of the house of God. 14 And Kore the son of Imnah the Levite, the porter toward the east, *was* over the freewill offerings of God, to distribute the oblations of the LORD, and the most holy things. 15 And next him *were* Eden, and Miniamin, and Jeshua, and Shemaiah, Amariah, and Shecaniah, in the cities of the priests, in *their* set office, to give to their brethren by courses, as well to the great as to the small.

Various other Levites were assigned as assistants in the oversight and administration of the offerings brought to the Temple storehouse

16 Beside their genealogy of males, from three years old and upward, *even* unto every one that entereth into the house of the LORD, his daily portion for their service in their charges according to their courses; 17 Both to the genealogy of the priests by the house of their fathers, and the Levites from twenty years old and upward, in their charges by their courses; 18 And to the genealogy of all their little ones, their wives, and their sons, and their daughters, through all the congregation: for in their set office they sanctified themselves in holiness: 19 Also of the sons of Aaron the priests, *which were* in the fields of the suburbs of their cities, in every several city, the men that were expressed by name, to give portions to all the males among the priests, and to all that were reckoned by genealogies among the Levites.

The offerings of the Temple were therefore duly given to the Levites and Priests for assistance in their livelihood in the ministry. Listed here are the various groupings and family lineages which were to receive of the offerings from the Temple storehouse.

31:20-21 And thus did Hezekiah throughout all Judah, and wrought *that which was* **good and right and truth before the LORD his God. 21 And in every work that he began in the service of the house of God, and in the law, and in the commandments, to seek his God, he did** *it* **with all his heart, and prospered.** An overview of Hezekiah's ministry is here recorded. He "wrought that which was good and right and truth before the LORD his God. And in every work that he began in the service of the house of God, and in the law, and in the commandments, to seek his God, he did it with all his heart, and prospered." As this godly king totally dedicated himself to serve the Lord with all his heart, that which he did prospered. A lesson remains therein to this day.

* * * * *

Overview of II Chronicles 32: *This last chapter chronicling Hezekiah's life is instructive. Perhaps the key principle is found in verse 31 where we read, "God left him, to try him, that he might know all that was in his heart." This chapter presents several major trials in the life of Hezekiah. God on occasion may test His people for His own divine purposes. In II Chronicles 32, an immense amount of history is summarized.*

The Assyrian empire was threatening the entire Middle East. It was the major world "super-power" of its day. During the reign of Hezekiah, the Assyrians under the leadership of Sennacherib had attacked, defeated and deported the northern kingdom of Israel. II Kings 17 details how God allowed the Assyrians to deport and chasten the northern kingdom for their apostasy. Now, Sennacherib and the Assyrians were engaged in military operations against Judah. They invaded Judah and laid siege to outlying military outposts of the kingdom.

There is a latent spiritual principle clearly surfacing here. Hezekiah had been a godly man and had sought to serve the Lord with all his heart. God in turn had prospered and blessed him. Now, he faced a severe test. The principle illustrated herein is that God almost always will allow a time of trial to come to those who serve Him. In observing virtually any great godly individual in the Bible, sooner or later, trouble came in their lives. Hezekiah was no exception. God allows trials for various reasons: (1) to test His people to see what they are made of when trouble comes; (2) to teach lessons one would never learn when all is going well; (3) to strengthen—steel is tempered only by fire.

32:1 After these things, and the establishment thereof, Sennacherib king of Assyria came, and entered into Judah, and encamped against the fenced cities, and thought to win them for himself. About thirteen years after the events of the

Understanding II Chronicles 667

preceding two chapters, Assyria attacked and invaded Judah under the leadership of Sennacherib. The time was about 713 B.C. Assyria had already overrun the northern kingdom of Israel and deported it into captivity. Now, Sennacherib thought to conquer Judah as well. The fenced cities refer to cities with walls and thus having military fortification. The Assyrians thus attacked and besieged the major outlying cities of Judah, hoping to take them before attacking Jerusalem.

32:2-6 And when Hezekiah saw that Sennacherib was come, and that he was purposed to fight against Jerusalem, 3 He took counsel with his princes and his mighty men to stop the waters of the fountains which *were* without the city: and they did help him. 4 So there was gathered much people together, who stopped all the fountains, and the brook that ran through the midst of the land, saying, Why should the kings of Assyria come, and find much water?

Realizing that Jerusalem was next on Sennacherib's hit list, Hezekiah consulted his upper echelon leaders and planned a defense strategy. Knowing the Assyrians would besiege Jerusalem, Hezekiah planned to use water as a strategic weapon. There is little available water around Jerusalem. The primary source of water for the entire region is the spring of Gihon, located on the east side of the City of David. It actually was the headwaters of the brook Kidron. Hezekiah's plan was simple. They would cover the fountainhead of the spring with some sort of building and divert the water through an underground tunnel into the city. The Assyrians would thus be deprived of water and the city was have an ample supply.

Jewish engineers therefore conducted a marvel of engineering. A tunnel was carved through solid rock under the city from Gihon to what later would be called the pool of Siloam, inside the city. What is even more amazing is that they commenced tunneling from both ends at once and met in the middle—without modern instruments. The tunnel—ever since called Hezekiah's conduit—remains to this day. The Jews therefore had adequate water when the Assyrians arrived and the Assyrians never discovered the headwaters of Gihon.

5 Also he strengthened himself, and built up all the wall that was broken, and raised *it* up to the towers, and another wall without, and repaired Millo *in* the city of David, and made darts and shields in abundance. 6 And he set captains of war over the people, and gathered them together to him in the street of the gate of the city, and spake comfortably to them, saying.

Hezekiah made further military preparations for the coming battle. Sections of the wall of Jerusalem which were in disrepair were rebuilt and fortified. Additional defensive towers were built along the wall and an additional wall was built across the northern face of the city because this was whence the attack undoubtedly would come. (The other three sides of the city were protected by deep valleys.) Millo was a fortified wall across central Jerusalem (running east to west) which separated the upper city from the lower city (i.e., the City of David). This crucial defensive line was rebuilt and strengthened. Darts refers to missiles whether arrows or spears along with shields which were manufactured in abundance in preparation for war. Hezekiah also organized the city into militias with military officers over the entire city. He thus gathered his people in the 'civic plaza' of the eastern gate of the city to encourage them.

32:7-8 Be strong and courageous, be not afraid nor dismayed for the king of Assyria, nor for all the multitude that *is* with him: for *there be* more with us than with him: 8 With him *is* an arm of flesh; but with us *is* the LORD our God to help us, and to fight our battles. And the people rested themselves upon the words of Hezekiah king of Judah.

Notice the great faith and encouragement found in verses 7-8. Hezekiah urged his people to be strong, courageous and not afraid of the king of Assyria nor the multitude with him, "For there be more that is with us than with him." We are not given any specifics of the size of the forces on either side. However, Judah was a tiny nation not much larger than the size of several counties in American geography. Assyria, in contrast, was comprised of the area which today encompasses the modern state of Iraq and Syria. In all likelihood, Judah was vastly outnumbered militarily. Yet, Hezekiah told his people there were more with them than the Assyrians. No doubt what he had in mind, as evidenced in verse 8, is that the Lord and the armies of heaven were on their side. (II Kings 19:35 indicates that the Assyrian army had 185,000 troops at hand.)

Sennacherib could only rely upon the arm of the flesh, that is, human strength. Hezekiah knew they could rely upon the Lord their God to help them fight their battles. It is noteworthy why Hezekiah had such confidence. He knew he had honored the Lord and lived for him. He knew he had done right in the sight of the Lord. He knew he was on praying ground. Therefore, he knew God would deliver them. The predicate of his great faith was the knowledge he had honored the Lord and done right in His sight. The people of his realm therefore "rested themselves upon the words of Hezekiah king of Judah."

32:9-16 After this did Sennacherib king of Assyria send his servants to Jerusalem, (but he *himself laid siege* against Lachish, and all his power with him,) unto Hezekiah king of Judah, and unto all Judah that *were* at Jerusalem, saying. Sennacherib sent a general by the name of Rabshakeh (see II Kings 18:17) and other officers to taunt and demand the surrender of Jerusalem. Sennacherib himself remained at Lachish (pronounced LaKEESH) which was about 30 miles southwest of Jerusalem. It was a strongly defended city atop a hill and

Sennacherib hoped to starve that city into submission by siege. Therefore, he sent subordinates to demand Jerusalem's surrender, seeking to intimidate them.

10 Thus saith Sennacherib king of Assyria, Whereon do ye trust, that ye abide in the siege in Jerusalem? 11 Doth not Hezekiah persuade you to give over yourselves to die by famine and by thirst, saying, The LORD our God shall deliver us out of the hand of the king of Assyria? 12 Hath not the same Hezekiah taken away his high places and his altars, and commanded Judah and Jerusalem, saying, Ye shall worship before one altar, and burn incense upon it? 13 Know ye not what I and my fathers have done unto all the people of *other* lands? were the gods of the nations of those lands any ways able to deliver their lands out of mine hand?

14 Who *was there* among all the gods of those nations that my fathers utterly destroyed, that could deliver his people out of mine hand, that your God should be able to deliver you out of mine hand? 15 Now therefore let not Hezekiah deceive you, nor persuade you on this manner, neither yet believe him: for no god of any nation or kingdom was able to deliver his people out of mine hand, and out of the hand of my fathers: how much less shall your God deliver you out of mine hand? 16 And his servants spake yet *more* against the LORD God, and against his servant Hezekiah.

Rabshakeh therefore taunted both the inhabitants of Jerusalem and their God. He along with messengers sent to Jerusalem who mocked Hezekiah's reliance upon the Lord their God. They attacked Hezekiah's removal of the various high places and idols throughout the land. They implied the impending disaster was because Hezekiah had forsaken these gods. They reminded Judah what they had done to the surrounding nations including Israel to the north. They informed Jerusalem how their God would not be able to deliver them out of their hand.

Understanding II Chronicles 671

The foolish Assyrian general then made another blasphemous blunder. This arrogant Assyrian therefore equated the Almighty God of Israel with the pagan deities of the surrounding nations. It was utter blasphemy. As the Assyrians had crushed neighboring countries, Rabshakeh impudently asked, where were the gods of those places? Could they deliver from the power of the mighty Assyrian army? Well, of course, those pagan idols had no power in any event. But, Rabshakeh had sealed his doom by implying the Jehovah God was no better than them. He asked, if the pagan idols of the various nations which Assyria had conquered could not deliver from the power of Sennacherib, how could Jehovah deliver them? That was a big mistake to equate the power of Jehovah to the impotent gods of the pagan nations around. Rabshakeh had sealed his own fate by challenging Jehovah.

32:17-19 He wrote also letters to rail on the LORD God of Israel, and to speak against him, saying, As the gods of the nations of *other* lands have not delivered their people out of mine hand, so shall not the God of Hezekiah deliver his people out of mine hand. 18 Then they cried with a loud voice in the Jews' speech unto the people of Jerusalem that *were* on the wall, to affright them, and to trouble them; that they might take the city. 19 And they spake against the God of Jerusalem, as against the gods of the people of the earth, *which were* the work of the hands of man.

Furthermore, Sennacherib used the "news media" by writing frightening letters. He clearly was engaging in psychological warfare. He sent also messengers who "cried with a loud voice in the Jew's speech unto the people of Jerusalem that were on the wall, to affright them and to trouble them." For further detail, see II Kings 19:9-13. Notice further how he railed "on the LORD God of Israel . . . and spake against the God of Jerusalem." The Assyrians in their arrogance had sealed their doom in insulting Hezekiah's God. They thus invited the wrath of the God of Hezekiah upon themselves. They had picked a fight with One far more powerful and sealed their fate.

32:20 And for this *cause* Hezekiah the king, and the prophet Isaiah the son of Amoz, prayed and cried to heaven. For details thereof, see II Kings 19:14-19 and Isaiah 37:15-20.

32:21 And the LORD sent an angel, which cut off all the mighty men of valour, and the leaders and captains in the camp of the king of Assyria. So he returned with shame of face to his own land. And when he was come into the house of his god, they that came forth of his own bowels slew him there with the sword. II Kings 19:35-36 gives graphic details how after Hezekiah's prayer God sent a death angel who killed 185,000 Assyrian soldiers the next night. Sennacherib completely defeated therefore slunk back to Nineveh. Shortly thereafter, he was assassinated by his own sons while in the temple of his pagan god. See II Kings 19:36-37 for more details.

32:22-23 Thus the LORD saved Hezekiah and the inhabitants of Jerusalem from the hand of Sennacherib the king of Assyria, and from the hand of all *other*, and guided them on every side. 23 And many brought gifts unto the LORD to Jerusalem, and presents to Hezekiah king of Judah: so that he was magnified in the sight of all nations from thenceforth. God thus miraculously delivered Hezekiah and Jerusalem from the Assyrians and deterred any other country from molesting him. Moreover, God "guided them on every side." Furthermore, God so magnified Hezekiah that numerous nations of the region brought tribute gifts to him, seeking his friendship "so that he was magnified in the sight of all nations from thenceforth." Indeed, God blesses the righteous. See Psalm 5:12.

Understanding II Chronicles 673

32:24-26 In those days Hezekiah was sick to the death, and prayed unto the LORD: and he spake unto him, and he gave him a sign. It seems that when God richly blessed Hezekiah that his estimation of himself became inflated. Pride is a terrible thing and God takes a dim view thereof. God therefore chastened him with a grave illness. Nevertheless, Hezekiah poured out his heart to God in pray, begging for healing. That God did. See II Kings 20:1-11.

25 But Hezekiah rendered not again according to the benefit *done* unto him; for his heart was lifted up: therefore there was wrath upon him, and upon Judah and Jerusalem. Still, Hezekiah lapsed back into a smug and proud attitude. He became afflicted by ingratitude and apparently did not acknowledge the God who had so blessed him. Many a ministry from that day to this has been brought low when after reaching great heights of success become infected with pride and self-acclaim. "Therefore there was wrath upon him, and upon Judah and Jerusalem."

The reference to his heart being lifted up is a clear indication of pride. Proverbs 16:18 warns how "pride goeth before destruction." Hezekiah was perilously close. Notice also how his sin brought others into jeopardy. One's sin always affects others. Part of Hezekiah's folly may have been allowing the Babylonians to view the wealth of the temple as recorded in II Kings 20:12-19. Babylon, as Hezekiah no doubt knew, was just as wicked as Assyria. He had foolishly compromised in cooperating with them.

26 Notwithstanding Hezekiah humbled himself for the pride of his heart, *both* he and the inhabitants of Jerusalem, so that the wrath of the LORD came not upon them in the days of Hezekiah. Apparently, Hezekiah realized the err of his ways and humbled himself. God had evidently gotten his attention through unspecified chastening. Therefore, God stayed further judgment during his lifetime.

32:27-30 And Hezekiah had exceeding much riches and honour: and he made himself treasuries for silver, and for gold, and for precious stones, and for spices, and for shields, and for all manner of pleasant jewels; 28 Storehouses also for the increase of corn, and wine, and oil; and stalls for all manner of beasts, and cotes for flocks. 29 Moreover he provided him cities, and possessions of flocks and herds in abundance: for God had given him substance very much.

The blessing of God upon Hezekiah and his subsequent prospering is thus recorded. In addition to his success as king and in international politics, he became a wealthy man, "for God had given him substance very much." It evidently is for this that Hezekiah had been ungrateful earlier.

30 This same Hezekiah also stopped the upper watercourse of Gihon, and brought it straight down to the west side of the city of David. And Hezekiah prospered in all his works. Further details of Hezekiah's strategic 'conduit' are recorded. It remains to this day with its southerly terminus at the pool of Siloam. Recall 31:20-21. Hezekiah began his reign by serving the Lord with all heart. Accordingly, he "prospered in all his works." God honors righteousness, obedience, and total dedication to this day.

32:31 Howbeit in *the business of* the ambassadors of the princes of Babylon, who sent unto him to enquire of the wonder that was *done* in the land, God left him, to try him, that he might know all *that was* in his heart.

Though a great and godly man, Hezekiah had feet of clay and made a very foolish decision. He allowed ambassadors of Babylon to view the wealth of the Temple treasuries. The Babylonians in turn would return about one-hundred years later and appropriate the same to themselves. For further details thereof, see II Kings 20:12-19.

Understanding II Chronicles

32:32-33 Now the rest of the acts of Hezekiah, and his goodness, behold, they *are* written in the vision of Isaiah the prophet, the son of Amoz, *and* in the book of the kings of Judah and Israel. 33 And Hezekiah slept with his fathers, and they buried him in the chiefest of the sepulchres of the sons of David: and all Judah and the inhabitants of Jerusalem did him honour at his death. And Manasseh his son reigned in his stead.

Further details of the reign of Hezekiah are recorded in the Isaiah 36-39 as well as II Kings 18-20. Of interest is the word translated as **goodness** (חסד *checed*). It is primarily and overwhelmingly rendered otherwise as 'mercy,' 'kindness,' and 'lovingkindness.' This king was not only great, but quite evidently kind. Upon his death at age 54, he was buried " in the chiefest of the sepulchres of the sons of David." His subjects knew that their king was one of the greatest descendants of David. Accordingly, he was buried in the select site available in the royal cemetery in Jerusalem. A royal funeral thus was held on his behalf. Sadly, his son Manasseh was nothing like his father. He did evil in the sight of the Lord.

* * * * *

Overview of II Chronicles 33: In the reign of Manasseh, the beginning of the end of the kingdom of Judah commences. Though his grandson Josiah was a bright light spiritually, the remainder of the kings of Judah were spiritually dark. Manasseh restored the wickedness his father Hezekiah had purged and allowed even greater abominations. The end of the chapter also provides a brief synopsis of the reign of his son Amon who was even worse. In II Chronicles 33, record is made that Manasseh reigned for fifty-five years, "but did that which was evil in the sight of the LORD, like unto the abominations of the heathen, *whom the* LORD *had cast out before the children of Israel." What is implied is that he returned the debauchery of the Canaanites to the land.*

33:1-2 Manasseh *was* twelve years old when he began to reign, and he reigned fifty and five years in Jerusalem: 2 But did *that which was* evil in the sight of the LORD, like unto the abominations of the heathen, whom the LORD had cast out before the children of Israel.

Manasseh, Hezekiah's son, acceded the throne of Judah at age twelve and reigned until he was sixty-seven years old. However, he did "*that which was* evil in the sight of the LORD." During his wicked reign, the moral and spiritual condition of Judah deteriorated to that of the days of the Canaanites centuries earlier. His reign thus was the beginning of the end of Judah. Notwithstanding, he did repent later in life. See 33:11-13.

33:3-6 For he built again the high places which Hezekiah his father had broken down, and he reared up altars for Baalim, and made groves, and worshipped all the host of heaven, and served them. 4 Also he built altars in the house of the LORD, whereof the LORD had said, In Jerusalem shall my name be for ever. 5 And he built altars for all the host of heaven in the two courts of the house of the LORD.

Notice the litany of the spiritual abominations which Manasseh re-instituted. Baal worship was restored with all of its moral degeneracy. He "worshipped all the host of heaven and served them." What apparently is alluded herein is the adoption of the idolatrous practice of worshiping various heavenly bodies such as the sun, moon, and stars. He moreover had the brazen audacity to build blasphemous idolatrous altars even in the Temple of God at Jerusalem.

Understanding II Chronicles

In verse 4 a bitter irony is purposefully recorded that "the LORD had said, In Jerusalem shall my name be for ever." What is implied is that the Lord recalled with pathos the contradiction of the house built for His name now being a place of blasphemy and idolatry.

6 And he caused his children to pass through the fire in the valley of the son of Hinnom: also he observed times, and used enchantments, and used witchcraft, and dealt with a familiar spirit, and with wizards: he wrought much evil in the sight of the LORD, to provoke him to anger.

Record is made of Manasseh causing "his children to pass through the fire in the valley of the son of Hinnom." This is a reference to the unbelievable practice of offering infant children to the god Molech. The Scripture is not clear. However, causing children to pass through the fire was at the least an ordeal of "purification." There an infant was literally passed through the fire of the altar of Molech. It also on other occasions involved the actual sacrifice of infants to the god Molech.

Though the Scripture does not provide the details, other historical sources record that a metallic idol was hollow-cast in the form of a seated man or upright animal. Its head was that of a bull. The idol had out-stretched arms held at an upward angle causing a child laid thereon to roll into the its large open mouth. A hot fire was stoked within the metallic idol until it glowed red-hot.

Pagans would then offer their children upon the out-stretched arms of the furnace-like idol devouring the infants. Loud music especially with drums blared drowning out the cries of the small children as they were burned to death. The heathen practice was thought to pacify and appease the wrath of the god Molech.

In the account of Manasseh in II Kings 21:16 it is recorded that "Manasseh shed innocent blood very much, til he had filled Jerusalem from one end to another." Though the practice of causing children to pass through the fire is not mentioned in that immediate context, it seems evident they were a part of such innocent blood. The parallels to modern abortion are only too obvious.

Notice in the immediate context how that Manasseh also "observed times, and used enchantments, and used witchcraft, and dealt with a familiar spirit, and with wizards." All of this is of the occult. The mention to "times and enchantments" may be a reference to astrology. Witchcraft, familiar spirits, and wizards are all direct dealings with demons and even the devil himself. Manasseh in fact worshiped the devil rather than God. Needless to say, "he wrought much evil in the sight of the LORD, to provoke him to anger."

33:7-8 And he set a carved image, the idol which he had made, in the house of God, of which God had said to David and to Solomon his son, In this house, and in Jerusalem, which I have chosen before all the tribes of Israel, will I put my name for ever: 8 Neither will I any more remove the foot of Israel from out of the land which I have appointed for your fathers; so that they will take heed to do all that I have commanded them, according to the whole law and the statutes and the ordinances by the hand of Moses.

Manasseh also had the blasphemous gall to not only have altars to his pagan deities at the Temple, he also erected a "carved image" in the Temple of God. Again, the irony of how and why that house had been built and dedicated to Jehovah God is recalled in verses 7 and 8. The sacred writer thus quoted what God had said to David and Solomon regarding the Temple. See II Samuel 7:13 and I Kings 8:29. Manasseh had thereby desecrated the very Temple built to worship Jehovah God. In placing His name at the Temple, God had promised to not remove Israel from their land. The condition of that promise however was obedience to His commandments.

33:9-10 So Manasseh made Judah and the inhabitants of Jerusalem to err, *and* to do worse than the heathen, whom the LORD had destroyed before the children of Israel. 10 And the LORD spake to Manasseh, and to his people: but they would not hearken.

Summary is made how that "Manasseh made Judah and the inhabitants of Jerusalem to err, and to do worse than the heathen whom the LORD had destroyed before the children of Israel." God had used Israel in an earlier era to cast the Canaanites out of the land for their abominations. The sad irony was that Judah under Manasseh introduced even worse abominations. Notice in verse 10 that "the LORD spake to Manasseh, and to his people: but they would not hearken." God sent prophets to Manasseh and Judah, warning them of coming judgment, lest they repent. See II Kings 21:10-15. With gross sin there often is an accompanying hardness of heart and stubbornness. Thus, Judah and Manasseh would not listen.

33:11-13 Wherefore the LORD brought upon them the captains of the host of the king of Assyria, which took Manasseh among the thorns, and bound him with fetters, and carried him to Babylon. Notice the cause and effect relationship between the events in the first ten verses of this chapter and verse 11. God severely chastened Manasseh by the king of Assyria. Manasseh was made a prisoner-of-war and taken in chains to Babylon. The word *wherefore* provides a sequential linkage of the preceding events to that which followed. Assyria was still the dominate power in the Middle East of that day. Manasseh was taken captive to Babylon, a city under Assyrian control.

12 And when he was in affliction, he besought the LORD his God, and humbled himself greatly before the God of his fathers, 13 And prayed unto him: and he was intreated of him, and heard his supplication, and brought him again to

Jerusalem into his kingdom. Then Manasseh knew that the LORD he *was* God.

Two amazing thoughts are found in verses 12 and 13. First is that Manasseh when facing such divine chastisement "besought the LORD his God, and humbled himself greatly before the God of his fathers." There is irony in how after such blasphemous departure from Jehovah God, God is referred to as Manasseh's God. God to this day likewise has ways of humbling rebellious Christians.

The second amazing thing is God's mercy and grace. When Manasseh humbled himself in repentance and prayed for God's forgiveness, God "heard his supplication, and brought him again to Jerusalem into his kingdom." Truly God's grace is amazing and truly His mercy is great above the heavens. Thank God for His mercy and grace. If God will forgive such an utter reprobate as Manasseh, He no doubt will deal kindly with those even to this day who come to Him in repentance with a contrite heart. See Psalm 51:17.

33:14-16 Now after this he built a wall without the city of David, on the west side of Gihon, in the valley, even to the entering in at the fish gate, and compassed about Ophel, and raised it up a very great height, and put captains of war in all the fenced cities of Judah. 15 And he took away the strange gods, and the idol out of the house of the LORD, and all the altars that he had built in the mount of the house of the LORD, and in Jerusalem, and cast *them* out of the city. 16 And he repaired the altar of the LORD, and sacrificed thereon peace offerings and thank offerings, and commanded Judah to serve the LORD God of Israel.

After Manasseh was allowed to return to Jerusalem, he repaired the city's defenses. Gihon was on the east side of Jerusalem. He thus rebuilt the wall of Jerusalem from just west of Gihon all the way around to the west side whence was the fish

Understanding II Chronicles

gate to Joppa. The 'Ophel' was a ridge along the east side of Jerusalem between the upper and lower cities. There, Manasseh further rebuilt the wall of the city. More importantly, he set out to eradicate the idolatry in Jerusalem and the Temple he had earlier allowed. He removed the idols and the major idol he had erected in the Temple along with all idolatrous altars. Moreover, "he repaired the altar of the LORD and sacrificed thereon peace-offerings and thank-offerings, and commanded Judah to serve the LORD God of Israel."

33:17 Nevertheless the people did sacrifice still in the high places, *yet* unto the LORD their God only. Though there was a semblance of a revival in Judah in the latter years of Manasseh's reign, the people continued to make private sacrifice atop the high places throughout Judah. Though they did so only to Jehovah, nevertheless, that was in violation of the Law of God. See Deuteronomy 12:5-15.

33:18-20 Now the rest of the acts of Manasseh, and his prayer unto his God, and the words of the seers that spake to him in the name of the LORD God of Israel, behold, they *are written* in the book of the kings of Israel. 19 His prayer also, and *how God* was intreated of him, and all his sin, and his trespass, and the places wherein he built high places, and set up groves and graven images, before he was humbled: behold, they *are* written among the sayings of the seers. Further details of the reign of Manasseh were written in non-canonical books which have been lost to history. Mention there was again made of his sin, his prayer of repentance, and God's mercy to him.

20 So Manasseh slept with his fathers, and they buried him in his own house: and Amon his son reigned in his stead. Once again the euphemism of sleeping with one's fathers is used for death. Manasseh was thence buried in the garden of his palace at Jerusalem rather than in the royal cemetery of the kings of Judah. His son Amon succeeded him on the throne.

33:21-23 Amon *was* two and twenty years old when he began to reign, and reigned two years in Jerusalem. 22 But he did *that which was* evil in the sight of the LORD, as did Manasseh his father: for Amon sacrificed unto all the carved images which Manasseh his father had made, and served them. The son of Manasseh, Amon, reigned for only two years. He did like his father had through much of his reign in doing "*that which was* evil in the sight of the LORD." The truth of Proverbs 28:2 is illustrated. Wicked kings often have unstable tenures. Amon pursued graven images in direct violation of God's commandments.

23 And humbled not himself before the LORD, as Manasseh his father had humbled himself; but Amon trespassed more and more. Unlike his father, Amon refused to humble himself before God and "trespassed more and more." The consequences thereof are recorded in the next verse. A lesson may be drawn of how that Manasseh repented of his sin and God forgave him. However, in the process, he lost his son to the devil. Repentance may invoke God's mercy, but it usually will not alter the harvest of sin already sown. That harvest usually comes in one's children. Herein is a classic example.

33:24-25 And his servants conspired against him, and slew him in his own house. Amon's own servants conspired against him and murdered him in his own house. Indeed sin is a reproach to any people. It brings even political instability.

25 But the people of the land slew all them that had conspired against king Amon; and the people of the land made Josiah his son king in his stead. In the uprising which ensued, the population of Judah killed the assassins of Amon

Understanding II Chronicles

and placed his son Josiah upon the throne of Judah. He was the final bright light of the kings of Judah before the end came.

* * * * *

Overview of II Chronicles 34: *The life and reign of Josiah is here commenced. Josiah was the last great king of Judah. In fact, it was his righteousness which stayed God's impending wrath against Judah. It came following his death. Josiah brought a great revival to the spiritual darkness prevailing in Israel. Yet in his final years, he, like others whom God had blessed, forgot to seek God's counsel. It led to his destruction and death.*

II Chronicles 34 details the rise of young king Josiah and the revival he brought to the land. He began his reign as an eight-year-old boy. By the time he was sixteen, he had matured to seek the Lord. He purged the idolatry of the land and restored the Temple. In reopening the Temple, a copy of the Law was found. In hearing the warnings of God's judgment for apostasy, Josiah made a covenant with his people to rededicate themselves to serve the Lord.

34:1-2 Josiah *was* eight years old when he began to reign, and he reigned in Jerusalem one and thirty years. 2 And he did *that which was* right in the sight of the LORD, and walked in the ways of David his father, and declined *neither* to the right hand, nor to the left. No record is made who was the mother of Josiah. He surely was not influenced to godliness and righteousness by his father. Nevertheless, God's summarized his life and reign as follows: "He did that which was right in the sight of the LORD, and walked in the ways of David his father, and declined neither to the right hand, nor to the left." Not only did he do right as a characteristic of life, he did not deviate therefrom. He stayed the course. He was not distracted to lessor matters on the right hand or left. He did not sacrifice the best upon the altar of the good. He walked in the ways of David his ancestor of nearly 400 years prior.

34:3-7 For in the eighth year of his reign, while he was yet young, he began to seek after the God of David his father: and in the twelfth year he began to purge Judah and Jerusalem from the high places, and the groves, and the carved images, and the molten images. The text well summarizes the uniqueness of Josiah's reign. As a young man of sixteen years "be began to seek after the God of David his father." What we are not told is who had such a profound influence upon his life. Perhaps it was his mother or maybe it was a godly tutor. The latter is likely. Tutors of that day were often Levites or priests, many of which remained faithful to God.

At age twenty, Josiah began to purge Judah of the pagan idolatry which had come to infest the land during Manasseh's and Amon's reigns. Josiah attacked the idolatry vehemently.

4 And they brake down the altars of Baalim in his presence; and the images, that *were* on high above them, he cut down; and the groves, and the carved images, and the molten images, he brake in pieces, and made dust *of them*, and strowed *it* upon the graves of them that had sacrificed unto them. 5 And he burnt the bones of the priests upon their altars, and cleansed Judah and Jerusalem. 6 And *so did he* in the cities of Manasseh, and Ephraim, and Simeon, even unto Naphtali, with their mattocks round about. 7 And when he had broken down the altars and the groves, and had beaten the graven images into powder, and cut down all the idols throughout all the land of Israel, he returned to Jerusalem.

Notice the thoroughness of his zeal. He broke down the altars of Baal in his presence. He not only destroyed the idols and their associated stuff, he ground them into dust and scattered it upon the graves of those who had sacrificed thereto. He even burnt the bones of the priests of Baal. In so doing, he "cleansed Judah and Jerusalem." Furthermore, he extended his campaign of eradicating sin into the remnant of the northern kingdom all the way to Naphtali which was in the Galilee region. (The northern kingdom by now had been taken captive and deported by the Assyrians.)

After he utterly destroyed "the altars and the groves, and had beaten the graven images into powder, and cut down all the idols throughout all the land of Israel, he returned to Jerusalem." Thus, as a young king, Josiah to the best of his ability, eradicated idolatry from not only Judah but much of the territory of the former northern kingdom as well.

34:8-13 Now in the eighteenth year of his reign, when he had purged the land, and the house, he sent Shaphan the son of Azaliah, and Maaseiah the governor of the city, and Joah the son of Joahaz the recorder, to repair the house of the LORD his God. 9 And when they came to Hilkiah the high priest, they delivered the money that was brought into the house of God, which the Levites that kept the doors had gathered of the hand of Manasseh and Ephraim, and of all the remnant of Israel, and of all Judah and Benjamin; and they returned to Jerusalem.

Record is made how that Josiah (at age twenty-six) turned his attention to repairing and restoring the Temple at Jerusalem. After purging the land and the Temple of all idolatry, he ordered repairs be made on the Temple. During the reign of his father and grandfather (Manasseh and Amon), the Temple had been allowed to deteriorate and even had been used for idolatry. Funds thus had been raised from Jews, even those who still lived in the defunct northern kingdom. Those funds were thereupon used to begin restoration and renovation of the Temple.

God's plan has always been for God's people to support the work of God and the funding of the house of God.

10 And they put *it* in the hand of the workmen that had the oversight of the house of the LORD, and they gave it to the workmen that wrought in the house of the LORD, to repair and amend the house. 11 Even to the artificers and builders gave they *it*, to buy hewn stone, and timber for couplings, and to floor the houses which the kings of Judah had destroyed. 12 And the men did the work faithfully: and the overseers of them *were* Jahath and Obadiah, the Levites, of the sons of Merari; and Zechariah and Meshullam, of the sons of the Kohathites, to set *it* forward; and *other of* the Levites, all that could skill of instruments of musick. 13 Also *they were* over the bearers of burdens, and *were* overseers of all that wrought the work in any manner of service: and of the Levites *there were* scribes, and officers, and porters.

Skilled craftsmen were hired to do the necessary repairs upon the Temple. These skilled tradesmen did the work of repair of the Temple faithfully. Implied is that they were honest in the use of Temple funds and were diligent in their work. Oversight was by Levites who were appointed over the work.

34:14-17 And when they brought out the money that was brought into the house of the LORD, Hilkiah the priest found a book of the law of the LORD *given* by Moses. 15 And Hilkiah answered and said to Shaphan the scribe, I have found the book of the law in the house of the LORD. And Hilkiah delivered the book to Shaphan. 16 And Shaphan carried the book to the king, and brought the king word back again, saying, All that was committed to thy servants, they do *it*. 17 And they have gathered together the money that was found in the house of the LORD, and have delivered it into the hand of the overseers, and to the hand of the workmen.

Understanding II Chronicles

Record is made how during the restoration of the Temple, a copy of the law of Moses was discovered. What is implied is that at this point in Old Testament history, the Word of God had basically disappeared. With the sin and corruption which had prevailed, this therefore is not surprising. Nevertheless, God preserves His Word and like a buried seed, it always sprouts back into the open. The notables at this time were Hilkiah the priest who found the book. Shaphan, the scribe, who was in charge of the renovation delivered the book to king Josiah. As Shaphan reported to the king of the progress of the work, he also noted a copy of the book of the Law had been discovered.

34:18-21 Then Shaphan the scribe told the king, saying, Hilkiah the priest hath given me a book. And Shaphan read it before the king. 19 And it came to pass, when the king had heard the words of the law, that he rent his clothes. 20 And the king commanded Hilkiah, and Ahikam the son of Shaphan, and Abdon the son of Micah, and Shaphan the scribe, and Asaiah a servant of the king's, saying, 21 Go, enquire of the LORD for me, and for them that are left in Israel and in Judah, concerning the words of the book that is found: for great *is* the wrath of the LORD that is poured out upon us, because our fathers have not kept the word of the LORD, to do after all that is written in this book.

An account of how the book of the Law was read to king Josiah is made. C. I. Scofield commented *"By the law is the knowledge of sin."* As Josiah heard the Law of God, likely from Leviticus or Deuteronomy, he was convicted of the sin of the nation and of his forefathers. He thus ripped his royal clothing as a demonstration of his despair and sorrow. It is apparent that even godly Josiah had not heretofore been directly exposed to the Word of God. What is implied is that portions of the Law (the Pentateuch) was read to him. That likely included Leviticus 26 and Deuteronomy 28. Both of those chapters present in unwavering clarity how God would judge His people if they departed from Him and served other gods. Both Leviticus 26 and Deuteronomy 28 made it very clear in specific detail how God would so judge Israel. Moreover, Josiah no doubt was well aware of how Israel, their ancestral brethren to the north, had been chastened and deported by the Assyrians. Josiah knew all too well the idolatrous abominations which had prevailed under his predecessors. He therefore realized the predicament Judah faced. God's wrath was impending against the nation.

34:22-28 And Hilkiah, and *they* that the king *had appointed*, went to Huldah the prophetess, the wife of Shallum the son of Tikvath, the son of Hasrah, keeper of the wardrobe; (now she dwelt in Jerusalem in the college:) and they spake to her to that *effect*. 23 And she answered them, Thus saith the LORD God of Israel, Tell ye the man that sent you to me. The fact that the royal delegation went to a female prophet indicates there was no other prophet or priest in the land which had any power with God. Apparently, Huldah was the only such godly person in the realm. The word translated as **college** (מִשְׁנֶה *mishneh*) is uncertain. In any event, the royal delegation turned to Huldah for word from God. Huldah clearly spoke on behalf of God with the declaration, "*Thus saith the LORD.*" She had a message from God to be delivered to the king.

24 Thus saith the LORD, Behold, I will bring evil upon this place, and upon the inhabitants thereof, *even* all the curses that are written in the book which they have read before the king of Judah: 25 Because they have forsaken me, and have burned incense unto other gods, that they might provoke me to anger with all the works of their hands; therefore my wrath shall be poured out upon this place, and shall not be quenched.

Judah had forsaken their God by turning to other idolatrous gods and thus provoking Him to anger. Therefore, His wrath was impending against Jerusalem. Moreover, nothing they could do would prevent God's wrath from falling upon them.

26 **And as for the king of Judah, who sent you to enquire of the LORD, so shall ye say unto him, Thus saith the LORD God of Israel** *concerning* **the words which thou hast heard; 27 Because thine heart was tender, and thou didst humble thyself before God, when thou heardest his words against this place, and against the inhabitants thereof, and humbledst thyself before me, and didst rend thy clothes, and weep before me; I have even heard** *thee* **also, saith the LORD. 28 Behold, I will gather thee to thy fathers, and thou shalt be gathered to thy grave in peace, neither shall thine eyes see all the evil that I will bring upon this place, and upon the inhabitants of the same. So they brought the king word again.**

However, Huldah offered this reprieve for Josiah. God was well aware of the godly character of Josiah and his attempts to restore righteousness to the kingdom. God had noticed that (1) Josiah had a tender heart and (2) how he had humbled himself before God. Because (3) of his godly sorrow over the sin of his kingdom, God informed Josiah that He had heard his prayer. The wrath of God would not be turned away from Judah. However, because of the righteous heart, humility, and godly sorrow of Josiah; God promised that His wrath would not come in Josiah's lifetime. It would be postponed. Though Josiah would die an untimely death, it would not be connected with God's wrath against Judah. His righteous spirit had deferred the judgment of God. It would still come, but not in Josiah's lifetime.

34:29-32 Then the king sent and gathered together all the elders of Judah and Jerusalem. 30 And the king went up into the house of the LORD, and all the men of Judah, and the inhabitants of Jerusalem, and the priests, and the Levites, and all the people, great and small: and he read in

their ears all the words of the book of the covenant that was found in the house of the LORD. 31 And the king stood in his place, and made a covenant before the LORD, to walk after the LORD, and to keep his commandments, and his testimonies, and his statutes, with all his heart, and with all his soul, to perform the words of the covenant which are written in this book. 32 And he caused all that were present in Jerusalem and Benjamin to stand** *to it*. **And the inhabitants of Jerusalem did according to the covenant of God, the God of their fathers.**

Josiah thus assembled the entire leadership as well as all of the men of Jerusalem and Judah to the Temple where he himself read to them "the words of the book of the covenant." Precisely which portions of the Law were read is not sure. But it likely may have been from Exodus 24 as well as portions of Deuteronomy, warning of God's chastening upon Israel if they forsook Him.

It may be that Josiah stood upon the brazen scaffold which Solomon had made for official appearances at the Temple. See II Kings 11:14. In any event, he there publicly recommitted himself to a covenant with the Lord (1) to walk after the Lord, (2) to obey His commandments, testimonies and statutes (i.e., all the laws of God, moral, civil, and ceremonial). Implicit in the text is that the king made this covenant with God on behalf of the nation so that they as well would obey all of God's word "with all *their* heart and all *their* soul." Furthermore, the king determined before his people (3) to perform the words of the covenant written in God's Word. Evidently, in standing to the covenant, the men of Judah showed respect to the Word of God and publicly agreed thereto.

34:33 And Josiah took away all the abominations out of all the countries that *pertained* **to the children of Israel, and made all that were present in Israel to serve,** *even* **to serve**

Understanding II Chronicles

the LORD their God. *And* all his days they departed not from following the LORD, the God of their fathers. Josiah therefore removed the abomination of idolatry from the entire land of Israel, including the territory of the northern kingdom. He "made all that were present in Israel to serve, *even* to serve the LORD their God." As king, he *made* his people serve the Lord and not pagan idols. He therefore departed not from following the Lord his entire life. What a testimony, especially in the midst of all the spiritual darkness surrounding his reign.

* * * * *

Overview of II Chronicles 35: *Two notable events are recorded. (1) The great passover observed by Josiah and (2) his folly leading to his death.*

35:1-6 Moreover Josiah kept a passover unto the LORD in Jerusalem: and they killed the passover on the fourteenth day of the first month. 2 And he set the priests in their charges, and encouraged them to the service of the house of the LORD. Though observance of the Passover was a prescribed holy day on the Hebrew calendar, this observance was special. Implicit is that observance thereof had faded into oblivion. However, after having read the Law of God, Josiah determined to re-institute its observance in a grand fashion. In fact, verse 18 says "And there was no passover like to that kept in Israel from the days of Samuel the prophet; neither did all the kings of Israel keep such a passover as Josiah kept, and the priests, and the Levites, and all Judah and Israel that were present, and the inhabitants of Jerusalem."

Josiah therefore reconstituted the priestly orders and their assigned duties in preparation for the massive Passover about to be observed. He thus encouraged them for the task ahead.

3 And said unto the Levites that taught all Israel, which were holy unto the LORD, Put the holy ark in the house which Solomon the son of David king of Israel did build; *it shall* **not** *be* **a burden upon** *your* **shoulders: serve now the LORD your God, and his people Israel.** Clearly implied is that the ark of the covenant had been removed from the holy of holies in the Temple. Where and by whom is not clear. However, Josiah ordered it returned to its rightful place. Josiah thus directed the Levites who evidently had taken care of the ark to return it and attend to other matter of Levitical service.

4 And prepare *yourselves* **by the houses of your fathers, after your courses, according to the writing of David king of Israel, and according to the writing of Solomon his son. 5 And stand in the holy** *place* **according to the divisions of the families of the fathers of your brethren the people, and** *after* **the division of the families of the Levites. 6 So kill the passover, and sanctify yourselves, and prepare your brethren, that** *they* **may do according to the word of the LORD by the hand of Moses.**

The Levites were thus ordered to prepare themselves in their proper orders for the observance of the coming Passover. They were therefore ordered to kill the Passover lamb and be prepared to serve at the Temple "according to the word of the LORD by the hand of Moses."

35:7-9 And Josiah gave to the people, of the flock, lambs and kids, all for the passover offerings, for all that were present, to the number of thirty thousand, and three thousand bullocks: these *were* **of the king's substance. 8 And his princes gave willingly unto the people, to the priests, and to the Levites: Hilkiah and Zechariah and Jehiel, rulers of the house of God, gave unto the priests for the passover offerings two thousand and six hundred** *small cattle***, and three hundred oxen. 9 Conaniah also, and Shemaiah and**

Nethaneel, his brethren, and Hashabiah and Jeiel and Jozabad, chief of the Levites, gave unto the Levites for passover offerings five thousand *small cattle*, and five hundred oxen. In preparation of this massive Passover celebration, Josiah himself provided 30,000 lambs for the people who were present in addition to 3,000 bullocks for burnt offerings. The princes of Judah also donated 2,600 animals for sacrifice (presumably lambs or kid goats) and 300 oxen for sacrifices. Josiah's brothers and the chief Levites also donated 5,000 animals (presumably lambs and kid goats) along with 500 oxen for sacrifices.

35:10-13 So the service was prepared, and the priests stood in their place, and the Levites in their courses, according to the king's commandment. 11 And they killed the passover, and the priests sprinkled *the blood* from their hands, and the Levites flayed *them*. 12 And they removed the burnt offerings, that they might give according to the divisions of the families of the people, to offer unto the LORD, as *it is* written in the book of Moses. And so *did they* with the oxen. 13 And they roasted the passover with fire according to the ordinance: but the *other* holy *offerings* sod they in pots, and in caldrons, and in pans, and divided *them* speedily among all the people.

After such massive preparations were made, the huge number of lambs (or kid goats) were slain, their blood was sprinkled and the Levites butchered the animals. The animals which were designated for burnt offerings as free-will, sweet-savor offerings to God were therefore set apart from the Passover lambs. These evidently were then offered separately and then cooked as noted below for other meats. The Passover lambs were then roasted according to the rules of the Law, the other meats were cooked (perhaps as stews) in pots and pans, and it all was speedily served to the throngs assembled.

35:14-17 And afterward they made ready for themselves, and for the priests: because the priests the sons of Aaron *were busied* **in offering of burnt offerings and the fat until night; therefore the Levites prepared for themselves, and for the priests the sons of Aaron.** Because the priests were so busy in preparing the Passover lambs that entire day, the Levites therefore prepared lambs for themselves and for the priests that day.

15 And the singers the sons of Asaph *were* **in their place, according to the commandment of David, and Asaph, and Heman, and Jeduthun the king's seer; and the porters** *waited* **at every gate; they might not depart from their service; for their brethren the Levites prepared for them.** Levites who had specific duties such as singing in the Temple choir that day or were guards assigned to Temple gates remained on duty all day. However, other Levites prepared Passover lambs for them as well.

16 So all the service of the LORD was prepared the same day, to keep the passover, and to offer burnt offerings upon the altar of the LORD, according to the commandment of king Josiah. 17 And the children of Israel that were present kept the passover at that time, and the feast of unleavened bread seven days. Thus, the entire ministry of the Temple was prepared that day to (1) observe the Passover and (2) to offer burnt offerings unto the Lord. The Israelites present (implying more than just the tribe of Judah) thus observed the Passover at Jerusalem and the feast of Unleavened Bread the following seven days.

35:18-19 And there was no passover like to that kept in Israel from the days of Samuel the prophet; neither did all the kings of Israel keep such a passover as Josiah kept, and the priests, and the Levites, and all Judah and Israel that were present, and the inhabitants of Jerusalem. 19 In the

eighteenth year of the reign of Josiah was this passover kept. The sacred chronicler thus notes that no Passover was observed in Israel like this one since the days of Samuel. That is remarkable for it includes the reigns of David, Solomon, Jehoshaphat, and Hezekiah. No king of Israel conducted a Passover such as did Josiah. This massive Passover was observed in the eighteenth year of Josiah when he was about twenty-six years old.

35:20-24 After all this, when Josiah had prepared the temple, Necho king of Egypt came up to fight against Carchemish by Euphrates: and Josiah went out against him. 21 But he sent ambassadors to him, saying, What have I to do with thee, thou king of Judah? *I come* **not against thee this day, but against the house wherewith I have war: for God commanded me to make haste: forbear thee from** *meddling with* **God, who** *is* **with me, that he destroy thee not. 22 Nevertheless Josiah would not turn his face from him, but disguised himself, that he might fight with him, and hearkened not unto the words of Necho from the mouth of God, and came to fight in the valley of Megiddo.**

23 And the archers shot at king Josiah; and the king said to his servants, Have me away; for I am sore wounded. 24 His servants therefore took him out of that chariot, and put him in the second chariot that he had; and they brought him to Jerusalem, and he died, and was buried in *one of* **the sepulchres of his fathers. And all Judah and Jerusalem mourned for Josiah.**

Verses 20-24 presents the final years of Josiah and the sad account of his untimely death. Egypt was at war with Babylon and the Egyptian army (under Necho) was on its way to fight Babylon at Carchemish on the Euphrates River. (Carchemish was located in what would be northern Syria today.) That took the Egyptians through the land of Israel. Josiah therefore went out to assert himself against the Egyptian army, perhaps to prevent the re-institution of Egyptian control in Palestine. The Egyptians told him their fight was not with him. Josiah would not listen. The date was 609 B.C.

In the ensuing battle at Megiddo, Josiah was mortally wounded and brought back to Jerusalem where he died. Perhaps the lesson which might be drawn is that Josiah made a major decision without enquiring of the Lord. He did not seek the Lord's face in the matter. The decision made, in his own understanding and without God's counsel, was his undoing and his destruction. In the aftermath of the battle, Egypt did in fact take control of the region of Israel as will be detailed in the following chapter.

35:25-27 And Jeremiah lamented for Josiah: and all the singing men and the singing women spake of Josiah in their lamentations to this day, and made them an ordinance in Israel: and, behold, they *are* written in the lamentations. 26 Now the rest of the acts of Josiah, and his goodness, according to *that which was* written in the law of the LORD, 27 And his deeds, first and last, behold, they *are* written in the book of the kings of Israel and Judah.

Record is thus made how in the early years of Jeremiah's ministry, the prophet lamented the death of Josiah. Mournful songs of remembrance were composed by musicians in Judah which were sung by Jews even to the days of the writing of Chronicles, perhaps by Ezra. Jamieson, Fausset, and Brown write, "The spot in the valley of Megiddo where the battle was fought was near the town of Hadad-rimmon; hence the lamentation for the death of Josiah was called 'the lamentation of Hadad-rimmon in the valley of Megiddo,' which was so great and so long continued, that the lamentation of Hadad passed afterwards into a proverbial phrase to express any great and extraordinary sorrow (see Zechariah 12:11).

Thus ended the truncated reign of Josiah, one of the truly great kings of Israel. Other record is made of him in other non-inspired books of Jewish history. The "book of the kings of Israel and Judah" most likely does not refer to the canonical Book of Kings.

* * * * *

Overview of II Chronicles 36: *This final chapter of II Chronicles is both a dark chapter in Old Testament history and at the same time a momentous one. The judgement God foretold (of which Josiah would outlive) now falls heavily. Four weak, wicked, and for the most part short-term kings comprised the final list of the kings of Judah. In this chapter, the Babylonian captivity begins. Israel (and Judah) as a sovereign kingdom ceased to exit until A.D. 1948. In fact, though Israel has been reconstituted as an independent nation, the kingdom still has not been restored. The mills of God grind slow, but they grind exceedingly fine.*

Contemporaneous with this chapter are the prophets Jeremiah, Daniel, and Ezekiel. The Babylonian captivity as noted here actually was in three phases. The first began in approximately 605 B.C. at which time Daniel and others were taken to Babylon. Then the Babylonians returned about eight years later and chastened the land, taking another quantity of Jews to Babylon.

Finally, in about 586 B.C. when Zedekiah the final king of Judah rebelled against his Chaldean overlords, the Babylonians returned with vengeance. Jerusalem was destroyed. The Temple was destroyed. The vast majority of the Jews were either killed or deported. The darkest days in the history of Israel began. It is during this time, the events of the books of Daniel, Jeremiah, and Ezekiel were written.

36:1-3 Then the people of the land took Jehoahaz the son of Josiah, and made him king in his father's stead in Jerusalem. 2 Jehoahaz *was* twenty and three years old when he began to reign, and he reigned three months in Jerusalem. 3 And the king of Egypt put him down at Jerusalem, and condemned the land in an hundred talents of silver and a talent of gold.

The short lived reign of Jehoahaz the son of Josiah is recorded. He was installed upon the throne of his father Josiah by the people of the land at the age of twenty three. Notice that he reigned only three months. After having prevailed at the battle of Carchemish, Necho, king of Egypt "put him down at Jerusalem" and further levied an annual tax upon Judah of "an hundred talents of silver and a talent of gold." The judgement prophesied by Huldah the prophetess in chapter 34 was beginning to come to pass. Jehoahaz was taken as a prisoner of war to Egypt. For the moment, Egypt was the dominant power of the region and Judah was forced to be its vassal state.

36:4-7 And the king of Egypt made Eliakim his brother king over Judah and Jerusalem, and turned his name to Jehoiakim. And Necho took Jehoahaz his brother, and carried him to Egypt. 5 Jehoiakim *was* twenty and five years old when he began to reign, and he reigned eleven years in Jerusalem: and he did *that which was* evil in the sight of the LORD his God.

In asserting himself over Judah, Necho, king of Egypt, removed Jehoahaz from the throne of Judah and replaced him with his brother Eliakim. Eliakim's name therefore was changed to Jehoiakim. Jehoahaz died in Egypt according to Jeremiah 22:10-12. Jehoiakim was placed on the throne of Judah at the age of twenty five and reigned for eleven years. His reign was characterized by the inspired chronicler as "evil in the sight of the LORD his God."

6 Against him came up Nebuchadnezzar king of Babylon, and bound him in fetters, to carry him to Babylon. **7** Nebuchadnezzar also carried of the vessels of the house of the LORD to Babylon, and put them in his temple at Babylon.

The tides of international politics thus changed and Babylon became the major power of the Middle East, surpassing the Egyptians and Assyrians. The new young king of Babylon was Nebuchadnezzar who promptly invaded Judah in 605 B.C., asserting himself over Egyptian influence. He captured Jerusalem and removed many of the sacred gold and silver vessels of the Temple, taking them to Babylon and depositing them in the temple of his god Belus (see Daniel 5:2).

It was also at this time that Daniel and his companions were deported to Babylon. It was the philosophy of the Babylonians to take the bright young people of conquered lands and train them in Babylonian culture. Their goal was to educate the cream of the crop of their conquered realm as Babylonians and use them to help rule their empire. Daniel and his companions were part of this venture. Daniel 1:1 reveals how this invasion took place in the third year of Jehoiakim's reign The first wave of the Jewish diaspora had begun. See Daniel 1.

36:8-10 Now the rest of the acts of Jehoiakim, and his abominations which he did, and that which was found in him, behold, they *are* written in the book of the kings of Israel and Judah: and Jehoiachin his son reigned in his stead. The reign of Jehoiakim is characterized as being abominable to God. Upon his death in his thirty-sixth year, his son Jehoiachin succeeded him upon the throne of Judah. He also is known as Jeconiah (or even, Coniah for short).

9 Jehoiachin *was* eight years old when he began to reign, and he reigned three months and ten days in Jerusalem: and he did *that which was* evil in the sight of the LORD.

Understanding II Chronicles

A supposed contradiction of details is imagined by some here when compared with II Kings 24:8 where that text reads "Jehoiachin *was* eighteen years old when he began to reign." John Gill makes this comment regarding the supposed discrepancy of Scripture. "In II Chronicles 36:9 he is said to be but eight years old; which may be reconciled by observing, that he might be made and declared king by his father, in the first year of his reign, who reigned eleven years, so that he was eight years old when he began to reign with him, and eighteen when he began to reign alone." This young king, in any event, is remembered as having done that which was evil before God even as his father had done. His reign was only three months because of events which took place in the next verse.

10 And when the year was expired, king Nebuchadnezzar sent, and brought him to Babylon, with the goodly vessels of the house of the LORD, and made Zedekiah his brother king over Judah and Jerusalem. In a second incursion against Jerusalem in about 597 B.C., Nebuchadnezzar once again invaded Judah and removed Jehoiachin from the throne and replaced him with his brother Zedekiah. In the invasion, the Jews resisted and the Babylonians proceeded to besiege Jerusalem. Precisely how long the siege lasted is not noted. However, it apparently was not long.

Perhaps because Jehoiachin had resisted Babylonian forces and perhaps Nebuchadnezzar thought that by granting the throne to Zedekiah he would have a loyal vassal, Jehoiachin was removed and Zedekiah was made king over Judah. Jehoiachin was therefore deported back to Babylon along with more sacred vessels of the Temple. At this time also Nebuchadnezzar also deported all the all nobles and most skilful artisans of Judea. It was also at this time that Ezekiel was taken to Babylon.

36:11-14 Zedekiah *was* one and twenty years old when he began to reign, and reigned eleven years in Jerusalem. 12

And he did *that which was* evil in the sight of the LORD his God, *and* humbled not himself before Jeremiah the prophet *speaking* from the mouth of the LORD. Zedekiah, brother of Jehoiachin was installed on the throne of Judah at the age of twenty one and reigned for eleven years. The inspired chronicler characterized him as doing "*that which was* evil in the sight of the LORD his God." Moreover, his reign was contemporaneous with the later ministry of Jeremiah the prophet who wrote and preached against his sin. However, even with a major prophet of God preaching against his sin, Zedekiah "humbled not himself before Jeremiah the prophet *speaking* from the mouth of the LORD." Notice also the divinely inspired source of Jeremiah's message: he spoke from the mouth of the LORD.

13 And he also rebelled against king Nebuchadnezzar, who had made him swear by God: but he stiffened his neck, and hardened his heart from turning unto the LORD God of Israel. 14 Moreover all the chief of the priests, and the people, transgressed very much after all the abominations of the heathen; and polluted the house of the LORD which he had hallowed in Jerusalem.

Not only did he rebel against the LORD, he also rebelled against Nebuchadnezzar, king of Babylon. Notice further that Zedekiah "hardened his heart from turning unto the LORD God of Israel." As the leader, so followed the people of the land in turning from the Lord. The Book of Jeremiah records the rebellious spirit of Pashur the priest and other leaders of Judah. They followed Zedekiah's lead in rebelling against the Lord. Like some of his forefather's, Zedekiah polluted the Temple by re-instituting idolatry there once again. Clearly implied is that in placing Zedekiah upon the throne of Judah, that he had sworn allegiance by God to Nebuchadnezzar to be a loyal subordinate. However, this foolish king rebelled against him as well. That would soon prove to be his undoing.

35:15-16 And the LORD God of their fathers sent to them by his messengers, rising up betimes, and sending; because he had compassion on his people, and on his dwelling place: 16 But they mocked the messengers of God, and despised his words, and misused his prophets, until the wrath of the LORD arose against his people, till *there was* no remedy.

The sacred chronicler pauses to insert a poignant comment. Notwithstanding the sin and rebellion of Judah, led by Zedekiah, God had compassion on them. He thus sent numerous prophets to them warning them, not the least of which were Isaiah, Jeremiah, and Ezekiel in Babylon, not to mention other lessor prophets. These prophets rose early in the morning and warned Judah. The thought is that they were diligent in doing the task to which God had sent them. With words of tragedy, the sacred writer records, "But they mocked the messengers of God, and despised his words, and misused his prophets, until the wrath of the LORD arose against his people, till *there was* no remedy." The persecution and imprisonment of Jeremiah certainly would be one illustration thereof. Judah had cooked its goose. The wrath of God was about to be poured out without remedy. Their end was at hand.

36:17-19 Therefore he brought upon them the king of the Chaldees, who slew their young men with the sword in the house of their sanctuary, and had no compassion upon young man or maiden, old man, or him that stooped for age: he gave *them* all into his hand. 18 And all the vessels of the house of God, great and small, and the treasures of the house of the LORD, and the treasures of the king, and of his princes; all *these* he brought to Babylon. 19 And they burnt the house of God, and brake down the wall of Jerusalem, and burnt all the palaces thereof with fire, and destroyed all the goodly vessels thereof.

Understanding II Chronicles   703

Upon learning of Zedekiah's treachery and rebellion (especially after having given the throne to him), Nebuchadnezzar returned with vengeance against Jerusalem. The sacred writer makes it clear that it ultimately was God who so sent the Babylonians against rebellious Zedekiah and Judah. Babylon besieged Jerusalem for eighteen months during which terrible starvation and disease ravaged the city. The Book of Lamentations is Jeremiah's mournful account of that terrible siege. Upon finally breaking into the city, the Babylonian forces killed multitudes, having compassion on no one—"young man or maiden, old man, or him that stooped for age." The Temple and king's palace was cleaned out of all valuables. Once all of value had been taken, the Babylonians set the Temple on fire and broke down the walls of Jerusalem—their line of military defence.

When the Babylonians finally pulled out of Jerusalem, virtually nothing was left standing. The city had been utterly destroyed. The few who survived the onslaught were taken prisoner to Babylon. Judah (and by extension greater Israel) ceased to exist as an independent state. Though there would eventually be a limited restoration of Jerusalem under Ezra and Nehemiah and a few feeble attempt of independence under the Maccabees, Israel went out of existence as a nation until A.D. 1948. This final deportation culminated in 586 B.C. Whereas the Jews called their diaspora from Jehoiakim and Jehoiachin their "servitude" and "captivity" respectively, from 586 B.C. the diaspora became known as the "desolation."

Jeremiah, who witnessed the awful devastation upon Jerusalem, said in Lamentations 3:1, "I am the man that hath seen affliction by the rod of his wrath." In fact, the entire book of Lamentations poetically, yet graphically describes the extent of God's wrath which was poured out by the Babylonians.

36:20-21 And them that had escaped from the sword carried he away to Babylon; where they were servants to

him and his sons until the reign of the kingdom of Persia: 21 To fulfil the word of the LORD by the mouth of Jeremiah, until the land had enjoyed her sabbaths: *for* as long as she lay desolate she kept sabbath, to fulfil threescore and ten years.

II Kings 25:4-8 describes the attempt by Zedekiah to flee Jerusalem and his execution. Most other Jews were rounded up and marched as prisoner of war back to Jerusalem. The official captivity lasted until "the reign of the kingdom of Persia." The specific length of the captivity was foretold by Jeremiah in Jeremiah 25:9-12 as seventy years. This was in recompense for the 490 years in which greater Israel had ignored the law of the sabbatical year. The latter totaled seventy sabbatical years which they had ignored.

Following those years backwards, the time when the sabbatical years was violated was when Saul became king over Israel. From that time onward, Israel had ignored the law of the sabbatical year. God thus gave the land rest for seventy years in recompense. The mills of God grind slow, but they grind exceedingly fine. Many in Israel no doubt thought the sabbatical year was no longer important. But God never abrogated that law and His judgment eventually came. It always does.

36:22-23 Now in the first year of Cyrus king of Persia, that the word of the LORD *spoken* by the mouth of Jeremiah might be accomplished, the LORD stirred up the spirit of Cyrus king of Persia, that he made a proclamation throughout all his kingdom, and *put it* also in writing, saying, 23 Thus saith Cyrus king of Persia, All the kingdoms of the earth hath the LORD God of heaven given me; and he hath charged me to build him an house in Jerusalem, which *is* in Judah. Who *is there* among you of all his people? The LORD his God *be* with him, and let him go up.

Because the sacred writer speaks of the decree of Cyrus in the past tense, many have conjectured that the author of Chron-

Understanding II Chronicles

icles was Ezra. That very well may be. The sacred text therefore records how that God "stirred up the spirit of Cyrus king of Persia." The decree of Cyrus recorded here is virtually identical with that which is recorded in Ezra 1:2-3. At that time, Cyrus decreed to his entire empire that he would allow the rebuilding of the Temple of God at Jerusalem. Any and all Jews in his realm would therefore be free to return to Jerusalem to rebuild the Temple. The details thereof are recorded in the following Book of Ezra.

EZRA

Introduction to Ezra: The book of Ezra is the chronological successor to II Chronicles. At the end of II Chronicles, Judah had been finally captured by Babylon. The time of the beginning book of Ezra is approximately fifty years later. Ezra records the beginning of the restoration and return of captive Israel to their home land. In some ways, there are parallels to the return of modern Israel to its homeland.

During the seventy year interval of the official exile, God inspired several prophets to write. Jeremiah completed his prophecies from the land of Judah including Lamentations. Ezekiel wrote his prophecies during this time as a captive within the Babylonian empire. Daniel also wrote from Babylon. Meanwhile back in Palestine, the small number of Jews not taken to Assyria or Babylon had intermarried with gentiles forming the nucleus of the later race of Samaritans. The land was little by little being claimed by neighboring gentile peoples. Jerusalem was utterly destroyed. The Temple was gone and little was left of what once was the proud nation of Israel. God had judged His people for their backslidden, sinful condition.

Ezra is the first of six post-captivity (restoration) books of the Bible. Following Ezra, Nehemiah wrote. Also the book of Esther was written at roughly the same time. As the restoration era continued, Haggai, Zechariah, and Malachi wrote. The book of Ezra forms the beginning of the restored nation of Israel which historically is the platform upon which New Testament times develop.

Specifically, the Book of Ezra records the return to Palestine of a remnant of Jews under the leadership of Zer-ubbabel in about 536 B.C. They laid the foundation of a new Temple. Approximately, seventy-eight years later in about 458 B.C., Ezra the priest himself returned and restored the Temple worship and ritual. (Later still, in 444 B.C. Nehemiah returned to rebuild the wall of Jerusalem.) Ezra writes of these events which predated his involvement as well as the years he himself was present. He records the difficulties, obstacles, opposition and success in doing a work for God. One thing is for sure. It was not easy. It never is. Ezra never had the privilege of ministering in a large, well established Temple. His was small, of modest proportions, and limited influence.

Though not addressed directly, there are profound implications of Ezra. Approximately 50,000 Jews including their servants returned to the land more or less as pioneers of the restoration. However, there undoubtedly were Jews numbering into seven digits who remained in the greater Babylonian empire. After the shock of dislocation and cultural adjustment, they had become prosperous and comfortable living in the gentile world.

Though they gave lip service to Judaism and their spiritual heritage, the majority were not interested in returning when the time came. They were comfortable making money in Babylon. They had their synagogue system which they had developed. Restoring the work of God at Jerusalem though having some importance was not at the top of their priority list. Many of them sent money to support the restoration, but they themselves were not willing to go. They were too comfortable where they were at. Parallels to modern Christianity and the fulfillment of the Great Commission are only too apparent. Ezra records the history of that feeble remnant which had a heart for God and the restoration of his work.

* * * * *

Understanding Ezra

Overview of Ezra 1: *Ezra one and two presents the historical background of the return of the initial remnant. God's providential preparation of the heart of Cyrus is evident.*

1:1 Now in the first year of Cyrus king of Persia, that the word of the LORD by the mouth of Jeremiah might be fulfilled, the LORD stirred up the spirit of Cyrus king of Persia, that he made a proclamation throughout all his kingdom, and *put it* also in writing, saying. International geopolitics are assumed in this verse. The Babylonian empire had absorbed the Assyrian empire. Not long before the events of Ezra, Babylon had been conquered by the Persian empire. The ruler of this large amalgamated realm was Cyrus. The reference to the first year of Cyrus refers not to the first year he was king, but rather the first year Babylon had been under his rule. The last two verses of II Chronicles (36:22-23) refers to the same providential detail.

Jeremiah had prophesied near the beginning of the Babylonian captivity that it would last for seventy years (Jeremiah 25:11-12). Now to fulfill that, an amazing thing happened. God Himself directly "stirred up the spirit of Cyrus king of Persia." God providentially put it into the heart of a pagan, gentile king to allow Jews to return to their homeland. Cyrus therefore issued a proclamation, put it in writing, and had it published throughout his vast empire.

1:2 Thus saith Cyrus king of Persia, The LORD God of heaven hath given me all the kingdoms of the earth; and he hath charged me to build him an house at Jerusalem, which *is* in Judah. Precisely how God influenced Cyrus, we are not told. However, approximately 175 years earlier, God had inspired Isaiah to write about Cyrus and how he would someday sponsor the rebuilding of Jerusalem and specifically the Temple there. See Isaiah 44:28 - 45:1-4. It is quite possible, Cyrus had been made aware of this prophecy and may have even read Isaiah himself. It may be that God stirred Cyrus' spirit through exposure to His Word.

1:3 Who *is there* among you of all his people? his God be with him, and let him go up to Jerusalem, which *is* in Judah, and build the house of the LORD God of Israel, (he *is* the God,) which *is* in Jerusalem. Cyrus therefore issued an open invitation throughout his entire empire for any of the Lord's people (i.e., Jews) to return to Jerusalem to assist in the restoration and rebuilding of the Temple. The providential hand of God is clear in its working. Cyrus was the ruler of the most powerful nation on the face of the earth of its day. This gentile despot nevertheless urged and invited Jewish people to return to their land. Moreover, in referring to Jehovah God, he noted how is He alone is God. That is a remarkable admission from a pagan who otherwise likely was an idolater. Nevertheless, God had so stirred His spirit for His own purposes, that Cyrus willingly invited Jews to rebuild their Temple.

1:4 And whosoever remaineth in any place where he sojourneth, let the men of his place help him with silver, and with gold, and with goods, and with beasts, beside the freewill offering for the house of God that *is* in Jerusalem. Moreover, Cyrus urged the Jews who chose to remain to send support for the efforts of those who would undertake the mission. The vast majority of the Jews who did not go were urged to provide whatever was necessary for the 'pilgrim pioneers' willing to make the sacrificial journey. Moreover, Cyrus urged the Jews of the realm to additionally give a "free-will offering for the house of God that is in Jerusalem."

1:5-6 Then rose up the chief of the fathers of Judah and Benjamin, and the priests, and the Levites, with all *them*

Understanding Ezra

whose spirit God had raised, to go up to build the house of the LORD which *is* in Jerusalem. God not only had stirred the heart of Cyrus, He also stirred in the hearts of dedicated Jews living in the expanded Persian empire. It is noted how the leaders of the tribes of Judah and Benjamin in the exile along with priests and Levites "rose up . . . to go up to build the house of the LORD which is in Jerusalem." God providentially put it in the heart of His own people to become a part of this great venture. Perhaps, He moved in the hearts of others who, because of sin and backsliddenness, did not respond.

6 And all they that *were* about them strengthened their hands with vessels of silver, with gold, with goods, and with beasts, and with precious things, beside all *that* was willingly offered. As Cyrus had urged, many other Jews began to contribute to the mission of rebuilding their Temple in the homeland of their fathers.

1:7-8 Also Cyrus the king brought forth the vessels of the house of the LORD, which Nebuchadnezzar had brought forth out of Jerusalem, and had put them in the house of his gods; 8 Even those did Cyrus king of Persia bring forth by the hand of Mithredath the treasurer, and numbered them unto Sheshbazzar, the prince of Judah.

Moreover, Cyrus learned how many of the gold and silver vessels used at the Temple, when it was captured by the Babylonians during their three invasions, were in fact in the houses of the pagan gods of the former Babylonian empire. He therefore ordered Mithredath, the 'Secretary of the Treasury' to send these sacred utensils back to Jerusalem. These were "numbered" (i.e., accounted to) "Sheshbazzar, the prince of Judah." The man Sheshbazzar is generally agreed to be the Babylonian name for Zerubbabel who was grandson of Jehoiachin, one of the final kings of Judah. (Cross reference Ezra 5:14,16 with Haggai 1:14.) He either (a) was one stirred in his heart to return to Jerusalem, or because he was direct descendant of the royal lineage of Judah, (b) was directed to return. However, assuming that Shesbazzar and Zerubbabel are the same individual, Haggai 1:14 makes it clear that God indeed stirred his spirit for the task ahead.

1:10-11 And this *is* the number of them: thirty chargers of gold, a thousand chargers of silver, nine and twenty knives, 10 Thirty basons of gold, silver basons of a second *sort* four hundred and ten, *and* other vessels a thousand. 11 All the vessels of gold and of silver *were* five thousand and four hundred. All *these* did Sheshbazzar bring up with *them of* the captivity that were brought up from Babylon unto Jerusalem

Because of their sacred as well as monetary value, careful record was made of exactly how many vessels were to be sent back to Jerusalem. The reference to the chargers of gold and silver may have been used at one time as the containers of water of purification at the Temple. The gold and silver basins may have been used in collecting the blood of the sacrifices which was to be sprinkled upon the altar. The gold and silver knives likely were those used in the ceremonial slaying and dressing of the sacrificial animals. Altogether, 5,400 sacred vessels were directed to be sent with Sheshbazzar (Zerubbabel) back to Jerusalem.

* * * * *

Overview of Ezra 2: *Chapter two details specifically those who returned in the initial remnant.*

2:1-2 Now these *are* the children of the province that went up out of the captivity, of those which had been carried

away, whom Nebuchadnezzar the king of Babylon had carried away unto Babylon, and came again unto Jerusalem and Judah, every one unto his city; 2 Which came with Zerubbabel: Jeshua, Nehemiah, Seraiah, Reelaiah, Mordecai, Bilshan, Mispar, Bigvai, Rehum, Baanah. The number of the men of the people of Israel.

The reference to the *province* may be a generic reference to the greater body of those who went. It is derived from a word having the sense of a jurisdiction. Mention is made of a Nehemiah and Mordecai along with others. Some have speculated if these were the notable Nehemiah who later rebuilt the wall or the Mordecai, uncle of Esther.

Chronologically, it would have been possible for the Mordecai mentioned to be the same one in Esther, though he would had to have returned. However, it was at least ninety years later that Nehemiah began his mission. That makes it highly unlikely they are one and the same man. It moreover is likely the Mordecai mentioned is not the same as the uncle of Esther either.

2:3-35 The enumeration of the basic remnant is noted. In some cases returnees are family names, in other cases the names of the towns in Israel whence they originated are listed such as kirjatharim, Bethlehem, Bethel, and Jericho.

2:36-39 Notably, 4,289 of the descendants of the priestly line returned. That approximates a large percentage of the total returning. Notice the name *Pashur* hearkens back to the priest at Jerusalem who so tormented and persecuted Jeremiah. See Jeremiah 20:1-6.

2:40-42 The Levites who returned are listed. Curiously, only 341 Levites are listed as returning, whereas, in the times of David, there were 38,000 of them. See I Chronicles 23:3.

2:43-54 The Nethinims were servants of the Levites, likely the assimilated Gibeonites of Joshua 9. Ezra 2:25 notes that 392 Nethinims (including servants of Solomon) returned. That likely was more than the Levites themselves.

2:55-60 Additional returning servants of Solomon and Nethinims are enumerated.

2:61-63 Other claiming priestly lineage but without the required documentation likewise are noted. They were not allowed to serve as priests. Moreover, the Tirshatha said they could not eat of the priestly meats "till there stood up a priest with Urim and with Thummim."

Evidently when a fully qualified high priest was anointed for service, he with the Urim and Thummin would discern who were true priests and of which pedigree they were. The reference to the *Tirshatha* is the Persian word for governor—evidently Zerubbabel.

2:64-65 The whole congregation together *was* forty and two thousand three hundred *and* threescore, 65 Beside their servants and their maids, of whom *there were* seven thousand three hundred thirty and seven: and *there were* among them two hundred singing men and singing women.

The enumerated "congregation," evidently including those of lessor status such as the Nethinims and the servants of Solomon, totaled 42,360. Additionally, they brought with them their own servants totaling another 7,330 plus another 200 "singing men and singing women." The grand total was 49,890. It is noteworthy that a running total of the specific categories enumerated throughout the chapter adds up to only 29,829. Jewish commentators take the position that the difference were Jews from other tribes who also returned.

Understanding Ezra

2:66-67 Their horses *were* seven hundred thirty and six; their mules, two hundred forty and five; 67 Their camels, four hundred thirty and five; *their* asses, six thousand seven hundred and twenty. Note is made of the livestock they brought. The returning exiles brought 736 horses, 245 mules, 435 camels, and 6,720 donkeys.

2:68-69 And *some* of the chief of the fathers, when they came to the house of the LORD which *is* at Jerusalem, offered freely for the house of God to set it up in his place: 69 They gave after their ability unto the treasure of the work threescore and one thousand drams of gold, and five thousand pound of silver, and one hundred priests' garments. Upon finally arriving at Jerusalem, "*some* chief of the fathers" gave from their own resources a sizeable amount of gold and silver (61,000 drams of gold and 5,000 pounds of silver) for the rebuilding of the Temple. They also presented one-hundred sets of priests' garments.

2:70 So the priests, and the Levites, and *some* of the people, and the singers, and the porters, and the Nethinims, dwelt in their cities, and all Israel in their cities. Upon arriving the priests, Levites, Nethinims, singers, porters, and the other Jews returned to live in the towns of their ancestry.

* * * * *

Overview of Ezra 3: The third chapter of Ezra records how the returning Jews immediately restored the prescribed Levitical offerings and observances. Plans were set in place for materials to be delivered and shortly thereafter, work began on rebuilding the Temple.

3:1 And when the seventh month was come, and the children of Israel *were* in the cities, the people gathered themselves together as one man to Jerusalem. The seventh month referred to likely is according to the Jewish calendar which would make it about October. The Jews evidently had departed from Babylon in the spring of that year and arrived back in the vicinity of Jerusalem during the summer. They no doubt had need to secure housing and get settled. The next major holy day on the Levitical calendar was the feast of Tabernacles which was around the first of October. They there "gathered themselves together as one man to Jerusalem."

3:2-3 Then stood up Jeshua the son of Jozadak, and his brethren the priests, and Zerubbabel the son of Shealtiel, and his brethren, and builded the altar of the God of Israel, to offer burnt offerings thereon, as *it is* written in the law of Moses the man of God. 3 And they set the altar upon his bases; for fear *was* upon them because of the people of those countries: and they offered burnt offerings thereon unto the LORD, *even* burnt offerings morning and evening.

It is recorded that *Jeshua* (also known as Joshua), who was a priest and evidently the ranking (high) priest, "stood up" (i.e., arose) along with the other priests; and *Zerubbabel* (the ranking descendant of the royal line) along with his brethren and they "builded the altar of the God of Israel, to offer burnt-offerings thereon, as it is written in the law of Moses the man of God." Ezra records how they "set the altar upon his bases." What is implied is that they placed the new altar in the exact place where the former Solomonic altar had been. It may even have been the actual base or pedestal of the former altar and they built the new altar thereupon.

Though trouble is not noted until chapter 4, the Jewish leadership already sensed opposition and apparently wanted to get the altar established before trouble arose. The "countries" noted

Understanding Ezra

likely is reference to the Samaritans as well as neighboring gentile lands, the historic enemies of Israel. They therefore began offering the regular Levitical offerings, including the morning and evening sacrifices. See Exodus 29:38-39.

3:4-6 They kept also the feast of tabernacles, as *it is* **written, and** *offered* **the daily burnt offerings by number, according to the custom, as the duty of every day required; 5 And afterward** *offered* **the continual burnt offering, both of the new moons, and of all the set feasts of the LORD that were consecrated, and of every one that willingly offered a freewill offering unto the LORD. 6 From the first day of the seventh month began they to offer burnt offerings unto the LORD. But the foundation of the temple of the LORD was not** *yet* **laid**

The first major holy day of the autumn season, the feast of Tabernacles (Succoth), was promptly observed. See Leviticus 23: 34-42. That feast lasted for eight days. They followed the prescribed scriptural offerings throughout those eight days. See Numbers 29:12-38.

They also carefully re-instituted each of the various offerings and sacrifices prescribed in the Law of Moses. It may be observed that these restoration pilgrims were determined to obey God's Word in every detail and be scriptural in every aspect. A powerful lesson remains to this day from these dedicated people of God.

From the first of the seventh month (October) which was as soon as they could get the altar ready, they began to systematically observe all which God had ordained for them in the law. Ezra notes, however, that the foundation of the Temple was not as yet laid.

3:7 They gave money also unto the masons, and to the carpenters; and meat, and drink, and oil, unto them of

Zidon, and to them of Tyre, to bring cedar trees from Lebanon to the sea of Joppa, according to the grant that they had of Cyrus king of Persia.

Funds which had been collected from their Jewish patrons back in Babylon and presumably funds sent by Cyrus were now put to use in securing the necessary work force and materials for the impending Temple rebuilding program. (Recall that the Babylonians had totally destroyed the Temple about 50 years earlier. The overall official captivity was 70 years beginning in 605 B.C. But the final destruction came in about 586.) Ezra records how that orders were sent to Tyre and Zidon (Sidon) in Lebanon for the necessary timbers and cedar lumber. Both Tyre and Sidon were within the Persian empire as well. It is not noted if separate orders had been sent by Cyrus to Lebanon. However, the Jews evidently were able to purchase the necessary materials therefrom. It is of interest that the payment apparently was by barter and not of silver or gold.

3:8-9 Now in the second year of their coming unto the house of God at Jerusalem, in the second month, began Zerubbabel the son of Shealtiel, and Jeshua the son of Jozadak, and the remnant of their brethren the priests and the Levites, and all they that were come out of the captivity unto Jerusalem; and appointed the Levites, from twenty years old and upward, to set forward the work of the house of the LORD. 9 Then stood Jeshua *with* his sons and his brethren, Kadmiel and his sons, the sons of Judah, together, to set forward the workmen in the house of God: the sons of Henadad, *with* their sons and their brethren the Levites.

The reference to the second year can refer either to the next spring or possibly to the year thereafter. There was much preparation work to be done. The original Temple site of Solomon had to be cleared of the rubble. Specific plans had to be drawn. Materials had to be transported from Lebanon. Local quarries

Understanding Ezra

had to cut and deliver stone work. It is possible that work could have begun the next spring. However, construction logistics probably dictate the work began the second spring after they had returned. The "second month" mentioned likely would correspond to our month of May.

Again, Zerubbabel (the royal prince) along with Jeshua (Joshua) the high priest led in the project. They along with the Levites from twenty years and older (see I Chronicles 23:24) oversaw the construction of the work. The word translated **set forward** (נצח *natsach*) has the literal sense of 'oversight.' In accordance with the Levitical custom prescribed in the law, the Levites took oversight of the construction. Evidently, the necessary manpower needed was drawn from "all they that were come out of the captivity unto Jerusalem." Though the Levites oversaw the work, all of the men who returned were drawn upon to help rebuild the Temple.

3:10-11 And when the builders laid the foundation of the temple of the LORD, they set the priests in their apparel with trumpets, and the Levites the sons of Asaph with cymbals, to praise the LORD, after the ordinance of David king of Israel. 11 And they sang together by course in praising and giving thanks unto the LORD; because *he is good, for his mercy endureth* for ever toward Israel. And all the people shouted with a great shout, when they praised the LORD, because the foundation of the house of the LORD was laid.

The builders therefore proceeded to lay the stone foundation of the re-built Temple. When that was complete, the priests donned their formal priestly regalia, along with the Levites, and they played upon trumpets with cymbals in praising the Lord as prescribed by David in I Chronicles 15:16, 25:1. The Levitical Temple choirs also sang "together by course" (which implies either responsively or sequentially) "in praising and giving thanks unto the LORD; because he is good, for his mercy endureth for ever toward Israel." The rest of the assembled restoration pilgrims joined in shouting for joy. (Think of the sound of a great stadium erupting in cheers as the home team scores.) The foundation of the house of the Lord had been laid. The work was underway. Israel collectively shouted praise to God.

3:12-13 But many of the priests and Levites and chief of the fathers, *who were* ancient men, that had seen the first house, when the foundation of this house was laid before their eyes, wept with a loud voice; and many shouted aloud for joy: 13 So that the people could not discern the noise of the shout of joy from the noise of the weeping of the people: for the people shouted with a loud shout, and the noise was heard afar off.

However, the senior priests, Levites, and other elderly returnees who had seen the original Solomonic Temple in its spectacular glory wept and openly wailed. (And some of the same shouted for joy). The final incursion against Jerusalem by the Babylonians had taken place approximately 52 years earlier. Some of these elderly returning pilgrims had seen the original Temple of Solomon which was one of the wonders of the world. What was being rebuilt was only a fraction of the size and grandeur of the original Temple. Seeing a modest reconstruction begun brought back memories of the former Temple in its glory and they wept as they remembered it. Zechariah who wrote of these general times and events noted, "Who hath despised the day of small things?" (Zechariah 4:10). That is, who is ashamed of a small beginning. The sounds in Jerusalem that day were a mixture of a part of the crowd roaring in approval and another part openly wailing in sorrow. As noted by Ezra, "and the noise was heard afar off"—perhaps by the enemies of God's people in the adjoining areas.

Understanding Ezra 721

Overview of Ezra 4*: As the Temple reconstruction project got underway, there soon came opposition. The subdivisions of the chapter are: (1) The adversaries of the Temple in verses 1-5; and, (2) the building of the Temple hindered in verses 6-24.*

4:1-3 Now when the adversaries of Judah and Benjamin heard that the children of the captivity builded the temple unto the LORD God of Israel; 2 Then they came to Zerubbabel, and to the chief of the fathers, and said unto them, Let us build with you: for we seek your God, as ye *do*; and we do sacrifice unto him since the days of Esarhaddon king of Assur, which brought us up hither.

3 But Zerubbabel, and Jeshua, and the rest of the chief of the fathers of Israel, said unto them, Ye have nothing to do with us to build an house unto our God; but we ourselves together will build unto the LORD God of Israel, as king Cyrus the king of Persia hath commanded us.

As the reconstruction of the Temple became evident to the neighboring peoples (Samaritans and neighboring gentiles), they came and wanted to get in on the action. They offered to join together in a cooperative effort. We have here a clear and developing example of biblical ecclesiastical separation. These were the Samaritans who were not scriptural in their worship of God.

Moreover, these were involved in idolatry along with a professed worship of Jehovah. They were spiritual compro-misers through and through. They were the half Jew, half gentile stock which had been settled in the northern kingdom after the Assyrian deportation in about 722 B.C. See II Kings 17:24.

The response of Zerubbabel and Joshua was essentially, nothing doing. "But we ourselves together will build unto the LORD God of Israel, as king Cyrus the king of Persia hath commanded us." Zerubbabel therefore demonstrated a clear example of biblical separation from apostasy. He would not cooperate with those walking unscripturally.

4:4-5 Then the people of the land weakened the hands of the people of Judah, and troubled them in building, 5 And hired counsellors against them, to frustrate their purpose, all the days of Cyrus king of Persia, even until the reign of Darius king of Persia.

Thus spurned (not on personal grounds, but by scriptural principle), "the people of the land weakened the hands of the people of Judah, and troubled them in building." Though not specifically recorded, they evidently threatened the workmen, sought to interfere with the delivery of material from Lebanon, and generally opposed the project. Moreover, they "hired counsellors against them." The thought is how they apparently retained attorneys to file petitions and injunctions against the project. In effect, they went to court to try and stop the work. This went on throughout the remainder of the reign of Cyrus who evidently ignored them. It continued with his successor however, who unfortunately was negatively influenced against the Jewish remnant. The greater picture is so typical of Satan and how he works. He will find any method to undercut and oppose God's work.

4:6-10 And in the reign of Ahasuerus, in the beginning of his reign, wrote they *unto him* an accusation against the inhabitants of Judah and Jerusalem. 7 And in the days of Artaxerxes wrote Bishlam, Mithredath, Tabeel, and the rest of their companions, unto Artaxerxes king of Persia; and the writing of the letter *was* written in the Syrian tongue, and interpreted in the Syrian tongue.

Meanwhile, Cyrus passed the scene. In verse 6, mention is made of *Ahasuerus*. This likely is the king of Persia otherwise known as Cambyses. The *Artaxerxes* of verse 7 is likely the same individual. Actually, the name *Artaxerxes* is more of a title given to Persian kings than a name similar to the title of Caesar of the later Romans.

8 Rehum the chancellor and Shimshai the scribe wrote a letter against Jerusalem to Artaxerxes the king in this sort: 9 Then *wrote* Rehum the chancellor, and Shimshai the scribe, and the rest of their companions; the Dinaites, the Apharsathchites, the Tarpelites, the Apharsites, the Archevites, the Babylonians, the Susanchites, the Dehavites, *and* the Elamites, 10 And the rest of the nations whom the great and noble Asnappar brought over, and set in the cities of Samaria, and the rest *that are* on this side the river, and at such a time.

The enemies of the Jews therefore filed a formal complaint with this new king making "accusation against the inhabitants of Judah and Jerusalem." Various notables joining party to the suit are noted. Also mention is made how the letter was written in *Syrian* (the common language of the region). This later would become the Aramaic language which was the everyday language of Jesus' day in Israel.

The reference to Samaria is the first post-restoration mention made thereof. It refers to the inter-racial peoples who have existed north and east of Jerusalem and who were so notable in Jesus' day. The mention of "this side of the river" is an idiom referring to the lands west of the Euphrates river. The Asnapper mentioned probably is Sennacherib of biblical reference or possibly Ashurbanipal, either of whom were Assyr-ian kings.

4:11-16 This *is* the copy of the letter that they sent unto him, *even* unto Artaxerxes the king; Thy servants the men on this side the river, and at such a time. 12 Be it known unto the king, that the Jews which came up from thee to us are come unto Jerusalem, building the rebel-lious and the bad

city, and have set up the walls *thereof*, **and joined the foundations.**

The letter of complaint was filled with distortions and outright dishonesty in making allegations against the Jews. It simply was not true. Apart from calling them "rebellious and bad," the allegation of them rebuilding the wall of Jerusalem was an outright lie. (The allegation of rebuilding the wall had powerful political and military implications. A city wall in ancient times was a major military defensive system and could allow a city to revolt politically.)

The Samaritan enemies further alleged if the work proceeded, the Jews would cease to pay their incumbent taxes thus damaging "the revenue of the kings." They sanctimoniously went on to hypocritically claim they did not want to see the Persian king dishonored. (The truth is, they probably detested him.) They therefore advised the Persian king to make a search of records and note how the Jews in the not-too-distant past had been a thorn in the side of the Babylonians. (This was true under the final Judean kings Jehoiachim and Zedekiah. See II Kings 24:1,20; 25:1,9.)

13 **Be it known now unto the king, that, if this city be builded, and the walls set up** *again,* *then* **will they not pay toll, tribute, and custom, and** *so* **thou shalt endamage the revenue of the kings. 14 Now because we have maintenance from** *the king's* **palace, and it was not meet for us to see the king's dishonour, therefore have we sent and certified the king; 15 That search may be made in the book of the records of thy fathers: so shalt thou find in the book of the records, and know that this city** *is* **a rebellious city, and hurtful unto kings and provinces, and that they have moved sedition within the same of old time: for which cause was this city destroyed. 16 We certify the king that, if this city be builded** *again***, and the walls thereof set up, by this means thou shalt have no portion on this side the river.**

Understanding Ezra

They ominously concluded their letter warning Ahasuerus (Cambyses) how if he did not intervene, "if this city be builded again, and the walls thereof set up, by this means thou shalt have no portion on this side of the river." It all was deceit and dishonesty. The Jews who had returned had done so strictly for spiritual reasons to rebuild and restore their Temple worship. No attempt had been made to rebuild the wall or to politically rebel. There was no attempt to avoid payment of taxes. To the contrary, they were grateful to Cyrus for assisting them and allowing them to proceed. However, a standard tactic of the devil is to lie and slander. The very term *devil* literally means slanderer. Indeed, he is a liar and the father of all lies.

4:17-22 *Then* **sent the king an answer unto Rehum the chancellor, and** *to* **Shimshai the scribe, and** *to* **the rest of their companions that dwell in Samaria, and** *unto* **the rest beyond the river, Peace, and at such a time. 18 The letter which ye sent unto us hath been plainly read before me. 19 And I commanded, and search hath been made, and it is found that this city of old time hath made insurrection against kings, and** *that* **rebellion and sedition have been made therein. 20 There have been mighty kings also over Jerusalem, which have ruled over all** *countries* **beyond the river; and toll, tribute, and custom, was paid unto them. 21 Give ye now commandment to cause these men to cease, and that this city be not builded, until** *another* **commandment shall be given from me. 22 Take heed now that ye fail not to do this: why should damage grow to the hurt of the kings?**

The letter was received by the king of Persia. He ordered a search be made of the historical archives of Babylon. He thus learned of the past problems with the kingdom of Judah as they struggled to maintain their independence from Babylon. He perhaps learned even of David and Solomon, their power, and their notable successors. He therefore issued an order for the Jews in Jerusalem to cease and desist in rebuilding the *city* until further orders were received from him. He may have been sincerely deceived. In any event he was mainly interested in his political base and tax revenues.

4:23-26 Now when the copy of king Artaxerxes' letter *was* read before Rehum, and Shimshai the scribe, and their companions, they went up in haste to Jerusalem unto the Jews, and made them to cease by force and power. 24 Then ceased the work of the house of God which *is* at Jerusalem. So it ceased unto the second year of the reign of Darius king of Persia.

When the decree from the king arrived back in Samaria, the Samaritan leaders, Rehum and Shimshai the scribe along with subordinates, rushed to Jerusalem and forcibly caused the work to stop. Sadly, Satan had hindered God's work. The Temple project would remain in abeyance for approximately fourteen years.

* * * * *

***Overview of Ezra 5**:After an interval of approximately fourteen years, work resumed on the Temple. Immediately, the local representatives of the Persians king demanded to know by whose authority the work was proceeding. The Jews explained how Cyrus had given a decree for the work and they were in compliance with it. Word was sent to Babylon. The decree of Cyrus was confirmed.*

5:1 Then the prophets, Haggai the prophet, and Zechariah the son of Iddo, prophesied unto the Jews that *were* in Judah and Jerusalem in the name of the God of Israel, *even* unto them. The events here synchronize with

Understanding Ezra

Haggai and portions of Zechariah. They, through their preaching, urged the Jews to get back to rebuilding their Temple. In the interim, they had built comfortable, nice homes; but the Temple remained in a dismal state of being partially started. Weeds no doubt had grown back up on the site. It was pathetic testimony of unfinished business. See Haggai 1. (The record of Zechariah being the son of Iddo when referenced with Zechariah 1:1 works out thus. Zechariah was the son of Berechiah and the grandson of Iddo.) In any event, these prophets stood and preached it was high time to begin work on the Temple once again. It is noteworthy how the decree to cease and desist by Cambyses (*a.k.a.* Ahaseurus and Artaxerxes) was specifically directed only at the rebuilding of the *city* and by assumption, its wall. See Ezra 4:21. Therefore, Haggai and Zechariah urged the Temple project be restarted.

5:2 Then rose up Zerubbabel the son of Shealtiel, and Jeshua the son of Jozadak, and began to build the house of God which *is* at Jerusalem: and with them *were* the prophets of God helping them. Therefore, Zerubbabel, the royal heir of the line of David, along with Jeshua (Joshua) the high priest assumed the leadership "and began to build the house of God which is at Jerusalem: and with them were the prophets of God helping them." The prophets mentioned certainly included Haggai and Zechariah, but probably included other lessor know prophets of the day. Ezra 4:24 notes that two years earlier, Darius I had assumed the throne of the Persian empire. Knowledge of this may have been some of the impetus for Haggai and Zechariah urging the work to recommence. A new ruler hopefully brought a new outlook, which indeed he did.

5:3-4 At the same time came to them Tatnai, governor on this side the river, and Shetharboznai, and their companions, and said thus unto them, Who hath commanded

you to build this house, and to make up this wall? 4 Then said we unto them after this manner, What are the names of the men that make this building?

Nevertheless, the local Persian authorities, Tatnai the governor "on this side the river" (i.e., west of the Euphrates River—probably the province of Syria having jurisdiction of Judaea and Samaria) along with another Persian official named Shetharboznai, immediately challenged the work. Though no direct mention is otherwise made of any rebuilding of the wall of Jerusalem (which had military-political implications of rebellion), it may have been in clearing the rubble in Jerusalem, the foundations of the former walls had been exposed raising the suspicion the Jews planned to rebuild them.

It is noteworthy in chapter 4 how the adversaries likewise accused the Jews of rebuilding the wall. It may be some work had been started thereon. More likely, the *wall* noted is in reference to the wall of the Temple under construction. In any event, they demanded to know who authorized it and they wanted to know the names of those involved.

5:5 But the eye of their God was upon the elders of the Jews, that they could not cause them to cease, till the matter came to Darius: and then they returned answer by letter concerning this *matter*. God's providential intervention and protection is evident. Where He guides He not only provides, but also protects and prospers. Though challenged by the Persian authorities, the work continued. God's hand was upon it. Indeed, there often comes opposition in God's work. Nevertheless, as God's servants forge ahead with what God has called them to do, He providentially intervenes and prospers. Note is made of the letter soon to be sent to Darius.

5:6-7 The copy of the letter that Tatnai, governor on this side the river, and Shetharboznai, and his companions

the **Apharsachites, which** *were* **on this side the river, sent unto Darius the king: 7 They sent a letter unto him, wherein was written thus; Unto Darius the king, all peace.** The letter prepared by Tatnai and Shetharboznai to Darius concerning the work is formally noted and introduced.

5:8-16 Be it known unto the king, that we went into the province of Judea, to the house of the great God, which is builded with great stones, and timber is laid in the walls, and this work goeth fast on, and prospereth in their hands. 9 Then asked we those elders, *and* **said unto them thus, Who commanded you to build this house, and to make up these walls?**

The letter sent by the Persian officials is noted in detail. There is not the hostile tone of the earlier letter of accusation in chapter 4. Tatnai seems to endeavor to accurately present the overall picture of events of recent history. Note in verse 8 how Tatnai makes reference to "the great God." The mention of "great stones" literally is of "rolling stones." The idea probably is how the stone work of the Temple was of such magnitude, rollers were necessary under them to move them. The implication is how that a massive project was underway.

10 We asked their names also, to certify thee, that we might write the names of the men that *were* **the chief of them. 11 And thus they returned us answer, saying, We are the servants of the God of heaven and earth, and build the house that was builded these many years ago, which a great king of Israel builded and set up. 12 But after that our fathers had provoked the God of heaven unto wrath, he gave them into the hand of Nebuchadnezzar the king of Babylon, the Chaldean, who destroyed this house, and carried the people away into Babylon. 13 But in the first year of Cyrus the king of Babylon** *the same* **king Cyrus made a decree to build this house of God. 14 And the vessels also of**

gold and silver of the house of God, which Nebuchadnezzar took out of the temple that *was* in Jerusalem, and brought them into the temple of Babylon, those did Cyrus the king take out of the temple of Babylon, and they were delivered unto *one*, whose name *was* Sheshbazzar, whom he had made governor.

Notice also how the Jews answered the inquiry of who they were and what they were doing. Their reply was, "We are the servants of the God of heaven and earth." Indeed they were. And indeed God is the God of heaven and earth. There is a forceful nuance of distinction implied. Most idolaters, including the Persians, had the idea that their gods were local and pertained to specific functions such as fertility or warfare etc. However, what clearly is implied here is that the God of the Jews was God of the entire earth and the entire universe which indeed He is. He therefore is far greater than any pagan idol. The "great king" noted in verse 11 is Solomon and his original Temple construction.

The Jews in continuing their reply to Tatnai's interrogation gave candid answer. They acknowledged that their deportation to Babylon was because they had provoked the "God of heaven." However, they also correctly pointed out how the authority for their work was vested in the decree of Cyrus some years earlier.

15 And said unto him, Take these vessels, go, carry them into the temple that *is* in Jerusalem, and let the house of God be builded in his place. 16 Then came the same Sheshbazzar, *and* laid the foundation of the house of God which *is* in Jerusalem: and since that time even until now hath it been in building, and *yet* it is not finished.

Once again, the Sheshbazzar mentioned in verse 16 is Zerubbabel. What is implied is though the work had formally stopped with the decree of Artaxerxes in 4:21, the decree of Cyrus had never been abrogated. They therefore had resumed work on that basis.

5:17 Now therefore, if *it seem* good to the king, let there be search made in the king's treasure house, which *is* there at Babylon, whether it be *so*, that a decree was made of Cyrus the king to build this house of God at Jerusalem, and let the king send his pleasure to us concerning this matter. Tatnai therefore requested of King Darius I that a search of the archives be made in Babylon whether Cyrus ever made such a decree. He thus requested a reply in the matter.

* * * * *

Overview of Ezra 6: In this next chapter, Darius confirms the decree of Cyrus, the work upon the Temple therefore continued to completion whereupon the Passover was conducted at the newly rebuilt Temple.

6:1-2 Then Darius the king made a decree, and search was made in the house of the rolls, where the treasures were laid up in Babylon. 2 And there was found at Achmetha, in the palace that *is* in the province of the Medes, a roll, and therein *was* a record thus written. The letter from Tatnai was delivered to Darius and a search was indeed made for a decree by Cyrus authorizing rebuilding of the Temple. At Achmetha, which was the capitol of Media and the summer palace of the kings of Persia, a *roll* (scroll) was found. In it was recorded the information which was sought. (It should be noted how humanly, it could have been very easy for such a document to be missed. Nevertheless, God undoubtedly providentially intervened and made sure the needed documentation was found.)

6:3-7 In the first year of Cyrus the king *the same* Cyrus the king made a decree *concerning* the house of God at Jerusalem, Let the house be builded, the place where they offered sacrifices, and let the foundations thereof be strongly laid; the height thereof threescore cubits, *and* the breadth thereof threescore cubits; 4 *With* three rows of great stones, and a row of new timber: and let the expenses be given out of the king's house: 5 And also let the golden and silver vessels of the house of God, which Nebuchadnezzar took forth out of the temple which *is* at Jerusalem, and brought unto Babylon, be restored, and brought again unto the temple which *is* at Jerusalem, *every one* to his place, and place *them* in the house of God.

It is noteworthy how specific details of Cyrus' original decree not mentioned earlier are here brought to light. Cyrus in fact dictated architectural details noting even the dimensions of the building. It was to be of significant height–sixty cubits (approximately ninety feet) which was a major building in ancient architecture. The "three rows of great stones" noted in verse 4 may be reference to three rows of columns fronting the edifice. Some have speculated if the "row of new timber" refers to interior paneling or wainscoting of interior walls. That is possible.

However, more likely, Cyrus specified how fresh structural timbers which the Aramaic word (אע *aw*) implies. Though stones could conceivably be reused, fresh structural timber bespoke proper and the best type of reconstruction. Seemingly, Cyrus wanted the job done right. Moreover, the sacred gold and silver vessels and utensils which Nebuchadnezzar had plundered from the Temple were to be returned.

Now *therefore*, Tatnai, governor beyond the river, Shetharboznai, and your companions the Apharsachites, which *are* beyond the river, be ye far from thence: 7 Let the work of this house of God alone; let the governor of the Jews and the elders of the Jews build this house of God in his place.

Darius therefore straightly ordered Tatnai, Shetharboznai, and anyone under their jurisdiction to stand clear and allow the

Jews to proceed with their work. God providentially moved Darius to write, "Let the work of this house of God alone; let the governor of the Jews and the elders of the Jews build this house of God in his place."

6:8-10 Moreover I make a decree what ye shall do to the elders of these Jews for the building of this house of God: that of the king's goods, *even* of the tribute beyond the river, forthwith expenses be given unto these men, that they be not hindered. 9 And that which they have need of, both young bullocks, and rams, and lambs, for the burnt offerings of the God of heaven, wheat, salt, wine, and oil, according to the appointment of the priests which *are* at Jerusalem, let it be given them day by day without fail: 10 That they may offer sacrifices of sweet savours unto the God of heaven, and pray for the life of the king, and of his sons.

Darius went even further. He ordered appropriations be made to the Jews from government resources so the work be not hindered. Moreover, he ordered sufficient animals and other supplies be provided so that adequate resources for sacrifices be available when worship began thereat. He then added how that the Jews might therefore make sweet savor offerings on his behalf and pray for him and his sons. How scriptural that was according to the Law of Moses is in doubt. However, the king's desire to be prayed for had the right motive.

6:11-12 Also I have made a decree, that whosoever shall alter this word, let timber be pulled down from his house, and being set up, let him be hanged thereon; and let his house be made a dunghill for this. 12 And the God that hath caused his name to dwell there destroy all kings and people, that shall put to their hand to alter *and* to destroy this house of God which *is* at Jerusalem. I Darius have made a decree; let it be done with speed. Finally, Darius ordered if any altered or obstructed his order that he should be hanged from timbers pulled from his own house and his house be destroyed. Moreover, he invoked God to destroy any other king or nation which would bring harm to the Temple at Jerusalem.

6:13-14 Then Tatnai, governor on this side the river, Shetharboznai, and their companions, according to that which Darius the king had sent, so they did speedily. 14 And the elders of the Jews builded, and they prospered through the prophesying of Haggai the prophet and Zechariah the son of Iddo. And they builded, and finished *it*, **according to the commandment of the God of Israel, and according to the commandment of Cyrus, and Darius, and Artaxerxes king of Persia.**

The Persian official in the region, Tatnai and associates, had no alternative but to comply. Ezra notes how they did so "speedily." Therefore the work prospered "through the prophesying" (i.e., preaching) "of Haggai the prophet and Zechariah." The work was completed. The Temple was finished. Of interest is the endnote how that the completion was in accordance with not only the several Persian kings who showed favor, but also "according to the commandment of the God of Israel." That commandment evidently was through Haggai and Zechariah. See Haggai and Zechariah 1 respectively.

6:15 And this house was finished on the third day of the month Adar, which was in the sixth year of the reign of Darius the king. The restoration project was completed approximately four years after it had recommenced. Cross reference Ezra 4:24. The month Adar corresponds roughly to modern March, the last month of the Jewish year.

6:16-18 And the children of Israel, the priests, and the Levites, and the rest of the children of the captivity, kept the

Understanding Ezra

dedication of this house of God with joy, 17 And offered at the dedication of this house of God an hundred bullocks, two hundred rams, four hundred lambs; and for a sin offering for all Israel, twelve he goats, according to the number of the tribes of Israel. 18 And they set the priests in their divisions, and the Levites in their courses, for the service of God, which *is* at Jerusalem; as it is written in the book of Moses.

The remnant of Jews in the land rejoiced. Reference to the children of Israel implies the entire twelve tribes of which there were evidently representatives of all. It is quite possible the large number of animals sacrificed were provided in part by the decree of Darius. Also reference is made to the twelve tribes through the "twelve he goats" offered as a sin offering. (There never were ten *lost* tribes as alleged by some.) The priests and Levites were once again organized in their respective courses and divisions to maintain Temple service as prescribed in Numbers 3:6, 8:11, 14-15. See also I Chronicles 24:1. The term *dedication* is translated from the Aramaic word (חנכה) *hanukka* which in the Maccabean era became the basis for the modern Jewish holiday of Hanukkah.

6:19-22 And the children of the captivity kept the passover upon the fourteenth *day* **of the first month. 20 For the priests and the Levites were purified together, all of them** *were* **pure, and killed the passover for all the children of the captivity, and for their brethren the priests, and for themselves.**

21 And the children of Israel, which were come again out of captivity, and all such as had separated themselves unto them from the filthiness of the heathen of the land, to seek the LORD God of Israel, did eat, 22 And kept the feast of unleavened bread seven days with joy: for the LORD had made them joyful, and turned the heart of the king of

Assyria unto them, to strengthen their hands in the work of the house of God, the God of Israel.

As the first month of the Jewish calendar came to pass, Israel for the first time in many years was able to observe the Passover and the feast of unleavened bread at the Temple. All the priests and Levites were ceremonially clean. The entire restored nation of Jews rejoiced in how God had blessed them and turned the heart of the king to help and assist them in the work of the house of God. The king of Assyria is another title for the king of Persia. The Persians had assimilated the Babylonians who in turn had assimilated the Assyrians.

* * * * *

Overview of Ezra 7: Chapter seven presents the actual coming of Ezra to Jerusalem. Again, there is remarkable evidence of God's providential intervention in prospering His work. God put into the heart of another Persian king to underwrite, protect, and further strengthen God's people and work. There is some conflict among commentators concerning the historical placement of events. Some take the position chapters seven and eight are about a year after the events of the chapter six and the completion of the Temple. (Contextually, that certainly is plausible.)

However, others based upon historical details pertain-ing to the kings of Persia place this time approximately fifty-eight years later or about B.C. 458. The conflict centers around exactly who is the Artaxerxes mentioned. Part of the problem rests in how the name Artaxerxes had become a generic title of Persian kings similar to the Roman use of the name/title, Caesar. Most recent commentators take the position this Artaxerxes was one who ruled later than at the time in chapter 6 and hence the interval of fifty-eight years.

Understanding Ezra

Insight into understanding these two chapters is in noting that the first ten verses of chapter 7 present a summary overview of the greater mission which is detailed in the rest of chapter seven and through chapter 8. From Ezra's perspective, the first six chapters of this book are historical. The final four are autobiographical.

7:1-5 Now after these things, in the reign of Artaxerxes king of Persia, Ezra the son of Seraiah, the son of Azariah, the son of Hilkiah, 2 The son of Shallum, the son of Zadok, the son of Ahitub, 3 The son of Amariah, the son of Azariah, the son of Meraioth, 4 The son of Zerahiah, the son of Uzzi, the son of Bukki, 5 The son of Abishua, the son of Phinehas, the son of Eleazar, the son of Aaron the chief priest. Though the context would seem to suggest a rather short interval after chapter six, we will proceed with the assumption that these proceedings took place fifty-eight years later. Ezra here presents his priestly pedigree, establishing his lineage back to Eleazar the son of Aaron.

7:6 This Ezra went up from Babylon; and he *was* a ready scribe in the law of Moses, which the LORD God of Israel had given: and the king granted him all his request, according to the hand of the LORD his God upon him. This verse fairly well summarizes the rest of the book of Ezra. He went from Babylon back to Jerusalem. Notice how he described himself as "a ready scribe in the law of Moses." The essence of that statement is that Ezra was a diligent scribe of the Scripture. In other words, he was a man of the Word. He knew it and understood it.

He goes on to summarize his undertakings and how "the king granted him all his request." As will be noted, Artaxerxes granted to him very substantial resources. It might be inferred that Ezra had some sort of royal relationship with this Persian king not unlike that of Nehemiah (the king's cup-bearer) or perhaps even Daniel (a royal advisor) who lived years earlier. However, Ezra makes it clear the assistance of Artaxerxes ultimately was because God's hand was upon him (Ezra). The idea of God's hand being upon one is found several times in Ezra and Nehemiah and has the sense of God's blessing.

7:7-9 And there went up *some* of the children of Israel, and of the priests, and the Levites, and the singers, and the porters, and the Nethinims, unto Jerusalem, in the seventh year of Artaxerxes the king. 8 And he came to Jerusalem in the fifth month, which *was* in the seventh year of the king. 9 For upon the first *day* of the first month began he to go up from Babylon, and on the first *day* of the fifth month came he to Jerusalem, according to the good hand of his God upon him.

Ezra further summarizes how in so going from Babylon to Jerusalem: (1) he was accompanied by priests, Levites, singers, porters, Nethinims (servants of the Levites); (2) the journey took approximately four months—traveling on foot in a large caravan was slow; (3) he again notes how their ultimate safe arrival was due "to the good hand of his God upon him." There is sound scriptural basis here for seeking journeying mercies of the Lord as we travel even to this day.

7:10 For Ezra had prepared his heart to seek the law of the LORD, and to do *it*, and to teach in Israel statutes and judgments. Here perhaps is the reason why God's hand was upon Ezra. (1) He "had prepared his heart to seek the law of the LORD." The word translated as **seek** (דרשׁ *dawrash*) has the sense to 'resort to', to 'frequent,' to 'consult,' and to 'enquire.' Ezra was a man whose heart was *determined* to seek God's Word. The idea is of frequent and regular study. (2) He had prepared his heart "to do it." He not only had a hunger for what

Understanding Ezra

God's Word had to say, he was determined to do it (i.e., obey it). (3) Moreover, he had prepared his heart "to teach in Israel God's Word"—its "statues and judgments."

7:11-12 Now this *is* the copy of the letter that the king Artaxerxes gave unto Ezra the priest, the scribe, *even* a scribe of the words of the commandments of the LORD, and of his statutes to Israel. 12 Artaxerxes, king of kings, unto Ezra the priest, a scribe of the law of the God of heaven, perfect *peace*, and at such a time. Ezra briefly summarized how king Artaxerxes issued a written decree on Ezra's behalf prescribing his authorization, his appropriations from the royal treasury, his authority, and in short, the royal blessing upon the expedition he was about to undertake. Verses 12-26 presents the details of this decree.

Artaxerxes describes himself as "king of kings" and notes Ezra as a scribe of the "God of heaven." It is remarkable how this pagan king of the mighty Persian empire (which at the time was the most powerful empire in the world) would acknowledge Jehovah God as the God of heaven, that is, God over all.

7:13-20 I make a decree, that all they of the people of Israel, and *of* his priests and Levites, in my realm, which are minded of their own freewill to go up to Jerusalem, go with thee. 14 Forasmuch as thou art sent of the king, and of his seven counsellors, to enquire concerning Judah and Jerusalem, according to the law of thy God which *is* in thine hand; 15 And to carry the silver and gold, which the king and his counsellors have freely offered unto the God of Israel, whose habitation *is* in Jerusalem, 16 And all the silver and gold that thou canst find in all the province of Babylon, with the freewill offering of the people, and of the priests, offering willingly for the house of their God which *is* in Jerusalem: 17 That thou mayest buy speedily with this

money bullocks, rams, lambs, with their meat offerings and their drink offerings, and offer them upon the altar of the house of your God which *is* in Jerusalem. 18 And whatsoever shall seem good to thee, and to thy brethren, to do with the rest of the silver and the gold, that do after the will of your God. 19 The vessels also that are given thee for the service of the house of thy God, *those* deliver thou before the God of Jerusalem. 20 And whatsoever more shall be needful for the house of thy God, which thou shalt have occasion to bestow, bestow *it* out of the king's treasure house.

Artaxerxes decreed (1) how "all they of the people of Israel, and of his priests and Levites" throughout the Persian empire were free to return to Israel with Ezra if they so desired. (Sadly, only a remnant chose to do so. Many were too comfortable making money in Babylon.) (2) He was authorized to bring funds from the royal Persian treasury for the Temple at Jerusalem. (3) He was authorized to receive a "freewill offering" from the people (i.e., Jews in the empire) for his expedition to Jerusalem. The purpose of these resources was to buy whatever necessary for proper sacrifices at the Temple. (4) He could do whatever with what was left over according to God's will. (5) Additional sacred vessels for Temple worship were to be sent for service of the Temple. (6) For *anything else* he needed for the Temple in Jerusalem, he was authorized to appropriate from the king's treasure house (i.e., treasury). The generosity of this pagan king toward the work of God and His worship is most remarkable. God indeed had providentially worked in his heart.

7:21-23 And I, *even* I Artaxerxes the king, do make a decree to all the treasurers which *are* beyond the river, that whatsoever Ezra the priest, the scribe of the law of the God of heaven, shall require of you, it be done speedily, 22 Unto an hundred talents of silver, and to an hundred measures of

wheat, and to an hundred baths of wine, and to an hundred baths of oil, and salt without prescribing *how much*. 23 Whatsoever is commanded by the God of heaven, let it be diligently done for the house of the God of heaven: for why should there be wrath against the realm of the king and his sons?

Artaxerxes further issued a decree to all royal officers "beyond the river" (i.e., west of the Euphrates, or toward Jerusalem) to give to Ezra whatever he required "speedily" to the limit noted. Moreover, whatever Ezra was commanded by "the God of heaven" concerning the Temple at Jerusalem, he was authorized to do. Part of Artaxerxes motive in all of this was that he feared the wrath of God against him and his sons. Indeed, the fear of the Lord had been instilled into Artaxerxes. The question therefore arises, how did this come to be? Did God directly intervene and so convict his heart? Or, had Ezra or other high ranking Jews 'witnessed' to him from the Old Testament Scripture, instructing him of the God of heaven. There probably was a combination of both. As God's Word was presented to Ezra, God's Spirit convicted his heart of the need of God's work.

7:24 Also we certify you, that touching any of the priests and Levites, singers, porters, Nethinims, or ministers of this house of God, it shall not be lawful to impose toll, tribute, or custom, upon them. He also granted tax-exempt status to the priests, Levites and their attendants in the Temple service. This is a clear scriptural example of tax-exempt status by a secular government for God's work.

7:25-26 And thou, Ezra, after the wisdom of thy God, that *is* in thine hand, set magistrates and judges, which may judge all the people that *are* beyond the river, all such as know the laws of thy God; and teach ye them that know

them not. 26 And whosoever will not do the law of thy God, and the law of the king, let judgment be executed speedily upon him, whether *it be* unto death, or to banishment, or to confiscation of goods, or to imprisonment. Moreover, Ezra was authorized to establish a judicial system in and about Jerusalem to teach and enforce the Law of Moses. Additionally, he was given the authority to prosecute those who ignored the Scripture, ranging from imprisonment to even death.

7:27-28 Blessed *be* the LORD God of our fathers, which hath put *such a thing* as this in the king's heart, to beautify the house of the LORD which *is* in Jerusalem: 28 And hath extended mercy unto me before the king, and his counsellors, and before all the king's mighty princes. And I was strengthened as the hand of the LORD my God *was* upon me, and I gathered together out of Israel chief men to go up with me.

Ezra concluded the chapter by thanking and praising God for having put such things into the heart of the king for the further beautification of the Temple. Moreover, he thanked God for granting such mercy before the rulers of Persia. He again noted God's hand upon him. Therefore, he began to gather together out of Israel chief men to go up with him to Jerusalem.

* * * * *

Overview of Ezra 8: *Details of the actual expedition to Jerusalem are listed including: (1) the companions of Ezra in verses 1-20; (2) Ezra beseeching God's blessing in verses 21-23; (3) the funds appropriated to the priests in verses 24-30; and, (4) Ezra arrival at Jerusalem in verses 31-36.*

Understanding Ezra

8:1-14 Ezra lists the men (and their families) who would make the journey back to Jerusalem with him. Only men are noted, though it is clear entire families were involved from 8:21. The number of men noted totals 1,496 (not including their families and some presumed servants). The total migration no doubt therefore totaled well over five thousand people.

8:15-20 And I gathered them together to the river that runneth to Ahava; and there abode we in tents three days: and I viewed the people, and the priests, and found there none of the sons of Levi. 16 **Then sent I for Eliezer, for Ariel, for Shemaiah, and for Elnathan, and for Jarib, and for Elnathan, and for Nathan, and for Zechariah, and for Meshullam, chief men; also for Joiarib, and for Elnathan, men of understanding.**

17 **And I sent them with commandment unto Iddo the chief at the place Casiphia, and I told them what they should say unto Iddo, *and* to his brethren the Nethinims, at the place Casiphia, that they should bring unto us ministers for the house of our God.** 18 **And by the good hand of our God upon us they brought us a man of understanding, of the sons of Mahli, the son of Levi, the son of Israel; and Sherebiah, with his sons and his brethren, eighteen;** 19 **And Hashabiah, and with him Jeshaiah of the sons of Merari, his brethren and their sons, twenty;** 20 **Also of the Nethinims, whom David and the princes had appointed for the service of the Levites, two hundred and twenty Nethinims: all of them were expressed by name.**

As the expedition assembled for departure, they met along the river Ahava (somewhere in the region of Babylon). There, in getting organized for final departure, Ezra discovered that there were no Levites with them. He therefore sent word back to what evidently was a place where many Levites lived (Casiphia) and sought for volunteers to join with them. As a result, a total of thirty-eight Levites agreed to go. Also two hundred-twenty Nethinims (official servants of the Levite and the Temple) volunteered to go. (This was in addition to the numbers mentioned above.)

8:21-23 Then I proclaimed a fast there, at the river of Ahava, that we might afflict ourselves before our God, to seek of him a right way for us, and for our little ones, and for all our substance.

22 For I was ashamed to require of the king a band of soldiers and horsemen to help us against the enemy in the way: because we had spoken unto the king, saying, The hand of our God *is* upon all them for good that seek him; but his power and his wrath *is* against all them that forsake him. 23 So we fasted and besought our God for this: and he was intreated of us.

Ezra therefore "proclaimed a fast there . . . that we might afflict ourselves before our God, to seek of him a right way for us, and for our little ones, and for all our substance." Though, God had obviously blessed thus far, Ezra nevertheless urged the expedition to seek God's continual help and protection. He noted that he was ashamed to ask for soldiers to guard them and the large sums of money they were carrying. He had told the king that God would protect them.

Notice Ezra's statement, "The hand of our God is upon all them for good that seek him; but his power and his wrath is against all them that forsake him." Pause to consider that remains to this day. The greater principle is how Ezra exercised great faith in trusting the Lord for protection and deliverance. Though fasting is a means of denying oneself of simple physical pleasure such as food for a season, the greater principle is that of faith. In fasting, they "besought our God for this: and he was intreated of us." In other words, God noted their reliance (trust) in Him and helped them.

Understanding Ezra

8:24-30 Then I separated twelve of the chief of the priests, Sherebiah, Hashabiah, and ten of their brethren with them, 25 And weighed unto them the silver, and the gold, and the vessels, *even* the offering of the house of our God, which the king, and his counsellors, and his lords, and all Israel *there* present, had offered: 26 I even weighed unto their hand six hundred and fifty talents of silver, and silver vessels an hundred talents, *and* of gold an hundred talents; 27 Also twenty basons of gold, of a thousand drams; and two vessels of fine copper, precious as gold.

28 And I said unto them, Ye *are* holy unto the LORD; the vessels *are* holy also; and the silver and the gold *are* a freewill offering unto the LORD God of your fathers. 29 Watch ye, and keep *them*, until ye weigh *them* before the chief of the priests and the Levites, and chief of the fathers of Israel, at Jerusalem, in the chambers of the house of the LORD. 30 So took the priests and the Levites the weight of the silver, and the gold, and the vessels, to bring *them* to Jerusalem unto the house of our God.

Ezra therefore took immediate steps to entrust the considerable monies they were carrying to the oversight of the priests and Levites. The sums were enormous. Record is noted of 650 talents of silver, plus 100 talents of silver vessels, plus 100 talents of gold. Translating that into modern numbers is difficult. However, if a talent is assumed to be approximately 100 pounds American weight (there were several measures of ancient talents ranging from sixty to one hundred-twenty pounds), that would approximate 1,600 ounces of gold per talent.

If a conservative figure of $350 per ounce of gold is assumed, the sum of one talent of gold would exceed a $500,000. One-hundred talents of gold would be more than *fifty million* dollars. That does not include the 750 talents of silver, nor the 20 basons of gold or the vessels of fine copper (high grade brass) which was as precious as gold. Ezra therefore enjoined the priests and Levites as holy men of God to "watch ye, and keep them" until it all arrives at the Temple at Jerusalem. The priests and Levites therefore counted the funds, recorded it, and accounted of it upon delivery to the Temple.

8:31-32 Then we departed from the river of Ahava on the twelfth *day* **of the first month, to go unto Jerusalem: and the hand of our God was upon us, and he delivered us from the hand of the enemy, and of such as lay in wait by the way. 32 And we came to Jerusalem, and abode there three days**.

The expedition therefore formally departed on the twelfth day of the first month (Nisan) which is approximately April and arrived around the first of August (see 7:9). Ezra notes again that "the hand of our God was upon us, and he delivered us from the hand of the enemy, and of such as lay in wait by the way." (Highway robbery was common then.) They rested three days upon arriving at Jerusalem.

8:33-36 Now on the fourth day was the silver and the gold and the vessels weighed in the house of our God by the hand of Meremoth the son of Uriah the priest; and with him *was* **Eleazar the son of Phinehas; and with them** *was* **Jozabad the son of Jeshua, and Noadiah the son of Binnui, Levites; 34 By number** *and* **by weight of every one: and all the weight was written at that time.**

35 *Also* **the children of those that had been carried away, which were come out of the captivity, offered burnt offerings unto the God of Israel, twelve bullocks for all Israel, ninety and six rams, seventy and seven lambs, twelve he goats** *for* **a sin offering: all** *this was* **a burnt offering unto the LORD. 36 And they delivered the king's commissions unto the king's lieutenants, and to the governors on this side the river: and they furthered the people, and the house of God.**

Understanding Ezra

The vast sums designated for the Temple were delivered on the fourth day and those arriving in Jerusalem offered sacrifices at the Temple for the first time in their lives. It must have been a time of great rejoicing for all. For the priests, Levites, and other Jews living around Jerusalem, an unbelievable sum had been delivered for the beautification, redecorating, and improvement to their Temple. For the pilgrims arriving, it must have been a time of great joy in returning to the land God had promised their forefathers. Furthermore, they were able to offer a proper sacrifice to Jehovah God at *the* Temple in Jerusalem.

Finally, the appropriate officials of the Persian empire in the region were notified of the decrees and authorizations which Artaxerxes had made to Ezra and his people. The word translated as **furthered** (נשא *nasaw*) as conjugated has the sense of 'lifting' (the load) or easing the way for the Jews. As the decrees from Artaxerxes were presented, the governmental officials did all they could to assist and remove obstacles for the improvements to the Temple.

* * * * *

Overview of Ezra 9: *The final two chapters of Ezra present a thorny, difficult problem and the courage of Ezra in confronting it. He learned that the restored remnant had intermarried with pagan people of the nations round about Jerusalem. This was a direct violation of God's Law (see Deuteronomy 7:3). There is record here of a powerful intercessory prayer on the part of Ezra. The subdivisions of the chapter are: (1) Ezra's mourning for the Jews' conduct in verses 1-4); and, Ezra's confession of their sins in verses 5-15.*

9:1-2 Now when these things were done, the princes came to me, saying, The people of Israel, and the priests,

and the Levites, have not separated themselves from the people of the lands, *doing* according to their abominations, *even* of the Canaanites, the Hittites, the Perizzites, the Jebusites, the Ammonites, the Moabites, the Egyptians, and the Amorites. 2 For they have taken of their daughters for themselves, and for their sons: so that the holy seed have mingled themselves with the people of *those* lands: yea, the hand of the princes and rulers hath been chief in this trespass.**

Not long after Ezra's arrival in Jerusalem and his grant to the Temple, portions of the leadership of Israel came to him with a disturbing problem. "The people of Israel, including the priests, and the Levites, have not separated themselves from the people of the lands." In joining into a covenant with God centuries earlier, Israel had agreed to be a *separated* people. See Exodus 33:16. They had directly violated that promise.

Specifically, they had begun to inter-marry with the "Canaanites, the Hittites, the Perizzites, the Jebusites, the Ammonites, the Moabites, the Egyptians and the Amorites." When Israel had conquered the land centuries earlier, God had forbade them to have contact, socially or otherwise, with local inhabitants. They are noted here as practicing abominations. Not only were they idolaters, they were degenerate in their various immoral sexual practices. In short, God had commanded His people to be separate from the world and its people. Israel in Ezra's day had violated not only the spirit but the very letter of God's Word in this matter.

9:3-4 And when I heard this thing, I rent my garment and my mantle, and plucked off the hair of my head and of my beard, and sat down astonied. 4 Then were assembled unto me every one that trembled at the words of the God of Israel, because of the transgression of those that had been carried away; and I sat astonied until the evening sacrifice.

Understanding Ezra 749

insight into the holy mind and spirit of Ezra are evidenced. Upon hearing this troubling news, he rent his garments, plucked out hair and beard "and sat down astonied." The word translated as **astonied** (שמם *shamem*) has the sense of being 'appalled' or 'stunned.' Ezra along with others in Israel who were also likewise vexed sat down with him and "trembled at the words of the God of Israel, because of the transgression of those that had been carried away." They sat together until the evening sacrifice—approximately 3 p.m. Rending ones clothes was a symbol of utter grief, anger, or consternation.

9:5 And at the evening sacrifice I arose up from my heaviness; and having rent my garment and my mantle, I fell upon my knees, and spread out my hands unto the LORD my God. Late that day, Ezra fell on his knees and began to pour out his heart to God in one of the great intercessory, penitent prayers in the Bible. There is great fervency and deep distress in his prayer. Ezra's solemn prayer occupies the remainder of the chapter. In fashion like unto Daniel in Daniel 9, Ezra confessed and interceded on behalf of his sinful nation.

9:6-7 And said, O my God, I am ashamed and blush to lift up my face to thee, my God: for our iniquities are increased over *our* head, and our trespass is grown up unto the heavens. 7 Since the days of our fathers *have* we *been* in a great trespass unto this day; and for our iniquities have we, our kings, *and* our priests, been delivered into the hand of the kings of the lands, to the sword, to captivity, and to a spoil, and to confusion of face, as *it is* this day. Ezra began his grim prayer by an utter humbling of himself before a holy and just God. As he prayed with his face to the ground, he noted how he was "ashamed and blush to lift up my face to thee, my God: for our iniquities are increased over our head, and our trespass is grown up into the heavens." With great eloquence, he confessed the sin of his people. Yet, it is evident, he truly was smitten and contrite before His God.

He acknowledged how Israel as a people had been judged for their prior sin, ranging from the kings and priests to the common people. It is clear that at least some in Israel were very much aware of why God had sent them into captivity.

9:8-9 And now for a little space grace hath been *shewed* from the LORD our God, to leave us a remnant to escape, and to give us a nail in his holy place, that our God may lighten our eyes, and give us a little reviving in our bondage. 9 For we *were* bondmen; yet our God hath not forsaken us in our bondage, but hath extended mercy unto us in the sight of the kings of Persia, to give us a reviving, to set up the house of our God, and to repair the desolations thereof, and to give us a wall in Judah and in Jerusalem.

Ezra continued to acknowledge that for a relatively short time God had been gracious to them in allowing a remnant to return and resume His work at Jerusalem. The reference to them being given "a nail in this holy place" has the idea of re-establishing a 'beach-head' as it were. One nail had been set to fasten them back in their land. The idea is how precarious their situation was. God had been gracious in allowing them return and they had flagrantly disregarded His Word.

Ezra continued to acknowledge that God had not forsaken His people even in their captivity. He had been merciful to them in stirring the heart of the Persian kings in allowing them to return with their blessing.

9:10-11 And now, O our God, what shall we say after this? for we have forsaken thy commandments, 11 Which thou hast commanded by thy servants the prophets, saying, The land, unto which ye go to possess it, is an unclean land with the filthiness of the people of the lands, with their

abominations, which have filled it from one end to another with their uncleanness.

Ezra directly confessed the present sin. Israel had forsaken His commandments. God through Moses had clearly ordered His people not to inter-marry with 'unsaved' people of the world. See Deuteronomy 7:3. This command was alluded to by both Joshua (23:12) and the writer of Judges (2:2). God was concerned with not only preserving the identity of His people, but more importantly the principle of separation from sin. In II Corinthians 6:17, the command is *"Come out from among them,"* (i.e., the people of the world). When God's people walk in the counsel of the ungodly, stand in the way of sinners, and sit in the seat of the scornful; before long they 'catch' the attitudes of the world's crowd. They soon are infected with the same sin and spiritual rebellion so characteristic of the world.

Ezra noted the **filthiness** of the people of the land. The word so translated (נדה *niddah*) has the sense of moral filthiness. It pertains to sexual perversity and all that implies. Leviticus 18 details the perverse immorality of the same nations mentioned in verse 1 of Ezra 9. There, God condemned such sin of the Canaanites as incest, bestiality, homosexuality, not to mention fornication and adultery. The *abominations* noted may refer to not only the degenerate moral practices but also their idolatry. He summarizes how these nations had filled the land from one end to the other "with their uncleanness."

9:12 Now therefore give not your daughters unto their sons, neither take their daughters unto your sons, nor seek their peace or their wealth for ever: that ye may be strong, and eat the good of the land, and leave *it* for an inheritance to your children for ever.

Ezra continued in his prayer, recalling that God had specifically commanded His people not to inter-marry with the neighboring nations of the world.

9:13-14 And after all that is come upon us for our evil deeds, and for our great trespass, seeing that thou our God hast punished us less than our iniquities *deserve*, and hast given us *such* deliverance as this; 14 Should we again break thy commandments, and join in affinity with the people of these abominations? wouldest not thou be angry with us till thou hadst consumed *us*, so that *there should be* no remnant nor escaping?

Ezra noted that even after all God had done in chastening His people for their prior sin, yet He had punished them "less than our iniquities deserve, and has given us such deliverance." Again, Ezra in effect thanked God for not having punished them any more than He had. He defined God's mercy in not giving them what they really deserved.

Ezra therefore posed the question in his prayer, "Should we again break thy commandments, and join in affinity with the people of these abominations?" He in so many words asked, have we not learned our lesson? Then he went on to note that God could very easily be angry with them to the point they were consumed by His wrath altogether. He feared God's wrath would be provoked "so that there should be no remnant nor escaping."

9:15 O LORD God of Israel, thou *art* righteous: for we remain yet escaped, as *it is* this day: behold, we *are* before thee in our trespasses: for we cannot stand before thee because of this.

He concluded his prayer with the simple but profound confession, "O LORD God of Israel, thou are righteous." Indeed He is. Throughout His Word He is frequently so described. The remnant remained a people at His mercy and escaped only by His grace. He one more time admitted and confessed on behalf of His people their sin and acknowledged how they could not stand before God in such a state. Indeed, sin removes our fellowship before God. It short-circuits prayer. It aborts God's blessing. It places one in the line of fire of God's chastening judgment.

* * * * *

Overview of Ezra 10: *In this final chapter, Ezra (1) demanded separation in verses 1-5; (2) He assembled the people in verses 6-14; and, (3) Separation was implemented in 15-44.*

10:1 Now when Ezra had prayed, and when he had confessed, weeping and casting himself down before the house of God, there assembled unto him out of Israel a very great congregation of men and women and children: for the people wept very sore. Further insight into the intensity of Ezra's prayer is noted in that he had "confessed, weeping and casting himself down before the house of God." One thing is for sure. Ezra had understanding of God's holiness. Because of his adherence to God's holy nature, he himself was deeply vexed by the sin he had discovered. Upon rising from his heart-wrenching prayer, he found others of Israel, "a very great congregation of men and women and children," had joined him and with him "wept sore." To their credit, a large number of God's people joined in the godly sorrow over sin in their ranks.

10:2-4 And Shechaniah the son of Jehiel, *one* **of the sons of Elam, answered and said unto Ezra, We have trespassed against our God, and have taken strange wives of the people of the land: yet now there is hope in Israel concerning this thing. 3 Now therefore let us make a covenant with our God to put away all the wives, and such as are born of them, according to the counsel of my lord, and of those that tremble at the commandment of our God; and let it be done according to the**

law. 4 Arise; for *this* matter *belongeth* unto thee: we also *will be* with thee: be of good courage, and do *it*.

Evidently, some of those who joined with Ezra in penance were guilty parties. One named *Shechaniah* stood and likewise confessed the sin of the people. Exactly who Shechaniah was is not clear. In chapter 8:3,5, sons of Shechaniah are mentioned among those who returned with Ezra. Implied is he was of that party. However, he uses the first person plural *we* in confessing the sin. Whether that is an *editorial* we or whether he himself was involved in the sin is not clear. In any event, he saw hope in the matter.

Shechaniah proposed putting away all the alien wives and even the children born of them. This presents thorny issues. First, what he proposed would be of profound emotional distress. Yet, he was willing to do something very difficult in order to return to a holy and right position before God. Moreover, he proposed how this be "done according to the law" (i.e., of Moses).

This leads us to the difficult matter of divorce. What he may have had in mind is Deuteronomy 24:1 where in the law of Moses, divorce was allowed if and only if there was found "uncleanness" in the woman. (It was a patriarchal culture with the man holding the majority of the rights.) The word *uncleanness* there seemed to imply moral impurity (i.e., adultery, fornication, lesbian activity etc. See notes on Deuteronomy 24:1.) It may be Shechaniah took the position that these pagan, gentile women were by their very class unclean, if not personally so. They therefore had grounds under the law of Moses to so proceed. In any event, it was a very difficult situation.

Finally, Shechaniah urged Ezra to so order this position and the people would back him. He urged him to "be of good courage, and do it."

Understanding Ezra

10:5-6 Then arose Ezra, and made the chief priests, the Levites, and all Israel, to swear that they should do according to this word. And they sware. 6 Then Ezra rose up from before the house of God, and went into the chamber of Johanan the son of Eliashib: and *when* he came thither, he did eat no bread, nor drink water: for he mourned because of the transgression of them that had been carried away.

Therefore, first of all Ezra enjoined the chief priests and the Levites "to swear that they should do according to this word." He then went to see Johanan who quite evidently had not joined with the congregation in weeping with Ezra before the Temple. Johanan was not the high priest, but was of his family and a man of high influence.

Evidently, Ezra sought to get Johanan to 'sign on' to the proposal at hand. We are not told of his response. However, the fact Ezra would eat nor drink anything after departing from Johanan's chamber gives some clue to his attitude. Ezra's fasting may have only been for the rest of the day, but in any event, "he mourned because of the transgression of them that had been carried away."

10:7-8 And they made proclamation throughout Judah and Jerusalem unto all the children of the captivity, that they should gather themselves together unto Jerusalem; 8 And that whosoever would not come within three days, according to the counsel of the princes and the elders, all his substance should be forfeited, and himself separated from the congregation of those that had been carried away.

Therefore a proclamation was sent through Judah and Jerusalem ordering "all the children of the captivity" to assemble at Jerusalem within three days. If they would not come, Ezra had authority from the king of Persia to inflict any penalty he deemed necessary. He therefore warned that anyone ignoring this injunction would (1) have all their property confiscated and

(2) they themselves would be separated from the congregation (i.e., kicked out of Israel).

10:9 Then all the men of Judah and Benjamin gathered themselves together unto Jerusalem within three days. It *was* the ninth month, on the twentieth *day* of the month; and all the people sat in the street of the house of God, trembling because of *this* matter, and for the great rain.

It was the ninth month of the Jewish year (December) and the twentieth day. It therefore was cool weather at the least. The entire congregation of the returned remnant came to Jerusalem and sat in the street (or courtyard) of the house of God.

Moreover, they were "trembling because of this matter, and of the great rain." Word had quickly spread as to why they were being assembled. They no doubt had heard of the wrath of Ezra with the authority of the king of Persia backing him. Moreover, they sat out in the open in a pouring, cold, December rain.

10:10-11 And Ezra the priest stood up, and said unto them, Ye have transgressed, and have taken strange wives, to increase the trespass of Israel. 11 Now therefore make confession unto the LORD God of your fathers, and do his pleasure: and separate yourselves from the people of the land, and from the strange wives.

Ezra stood and wasted no time in getting to the point. "Ye have transgressed, and have taken strange wives, to increase the trespass of Israel." His remedy was simple.(1) "Now therefore make confession unto the LORD God of your fathers," (2) "do his pleasure" (i.e., do His will or what is pleasing to Him), (3) "and separate yourselves from the people of the land, and from the strange wives." The injunction was simple: divorce.

10:12-15 Then all the congregation answered and said with a loud voice, As thou hast said, so must we do. 13 But the

people *are* many, and *it is* a time of much rain, and we are not able to stand without, neither *is this* a work of one day or two: for we are many that have transgressed in this thing.

14 Let now our rulers of all the congregation stand, and let all them which have taken strange wives in our cities come at appointed times, and with them the elders of every city, and the judges thereof, until the fierce wrath of our God for this matter be turned from us. 15 Only Jonathan the son of Asahel and Jahaziah the son of Tikvah were employed about this *matter*: and Meshullam and Shabbethai the Levite helped them.

The congregation agreed. However, they suggested this was a matter which could not be resolved in a day or two "for we are many that have transgressed in this thing." A systematic procedure was therefore appointed in which those who were guilty would come at an appointed time along with the elders and judges of each city and settle each marriage in an orderly manner, "until the fierce wrath of our God for this matter be turned from us."

What is implied is that God apparently already had begun to bring judgment upon the people and they were aware of it. A small number of men were appointed to oversee the administration of this difficult matter.

10:16-17 And the children of the captivity did so. And Ezra the priest, *with* certain chief of the fathers, after the house of their fathers, and all of them by *their* names, were separated, and sat down in the first day of the tenth month to examine the matter. 17 And they made an end with all the men that had taken strange wives by the first day of the first month.

About ten days later ("the first day of the tenth month"), Ezra along with others in leadership sat down one by one with those who were separated "to examine the matter." It took them three full months to make "an end with all the men that had taken strange wives."

10:18-43 A listing of those who were so processed is listed. It is of note that in verse 18, the sons of Jeshua are named. In Zechariah 3:3, Jeshua is represented in a vision as having filthy skirts. It may be he was acquiescent in allowing his sons to intermingle with the ungodly. Other sons of priests were also among the guilty parties along with some Levites. Nevertheless, they all agreed "that they would put away their wives; and being guilty, they offered a ram of the flock for their trespass."

10:44 All these had taken strange wives: and *some* of them had wives by whom they had children. The question remains if they did so out of a heart of repentance before God, or if they merely acquiesced to the absolute authority granted to Ezra to execute judgment as he saw fit in Israel. In any event, the impurity was purged from Israel. Observant Jews to this day seek to marry only of the stock of Israel.

THE BOOK OF
NEHEMIAH

Introduction: *The book of Nehemiah is the historical successor to Ezra. Though there clearly is a new personality, a new leader, new circumstances, and a new author in Nehemiah, Jews traditionally have viewed the book of Nehemiah as "the second book of Ezra." Indeed, it continues the history of the restoration of the remnant of God's people back to the land of promise. The events of the book cover approximately twelve years based on the chronological indicators of Nehemiah 1:1 and 13:6.*

The essence of the book is how Nehemiah, a Jewish court official of the Persian king Artaxerxes is allowed to return with the king's blessing to rebuild the wall and city of Jerusalem. (Zerbubbabel and Ezra had been granted permission to rebuild only the Temple.) Though having official permission to rebuild the wall, there immediately came opposition from adversaries displeased to see God's people prosper. There also is record of the internal problems of selfishness, discouragement and the difficulty of the work along with further external troubles. Nevertheless, the work of rebuilding the wall was completed.

The remainder of the book presents how God's Word was preached to the people by Ezra. There was repentance and revival and how the problem of separation was once again addressed. Nehemiah also presents genealogical details of the Jews of the remnant who had returned over the years.

On a broader spiritual level, the book of Nehemiah, like Ezra, presents how that the enemy will always seek to oppose God's work. No sooner had they endeavored to serve God than the adversary sought any way possible to stop them. To one degree or another, that remains true to this day. It is never easy to do a work for God, then or now.

* * * * *

Overview of Nehemiah 1: *Chapter 1 of Nehemiah presents the historical setting and Nehemiah's determination to help his people and their homeland. Over ninety years had passed since the first group of the remnant Jews had returned. Though the Temple had been rebuilt, the rest of Jerusalem was still largely destroyed. The rubble and desolation of the earlier Babylonian conquests remained. As Nehemiah obtained word of the continuing desolation, he asked and received permission to return.*

1:1 The words of Nehemiah the son of Hachaliah. And it came to pass in the month Chisleu, in the twentieth year, as I was in Shushan the palace. Nehemiah presents the setting for the events to be recorded. It was the twentieth year of the rule of Artaxerxes and about December (the Hebrew month Chisleu). He was employed at the palace of the king at Shushan (in modern archaeology, called Susa) which was the winter palace of the Persian empire. (In modern geography, Susa is in southwestern Iran.) Apart from his father's name, little else is known about the background of Nehemiah.

1:2-4 That Hanani, one of my brethren, came, he and *certain* **men of Judah; and I asked them concerning the Jews that had escaped, which were left of the captivity, and concerning Jerusalem. 3 And they said unto me, The**

Understanding Nehemiah

remnant that are left of the captivity there in the province *are* **in great affliction and reproach: the wall of Jerusalem also** *is* **broken down, and the gates thereof are burned with fire.** Nehemiah refers to Hanani as one his brethren. Based upon comments made in 7:2, it seems he was his literal brother in distinction to the more generic reference of other Jewish brethren. Evidently, he and other Jews had returned from a trip to Jerusalem. Nehemiah, as a Jew, was very much interested in the welfare of his homeland and the Jews who had been living there now for over ninety years.

His brother and associates bore bad news. They reported how "the remnant of the captivity there in the province are in great affliction and reproach: the wall of Jerusalem also is broken down, the gates thereof are burned with fire." Evidently, the city of Jerusalem lay much as it had since the final destruction by the Babylonians in 586 B.C. Moreover, the Jews who had returned earlier apparently had fallen upon hard times from the hostility of the surrounding peoples.

4 And it came to pass, when I heard these words, that I sat down and wept, and mourned *certain* **days, and fasted, and prayed before the God of heaven.** Upon hearing such discouraging news, Nehemiah (1) "sat down and wept and mourned certain days." (2) He began to fast. And (3) he went to prayer "before the God of heaven." There is a tremendous lesson that when there seems to be no recourse for God's people, there always is room at the throne of grace.

1:5-11 And said, I beseech thee, O LORD God of heaven, the great and terrible God, that keepeth covenant and mercy for them that love him and observe his commandments. Recorded is one of the great prayers in the Bible. Nehemiah prayed (1) with great intensity and fervency. See James 5:16. (2) There is great eloquence. (3) There is confession on behalf of his people. (4) There is intercessory pleading by him on behalf of his people. (5) Finally, there is a direct request for God's help. Nehemiah evidently already had in mind to approach Artaxerxes the king with a request to return and rebuild Jerusalem. He therefore first asked God to intercede on his behalf and prosper his request before the king.

6 Let thine ear now be attentive, and thine eyes open, that thou mayest hear the prayer of thy servant, which I pray before thee now, day and night, for the children of Israel thy servants, and confess the sins of the children of Israel, which we have sinned against thee: both I and my father's house have sinned. 7 We have dealt very corruptly against thee, and have not kept the commandments, nor the statutes, nor the judgments, which thou commandedst thy servant Moses.

Notice the eloquence, yet fervent reverence in how Nehemiah approached God. "I beseech thee, O LORD God of heaven, the great and terrible God, that keepeth covenant and mercy for them that love him and observe his commandments." In effect, he began his prayer by praising God. He then begged God to hear his prayer. Though God certainly can hear our prayer, He is under no obligation to answer it. Nehemiah, knowing the sin of his people, was acutely aware of this. Notice that he was already in the practice of praying for his people "day and night." In fashion quite similar to Daniel and Ezra, he proceeded to intercede on their behalf and confessed their collective sin before God. (See Daniel 9 and Ezra 9:5.)

Remember, I beseech thee, the word that thou commandedst thy servant Moses, saying, *If* ye transgress, I will scatter you abroad among the nations: 9 But *if* ye turn unto me, and keep my commandments, and do them; though there were of you cast out unto the uttermost part of the heaven, *yet* will I gather them from thence, and will bring them unto the place that I have chosen to set my name

Understanding Nehemiah

there. **10 Now these *are* thy servants and thy people, whom thou hast redeemed by thy great power, and by thy strong hand.**

Nehemiah then reminded God of His promises. In reminding God of His Word, Nehemiah alluded to Deuteronomy 28:63-67 and 30:1-5. He reminded God that He had promised to restore His people to their land if they would return to Him and obey Him. He reminded God that He had already allowed some to return. Notice how he referred to them as "thy servants and thy people, who thou hast redeemed by thy great power, and by thy strong hand." God had allowed them to return. To that degree He had redeemed them by His power which indeed He had.

11 O Lord, I beseech thee, let now thine ear be attentive to the prayer of thy servant, and to the prayer of thy servants, who desire to fear thy name: and prosper, I pray thee, thy servant this day, and grant him mercy in the sight of this man. For I was the king's cupbearer.

Finally, Nehemiah got down to the heart of His prayer. He asked God to prosper and grant mercy to him as he approached Artaxerxes. For the first time, it is noted that Nehemiah was the cupbearer for the king. It was a position of high degree. It was his job to sample all drink before the king drank it to verify there was no poison therein. He therefore held a position of high trust and personal contact with the king. He accordingly intended to approach Artaxerxes with a plan to rebuild Jerusalem. He therefore besought the Lord for his divine intervention and prospering in the matter.

* * * * *

Overview of Nehemiah 2: *Three developments are contained in this chapter: (1) Nehemiah's request to the king in* verses 1-10; (2) Nehemiah arrival in Jerusalem in verses 11-16; and (3) Nehemiah encourages the people to rebuild the wall in verses 17-20.

2:1-2 And it came to pass in the month Nisan, in the twentieth year of Artaxerxes the king, *that* wine *was* before him: and I took up the wine, and gave *it* unto the king. Now I had not been *beforetime* sad in his presence. 2 Wherefore the king said unto me, Why *is* thy countenance sad, seeing thou *art* not sick? this *is* nothing *else* but sorrow of heart. Then I was very sore afraid.

By now, it was spring (the month Nisan, approximating April). Precisely at what time or how long Nehemiah had prayed along the lines noted above we are not told. However, it is clear that approximately four months had passed since he first received the news concerning Jerusalem. However, it is clear from 1:11, that the very day he was to make his request before Artaxerxes, he had prayed about the matter. He notes that in appearing before the king he was distraught. In all likelihood, his evident distress was more than just sorrow over the affairs of Jerusalem (he had known thereof for four months). He was likely very anxious and it showed.

The king in knowing Nehemiah personally, immediately picked up upon his demeanor and asked him about it. This only agitated Nehemiah all the more. Part of his job description was to be of good cheer in the presence of the king. He was not. Moreover, the king wondered if he were not sick which likewise had profound implications for a cupbearer. But Artaxerxes perceptively discerned Nehemiah's anxiety was in his heart.

2:3-4 And said unto the king, Let the king live for ever: why should not my countenance be sad, when the city, the place of my fathers' sepulchres, *lieth* waste, and the gates thereof are consumed with fire? 4 Then the king said unto

Understanding Nehemiah

me, **For what dost thou make request? So I prayed to the God of heaven.** Nehemiah therefore recounted to the king how that his homeland and the place of his ancestors was desolate. Whereupon, the king asked him what his request was.

Of interest was how at that moment, Nehemiah prayed in his spirit on the spot for God's help. It is evident he did not pray verbally or out loud. In that instant, however, he pled with God for help in what he was about to ask. He truly was instant in prayer.

2:5-6 And I said unto the king, If it please the king, and if thy servant have found favour in thy sight, that thou wouldest send me unto Judah, unto the city of my fathers' sepulchres, that I may build it. 6 And the king said unto me, (the queen also sitting by him,) For how long shall thy journey be? and when wilt thou return? So it pleased the king to send me; and I set him a time.

Nehemiah therefore directly requested permission to go to Jerusalem and rebuild the city. The king therefore asked him how long this journey would be and when he would return. Nehemiah's reply is not specifically noted, though he did "set him a time." The length of the book is twelve years. It is likely that is not what Nehemiah requested. Rather, it seems that he went to Jerusalem, got the job done, and then returned. Though not explicitly noted, he evidently was then sent back to Jerusalem as a duly appointed governor.

2:7-8 Moreover I said unto the king, If it please the king, let letters be given me to the governors beyond the river, that they may convey me over till I come into Judah; 8 And a letter unto Asaph the keeper of the king's forest, that he may give me timber to make beams for the gates of the palace which *appertained* to the house, and for the wall of the city, and for the house that I shall enter into. And the

king granted me, according to the good hand of my God upon me. Nehemiah further requested from king Artaxerxes letters verifying and authorizing his mission for the local authorities "beyond the river" (west of the Euphrates). He also requested permission for timber to be cut and prepared from the king's forest (likely in Lebanon). His need for such timbers is noted for the palace (adjacent to the Temple) the gates, and other necessary construction.

Artaxerxes granted all he requested. However, Nehemiah notes that the greater reason was "according to the good hand of my God upon me."

2:9-10 Then I came to the governors beyond the river, and gave them the king's letters. Now the king had sent captains of the army and horsemen with me. 10 When Sanballat the Horonite, and Tobiah the servant, the Ammonite, heard *of it,* **it grieved them exceedingly that there was come a man to seek the welfare of the children of Israel.** Nehemiah therefore made the journey from Persia to the region of Jerusalem and delivered his letters of authorization to the local authorities. He also notes that Artaxerxes had sent officers and horsemen from the Persia army for protection and no doubt to further authenticate the royal authority by which he came.

Nevertheless, note is made that the enemies of God's people were not happy upon hearing of the coming strengthening of God's work. Little is known of Sanballat and Tobiah. They evidently were Ammonites. They likely were local governmental officials of the Persian Empire because they were made aware of the mission even before anyone in Jerusalem knew anything about it.

Notice how that they were grieved that someone would come to "seek the welfare of the children of Israel." There may have been anit-Semitism involved. It had have been the long historic enmity between Jews and local gentiles. It may have been motivated by pagan disdain for the worship of Jehovah God by the Jews. In any event, their hatred and soon opposition is all too typical of Satan and how he operates. He will always do everything at his disposal to hinder God's work.

2:11-16 So I came to Jerusalem, and was there three days. 12 And I arose in the night, I and some few men with me; neither told I *any* man what my God had put in my heart to do at Jerusalem: neither *was there any* beast with me, save the beast that I rode upon. 13 And I went out by night by the gate of the valley, even before the dragon well, and to the dung port, and viewed the walls of Jerusalem, which were broken down, and the gates thereof were consumed with fire. 14 Then I went on to the gate of the fountain, and to the king's pool: but *there was* no place for the beast *that was* under me to pass. 15 Then went I up in the night by the brook, and viewed the wall, and turned back, and entered by the gate of the valley, and *so* returned.

Nehemiah records how upon arriving at Jerusalem, he evidently rested three days and then proceeded to secretly survey the situation. He arose in the middle of the night. Though not stated, there very well may have been good moonlight for the nocturnal mission. He along with companions of the mission rode on horseback around the city and surveyed the continuing desolation of the city.

Ancient cities relied upon fortified walls for their defense. Jerusalem's walls had been torn down by the Babylonians many years earlier. The remnants of the gates of the city remained charred from their burning. Jerusalem was defenseless and apparently at the mercy of unfriendly neighboring peoples. No doubt part of their continuing distress was related to their lack of defense. Marauding bands of outlaws and local tyrants could and apparently did pillage them at will.

Nehemiah's nocturnal survey of the city apparently began a gate opening to the Tyropoeon Valley to the southwest and circled around to the Kidron Valley. He thus surveyed the southern portion of the city and then returned to whence he began. It clearly was an arduous task, such that his steed could not pass for all the rubble, especially at night.

16 And the rulers knew not whither I went, or what I did; neither had I as yet told *it* to the Jews, nor to the priests, nor to the nobles, nor to the rulers, nor to the rest that did the work. To this point, Nehemiah had not told anyone at Jerusalem why he had come. His survey of the city by night was in secret. Evidently, the local political leadership of the city were gentiles appointed by the Persians. It may have even been under the jurisdiction of Sanballat and Tobiah. They evidently had little interest in the welfare of the Jewish remnant there. Nehemiah had not informed them or the Jews of his mission. But now he had a clear sense of the magnitude of the project which lay ahead.

2:17-18 Then said I unto them, Ye see the distress that we *are* in, how Jerusalem *lieth* waste, and the gates thereof are burned with fire: come, and let us build up the wall of Jerusalem, that we be no more a reproach. 18 Then I told them of the hand of my God which was good upon me; as also the king's words that he had spoken unto me. And they said, Let us rise up and build. So they strengthened their hands for *this* good *work*. Shortly thereafter, maybe even the next day, Nehemiah revealed his mission. He reminded those who had become accustomed to the desolation just how bad it really was. Often someone coming in from the outside will have a better perspective of a situation than those who have lived with it for a long period.

Nehemiah therefore announced his plan to rebuild the wall of the city. With the authority of the Persian Empire backing him, he urged his Jewish brethren to "come, and let us build up

Understanding Nehemiah

the wall of Jerusalem, that we be no more a reproach" The word translated as **reproach** (חרפה *cherpah*) has the sense of being an object of shame.

He further revealed to them of "the hand of my God which was good upon me; as also the king's words that he had spoken unto me." They therefore united together and said, "Let us rise up and build." The reference to their hands being strengthened has the idea: they were encouraged to proceed.

2:19 But when Sanballat the Horonite, and Tobiah the servant, the Ammonite, and Geshem the Arabian, heard *it*, they laughed us to scorn, and despised us, and said, What *is* this thing that ye do? will ye rebel against the king? Nevertheless, their enemies immediately began to cause trouble. Initially, it was by mocking them, snickering at them and sowing doubt. They insinuated how their impending work would be viewed as rebellion against the king. Satan always lies. Their work was with the blessing of the king. Yet Satan will use any device he can muster to hinder God's work. Deceit is a common satanic tactic.

2:20 Then answered I them, and said unto them, The God of heaven, he will prosper us; therefore we his servants will arise and build: but ye have no portion, nor right, nor memorial, in Jerusalem. In response, Nehemiah hit the nail on the head. He noted that "the God of heaven, he will prosper us; therefore we his servants will arise and build." He warned the opponents that they had no historic portion (i.e., inheritance in Jerusalem), no rights there, and no memorial (no family ancestors). The opposition is not unlike that which modern Israel has faced from disgruntled Palestinians in the twentieth century.

* * * * *

***Overview of Nehemiah 3:** After urging the people at Jerusalem to begin building the wall, the work commences and virtually all join together in the project. Nevertheless, the project is not easy. The essence of chapter 3 is how virtually all of the Jews of Jerusalem threw themselves into the work of rebuilding the wall of the city. Nehemiah records the work of the various groups from the beginning of the work at the sheep gate sequentially around the circumference of the city back to the starting point of the work (verses 1-32).*

Several remarks are of note. In verse 5, comment is made how for whatever reason, the "nobles of the Tekoites put not their necks to the work of their Lord." Precisely who these Tekoite nobles were or what their problem was, they were happy to let others work, but they themselves would not participate. They let others serve the Lord, but they were indifferent thereto. (Tekoa was a city of Judah, about 15 miles south and east of Jerusalem.) In contrast, there were several groups who did not only what was assigned to them, but volunteered for extra duty. For example, note "Meremoth the son of Urijah" in verse 4 and again in verse 21 and Meshullam in verses 6 and 30. Even some women joined in the work as noted in verse 12.

Also of interest is the mention of the Nethinims (which were servants to the Levites.) Though they are mentioned twice in the chapter (verses 26 and 31) no mention is made of them participating in the work. Chapter 3 is a lesson how there was great team work and willingness to serve the Lord. However, there were notable exceptions of those who avoided God's work.

The wall of the ancient city of Jerusalem is described in considerable detail. (The details will be presented in counterclockwise order.) The sheep gate mentioned in verse 1 was at the northeast corner of the city, near the Temple. Accordingly, priests joined in the work in that area. The tower

Understanding Nehemiah 771

of Hananeel was in the center of the northern wall of the city. This area was the most vulnerable to military attack and therefore a defensive tower was built there. The fish gate was just to the west of the tower of Hananeel. This is whence fish from Galilee and Joppa were brought into the city. In verses 4-5, further sections of the northern wall are mentioned.

The old gate (verse 6) was at the northwest corner of the old city of Jerusalem. There, the wall turned southward. The western wall was also known as the broad wall. See verse 8. The tower of the furnaces (i.e., ovens) was further to the south and east (verse 11). The valley gate (verse 13) opened to the Tyropoeon valley. The dung gate (verse 14) was the southern extremity of the city and opened to the valley of Hinnom to the west. The gate of the fountain (verse 15) was where the pool of Siloam was at the southern end of the city and now on the east wall as it ascended toward the Ophel. The wall thence ascended to the City of David (verse 16). There was the royal cemetery of the kings of Judah (verse 16).

At the Ophel (fortifications between the lower and upper city) was an armory (verse 19). Along the eastern wall were several bends and turns as noted in verse 17-25. The water gate was whence the original source of the Kidron brook was as noted in verse 26. Fortress towers were erected in this area (verses 25-27). These all were in the vicinity of the Ophel. The horse gate (verse 28) was farther north along the eastern wall, just below the Temple. The east gate (verse 29) was the major eastern entrance to the city and in front of the Temple entrance. The gate of Miphkad was near the northeastern corner of the city (verse 32). The sheep gate completed the circumference as noted in verse 1. Thus, the circumference of the city wall was described and those who rebuilt each section thereof.

* * * * *

Overview of Nehemiah 4: *There immediately arose opposition from without. The enemies of God's people threatened them to such a degree that the work was done with weapons at their side to defend themselves. Moreover, there comes trouble from within. The work is extremely difficult and there soon came weariness and discouragement. Subdivisions of the chap-ter are: (1) the opposition of Sanballat and others in verses 1-6; (2) the conspiracy of the adversaries in verses 7-15; and (3) Nehemiah's precautions in verses 16-23.*

4:1-3 But it came to pass, that when Sanballat heard that we builded the wall, he was wroth, and took great indignation, and mocked the Jews. 2 And he spake before his brethren and the army of Samaria, and said, What do these feeble Jews? will they fortify themselves? will they sacrifice? will they make an end in a day? will they revive the stones out of the heaps of the rubbish which are burned? 3 Now Tobiah the Ammonite *was* by him, and he said, Even that which they build, if a fox go up, he shall even break down their stone wall.

As is often so typical of Satan, opposition quickly arose to God's work. It began from without. Though not expressly noted, Sanballat evidently was a Samaritan official. As he heard of the commencement of the reconstruction of the wall of Jerusalem, "he was wroth, and took great indignation, and mocked the Jews." He not only was angry that Jerusalem (the historic rival of Samaria) was being fortified, he retaliated immediately with mockery of the project. A comparable modern example might be a politician publicly ridiculing a project he opposes.

Moreover, he conferred not only with his cohorts (his brethren), but also of the army of Samaria. Evidently, the Persian government had allowed Samaria a small standing army for local defense. He sarcastically and derisively spoke publicly

Understanding Nehemiah

against the wall project. He mocked the Jews calling them *feeble*. By his rhetorical questions, he implied, they would never get the job done. They would never be able to rebuild the wall from the accumulated decades of rubbish and burned debris. He no doubt sought to dishearten his Jewish adversaries by publicly predicting they would fail.

Tobiah the Ammonite (from neighboring Ammon—modern Jordan), evidently an ally of Sanballat and the Samaritans, joined in condemning the project. He too ridiculed it publicly. The morning paper the next day (as it were) perhaps had the headline, "Tobiah: even a fox will knock down their work." The implication was the workmanship of the Jews was so inferior that even the weight of a small animal would knock it over.

4:4-5 Hear, O our God; for we are despised: and turn their reproach upon their own head, and give them for a prey in the land of captivity: 5 And cover not their iniquity, and let not their sin be blotted out from before thee: for they have provoked *thee* to anger before the builders.

The public ridicule and opposition from established local governmental officials was not unnoticed by Nehemiah. Though they evidently had not actually physically intervened, their public ridicule and opposition had an effect. It certainly brought discouragement and anxiety. To that degree, the verbal attack of the adversaries was successful. Nehemiah likely had not anticipated such opposition in planning and embarking on his mission. Therefore, he turned to the only resource he had—the Lord.

He therefore prayed and asked God to take note of their peril. Moreover, he asked God to deal with them, that is, make them captive even as we have been a captive people. The simple lesson is to take our problems to the Lord and ask Him to deal with them.

4:6 So built we the wall; and all the wall was joined together unto the half thereof: for the people had a mind to work. Nevertheless, the work went ahead. In the face of much opposition, they did what God had called them to do. "So we built the wall!" The mention of "unto the half thereof" most likely refers to building it to half its total height (or possibly half way around, though that does not seem to mesh with the detail presented in chapter three). Nehemiah gives the simple reason: "for the people had a mind to work." They had, almost to a man, joined the work with great enthusiasm, notwithstanding the prevailing opposition.

4:7-8 But it came to pass, *that* when Sanballat, and Tobiah, and the Arabians, and the Ammonites, and the Ashdodites, heard that the walls of Jerusalem were made up, *and* that the breaches began to be stopped, then they were very wroth, 8 And conspired all of them together to come *and* to fight against Jerusalem, and to hinder it. As the various traditional enemies of God's people in the region (the Samaritans, the Ammonites, the Arabians, and Philistines {Ashdodites}) received word that the wall of Jerusalem was underway and its breaches being rebuilt, there was great anger. These historic enemies of Israel therefore "conspired all of them together to come and to fight against Jerusalem, and to hinder it."

4:9 Nevertheless we made our prayer unto our God, and set a watch against them day and night, because of them. Nehemiah did the two things he could do. (1) He prayed and asked for God's providential protection. God quite evidently answered his prayer. For though their enemies did huff and puff, threatening the work, they did not in fact attack. (2) At the time, not knowing exactly what would happen, Nehemiah therefore "set a watch day and night, because of them."

4:10 And Judah said, The strength of the bearers of burdens is decayed, and *there is* much rubbish; so that we are not able to build the wall. In addition to the opposition from without came trouble from within the ranks. As the project continued, the workers became worn out. The undertaking was immense. Just clearing the accumulated debris from the destruction of the Babylonians years earlier, plus all the assorted other rubble of the years became more than they anticipated. The workmen were therefore tired and discouraged.

4:11-12 And our adversaries said, They shall not know, neither see, till we come in the midst among them, and slay them, and cause the work to cease. 12 And it came to pass, that when the Jews which dwelt by them came, they said unto us ten times, From all places whence ye shall return unto us *they will be upon you*.

If that were not enough, the external adversaries continued their "psychological operations" against the Jews. They schemed how they would slip in undetected, attack the workmen, and force the project to a halt. Apparently even some Jews living in outlying areas were used (whether wittingly or not is unclear) to influence the work in Jerusalem. On ten separate occasions, Jews who lived near the enemy came with propaganda.

The translation of the end of verse 12 is uncertain. It may be a subtle invitation to join in alliance with the allied adversaries and they would leave them alone. Or, it may have been continued threats. The final phrase is interpolated by the translators and is not in the Hebrew text. In any event, it was war-time propaganda intended to alter the course of events by influencing their adversary, the Jews, through reports intended to unsettle them.

4:13-14 Therefore set I in the lower places behind the wall, *and* on the higher places, I even set the people after their families with their swords, their spears, and their bows. 14 And I looked, and rose up, and said unto the nobles, and to the rulers, and to the rest of the people, Be not ye afraid of them: remember the Lord, *which is* great and terrible, and fight for your brethren, your sons, and your daughters, your wives, and your houses.

When Nehemiah heard of the plans of the enemy, he therefore took further precautions. He assigned added forces behind the lower, unfinished portions of the wall which were most vulnerable. It was a citizen's militia. Families were assigned to guard duty with their weapons. Moreover, he sought to encourage the leadership of the people reminding them how the Lord is "great and terrible." The word translated as **terrible** (ירא *yawray*) has the sense of 'awesome.' In other words, he reminded them that God was on their side and He is awesome. He urged them to fight, if need be, for their heritage.

4:15 And it came to pass, when our enemies heard that it was known unto us, and God had brought their counsel to nought, that we returned all of us to the wall, every one unto his work. As word leaked back to the enemies that the Jews would fight to protect themselves, they backed off. The work therefore continued.

4:16-18 And it came to pass from that time forth, *that* the half of my servants wrought in the work, and the other half of them held both the spears, the shields, and the bows, and the habergeons; and the rulers *were* behind all the house of Judah. 17 They which builded on the wall, and they that bare burdens, with those that laded, *every one* with one of his hands wrought in the work, and with the other *hand* held a weapon. 18 For the builders, every one had his sword

girded by his side, and *so* builded. And he that sounded the trumpet *was* by me.

Nevertheless, the Jews were forewarned and thus forearmed. The work therefore continued. However, now the workmen did so with their weapons at their sides ready to pick them up at a moments notice. Others (up to half) were on guard duty while the rest worked on the wall.

4:19-20 And I said unto the nobles, and to the rulers, and to the rest of the people, The work *is* great and large, and we are separated upon the wall, one far from another. 20 In what place *therefore* ye hear the sound of the trumpet, resort ye thither unto us: our God shall fight for us. As the work progressed and the wall rose, it became evident from a military perspective that the defenders were thinly spread. Therefore, Nehemiah implemented a signal system. If trouble should appear at one side of the city, trumpets would sound signals. Forces could then rush to that side of the wall. Moreover, he encouraged his people with the truth, "Our God shall fight for us." To this day, as God's people do God's work, though the opposition be fierce, God will protect and help His people.

4:21-23 So we laboured in the work: and half of them held the spears from the rising of the morning till the stars appeared. 22 Likewise at the same time said I unto the people, Let every one with his servant lodge within Jerusalem, that in the night they may be a guard to us, and labour on the day. 23 So neither I, nor my brethren, nor my servants, nor the men of the guard which followed me, none of us put off our clothes, *saving that* every one put them off for washing.

The intensity of the activity is noted in how they worked from dawn to dark. All workers and their servants were ordered not to leave the city for their homes at night. Nehemiah and his associates did not even take their clothes off to sleep. He notes that they in fact did not change clothes during the project except for occasional laundering. The atmosphere was so tense, their only goal was to finish the wall.

* * * * *

Overview of Nehemiah 5: *As the work of the reconstruction continued, it was a hard time economically and the people had to borrow to survive. Some unscrupulous Jews were charging exorbitant interest rates of their brethren who needed funds to buy food. Finally, Nehemiah set an example of living from his own resources, not requiring the customary support tax of the people he governed. The subdivisions of the chapter are: (1) the Jews complain of their troubles in verses 1-5; (2) Nehemiah addresses their grievances in verses 6-13; and, (3) Nehemiah's example of unselfishness in verses 14-19.*

5:1-5 And there was a great cry of the people and of their wives against their brethren the Jews. 2 For there were that said, We, our sons, and our daughters, *are* many: therefore we take up corn *for them*, that we may eat, and live. 3 *Some* also there were that said, We have mortgaged our lands, vineyards, and houses, that we might buy corn, because of the dearth. 4 There were also that said, We have borrowed money for the king's tribute, *and that upon* our lands and vineyards. 5 Yet now our flesh *is* as the flesh of our brethren, our children as their children: and, lo, we bring into bondage our sons and our daughters to be servants, and *some* of our daughters are brought unto bondage *already*: neither *is it* in our power *to redeem them*; for other men have our lands and vineyards.

Understanding Nehemiah

If the threat of the enemy coupled with the backbreaking labor were not enough, new trouble erupted from within. Greed, selfishness, and a lack of concern for neighbors going through hard times added to problems which already were great. Details are not enumerated, but clearly the inhabitants of the land were going through a hard time. It may have been from crop failure caused by famine. It may have been the war-time conditions had impressed the available labor force into the defense and building of the wall rather than tending to crops. In any event, a crisis had developed.

The poorer of the land could not feed their families. Some had gone so far as to mortgage their homes to buy food from Jewish merchants who evidently were charging exorbitant prices. Others had to chose between using money from mortgaging their homes to either buy groceries or pay the required tax to the Persian government. Some had been forced to sell their children as servants to obtain resources to buy food to live. Moreover, is it clear more prosperous Jews were taking advantage of their less fortunate brethren.

5:6-10 And I was very angry when I heard their cry and these words. 7 **Then I consulted with myself, and I rebuked the nobles, and the rulers, and said unto them, Ye exact usury, every one of his brother. And I set a great assembly against them.** 8 **And I said unto them, We after our ability have redeemed our brethren the Jews, which were sold unto the heathen; and will ye even sell your brethren? or shall they be sold unto us? Then held they their peace, and found nothing** *to answer.*

9 **Also I said, It** *is* **not good that ye do: ought ye not to walk in the fear of our God because of the reproach of the heathen our enemies?** 10 **I likewise,** *and* **my brethren, and my servants, might exact of them money and corn: I pray you, let us leave off this usury.**

Upon hearing this, Nehemiah was angered. He rebuked the nobles and rulers who evidently were the guilty parties. They were charging exorbitant interest of their own Jewish brethren which was a violation of Jewish law. (In Exodus 22:25, Jews were forbidden from charging usury to their own brethren who were in distress. The business of paying interest per se is not unscriptural. What is at hand is exorbitant interest charged to *brethren* who are going through hard times.) Nehemiah noted how that he himself as governor could do the same, but refused to do so. He therefore urged them to stop the practice.

5:11-13 Restore, I pray you, to them, even this day, their lands, their vineyards, their oliveyards, and their houses, also the hundredth *part* of the money, and of the corn, the wine, and the oil, that ye exact of them. 12 Then said they, We will restore *them*, and will require nothing of them; so will we do as thou sayest. Then I called the priests, and took an oath of them, that they should do according to this promise. 13 Also I shook my lap, and said, So God shake out every man from his house, and from his labour, that performeth not this promise, even thus be he shaken out, and emptied. And all the congregation said, Amen, and praised the LORD. And the people did according to this promise.

In addition, Nehemiah urged those who had taken collateral for mortgages of lands, vineyards, olive groves, and homes to return them and release any mortgages they held. Notices in verse 11 the mention of "the hundredth part of the money." They were charging interest in what was one percent per month on the loans and mortgages they had issued. Nehemiah ordered this practice stopped and restoration made.

Nehemiah therefore made an oath before the priests of the Temple enjoining God to shake out even as he had shaken out his robe, any man who would not fulfill his injunction to release his brethren, the Jews, from their debts. The entire congregation of Jews of Jerusalem was assembled before the Temple. Upon hearing Nehemiah's injunction and oath of the matter, they said, "Amen, and praised the LORD." The problem from within was thus resolved.

5:14 Moreover from the time that I was appointed to be their governor in the land of Judah, from the twentieth year even unto the two and thirtieth year of Artaxerxes the king, *that is***, twelve years, I and my brethren have not eaten the bread of the governor.** Though the book of Nehemiah is basically chronological, what is implied here is that Nehemiah, after the completion of the wall, returned to Artaxerxes with a report of his mission. At that time, he evidently was sent back again as governor. His rule was for twelve years. The final verses of chapter five apparently are written as an epilogue after the fact.

5:15-18 But the former governors that *had been* **before me were chargeable unto the people, and had taken of them bread and wine, beside forty shekels of silver; yea, even their servants bare rule over the people: but so did not I, because of the fear of God. 16 Yea, also I continued in the work of this wall, neither bought we any land: and all my servants** *were* **gathered thither unto the work. 17 Moreover** *there were* **at my table an hundred and fifty of the Jews and rulers, beside those that came unto us from among the heathen that** *are* **about us. 18 Now** *that* **which was prepared** *for me* **daily** *was* **one ox** *and* **six choice sheep; also fowls were prepared for me, and once in ten days store of all sorts of wine: yet for all this required not I the bread of the governor, because the bondage was heavy upon this people.**

The point being made is that Nehemiah, as the duly appointed representative of the king of Persia and then governor of Judah in deference to the situation, did not receive the tribute customary of Persian governors. Typically, the people would be taxed a certain rate to support their governor. Nehemiah did not, but supported himself largely through his own resources.

His focus was upon doing the work of God. He supported over one-hundred-and-fifty people at his own expense. However, verse 18 indicates he did receive some remuneration for his expenses amounting to a butchered ox each day, six choice sheep, various poultry, and wine every ten days. However, he pointed out that this was nothing compared to what other governors of the kingdom extracted from their people. He had a heart for his people and the labor which was heavy upon them. The word translated as **bondage** (עבדה *abodah*) has the sense of labor or service. Because he understood their service in the mission of rebuilding the city and its walls, he therefore did not receive of them what he could as a gov-ernor.

5:19 Think upon me, my God, for good, *according* to all that I have done for this people. Though he did not receive the earthly reward others of his rank did, Nehemiah therefore besought the Lord to remember how he had served Him and helped His people. God will honor those who honor Him and His work!

* * * * *

Overview of Nehemiah 6: *Opposition to God's work continued. Satan now sought to undermine from within as well as from without. Not only did the 'psychological warfare' continue from the enemies without, they also found willing sympathizers from within. Nevertheless, the work was accomplished because God's hand was upon them.*

6:1-4 Now it came to pass, when Sanballat, and Tobiah, and Geshem the Arabian, and the rest of our enemies, heard that I had builded the wall, and *that* there was no breach left therein; (though at that time I had not set up the doors upon the gates;) 2 That Sanballat and Geshem sent unto me, saying, Come, let us meet together in *some one of the villages in the plain of Ono*. But they thought to do me mischief.

3 And I sent messengers unto them, saying, I *am* doing a great work, so that I cannot come down: why should the work cease, whilst I leave it, and come down to you? 4 Yet they sent unto me four times after this sort; and I answered them after the same manner.

As the work proceeded, the enemies (Sanballat, Tobiah, Geshem, and others) continued to undermine the work. The breaches of the ruined wall had been closed though the gates had yet to be hung upon their hinges in the gateways. Therefore, these opponents changed their strategy. Rather than threaten and publicly oppose it, they decided to have a 'peace conference.' In effect they invited Nehemiah to come and enter into 'dialogue' with them. They in effect said, "Let's negotiate." Nehemiah had nothing to negotiate. He had come to do a job and, by the grace of God, he intended to finish it! Moreover, he quickly perceived, "they thought to do me mischief."

The word translated as **mischief** (רע *ra*) is the common Hebrew word for 'evil.' Nehemiah therefore sent word, "I am doing a great work, so that I cannot come down: why should the work cease whilst I leave it, and come down to you." Insight into the character of Nehemiah is clear. He was a man of determination, singleness of purpose, and would not be intimidated or distracted. He knew what God had called him to do and he kept on doing it. Nevertheless, the enemies did not give up. They sent word on four different occasions for Nehemiah to come negotiate. He would not!

6:5-7 Then sent Sanballat his servant unto me in like manner the fifth time with an open letter in his hand; 6 Wherein *was* **written, It is reported among the heathen, and Gashmu saith** *it, that* **thou and the Jews think to rebel: for which cause thou buildest the wall, that thou mayest be their king, according to these words. 7 And thou hast also appointed prophets to preach of thee at Jerusalem, saying,** *There is* **a king in Judah: and now shall it be reported to the king according to these words. Come now therefore, and let us take counsel together.**

Therefore, Sanballat modified his plan again, having failed thus far. He sent his servant under his own name with an open letter designed to intimidate Nehemiah. In the letter, he alleged that Nehemiah *really* was planning to rebel against the king of Persia and that is why he was building the fortifications of the city. Moreover, Sanballat noted that "It is reported among the heathen and Gashmu saith it." (The *Gashmu* noted is another rendering of the name Geshem mentioned in verse 2. Also the word translated as **heathen** { גוי *goy* or גוים *goyim* plural} is the more common word for 'gentiles' or 'other nations.') In other words, Sanballat wrote to Nehemiah and tried to further intimidate him with the idea how "everybody thinks this." This is what 'they' are all saying.

Moreover, 'they' all are saying he had appointed prophets to preach that Nehemiah was going to be the new king of Judah. Furthermore, he planed to report all of this to the king. "Come now therefore, and let us take counsel together." Sanballat therefore tried to intimidate Nehemiah to negotiate. Though 'everybody' might have been saying it, Nehemiah knew the truth of the matter. Rumor, innuendo, gossip and 'public opinion' would not deter him.

6:8 Then I sent unto him, saying, There are no such things done as thou sayest, but thou feignest them out of

thine own heart. Nehemiah sent a simple reply back to the effect, "You don't know what you are talking about. You have fabricated the charges out of whole cloth." The truth of the matter was, Nehemiah had a personal friendship with the king of Persia and had come because of the good graces of the king. He had no intention to betray his benefactor.

6:9 For they all made us afraid, saying, Their hands shall be weakened from the work, that it be not done. Now therefore, *O God*, strengthen my hands. Nevertheless, the innuendo and intimidation tactics worked to the extent they frightened the loyal Jews. Their intent was that "their hands shall be weakened from the work, that it be not done." It almost worked. However, Nehemiah turned to the one Resource which never fails. He sought help from God. He therefore pled with obvious fervency, "O God, strengthen my hands." The lesson remains to this day.

6:10-14 Afterward I came unto the house of Shemaiah the son of Delaiah the son of Mehetabeel, who *was* shut up; and he said, Let us meet together in the house of God, within the temple, and let us shut the doors of the temple: for they will come to slay thee; yea, in the night will they come to slay thee. 11 And I said, Should such a man as I flee? and who *is there*, that, *being* as I *am*, would go into the temple to save his life? I will not go in. 12 And, lo, I perceived that God had not sent him; but that he pronounced this prophecy against me: for Tobiah and Sanballat had hired him. 13 Therefore *was* he hired, that I should be afraid, and do so, and sin, and *that* they might have *matter* for an evil report, that they might reproach me. 14 My God, think thou upon Tobiah and Sanballat according to these their works, and on the prophetess Noadiah, and the rest of the prophets, that would have put me in fear.

An even more insidious enemy began to come out of the woodwork. Some of the Jews, even those in high places, were found to be in sympathy with the enemy. Someone connected with the Temple, possibly a priest, tried therefore to induce Nehemiah to seclude himself 'for his own safety.' He sought to get Nehemiah to 'hide' in the Temple and have meetings about the whole matter. He intimated how Nehemiah's life was at risk. His opponents might come by night and seek his life. (1) Nehemiah remained resolute. "Should such a man as I flee?" He realized that if he as leader absented himself, the work would grind to a halt. He refused to 'hide' in the Temple.

(2) Nehemiah perceived this fellow was actually working for Tobiah and Sanballat who had hired him. The relentlessness of the enemies is so typical of the chief adversary who undoubtedly was motivating them. Satan never stops trying to oppose God's work. When the devil is attacking, it is a pretty good indication one is doing what God would have him to do. Satan does not hinder those out of God's will. Nehemiah discerned how even an apparent priest had been enlisted by the enemy. (3) Even more enemies from within were uncovered. A prophetess named Noadiah and other prophets were part of the conspiracy.

6:15 So the wall was finished in the twenty and fifth *day* of *the month* Elul, in fifty and two days. Notwithstanding the endless opposition, "the wall was finished" in September of that year in fifty-two days. Some have questioned if the figure of fifty-two days is accurate. (1) God's Word says it, therefore that settles it. (2) From a human perspective, there were upwards of at least fifty-thousand motivated men working on the project who worked from sun-up to sun-down during the project. (3) Furthermore, the original walls had not been totally destroyed. Mention is made several times of the 'breaches' in the wall. The foundation was intact. The original stones were laying nearby.

Understanding Nehemiah

The Babylonians evidently had not totally razed the walls, but had broken various breaches into it thus rendering its military value useless. (4) God's blessing was upon the effort. The initial purpose of Nehemiah's coming was thus complete.

6:16-19 And it came to pass, that when all our enemies heard *thereof*, and all the heathen that *were* about us saw *these things*, they were much cast down in their own eyes: for they perceived that this work was wrought of our God. 17 Moreover in those days the nobles of Judah sent many letters unto Tobiah, and *the letters* of Tobiah came unto them. 18 For *there were* many in Judah sworn unto him, because he *was* the son in law of Shechaniah the son of Arah; and his son Johanan had taken the daughter of Meshullam the son of Berechiah. 19 Also they reported his good deeds before me, and uttered my words to him. And Tobiah sent letters to put me in fear.

Further insight into the web of intrigue and conspiracy used by the enemies becomes evident. They were disheartened that their opposition to the work had failed. They grudgingly had to admit the success of the work was wrought of God. Nevertheless, many communiques were written back and forth between disloyal Jews and Tobiah. They, writing from within, kept Tobiah abreast of what was going on. It turns out that Tobiah and others had intermarried with Jews. He had become influential. He, through family and other connections, had sought to hinder God's work. There is a clear example how intertwining between God's people and the world winds up becoming major trouble for God's work. Ezra had dealt with it (Ezra 9-10). Nehemiah would later deal with the same problem. Separation therefore is a very practical benefit for God's people.

* * * * *

Overview of Nehemiah 7: *Nehemiah, upon completion of the wall, therefore appointed leadership of the city. He evidently shortly thereafter returned to Babylon for a time. He also prepared another formal register of the Jews who were a part of the restoration of the city.*

7:1-2 Now it came to pass, when the wall was built, and I had set up the doors, and the porters and the singers and the Levites were appointed, 2 That I gave my brother Hanani, and Hananiah the ruler of the palace, charge over Jerusalem: for he *was* a faithful man, and feared God above many. The initial work was completed. The wall was done and the gates had been hung (though much internal work in rebuilding the city remained). Nehemiah therefore re-appointed the Levites, porters, and singers to their respective duties at the Temple. They recently had been assigned to the wall work.

He therefore also appointed two men to rule Jerusalem. Though not explicitly noted, shortly hereafter it seems Nehemiah returned to the king of Persia and reported on the mission. He then apparently was appointed governor and returned.

The men appointed were (1) his brother Hanani (who had brought the initial report to Nehemiah of the condition of Jerusalem in 1:2) and (2) Hananiah the ruler of the palace. Which palace Hananiah ruled over is not clear. It may be he, like Nehemiah, had had a high position under the king of Persia and returned to the land. In any event, "he was a faithful man and feared God above many." Though Hananiah evidently had leadership and administrative ability, the reason he was appointed was the spiritual virtue of faithfulness and that he feared God. He was a faithful man. See I Corinthians 4:2.

7:3-4 And I said unto them, Let not the gates of Jerusalem be opened until the sun be hot; and while they

Understanding Nehemiah

stand by, let them shut the doors, and bar *them*: and appoint watches of the inhabitants of Jerusalem, every one in his watch, and every one *to be* over against his house. 4 Now the city *was* large and great: but the people *were* few therein, and the houses *were* not builded.

Insight into the continuing hostile environment is noted. Nehemiah instructed Hanani and Hananiah to not open the gates of the city each day "until the sun be hot," that is, broad day light. Opponents could lurk in the shadows and rush an open gate. Furthermore, there always was to be a watch set, especially at dusk, when the gates were shut. A battle had been won, but opposition remained. Furthermore, though the city was now enclosed, it was not much inhabited. The returning restoration Jews had located in the surrounding communities and countryside. It has been estimated the circumference of the completed wall was six miles.

7:5-6 And my God put into mine heart to gather together the nobles, and the rulers, and the people, that they might be reckoned by genealogy. And I found a register of the genealogy of them which came up at the first, and found written therein, 6 These *are* the children of the province, that went up out of the captivity, of those that had been carried away, whom Nebuchadnezzar the king of Babylon had carried away, and came again to Jerusalem and to Judah, every one unto his city.

Before leaving to return to Babylon, Nehemiah first assembled the leaders of the nation to make an accurate registry of the Jews which had returned to the land from Babylon and captivity.

7:7-62 Nehemiah therefore embarked to find and record the register of all the Jews which had come in the original return years earlier. In comparing this list with that found in Ezra there will be discrepancies noted. No doubt, in the original journey some had died. Others came later with Ezra.

7:63-65 And of the priests: the children of Habaiah, the children of Koz, the children of Barzillai, which took *one* of the daughters of Barzillai the Gileadite to wife, and was called after their name. 64 These sought their register *among* those that were reckoned by genealogy, but it was not found: therefore were they, as polluted, put from the priesthood. 65 And the Tirshatha said unto them, that they should not eat of the most holy things, till there stood *up* a priest with Urim and Thummim. This refers to the same incident recorded in Ezra 2:61-63. See notes thereto.

7:66-67 The whole congregation together *was* forty and two thousand three hundred and threescore, 67 Beside their manservants and their maidservants, of whom *there were* seven thousand three hundred thirty and seven: and they had two hundred forty and five singing men and singing women. As noted in Ezra 2:64-65, a total of 42,360 Jews had returned from Babylon along with 7,337 servants. See notes for Ezra 2:64-65.

7:68-70 Their horses, seven hundred thirty and six: their mules, two hundred forty and five: 69 *Their* camels, four hundred thirty and five: six thousand seven hundred and twenty asses. 70 And some of the chief of the fathers gave unto the work. The Tirshatha gave to the treasure a thousand drams of gold, fifty basons, five hundred and thirty priests' garments. See comments for Ezra 2:66-68

7:71-72 And *some* of the chief of the fathers gave to the treasure of the work twenty thousand drams of gold, and two thousand and two hundred pound of silver. 72 And *that*

which the rest of the people gave *was* twenty thousand drams of gold, and two thousand pound of silver, and threescore and seven priests' garments. The account here differs from that of Ezra 2:69-70. The difference evidently is different sum-totals for differing unnamed individuals at two separate occasions. However, the amounts of gold and silver given were substantial. This evidently was given for the ministry of the Temple.

7:73 So the priests, and the Levites, and the porters, and the singers, and *some* of the people, and the Nethinims, and all Israel, dwelt in their cities; and when the seventh month came, the children of Israel *were* in their cities. Nehemiah noted that the returned remnant (including "all Israel" implying representatives of all twelve tribes) dwelt in their various cities in Palestine. The seventh month noted (late September or early October) sets the time for chapter eight.

* * * * *

Overview of Nehemiah 8: Ezra the priest gathered the restoration Jews together and read to them the Word of God and re-instituted the Feast of Tabernacles altogether. The subdivisions of the chapter are: (1) the reading and exposition of the Law in verses 1-8; (2) the people called upon to be joyful in verses 9-13; and, (3) the Feast of Tabernacles re-instituted in verses 13-18.

8:1-4 And all the people gathered themselves together as one man into the street that *was* before the water gate; and they spake unto Ezra the scribe to bring the book of the law of Moses, which the LORD had commanded to Israel. 2 And Ezra the priest brought the law before the congre-

gation both of men and women, and all that could hear with understanding, upon the first day of the seventh month. 3 And he read therein before the street that *was* before the water gate from the morning until midday, before the men and the women, and those that could understand; and the ears of all the people *were attentive* unto the book of the law. 4 And Ezra the scribe stood upon a pulpit of wood, which they had made for the purpose; and beside him stood Mattithiah, and Shema, and Anaiah, and Urijah, and Hilkiah, and Maaseiah, on his right hand; and on his left hand, Pedaiah, and Mishael, and Malchiah, and Hashum, and Hashbadana, Zechariah, *and* Meshullam.

The latter portion of Ezra's ministry overlapped with the initial work of Nehemiah. The wall was done. The Temple worship had been restored and the Levites returned to their ministries. It was the first of the seventh month of the year. Therefore the people requested Ezra to come forth and publicly read the Word of God to them from "the book of the law of Moses." Ezra therefore publicly read the Scripture from a wooden pulpit (or platform) located at the street before the water gate (a large street suitable for a large gathering). It is noted that he read from morning (shortly after sunrise) to midday. The listing of the other names in verse 4 may be other priests who assisted him in the reading of the law.

8:5-7 And Ezra opened the book in the sight of all the people; (for he was above all the people;) and when he opened it, all the people stood up: 6 And Ezra blessed the LORD, the great God. And all the people answered, Amen, Amen, with lifting up their hands: and they bowed their heads, and worshipped the LORD with *their* faces to the ground. 7 Also Jeshua, and Bani, and Sherebiah, Jamin, Akkub, Shabbethai, Hodijah, Maaseiah, Kelita, Azariah, Jozabad, Hanan, Pelaiah, and the Levites, caused the

people to understand the law: and the people *stood* in their place.

As Ezra stood upon the elevated pulpit platform, he visibly opened the book, "and when he opened it, all the people stood up." Their standing evidently showed respect for God's Word. Before reading, Ezra first prayed a short prayer of invocation blessing the Lord, "the great God." And all the people answered, "Amen." Amen is part of worshiping God. The list of other names noted evidently were other priests who that day assisted Ezra in the reading and teaching of God's Word. They thus "caused the people to understand the law."

8:8 So they read in the book in the law of God distinctly, and gave the sense, and caused *them* to understand the reading. A profound example of the ministry of God's Word to this day is set forth. (1) "They read in the book in the law of God distinctly." (2) They "gave the sense." (3) And they "caused them to understand the reading." In other words, these priests not only read the Word of God, they explained its essence so that the listeners could understand the Word of God. That is the essence of this commentary. It should be a major goal of every pastor.

8:9-13 And Nehemiah, which *is* the Tirshatha, and Ezra the priest the scribe, and the Levites that taught the people, said unto all the people, This day *is* holy unto the LORD your God; mourn not, nor weep. For all the people wept, when they heard the words of the law. 10 Then he said unto them, Go your way, eat the fat, and drink the sweet, and send portions unto them for whom nothing is prepared: for *this* day *is* holy unto our Lord: neither be ye sorry; for the joy of the LORD is your strength. 11 So the Levites stilled all the people, saying, Hold your peace, for the day *is* holy; neither be ye grieved. 12 And all the people went their way to eat,

and to drink, and to send portions, and to make great mirth, because they had understood the words that were declared unto them. 13 And on the second day were gathered together the chief of the fathers of all the people, the priests, and the Levites, unto Ezra the scribe, even to understand the words of the law.

(Once again, the title *Tirshatha* means governor which was Nehemiah.) As God's Word was read and expounded that day, many wept, perhaps convicted of their sin. Yet, Nehemiah and Ezra, along with the Levites and priests assisting, encouraged them to rather rejoice and celebrate God's blessing for that day was holy unto the Lord. "For the joy of the LORD is your strength." Leviticus 23:24 notes that the first day of the seventh month was the Feast of Trumpets, "a sabbath, a memorial of blowing of trumpets, an holy convocation." The day evidently was a feast day and thus a special holy day to rejoice. Therefore, the leadership admonished the people to rejoice in the Lord for indeed, as we rejoice in Him, there is strength. They had just come through a time of great stress and trouble. God had given the victory. Nehemiah therefore urged them rejoice in the Lord for it indeed brings God's strength.

The people therefore rejoiced that day. The next day, the spiritual leadership of Israel gathered unto Ezra to hear more of the Word of God. A revival was underway. Nehemiah had returned. He immediately had undertaken the work notwithstanding great opposition. Now the initial phase was done and as the people heard the Word of God, there was a revival in their hearts.

8:14-18 And they found written in the law which the LORD had commanded by Moses, that the children of Israel should dwell in booths in the feast of the seventh month: 15 And that they should publish and proclaim in all their cities, and in Jerusalem, saying, Go forth unto the mount, and

fetch olive branches, and pine branches, and myrtle branches, and palm branches, and branches of thick trees, to make booths, as *it is* written. 16 So the people went forth, and brought *them*, and made themselves booths, every one upon the roof of his house, and in their courts, and in the courts of the house of God, and in the street of the water gate, and in the street of the gate of Ephraim.

17 And all the congregation of them that were come again out of the captivity made booths, and sat under the booths: for since the days of Jeshua the son of Nun unto that day had not the children of Israel done so. And there was very great gladness. 18 Also day by day, from the first day unto the last day, he read in the book of the law of God. And they kept the feast seven days; and on the eighth day *was* a solemn assembly, according unto the manner.

As the Word of God had been presented, it was noted that the Feast of Tabernacles was at hand. Israel, in the Law, had been commanded to actually live in **booths**. The word so translated is (סכה) *sukkah* which literally means a hut or a 'lean-to.' The Feast of Tabernacles was intended to be a time each year in which Israel recalled how they in the exodus had lived in tents and the humblest of housing. It was intended not only as a memorial but also of humbling themselves before God. Over the centuries, they had continued to observe the Feast of Tabernacles, but it had not been since the time of Joshua that they had actually gone to the trouble of pitching the 'booths' or humble lean-to type of dwellings. Under Nehemiah's leadership they returned to directly and literally obeying the Word of God.

The congregation of Israel therefore gathered the necessary branches and brush to construct the *booths* thus noted in the law of Moses. They built them on the roofs or courtyards of their homes, even in the streets. In obeying God's Word altogether, "there was very great gladness." There always is. One reason

God's people have problems with discouragement is their lack of total obedience to God.

The Feast of Tabernacles (*succoth*) lasted for eight days. During that time, Ezra publicly read "the book of the law of God." Thus, they kept the solemn assembly "according to the manner, that is according to the law."

* * * * *

Overview of Nehemiah 9: *As the observance for the completion of the wall continued, the leadership of Judah publicly worshiped God. They openly and publicly praised God, confessed the collective sin of the nation, and entered into a renewed covenant to serve the Lord.*

9:1-3 Now in the twenty and fourth day of this month the children of Israel were assembled with fasting, and with sackclothes, and earth upon them. 2 And the seed of Israel separated themselves from all strangers, and stood and confessed their sins, and the iniquities of their fathers. 3 And they stood up in their place, and read in the book of the law of the LORD their God *one* fourth part of the day; and *another* fourth part they confessed, and worshipped the LORD their God.

Two days after the Feast of Tabernacles was over, the restoration remnant "assembled with fasting, and with sackclothes, and earth upon them." This all was symbolic of contrition and repentance. They separated themselves from ungodly associates (i.e., "strangers") and "stood and confessed their sins, and the iniquities of their fathers." A spirit of revival swept across the people. Moreover, they spent a quarter of a day (probably three hours) publicly reading the "book of the law of the LORD their God." They spent another quarter of the day confessing and worshiping "the LORD their God." There was nothing shallow or of pretense. These people truly were revived in their spirit to honor the Lord and serve Him.

9:4-5 Then stood up upon the stairs, of the Levites, Jeshua, and Bani, Kadmiel, Shebaniah, Bunni, Sherebiah, Bani, *and* Chenani, and cried with a loud voice unto the LORD their God. 5 Then the Levites, Jeshua, and Kadmiel, Bani, Hashabniah, Sherebiah, Hodijah, Shebaniah, *and* Pethahiah, said, Stand up *and* bless the LORD your God for ever and ever: and blessed be thy glorious name, which is exalted above all blessing and praise.

Chief Levites stood upon an elevated place in the Temple area and urged Israel to "stand up and bless the LORD you God for ever and ever." Beginning at the middle of verse 5 and then ranging to the end of the chapter is a powerful prayer of worship, confession, praise, and rededication. Notice how in beginning the prayer, God was worshiped and praised. "Blessed by thy glorious name, which is exalted above all blessing and praise." In the 'Lord's prayer,' Jesus taught His disciples to follow the same procedure. As this lengthy public prayer unfolds, the Levites essentially rehearse Old Testament history to that point, praising God for how He had delivered His people in the past.

9:6 Thou, *even* thou, *art* LORD alone; thou hast made heaven, the heaven of heavens, with all their host, the earth, and all *things* that *are* therein, the seas, and all that *is* therein, and thou preservest them all; and the host of heaven worshippeth thee. Clear acknowledgment of God as Creator is noted. Creation in the Bible far transcends the first several chapters of Genesis. Of note also is the comment how that "the host of heaven worshippeth thee." That probably is a reference to the angelic host of heaven.

9:7-8 Thou *art* the LORD the God, who didst choose Abram, and broughtest him forth out of Ur of the Chaldees, and gavest him the name of Abraham; 8 And foundest his heart faithful before thee, and madest a covenant with him to give the land of the Canaanites, the Hittites, the Amorites, and the Perizzites, and the Jebusites, and the Girgashites, to give *it, I say*, to his seed, and hast performed thy words; for thou *art* righteous.

In recording that God chose Abraham, notice how it is noted, God "foundest his heart faithful before thee." There is nothing complicated about faithfulness. It remains a spiritual virtue to this day. Almost two and one-half thousand years ago, these Jews recalled how God had even much earlier given the land of Palestine to Abraham and his descendants. They noted how God "performed" His Word which He always does. And then noted that "thou are righteous." The righteousness of God is truly one of His most basic attributes. It is one of the most repeated attributes of God in the Bible.

9:9-11 And didst see the affliction of our fathers in Egypt, and heardest their cry by the Red sea; 10 And shewedst signs and wonders upon Pharaoh, and on all his servants, and on all the people of his land: for thou knewest that they dealt proudly against them. So didst thou get thee a name, as *it is* this day.

11 And thou didst divide the sea before them, so that they went through the midst of the sea on the dry land; and their persecutors thou threwest into the deeps, as a stone into the mighty waters.

They recalled how that God providentially and miraculously delivered their forefathers from Egypt. They also noted that the Egyptians had "dealt proudly." God is never impressed with human pride. To the contrary, He deals against it.

Understanding Nehemiah

9:12-15 Moreover thou leddest them in the day by a cloudy pillar; and in the night by a pillar of fire, to give them light in the way wherein they should go. 13 Thou camest down also upon mount Sinai, and spakest with them from heaven, and gavest them right judgments, and true laws, good statutes and commandments: 14 And madest known unto them thy holy sabbath, and commandedst them precepts, statutes, and laws, by the hand of Moses thy servant: 15 And gavest them bread from heaven for their hunger, and broughtest forth water for them out of the rock for their thirst, and promisedst them that they should go in to possess the land which thou hadst sworn to give them.

They began to systematically recall how that God was merciful and helped them at every step of the great exodus. He provided the pillar of cloud and fire for guidance. He gave them His Law. Notice how they described it. It is characterized as right(eous), true, and good. The issuing of the sabbatical command was in fact an act of goodness by God for His people that they might have a day of rest. He miraculously provided their every need: "bread from heaven . . . water for them out of the rock for their thirst" and promised them a land which He swore would be theirs.

9:16-19 But they and our fathers dealt proudly, and hardened their necks, and hearkened not to thy commandments, 17 And refused to obey, neither were mindful of thy wonders that thou didst among them; but hardened their necks, and in their rebellion appointed a captain to return to their bondage: but thou *art* a God ready to pardon, gracious and merciful, slow to anger, and of great kindness, and forsookest them not. 18 Yea, when they had made them a molten calf, and said, This *is* thy God that brought thee up out of Egypt, and had wrought great provocations; 19 Yet thou in thy manifold mercies

forsookest them not in the wilderness: the pillar of the cloud departed not from them by day, to lead them in the way; neither the pillar of fire by night, to shew them light, and the way.
Though upwards of nine-hundred years had passed, these restoration Jews again confessed the collective sin of their forefathers. Notice the simple basics of the sin of Israel past. (1) They were proud before God. (2) They hardened their necks (i.e., their hearts). (3) They ignored His commandments. (4) They refused to obey Him. (5) They forgot His salvation, and (6) they rebelled. People do not change nor does the nature of sin. The same basic sin of Israel is alive and well in God's people to this day. Nevertheless, they recalled how God remained "ready to pardon, gracious and merciful, slow to anger, and of great kindness, and forsookest them not." Truly His mercy endures for ever. Even in their great provocation against God, He mercifully forsook them not.

9:20-21 Thou gavest also thy good spirit to instruct them, and withheldest not thy manna from their mouth, and gavest them water for their thirst. 21 Yea, forty years didst thou sustain them in the wilderness, *so that* they lacked nothing; their clothes waxed not old, and their feet swelled not. Nevertheless God gave His "good spirit to instruct them." He did not withhold either manna from heaven nor water for their thirst. He provided their every need "so that they lacked nothing." The same God is still on the throne.

9:22-25 Moreover thou gavest them kingdoms and nations, and didst divide them into corners: so they possessed the land of Sihon, and the land of the king of Heshbon, and the land of Og king of Bashan. 23 Their children also multipliedst thou as the stars of heaven, and broughtest them into the land, concerning which thou hadst promised to their fathers, that they should go in to possess

it. **24 So the children went in and possessed the land, and thou subduedst before them the inhabitants of the land, the Canaanites, and gavest them into their hands, with their kings, and the people of the land, that they might do with them as they would. 25 And they took strong cities, and a fat land, and possessed houses full of all goods, wells digged, vineyards, and oliveyards, and fruit trees in abundance: so they did eat, and were filled, and became fat, and delighted themselves in thy great goodness.**

God furthermore gave them victory to possess the land He had promised them. He multiplied their posterity as He had promised them. He gave them a land which was developed and prosperous. The reference to "a fat land" has the idea of a rich land or a prosperous land. The land of Palestine then was not the barren, semi-arid, and more or less treeless land it has been in recent centuries. It truly was a rich land, flowing with milk and honey. As they conquered the land they assumed possession of homes already built, priceless wells already dug, "vineyards, oliveyards, and fruit trees in abundance." In possessing the land, "they did eat, and were filled, and became fat, and delighted themselves in thy great goodness." God not only gave them a land, it was one of the most prosperous places on the face of the earth in that time. They essentially inherited it all.

9:26-27 Nevertheless they were disobedient, and rebelled against thee, and cast thy law behind their backs, and slew thy prophets which testified against them to turn them to thee, and they wrought great provocations. 27 Therefore thou deliveredst them into the hand of their enemies, who vexed them: and in the time of their trouble, when they cried unto thee, thou heardest *them* from heaven; and according to thy manifold mercies thou gavest them saviours, who saved them out of the hand of their enemies.

Some of the most profound comments in the entire Bible are noted. Notwithstanding all that God had done for them, "nevertheless they were disobedient, and rebelled against thee, and cast thy law behind their backs, and slew thy prophets which testified against them to turn to thee." That they in so doing "wrought great provocations" is a profound understatement.

God therefore chastened them. They, thus in their trouble, would cry to God for help, "and according to thy manifold mercies thou gavest them saviors, who saved them out of the hand of their enemies." This referred to the era of the judges.

9:28-31 But after they had rest, they did evil again before thee: therefore leftest thou them in the hand of their enemies, so that they had the dominion over them: yet when they returned, and cried unto thee, thou heardest *them* from heaven; and many times didst thou deliver them according to thy mercies; 29 And testifiedst against them, that thou mightest bring them again unto thy law: yet they dealt proudly, and hearkened not unto thy commandments, but sinned against thy judgments, (which if a man do, he shall live in them;) and withdrew the shoulder, and hardened their neck, and would not hear.

30 Yet many years didst thou forbear them, and testifiedst against them by thy spirit in thy prophets: yet would they not give ear: therefore gavest thou them into the hand of the people of the lands. 31 Nevertheless for thy great mercies' sake thou didst not utterly consume them, nor forsake them; for thou *art* a gracious and merciful God.

The Levites continued to rehearse in their prayer how their forefathers had provoked God and how He continued to be patient with them. He sent prophets to further warn them. They ignored them and God allowed them to be dispersed among gentile nations as most remained in that day. Yet God did not forget His people. Because of His "great mercies' sake thou didst not utterly consume them, nor forsake them; for thou are a gracious and merciful God."

9:32 Now therefore, our God, the great, the mighty, and the terrible God, who keepest covenant and mercy, let not all the trouble seem little before thee, that hath come upon us, on our kings, on our princes, and on our priests, and on our prophets, and on our fathers, and on all thy people, since the time of the kings of Assyria unto this day. The character of the prayer changes. The Levites therefore began to plead for God to once again intervene on their behalf. In further praising Him, they pled with Him to "let not all the trouble seem little before thee, that hath come upon us . . . since the time of the kings of Assyria unto this day."

9:33-34 Howbeit thou *art* just in all that is brought upon us; for thou hast done right, but we have done wickedly: 34 Neither have our kings, our princes, our priests, nor our fathers, kept thy law, nor hearkened unto thy commandments and thy testimonies, wherewith thou didst testify against them. They further acknowledged how God has been "just in all that is brought upon us; for thou hast done right, but we have done wickedly." They again further confessed the sins of their more recent fore-bearers in how they had disobeyed God.

9:35-37 For they have not served thee in their kingdom, and in thy great goodness that thou gavest them, and in the large and fat land which thou gavest before them, neither turned they from their wicked works. 36 Behold, we *are* servants this day, and *for* the land that thou gavest unto our fathers to eat the fruit thereof and the good thereof, behold, we *are* servants in it: 37 And it yieldeth much increase unto

the kings whom thou hast set over us because of our sins: also they have dominion over our bodies, and over our cattle, at their pleasure, and we *are* in great distress.

The Levites acknowledged they were servants in the good land God had long before promised them. The word translated as **servants** (עבד *ebed*) has the sense of 'slavery' or 'bondmen.' They acknowledged that their lack of freedom even in their own land was "because of our sins" and therefore they were "in great distress."

9:38 And because of all this we make a sure *covenant*, and write *it*; and our princes, Levites, *and* priests, seal *unto it*. Because of all of this, they therefore vowed to renew their covenant with God and put it in writing. The reference to their "princes, Levites, and priests, seal *unto* it" has the sense that the leadership therefore signed the renewed written covenant they made with God.

* * * * *

Overview of Nehemiah 10: *Chapter 10 records those who signed the renewed covenant with God. The subdivisions of the chapter are: (1) those who signed the covenant with God (along with a few details thereof) in verses 1-29; and, (2) the restoration of scriptural practices in verses 30-39.*

10:1-27 The list of the leadership of restoration Israel who signed the covenant to once again serve the Lord is recorded. The note of "Nehemiah the Tirshatha" refers to how he was the governor under the Persians.

10:28-29 And the rest of the people, the priests, the Levites, the porters, the singers, the Nethinims, and all they

that had separated themselves from the people of the lands unto the law of God, their wives, their sons, and their daughters, every one having knowledge, and having understanding; 29 **They clave to their brethren, their nobles, and entered into a curse, and into an oath, to walk in God's law, which was given by Moses the servant of God, and to observe and do all the commandments of the LORD our Lord, and his judgments and his statutes**.

The rest of the restoration remnant likewise "clave to their brethren, their nobles . . . to walk in God's law, which was given by Moses the servant of God, and to observe and to do all the commandments of the LORD our Lord." The mention of a curse and oath likely is how that they vowed a curse by an oath upon themselves if they should violate this renewed covenant. The essence of the covenant they entered into is summarized as follows.

10:30 And that we would not give our daughters unto the people of the land, nor take their daughters for our sons. They vowed to not allow their children inter-marry with gentiles (i.e., ungodly people).

10:31 And *if* the people of the land bring ware or any victuals on the sabbath day to sell, *that* we would not buy it of them on the sabbath, or on the holy day: and *that* we would leave the seventh year, and the exaction of every debt. They vowed to not do business on the Sabbath Day. They further would once again observe the sabbatical year in allowing the land to lie fallow on that year. They furthermore would release all debts on that year as prescribed in the law of Moses. See Leviticus 25:4-7 and Deuteronomy 15:2.

10:32-33 Also we made ordinances for us, to charge ourselves yearly with the third part of a shekel for the

service of the house of our God; 33 For the shewbread, and for the continual meat offering, and for the continual burnt offering, of the sabbaths, of the new moons, for the set feasts, and for the holy *things*, and for the sin offerings to make an atonement for Israel, and *for* all the work of the house of our God.

They vowed to once again pay even more than the annual Temple offering as prescribed by the Law. This was the third of a shekel above the prescribed half-shekel required. They realized these funds were needed for the on-going daily maintenance of the Temple and its sacrifices.

10:34 And we cast the lots among the priests, the Levites, and the people, for the wood offering, to bring *it* into the house of our God, after the houses of our fathers, at times appointed year by year, to burn upon the altar of the LORD our God, as *it is* written in the law. They vowed to again share the burden of supplying the Temple altar with wood for the fire there.

10:35 And to bring the firstfruits of our ground, and the firstfruits of all fruit of all trees, year by year, unto the house of the LORD. They vowed to bring again the first fruit offering to the Temple as prescribed in Exodus 23:19.

10:36 Also the firstborn of our sons, and of our cattle, as *it is* written in the law, and the firstlings of our herds and of our flocks, to bring to the house of our God, unto the priests that minister in the house of our God. They vowed to once again present their first-born at the Temple to God. In Exodus 13, God laid claim to all the first-born after He had so dealt with Egypt. However, He allowed His people to redeem their first-born by the sacrifice of a lamb. See Exodus 13:1-15 and Leviticus 27:26-27.

10:37-38 And *that* we should bring the firstfruits of our dough, and our offerings, and the fruit of all manner of trees, of wine and of oil, unto the priests, to the chambers of the house of our God; and the tithes of our ground unto the Levites, that the same Levites might have the tithes in all the cities of our tillage. 38 And the priest the son of Aaron shall be with the Levites, when the Levites take tithes: and the Levites shall bring up the tithe of the tithes unto the house of our God, to the chambers, into the treasure house. They further vowed to honor the Lord with not only the first fruits of their produce, but also the tithe of their crops.

10:39 For the children of Israel and the children of Levi shall bring the offering of the corn, of the new wine, and the oil, unto the chambers, where *are* the vessels of the sanctuary, and the priests that minister, and the porters, and the singers: and we will not forsake the house of our God. They finally vowed to be faithful in bringing all of their offerings to the sanctuary storehouse. In conclusion, they vowed to "not forsake the house of our God." The preceding context seems to lend credence to how they would faithfully support the house of God in a financial way as well as in personal attendance. The gravity of their renewed covenant with God to honor and obey Him is evident. It is particularly so as they specifically noted the various offerings, necessary support of the Temple, and their tithes. When dedication reaches to the pocket-book, a man is truly right with God! All the rest is just religious talk.

* * * * *

Overview of Nehemiah 11: *In Nehemiah 11 is record of the Jews who moved into Jerusalem,*

11:1-2 And the rulers of the people dwelt at Jerusalem: the rest of the people also cast lots, to bring one of ten to dwell in Jerusalem the holy city, and nine parts *to dwell* **in** *other* **cities. 2 And the people blessed all the men, that willingly offered themselves to dwell at Jerusalem.** As the wall was completed, Jerusalem was once again a viable city, able to protect itself. To this point, the returned restoration Jews had lived in outlying areas. Jerusalem had been without walls with only the reconstructed Temple in the city. Therefore it was determined "to bring one of ten to dwell in Jerusalem the holy city, and nine parts to dwell in other cities." Evidently, at least ten percent of the people volunteered to dwell in Jerusalem.

11:3-19 A listing of those who chose to locate in Jerusalem is recorded as a memorial of those who made the sacrificial move into the otherwise desolate city.

11:20-36 A record is also made of "the residue of Israel." Note is made of the Nethinims dwelling in *Ophel*, a ridge once used as a military fortification on the east edge of the city. In verse 23 note is made that the king had made a commandment concerning the singing Levites that they should receive a salary. Some take the position that the king in question was David, while others think it was the king of Persia, wishing proper worship at the Temple. Also a *Pethahiah* is mentioned in verse 24 as an apparent ambassador in Persia to the king on behalf of the Jews. Note is then made of where the residue of Israel lived across the land apart from Jerusalem.

* * * * *

Overview of Nehemiah 12: *Record is made of the priests and Levites who had come back in the initial return with Zer-*

ubbabel. Record is also made of the dedication of the completion of the wall.

12:1-7 Now these *are* the priests and the Levites that went up with Zerubbabel the son of Shealtiel, and Jeshua: Seraiah, Jeremiah, Ezra, 2 Amariah, Malluch, Hattush, 3 Shechaniah, Rehum, Meremoth, 4 Iddo, Ginnetho, Abijah, 5 Miamin, Maadiah, Bilgah, 6 Shemaiah, and Joiarib, Jedaiah, 7 Sallu, Amok, Hilkiah, Jedaiah. These *were* the chief of the priests and of their brethren in the days of Jeshua.

In this initial list, chief priests representing twenty-two of the original twenty-four orders of Levites are enumerated as having returned with Zerubbabel. See also Nehemiah 7:39-42 and Ezra 2:36-39. Jamieson, Fausset, and Brown comments, "Twenty-two only are enumerated here, and no more than twenty in Nehemiah 12:12-21. The discrepancy is due to the extremely probable circumstance that two of the twenty-four courses had become extinct in Babylon; for none belonging to them are reported as having returned (Nehemiah 12:2-5)."

12:8-9 Moreover the Levites: Jeshua, Binnui, Kadmiel, Sherebiah, Judah, *and* Mattaniah, *which was* over the thanksgiving, he and his brethren. 9 Also Bakbukiah and Unni, their brethren, *were* over against them in the watches. Significant Levites who returned with Zerubbabel are also listed here.

12:10-21 Listed is the succession of the high priests in the second Temple. Josephus claims that the list continues to the time when Alexander the Great invaded the land. If that be the case, then another inspired chronicler other than Nehemiah must have compiled the list.

12:22-25 Listed are Levites "in the days of Eliashib" the third high priest of the second Temple. These priests continued to the "reign of Darius the Persian," whom Alexander conquered. The reference to the "book of chronicles" in verse 23 is thought by some to refer to I Chronicles 9:14. Other divisions of Levites of the second Temple are listed included those who were charged "to praise *and* to give thanks, according to the commandment of David the man of God, ward over against ward" (verse 24). These were Levitical singers, the rotating of whose shifts (i.e., orders) was organized by David before the first Temple was built. Levitical porters (i.e., guards) are also noted who served in the days of days of "Nehemiah the governor, and of Ezra the priest, the scribe."

12:27-30 And at the dedication of the wall of Jerusalem they sought the Levites out of all their places, to bring them to Jerusalem, to keep the dedication with gladness, both with thanksgivings, and with singing, *with* cymbals, psalteries, and with harps. 28 And the sons of the singers gathered themselves together, both out of the plain country round about Jerusalem, and from the villages of Netophathi; 29 Also from the house of Gilgal, and out of the fields of Geba and Azmaveth: for the singers had builded them villages round about Jerusalem. 30 And the priests and the Levites purified themselves, and purified the people, and the gates, and the wall.

The preparations for the dedication of the wall are recorded. Levites were brought from throughout Judah to sing and provide musical accompaniment for the festivities at hand. The priests and Levites therefore made themselves ceremonially clean.

12:31-36 Then I brought up the princes of Judah upon the wall, and appointed two great *companies of them that gave* thanks, *whereof one* went on the right hand upon the wall toward the dung gate: 32 And after them went

Hoshaiah, and half of the princes of Judah, 33 And Azariah, Ezra, and Meshullam, 34 Judah, and Benjamin, and Shemaiah, and Jeremiah, 35 And *certain* of the priests' sons with trumpets; *namely*, Zechariah the son of Jonathan, the son of Shemaiah, the son of Mattaniah, the son of Michaiah, the son of Zaccur, the son of Asaph: 36 And his brethren, Shemaiah, and Azarael, Milalai, Gilalai, Maai, Nethaneel, and Judah, Hanani, with the musical instruments of David the man of God, and Ezra the scribe before them.

Nehemiah therefore brought up onto the finished wall the princes of Judah. He split them into two companies, evidently half on the western section of the wall and the other half on the eastern section.

The dung gate was at the southern extremity of the city where the western wall and the eastern wall met in a "V" pointing southward. There a gate was built to take refuse out into the valley of Hinnom which was adjacent thereto. Thus the dedication of the wall began at its southern extremity, which also was its lowest elevation. The wall rose upward on both sides of the city to the north. The wall evidently was wide enough at the top that the respective companies could walk as a group thereon.

12:37-40 And at the fountain gate, which was over against them, they went up by the stairs of the city of David, at the going up of the wall, above the house of David, even unto the water gate eastward. 38 And the other *company of them that gave* thanks went over against *them*, and I after them, and the half of the people upon the wall, from beyond the tower of the furnaces even unto the broad wall; 39 And from above the gate of Ephraim, and above the old gate, and above the fish gate, and the tower of Hananeel, and the tower of Meah, even unto the sheep gate: and they stood still in the prison gate. 40 So stood the two *companies of them that*

gave **thanks in the house of God, and I, and the half of the rulers with me**.

The fountain gate was located on the eastern wall, not far from the dung gate. It was near the pool of Siloam. These assembled officials of Judah therefore began to ascend up the wall in elevation northward toward the water gate which was on the east wall and north of the fountain gate.

The other company of officials began their tour of the western wall, continuing northward and upward to the gate of the furnaces (i.e., baker's ovens) as noted in verse 38. The two companies of princes of Judah thus ascended northward and upward along the rebuilt eastern and western walls of Jerusalem until they met at the northeast corner thereof by the sheep and prison gates. They then assembled into the adjacent Temple and gave thanks to God (verse 40).

12:41-43 And the priests; Eliakim, Maaseiah, Miniamin, Michaiah, Elioenai, Zechariah, *and* Hananiah, with trumpets; 42 And Maaseiah, and Shemaiah, and Eleazar, and Uzzi, and Jehohanan, and Malchijah, and Elam, and Ezer. And the singers sang loud, with Jezrahiah *their* overseer.

43 Also that day they offered great sacrifices, and rejoiced: for God had made them rejoice with great joy: the wives also and the children rejoiced: so that the joy of Jerusalem was heard even afar off.

In the official dedication service at the Temple, the priests and Levites sang aloud with great joy. Many sacrifices were offered and they openly rejoiced "for God had made them rejoice with great joy." The entire congregation of Judah thus cheered and rejoiced to such a degree "that the joy of Jerusalem was heard even afar off." Their singing, rejoicing, and cheering was heard for miles around Jerusalem. No doubt their enemies heard them as well.

12:44-47 And at that time were some appointed over the chambers for the treasures, for the offerings, for the firstfruits, and for the tithes, to gather into them out of the fields of the cities the portions of the law for the priests and Levites: for Judah rejoiced for the priests and for the Levites that waited. 45 And both the singers and the porters kept the ward of their God, and the ward of the purification, according to the commandment of David, *and* **of Solomon his son.**

46 For in the days of David and Asaph of old *there were* **chief of the singers, and songs of praise and thanksgiving unto God. 47 And all Israel in the days of Zerubbabel, and in the days of Nehemiah, gave the portions of the singers and the porters, every day his portion: and they sanctified** *holy things* **unto the Levites; and the Levites sanctified** *them* **unto the children of Aaron.**

Further structuring and ordering of the Temple ministry was implemented. The financial support system of the Temple was also re-instituted under the leadership of Nehemiah. The priests and Levites were restored as best as could be re-established into their original 'orders' and divisions. Levitical choirs were again organized and gatekeepers (i.e., porters) were again organized into their respective shifts even as David and Solomon had organized them centuries earlier. Also the system of greater Israel, bringing material and financial support to the Temple for the support of the Levites and priests on duty, was again re-established. The Levites therefore ceremonially cleansed themselves for service at the Temple, in serving the priests.

* * * * *

Overview of Nehemiah 13: *Chapter 13 presents the spiritual problems which had crept back during the absence of Nehemiah and his unflinching stand for righteousness.*

13:1-3 On that day they read in the book of Moses in the audience of the people; and therein was found written, that the Ammonite and the Moabite should not come into the congregation of God for ever; 2 Because they met not the children of Israel with bread and with water, but hired Balaam against them, that he should curse them: howbeit our God turned the curse into a blessing. 3 Now it came to pass, when they had heard the law, that they separated from Israel all the mixed multitude.

There is some difference of opinion as to when the events of this chapter take place. Some take the position it was a continuation of the events of the dedication as noted in chapter 12. The immediate context would seem to indicate this. Others, take the position chapter 13 is some time later after Nehemiah had gone to Babylon and returned. The latter view seems to make more sense in the greater context.

In any event, there was a day of public convocation of the people at the Temple, perhaps upon Nehemiah's return. Then "they read in the book of Moses in the audience of the people . . . that the Ammonite and Moabite should not come into the congregation of God for ever." (See Deuteronomy 23:3-4.) As will be quickly noted, there had been flagrant violation of this command. Under Nehemiah's leadership, they thus "separated from Israel all the mixed multitude." Pagan, unbelieving gentiles had intermingled with God's people. They therefore were told to leave.

13:4-5 And before this, Eliashib the priest, having the oversight of the chamber of the house of our God, *was* allied unto Tobiah: 5 And he had prepared for him a great

chamber, where aforetime they laid the meat offerings, the frankincense, and the vessels, and the tithes of the corn, the new wine, and the oil, which was commanded *to be given* to the Levites, and the singers, and the porters; and the offerings of the priests.** Furthermore, prior to this, Eliashib the priest had made an apartment for Tobiah in the Temple. Recall from Nehemiah 4:3 that Tobiah was an Ammonite. He had in fact married a daughter of a priest (6:18) and now was actually living in the Temple. The compromising Eliashib had cleared out rooms in the Temple used for grain offerings, storage of tithes, and other necessary purposes to make a substantial apartment for Tobiah. This was a gross violation of the law. Not only was there intermarrying by a priest's daughter of an enemy of God's work, they had been allowed to live in the Temple in direct violation of the Law (Deuteronomy 23:3-4).

13:6 But in all this *time* was not I at Jerusalem: for in the two and thirtieth year of Artaxerxes king of Babylon came I unto the king, and after certain days obtained I leave of the king. Nehemiah notes how all of this took place while he was gone. He evidently had returned to Babylon, perhaps to report to the king on the status of things in Jerusalem. Some take the position, Nehemiah was gone for twelve years (based upon 5:14). However, it seems more likely his leave of absence was much shorter than that. He indeed had been the official governor during that time, but events seem to indicate he was not gone long from Jerusalem, perhaps a year or so. He then was given permission by the king to return. During his absence however, major problems developed.

**13:7-9 And I came to Jerusalem, and understood of the evil that Eliashib did for Tobiah, in preparing him a chamber in the courts of the house of God. 8 And it grieved

816   *Understanding Nehemiah*

me sore: therefore I cast forth all the household stuff of Tobiah out of the chamber. 9 Then I commanded, and they cleansed the chambers: and thither brought I again the vessels of the house of God, with the meat offering and the frankincense.

Upon returning from Babylon, Nehemiah learned that Tobiah had been moved into the Temple, displacing necessary rooms used for God's service. He therefore threw Tobiah out along with his household stuff. He then ordered the chambers ceremonially cleansed and restored them to their prior and intended purposes.

13:10-14 And I perceived that the portions of the Levites had not been given *them*: for the Levites and the singers, that did the work, were fled every one to his field. 11 Then contended I with the rulers, and said, Why is the house of God forsaken? And I gathered them together, and set them in their place. 12 Then brought all Judah the tithe of the corn and the new wine and the oil unto the treasuries. 13 And I made treasurers over the treasuries, Shelemiah the priest, and Zadok the scribe, and of the Levites, Pedaiah: and next to them *was* Hanan the son of Zaccur, the son of Mattaniah: for they were counted faithful, and their office *was* to distribute unto their brethren. 14 Remember me, O my God, concerning this, and wipe not out my good deeds that I have done for the house of my God, and for the offices thereof.

Nehemiah further learned that in his absence, the Levites no longer were being paid their prescribed **portion** (i.e., salary). They therefore were forced to return to farming to make a living. In learning of this, Nehemiah "contended with the rulers and said, Why is the house of God forsaken?" After being chastened by Nehemiah, Judah again tithed to the Temple and its support. He furthermore appointed treasurers who "were

Understanding Nehemiah

counted faithful." They were expressly directed to distribute the tithe to their brethren the other priests and Levites.

In so doing, Nehemiah besought the Lord to remember the good he had done for God's house. It might be inferred that he did not make himself popular by forcing the matter of tithing and setting things aright. However, in so doing, he asked God to not forget the good he had done for His house and its ministry. No doubt, God did not overlook his faithful service.

13:15-22 In those days saw I in Judah *some* treading wine presses on the sabbath, and bringing in sheaves, and lading asses; as also wine, grapes, and figs, and all *manner of* burdens, which they brought into Jerusalem on the sabbath day: and I testified *against them* in the day wherein they sold victuals. 16 There dwelt men of Tyre also therein, which brought fish, and all manner of ware, and sold on the sabbath unto the children of Judah, and in Jerusalem. 17 Then I contended with the nobles of Judah, and said unto them, What evil thing *is* this that ye do, and profane the sabbath day?

18 Did not your fathers thus, and did not our God bring all this evil upon us, and upon this city? yet ye bring more wrath upon Israel by profaning the sabbath. 19 And it came to pass, that when the gates of Jerusalem began to be dark before the sabbath, I commanded that the gates should be shut, and charged that they should not be opened till after the sabbath: and *some* of my servants set I at the gates, *that* there should no burden be brought in on the sabbath day. 20 So the merchants and sellers of all kind of ware lodged without Jerusalem once or twice. 21 Then I testified against them, and said unto them, Why lodge ye about the wall? if ye do *so* again, I will lay hands on you. From that time forth came they no *more* on the sabbath. 22 And I commanded the Levites that they should cleanse themselves, and *that* they

should come *and* keep the gates, to sanctify the sabbath day. Remember me, O my God, *concerning* this also, and spare me according to the greatness of thy mercy.

Other problems had sprouted in Nehemiah's absence. The Sabbath was being ignored. Jews were working as usual on the Sabbath. Moreover, gentile merchants were doing brisk business with Jews thereon. Nehemiah therefore first "contended with the nobles of Judah." He reminded them that God had judged them in the past for similar sins (ignoring the sabbatical year). He then ordered the gates of the city closed at the beginning of the Sabbath on Friday evening and not opened again until the Sabbath was complete. He further policed it with his own servants. Yet, the gentile merchants waited outside the wall on the Sabbath for several weeks.

Nehemiah therefore warned them, "if ye do so again, I will lay hands on you." After being threatened with force, they stopped trying to sell their wares even outside the wall on the Sabbath. He further ordered the Levites to henceforth present themselves ceremonially clean and to police the gates of the city on the Sabbath day. Again, Nehemiah besought God's remembrance for enforcing His Word. He no doubt was not popular in his decisions, but he was right!

13:23-29 In those days also saw I Jews *that* had married wives of Ashdod, of Ammon, *and* of Moab: 24 And their children spake half in the speech of Ashdod, and could not speak in the Jews' language, but according to the language of each people. 25 And I contended with them, and cursed them, and smote certain of them, and plucked off their hair, and made them swear by God, *saying*, Ye shall not give your daughters unto their sons, nor take their daughters unto your sons, or for yourselves.

26 Did not Solomon king of Israel sin by these things? yet among many nations was there no king like him, who was

beloved of his God, and God made him king over all Israel: nevertheless even him did outlandish women cause to sin. 27 Shall we then hearken unto you to do all this great evil, to transgress against our God in marrying strange wives? 28 And *one* of the sons of Joiada, the son of Eliashib the high priest, *was* son in law to Sanballat the Horonite: therefore I chased him from me. 29 Remember them, O my God, because they have defiled the priesthood, and the covenant of the priesthood, and of the Levites.**

Nehemiah also discovered that restoration Jews were intermarrying and assimilating with pagan gentile peoples of the region. The children of such unions could not even speak proper Hebrew. He therefore fiercely verbally chastised them and even physically punished some of them.

He forced the nation to swear before God that they would not inter-marry with the ungodly. He reminded them of the sin of Solomon and his intermarriage with ungodly women. Solomon's breach of the principle of separation led to sin in his life which brought God's judgment upon him. Again, Nehemiah's position likely was not popular. Yet he noted, "Shall we then hearken unto you to do all this great evil, to transgress against our God in marrying strange wives."

Moreover, Nehemiah discovered that one of the sons of the high priest had become the son-in-law of Sanballat the Horonite. (Recall that Sanballat had been an archenemy to the rebuilding of the wall and the restoration of God's work.) When Nehemiah found out, he notes that "therefore I chased him from me." One thing is sure. Nehemiah had no time for those who compromised the Scriptures. His actions no doubt made him unpopular. However, he knew what he did was right before God. Again, he enjoined God to remember that he had stood for right.

13:30-31 Thus cleansed I them from all strangers, and appointed the wards of the priests and the Levites, every

one in his business; 31 And for the wood offering, at times appointed, and for the firstfruits. Remember me, O my God, for good. In concluding the book, Nehemiah notes how that he cleansed the impurity from Israel and re-appointed the prescribed *wards* (courses and shift assignments) of the Levites. He ends the book with a final invocation for God to remember him for good. He had come and done what was not popular but what was right. A similar prayer remains in order to this day. To so serve the Lord that He remembers us for good will be a blessing indeed. To hear Him say, "Well done, thou good and faithful servant," will be worth it all.

THE BOOK OF
ESTHER

Introduction: The Book of Esther, though not pertaining to the restoration projects in Jerusalem, takes places at the same general time back in the former Babylonian and now Media/Persian empire. Some have placed the book at the same time as the rebuilding of the Temple. Others place it closer to the time when Ezra actually arrived in Jerusalem. In any event, the general events are in Persia and contemporaneous to the general restoration in the Book of Ezra. The key to its date rests in deciding who the Ahasuerus is. The problem is, the term Ahasuerus is more of a title than a name (similar to Caesar in the Roman era). Recent historians generally acknowledge him to be Xerxes. Though the book is titled Esther, it is doubtful that she herself wrote it. (There is no claim in the text hat she did.) Others have thought it may well have been written by Mordecai and some even suggest Ezra. It would seem that Mordecai would be the most likely prospect.

The book is unusual in several regards. First, there is no mention of God or any of His various Old Testament names. For that reason, some Jews questioned its authenticity as Scripture. However, the invisible hand of God's providence is so conspicuous, it was obviously ordained of God. It truly illustrates the principle of Romans 8:28. The book also demonstrates God's providential protection and preservation of His people.

The setting of the book is within Media/Persia and the Jews dispersed therein from the Babylonian captivity. Jews with a heart for the things of God had largely returned to begin the restoration of the Temple. The rest had become comfortable living in the Persian Empire. It would seem that Mordecai was such a Jew. Though he may not have had a desire to return to Jerusalem, yet he remained a Jew and identified with his heritage, though perhaps privately. There is insight into the social customs of ancient Persia. It will be helpful in understanding the book of Esther that events are presented from the perspective of Persian social culture. There is evident divorce, concubines, what amounts to a harem, and remarriage. There is no basis to build any case for biblical principles of marriage. Rather, the practice of the king of Persia is recounted historically.

* * * * *

Overview of Esther 1: As the book unfolds, the setting is established how that Ahasuerus essentially divorced his wife for insubordination.

1:1-2 Now it came to pass in the days of Ahasuerus, (this *is* Ahasuerus which reigned, from India even unto Ethiopia, *over* an hundred and seven and twenty provinces:) 2 *That* in those days, when the king Ahasuerus sat on the throne of his kingdom, which *was* in Shushan the palace The setting is the Persian empire under a king called Ahasuerus. This likely is Xerxes. The Shushan noted was the winter palace of the kings of Persia. Shushan also was known as Susa and was located in

Understanding Esther

what today would be southwestern Iran in Elam. The extent of the vast Persian Empire is thus noted stretching from India on the east to Ethiopia on the west. There were now seven more provinces under their jurisdiction than were in the times of Darius the Mede. See Daniel 6:1.

1:3-8 In the third year of his reign, he made a feast unto all his princes and his servants; the power of Persia and Media, the nobles and princes of the provinces, *being* **before him: 4 When he shewed the riches of his glorious kingdom and the honour of his excellent majesty many days,** *even* **an hundred and fourscore days.**

5 And when these days were expired, the king made a feast unto all the people that were present in Shushan the palace, both unto great and small, seven days, in the court of the garden of the king's palace; 6 *Where were* **white, green, and blue,** *hangings***, fastened with cords of fine linen and purple to silver rings and pillars of marble: the beds** *were of* **gold and silver, upon a pavement of red, and blue, and white, and black, marble.**

7 And they gave *them* **drink in vessels of gold, (the vessels being diverse one from another,)and royal wine in abundance, according to the state of the king. 8 And the drinking** *was* **according to the law; none did compel: for so the king had appointed to all the officers of his house, that they should do according to every man's pleasure**.

In the third year of his reign, Xerxes determined to celebrate the greatness of his kingdom. He made feasts for not only the nobility of the kingdom but also even the common people at Shushan. The latter feast lasted seven days, though 180 days were spent in the general preparations thereof. The splendor of the Persian court is thus described: "white, green, and blue, *hangings*, fastened with cords of fine linen and purple to silver rings and pillars of marble: the beds *were of* gold and silver, upon a pavement of red, and blue, and white, and black, marble." Note is made of the drinking which took place at the feast. It appears that getting drunk was a primary feature of this so-called great feast. The splendor of the feast is noted in the golden cups used for the drinking. The thought of the drinking being "according to the law; none did compel" likely has the thought that men could drink as little or as much as they chose. There were no limits. That thought is furthered in the comment "that they should do according to every man's pleasure." Thus, this great feast prepared by Xerxes degenerated into a drunken orgy.

1:9-12 Also Vashti the queen made a feast for the women *in* the royal house which *belonged* to king Ahasuerus. 10 On the seventh day, when the heart of the king was merry with wine, he commanded Mehuman, Biztha, Harbona, Bigtha, and Abagtha, Zethar, and Carcas, the seven chamberlains that served in the presence of Ahasuerus the king, 11 To bring Vashti the queen before the king with the crown royal, to shew the people and the princes her beauty: for she *was* fair to look on. 12 But the queen Vashti refused to come at the king's commandment by *his* chamberlains: therefore was the king very wroth, and his anger burned in him.

Meanwhile, the sitting queen, a woman by the name of Vashti, separately entertained the women. As the seventh day of the royal feast neared its end, and as the king was "merry with wine" (i.e., quite drunk), he sent word for his queen to come. His intent was "to shew the people and the princes her beauty: for she was fair to look on." It might be surmised that the king in his drunkenness had less than appropriate ideas in displaying his wife before his drunken audience. She evidently sensed that and refused to come. Upon learning of this, "the king was wroth, and his anger burned within him."

1:13-18 Then the king said to the wise men, which knew the times, (for so *was* the king's manner toward all that knew law and judgment: 14 And the next unto him *was* Carshena, Shethar, Admatha, Tarshish, Meres, Marsena, *and* Memucan, the seven princes of Persia and Media, which saw the king's face, *and* which sat the first in the kingdom;) 15 What shall we do unto the queen Vashti according to law, because she hath not performed the commandment of the king Ahasuerus by the chamberlains?

16 And Memucan answered before the king and the princes, Vashti the queen hath not done wrong to the king only, but also to all the princes, and to all the people that *are* in all the provinces of the king Ahasuerus. 17 For *this* deed of the queen shall come abroad unto all women, so that they shall despise their husbands in their eyes, when it shall be reported, The king Ahasuerus commanded Vashti the queen to be brought in before him, but she came not. 18 *Likewise* shall the ladies of Persia and Media say this day unto all the king's princes, which have heard of the deed of the queen. Thus *shall there arise* too much contempt and wrath.

The king, therefore publicly embarrassed by his wife, sought counsel on what he should do. He was counseled how that his wife had not only done wrong to him, but to all the men of the kingdom. They reasoned that when the women of the kingdom learned of the queen's insubordination, they too would become insubordinate to their husbands.

1:19-22 If it please the king, let there go a royal commandment from him, and let it be written among the laws of the Persians and the Medes, that it be not altered, That Vashti come no more before king Ahasuerus; and let the king give her royal estate unto another that is better than she. 20 And when the king's decree which he shall make shall be published throughout all his empire, (for it is great,)all the wives shall give to their husbands honour, both to great and small. 21 And the saying pleased the king and the princes; and the king did according to the word of Memucan: 22 For he sent letters into all the king's provinces, into every province according to the writing thereof, and to every people after their language, that every man should bear rule in his own house, and that *it* should be published according to the language of every people.

Therefore, the king's counselors advised him to issue a commandment which in effect would divorce Vashti. They further counseled that this should be published throughout the kingdom as a warning to other women lest they also rebel against their husbands. The conclusion of leadership by a husband in the home was right. Just about everything else in this matter was not.

* * * * *

Overview of Esther 2: *Two major subjects are recorded in chapter 2: (1) Esther chosen as queen in verses 1-20; and, (2) Mordecai discovered a plot against the king in verses 21-23.*

2:1-4 After these things, when the wrath of king Ahasuerus was appeased, he remembered Vashti, and what she had done, and what was decreed against her. 2 Then said the king's servants that ministered unto him, Let there be fair young virgins sought for the king: 3 And let the king appoint officers in all the provinces of his kingdom, that they may gather together all the fair young virgins unto Shushan the palace, to the house of the women, unto the

custody of Hege the king's chamberlain, keeper of the women; and let their things for purification be given *them*: 4 And let the maiden which pleaseth the king be queen instead of Vashti. And the thing pleased the king; and he did so.

After the dust settled and Vashti had been deposed as queen, Xerxes counselors therefore came up with a plan. They suggested that "there be fair young virgins sought for the king." Word was to be sent throughout the kingdom for beautiful young virgins to be brought to Shushan and placed under the supervision of "Hege the king's chamberlain, keeper of the house of the women." This likely was the equivalent of a harem for the king. Cosmetics and soaps for cleansing, hygiene, and beautifying were to be provided for each young woman. Upon finding a young woman which particularly pleased the king, she would become the queen. Xerxes liked the idea and the plan was implemented.

2:5-7 *Now* in Shushan the palace there was a certain Jew, whose name *was* Mordecai, the son of Jair, the son of Shimei, the son of Kish, a Benjamite; 6 Who had been carried away from Jerusalem with the captivity which had been carried away with Jeconiah king of Judah, whom Nebuchadnezzar the king of Babylon had carried away. 7 And he brought up Hadassah, that *is*, Esther, his uncle's daughter: for she had neither father nor mother, and the maid *was* fair and beautiful; whom Mordecai, when her father and mother were dead, took for his own daughter

Meanwhile in Shushan was a Jew by the name of Mordecai. Though some think this is the same Mordecai mentioned in Ezra 2:2 or Nehemiah 7:7, that is not likely. In any event, he was a Benjamite, the descendant of Kish. His family, along with many others of Judah-Benjamin, had been taken in the second wave of the Babylonian captivity. His uncle before his death had a daughter. Jewish tradition says the man died prior to Esther's birth and her mother died in child birth. Therefore, Mordecai 'adopted' the little girl whose Jewish name was Hadassah. Her Persian name was Esther. In Hebrew, *Hadassah* means 'myrtle.' There has been much speculation as to what 'Esther' means in Persian, though it seems to likewise mean 'myrtle,' a fragrant flowering tree. Others suggest the name meant a 'star.'Mordecai therefore brought up the orphaned Esther. Moreover, it is noted that she was "fair and beautiful."

2:8-11 So it came to pass, when the king's commandment and his decree was heard, and when many maidens were gathered together unto Shushan the palace, to the custody of Hegai, that Esther was brought also unto the king's house, to the custody of Hegai, keeper of the women. 9 And the maiden pleased him, and she obtained kindness of him; and he speedily gave her her things for purification, with such things as belonged to her, and seven maidens, *which were* meet to be given her, out of the king's house: and he preferred her and her maids unto the best *place* of the house of the women. 10 Esther had not shewed her people nor her kindred: for Mordecai had charged her that she should not shew *it*. 11 And Mordecai walked every day before the court of the women's house, to know how Esther did, and what should become of her.

As beautiful young women were sought for the king, Esther was brought to the palace. It is noted that she pleased the keeper of the women and thus obtained kindness of him. Each of these women were given the various items "for purification." The idea is of cosmetic beautifying. She was even given seven maid girls to help her prepare herself. The keeper of the 'harem' therefore placed Esther at the best place in the house of the women. However, Esther did not reveal her Jewish heritage upon instructions of Mordecai. It would seem there was present anti-

Understanding Esther

Semitism in the kingdom which became open with Haman. Meanwhile, Mordecai checked daily upon Esther "and what should become of her."

2:12-14 Now when every maid's turn was come to go in to king Ahasuerus, after that she had been twelve months, according to the manner of the women, (for so were the days of their purifications accomplished, *to wit*, six months with oil of myrrh, and six months with sweet odours, and with *other* things for the purifying of the women;) 13 Then thus came *every* maiden unto the king; whatsoever she desired was given her to go with her out of the house of the women unto the king's house. 14 In the evening she went, and on the morrow she returned into the second house of the women, to the custody of Shaashgaz, the king's chamberlain, which kept the concubines: she came in unto the king no more, except the king delighted in her, and that she were called by name.

A description is made how these various young women were detained for one year to ensure their virginity. They each were offered various toiletries to enhance their natural beauty. They then, each by turn, were sent in to the king in the evening to spend the night with him. Afterwards they were sent to a "second house of women." This essentially was for concubines. Unless the king requested her, she no longer was received by him.

2:15-18 Now when the turn of Esther, the daughter of Abihail the uncle of Mordecai, who had taken her for his daughter, was come to go in unto the king, she required nothing but what Hegai the king's chamberlain, the keeper of the women, appointed. And Esther obtained favour in the sight of all them that looked upon her. 16 So Esther was taken unto king Ahasuerus into his house royal in the tenth

month, which *is* the month Tebeth, in the seventh year of his reign. 17 **And the king loved Esther above all the women, and she obtained grace and favour in his sight more than all the virgins; so that he set the royal crown upon her head, and made her queen instead of Vashti. 18 Then the king made a great feast unto all his princes and his servants,** *even* **Esther's feast; and he made a release to the provinces, and gave gifts, according to the state of the king.**

The turn for Esther came. It is noted as being in the seventh year of the king's reign. (Four years therefore had passed since the incident of Vashti.) It is noted that though Esther asked for nothing but the standard beauty aides, she "obtained favor in the sight of all them that looked upon her." The king was smitten with Esther's beauty and loved her above all the women. He therefore made her his queen. This was followed by a great feast with the nobility of the realm. Also a national holiday was declared. The word *rest* in verse 18 has the sense of 'rest' as in a holiday or perhaps a release of taxes for a short time in honor of Esther. In any event, there was a great celebration over Esther.

2:19-20 And when the virgins were gathered together the second time, then Mordecai sat in the king's gate. 20 Esther had not *yet* **shewed her kindred nor her people; as Mordecai had charged her: for Esther did the commandment of Mordecai, like as when she was brought up with him.**

The second gathering of the women likely refers to a second gathering of young virgins for the king. Though Esther was morally pure, it is clear that Xerxes was not. Moreover, his actions quite evidently were socially acceptable for a king.

It is also noted how Mordecai now "sat in the king's gate." This is a reference to a position of royal authority, perhaps as an officer of some type in the royal court. It may have been through

Understanding Esther

the influence of Esther that he was so promoted. Nevertheless, Esther did not reveal her ancestry and heritage as a Jewess. She remained in obedience to her 'step father' Mordecai.

2:21-23 In those days, while Mordecai sat in the king's gate, two of the king's chamberlains, Bigthan and Teresh, of those which kept the door, were wroth, and sought to lay hand on the king Ahasuerus. 22 And the thing was known to Mordecai, who told *it* unto Esther the queen; and Esther certified the king *thereof* in Mordecai's name. 23 And when inquisition was made of the matter, it was found out; therefore they were both hanged on a tree: and it was written in the book of the chronicles before the king.

Meanwhile, two officials of the royal court (Bigthan and Teresh) plotted to overthrow the king. Mordecai became aware of their conspiracy and reported it to Esther. Upon investigation, it was found to be true. The conspirators were therefore hanged. The incident was thus duly recorded in the official chronicles of the king.

* * * * *

Overview of Esther 3: *This next chapter records the conspiracy of Haman against the Jews. The subdivisions of the chapter are: (1) Haman's conspiracy to destroy the Jews in verses 1-6; and, (2) his procural of a decree against them in verses 7-15.*

3:1-3 After these things did king Ahasuerus promote Haman the son of Hammedatha the Agagite, and advanced him, and set his seat above all the princes that *were* with him. 2 And all the king's servants, that *were* in the king's gate, bowed, and reverenced Haman: for the king had so

commanded concerning him. But Mordecai bowed not, nor did *him* reverence. 3 Then the king's servants, which *were* in the king's gate, said unto Mordecai, Why transgressest thou the king's commandment?

In the course of events, at least five years later (see verse 7), the king promoted a court official by the name of Haman, to what amounted, to be prime minister of the kingdom. He was higher in position than any other official except the king. All other officers and servants therefore bowed and reverenced Haman. It was customary in Persia to so honor a high ranking official as a god. The king therefore ordered all to bow to Haman. However, Mordecai refused to bow or so reverence Haman. It may be surmised that Mordecai's refusal was based upon his conviction, that reverence was due only to God. Other of the king's servants therefore asked Mordecai why he disobeyed this commandment of the king.

3:4-5 Now it came to pass, when they spake daily unto him, and he hearkened not unto them, that they told Haman, to see whether Mordecai's matters would stand: for he had told them that he *was* a Jew. 5 And when Haman saw that Mordecai bowed not, nor did him reverence, then was Haman full of wrath. Other court officials spoke daily to Mordecai about the matter, but he refused to bow. Therefore, they told Haman of the matter to see if Mordecai would continue to refuse. It is noted that he had revealed by now he was Jew. When Haman observed that Mordecai refused to bow or reverence him, he was "full of wrath."

3:6-7 And he thought scorn to lay hands on Mordecai alone; for they had shewed him the people of Mordecai: wherefore Haman sought to destroy all the Jews that *were* throughout the whole kingdom of Ahasuerus, *even* the people of Mordecai. 7 In the first month, that *is*, the month

Nisan, in the twelfth year of king Ahasuerus, they cast Pur, that *is*, the lot, before Haman from day to day, and from month to month, *to* the twelfth *month*, that *is*, the month Adar.

Haman's hatred and revenge was such that he sought to do more than merely vent his wrath upon Mordecai. Upon learning he was a Jew, Haman sought to "destroy all the Jews that were throughout the whole kingdom of Ahasuerus, even the people of Mordecai." Therefore, Haman and his associates cast lots to determine which would be the 'luckiest' month to deal with the Jews. (It would be akin to rolling dice.) The time was noted as the twelfth year of the king. In casting their lots, they decided the twelfth month would be the month to execute their plan. (It was still the first month of the year at the time.)

3:8-11 And Haman said unto king Ahasuerus, There is a certain people scattered abroad and dispersed among the people in all the provinces of thy kingdom; and their laws *are* diverse from all people; neither keep they the king's laws: therefore it *is* not for the king's profit to suffer them. 9 If it please the king, let it be written that they may be destroyed: and I will pay ten thousand talents of silver to the hands of those that have the charge of the business, to bring *it* into the king's treasuries. 10 And the king took his ring from his hand, and gave it unto Haman the son of Hammedatha the Agagite, the Jews' enemy. 11 And the king said unto Haman, The silver *is* given to thee, the people also, to do with them as it seemeth good to thee.

Haman therefore approached the king and accused the Jewish race. Though they are not noted specifically as such, there is little doubt, the king knew who he was talking about. As is so typical of Satan, the accuser of the brethren, Haman distorted the truth and portrayed the Jews as an evil and a blight upon the kingdom. He therefore proposed to the king that the Jewish race be destroyed. He furthermore promised to pay the king for his trouble in destroying the Jews (i.e., his loss of tax revenue).

The king therefore agreed and gave his ring to Haman. This probably was to allow him to place the king's signet (signature) upon the wax seals of the documents which would be sent throughout the realm. Moreover, the king either refused Haman's offer of money for his loss, or it was returned to him.

3:12-13 Then were the king's scribes called on the thirteenth day of the first month, and there was written according to all that Haman had commanded unto the king's lieutenants, and to the governors that *were* over every province, and to the rulers of every people of every province according to the writing thereof, and *to* every people after their language; in the name of king Ahasuerus was it written, and sealed with the king's ring. 13 And the letters were sent by posts into all the king's provinces, to destroy, to kill, and to cause to perish, all Jews, both young and old, little children and women, in one day, *even* upon the thirteenth *day* of the twelfth month, which is the month Adar, and *to take* the spoil of them for a prey.

Therefore on the thirteenth day of the first month of the year (comparable to modern April) orders were sent to the every officer and governor of every province of the Persian Empire in the king's name. It was officially declared that on the thirteenth day of the twelfth month of the year (modern March), orders were given "to destroy, to kill, and to cause to perish, all Jews, both young and old, little children and women, in one day . . . and to take the spoil of them for a prey." The Jewish nation was to be exterminated and their possessions taken on one day, the thirteenth day of the last month of that year.

3:14-15 The copy of the writing for a commandment to be given in every province was published unto all people,

Understanding Esther 835

that they should be ready against that day. 15 The posts went out, being hastened by the king's commandment, and the decree was given in Shushan the palace. And the king and Haman sat down to drink; but the city Shushan was perplexed.

These documents were published and sent throughout the kingdom, instructing the empire to be prepared to execute the orders on the given day. Thus, "the king and Haman sat down to drink; but the city of Shushan was perplexed." Perhaps a banquet was prepared by Haman in which to celebrate with the king. However, there was confusion in the city of Shushan. The people of the city knew there were many Jews in high places. They perhaps were astounded at the barbarity of the decree. Moreover, it may well be assumed though the king did not know Esther's heritage, it was known in the city who had watched her grow up.

* * * * *

Overview of Esther 4*: The decree to destroy the Jews is issued. Mordecai goes into mourning and seeks Esther to intervene on behalf of her people. Though refusing at first, she therefore determines to risk her life in approaching the king on their behalf. The subdivisions of the chapter are: (1) the Jews lament their crisis in verses 1-4; and, (2) Esther undertakes to intercede for her people in verses 5-17.*

4:1-4 When Mordecai perceived all that was done, Mordecai rent his clothes, and put on sackcloth with ashes, and went out into the midst of the city, and cried with a loud and a bitter cry; 2 And came even before the king's gate: for none *might* enter into the king's gate clothed with sackcloth. 3 And in every province, whithersoever the king's com-

mandment and his decree came, *there was* great mourning among the Jews, and fasting, and weeping, and wailing; and many lay in sackcloth and ashes. 4 So Esther's maids and her chamberlains came and told *it* her. Then was the queen exceedingly grieved; and she sent raiment to clothe Mordecai, and to take away his sackcloth from him: but he received *it* not.

Mordecai, upon learning of the decree contrived by Haman, went into mourning. As was customary of Jews in great sorrow, he tore his clothing, put on sackcloth of ashes, and cried with a loud and bitter voice. Rending of clothing along with sackcloth and ashes was an oriental custom of showing great distress. It was a visual aide in putting on crude work clothes along with ashes as a symbol of a troubled heart.

Throughout the Persian Empire Jews did similarly as the decree spread. It was reported to Esther how Mordecai was so behaving. It seems from the succeeding context, she as yet was unaware of the crisis. She therefore sent appropriate clothes for Mordecai to return unto the court. He refused.

4:5-9 Then called Esther for Hatach, *one* of the king's chamberlains, whom he had appointed to attend upon her, and gave him a commandment to Mordecai, to know what it *was*, and why it *was*. 6 So Hatach went forth to Mordecai unto the street of the city, which *was* before the king's gate. 7 And Mordecai told him of all that had happened unto him, and of the sum of the money that Haman had promised to pay to the king's treasuries for the Jews, to destroy them.

8 Also he gave him the copy of the writing of the decree that was given at Shushan to destroy them, to shew *it* unto Esther, and to declare *it* unto her, and to charge her that she should go in unto the king, to make supplication unto him, and to make request before him for her people. 9 And Hatach came and told Esther the words of Mordecai.

Esther therefore sent a chamberlain named Hatach which was assigned to her unto Mordecai to find out what was going on. The word translated as **chamberlain** (סריס *cariyc*) is more commonly rendered as 'eunuch' and literally means one who has been castrated. Hatach found Mordecai, who told him all which had transpired. Note is made again how that Haman had promised to reimburse the royal treasury for whatever lack the empire incurred from the loss of taxes collected from Jews. Mordecai further sent a copy of the decree with Hatach to deliver to Esther. He sent also word urging her "that she should go in unto the king, to make supplication unto him, and to make request before him for her people." Hatach therefore returned to Esther and duly repeated what Mordecai had told him.

4:10-12 Again Esther spake unto Hatach, and gave him commandment unto Mordecai; 11 All the king's servants, and the people of the king's provinces, do know, that whosoever, whether man or woman, shall come unto the king into the inner court, who is not called, *there is* one law of his to put *him* to death, except such to whom the king shall hold out the golden sceptre, that he may live: but I have not been called to come in unto the king these thirty days. 12 And they told to Mordecai Esther's words.

Esther returned word through Hatach. She noted how even she could not come into the king's inner court without being invited. Unless bidden by the king's scepter, the penalty for so doing was death. Furthermore, she indicated that the king had not invited her into his presence for thirty days, implying that she might not be as close to the king as Mordecai might think.

4:13-14 Then Mordecai commanded to answer Esther, Think not with thyself that thou shalt escape in the king's house, more than all the Jews. 14 For if thou altogether holdest thy peace at this time, *then* shall there enlargement

and deliverance arise to the Jews from another place; but thou and thy father's house shall be destroyed: and who knoweth whether thou art come to the kingdom for *such* a time as this?

Mordecai sent word back again. He warned that even she would not escape the planned holocaust against the Jews. He intimated how that even if she did not intervene, deliverance for the Jews might otherwise arise by divine providence, though she and her relatives would be destroyed. Mordecai then added the fateful words, "and who knoweth whether thou art come to the kingdom for such a times this?" Without mentioning God by name, Mordecai clearly implied that by God's providence, she had become queen for this very crisis. Indeed, God had providentially placed Esther into the position she was in to provide a miraculous deliverance.

4:15-17 Then Esther bade *them* return Mordecai *this* answer, 16 Go, gather together all the Jews that are present in Shushan, and fast ye for me, and neither eat nor drink three days, night or day: I also and my maidens will fast likewise; and so will I go in unto the king, which *is* not according to the law: and if I perish, I perish. 17 So Mordecai went his way, and did according to all that Esther had commanded him.

Evidently, upon thinking it over, Esther changed her mind. She presented a simple plan for Mordecai. It was to gather all the Jews in Shushan to fast for three days. Fasting in the Scripture is usually not specifically defined. However, the crisis was so grave, she ordered them to not eat or drink for three days. The word translated as **drink** (שתה *shathah*) is related to drinking of wine and may not imply the intake of water. Often Jewish fasts were a denial of prepared food and beverages, excluding water and the simplest of bread. Though not mentioned, the implication is that they prayed to God during those three days seeking His deliverance. Esther evidently had been allowed to bring other Jewish ladies to be her maidens. They likewise would be impressed into the fasting (and praying). At the conclusion of their fasting, she would go to the king even though it was illegal—"And if I perish, I perish." Esther seemingly came to understand why she was where she was and prepared for the worst if that in fact came to pass. Mordecai therefore did as she instructed.

* * * * *

Overview of Esther 5: *This next chapter records the courage of Esther. Esther's appeals to the king in verses 1-8; and, (2) Haman prepares to hang Mordecai in verses 9-14.*

5:1-2 Now it came to pass on the third day, that Esther put on *her* royal *apparel*, and stood in the inner court of the king's house, over against the king's house: and the king sat upon his royal throne in the royal house, over against the gate of the house. 2 And it was so, when the king saw Esther the queen standing in the court, *that* she obtained favour in his sight: and the king held out to Esther the golden sceptre that *was* in his hand. So Esther drew near, and touched the top of the sceptre. On the third day, Esther changed from her garments of fasting into her royal apparel and entered the king's inner court. It might be inferred how she stood in a meek and demur pose which touched the heart of the king. He graciously extended to her his golden scepter. She therefore humbly approached with gratitude and respect touching the top of the scepter.

5:3-8 Then the king said, Cause Haman to make haste, that he may do as Esther hath said. So the king and Haman

came to the banquet that Esther had prepared. 6 And the king said unto Esther at the banquet of wine, What *is* thy petition? and it shall be granted thee: and what *is* thy request? even to the half of the kingdom it shall be performed. 7 Then answered Esther, and said, My petition and my request *is*; 8 If I have found favour in the sight of the king, and if it please the king to grant my petition, and to perform my request, let the king and Haman come to the banquet that I shall prepare for them, and I will do to morrow as the king hath said.

It is evident that Esther had thought through what she planned to do. She invited the king and Haman to a banquet she had prepared for that day. The king therefore sent word for Haman to come and they both came to Esther's banquet. It also is called a banquet of wine. This referred to the latter part of a Persian banquet when wine was served. The king drank and evidently became 'loosened up' thereby. He intuitively perceived how that Esther wanted something. Therefore, he asked, "What is thy request? Even to the half of the kingdom it shall be performed." Curiously, Esther declined to broach the main reason she wanted to see the king. Could it be she got cold feet? Or, did she understand the king well enough to let him puzzle over her wish that night? The Scripture does not indicate. The latter might be more likely.

She therefore invited the king and Haman to attend another banquet the next day. At that meal, she would inform the king of her request.

5:9-14 Then went Haman forth that day joyful and with a glad heart: but when Haman saw Mordecai in the king's gate, that he stood not up, nor moved for him, he was full of indignation against Mordecai. 10 Nevertheless Haman refrained himself: and when he came home, he sent and called for his friends, and Zeresh his wife. 11 And Haman

told them of the glory of his riches, and the multitude of his children, and all *the things* wherein the king had promoted him, and how he had advanced him above the princes and servants of the king.

12 Haman said moreover, Yea, Esther the queen did let no man come in with the king unto the banquet that she had prepared but myself; and to morrow am I invited unto her also with the king. 13 Yet all this availeth me nothing, so long as I see Mordecai the Jew sitting at the king's gate. 14 Then said Zeresh his wife and all his friends unto him, Let a gallows be made of fifty cubits high, and to morrow speak thou unto the king that Mordecai may be hanged thereon: then go thou in merrily with the king unto the banquet. And the thing pleased Haman; and he caused the gallows to be made.

Haman therefore headed for home. On the way, he noted once again that Mordecai still showed him no deference. Though, he was excited about being invited back to dinner with the king and queen, he was enraged by Mordecai's snub. "Nevertheless Haman refrained his anger" against Mordecai, went home, called his friends and wife together, and told them what had happened that day. He pompously rehearsed all his accomplishments and how the king had promoted him. Moreover, he could not resist bragging about how he was the only one invited to a dinner with the king and queen. Furthermore, he was invited again the next day.

Still, he confided that he was snubbed by Mordecai the Jew. Therefore, his wife and friends urged him to build a tall gallows to hang Mordecai upon. A fifty-cubit-tall gallows was intended so all could see who hung thereon. It would approximate seventy-five feet in height. Then he could go to the banquet the next day *merrily*. Haman therefore ordered such a gallows to be built over night.

* * * * *

Overview of Esther 6: *The plot of Haman is about to backfire. The subdivisions of the chapter are: (1) God providentially enabled Mordecai to find the king's favour in verses 1-3; (2) Haman's is compelled to honor Mordecai in verses 4-11; and, (3) Haman is warned of impending danger in verses 12-14.*

6:1-3 On that night could not the king sleep, and he commanded to bring the book of records of the chronicles; and they were read before the king. 2 And it was found written, that Mordecai had told of Bigthana and Teresh, two of the king's chamberlains, the keepers of the door, who sought to lay hand on the king Ahasuerus. 3 And the king said, What honour and dignity hath been done to Mordecai for this? Then said the king's servants that ministered unto him, There is nothing done for him.

The providential working of God is once again clearly evident. That night, the king could not sleep. (That was not coincidence, but God's providence.) Instead of seeking other amusements (he had numerous concubines and court entertainers), he rather ordered "the book of records of the chronicles be brought and read." (Again, God's working is evident.) As the records were read, he was reminded that Mordecai had saved his life in reporting the sedition of Bigthana and Teresh. The king therefore enquired, "What honour and dignity hath been done to Mordecai for this?" He was told that nothing had been done. (Further, providential leading is obvious in how the very section pertaining to Mordecai was read.)

6:4-5 And the king said, Who *is* in the court? Now Haman was come into the outward court of the king's house, to speak unto the king to hang Mordecai on the gallows that he had prepared for him. 5 And the king's servants said unto him, Behold, Haman standeth in the

court. **And the king said, Let him come in.** It is not clear if the night had passed and morning had come or if the time was still the middle of the night. The context seems to indicate morning had come. In any event, Haman had arrived in the outer court of the king to seek permission to hang Mordecai on the gallows he had prepared overnight. The king apparently perceived someone was waiting to see him, and enquired who was there. He was told Haman and therefore invited him in.

6:6-9 So Haman came in. And the king said unto him, What shall be done unto the man whom the king delighteth to honour? Now Haman thought in his heart, To whom would the king delight to do honour more than to myself? 7 And Haman answered the king, For the man whom the king delighteth to honour, 8 Let the royal apparel be brought which the king *useth* to wear, and the horse that the king rideth upon, and the crown royal which is set upon his head: 9 And let this apparel and horse be delivered to the hand of one of the king's most noble princes, that they may array the man *withal* whom the king delighteth to honour, and bring him on horseback through the street of the city, and proclaim before him, Thus shall it be done to the man whom the king delighteth to honour.

Before Haman could say a word, the king asked him what should be done to one the king intended to honor. Haman vainly thought the king was referring to him. Therefore, he suggested the highest honor of which he could think. Under Persian custom and law, only the king could wear a royal purple robe. Furthermore, a highly prized breed of horses was reserved for the exclusive use of the king. Only the king could ride upon the royal horse. To ride upon that horse with the royal robe was tantamount to being king. It at least conveyed the appearances thereof. Haman therefore suggested that such an one be honored with the king's robe and horse. Additionally, this one was to be led through the streets of the city with a herald proclaiming "thus shall it be done to the man whom the king delighteth to honour."

6:10-11 Then the king said to Haman, Make haste, *and* take the apparel and the horse, as thou hast said, and do even so to Mordecai the Jew, that sitteth at the king's gate: let nothing fail of all that thou hast spoken. 11 Then took Haman the apparel and the horse, and arrayed Mordecai, and brought him on horseback through the street of the city, and proclaimed before him, Thus shall it be done unto the man whom the king delighteth to honour.

To his shock and dismay, the king ordered Haman to do exactly that to "Mordecai the Jew: let nothing fail of all that thou hast spoken." The irony was profound. The one Haman wished to execute that very day had in fact been exalted by the king. His plot was thwarted. He no doubt was thoroughly chagrined and humiliated.

6:12-14 And Mordecai came again to the king's gate. But Haman hasted to his house mourning, and having his head covered. 13 And Haman told Zeresh his wife and all his friends every *thing* that had befallen him. Then said his wise men and Zeresh his wife unto him, If Mordecai *be* of the seed of the Jews, before whom thou hast begun to fall, thou shalt not prevail against him, but shalt surely fall before him.

14 And while they *were* yet talking with him, came the king's chamberlains, and hasted to bring Haman unto the banquet that Esther had prepared.

After the procession was over, Mordecai returned to his regular position at the king's gate. Haman however went home utterly humiliated over what had happened. Having his head covered was a symbol of being ashamed to be seen.

Understanding Esther 845

He ignominiously rehearsed what had happened to him that day. His friends and wife however, saw an ominous omen in it all. They reasoned that if Mordecai, as a Jew, was the target of Haman's wrath, his scheme to destroy the Jews would fail. Moreover, they predicted that he himself would fall before Mordecai (which indeed happened that very day).

Apart from the obvious providential intervention by God to protect His people, there is another moral to the story. As noted in Proverbs 26:27, "Whoso diggeth a pit shall fall therein: and he that rolleth a stone, it will return upon him." Haman would be caught in the trap he had set for Mordecai. His pride brought him low and eventually destroyed him.

Meanwhile, "came the king's chamberlains, and hasted to bring Haman unto the Banquet that Esther had prepared." It might be implied that Haman in his dejection had missed his appointment with the royal couple and messengers were sent to bring him. Things would swiftly go from bad to worse.

*****

Overview of Esther 7*: With Haman's cup of iniquity full, God turned the tables upon him. Esther informed the king how Haman's plot involved her and her people. The king in rage ordered Haman hanged. The subdivisions of the chapter are: (1) Esther accuses Haman in verses 1-6; and, (2) Haman is hanged on his own gallows in verses 7-10.*

7:1-4 So the king and Haman came to banquet with Esther the queen. 2 And the king said again unto Esther on the second day at the banquet of wine, What *is* **thy petition, queen Esther? and it shall be granted thee: and what** *is* **thy request? and it shall be performed,** *even* **to the half of the kingdom. 3 Then Esther the queen answered and said, If I**

have found favour in thy sight, O king, and if it please the king, let my life be given me at my petition, and my people at my request: 4 For we are sold, I and my people, to be destroyed, to be slain, and to perish. But if we had been sold for bondmen and bondwomen, I had held my tongue, although the enemy could not countervail the king's damage.

The king, along with Haman, therefore came to Esther's banquet. The king again asked Esther of her request. Esther therefore revealed to him that she and her people were in line to be destroyed. She noted how if it were just a matter of servitude, she could bear with it. But it was more than that. Moreover, the promise to pay ten thousand pieces of silver to the king to make up his loss of tax revenue from the destruction of the Jews would not begin to equal the loss the king's treasury would suffer.

7:5-7 Then the king Ahasuerus answered and said unto Esther the queen, Who is he, and where is he, that durst presume in his heart to do so? 6 And Esther said, The adversary and enemy *is* this wicked Haman. Then Haman was afraid before the king and the queen. 7 And the king arising from the banquet of wine in his wrath *went* into the palace garden: and Haman stood up to make request for his life to Esther the queen; for he saw that there was evil determined against him by the king.

The king therefore indignantly enquired, "Who is he, and where is he, that durst presume in his heart to do so?" Esther revealed it was Haman. The trap Haman had laid snared him. He knew the jig was up. Meanwhile, the king stormed out into the garden to collect his thoughts. No doubt, it all came together in his mind. Now he understood who Haman had in mind in his scheme. Haman stood from the table to plead his life before the queen. He perhaps lost his balance and fell on the couch upon which Esther reclined at the table.

7:8-10 Then the king returned out of the palace garden into the place of the banquet of wine; and Haman was fallen upon the bed whereon Esther *was*. Then said the king, Will he force the queen also before me in the house? As the word went out of the king's mouth, they covered Haman's face. 9 And Harbonah, one of the chamberlains, said before the king, Behold also, the gallows fifty cubits high, which Haman had made for Mordecai, who had spoken good for the king, standeth in the house of Haman. Then the king said, Hang him thereon. 10 So they hanged Haman on the gallows that he had prepared for Mordecai. Then was the king's wrath pacified.

At that moment, the king returned and saw Haman sprawled upon Esther. Though he probably did not really think Haman would actually assault his queen then and there, nevertheless, seeing him such only magnified his anger. It gave the king further excuse to execute him. It probably brought to mind that a man capable of devising such a cruel plot was capable of raping his wife.

The king's servants understood what was about to happen. They therefore covered Haman's face which was the custom of one condemned to die. The king was then reminded that Haman had made a gallows for Mordecai the king's benefactor. He therefore ordered Haman to be hanged thereon. "Then was the king's wrath pacified."

* * * * *

Overview of Esther 8*: The plot of Haman had backfired in his face. The king allowed Esther along with Mordecai to write a decree reversing Haman's plot, allowing the Jews to destroy their enemies. The subdivisions of this chapter are: (1) Mordecai is promoted in verses 1-2; Esther intercedes for the Jews in* verses 3-14; and, (3) Mordecai is honored and the Jews rejoice in verses 15-17.

8:1-2 On that day did the king Ahasuerus give the house of Haman the Jews' enemy unto Esther the queen. And Mordecai came before the king; for Esther had told what he *was* unto her. 2 And the king took off his ring, which he had taken from Haman, and gave it unto Mordecai. And Esther set Mordecai over the house of Haman. The king therefore also ordered Haman's house given to Esther. Also that day she revealed to the king her relationship to Mordecai—her uncle and *defacto* step father. The king therefore gave his royal ring to Mordecai and gave him the oversight of Haman's house.

8:3-6 And Esther spake yet again before the king, and fell down at his feet, and besought him with tears to put away the mischief of Haman the Agagite, and his device that he had devised against the Jews. 4 Then the king held out the golden sceptre toward Esther. So Esther arose, and stood before the king, 5 And said, If it please the king, and if I have found favour in his sight, and the thing *seem* right before the king, and I *be* pleasing in his eyes, let it be written to reverse the letters devised by Haman the son of Hammedatha the Agagite, which he wrote to destroy the Jews which *are* in all the king's provinces: 6 For how can I endure to see the evil that shall come unto my people? or how can I endure to see the destruction of my kindred?

Still, Queen Esther humbly prostrated herself before her husband, tearfully requesting him to "put away the mischief of Haman" and what he had plotted against her people the Jews. He bade her audience and she requested the king to issue a written order reversing Haman's plot. She further bared her heart with the comment, "for how can I endure to see the evil that shall come unto my people? Or how can I endure to see the destruction of my kindred?" Her humble spirit coupled with her heart felt distress, no doubt touched the heart of her husband, the king.

8:7-10 Then the king Ahasuerus said unto Esther the queen and to Mordecai the Jew, Behold, I have given Esther the house of Haman, and him they have hanged upon the gallows, because he laid his hand upon the Jews. 8 Write ye also for the Jews, as it liketh you, in the king's name, and seal *it* **with the king's ring: for the writing which is written in the king's name, and sealed with the king's ring, may no man reverse.**

9 Then were the king's scribes called at that time in the third month, that *is*, **the month Sivan, on the three and twentieth** *day* **thereof; and it was written according to all that Mordecai commanded unto the Jews, and to the lieutenants, and the deputies and rulers of the provinces which** *are* **from India unto Ethiopia, an hundred twenty and seven provinces, unto every province according to the writing thereof, and unto every people after their language, and to the Jews according to their writing, and according to their language. 10 And he wrote in the king Ahasuerus' name, and sealed** *it* **with the king's ring, and sent letters by posts on horseback,** *and* **riders on mules, camels,** *and* **young dromedaries.**

The king therefore gave Esther and Mordecai permission to issue a decree in the king's name as they wished. It was issued in the third month of the year (June) through Mordecai to the various governmental officials throughout the one-hundred-twenty-seven provinces of the Persian empire.

8:11-14 Wherein the king granted the Jews which *were* **in every city to gather themselves together, and to stand for their life, to destroy, to slay, and to cause to perish, all the**

power of the people and province that would assault them, *both* little ones and women, and *to take* the spoil of them for a prey, 12 Upon one day in all the provinces of king Ahasuerus, *namely*, upon the thirteenth *day* of the twelfth month, which *is* the month Adar. 13 The copy of the writing for a commandment to be given in every province *was* published unto all people, and that the Jews should be ready against that day to avenge themselves on their enemies. 14 *So* the posts that rode upon mules *and* camels went out, being hastened and pressed on by the king's commandment. And the decree was given at Shushan the palace.

The decree gave the Jews of the empire the right to stand and defend themselves against their enemies. Moreover, they were granted express permission to destroy those who sought to do them harm. This was to be enacted upon the thirteenth day of the twelfth month, the same day Haman had originally planned to execute his plot against the Jews. The decree was published from the Shushan the palace to the ends of the empire.

8:15-17 And Mordecai went out from the presence of the king in royal apparel of blue and white, and with a great crown of gold, and with a garment of fine linen and purple: and the city of Shushan rejoiced and was glad. 16 The Jews had light, and gladness, and joy, and honour. 17 And in every province, and in every city, whithersoever the king's commandment and his decree came, the Jews had joy and gladness, a feast and a good day. And many of the people of the land became Jews; for the fear of the Jews fell upon them.

To show his pleasure toward Mordecai, the king granted him to wear royal apparel of blue and white, with a magnificent crown and additional trappings of royal purple. Few if any others in the empire were ever allowed to wear apparel which otherwise was reserved for the king.

Understanding Esther

As the decree arrived throughout the empire in each province, "the Jews had light, and gladness, and joy, and honour." The sense of the word translated as **light** (אורה *owrah*) can have the idea of happiness or prosperity in contrast to the trouble of darkness. In every province the Jews celebrated and declared a feast. Moreover, gentiles became Jews as fear of their special prerogative fell upon them. Significant is the comment how that " in every province" the Jews had light and gladness etc. Implicit is that even this relatively early date of the diaspora, Jews had scattered to the entire 127 provinces of the Persian Empire stretching from India to Ethiopia. Moreover, as a result of the clear working of Jehovah God on behalf of His people, many gentiles across the Persian Empire became Jewish proselytes. Powerful indeed was the testimony of God's people and the grace of their God.

* * * * *

Overview of Esther 9: *The retribution against the enemies of the Jews was therefore executed. In memorial thereof, a national Jewish holiday was instituted called Purim. The subdivisions of the chapter are: (1) the prospering of the Jews in the Persian Empire in verses 1-19; and, (2) the Feast of Purim instituted as a memorial in verses 20-32.*

9:1-3 Now in the twelfth month, that *is*, the month Adar, on the thirteenth day of the same, when the king's commandment and his decree drew near to be put in execution, in the day that the enemies of the Jews hoped to have power over them, (though it was turned to the contrary, that the Jews had rule over them that hated them;) 2 The Jews gathered themselves together in their cities throughout all the provinces of the king Ahasuerus, to

lay hand on such as sought their hurt: and no man could withstand them; for the fear of them fell upon all people. 3 And all the rulers of the provinces, and the lieutenants, and the deputies, and officers of the king, helped the Jews; because the fear of Mordecai fell upon them.

The fateful thirteenth day of the twelfth month (March) came. Jews throughout the Persian empire gathered themselves against any which would attack them, yet "no man could withstand them; for the fear of them fell upon all people." Furthermore, they had the backing and sympathy of the Persian government which by now were aware of Queen Esther's Jewish background.

9:4-12 For Mordecai *was* great in the king's house, and his fame went out throughout all the provinces: for this man Mordecai waxed greater and greater. 5 Thus the Jews smote all their enemies with the stroke of the sword, and slaughter, and destruction, and did what they would unto those that hated them. 6 And in Shushan the palace the Jews slew and destroyed five hundred men. 7 And Parshandatha, and Dalphon, and Aspatha, 8 And Poratha, and Adalia, and Aridatha, 9 And Parmashta, and Arisai, and Aridai, and Vajezatha, 10 The ten sons of Haman the son of Hammedatha, the enemy of the Jews, slew they; but on the spoil laid they not their hand. 11 On that day the number of those that were slain in Shushan the palace was brought before the king. 12 And the king said unto Esther the queen, The Jews have slain and destroyed five hundred men in Shushan the palace, and the ten sons of Haman; what have they done in the rest of the king's provinces? now what *is* thy petition? and it shall be granted thee: or what *is* thy request further? and it shall be done.

Rather than be the vanquished, the Jews rose up against those of anti-Semitic persuasion and became the victors. In the city of Shushan alone, five hundred were slain including the ten sons of Haman. It is noteworthy that the Jews decided not to profit from the spoil of the estates or property of their enemies. They could have done so, but they elected not to. Perhaps there was concern they be viewed as destroying enemies for gain at their expense.

The king thus noted their victory at Shushan. He was curious as to what degree their victories had gone across the rest of the empire. Nevertheless, he told Esther she could make any further petition in the matter and he would grant it.

9:13-19 Then said Esther, If it please the king, let it be granted to the Jews which *are* in Shushan to do to morrow also according unto this day's decree, and let Haman's ten sons be hanged upon the gallows. 14 And the king commanded it so to be done: and the decree was given at Shushan; and they hanged Haman's ten sons. 15 For the Jews that *were* in Shushan gathered themselves together on the fourteenth day also of the month Adar, and slew three hundred men at Shushan; but on the prey they laid not their hand. 16 But the other Jews that *were* in the king's provinces gathered themselves together, and stood for their lives, and had rest from their enemies, and slew of their foes seventy and five thousand, but they laid not their hands on the prey, 17 On the thirteenth day of the month Adar; and on the fourteenth day of the same rested they, and made it a day of feasting and gladness. 18 But the Jews that *were* at Shushan assembled together on the thirteenth *day* thereof, and on the fourteenth thereof; and on the fifteenth *day* of the same they rested, and made it a day of feasting and gladness. 19 Therefore the Jews of the villages, that dwelt in the unwalled towns, made the fourteenth day of the month Adar *a day of* gladness and feasting, and a good day, and of sending portions one to another.

Esther requested the bodies of the sons of Haman be hung on ten gallows. Furthermore, the next day, an additional three-hundred enemies of the Jews were slain in Shushan. Yet they scrupulously avoided profiting from their enemies. "On the prey they laid not a hand." Across the empire, seventy-five thousand enemies of the Jews were killed.

The following day (the fourteenth), Jews throughout the realm made a day of feasting in celebration of their victory (though those in Shushan celebrated from the thirteenth to the fifteenth). They not only feasted, but they observed it as a good day, sending portions one to another. That is, they sent gifts to each other in celebration thereof.

9:20-25 And Mordecai wrote these things, and sent letters unto all the Jews that *were* in all the provinces of the king Ahasuerus, *both* nigh and far, 21 To stablish *this* among them, that they should keep the fourteenth day of the month Adar, and the fifteenth day of the same, yearly, 22 As the days wherein the Jews rested from their enemies, and the month which was turned unto them from sorrow to joy, and from mourning into a good day: that they should make them days of feasting and joy, and of sending portions one to another, and gifts to the poor. 23 And the Jews undertook to do as they had begun, and as Mordecai had written unto them; 24 Because Haman the son of Hammedatha, the Agagite, the enemy of all the Jews, had devised against the Jews to destroy them, and had cast Pur, that *is*, the lot, to consume them, and to destroy them; 25 But when *Esther* came before the king, he commanded by letters that his wicked device, which he devised against the Jews, should return upon his own head, and that he and his sons should be hanged on the gallows.

Thereafter, Mordecai sent letters to the Jewish communities scattered throughout the Persian Empire, instructing them

Understanding Esther

from thenceforth to observe the fourteenth and fifteenth day of the month Adar (i.e., essentially March) yearly. It was designed to commemorate the providential events how their persecution had been turned into a great victory.

9:26-32 Wherefore they called these days Purim after the name of Pur. Therefore for all the words of this letter, and *of that* which they had seen concerning this matter, and which had come unto them, 27 The Jews ordained, and took upon them, and upon their seed, and upon all such as joined themselves unto them, so as it should not fail, that they would keep these two days according to their writing, and according to their *appointed* time every year; 28 And *that* these days *should be* remembered and kept throughout every generation, every family, every province, and every city; and *that* these days of Purim should not fail from among the Jews, nor the memorial of them perish from their seed.

29 Then Esther the queen, the daughter of Abihail, and Mordecai the Jew, wrote with all authority, to confirm this second letter of Purim. 30 And he sent the letters unto all the Jews, to the hundred twenty and seven provinces of the kingdom of Ahasuerus, *with* words of peace and truth, 31 To confirm these days of Purim in their times *appointed*, according as Mordecai the Jew and Esther the queen had enjoined them, and as they had decreed for themselves and for their seed, the matters of the fastings and their cry. 32 And the decree of Esther confirmed these matters of Purim; and it was written in the book.

This Jewish holiday became known as Purim. The word *Purim* is the Hebrew plural for (פור) *pur* (pronounced pur-EEM). That word had the sense of casting of lots. It was based upon how Haman had cast lots (i.e., rolled dice) to determine which month would be the luckiest for him to execute his plot.

Haman's decree had originally been issued on the thirteenth day of the month. Therefore, the Jews took the very name of the fateful event—the casting of a lot (*pur*), made it plural (*purim*), and named a holiday thereafter which is observed to this day.

Both Mordecai, who by now had great authority, along with Esther the Queen added "all authority to confirm this second letter of Purim." A second letter was sent throughout the empire granting official governmental status to the day.

* * * * *

Overview of Esther 10: *Mordecai was promoted to second in command in the kingdom.*

10:1-3 And the king Ahasuerus laid a tribute upon the land, and *upon* the isles of the sea. 2 And all the acts of his power and of his might, and the declaration of the greatness of Mordecai, whereunto the king advanced him, *are* they not written in the book of the chronicles of the kings of Media and Persia? 3 For Mordecai the Jew *was* next unto king Ahasuerus, and great among the Jews, and accepted of the multitude of his brethren, seeking the wealth of his people, and speaking peace to all his seed.

Meanwhile, Mordecai was made second to the king. In modern parlance, he perhaps would be called the prime minister of Persia. Though the name of God is not mentioned in Esther, perhaps because of Persian governmental complications, nevertheless, the providential hand of God is clear. He not only proved just in protecting an innocent people, He providentially vindicated them. Anti-Semitism is nothing new. It is as old as the adversary. Nevertheless, God's hand of providential protection remains upon His people to this day.

Notes

Notes

Notes

Notes

Notes

Notes

Notes

Notes